theology of revelation

by rené latourelle, s. j.

alba house
DIVISION OF THE SOCIETY OF ST. PAUL
STATEN ISLAND, N.Y. 10314

theology of revelation

including a commentary on the constitution "dei verbum"
of vatican II

8th printing - March 1987

Original title: *Théologie De La Révélation* (Desclée de Brouwer)

Nihil Obstat:
Gall Higgins, O.F.M.Cap.
Censor Librorum
Imprimatur:
✠ Terence J. Cooke, D.D., V.G.

New York, N.Y. — March 4, 1966

Library of Congress Catalog Card Number: 65-15734

contents

Part 2
THE THEME OF REVELATION IN THE
WRITINGS OF THE FATHERS OF THE CHURCH

Part 3
THE NOTION OF REVELATION IN THE THEOLOGICAL TRADITION

Part 4
NOTION OF REVELATION AND CHURCH MAGISTERIUM

Part 5
THEOLOGICAL REFLECTION

INTRODUCTION

God is not an absent Presence. "God, who at sundry times and in divers manners spoke in times past to the fathers by the prophets, last of all in these days has spoken to us by His Son" (Heb. 1:1). "No one has ever seen God; the only-begotten Son who is in the bosom of the Father, he has revealed Him" (Jn. 1:18). God broke the silence; God came out of His mystery; He addressed Himself to man and unveiled for him the secrets of His personal life; to man He communicated His unheard-of plan for a covenant with man, offering him a share in life. God, the living God, *has spoken* to humanity. This is the immense fact that dominates both testaments. This word, distant at first, confused, intermittent, like a series of unconnected sounds whose unity the ear can barely grasp, is delivered in its fullness, in Jesus Christ, Son of the Father, Word of the Father; it becomes Gospel and echoes, clear and distinct, like a message: "The word of the Gospel" (Acts 15:7), the "Word of the Lord" (1 Thess. 1:8; 2 Thess. 3:1), the "Word of God" (1 Thess. 2:13), the "Word of Truth" (2 Cor. 6:7; Eph. 1:13; Col. 1:5; 2 Tim. 2:15), the "Word of Life" (Phil. 2:16), the "message of salvation" (Acts 13:26), "Gospel of Grace" (Acts 20:24).

The revelation or God's word to humanity is the first Christian reality: the first fact, the first mystery, the first category. The whole economy of salvation, in the order of knowledge, rests upon this *mystery* of God's self-manifestation in trust and love. Revelation is the original mystery; it communicates every other mystery; it is the manifestation of the plan for salvation which God had in mind from all eternity and which He has realized in Jesus Christ (Eph. 1:9-10; Rom. 16:25-27); it is through revelation that we know the gifts of salvation and the means that can assure its possession. Revelation is the decisive and first *event* of Christianity, the event which conditions our decision to believe; for, if God has spoken to humanity and if the fact of this word is solidly established, the decision to believe is no longer blind, but a human decision, in keeping with the nature of a free and intelligent being. Revelation, finally, is the first of these *categories* which are the basis of all theological research. For the science of theology, it is revelation, inspiration, and tradition which represent what are, for the human sciences, fundamental notions. Necessarily implied in every scientific progress, these categories are the first that the scholar must recognize, define, explain.

Revelation is the first fact, the first mystery, and the first category of Christianity. But, this reality is not a much studied subject. In 1911, J. Lebreton already pointed out that the theologians have too much neglected the "fundamental concept of revelation and faith".[1] Some fifty years later, in 1961, A. Leonard, in his introduction to a collective work on the theology of the Word of God, makes the same lament. Revelation, he points out, is "the first and fundamental reality" of Christianity. "Thus it is all the more strange to note that Catholic theology has in no way treated and developed all the variations of this theme. . . . It seems to have played, in theology, the role of one of these fundamentally obvious truths which, without ever being expressed, run the whole length and breadth of everything that is said. . . . In theology everything depends on divine revelation, everything goes back to divine revelation; nothing can be explained without its light, and that is perhaps the very reason why revelation remains, paradoxically enough, one of these great implicit truths which are so brilliant and so certain that they do not need to be made explicit".[2] It is equally significant that the theme of revelation has been regularly passed over in silence by the historians of dogma. Harnack, Schwane, Tixeront, De Groot, Loofs, Seeberg and Landgraf do not have so much as a chapter on the question.

Still, in theology there is a treatise on revelation. This treatise studies the *fact of revelation* and the evidence of the signs which permits us to conclude with certainty to the existence of this fact. This reflection on the fact of revelation, which goes back to the *apologetic* function of theology, is a necessary reflection in the Church; for if the Church should cease to reflect upon the intervention of God in history and upon the signs of this intervention, she would eventually expose her teaching to the perils of fideism. Intimately bound up in the adventure of faith, she would no longer know why nor how she found herself involved.

Yet, the apologetic study of the fact of revelation, solid as it may be, could never exhaust the richness of reality; for this reality, as we have pointed out, is not only a fact, but a mystery. Once we have established the fact that God has spoken, and that the appearance of Christ in history constitutes the most concentrated point of this intervention, we have accomplished very much; but we have not yet finished. We have established that revelation *exists*, but we have not yet said *everything that it is*. We are still on the outer margin of revelation. We still need to discover its nature, aspects, dimensions, depths. Side by side with the apologetic study of revelation, there is thus room for a dogmatic study of revelation, just as side by side with the apologetic study of Church and Resurrection, there is a dogmatic treatise on Church and Resurrection.

The present study would like to be a contribution to this dogmatic study of revelation. It looks upon revelation from the point of view of revelation, just like all the other mysteries of faith: creation, incarnation, redemption, etc. It proceeds from faith to the understanding of faith, based on scripture as an inspired source and on the Church as a divine institution. *Fides quaerens intellectum*: it is a search of the mind, an examination into the mystery already welcomed in the act of faith.

The theology of revelation understood in this way, seems to answer the desires of our age, which has rediscovered the mystery of the Word of God. From every side, there is a proliferation of studies on scripture, tradition, preaching, liturgy, understood as the Word of God or as effects of the Word of God. The term "Word of God" serves to designate almost all the mysteries of salvation and all the Christian realities. This is already evidence enough that we are trying to restore the Word of God to the place of honor which it deserves in Christian faith and in Christian life.

The term *Word of God* is applied primarily to *revelation*, that is, to this first intervention by which God comes out of His mystery, addresses Himself to humanity, and communicates His plan for salvation. Scripture and tradition contain this word; the preaching of the Church transmits it; the liturgy celebrates and actualizes it. But all this derives from the original word spoken *through* God.

This theology of the revelation of the Word of God, in the present-day state of theological studies, presents a formidable undertaking. In the biblical and patristic renewal of the twentieth century, in the reflections on the nature and status of theology, in the criticisms and efforts of kerygmatic theology, in the researches on the meaning of the Church's preaching ministry, in the studies on dogmatic progress and in the monographs on revelation and faith, there are all the elements of a vast synthesis. It appears that a new dogmatic treatise is in the making, a treatise on revelation, destined to take its place among the great theological treatises such as those on faith and the sacraments. This dogmatic treatise on revelation will appear as a complement to the treatise on apologetics and also as a preparation to the treatise on faith.

"What is important," writes John Baillie, "is to have a correspondence on all points between the understanding of revelation and the understanding of the faith which receives it".[3] Since faith and revelation are correlative notions, like word and answer, any reflection on revelation can only contribute to the fertility and vitality of a theology of faith.

A dogmatic treatise on revelation, apart from its contribution to enriching theological thought, has also found a place for itself in the area of ecumenical efforts. Ecumenism is actually not only a problem of ecclesiology but also a problem in methodology. A theology that is ecumenical in tone and intention must be concerned with presenting the doctrine of the Church with fidelity, but a fidelity that promotes dialogue with separated Christians. Now among the Protestants primarily, since Scripture is the only center of attention, we can see that the Word of God is the foundation of their spiritual life just as it is at the foundation of theological research. In Protestant teaching man is alone before the Word of God; this is the medium and environment for his interior life, which is nourished and renewed by daily contact with Scripture. The theology of the Word of God, consequently, stands out in boldest relief and receives a privileged treatment. As a matter of fact, all the great names of contemporary Protestant theology (K. Barth, R. Bultmann, E. Brunner, P. Tillich, R. Niebuhr, H. W. Robinson, etc.) have devoted chapters and even entire works to the theme of revelation. Thus, giving the Word of God all the importance it deserves among the Christian realities means contributing in some manner to an understanding among Christians.

Our study is made up of five successive parts, following the normal method of theology, the speculative function following upon the positive function to further elaborate the data of revelation:

1. *Biblical notion of revelation.*[4]
2. *The theme of revelation in the Fathers of the Church.*
3. *Notion of revelation in the theological tradition.*
4. *Notion of revelation and Church Magisterium.*
5. *Theological reflection.*

In the second and third parts of the book, there can obviously be no question of consulting all the Fathers of the Church and all the theologians who have written upon the theme of revelation. This would be an immense and actually an impossible research; for as yet there are only rare monographs on this subject. Rather than multiplying the authors consulted and offering only fragments from each, we have preferred to make a more attentive examination of a certain number of masters in whom the thinking of an era is well summed up. Thus our investigation, for the patristic period, has focused upon some twenty authors and, for the theological tradition, upon some fifteen of the most important names. Our constant point of reference has been revelation in so far as it is correlative to faith.

The fourth part studies the notion of revelation in the documents of the magisterium: the documents of the extraordinary magisterium by way of the councils; and also the ordinary magisterium, particularly in the encyclicals. These documents for the most part belong to the nineteenth and twentieth centuries. They sanction and extend the theological elaboration of preceding centuries, and at the same time they reflect the actual preoccupations of the Church today. From the historical point of view, this part is closely connected with the preceding sections.

This study makes no pretense to being exhaustive. It is presented, we repeat, as a *simple approach* to a dogmatic treatise on revelation. If, under this guise, it can render some little service and make it possible for others to push farther along in the same direction, we shall feel amply rewarded.[5]

---

1. J. Lebreton, "Son Éminence le Cardinal Billot," *Études*, 129 (1911): 521-522.
2. A. Leonard, "Vers une théologie de la parole de Dieu," in *La Parole de Dieu en Jésus-Christ* (Paris, 1961), p. 12.
3. J. Baillie, *The Idea of Revelation in Recent Thought* (London, 1956), p. 99.
4. Here we give the term *notion* the force it has in German (*Begriff*). Notion in this context, is used to designate the whole reality of revelation, under its manifold aspects.
5. The present edition is a translation from the French: *Théologie de la Révélation* (Desclée de Brouwer, Bruges, 1963). Two important passages have been added: one section on the Epistle to the Hebrews and a whole chapter on the second Vatican Council and revelation.

part 1
biblical notion of revelation

CHAPTER I

REVELATION IN THE OLD TESTAMENT

What characterizes the religion of the Old Testament is its claim of an intervention on the part of God in history, an intervention due solely to God's free choosing. This intervention is conceived of under the form of an encounter between two people: one person speaking and the other person listening and answering. God addresses man, as a master his servant; He asks a question; man, hearing God, answers by faith and obedience. The fact and content of this communication are called *revelation*.[1]

Taken in its totality, as a complex phenomenon including a multiplicity of forms and mediums, this revelation is presented primarily as the experience of the activity of a sovereign power, changing the normal course of history and individual existence. Still, this activity is not a brute display of power; it is always incorporated in words: this power is the dialogue, the announcement, the explanation, the manifestation of a plan. God does not speak to the whole mass of humanity; He chooses first of all one people, then, in this people, intermediaries who will transmit His word and demand an answer in His name.

If the Old Testament lacks a technical term for the idea of revelation,[2] the expression "Word of Yahweh" remains a favorite expression, the most frequent and the most significant to express the divine communication. In the theophanies, the visible manifestation is always subservient to the word.[3] What is primary here is not the fact of seeing the divinity, but the fact of hearing His word. God's call to Abraham is presented as a pure act of speaking on the part of God (Gen. 12:1 ff). It is equally significant that Moses, who was privileged to converse with God as a friend speaks with his friend (Ex. 33:11), could not see his face (Ex. 33:21-23). In the revelation on Sinai, the whole burden of the story rests on the word of God. Among the prophets, "it is remarkable," says Mowinckel, "that even in their visions, it is the words that are the essential thing".[4] Revelation through visions, observes Kohler, is also a revelation through the word.[5] It is through His word that God, progressively, introduces man to the knowledge of his intimate being. "The word of God, in the Old Testament, directs and inspires a history which begins with the word of God pronounced at the time of creation and ends up with the Word made flesh".[6] To outline the history of the word of God is thus at the same time to outline the history of révélation.[7]

I. THE MOMENTS OF THE HISTORY OF REVELATION

1. On the most ancient phase of revelation, research is still hesitant. This phase seems to be primarily bound up with theophanies and manifestations of an oracular nature.

Genesis recounts that Yahweh appeared under a human form to Abraham, near the terebinths of Mambre (Gen. 18:1 ff), announcing the birth of Isaac and the destruction of Sodom. Yahweh appeared once again to conclude a covenant with him and change his name from Abram to Abraham (Gen. 17:1 ff). Isaac and Jacob were favored with similar apparitions (Gen. 26:2; 32:25-31; 35:9). Still it is impossible to determine the exact nature of these manifestations, which could have been sense visions affecting the external senses, or interior visions, the anthropomorphic personification serving then to express the intense and direct character of the interior experience. These traditions concerning the patriarchs have been preserved for us in texts which contemporary research dates in the neighborhood of the tenth century (J) or the ninth-eighth century (E); but these texts relate traditions which are far older. Obviously, we might expect some editing of these accounts by the narrators.

The original milieu had certain techniques for discovering the secrets of the gods: divination, dreams, drawing lots, omens, etc. The Old Testament, for a long time, preserved something of these techniques, purifying them of their polytheistic or magical overtones (Lev. 19:26; Deut. 18:10 ff; 1 Sam. 15:23; 28:3), but always attributing a certain value to them. In important or difficult circumstances, for example before deciding upon a war or an alliance, Israel consults Yahweh her God, whom she knows to be present in all her activities (1 Sam. 9:1-10; Jos. 7:6-15; 1 Sam. 10:20-21). But whereas, among the neighboring Semitic tribes or among the Egyptians, the soothsayer tries to constrain the gods by rites which are considered infallibly effective, Israel waits for an answer simply from the good pleasure of Yahweh. These consultations, most frequently made in behalf of the nation's rulers, are the work of seers and particularly priests (1 Sam. 14:36;

22:15). The priest, in giving his oracles, makes use of the *Urim* and *Thummim,* which he carries in the *ephod,* and answers the questions put to him in brief formulas, affirmative or negative (Deut. 33:8; Ex. 28:30; Lev. 8:8; Num. 27:21; 1 Sam. 14:41; 23:10 ff).[8] It is equally significant that Israel always refused to accept certain classical forms of oracular technique for revealing divine thought, such as hepatoscopy, which was widely used in sacrificial prophecy throughout the ancient orient.

Like the majority of ancient peoples, the Hebrews admitted that God could make use of dreams to make known His will (Gen. 20:3; 28:12-15; 37:5-10; Jgs. 7:13ff; 1 Sam. 28:6; 1 Kgs. 3:5-14). Joseph has a divining cup (Gen. 44:2-5) and he excels in the interpretation of dreams (Gen. 40-41). But, progressively, there comes a distinction between the dreams which God sends to the authentic prophets (Num. 12:6; Deut. 13:2) and those of the professional seers who prophesy on the basis of false dreams (Jer. 23:25-32; Is. 28:7-13).

In the prophets these ancient techniques tend to disappear, giving way to an increased experience of the word itself.[9]

2. The covenant of Sinai is a decisive moment in the history of revelation. It can be understood only in the light of the whole historic process of which it is the goal and fulfillment.[10] Through this covenant Yahweh, who had proved His power and faithfulness to Israel and delivered her from her Egyptian masters, makes this people His property and becomes the head of the nation. All the traditions attach certain laws to this covenant which are the conditions of Yahweh, the clauses imposed by Him on Israel.[11] These laws are the "words" of the covenant (Ex. 20: 1-17) or the "ten words" (Ex. 34:28). What characterizes these *debarim* which, originally, could have existed under a much more simple form and one not involving the number 10, is the apodictic style which is found only in Israel and in certain Hittite treaties of the second millenium.[12] The words of the covenant are the revelation of the divine will; respect or transgression brings blessing or curse; they express the exclusivity of Israel's God and His demands in the area of morality. The covenant made the tribes which came out of Egypt into a community with a law, a worship, a God, a religious conscience. Israel becomes a people governed by Yahweh. All her destiny, ever after, is bound up with this will of God historically expressed and based on the event of deliverance.[13]The prophets never stop applying to the events of their own times the implications of being ruled under a covenant.[14] The *mishpatim* or common code of the covenant (Ex. 20: 22-23, 19), even though they belonged to a subsequent phase which presupposes a canonization of the common law established by antiquity, are also

considered as the expression of God's will. By their imperative formulas, though more casuistic and circumstantial in nature, they are a prolongation of the decalogue.

3. Prophecy represents a new stage in the history of the word. Already the Elohist and even the Yahwist, in recounting the history of the nation's origins, assume a prophetic point of view. They envision certain facts as "judgments" and consider the patriarchs as charismatic men, directed by the word of Yahweh (Gen. 12; 13; 15; 16; 18; 26; 28). Balaam, even though a pagan, enjoys the role of inspired prophet (Num. 22-23). Moses above all is considered as the prototype of prophets (Deut. 34:10-12; 18:15. 18). But even if Joshua already appears as the confidant and mouthpiece of Yahweh, it is only beginning with Samuel (1 Sam. 3:1-21) that prophecy becomes frequent; it seems almost a permanent institution, even though it is always charismatic rather than institutional in nature, up until the fifth century.

In the era of the writing prophets, the word of Yahweh stands out more and more as the expression of the divine will and as a decisive power in Israel's history. The prophets before the exile (Amos, Hosea, Micah, Isaiah) are guardians and defenders of the moral order prescribed by the covenant. Their preaching is an appeal to justice, to fidelity, to the service of the almighty and thrice holy God, but, since Israel is unfaithful to the conditions of the covenant, the divine *dabar* most frequently pronounces condemnations and announces punishments (Am. 4:1; 5:1; 7:10-11; Hos. 8:7-14; 13:15; Mi. 6-7; Is. 1:10-20; 16: 13; 28:13-14; 30:12; 37:22; 39:5. 8). These punishments will not be revoked. The theme of the irreversibility and dynamism of the divine word is nicely asserted in Is. 31:2; Hos. 6:5 and more explicitly still in Is. 9:8: "The Lord sent a word into Jacob and it has lighted upon Israel." The word appears here as pure dynamism. It is hurled down like a thunderbolt and works out its effects in successive stages.

In theological reflection on revelation, Jeremiah occupies an important place; he tried to determine the criteria of the authentic word of God. His criteria are: accomplishment of the word of the prophet (Jer. 28:9; 32:6-8; Deut. 18:21-22), fidelity to Yahweh and the traditional religion (Jer. 23:13-32), finally the often heroic testimony of the prophet himself in behalf of his vocation (Jer. 1:4-6; 26:12-15). Jeremiah was consecrated prophet by a sort of ritual: God sent His words into his mouth like a material object (Jer. 1:9). At once sweet food (Jer. 15:16) and source of torment (Jer. 20:9. 14), the word of God made him subject, put him under constraint like an objective and higher reality. The word of which he was recipient or organ is ordinarily concerned with the faithfulness which Israel owes the covenant of Yahweh. Jeremiah is the defender of the law of the covenant. Like the other prophets, he exhorts, he promises, he threatens (Jer. 2:4; 7:2; 17:20; 22:2. 19; 34:4; 22:5; 26:12-13; 19:2; 20:1). In him too, the word is represented as an independent entity, endowed with irresistible dynamism (Jer. 5:14; 23:29; 25:13; 26:12).[15]

4. Deuteronomy, the product of northern circles which had been touched by the prophetic teaching of the ninth and eighth centuries (according to Welch, Alt, von Rad), stands at the confluence of two currents: the legalist current which is the expression of the priesthood, and the prophetic current. Under this double influence, both theology and law gain in depth. Deuteronomy, in an effort to correct the present in the light of the past, attaches the law much more closely than before to the theme of the covenant. The history of Israel, with all her misfortunes, appears thus as the logical consequence of her constantly renewed infidelity. Yahweh, in revealing his will, had promised his blessing upon obedience: the punishment of Israel is God's judgment on the disobedience of His people.[16] If Israel wants to live, she must put into practice all the words of the law (Deut. 29:28); for this law, coming from the mouth of Yahweh Himself, is a source of life (Deut. 32:47). Deuteronomy enlarges the divine *dabar* in many senses. The accounts of Sinai use the word *debarim* for the decalogue (Ex. 20). Deuteronomy, which also calls the decalogue the "ten words" (Deut. 4:13; 10:4), further extends the expression to all the clauses of the covenant (Deut. 28:69), that is, the whole complex of moral, civil, religious, and criminal legislation. The inner unity of all these prescriptions is so strongly expressed that the "word" ends up by designating the whole Mosaic law (Deut. 28:69; 30:14; 32:47). In the prescriptions of Sinai, the divine *dabar* was a pure commandment, without commentary. In Deuteronomy, however, the expression of precept is accompanied by historical flashbacks, promises, threats (Deut. 4:32), whose object is to inspire love and respect for the law. Finally, the word of faith becomes interior. The "commandments and laws" which Yahweh has prescribed (Deut. 27:10) are no longer conceived of as a simple imperative, but as an intimate reality in the heart of man: "The word is very nigh unto thee, in thy mouth and in thy heart, that thou mayest do it" (Deut. 30:11-14). The law consists in loving God with all one's heart and all one's soul (Deut. 4:29).[17]

5. Parallel with the prophetic and the deuteronomic currents, an historical literature is gradually elaborated (Judges, Samuel, Kings) which incorporates sources and documents that are far more ancient. This historical literature is in fact a history of salvation and a theology of history. The book of Judges sees in the misfortunes and successes

of Israel an illustration of the rule of the covenant. In the book of Kings particularly, the concept of the divine *dabar* is developed as something present at the heart of history, in order to direct it. The covenant concluded by Yahweh and the conditions imposed by Him presuppose that the course of human events is regulated by the divine will, in terms of the attitudes of the chosen people. Israel never again divorced her religious thinking from a category of history. In the last analysis, it is the word of God that makes history and renders it intelligible. All throughout the history of the Kings, the words of Yahweh range over the course of events and express their religious import (1 Kgs. 2:4; 3:11-14; 6:11-13; 8:46-52; 9:3-9; 11:31-39; 12:15; 14:6-16; 15:29-30; 16:1-4. 7; 2 Kgs. 9:7-10; 21:10-15; 22:16-20; 24:2-4).

An important text of this historical literature is the prophecy of Nathan (2 Sam. 7) who makes the covenant royal and establishes the foundation of royal Messianism. Through this prophecy, the dynasty of David becomes directly and forever the ally of Yahweh (2 Sam. 7:16; 23:5); it becomes the pivot for the axis of salvation. Ever after, the hope of Israel will rest upon a king: a present king first of all, and then a king to be, eschatological, as the infidelities of the historical kings gradually dim the hope for a king according to the Davidic ideal. This prophecy is the point of departure for a theology, elaborated by the prophets, which is primarily a *promise*, constantly turning to the *future*, much more so than the theology of the Sinai covenant, whose demands are more a matter of everyday concern.[18]

6. At the time of the exile, the prophetic word, without ceasing to be a living word, becomes more and more a written word. It is significant that the word entrusted to Ezekiel is written on a scroll which the prophet must swallow before he can preach its contents (Ez. 3: 1 ff). His messages will have, in writing, the fixed character of divine decrees. Ezekiel is the minister of an irrevocable word, which announces events and makes their accomplishment infallible (Ez. 12:25-28; 24:14). At times, the *dabar*, in Ezekiel, is no longer a message but a vehement command, a power that operates physical effects. A primary characteristic of the prophecy of Ezekiel is the number and breadth of the visions (Ez. 1; 2:8-3, 9; 8-11; 37; 40:1-48, 35). There are words to serve as commentary on these visions, themselves constituting a teaching. A second characteristic is the pastoral tone of the word of Ezekiel. After the fall of Jerusalem (Ez. 33:1-21), Israel no longer exists as a nation. The word of Yahweh becomes a word of comfort and hope for the shattered exiles. Ezekiel undertakes the formation of a new Israel, like a spiritual director (Ez. 33:1-9). In showing that the word which has decreed and realized their punishment remains a promise for them,

Ezekiel is still concerned with avoiding every misunderstanding as to its nature and demands: it is not enough to hear the word, it must be lived (Ez. 33:30). Ezekiel "orients us nicely towards a sapiential notion of the word, by the place he gives the *mashal*, the moral and individual teaching, cold reflection".[19]

Deutero-Isaiah (Is. 40-55), who must be read in the background of the exile, considers the divine *dabar* in its dynamism, which is at once cosmic and historic. The transendence of Yahweh is manifested first of all in nature. The hosts of heaven obey the Creator: Yahweh calls the stars by their name and they obey Him (Is. 40:26; 45:12; 48:13). His absolute sovereignty over creation is the foundation and guarantee of His all-powerful activity in history: it is because Yahweh, through His word, has called everything out of nothingness that He is lord of nations just as He is master over the forces of nature. The historic aspect of the *dabar* inspires the whole first part of the collection (Is. 40:1-48, 22). The word dominates history and, far in advance, reveals its course (Is. 45:19; 48:16). It is at the beginning and at the end of all events: it predicts them, calls them into being, accomplishes. In Isaiah 48:3-8, the accomplishment of earlier prophecies appears as the guarantee of future things, equally predicted; that is, deliverance, return, restoration, eschatological universalism. God holds the poles of history (Is. 41:4; 44:6; 48:12). History is intelligible because it unfolds according to a plan that the word reveals progressively to men. Finally, in Is. 55, the author celebrates the infallible efficacy of the word which executes the divine will with the same fidelity as the elements of nature: "As the rain and the snow come down from heaven, and return no more thither, but soak the earth and water it, and make it to spring new seed to the sower and bread to the eater: so shall my word be, which shall go forth from my mouth. It shall not return to me void, but it shall do whatsoever I please and shall prosper in the things for which I sent it" (Is. 55:10-11). A bold personification, presenting the word as a dynamic reality, creator of history.[20]

7. The sapiential literature represents a very ancient tradition in Israel (1 Kgs. 5:9-14; 10:1-13. 23-25); but, in the Persian and Hellenistic era, it enjoys a new popularity: the existing collections (for example Prov. 10:1-22, 16; 25-29) are augmented by numerous creations (Job, Ecclesiastes, Sirach, Wisdom). Even though the sapiential literature of the Old Testament belongs to an international current of thought (Greece, Egypt, Babylon, Phoenicia), attested already from the beginning of the second millenium,[21] this current of thought was soon transformed by Israel into an instrument of revelation. The same God who gives light to the prophets made use of human experience to reveal man to

himself (Prov, 2:6; 20:27). At the beginning, this wisdom is simple
reflection, positive and realistic, on man and his conduct, to help him
direct his life with prudence and discretion (Prov. 1:1-6). In Greece, this
reflection will take a more speculative trend and change into philosophy.
In Israel, the treasure of human experience and wisdom was quickly
animated by the breath of Yahweh's religion. Israel takes up human
experience, but interprets it and gives it a greater depth in the light of
her faith in Yahweh, master of man and life.[22] What is more, the experience from which this sapiential reflection is refined frequently belongs
to revelation: creation (Sir. 43), history which makes known the ways
of God (Sir. 44-50), the historical books, the Law and the prophets
(Sir. 39:1 ff). Under the influence of this faith in Yahweh, the opposition between wisdom and folly progressively turns into an opposition
between justice and iniquity, between piety and impiety. The sage is
the man who accomplishes God's law (Sir. 15:1; 19:20; 24:23; Eccl. 12:
13); for all wisdom comes from God (Prov. 2:6). He alone possesses
wisdom in its fullness; He manifests wisdom in His works and communicates it to those who love Him (Sir. 1:8-10; Wis. 9:4; Job 28:
12-27). Wisdom, like His word, comes from the mouth of the Most
High; it was at work from the beginning of creation and it has come
to establish itself in Israel (Sir. 24:3-31). Thus, wisdom, finally, is
identified with the word of God, creator and revealer (Wis. 7-9).

8. The Psalter, which grew up gradually to its present form over the
course of history, is primarily an answer to revelation; but it is revelation too, for the prayer of men, through the sentiments which it expresses, gives revelation its full scope and breadth. The grandeur, the
majesty, the power, the faithfulness, the holiness of Yahweh, revealed
through the prophets, are reflected in the attitudes of the believer and in
the intensity of his prayer.[23] Mirror of revelation, the psalms are also
a daily re-actualization of the Temple worship. Thus it is not surprising
that the psalms reflect the different aspects of the word already noted.
The word of Yahweh frequently means the prescriptions imposed by
God upon His people (Ps. 17:4; 107:11). Psalm 119, elaborating upon
this vision, celebrates the Torah as the incarnation of all divine revelation which is either a source of order or else a curse or promise.
The Psalter also contains oracles which hark back to Yahweh's previous
involvement in history (Ps. 99:7; 85:9; 89:20; 12:6; 62:12; 60:8;
105:11; 68:23). The psalmist stresses once again the veracity and the
faithfulness of the word of Yahweh, always sure and always without
alloy. Even where the *dabar* is not promulgated in oracular form, it
frequently has the force of a promise. Thus, in psalm 56, the faithful
Israelite puts his hope in the word of Yahweh whose veracity is without

fail. Finally, many psalms celebrate the word of Yahweh as creator: the world rises up from nothingness on the order of His word which produces, organizes, governs (Ps. 33:6. 9). The elements of nature, even the tempest, obey the commandment of God (Ps. 147:15-18; 107: 25; 148:8). In brief, for the psalmist, the word of God is at once law, promise, and power, exercised in nature and throughout history.[24]

9. Concluding this brief sketch, let us stress the role of Scripture in the history of revelation. The process of putting the word into a fixed form was at first a very slow process. Up to the end of the royal period, the writing down of ancient traditions and prophetic oracles was only occasional and seems not to have been directed by any fixed idea to set up a canon. It is only after the exile that the great collections were completed and edited in successive strata, and on a very ancient foundation, which was called the Deuteronomic and Priestly code. This fixed format made it possible to read and meditate the word of God, to contemplate His faithful accomplishment of His promises. In its written form, the word of God takes on a quality of durability and eternity: it abides, irrevocable and infallible. On the other hand, in its fixed form, it runs the risk of losing something of the dynamism that it had in the prophets.[25] It always needs to be actualized and applied to new situations in history, by a constant re-reading, which is itself the key to a new depth of understanding.

II. NOETIC AND DYNAMIC FORCE OF THE WORD OF GOD

This outline of the history of revelation has already shown us the meaning and force of the word of God in Israel. If the etymology of the word *dabar* is contested,[26] popular usage can teach us the precise implication of the term. The *dabar* is "what comes out of the mouth" (Num. 30:13) or "the lips" (Jer. 17:16) of man, but it also has its source in the heart of the man. The *dabar* expresses, exteriorizes what the man has already said in his heart (Gen. 17:17; Ps. 14:1), or what rises to his heart (Jer. 3:16; Is. 65:17) or his mind (Ex. 11:5; 20:32). The word is thus not the pure expression of abstract ideas; it is full of meaning, it has a noetic content, resulting from a man's concentration on an object or the rising up within him of thoughts which seize upon him, but at the same time it expresses a state of soul; something of his soul impregnates the spoken, articulated word.[27] Pedersen is right in saying the "word ... is the corporal expression of the soul's content ... ; behind the word there subsists the totality of the soul which has created it. If the person who expresses the word is an energetic soul, then his word will express more reality than that of a feeble soul. The man who addresses a word to another has created something of his soul in the soul of the other".[28] That is why the word is effective, capable of realizing: it acts as a prolongation and extension of the psychic energy from which it emanates.

For Israel, the word possesses a double force: *noetic* and *dynamic*. On the one hand, it is the expression of thoughts, intentions, projects, decisions; it is intelligible discourse; it enlightens the meaning of events; it "names" things, for name is reality in so far as reality is intelligible. And on the other hand, it is an active force, a power which accomplishes what it signifies; it effects what man thinks and decides in his heart. The word of desire, promise, commandment—its activity abides throughout the whole process it sets in motion. Its efficacy is as great as the power of the will which expresses it (as in the case of Kings, or God); as deep as the source from which it springs (hate, love). The word sets loose an energy which cannot be recovered; its efficacy is shown primarily in the changes of name which are the sign of a new call, a new vocation (Gen. 17:5. 15; 35:10); and in the formulas of blessing and cursing (Gen. 27; Jud. 17:1-2; 2 Sam. 12:1-8; Num. 5:12-31). The realism of the word is attested further by the fact that *dabar* designates not only the word, but also the thing, the reality, the event set in motion (Gen. 22:1; 24:66; 1 Kgs. 11:41). Finally, the word is an active force whose dynamism is rooted in the very dynamism of the person who pronounces it. It is hardly distinct from the person whose mode of being and activity it represents. That is why the word is a revealer. No one speaks without revealing himself.[29]

Such is the word of Yahweh, at once noetic and dynamic: it is the discourse of the God of truth and the salvific act of the living God; proclamation and realization of salvation; light and power. On the one hand, the word of God creates the world, imposes His law, sets history in motion; and on the other hand it manifests the will of God, His salvific plan. The word of God infallibly effects what it says. God sends out His word as a living messenger and He keeps guard over it in order to accomplish it. The word of God abides forever, faithful and efficacious.

III. COSMIC REVELATION AND HISTORIC REVELATION

Interest in the word as creative represents, in Israel, a rather late stage of inspired reflection (even though the idea of creation might have risen and circulated long before it found its way into the sacred text). It is through her history primarily that Israel came to know Yahweh, when in Egypt she experienced His power to deliver. Constant meditation on this unlimited power of Yahweh, using the elements of nature for the salvation of His people (the plagues of Egypt, the passage through the Red Sea, the theophany on Sinai), ended up, in homogeneous organic maturation and under the influence of environment, as a belief in creation. Israel understood that the same God who had raised Israel from the nothingness of slavery had also raised the cosmos from nothingness. His sovereignty is universal. Gen. 1 asserts that God has created everything by His word: He names created things and, at His call, creation rises out of nothingness; the word of God gives it existence and subsistence. Psalm 33 is still more expressive: "Through His word the Heavens are made, through the breath of His mouth all their power. . . . He speaks and it is, He demands and it rises to being" (Ps. 33:6. 9). Since creation is something said by God it is also revelation. Created things are an echo of the word of Him who called them into being; they manifest His presence, His majesty, His wisdom (Ps. 19:2-5; Job 25:7-14; Prov. 8:22-31; Sir. 42:15-43, 33; Wis. 13:1-9). God appears veiled in a cloud (Ex. 13:21), burning like a burning fire (Ex. 3:2; Gen. 15:17), thundering in the tempest (Ex. 19:16; Ps. 29: 2 ff), gentle as a light breeze (1 Kgs. 19:12 ff).[30]

What is more, the source of the priestly tradition, which rethinks creation in liturgical terms, sees in the universe an expression of the will of God which, through the stars and the seas, determines the liturgical times, the Sabbath and the feasts (Gen. 2:2-3). By His word too, God rules all the phenomena of nature, the snow, the frost, the winds (Ps. 107:25; 147:15-18; 148:8; Job 37:5-13), the waters of the abyss (Is. 44: 27; 50:2). At His command, the stars and elements fight for Israel (Ps. 46:7; 106:9-12; 107:25).

Apart from the primitive revelation which is recorded in the first chapters of Genesis, *historical* revelation (as distinguished from cosmic revelation) begins with Abraham, Moses, and the prophets. The word now becomes fully intelligible. God addresses Himself to man, asks him a question, makes him the partner of His plan, speaks to him. Revelation becomes the mystery of a personal *meeting* between the living God and man. Law and prophetic word are the favorite forms of this revelation.[31]

When the word is imposed on things, it creates; when it is imposed on man, it becomes *law*. The "ten words of Sinai" (Ex. 34:28; Deut. 4: 13; 10:4), pronounced by Yahweh on the mountain top, in the midst of fire, are a revelation of the will of the God of the covenant: Yahweh there asserts Himself as Lord. The term *word* as applied to the common law of the code of the covenant (Ex. 20:22-23, 19), means that the whole daily life of the Hebrews is subject to the will of Yahweh, enacted in His presence.[32] Deuteronomy, in its turn, extends the term word to cover all the prescriptions of the covenant, so that the word eventually comes to designate the whole Mosaic Law (Deut. 28:69). Finally, the whole complex of the sacred books, and particularly the Law, will come to be considered as the word of God.[33] In this stage, the Law absorbs everything: law, wisdom, prophecy. As expression of the will of God, it is the way of life and salvation (Deut. 30:14; 32:47; 8:3). Accordingly as it is accepted or refused, it is absolution or judgment, life or death.

The *prophetic* revelation is the other form of historical revelation. The expression "word of God" in 225 cases out of 241, means the word received or addressed by the prophet. Because of its importance, this form of revelation demands a special treatment.

IV. PROPHETIC REVELATION

The revelation of Sinai always remains the central bloc of revelation; but if it lasted throughout the Old Testament, particularly during the royal era and the exile, and if it acquired new depth and development, all this is the work of the prophets. Their restatement of the laws and demands of the covenant is often so vigorous as to give the impression that they are creating something new, that they are the bearers of a religion which surpasses that of the Law and sometimes even goes counter to it. The reason is that they all have their secret source. What really constitutes the authority and originality of the prophet is the fact that he has been the object of a privileged experience: he knows Yahweh, for Yahweh has spoken to him and entrusted His word to him. He has been admitted to a particular intimacy with God: he has been called to share His knowledge, His plans, His will, to be His interpreter among men.[34] Just as the angels who stand in the divine counsel (Job 1:6; 2:1; Zech. 1:11 ff), the prophet "has stood in the counsel of Yahweh" (Jer. 23:18. 22; 1 Kgs. 22:19-23) and Yahweh has revealed His plans (Amos 3:7). He knows the secrets of the Most High (Num. 24:16-17), for he has understood the words of Yahweh (1 Sam. 15:16). Yahweh has spoken to him and he possesses Yahweh's word.

This experience is the fundamental experience of the prophet. The word of Yahweh is in him (Jer. 5:13). It has been placed in his mouth (Jer. 1:9; 5:14) and he has assimilated it like food (Ez. 3:1-3). Jeremiah repeats on many occasions that it is the possession of this word that makes the decisive difference between the true prophet and the false (Jer. 23:16-31). "Thus speaks Yahweh" is the habitual introduction to the prophetic message, or: "I hear the voice of the Lord" (Is. 6:8), or: "thus Yahweh spoke to me" (Is. 8:11; Jer. 11:21; 15:1), or: "my ears have received this revelation" (Is. 22:14), or "the word of Yahweh came to me".[35]

Whether this word of God in the prophet is a sudden thought or an idea slowly formed, it is always "given to Him"; it always "comes to Him." This coming is a supernatural event. The experience of God's word forces upon the prophet the very firm conviction that the word He hears is of divine and not human origin. The prophet is aware that he has not created this word which is in him, but not of him (Jer. 1:4-10), and which moreover frequently contradicts his own natural instincts and sentiments.[36] "This special knowledge of God, proper to the prophets," says Mowinckel "consists in this that they have received the word of Yahweh, that they know His will, His plans, and thus the side of His person that is turned towards the world".[37]

The prophet has received this word, not to keep it, but to transmit it, to publish it, to announce it. He is the *mouth* of Yahweh (Jer. 15:19; Ex. 7:1-2), just as Aaron is a prophet of Moses, because he announces His Words (Ex. 4:16). Jeremiah is established as prophet because God sends him and puts His words in his mouth. The prophet is the herald of Yahweh, chosen, called by Him, to proclaim the words which he has received or understood from Yahweh. The prophet is *the man of the word* (Jer. 18:18).[38] Among men, his position is that of *interpreter* authorized by God, to explain everything that happens in the universe (storm, cataclysm, famine, prosperity), among men (sin, death, hardening of heart), and in history (defeat, success, succession of empire).[39]

It is important to stress the objective and dynamic character of the word. Yahweh *addresses* His word to the prophet. In the prophet this word is an active reality, charged with the very power of God who communicates. The first effect of this word is in the prophet who receives it. The prophet is seized by a strange power which floods his whole being and puts him under constraint. Sometimes it is a source of joy (Jer. 15:16), sometimes a source of shame (Jer. 20:7-9); the word acts like a consuming fire (Jer. 20:8-9), as an indomitable power (Jer. 6:11). It is impossible to run away from it. Yahweh has spoken: the prophet must give his witness. In him the word is like a light and an energy. Such is the experience of Amos (Am. 3:8), of Jeremiah (Jer. 20: 7-9), of Isaiah (Is. 8:11), of Ezekiel (Ez. 3:14), of Elijah (1 Kgs. 18:46), of Elisha (2 Kgs. 3:15).[40] The prophet is bound to God by His word.

In addition to its activity in the prophet, the word of God possesses an efficacy of its own, independent of the prophet: a sacramental force. When Yahweh sends forth His word, nothing can hinder its movement: it follows out its way and accomplishes its work.[41] Destruction, death, famine, salvation, the flight of armies: everything happens in conformity with his word which is truth (1 Kgs. 15:29; 16:12; 2 Kgs. 1:17; 7:16; 9:26; 10:17). The word of the prophet, which is the word of God in human speech, shares this same efficacy. Jeremiah receives power "over nations and kingdoms, to root up and to pull down, to waste and destroy" (Jer. 1:10; 1 Sam. 16:4; 2 Kgs. 2:24). The word of God is like a hammer which shatters the rock (Jer. 5:14; 23:29), or like a sword which slays (Hos. 6:5). It is never barren (Is. 45:23; 31:2). It "abides forever," like Yahweh himself (Is. 40:6-8).[42] This does not mean it is an uncontrollable force. God always remains Master, controlling its effects according to His plans; but this plan, which He reveals little by little, is the salvation and life of man. That is why, throughout the Old Testament, God, in His patience, is willing to listen, to be bent, to pardon, even to "repent."

The prophetic word finds its field of activity in history. The prophetic word is *creator* and *interpreter* of history. The revelation of God actually came to the Hebrew people by means of the divine experience at work on its behalf. Biblical religion is essentially a matter of believing in the divine facts, in the interventions of God in the course of human history.[43] These facts are principally those which have marked the birth of Israel as a nation: her deliverance from the slavery of Egypt, her wandering through the desert, her conquest of the promised land. Throughout forty years, Yahweh marches through the desert with His people, leading them as a shepherd. He alone protected Israel, defended, saved. The faith of Israel is based on these salvific events, and her creed consists in reciting them (Deut. 26:5-10). In the time that follows, the prophets constantly refer to these events, either to remind Israel of the faithfulness she owes the covenant, or, during the time of exile, to proclaim a new exodus, a new covenant (Ex. 36-37; Is. 54-55).[44]

The activity of God, which makes history a work of salvation or reprobation, is doubly the work of His word: it is the word of Yahweh that begins and directs all events, just as it is the word of Yahweh which interprets their meaning. Through His word, God anticipates and announces the event, for He is first and last; He knows what will happen in the end (Is. 41:4; 43:10; 44:6; 48:12). "The Lord God does nothing without revealing His secret to His servants the prophets" (Am. 3:7). All the decisive stages of Israel's history are preceded by God's word: creation (Gen. 1:3), deluge (Gen. 6:7), the call of Abraham (Gen. 12:1), the call of Moses and deliverance from Egypt (Ex. 3; 14:30-31), the trek from Horeb to Chanaan (Deut. 1:6; 6:2. 18. 31; 3:1. 27. 28), the call of Samuel (1 Sam. 3), the establishment of the kingdom (1 Sam. 8:7; 9:17; 10:17-24), the election of David (1 Sam. 15:10; 16:12), the covenant with the dynasty of David through the prophecy of Nathan (2 Sam. 7), the division of the Kingdom of Israel (1 Kgs. 11: 31 ff), the fall of the house of Ahab (1 Kgs. 21:17-24), exile (Jer. 25: 1-13), the destruction of Jerusalem (Ez. 1-23), the return from captivity (Is. 40:2; 43:1-5; 44:21-23; 48:20-21). For Israel, history is a process directed by Yahweh, towards a goal willed by Him.[45]

The prophetic word not only announces history and puts it in motion, but also interprets it. The prophet is steeped in the history of his time, and it is in the actuality of this history that God reveals His will to him, His plan of salvation. The God of the Old Testament is a God who intervenes, and the prophet is the man who meditates upon these interventions, who grasps and proclaims their meaning for salvation. The prophet perceives the divine meaning of events and makes it known to the men of his time. He interprets history from the point of view of God.[46]

If the realization of salvation in history is already the word of God, the precise content of this word becomes intelligible only through the word of the prophet. Revelation-event and revelation-word are, as it were, the two faces of the word of God. The history of salvation is a series of divine interventions interpreted by the prophet. For an Israelite. to tell the story of history means to interpret history in the light of God's communications to His confidants. Thus, through the events of the exodus, as interpreted by Moses, the Hebrew people learned to know Yahweh as a living, personal God, unique, all-powerful, faithful, who saves His people and makes a covenant with them so that His chosen people will be faithful to Him in view of the common work of salvation (Deut. 6:20-24). It follows then that God, His attributes, His plan, are revealed not abstractly, but concretely, in history and through history. The message of revelation is incorporated in history. There is progress in the knowledge of God, but this progress is bound up with events which the word of God announces, realizes, and interprets.[47]

V. THE OBJECT OF REVELATION

We might say that the object or content of Old Testament revelation is twofold: it is the revelation of God Himself and the revelation of His plan for salvation. The God of the Old Testament reveals Himself first of all as a living and personal God, as He who *is* (efficaciously), in opposition to the dumb and dead idols; as an all-powerful God, Master of the cosmos and Lord of nations, who demands obedience to His laws. Little by little, the prophets raise Israel to a more and more profound understanding of the attributes of God: Amos casts light on His justice; Hosea on His tender and even jealous love; Isaiah on His grandeur and transcendence; Jeremiah teaches a more interior religion; Ezekiel recalls the demands imposed by the holiness of God; Deutero-Isaiah towards a more universalist religion. At the same time that Israel refines this idea of the transcendence of God, there is also a development in her awareness of His nearness and intimacy. For the Most High, the thrice-holy and mysterious God, is also a God who comes out of His mystery, who enters into dialogue with man: He becomes Emmanuel and Bride-groom. This is an evolution which shows clearly in the theme of the covenant. Between the transcendent God and the God of the covenant, between the hidden God and the God of the word, there exists a sort of constant tension which constitutes a sort of dynamic of Old-Testament revelation. The two poles exercise an equal attraction. A delicate equi-librium is established between the God of mystery and the God of revelation. It is the solution of this contrast which results, finally, in the harmony of religious feeling in the faithful of the Old Testament.

Salvation is the other aspect of Old-Testament revelation. The cove-nant, actually, is bound up with a divine plan (a mystery, St. Paul will call it), which has remained hidden until the fullness of time, although God has progressively revealed the first sketches of this plan in the Old Testament.

Already in the protoevangelium, there shines a promise of salvation (Gen. 3:15). Since exodus, the God whom Israel knew is a God who saves his people from bondage, fights together with them, and delivers the promised land into their hands. The covenant is sealed in an atmos-phere of salvation. Later, the idea of the covenant extends into the idea of kingdom. Through the prophecy of Nathan (2 Sam. 7:16), Yahweh makes an eternal covenant with David and with his dynasty. Still, the experience of the kingdom, just like that of the covenant, meets with a violent check. It appears so, at least, for God pursues His plan with a mysterious continuity, revealing, even in this checkmate, a new dimension of His economy of salvation. Despite the infidelity of Israel and her kings, Yahweh, through His prophets, proclaims a new covenant, a new kingdom, a new king (Jer. 11:3. 5; 24: 5-7; Ez. 11:19-20; Joel 2:17; Zech. 8:1-17; 13:9; Is. 2:3; 11). In the periods of crisis, too, it is from a king that Israel looks for salvation. Some think that Yahweh Himself will establish His kingdom, without the cooperation of any human king; this is a thought which appears in the kingdom psalms (Ps. 97; 98; Zech. 14:16). For others, salvation will come from that mysterious "son of man" who approaches on the clouds of heaven to receive investiture and mission. In certain priestly circles of Jerusalem and at Qumrân, they were waiting for a Messiah from the priestly line.

Still others, finally, look for salvation from the servant of Yahweh, prophet and king, who will save through suffering. Israel came to live upon this hope of a salvation which is to come.

VI. MAN'S RESPONSE TO REVELATION

If God speaks, man must *listen*. Biblical revelation does not come from a contemplation of the divinity as in the Greek mysteries and the oriental gnosis, but through attention to God's word. Here below, no man can see God (Ex. 33:20). God gives witness to Himself, communicating Himself to man through His word; but He is hidden from the eyes of men. In His innermost reality, He always remains the unfathomable God, completely other: His mystery escapes us. When God called him, Samuel answered: "Speak, for your servant listens" (1 Sam. 3:10). *Listening* expresses the first attitude of man in the face of revelation: not in a material and passive way, but with an active willingness. Once the word is heard, it asks to be assimilated by faith and submission, in a total self-commitment of which Abraham remains a perfect model (Gen. 15:6; 24:7). The response to the word must be docility of mind and docility of conduct (Mi. 6:8).

Through revelation, Israel knew God, that is to say, Israel was admitted, through His grace, to a communion of thought and will with Yahweh. Such a knowledge implies, in return, on Israel's part, a total attachment to Yahweh through the bonds of faith, obedience, and love. The man who has heard the word of Yahweh must accomplish that word, that is, he must live according to the demands of the covenant. Such is the constant preaching of the prophets (Mi. 6:8; Hos. 6:6; Jer. 5:1-9; 9:2-5; 22:15 ff).[48] Man must constantly renew this fidelity to Yahweh, in keeping with his changing situation.[49]

Revelation and faith are correlative. The faith of the Old Testament is an exact response to the type of revelation addressed to it. The revelation of the Old Testament was essentially *law* and *promise* of salvation; its faith is made up principally of *obedience* and *confidence*. In addressing Abraham, God orders him to leave his country and at the same time promises him a numerous posterity (Gen. 12:1-3; 15:5-6). At the same time that He gives His law to the people of Israel, God insures their faithfulness (Ex. 19:3-8). Believing, from that time on, for a Hebrew, means obeying and having trust; it means recognizing Yahweh as the only God and Savior of Israel, as He has given His law and promised salvation; it means accepting the will of God and trusting in His promises. In Mary, the flower of the Old Testament, faith is complete obedience and trust: the obedience of the handmaid of the Lord (Lk. 1:38) and the trust of a woman whom God, faithful to His promises, has "magnified".[50]

VI. TRAITS AND CHARACTERISTICS OF REVELATION

Old-Testament revelation has certain very specific traits which distinguish it from every other type of knowledge:

1. Revelation is essentially interpersonal. Much more than the manifestation of *some thing*, it is the manifestation of *some one* to *some one*. Yahweh is at once subject and object of revelation, God revealing and God revealed, God who lets Himself be known and God who makes Himself known. Yahweh, living God, enters into personal relationship with man. He makes a covenant with him, like a Lord with his servant, and then, progressively, like a father with his son, like a man with his friend, like a bridegroom with his bride. The word of God introduces man to a *koinōnia*, a communion with God in view of man's salvation.

2. Biblical revelation proceeds from the divine initiative. It is not man who discovers God: it is rather Yahweh who shows Himself, when He wills, to whom He wills, and because He wills. Yahweh is absolute freedom. It was He at first who chose, promised, sealed the covenant. His word, which went counter to the human and earthly hopes of Israel, is a further light upon the freedom and continuity of His plan. The freedom of God is manifest again in the variety of the means He chooses to reveal Himself: the way of nature, human existence and history; the variety of personalities He chooses (priests, sages and prophets, kings and aristocrats, peasants and shepherds); the diversity in His way of communication (theophanies, dreams, consultations, visions, ecstasies, trances, etc.); the diversity in His way of expression or literary genre (oracle, exhortation, autobiography, description, hymn, sapiential literature, meditation, etc.).

3. What gives the economy of revelation its unity is the word. This primacy of the word is not a postulate of faith, but a fact that can be perceived on the same level as historical knowledge. The Greek philosophies and the religions of the Hellenistic era tend towards a vision of the divinity. The religion of the Old Testament, on the contrary, is a religion of hearing the word. God reveals and is revealed by His word. This prevalence of hearing over seeing expresses one of the essential characters of biblical revelation. Since the fall, it is through faith in His word that God effects the return of humanity to vision. God speaks to the prophet and sends him out to speak. The prophet communicates the plan and will of God and man is invited

to the obedience of faith. Still, vision is not completely excluded because, according to its varying degrees, the word already begins to lift aside the veil which darkens the mind, as harbinger of vision. If man cannot yet make his way into the intimacy of the mysteries, he still has, through the word, a certain approach to this mystery. Let us note once more that if the word presupposes, on the part of the man, more attention than the vision, this is a sign of greater respect for human freedom on the part of God: God addresses Himself to man, asks him a question, but man remains free to answer or refuse. The spoken word which, among men, is the most spiritual human exchange, is also the preferred medium for spiritual exchange between God and man.

4. Through revelation, man is confronted with the word, a word which demands faith and accomplishment. Sin, in this respect, consists in not wanting to listen, in not answering the calls of God, hardening one's heart in resistance (Jer. 7:13; Hos. 9:17). According to whether it is accepted or refused, revelation becomes for man grace or judgment, life or death (Is. 1:20). The lot of man is bound up with the decisive choice he makes for or against the word. But the goal and end of revelation is the life and salvation of man, his communion with God (Is. 55:2).

5. All revelation is "finalized" through the hope of a salvation to come. It takes its first great step with the promise made to Abraham and tends toward its accomplishment. For the prophet, the present is only the partial realization of the future which is proclaimed, awaited, prepared, and promised, but still hidden. What is present acquires its whole weight only through the promise, in the past, of what will be in the future. Each prophetic revelation marks an accomplishment of the word, but at the same time leaves hope for a still more decisive accomplishment. Biblical time is thus not cyclic, but linear: something new is happening in history, under the direction of God. History tends toward the fullness of time, which is the accomplishment of God's plan in Christ and through Christ.

VIII. CONCLUSION

This brief research gives us a more precise view of the notion of revelation in the Old Testament. Revelation appears as the free and gratuitous intervention by which the holy and hidden God—in the field of history, and in relation with the events of history as interpreted through the word addressed to the prophets, in accordance with the most manifold media of communication—progressively makes Himself known, together with His plan for salvation, which is to make a covenant with Israel, and then with all the nations, to accomplish finally in the person of His Anointed the promise given of old to Abraham, that in his posterity all the people of the earth would be blessed. In terms of the prophetic mystique, revelation is the progressive unveiling, through the spoken word, of the plan of grace through which Yahweh becomes a bridegroom to His people, and then to all humanity, to join with them forever in the person of his Anointed. Such an activity is conceived of as a word of God inviting to faith and obedience; a word essentially dynamic, which *effects* salvation at the same time as it *proclaims* salvation.[51]

1. On the theme of revelation in the Old Testament, the fundamental works are the following: O. GRETHER, Name und Wort Gottes im Alten Testament (Giessen,, 1934); L. DUERR, Die Wertung des gottlichen Wortes im A. T. und im Antiken Orient (Leipzig, 1938); H. NIEBECKER, Wesen und Wirklichkeit der ubernaturlichen Offenbarung (Freiburg, 1940); W. EICHRODT, Theologie des Alten Testaments (2 vol., Berlin, 1948), 2:32-38; A. ROBERT, "La parole divine dans l'Ancien Testament," Dictionnaire de la Bible, Supplément, 5:442-465; S. MOWINCKEL, "La connaissance de Dieu chez les prophètes de l'Ancien Testament," Revue d'histoire et de philosophie religieuses, 22 (1942): 69-106; C. LARCHER, "La parole de Dieu en tant que révé-lation dans l'Ancien Testament," in La Parole de Dieu en Jésus-Christ (Paris, 1961), pp. 35-67; G. E. MENDENHALL, Law and Covenant in Israel and the Ancient Near East (Pittsburgh, 1955); W. MORAN, "De Foederis mosaici Traditione," Verbum Domini, 40 (1962): 3-17; A. OEPKE, "Apokaluptó," Theologisches Worterbuch, 3:565-597; O. PROCKSCH, "Wort Gottes im A. T.," Theologisches Worterbuch, 4:89-100; W. E. WRIGHT, God who acts (London, 1952); P. VAN IMSCHOOT, Théologie de l'Ancien Testament (2 vol., Paris-Tournai-New York-Rome, 1954 et 1956), 1:142-255; E. JACOB, Théologie de l'Ancien Testament (Paris, 1955), pp. 103-109, 148-184; L. KOEHLER, Old Testament Theology (London, 1957), pp. 99-126; J. L. McKENZIE, "The Word of God in the Old Testament," Theological Studies, 21 (1960): 183-206; TH. C. VRIEZEN, An Outline of the Old Testament Theology (Oxford, 1958), pp. 233-267; A. BARUCQ, "Oracle," Dictionnaire de la Bible, Supplément, 6:752-787; H. W. ROBINSON, Inspiration and Revelation in the Old Testament (Oxford, 1946); J. LEVIE, La Bible, parole humaine et message de Dieu (Paris-Louvain, 1958); H. H. ROWLEY, The Faith of Israel (London, 1958), pp. 23-47; R. B. Y. SCOTT, The Relevance of the Prophets (New York, 1960); JAMES G.S.S. THOMSON, The Old Testament View of Revelation (Grand Rapids, Michigan, 1960); W. BULST, Offenbarung (Dusseldorf, 1960); P. GRELOT, Sens chrétien de l'Ancien Testament (Paris-Tournai-New York-Rome, 1962), pp. 126-134.

2. H. SCHULTE, Der Begriff der Offenbarung im Neuen Testament (Munchen, 1949), pp. 38-40; P. VAN IMSCHOOT, Théologie de l'Ancien Testament, 1:142.

3. S. MOWINCKEL, "La connaissance de Dieu chez les prophètes de l'Ancien Testament," Rev. d'hist. et de ph. rel., 22 (1942): 79.

4. Ibid., p. 83.

5. L. KOEHLER, Theologie des Alten Testaments (1953), p. 87.

6. E. JACOB, Théologie de l'Ancien Testament, p. 104. "If we except the name of God," as F. J. LEENHARDT points out, "there is no word which occupies a place or enjoys a role comparable to those which refer to the term Word in the whole of Christian tradition, and, before the time of Christ, in Hebrew thinking from which the Christian tradition developed" (F. J. LEENHARDT, "La signification de la notion de parole dans la pensée chrétienne," Rev. d'hist. et de ph. rel., 35 (1955): 261.

7. A. ROBERT, "La parole divine dans l'Ancien Testament," Dict. de la Bible, Suppl., 5: 442-465; C. LARCHER, "La parole de Dieu en tant que révélation dans l'Ancien Testament," in: La Parole de Dieu en Jésus-Christ, pp. 35-67.

8. P. VAN IMSCHOOT, Théologie de l'Ancien Testament, 1:148-154; H. H. ROWLEY, The Faith of Israel, pp. 28-29; A. BARUCQ, "Oracle," Dict. de la Bible, Suppl., 6:679-681; H. W. ROBINSON, Inspiration and Revelation in the Old Testament, pp. 202-204.

9. Still, we find dreams of an apocalyptic nature (Daniel, Zachary); they are then very meaningful and become the equivalent of words themselves.

10. H. W. ROBINSON, *Inspiration and Revelation in the Old Testament*, p. 153.

11. W. EICHRODT, *Theology of the Old Testament* (trad. J. A. Baker, London, 1961), 1:37-38; G. E. MENDENHALL, *Law and Covenant in Israel and the Ancient Near East*, pp. 37 et 43; W. MORAN, "De Foederis mosaici Traditione," *Verbum Domini*, 40 (1962) : 7-13.

12. W. EICHRODT, *Theology of the Old Testament*, 1:71-72; G. E. MENDENHALL, *Law and Covenant in Israel and the Ancient Near East*, pp. 7. 10. 27. 28; A. ALT, *Die Ursprunge des israelitischen Rechts* (Leipzig, 1934); W. KORNFELD, *Studien zum Heiligkeitsgesetz* (Wien, 1952), pp. 53-66.

13. W. EICHRODT, *Theology of the Old Testament*, 1:39; G. E. MENDENHALL, *Law and Covenant in Israel and the Ancient Near East*, p. 5. We might add that, through the covenant, Israel realizes that she is engaged in a *dialogue*; Israel is now situated in a context of question and answer.

14. W. EICHRODT, *Theology of the Old Testament*, 1:42; A. ROBERT, "La parole divine dans l'Ancien Testament," *Dict. de la Bible Suppl.*, 5:444.

15. A. ROBERT, *ibid.*, 5:446-447.

16. G. VON RAD, *Studies in Deuteronomy* (London, 1956), p. 77.

17. A. ROBERT, "La parole divine dans l'Ancien Testament," *Dict. de la Bible*, *Suppl.*, 5:448; G. VON RAD, *Studies in Deuteronomy*, pp. 77-91; C. LARCHER, "La parole de Dieu en tant que révélation dans l'Ancien Testament," dans: *La Parole de Dieu en Jésus-Christ*, pp. 59-60.

18. A. GELIN, art. "Messianisme," *Dict. de la Bible Suppl.*, 5:1174-1177; H. VAN DEN BUSSCHE, "Le texte de la prophétie de Nathan sur la dynastie davidique, *Eph. theol. low.* (1948): 354-394.

19. A. ROBERT, "La parole divine dans l'Ancien Testament," *Dict. de la Bible Suppl.* 5:451.

20. *Ibid.*, 5:453-455.

21. H. W. ROBINSON, *Inspiration and Revelation in the Old Testament*, pp. 235-237.

22. *Ibid.*, pp. 252-253.

23. *Ibid.*, pp. 262-265.

24. A. ROBERT, "La parole divine dans l'Ancien Testament," *Dict. de la Bible*, Suppl. 5:458-461.

25. E. JACOB, *Théologie de l'Ancien Testament*, p. 108.

26. O. Procksch and E. Jacob give it the basic meaning of "being behind and pushing." Jacob says: "*The dabar* could be defined as a forward projection of what is behind, that is to say, the passage into activity of what is first of all in the heart" (*Théologie de l'Ancien Testament*, p. 104). And O. Procksch: "The *dabar* is the background of a thing, the meaning which is proper to it; and this meaning finds its expression in the word.... Each word contains not only a meaning, but also an energy" (*Theologie des Alten Testaments*, p. 469). This explanation justifies, in his eyes, the noetic and dynamic aspect of the word. A. Robert concludes that "the surest solution is to suppose here, as in so many other cases, the existence of two parallel roots, one signifying to speak, and the other to be behind." (*Dict. de la Bible*, Suppl., 5:442). See also F. J. Leenhardt, "La signification de la notion de parole dans la pensée chrétienne," *Rev. d'hist. et phil. rel.*, 35 (1955): 263-264. The method of O. Procksch has been criticized by J. Barr, "Hypostatization of Linguistic Phenomena in modern Theological Interpretation," *Journal of Semitic Studies*, 7 (1962): 88-92.

27. C. LARCHER, "La parole de Dieu en tant que révélation dans l'Ancien Testament," *La Parole de Dieu en Jésus-Christ*, pp. 37-40.

28. J. PEDERSEN, *Israel, its Life and Culture* (London, 1946), p. 107.

29. J. L. McKenzie, "The Word of God in the Old Testament," Theological Studies, 21 (1960): 187-191; E. JACOB, *Théologie de l'Ancien Testament*, pp. 103-104; P. VAN IMSCHOOT, *Théologie de l'Ancien Testament*, 1:201-202; L. DUERR, *Die Wertung des gottlichen Wortes im A. T. und antiken Orient* (Leipzig, 1938), pp. 149 ff.; VAN DER LEEUW, *La religion dans son essence et ses manifestations* (Paris, 1948), pp. 395-397.

30. Still, Israel does not confuse God with the tempest, or God with the cloud, etc. The word of God is not always intelligible, but it always remains the manifestation of a *personal* God. The cloud, the tempest, the fire, the gentle breeze, all manifest the presence of God and his attributes.

31. E. JACOB, *Théologie de l'Ancien Testament*, p. 104.

32. H. W. ROBINSON, *Inspiration and Revelation in the Old Testament*, p. 212.

33. A. ROBERT, "Le sens du mot Loi dans le psaume 119," *Revue Biblique* (1937), pp. 182-206.

34. S. MOWINCKEL, "La connaissance de Dieu chez les prophètes de l'Ancien Testament," *Revue d'hist. et de phil. rel.*, 22 (1942): 75-76; H. W. ROBINSON, *Inspiration and Revelation in the Old Testament*, pp. 166-170; W. EICHRODT, *Theology of the Old Testament*, 1:344.

35. In these expressions, we must obviously be on the lookout for editorial formulae, but

their very frequency is already significant. The prophets assert that God has spoken to them and that His word has come to them. It must also be noted that the term *word of God* is not everywhere verified in the same manner, nor with the same intensity. There are, in the life of the prophets, privileged moments, where the mastery of the word upon them has been more intense. The most significant moment is that of their vocation. For different reasons, the word of Yahweh is not to be identified with every direct and formal revelation. The reasons are the following: *a.* The oracles received by the prophets could have been very short, just as a vision can demand a considerable explanation. *b.* The prophet, normally, is called to comment on the word of God in a verbal prolongation of the interior impulse he has received. *c.* Often, there is only a new awareness of truths already known, because of some new situation. *d.* It can happen that the prophets are giving a fuller expression to truths already communicated to other prophets; often, actually, one prophet depends spiritually on another (Jeremias and Osee). Some prophets have had disciples, who took up their master's themes and made them more explicit. *e.* The word received is actualized frequently on the occasion of concrete fact, as a function of the events of history. The word of the prophet is a light upon history, either in dwelling upon Israel's past, particularly on the covenant, or on putting Israel's history in relation to that of other people, or in unveiling the purposes of God in history. On this subject see: C. Larcher, "La parole de Dieu en tant que révélation dans l'Ancien Testament," *La Parole de Dieu en Jésus-Christ*, pp. 56-58.

36. S. Mowinckel, "La connaissance de Dieu chez les prophètes de l'Ancien Testament," *Rev. d'hist. et de ph. rel.*, 22 (1942): 81-83. The subjective criterion which is the prophet's guarantee that he has really been the object of a divine communication is the experience of the word itself. This experience strikes the prophet with such force that he necessarily, in one and the same judgment which is both intuitive and immediate, recognizes both the word itself and the fact that God is author of that word. Someone is speaking in him, whereas there is no one speaking in the false prophets (Jer. 5:13; 14:14; 23; 29:8-9; Ez. 13:1-16). He has the criterion along with the word. In the effect produced within himself, the prophet, without any explicit reasoning process, grasps both the divine cause and its effect. In the word he recognizes the author of the word. The divine origin of the word is not deduced, but rather experienced in a living way, immediately and simultaneously. Cf. H. W. Robinson, *Inspiration and Revelation in the Old Testament*, pp. 194 and 274; J. Skinner, *Prophecy and Religion* (Cambridge, 1949), p. 196; I Seierstad, *Die Offenbarungserlebnisse der Propheten Amos, Jesaja und Jeremia* (Oslo, 1946), pp. 236-237.

37. S. Mowinckel, "La connaissance de Dieu chez les prophètes de l'Ancien Testament," *Rev. d'hist et de phil. rel.*, 22 (1942): 85.

38. Th. C. Vriezen, *An Outline of Old Testament Theology*, p. 241.

39. H. W. Robinson, *Inspiration and Revelation in the Old Testament*, pp. 161-164.

40. P. Van Imschoot, *Théologie de l'Ancien Testament*, 1:171-172; S. Mowinckel, "La connaissance de Dieu chez les prophètes de l'Ancien Testament," *Rev. d'hist. et de ph. rel.*, 22 (1942) : 77; E. Jacob, *Théologie de l'Ancien Testament*, pp. 105-106.

41. H. W. Robinson, *Inspiration and Revelation in the Old Testament*, p. 170.

42. J. L. McKenzie, "The Word of God in the Old Testament," *Theological Studies*, 21 (1960) : 196-197; E. Jacob, *Théologie de l'Ancien Testament*, p. 106; P. Van Imschoot, *Théologie de l'Ancien Testament*, 1:203; Th. C. Vriezen, *An Outline of Old Testament Theology*, pp. 238-239.

43. E. Jacob, *Théologie de l'Ancien Testament*, pp. 153-154.

44. *Ibid.*, 154-155.

45. J. L. McKenzie, "The Word of God in the Old Testament," *Theological Studies*, 21 (1960) : 198-199.

46. H. W. Robinson, *Inspiration and Revelation in the Old Testament*, pp. 125-128; Id., *Record and Revelation* (Oxford, 1951), pp. 303-304; H. Butterfield, *Christianity and History* (London, 1954), p. 3; G. E. Wright, *God who acts*, p. 13.

47. W. Eichrodt, "'Offenbarung und Geschichte im Alten Testament," *Theol. Zeitschrift*, 4 (1948): 322-323; Th C. Vriezen, *An Outline of Old Testament Theology*, pp. 31-34; H. M. Feret, *Connaissance biblique de Dieu* (Paris, 1955), pp. 36-40.

48. S. Mowinckel, "Connaissance de Dieu chez les prophètes de l'Ancien Testament," *Rev. d'hist. et de ph. rel.*, 22 (1942); 88-89; W. Eichrodt, *Theology of the Old Testament*, 1:389.

49. Th. C. Vriezen, *An Outline of Old Testament Theology*, p. 240.

50. P. Demann, "Foi juive et foi chrétienne," *Cahiers Sioniens*, 6 (1952): 89-103. In this respect, the faith of the New Testament marks a shift in emphasis. The aspect of obedience remains, but the aspect of trust is no longer manifest to the same degree. What prevails in the New Testament is the aspect of knowledge. The faith of the Old Testament tended towards a promised salvation, still obscure, the object of hope and trust. With the coming of Christ, this

salvation is an accomplished fact. Our faith, hereafter, has an explicit and actual content: Christ is the Son of God, sent by the Father, who has suffered and died for our sins, risen from the dead, is seated at the right of the Father from where He sends His Spirit. All this is the object, not only of hope and trust, but of knowledge and recognition. For the New Testament, *believing* means accepting the preaching of the Apostles relative to these facts; faith is accepting the *kerygma* as true (Acts 2:44; 4:4. 32; 8:13). New-Testament faith, following upon the coming of Christ, thus has a more explicit and doctrinal character than the faith of the Old Testament. Cf. J. ALFARO, "Fides in terminologia biblica," Gregorianum, 42 (1961): 504-505. See also: P. GRELOT, *Sens chrétien de l'Ancien Testament*, pp. 142-145.

51. In order to remain in the framework of our study, we have grouped the elements of this chapter according to the *via expositionis*. We might also have grouped them according to the *via inventionis*. The order of progress would have been: 1. Introduction: the first view of the Old Testament as revelation; absence of technical vocabulary, but presence of a common element encountered everywhere, that is, the divine *dabar;* what is the exact implication of this *dabar?* 2. Descriptive part: the stages of revelation, forms and media of revelation, literary genres; 3. Examination of results: the omnipresence of the dialogue, as a setting for the events of salvation; relationship of the word to the covenant and to prophecy; the power of the word in the mouth of Yahweh (word of creation, salvation, judgment) and in the mouth of His messengers; content of the word; the *dabar* is more than our "word"; 4. Resume of these elements according to the *via expositionis*: cosmic and historic revelation; prophetic revelation; human response; 5. Synthesis.

CHAPTER II

REVELATION IN THE NEW TESTAMENT

The notion of revelation, in the New Testament, presents a complexity and richness of tone far superior to that of the Old Testament. Between the two covenants, one pivotal event has taken place: "God, who at sundry times and in divers manners spoke in times past to the fathers by the prophets, last of all in these days has spoken to us by His Son" (Heb. 1:1). In Jesus Christ, the inner Word of God, in whom God expresses Himself totally and knows all things, was made flesh and became Gospel, word of salvation, to call man to salvation. In Jesus Christ, Incarnate Word, the Son is present in our midst and, in human terms that we can understand and assimilate, He speaks, preaches, teaches, testifies to what He has seen and heard in the bosom of the Father. Christ is the summit and fullness of revelation. Inexhaustible mystery, whose splendor the sacred writers can portray only by concentrating on one individual aspect. The synoptic tradition describes primarily the economy of the historic manifestation of Christ, binding up His activity of revelation with His title of Messiah, teacher, and preacher. Acts represents the apostles as the witnesses and heralds of Christ. St. Paul sets out the idea of revelation beginning with the theme of mystery and Gospel. The Epistle to the Hebrews compares the revelation of the two Covenants and extols that profferred by Christ, the Son of God. For St. John, the revealing activity of Christ is rooted in his quality as Logos and Son. These approaches to the central mystery are like complementary views of the same cathedral: they let us grasp the entire reality in its unity and in its complexity.

The New Testament makes use of a great number of words to express this economy of revelation.[1] The most frequent words are, among the verbs: *apokaluptein, phaneroun, gnôrizein, phôtizein, kèrussein, euangelizesthai, katangellein, didaskein, marturein, legein, lalein.* And among the substantives: *apokalupsis, epiphaneia kèrugma, euangelion martus, marturia, marturion, didaskalos, didachè, epistatès, gnôsis, mustèrion, logos, alètheia.* The study of one single word, *apokaluptein,* for example, would be quite inadequate to express the notion of revelation. If the presence of words tends to keep us on the alert, it must never serve as our exclusive guide. Even more than the *words* of revelation, we must be attentive to the *theme* of revelation, to the reality of revelation and the reality which makes a response to it, namely faith. This is the only adequate way to study the problem.

I. THE SYNOPTIC TRADITION

1. *The Words*

The terms which describe the revealing activity of Christ, in the synoptic tradition, are primarily: preaching, in the sense of proclaiming (*kèrussein*), preaching the Gospel (*kèrussein to euangelion*), evangelizing (*euangelizesthai*), teaching (*didaskein*), revealing (*apokaluptein*).[2] Christ is the rabbi, the doctor (teacher) who interprets the Scriptures with the authority of a master in Israel. These titles are witness to the respect of His disciples and the crowd for the eminently wise words of Jesus. In the eyes of the people, Christ also passes for a prophet: He is filled with the Spirit and the words of God are in His mouth. Like the prophets, He preaches, He works signs. These titles Christ never refuses; what is more, He claims them for Himself. For He is more than a prophet and more than a rabbi: He is the Son who shares the secrets of the Father. The events of His passion and resurrection, which unveil His true identity, led the first Christians to replace the inadequate titles of rabbi, doctor, prophet, by those of Christ, Lord, and Son of God. The fact that the synoptics have preserved these earlier titles, despite their archaic character, is already witness to their historical fidelity.[3]

In the most common perspective of the synoptics, Christ preaches and teaches: *kèrussein* and *didaskein* are easily predominant. Matthew and Luke sometimes join them in the same sentence: "He went about throughout all of Galilee, teaching in the synagogues, proclaiming the good news of the kingdom" (Mt. 4:23; 11:1; Lk. 20:1). They could also be found joined in several passages from Acts (Acts. 4:2; 5:42; 15:35; 28:31). Mark says equivalently that Christ *teaches* (Mk. 1:22) or *preaches* in the synagogues (Mk. 1:39), that He goes through the villages *teaching* (Mk. 6:6) or *preaching* (Mk. 1:38). According to Luke, Christ *teaches* or *proclaims the good news* in the Temple (Lk. 19:47; 20:1), He *preaches* or *teaches* throughout the towns and villages, on the roads and in the countryside (Lk. 13:22; 23:5). Still, it is possible to discover different nuances in these two terms. *Kèrussein* means to proclaim (in its full entirety) the unheard-of news of the Kingdom of God accomplished in Jesus Christ, whereas *didaskein* means to instruct by calling attention to the individual mysteries of faith and precepts of moral life. Whereas the *kerygma* stresses primarily the dynamic attributes of the word, the *didachè* stresses its noetic attributes. Normally, the teaching follows the impact of the first proclamation of salvation.[4]

2. *Christ as Preacher*

Through His preaching, Christ appears in continuity with the prophetic tradition. The prophets are the heralds of God, messengers and interpreters of His word (Ex. 4:15-16; 7:1; Jer. 1:9). God sends them to cry out the news (Jer. 2:2; Is. 58:1), to publish, promulgate, (Jer. 4:5; 50:2; Zech. 1:14. 17), to proclaim His Day, His will, His intentions, His promises, His threats. *Kèrussein* is frequent in Joel and Jonah to express the call to penance. Jonah, the type of the herald in the Old Testament, preaches (3:4) and, in Ninive, a public fast is promulgated (3:5), public penance is proclaimed (3:7). John the Baptist, "the prophet of the Most High" (Lk. 1:76-77), is the voice spoken of by Isaiah (Is. 40:3. 6), who precedes Yahweh and announces His coming. John is an echo of the word of God. In a powerful activity of the Spirit, John "proclaims a baptism of penance for the remission of sins" (Lk. 3:3). He is the herald of the Messiah who is to come (Mk. 1:6-8; Mt. 3:11-12; Lk. 3:16-17). The Synoptics characterize the mission of John the Baptist by the verb *kèrussein* (Mt. 3:1; Mk. 1:4. 7; Lk. 3:3).[5]

Christ inaugurates His ministry in the same manner as the prophets and the Baptist, by preaching the good news of the Kingdom and the penance which leads to the Kingdom: "Jesus began to preach and to say: Repent, for the Kingdom of Heaven is at hand" (Mt. 4:17; Mk. 1:14-15). In the synagogue at Nazareth, He applies the words of Deutero-Isaiah to Himself, words which show the Messiah as a prophet dedicated to evangelizing the poor (Lk. 4:18-19; Is. 61:1-2). In Matthew, Christ cites as a sign of His Messianic authenticity the fact that "the poor have the Gospel preached to them" (Mk. 11:5).

The essential content of His preaching is the Gospel of the Kingdom: Christ announces the inauguration of this Kingdom after John the Baptist had proclaimed its imminence (Mk. 1:15).

The people, recognizing the style of the great prophets in the preaching and miracles of Jesus, consider Him as one of the prophets. After the resurrection of the widow's son at Naim, the crowds cry out: "A great prophet has risen among us" (Lk. 7:16). Some see in Him John the Baptist, others Elijah, others Jeremiah or one of the prophets (Mt. 16:14). The Pharisees and the priests are afraid to arrest Him; the crowds take Him for a prophet (Mt. 21:46). The disciples from Emmaus speak of Jesus of Nazareth as "a prophet mighty in word and deed" (Lk. 24:19). What is more, on the basis of Deut. 18:18, the crowds refer to Jesus as *the* Prophet expected at the end of time (Mk. 6:14 ff; 8:28; Mt. 21:11). In John, those who witnessed the miracle of the multiplication of the loaves exclaim: "Truly He is *the* Prophet who is to come into the world" (Jn. 6:14).

Still, Christ, when He speaks of Himself, does not claim the title of prophet. He is aware of His affinity with the prophets: like them He penetrates the secrets of God (Mk. 4:11), and foresees for Himself the lot reserved for prophets (Mt. 13:57; Lk. 13:33). But insofar as He is a revealer, He goes far beyond all the prophets through the excellence of His person. He is greater than Jonah (Mt. 12:40), greater than Moses and Elijah (Mk. 9:2-10; Mt. 17:1-3; Lk. 9:28-36), greater than David (Mk. 12:35-37; Mt. 22:41-46; Lk. 20:41-44) and John the Baptist (Lk. 7:18-23; Mt. 11:2-6). In the parable of the vinedressers, He places Himself above the prophets just as the son is above the servants (Mk. 12:1-12). He accomplishes the law and the prophets (Mt. 5:17). He does not say: "Thus speaks Yahweh"; He says: "But I say to you" (Mt. 5:22, 28, 32).[6]

Not only does Christ preach, He also calls other men to share His mission: "And He appointed twelve that they might be with Him and that He might send them forth to preach" (Mk. 3:14). He sends them out "to proclaim the Kingdom of God and to cure the sick" (Lk. 9:2; Mt. 10:7-8). Jesus grants this power from the beginning of His life, but primarily after His resurrection: "Go out into the entire world, preach the Gospel to every creature" (Mk. 16:15. 20). The Gospel must not remain hidden: it must be "preached to all the nations" (Mk. 13:10), "throughout the entire world" (Mt. 24:14). Those who receive the message of the Apostles will be saved, the others will be condemned (Mk. 16:16; Mt. 10:14; Lk. 10:12-17). Between the preaching of Christ and that of His Apostles there is continuity.

3. *Christ as Teacher*

Christ *teaches*: He receives the title of *rabbi* (Mk. 9:5; 11:21; 14:45; Mt. 23:7; 26:25), of *didaskalos* or *epistátès* (proper to Luke, who uses it six times). *Didaskalos* is attributed to Jesus some forty times, either by the crowds or by the doctors of the law; *didaskein* comes up almost fifty times to describe His ministry. From the age of twelve, Jesus teaches in the Temple among the doctors of the Law (Lk. 2:46-47). During His public life, He teaches in the synagogue (Mk. 1:21; Mt. 4:23; 9:35); He teaches on the mountain (Mt. 5:1-2). On the eve of His passion, the evangelists show Him "teaching in the Temple" (Mk. 12:35; Lk. 19:47; 20:1; Mt. 21:23). Christ protests against those who come to arrest Him: "Everyday I was seated in the Temple teaching, and you did not arrest Me" (Mt. 26:55; Mk. 14:49). Like the other doctors in Israel, He has His disciples (Mk. 4:34; 6:37-41; 11:1-6) whom He forms and instructs in the manner of the rabbis of His time. This instruction is frequently occasional in character. Christ answers the questions of His disciples, comments on their attitudes (jealousy, vengeance, vanity, violence). He inculcates the principles of the new morality: poverty, humility, charity. Outside this occasional teaching, He also gives His apostles a more systematic instruction. He explains the meaning of His parables, for to them "It has been given to know the mysteries of the Kingdom of Heaven" (Mt. 13:10-12; Lk. 8:9-10). He enlightens them on the subject of His passion and resurrection (Mk. 8:31; 9:30-31). He has privileged conversations with them, such as the discourse following the Last Supper, where He instructs them on the essentials of His teaching. He also instructs the crowd: He sits down, explains, asks questions (Mt. 13:1-53; Mk. 10:1; 4:1-10). With the scribes and Pharisees He carries on discussions and debates (Mk. 8:11; 10:2; 3:22-30).

Christ teaches, but His teaching has an absolutely unique character. From the very beginning, His hearers are struck by this: "They were astonished at His teaching, for He taught as one having authority" (Mk. 1:22; 11:28; Lk. 4:31-32; Mt. 7:28-29). Christ stands out by the wisdom of His doctrine as well as the authority of His person. "He stirs up the people," His accusers will one day say of Him, "teaching through all Judea, from Galilee where He began, even to Jerusalem" (Lk. 23:5). Christ is not a simple rabbi: He is the Master (Mt. 23:10). The doctors of Israel are limited to commenting on the Law; Christ interprets, corrects, gives new depth. For the prescriptions

of an imperfect morality, He substitutes demands which make their
way to the very depth of the human heart. He speaks with the authority of Yahweh: "But I say to you" (Mt. 5:22. 28. 32). The man who
builds upon His words builds upon a rock foundation; otherwise, he
courts disaster (Mt. 7:24-28). "Heaven and earth will pass away,
but My words will not pass away" (Mt. 24:35). Never did He take
back a single one of His words. At the end of His ministry, He sends
out His Apostles to teach everything that He has commanded, and
He is with them "even to the consummation of the world" (Mt. 28:20).

4. Christ as the Son of the Father

If Christ, in His person, constitutes the highest possible prophetic
manifestation, if He teaches with such authority, it is because He is
the only Son, the heir (Mk. 12:6), to whom the Father has delivered
everything (Mt. 11:27), and whom the Father sends out after His
servants the prophets (Mk. 12:6). He calls God His "Father" (Mt.
7:21; 10:32-33; 11:27; 12:50), as a well-beloved son (Mk. 1:11;
12:6). "No one knows the Son excepting the Father, just as no one
knows the Father excepting the Son and He to whom the Son has
willed to reveal Him" (Mt. 11:25-27). No one knows (Lk.: *ginôskein*;
Mt.: *epiginôskein*), with that knowledge which is also experience, the
real character and intimate life of the Son, excepting the Father; and
no one knows the real character and intimate life of the Father excepting the Son. The two know each other, simply because they are
present to each other, like two equal magnitudes, of the same order.
But no one can share in this mystery of mutual knowledge without
gratuitous revelation. Christ, who is the Son, is the perfect Revealer
of the Father: He alone knows the Father and His secrets, and He
communicates this knowledge to whomever He will.[7] To the disciples
whom He has chosen, it has been "given" as a grace, to "know the
mysteries of the Kingdom of Heaven" (Mt. 13:11; Mk. 4:10-12).

The Father also reveals the Son: to the "little ones" who know
their need in the face of God, He reveals the mystery of the person of
Christ; it is through a revelation of the Father that Peter confessed
Christ for what He is (Mt. 16:17). The two revelations are complementary: the revelation of the Father makes men accept the
revelation of Jesus concerning the Father and the mysteries of the
Kingdom. Jesus teaches and preaches in vain if the Father does not
give souls the understanding of what He says. The Son cannot be
recognized for what He is without a light granted by the Father: this

grace is refused to the pride of the "wise." Acceptance of divine revelation is the work of grace.

5. Faith, the Response of Man

The Apostles, introduced by Christ into the mystery of the Father and the Son, received His word with Faith. Faith is the response which is proper to the teaching of the good news (Mk. 16:15-16). Men are invited to hear the word and to understand (Mt. 13:23), that is, to welcome the word of God in faith and live in conformity with this word (Mk. 4:20; Mt. 7:24-27; Lk. 6:47-49; 8:21; 11:28). Christ contrasts those who hear the word and put it into practice with those who hear the word without putting it into practice: He contrasts the house built on rock with the house built on sand (Mt. 7:24-27).

For many people, unfortunately, the word remains barren (Mk. 4:15-19). God reveals Himself in such an extraordinary way that revelation can become a stumbling block for men, the occasion for disbelief. The people who live in Nazareth reject Christ, for they are aware of His modest origin (Mk. 6:3). The words of Christ on the danger of riches (Mk. 10:23-27), on the suffering Messiah (Mk. 8:31; 9:31), are incomprehensible, even to the disciples. The attitudes of Christ with regard to the Jewish customs (Mk. 7:1 ff; Lk. 11:38-40) and with regard to the Sabbath (Mk. 3:1-6; Lk. 13:10-17; 14:1-6), His intercourse with publicans and sinners (Mt. 11:19; Lk. 7:34; Mk. 2:16), His claim to forgive sins (Mk. 2:5 ff; Lk. 7:48), His death on the cross (Mk. 15:29-32): all this can be a stumbling block.

Each man will be judged on his attitude towards the word. Revelation, being the proclamation of salvation, confronts men with a choice upon which depends their salvation or their condemnation: "preach the Gospel to every creature. He who believes and is baptized will be saved; he who does not believe will be condemned" (Mk. 16:15-16). The proclamation of the Kingdom is thus bound up with the call to conversion, that is to say, a return of the whole person towards God. Jesus begins His preaching with these words: "The Kingdom of God is at hand; be converted and believe in the Gospel" (Mk. 1:15; Mt. 3:2; 4:17). Tyre and Sidon, on the day of judgment, will be judged less severely than the towns of Galilee who refused to believe in the miracles of Christ (Mt. 11:20-24; Lk. 10:13-15). The Ninivites will rise up in judgment against the refusal of the Jews to accept Him who is greater than Jonah and Solomon (Mt. 12:41; Lk.

11:31). The preachers of the faith, on the day of judgment, will bear witness against those who refused their message (Mk. 6:11; 13:9; Mt. 10:15; Lk. 10:12).[8]

6. Conclusion

Thus, in the Synoptic tradition, Christ is Revealer because He proclaims the good news of the Kingdom of Heaven and teaches the word of God with authority. In the last analysis, if He reveals, it is because He is the Son who knows all the secrets of the Father. When Christ has finished His work, the Apostles, in their turn, must reveal what their Master has entrusted to them; they have to preach the Gospel of salvation, to teach, to invite men to faith. Faith, the gift of God, revelation of the Father, is man's response to the preaching of the Gospel. The essential content of revelation is the salvation offered to humanity under the figure of the Kingdom of God as preached and inaugurated by Christ. The time is accomplished: in Jesus Christ, the Kingdom of God is present and at work.[9] Christ is at once He who announces the Kingdom and He in whom the Kingdom is realized.

II. THE ACTS OF THE APOSTLES

Acts reflects the language of the primitive Church and its new faith. Little by little, beginning with the expressions of Jesus and the usage of the Septuagint, the religious vocabulary of the New Testament becomes more precise.[10]

Christ gave His apostles the mission of "preaching the Gospel" (*kèrussein to euangelion*) throughout the entire world (Mk. 16:15), "making disciples" (Mt. 28:19) and "teaching" (*didaskein*) all that He had commanded (Mt. 28:20). At the Ascension, He promised them His Spirit: "You will be witnesses to Me (*martures*) in Jerusalem, in all Judea and Samaria, and up to the very ends of the earth" (Acts 1:8). Peter declares before the centurion Cornelius that Christ ordered them to "*preach* to the people (*kèrussein*) and *witness* (*diamartu-resthai*)" that He is judge over the living and the dead (Acts 10:42). To be a witness, to preach the Gospel, to teach—this is the apostolic mission. Docile to the word of the Lord, His apostles actually do go out and "preach" (Mk. 16:20), "teach" (Acts 2:42; 4:2. 18; 5:25. 42; 11:26; 17:19; 18:11; 21:21), "witness" (1:22; 2:32; 3:15; 5:30-32; 10:39; 13:31).

1. *The Apostles Witness*

The first part of Acts insists on the terms *witness* and *bear witness*. Witness characterizes the apostolic activity immediately after the Resurrection. Those who have seen the risen Christ give witness to His return to life, stand up for Him in the face of hostile opposition.[11] Witnessing is an activity whose force is at once religious and juridic.[12]

The title of witness, in the first place, is proper to the apostles (Acts 1:8. 22; 2:32; 3:15; 5:32; 10:39. 41; 13:31). There are three characteristic traits about the apostles.[13] They were first of all chosen by God (Acts 10:41; 1:26).[14] Then, they were associates of Christ during His life and saw Him after His Resurrection. Matthias, who lived with Christ during His public life, becomes, together with the apostles, a "witness of His Resurrection" (Acts 1:22). The very best witness is one who has known the whole work of Christ, from his baptism to His resurrection, which is the crown and achievement of one single process of salvation.[15] The apostles, who followed Christ everywhere, who "ate and drank with Him after His resurrection" (Acts 10:41), will be witnesses throughout the entire world (Acts 1:8). Luke calls them "eye-witnesses and ministers of the word" (Lk. 1:2). Witness is thus the activity proper to those who have seen and heard Christ, who have lived in intimacy with Him and, as a result, possess a direct and living experience of His person, His doctrine, and His work. This is a necessary experience, for Christ did not write any book; He entrusted His living word to His apostles. Thus, only those who have seen and heard Christ, at the time of His earthly ministry, only those whom Christ long and patiently prepared, can be witness to what He did and said.[16] That is why St. John declares: "What we have seen and heard, that we announce to you" (1 Jn. 1:3). Revelation is formed by the deposition of this apostolic witness. The third trait of a witness is the mission or mandate he receives to be a witness (Acts 1:8).[17] Paul, like the apostles, is called to be a *witness*, for he was the object of a particular election: he saw the glorified Christ and received His teaching; he was sent to give witness before men (Acts 22:14-15). Christ appeared to him to make him "servant and witness" of the glory of the Risen One (Acts 26:16). In him too are verified the three conditions essential for a witness.[18] It is true that Paul was not an eye-witness of the whole earthly career of Christ, but Christ showed him the reality of His glorified life and made him understand at the same time His indentity with Jesus of Nazareth (Acts 22:6-8): this Jesus who died is now living (Acts 25:19). Paul is thus truly a witness to Christ of Nazareth, dead and risen.[19]

The apostles are first of all witnesses to the Resurrection, for the Resurrection is the essential fact which authorizes everything that comes before and everything that follows (Acts 1:22; 2:32; 3:13-16; 4:2. 33; 5:30-31; 10:39. 41. 42; 13:31); but, in a more general way, they are a witness to everything that they have seen and heard of Christ (Acts 4:20), His actions as well as His teachings (Acts 1:1). They are witnesses to His whole career (Acts 1:21), from baptism to Resurrection: "We are witnesses to everything He did in the country of the Jews and in Jerusalem" (Acts 10:39). They are witnesses to the work of salvation inaugurated by His death and Resurrection: God raised Him up "to grant repentance to Israel and forgiveness of sins. And we are witnesses of these things." (Acts 5:31). God "charged us to preach to the people and to testify that He it is who has been appointed by God to be judge of the living and the dead" (Acts 10:42). The apostles are witnesses to the whole of Christ's work: the activity that led towards His passion and Resurrection and the work that the passion and Resurrection set in motion.[20]

The testimony of the apostles is accomplished in the power of the Holy Spirit: "You will receive a power, that of the Holy Spirit. . . . You will then be My witnesses" (Acts 1:8), that is, the Holy Spirit, teaching you and strengthening you, will give you power to bear witness to Me. This, according to Acts, is the activity of the Spirit.[21] He instructs the apostles: their testimony gives evidence of a superior knowledge of Scripture and surpasses what one might expect of mere men "without education or culture" (Acts 4:13). The Spirit gives them courage and constancy to be witnesses despite the hostility they encounter (Acts 4:8. 31; 5:32; 6:10). Having received the Spirit, the apostles "with much power, bore witness to the Resurrection" (Acts 4:33). When they bear witness, the Spirit bears witness with them (Acts 5:32); His power sustains them and acts upon their listeners to attract them, to convince them, to overcome their arguments if they resist. The Spirit helps them, sustains them with His power, particularly in times of persecution, when they must confess Christ not only with their lips, but by their suffering. The Holy Spirit is with the Apostles who suffer persecution before the Sanhedrin (Acts 4:8; 5:41). He is with Stephen (Acts 6:1-15) whose confession and condemnation call to mind the testimony of Christ (Acts 7:54-60). Clothed thus in the Spirit, intrepid and invulnerable in the midst of their enemies, supported by the strength of God, the apostles belong to the prophets of the Old Testament. The prophets bore witness to the salvation that was to come, in an atmosphere of hostility and persecution; the apostles bear witness to the salvation that has been accomplished (Acts 10:43; 26:22), also in an atmosphere of persecution (Acts 4:7; 5:27; 7:58). One day, like Christ their Master, they will have to confess Christ to the point of martyrdom (Jn. 21:19), completing thus in themselves the image of Christ, the perfect Witness, (1 Tim. 6:13). In the Apocalypse (11:3), when the "two witnesses," that is, the prophets and the apostles, have given their witness, the Beast rises out of the abyss and puts them to death (Apoc. 11:7). But three days later they rise into Heaven, in the face of their enemies (Apoc. 11:12). Between Christ, Witness of the Father, and the apostles, witnesses to Christ, there is a continuity in mission, in testimony, in death, in glory.[22]

2. The Apostles Proclaim the Gospel

The *witness* of the apostles is spread by their *preaching* or *kerygma*. If these terms overlap in the concrete activity of the Apostles, it remains true that *bearing witness* is a properly apostolic activity, based on a privileged situation (that of those who have seen and heard), whereas *kèrussein* stresses the dynamic and public character of this testimony and can be just as well applied to preachers other than the apostles (Acts 15:35; 18:25). *Testimony* implies fidelity to an experience and courage to make it known. *Kerygma* implies the element of publicity, power, spread, public notice. Thus, Peter, on the day of Pentecost, stands before the crowd and calls out the good news of salvation through Christ at the top of his voice; he wants to make it public, known, official (Acts 2:14). Philip "proclaims" Christ to the Samaritans (Acts 8:5). The apostles receive the order to "preach to the people" (Acts 10:42). From the time of his conversion, Paul "proclaims" that Jesus is Son of God (Acts 9:20); he "proclaims the Kingdom" (Acts 20:25), the "Kingdom of God" (Acts 28:31). The word *euangelizesthai* is also found with the same meaning as *kèrussein*. Peter and John "evangelize" numerous Samaritan villages (Acts 8: 25). Philip "announces the good news of Jesus" to the Ethiopian eunuch (Acts 8:35). Paul and Barnabas "evangelize" the village of Derbe (Acts 14:21). In a vision, Paul understands that he must "evangelize" Macedonia (Acts 16:10).

Evangelize and *teach* are often paired together. The apostles, released by the Sanhedrin, do not cease "teaching and proclaiming the good news of Jesus" in the Temple and in private homes (Acts 5:42). Paul and Barnabas, at Antioch, "teach and announce the good news"

(Acts 15:35). Apollo "preaches and teaches" whatever concerns Jesus (Acts 18:25). At Rome, Paul "proclaims" the Kingdom of God and "teaches more about the Lord Jesus Christ" (Acts 28:31).[23]

The official public intention of the kerygma is obvious in many ways. Peter and Paul address themselves to the crowds (Acts 1:15-22; 3:12; 13:16) or to groups (Acts 10:44). They speak in the open air, in the synagogues, before the Sanhedrin. The preaching of the apostles is clear and open and begins to spread through both Jewish and Gentile circles. The attitudes of Peter and Paul are those of heralds. Peter "stands up" with the eleven and raises his voice (Acts 2:14). Their public discourse abounds in calls for attention, official summons in the name of God: lend you ear (Acts 2:14), hear (Acts 2:22), do penance (Acts 2:38), save yourselves (Acts 2:40). Everything about the apostles shows their consuming desire to spread the word of God everywhere and to everybody. Paul tries to reach the great cultural centers: Damascus, Corinth, Ephesus, Athens, Rome. After Pentecost, men from all nations hear the word (Acts 2:5). In the person of Cornelius, it is the world of the Gentiles to whom Peter addresses his message (Acts 10:35. 45). The word of the Gospel is dynamic, explosive. It is the will of Christ that His preachers reach the whole universe and all its inhabitants. The heralds of *Acts*, under the influence of the Spirit, are seized with a sort of fever, which forces them to cry out, to proclaim, to announce, to evangelize. They cannot keep silence about the salvation given through Christ.[24]

The proclamation of the Gospel is a work performed with sovereign assurance, for it is confirmed and sustained by signs of power (Acts 2:43; 3:16; 5:12. 14; 8:6; 9:35. 42; 13:12). Strong with the promise of Christ, the Apostles are not afraid to perform or request these signs (Acts 4:30). Scenes from the life of Christ are reviewed in their activity: "And there came also multitudes from the towns near Jerusalem, bringing the sick and those troubled with unclean spirits, and they were all cured" (Acts 5:16; 8:6-8; 19:11-12). God, through these signs, *accredits* His envoys before the hearers of the word and fills them with *assurance*: "Paul and Barnabas prolonged their sojourn for some time (at Iconium), *full of assurance* in the Lord who *bore witness* to their preaching with His grace, by working signs and wonders through their hands (Acts 14:3; 19:8). More precisely, these miracles confirm the testimony of those who claim to have seen Christ risen. The power at their disposal is proof of the fact that, really arisen and glorified by God, Jesus has once again put on omnipotence. Worked *in the name of Jesus* (Acts 3:6; 4:30), these wonders manifest the glory which is conferred on Him at the moment of His Resurrection. Jesus has a name which can operate miracles for those who believe in Him.[25]

3. The Object of Witness and Preaching

What the Apostles preach, teach, witness to, and what their hearers are invited to listen to and receive, is Christ (Acts 5:42; 8:5.35; 9:20; 18:5) or the word of Christ (Acts 15:35) or the word about Christ (Acts 18:25; 28:31). This word, as in the Old Testament, is the word of God (Acts 18:11; 4:29-31), the word of the Lord (Acts 13:48; 16:32). More precisely, what the Apostles preach, teach, witness to, is the good news of salvation through Christ. Englightened by the fact of Easter, the Apostles proclaim "that there is no other Name under heaven given to men by which we must be saved" (Acts 4:12). Peter tells Cornelius: "God has sent His word to the children of Israel, announcing the good news of peace through Jesus Christ: it is He who is Lord of all" (Acts 10:36; Heb. 1:1-2). In Jesus Christ, glorified by His Resurrection and made Lord of all, mankind is now reconciled. Peter speaks of "the word of the Gospel" (Acts 15:7) and Paul, of the "Gospel of grace" (Acts 20:24). Concretely, the word of God is thus the Gospel message (Acts 8:4; 14:7), the "message of salvation" (Acts 13:26), that is, the word which announces and leads to salvation.

In more explicit terms, the content of this word is first of all the fact that Jesus is risen (Acts 2:32; 3:15; 5:30; 10:41; 13:31) and that, by the Resurrection, He has been established judge of the living and the dead (Acts 10:42), Lord and Christ (Acts 2:36). It is through Him that salvation is granted: He is "Prince of life" (Acts 3:15), "Savior" (Acts 5:31; 13:23) outside of whom there is not any salvation (Acts 4:12; 5:31; 10:43). He is the culmination and fulfillment of the whole prophetic history (Acts 3:18. 21. 24. 25). Salvation is accomplished through faith in Christ and through baptism (Acts 2:41; 11:21; 18:8) which effects remission of sins (Acts 2:38; 5:31; 10:43; 13:38) and confers the Holy Spirit, the salvific gift (Acts 2:38). The mark of the Christian is to be "filled with the Spirit" (Acts 6:5; 9:17; 11:24; 13:52) and ruled by Him.[26]

4. Faith, Man's Response

The response proper to the kerygma and to the testimony of the apostles is faith.[27] Acts describes the constant growth in the number of believers under the activity of the word (Acts 2:41; 4:4; 5:14;

6:7; 9:42; 11:21; 13:43. 48; 14:1). At the beginning, there is preaching which presents faith with its object (Acts 11:20-21). To believe means to "receive the word" (Acts 2:41; 11:1), the "good news of the Kingdom" (Acts 8:12), the "good news of the Lord Jesus" (Acts 11:20), "the good news of Jesus" (Acts 8:35). Peter was chosen so that the pagans could hear from his mouth "the word of the good news and embrace the faith" (Acts 15:7). At Iconium, Paul and Barnabas "spoke in such a way that a great crowd of Jews and Greeks embraced the faith" (Acts 14:1). Many Corinthians "who heard Paul, embraced the faith and had themselves baptized" (Acts 18:8; 17:11-12. 34; 13:48).[28]

This faith, in Acts, has something global about it. It is adherence to Christ, absolute and total: it is faith in the Lord Jesus (Acts 16:31), faith in the Lord Jesus Christ (Acts 9:42; 11:17), faith in the Name of Jesus (Acts 3:16). It is giving to Christ; it accepts everything of Christ and everything He means. Also it implies a "conversion": a man believes in the Lord and is converted (Acts 11:21).

Faith is not a human work. Together with the invitation of the apostles' preaching, from without, strengthened with the signs that accompany it and give it divine credentials, God is at work within, to make His word assimilated in the soul. The apostle preaches, but God acts within through His grace, which *gives the power* to receive the word that is heard and cling to it in faith. Lydia heard the preaching of Paul: "The Lord opened her heart, such that she clung to the words of Paul" (Acts 16:14). Beginning with Pentecost, the apostles and the Spirit, the Church and the Spirit, work together to increase the Church (Acts 9:31). The mystery of the growth of the Church is the fruit of the word of preaching made fertile by the Spirit. This is because Christ, in making the apostles His witnesses and messengers, follows their mission with the sending of His Spirit (Acts 1:8).

The drama here is that man can close himself up in his own thinking and resist the word: such is the case of the Pharisee who is deliberately blind (Acts 4:16), and who stuffs his ears in order not to hear (Acts 7:57), or the Greek who jokes about the mystery (Acts 17:18. 32), or the dissolute man who hardens himself against faith (Acts 26:28), or the administrator who lacks purity of soul and sees only his own advantage in things (Acts 24:25-26), or the Jew who does not accept the universality of the divine plan (Acts 14:2). Self-sufficiency, whether it is religious, philosophical, or cultural in nature, gives rise to scorn, disdain, inattention. The call of God requires an attitude of attentiveness. Cornelius (Acts 10:1-2), Lydia (Acts 16:14), the proconsul Sergius Paulus (Acts 13:7-12): these all listen, receive, obey. Through His word, God lays bare the heart of man and forces him to take a stand. This is a tragic choice: one that either saves or condemns. It is a drama of light and shadows called into play by the coming of Christ and meeting with Him.

5. Conclusion

Acts describes the apostolic activity as a continuity with the activity of Christ. The Apostles heard Christ speak, preach, teach, reveal (Synoptic tradition). They receive from Him the mission to be witnesses to His Resurrection and to His work, to preach and teach what He had ordered and taught. Faithful to their mission, they give testimony to the risen Christ, Messiah and Lord; they preach the Gospel of Salvation, they announce the good news, they teach the doctrine of their Master. Their function is that of *witness* and *herald*. Their deposition, what they set down, makes up the object of our faith. The revelation handed down to the Church is contained in this apostolic testimony, that is, in the word of the Apostles inviting us to believe what Christ did and said. Faith, response to this teaching, is a divine work, set in motion by the Spirit who works within and makes fruitful the word that is heard from without.

III. SAINT PAUL

The theme of *mystery* and *Gospel* is the principal theme St. Paul uses to reach to the very heart of the idea of revelation. St. Paul is an Apostle in order to announce the good news of the mystery revealed by God.[29]

1. The Words

The very grouping of words already outlines the course of his thought on revelation. God unveils (*apokaluptein*), makes manifest (*phaneroun*), makes known (*gnôrizein*), casts light on (*phôtizein*). The apostles speak (*lalein*), preach (*kèrussein*), teach (*didaskein*), announce the good news (*katangellein*), give witness (*marturein*), and thus communicate the word (*logos*), the preaching (*kèrugma*), the witness (*marturion*), the mystery (*mustèrion*), the Gospel (*euangelion*).[30] The doxology which closes the letter to the Romans well illustrates this diversity and richness in the economy of revelation: "Now to Him who is able to strengthen you in accordance with my Gospel, and the preaching of Jesus Christ, according to the revelation of the mystery which has been kept in silence from eternal ages, which is manifested now through the writings of the prophets according to the precepts of the eternal God, and made known to all the Gentiles to bring about obedience and faith . . . to the only wise God, through Jesus Christ, be honor forever and ever. Amen" (Rom. 16:25-26). Thus, in Jesus Christ, the mystery which was heretofore hidden and kept secret (mustèrion), is now unveiled, revealed (apokaluptein) and made manifest (phaneroun); it has been brought to the knowledge of the nations (gnôrizein) through the Gospel (euangelion) and the preaching (kèrugma), in order to lead them to faith and obedience (upakoè pisteôs). The same language is found in the letter to the Colossians: "His minister I have become in virtue of the office that God has given me in your regard. For I am to fulfill the word of God —the mystery which has been hidden for ages and generations, but now is clearly shown through His saints" (Col. 1:25-26).

2. The Pauline Mystery

The theology of Saint Paul is a soteriology, whose fundamental intuition is summed up in the notion of mystery.[31] In all its fullness, the term appears principally in the captivity letters; there it refers to the divine plan of salvation as manifested and realized through Christ.[32] This meaning, however, is anticipated in 1 Cor. 2:7-8 and in Rom. 16:25. In the letter to the Corinthians, St. Paul stresses the "mysterious" character of the wisdom which had presided over the economy of salvation: secret wisdom, hidden in God and entirely supernatural, which has for its object the splendor of the good things that God has destined for His elect.[33] In the letter to the Romans, attention is concentrated on the Gentiles and their share in these blessings through faith (Rom. 16:25-27). Before this, the pagans had been, as it were, banned from salvation, which was reserved for the Jews. The divine plan to save them too and to call them to the "hope of glory" through union with Christ is finally revealed (Col. 1:25-28). The mystery is now unveiled: "Namely, that the Gentiles are joint heirs, and fellow-members of the same body, and joint partakers of the promise in Christ Jesus through the Gospel" (Eph. 3:6). The first chapter of the letter to the Ephesians enlarges upon this vision: the mystery is the reunion of all things in Christ, the submission of all persons to Christ, "to re-establish all things in Christ, both those in the heavens and those on the earth" (Eph. 1:10). Joining the different elements of these texts, we might say that the mystery of which St. Paul speaks is the divine plan of salvation, hidden from all eternity and now revealed, through which God establishes Christ as the center of His new economy of salvation, constituting Him, through His death and Resurrection, the one sole principle of salvation, both for Gentile and for Jew, the Head of all persons, angels and men; this is the whole divine plan (Incarnation, Redemption, election to glory) which, in the last analysis, all goes back to Christ, with His unfathomable riches (Eph. 3:8), His treasures of wisdom and knowledge (Col. 2:2-3). Concretely, the mystery is Christ (Rom. 16:25; Col. 1:26-27; 1 Tim. 3:16).[34] The world, created in unity, returns to unity through Christ, Savior and Head. Thus, in the description of the mystery, St. Paul, at the very outset lays great stress on the vocation of the Gentiles; then, in the captivity letters, the mystery becomes principally Christ and participation in Christ. Everything is "recapitulated" in Christ: in His manifestation, in the blessings which He represents, in the path He traces out towards God.[35]

3. Stages in the Revelation of the Mystery

This mystery can be studied on different levels: on the level of intention (the mystery of God); on the level of realization, in Christ and through Christ (the mystery of Christ); on the level of personal encounter (the mystery of the Gospel, the mystery of the word and of faith); on the level of its extension in humanity (the mystery of the Church). The revelation of the mystery is accomplished in successive stages which correspond to these different levels, describing the history of salvation.

In its initial phase, the mystery is hidden in God: a secret full of wisdom (1 Cor. 2:7), surrounded in silence during the times of eternity (Rom. 16:25), hidden from the generations who have passed (Eph. 3:5; Col. 1:26), hidden even from the heavenly spirits (Eph. 3:9-10). Wisdom inaccessible, knowledge reserved.

But "now" the mystery heretofore hidden is manifested, revealed (Rom. 16:25; Col. 1:26). Through the life, death, and Resurrection of Christ, the mystery has entered into its phase of realization; in Jesus Christ the salvific plan of God is once and for all accomplished and unveiled (Eph. 1:7-9); the mystery becomes an event of history (1 Tim. 3:16). In the divine economy, the mystery is communicated first of all to privileged witnesses: the Apostles and prophets in the Spirit (Eph. 3:5; Col. 1:26). These are the mediators and heralds of the mystery (Eph. 3:5). Through their preaching, they are the foundation of the Church, in which Christ is the cornerstone (Eph. 1:22-23; 2:20-21).[36] Paul belongs to this group of privileged souls: he is "a minister of the Church" (Col. 1:25-26) and, in the revelation of the mystery he occupies a choice position. That aspect of the mystery which concerns the Gentiles has been especially revealed to him: "Yes, to me, the very least of all the saints, there was given this grace, to announce among the Gentiles the good tidings of the unfathomable riches of Christ, and to enlighten all men as to what is the dispensation of the mystery which has been hidden from eternity in God" (Eph. 3:8-9). He has been called by God and "set apart" (Rom. 1:1) to be "preacher and Apostle..., teacher of the pagans in the faith and in the truth" (1 Tim. 2:7), "priest of the Gospel of God, so that the pagans will become an agreeable offering, sanctified in the Holy Spirit" (Rom. 15:16). By reason of this vocation, he has received a very deep understanding of the mystery (Eph. 3:3-4).

Once it is revealed to chosen witnesses, the mystery is made known to all who are called to the Church. The task of the Apostles is to proclaim the content of this mystery, the Gospel. St. Paul establishes a "concrete" equivalence between Gospel and mystery (Rom. 16:25; Col. 1:25-26; Eph. 1:9-13; 3:5-6). Both cases treat one and the same reality, that is, the divine plan of salvation, but as seen under two different aspects. On the one hand, there is a *secret*, unveiled, revealed, manifested, transmitted, or communicated; on the other hand, there is good news, a message announced and proclaimed.[37] The Gospel is made known just as the mystery is made known; we share in the Gospel (Eph. 3:6) just as we share in the mystery (Col. 1:27).[38] Divine plan hidden and revealed, divine plan proclaimed: Gospel and mystery have the same common object or content. This object is twofold: soteriological, that is, the whole economy of salvation through Christ (Eph. 1:1-10), and eschatological, that is, the promise of glory with all the blessings destined for the elect, the fruits of the cross and death of Christ (Col. 1:28; 1 Cor. 2:7; Eph. 1:18). The mystery made known to men through the preaching of the Gospel shows up as the plan for salvation arrived at the stage of personal event.

This good news of salvation St. Paul calls "Gospel," without further qualification (1 Thess. 2:4), or "Gospel of God" (Rom. 1:1; 15:16; 2 Cor. 11:7; 1 Thess. 2:2. 8-9), because it has God for author and object,[39] or, once again, "Gospel of Christ" (Rom. 15:19-20; 2 Cor. 2:12; 8:13; 10:14; Gal. 1:7; Phil. 1:27), "the Gospel of our Lord Jesus" (2 Thess. 1:8), "the Gospel of the glory of Christ" (2 Cor. 4:4).[40]

In the place of Gospel, but with the same technical meaning and Christian message, St. Paul also uses the term *word* (Col. 1:25-26; 1 Thess. 1:6), or word of God (1 Thess. 2:13; Rom. 9:6; 1 Cor.

14:36), or word of the Lord (1 Thess. 1:8; 4:15; 2 Thess. 3:1), or word of Christ (Rom. 10:17). Through this word, which is the message of God in a human mouth, it is always God who speaks and questions humanity (Rom. 10:14). St. Paul gives thanks to God because the Thessalonians have received the word announced through him, "not like a human word, but for what it really is, the word of God" (1 Thess. 2:13).[41] Because it is divine, this word is active. It is "word of salvation" (Eph. 1:13), "word of life" (Phil, 2:16), "word of truth" (2 Cor. 6:7; Col. 1:5; 2 Tim. 2:15), "word of reconciliation" (2 Cor. 5:19), not only because it has for its object truth, life, reconciliation, and salvation, but also because it offers and procures salvation, because it leads to life (Rom. 1:16; 1 Cor. 1:21; 1 Thess. 2:13; Eph. 1:13).[42] The work of God is twofold: at the same time that He effects the reconciliation of the world through Christ, God establishes the "word of reconciliation" (2 Cor. 5:18-19). "Side by side with what is done through Christ appears that which is done through His word. The two operations are salvific works of Christ".[43]

Since this mystery is the reunion of Jew and Gentile in Christ, in one and the same organism of salvation, the Church appears as the definitive terminus of this mystery, the striking realization of the divine economy, its visible and abiding expression. The plan of salvation is not only revealed and proclaimed by the Gospel, but also realized effectively in the Church. The objective establishment of the Church, which is the manifestation of this mystery, reveals to the powers of heaven the infinite wisdom of God's plan (Eph. 3:10) and announces that the time has come for the submission of all things to Christ (Col. 1:16). Just as Christ is the mystery of God made visible, so the Church is the mystery of Christ made visible.[44]

4. *Man's Response*

Access to the mystery, to the Gospel, to the word, is achieved through faith. Through faith man recognizes the plan of salvation, realized by God in the death and Resurrection of Christ, as true, even though it is embarrassing for human wisdom (1 Cor. 1:17-30; 2:1-4), and he clings to it completely. The preaching of the Gospel or the mystery revealed by God is aimed at "obedience to the faith" (Rom. 16:26; 2 Cor. 10:5). Faith is the specific response of man to the word of the Gospel. "This is what we preach and this is what you have believed," St. Paul reminds the Corinthians (1 Cor. 15:11). After having heard the "word of truth," the "good news" of their "salvation,"

the Ephesians believed (Eph. 1:13). It is through faith in this message
that Christians are open to salvation.[45]

The word demands to be heard, received, kept. Just as in the
Synoptic tradition and in the Acts of the Apostles, the good news is
meant for men who are not self-sufficient, men who are conscious of
their weakness, of their need, open to the gift that is offered. Faith is
possible only for those who want to hear the word of truth (Rom.
10:18: èkousan) and are ready to obey it (Rom. 10:16: upèkousan).
For St. Paul, faith is hearing the word (Rom. 10:16; Gal. 3:5: akoè
pisteôs) and obedience to the Gospel (Rom. 1:5; Rom. 16:26: upakoè
pisteôs).

This adherence and this submission to the Gospel message cannot
be accomplished by purely natural means. There must be a gift of
grace: an "illumination" from God comparable to the creation of
light on the first day (2 Cor. 4:5-6), an "anointing" of God (2 Cor.
1:21-22), stirring up faith in the hearts of those who hear the
Gospel.[46]

The word of God is not only the statement of truths; it is
primarily the presentation of Christ's person, as Lord and Savior,
with the meaning that such a personality implies for every man. The
preaching of the Gospel is thus the occasion and the setting for a
choice. For some, the Gospel is a scandal, a stumbling block (Rom.
9:32-33; 1 Cor. 1:23; Gal. 5:11), a folly (1 Cor. 1:18. 21. 23). It
remains veiled (2 Cor. 4:4). The unbelievers, those who are not docile
to the truth (Rom. 2:8; 10:21; 11:30-32; 15:31), those who have
no ears to hear the Gospel of salvation (Rom. 11:7-10), are on the
road to perdition (1 Cor. 1:19; 2 Cor. 4:3). All those who do not
believe, but take the side of iniquity, will be condemned (2 Thess.
2:11). The Gospel exercises its power of salvation and life only for
those who believe (Rom. 1:16-17; Gal. 3:11; 1 Cor. 1:18. 20; Phil.
2:16; 2 Tim. 1:10). The Gospel preaching is thus the prelude to the
day of final judgment.[47]

5. Depth of the Mystery

The knowledge of the mystery and the Gospel is a dynamic
knowledge, one that can always be perfected. It can constantly grow
in Christians, beginning with the initial knowledge that is given with
faith. Thus we can distinguish different levels in the knowledge of the
mystery. Still, this progress is bound up with certain conditions. The
man who wants to penetrate the wisdom of the divine plan and
measure its depth must bring to that work a soul transformed by the

Spirit: he needs a certain religious maturity. The Corinthians, imperfect and indocile, made themselves incapable of understanding the mysterious wisdom of God (1 Cor. 3:1-3). This knowledge is given only to the perfect (1 Cor. 2:6; Phil. 3:15; Eph. 4:12-13), to the spiritual (1 Cor. 13:1), that is, to Christians who are spiritually mature. These Christians, docile to the Spirit (1 Cor. 2:10. 15), lead a life in keeping with their faith. And the Spirit communicates to them a knowledge that is steeped in charity (Col. 2:2-3; 1 Cor. 2:6), which gives them the power to "understand" all the dimensions of the mystery and of the love of Christ which it manifests (Eph. 3:14-19; Col. 2:2-3), a knowledge which leads them to a constantly deeper understanding, a sort of super-knowledge of the economy of salvation (Phil. 1:9-11). This knowledge, in St. Paul, is of the mystical order. But every Christian is called to growth in the knowledge of this mystery. This wisdom is not a knowledge reserved for the initiated, but a gift which St. Paul asks for every Christian (Eph. 1:17-18).[48]

6. Historical Revelation and Eschatological Revelation

Outside this knowledge of faith and love, under the influence of the Spirit, there exists another revelation, an eschatological one, which will be full unveiling and full vision (1 Cor. 13:12). St. Paul vehemently longs for this final apocalypse. We can discover, in his thinking, a sort of tension between the first and last revelation. To understand this state of soul, we must examine the decisive experience in his life: the revelation of Christ on the road to Damascus (Gal. 1:16; Acts 9:3-9). At this moment, Paul was "seized by the Christ Jesus" (Phil. 3:12); he understood that Jesus of Nazareth, crucified, is now in His glory, exalted at the right hand of the Father. Paul was then converted through the vision of Christ risen and glorified (1 Cor. 15:3-8; 9:1; Gal. 1:15-16), exercising a divine power. He was honored with an apocalypse of the Son of God (1 Thess. 1:10; Col. 3:3-4). This is an anticipation in some way of the glorious epiphany of the end of time.[49]

This fundamental experience helps us to grasp the contrast which St. Paul sets up between the revelation of history and the revelation of the parousia, between the first and final epiphany of Christ, the first one veiled, the last one glorious (Phil. 2:5-11). The revelation which he announces is the revelation brought by the Christ of history: it is "now" that the mystery heretofore hidden is revealed (Rom. 16:25); it is "now" that the justice of God is manifest (Rom. 3:21); it is "now" that the preaching of the Gospel is accomplished. The revelation which constitutes the object of our faith is no longer something to be waited for: it is accomplished through Christ and in Christ. And St. Paul has received a mission, together with the Apostles, to proclaim this revelation. But he still has a much deeper desire for the eschatalogical revelation. Then will be realized in its fullness the "revelation of our Lord Jesus Christ" (1 Cor. 1:7; 2 Thess. 1:7). Men will witness the triumph of the Lord who will reveal before the eyes of all men the glory proper to the Son of God. Then also will appear the glory of all those who have become one with Christ (Rom. 8:17-19). This tension between history and eschatology, between the economy of the word and the economy of the vision, between humility and glory, is characteristic of St. Paul.

7. Finality of the Mystery

The immediate goal of the revelation of the mystery and the preaching of the Gospel is to lead men to obedience to the faith (Rom. 16:26), then to "make all men perfect in Christ" (Col. 1:28), to build up "a holy temple in the Lord," an "abode of God in the Spirit" (Eph. 2:21-22), to form "this body of Christ" which is the Church (Eph. 1:33; 6:16; 5:23. 30), this "perfect man" who "realizes the fullness of Christ" (Eph. 4:13). But, finally, the revelation of the mystery, as the letter to the Ephesians points out constantly, is "for the praise of the glory and the grace" of God (Eph. 1:6. 12. 14; Phil. 2:11). St. Paul, setting out the riches of the mystery (election, filiation, redemption), is overcome by the magnificence of this plan of salvation (Eph. 1:14), the work of the infinite wisdom of God (1 Cor. 2:7; Rom. 11:23; Col. 2:2-3) and the unheard-of manifestation of His charity towards man. The mystery reveals an abyss of wisdom and love: "God, who is rich in mercy, by reason of His very great love wherewith He has loved us even when we were dead by reason of our sins, brought us to life together with Christ . . . , that he might show in the ages to come the overflowing riches of His grace in kindliness towards us in Christ Jesus" (Eph. 2:4-7; 1:1-14). Response to such great wisdom and love must be the adherence of love to this plan and, in the example of St. Paul, a hymn of perpetual praise and thanksgiving.

8. Conclusion

Revelation, according to St. Paul, can thus be defined as the free and gratuitous activity through which God, in Christ and through Christ, manifests to the world His economy of salvation, that is, His eternal plan for re-uniting all things in Christ, Savior and Head of new creation. The communication of this plan is accomplished by the Gospel preaching, entrusted to the Apostles and prophets of the New Testament. The obedience of faith is man's response to the Gospel preaching, under the illuminating activity of the Holy Spirit. It is not a tyrannical demand on the part of God, but free consent of love to the plan of the infinite wisdom and charity of God. Faith inaugurates a constantly growing process of knowledge of this mystery, which will never be complete until the revelation of vision.

IV. THE EPISTLE TO THE HEBREWS

The Epistle to the Hebrews[50] is addressed to Judeo-Christians. It proposes to show the excellence of Christ as Mediator, and the superiority of His priesthood over that of the Old Covenant. The whole demonstration is based upon this play of contrasts, of opposites, between the two economies. The theme of revelation itself is impregnated by this climate and takes the form of a comparison between the revelation of the Old and New Testaments. The Judeo-Christians, whom the author addresses, are undergoing a crisis in their faith, and are tempted to return to the cult and liturgy of the Old Testament. Hence the pressing exhortation to faith, docility, obedience, endurance. The novelty of the Epistle to the Hebrews, insofar as it is related to the history of the very concept of revelation, lies in these two points: comparison between the revelation of the New and the Old Testament, the grandeur of the demands of the Word of God.

1. Revelation in the Old and New Testaments

The relationship between the revelation in the two Testaments is established from the very first verse of the Epistle: "God, who at sundry times and in divers manners spoke in times past to the fathers by the prophets, last of all in these days has spoken to us by His Son, a Son whom He has appointed to inherit all things" (1:1-2). This verse sets forth the authority of the revelation of the New Testament, as well as the historical relationship between the two phases of the history of salvation. Between these two economies, lies the relationship of *continuity* (God spoke), of *difference* (times, modes, mediators, recipients), and *excellence* (superiority of the new economy).

The element of *continuity* between the two revelations is *God* and *His word*, the word of the Son being the continuation and completion of the word of which the prophets were the instruments. This continuity is implicit in the very words: *God spoke*. This word, by which God intervened in history to manifest His will and His design for salvation, is a word of *authority*, uttered to be heard with attention (2:1; 12:25), to be believed (3:12-19; 4:2-3; 10:22. 38-39; 11; 13:7-9), to be obeyed (10:36; 11:8; 12:9). The absence of a direct object to the verb *lalein* stresses the interpersonal character of that word: communication between God and our fathers in the faith, between God and us, for the purpose of a personal communion. This word, finally, is essentially historical in character (an aspect pointed out by aorists), because it occurs at determined moments in time and is addressed to free beings whose free decision alters history. The word of God, in the Old Testament, announced and prepared the word of the Son, more eloquent than the blood of Abel (12:24).

Between the revelation of the Old and the New Testament, there is continuity and resemblance, but also *difference* and *surpassing*. Difference, firstly, as to *times* the same God, who once spoke to us in the long distant past, also spoke to us in this final stage of history in which we live. Secondly, difference in the modes of revelation in both Testaments: a successive, partial, fragmentary word in the Old Testament (*polumerôs*), where each communication brings out a sentence of the discourse or manifasts a part of God's plan; conversely, in the New Testament the total word of the Son. *Multiform* word (*polutropôs*) of the Old Testament, expressing itself in the form of promises, orders and threats; of terrible or familiar theophanies; of oracles, of dreams and visions; of rites and institutions. This multiplicity of forms resolves itself, in the New Testament, into the unity of the Person of the Son incarnate, expressing Himself by means of the flesh, that is, by gesture, word and action. Thirdly, difference in the *recipients*: in the Old Testament, God spoke to the fathers, that is, to the chosen people, to our ancestors in the faith, who transmitted to us the promises of which they were the depositaries; now it is to all those to whom the Gospel of Christ is addressed, preachers and listeners, that God speaks. Fourthly, difference in the *mediators* of the revelation. On the one hand, the multitude of the inspired: the prophets and all those whom God used to lead His people. God Himself spoke through them, instilling His words in them and making them His interpreters. On the other hand, the One Son, this Son, whose quality is then explained: heir of all things, through whom God created this world of time, the radiance of His glory, the full expression of His being (1:2-3). This Son is the sole Mediator in the New Testament, both on the level of revelation and on the level of priesthood. He is the sole and definitive Revealer in person. St. John will say: "No one has ever seen God; the only-begotten Son who is in the bosom of the Father, he has revealed Him" (Jn. 1:18). Ultimately, it is the Person of the Son who constitutes the superiority of the new revelation over the old.

The theme of the excellence of the new revelation reappears in the parenthesis of chapter 2:1-4, which is also linked with the introduction to the Epistle, with a nuance however. In the introduction, the parallel concerns the prophets and the Son; here, the angels and the Lord. It is a matter of the revelation of the Old Testament made through the intermediary of the angels, and of the revelation of the New Testament made by the Son and His witnesses. In order to stress the change of economy from one Testament to the other, the author of the Epistle opposes the *word* proclaimed by the angels to the *salvation* proclaimed by the Lord (2:2-3). Christ, in fact, brought us more than a word: he brought salvation itself, inaugurated by His own preaching. This salvation, accomplished and "notified" by the Lord, was attested to us by the immediate hearers of Christ (2:3; Lk. 1:2), God supporting their testimony by *signs* of His intervention, *prodigies* or extraordinary facts, *works of divine power* and by visible *charisms* or communications of the Spirit (2:4). This describes the whole economy of the new revelation: the revelation is the word of salvation proclaimed by the Lord or the Son, received and attested to by His direct witnesses, confirmed by God Himself by means of signs and charisms.

Other texts also stress how much the revelation of the Old Testament remains attached to the cosmic plan, in other words to a mediator belonging to the earthly world (12:21), to cosmic phenomena (mountain, fire, darkness, storm: 12:18-21. 25-26), to a cosmic, fabricated temple (9:1), whose rites reveal its insufficiency (9:8-10). The new revelation, on the contrary, comes to us from Heaven (12:22-24) and from a heavenly mediator, Jesus (12:24), who inaugurates a "new, a living approach" through the veil of His flesh (10:20).

2. Grandeur and Exigencies of the Word of God

The second theme stressed by the Epistle to the Hebrews is the theme of the grandeur and the exigencies of the word of God in an aspect of confrontation of the two Testaments.

At the beginning of the Epistle, after having illustrated, by a series of contrasts, the superiority of Christ over the angels (1:5-14), the author draws a practical conclusion for the intention of his readers: the necessity of a more attentive docility to the word of the Lord (2:1). We must obey the Gospel even more than the Law, in order not to risk drifting away, and be excluded from the economy of salvation. If, as a matter of fact, "all transgression and disobedience" to a Law proclaimed by angels only received its just retribution, how can we escape the just punishment if we neglect the salvation proclaimed by the Lord Himself (2:2-3)? If the ancestors were punished, how much more unfaithful Christians?

The second part of the Epistle begins with a comparison between fidelity to Moses and fidelity to Jesus. Moses was faithful, in the *household*, that is the people of God, in the role of *servant*, while Christ was faithful as the *Son* and the one who rules *over* the household (3:1-6). Christ, therefore, is entitled to a *fidelity* much superior to that which Moses deserves, because He is the *Son* set *over* the household. To underline this exigency, the author invokes Psalm 95 (3:7-11) which he comments (3:12-4:12) for his readers in grave danger of infidelity as were the Hebrews in the desert. Because of their *incredulity* (3:12; 3:19), the indocile Hebrews (3:18) could not enter the Promised Land (3:19; 4:1; 4:5). Christians, however, are invited to enter into the repose of the Lord, on condition, however, that "no one must fall away into the same kind of unbelief" (4:11; 4:6). Because indocility cannot boast itself to go unpunished. In fact, the word of God is endowed with fearful virtues: it is *living* as the living God Himself, *active* and even sharper than a double-bladed sword, so *subtle* that it *penetrates* to the line of separation of the soul and spirit; it *discerns* and *judges* the heart's dispositions and thoughts (4:12-13). "From Him, no creature can be hidden" (4:13). "Let us hold fast then, by the faith we profess" (4:14). This is the conclusion of the exhortation to follow docilely the Gospel of Christ, faithful Mediator, superior to Moses, superior to the angels, in His quality of the Son.

Thus, the word of God, in the Epistle to the Hebrews, is presented with traits which evoke those of the Old Testament, but with a character of greater urgency because of the presence and authority of the Son among us. This word is, at the same time, knowledge of the truth (10:26), teaching or message (2:1-2), promise (4:1), law (2:2). This word demands to be heard with attention (2:1), believed (3:12), obeyed (10:36). A word of comfort for those who subscribe to it (6:5), it is terrible for those who pay no heed to such a message

(2:3). A promise of rest (4:1; 4:5), it can become a menace (3:8; 4:7) and a judge (4:13). Active (4:12), efficacious (4:13), always present (3:7; 3:15; 4:7), it rings incessantly in the ears of Christians, and calls each soul, in a permanent today, to enter into the peace and rest of the Lord (3:7; 3:15; 4:11).[51]

3. Conclusion

Thus, in the Epistle to the Hebrews, the prevalent term to designate the revelation is the term *word*. In a comparison of the two phases of the economy of salvation, the Epistle stresses the continuity of the two revelations, as well as the excellency of the new revelation inaugurated by the Son's word of salvation. This word, received and transmitted by the Lord's witnesses, is further confirmed by the testimony of God, by means of signs and charisms. The excellency of this word exacts, on the part of Christians, a fidelity, an obedience proportionate to its origin and to the superiority of its Mediator.

V. SAINT JOHN

In the Synoptics, in the Acts of the Apostles, and in the letters of St. Paul, the word of God means the Gospel message. The great novelty introduced by St. John is the equation he establishes between Christ, Son of the Father, and Logos. Christ is the eternal, subsistent, personal Word, and revelation is accomplished when this Word becomes flesh to tell us about the Father.[52]

1. Jesus Christ, Word of God and Son of God

The Old Testament was already familiar with *Wisdom* and *Word*. In Job, Prov., Eccles., and particularly in Wis., *Wisdom* is found in God: it presides over creation and the organization of the world (Wis. 7-8); it sees everything, penetrates everything (Wis. 9:11), governs everything (Wis. 8:1); it instructs men (Wis. 8:7; 9:11), guides them (Wis. 9:11; 10.10), protects them (Wis. 9.11), assists them (Wis. 9:10); it emanates from God, it is the reflection of His image (Wis. 7:25-26). The Old Testament was also familiar with the *Word*, as Creator (Ps. 33:9) and Revealer, sent to earth to reveal the secrets of God and returning to Him once its mission was accomplished (Is. 55:10-11). But the Old Testament did not conceive (and could hardly conceive, because of its radical monotheism) of the *Wisdom* and *Word* of God as a really distinct person. Under the activity of the Holy Spirit, St. John recognized in the historic person of Christ this Wisdom and this Word of God of which the Old Testament is full. Jesus Christ is the eternal Word of God, exercising a role as creator and revealer, but always as a person. In Jesus Christ, the Word of God, which creates the universe, imposes a law upon it, announces salvation, and condescends to speak to man, finds its perfect accomplishment. For St. John, the Logos is a person, together with the Father, in the most intimate relationship: distinct from Him but still God equal to Him, Word of God (Jn. 1:1). This Word, incarnate among men (Jn. 1:14), is the Word of God, the only-begotten, because it is the terminus of a generation that is completely fertile. To this only Son, who lives in the bosom of the Father (Jn. 1:18) like the inner Word of God, St. John relates the whole of revelation.[53] In Jesus Christ, this inner Word of God echoes throughout the world and makes itself heard among men.

2. *Activity of the Logos*

The prologue of St. John's Gospel is presented as the activity of the Logos, as a brief history of the manifestations of God through His Word. In this economy, there are three stages. Creation constitutes God's first manifestation. "It is through your word that you have made the universe" (Wis. 9:1), writes the author of Wisdom. St. Paul, in his turn, asserts: "It is in Him that all things have been made . . . ; everything has been created through Him and for Him" (Col. 1:15-16). St. John echoes this when he says: "All things were made through Him and without Him nothing was made" (Jn. 1:3). Since the world has been created *through* the Logos (and *in* the Logos, for God sees and conceives all things in His Logos, which is the wisdom of God), the Word is in the world, with all His power and His wisdom. The world being a thing *spoken* (said) by God, it shows His presence and the invisible perfections of the God who speaks. Man, accordingly, should have recognized and glorified the author and architect of the world (Wis. 13:1-9; Rom. 1:18-23). But as a matter of fact, man remained deaf to the message of creation. This first manifestation of God met with stalemate: "The Word was in the world, and the world was made by Him, and the world did not recognize Him" (Jn. 1:10).[54] Next, God chose a people for His own and revealed Himself to them through the Law and prophets; but this revelation, like the first, met with an obstacle: "The Word came among His own and His own did not receive Him" (Jn. 1:11). Finally, after having spoken through the prophets, God speaks to us through His Son. (Heb. 1:1): "The Word was made flesh and pitched His tent among us" (Jn. 1:14). "No one has ever seen God; the only-begotten Son who is in the bosom of the Father has made Him known" (Jn. 1:18). Jesus Christ is the substantial Word of God, the only Son of the Father. Revelation is accomplished because the Word was made flesh and, thereby, becomes a divine message, speaking in human terms and propositions and telling us the secrets of the Father, especially the mystery of His love for His children.[55] There are three elements that make Christ the perfect Revealer of the Father: His pre-existence as Logos of God (Jn. 1:1-2), the incarnation of the Logos (Jn. 1:14), the permanent intimacy of life shared by Father and Son, before as well as after the Incarnation (Jn. 1:18).[56] Because St. John sees Christ as the Incarnate Word, the Son living in the bosom of the Father, He gives revelation its maximum extension and meaning. Christ is ontologically qualified as the only perfect Revealer: His mission as Revealer is rooted in the life that exists in the very bosom of the Trinity. He who, in the bosom of the Trinity, is already Word and Wisdom of God, becomes, in the concrete economy of the Incarnation, the source of light and truth for men. Thus St. John gives us the last word on Christ's mission as Revealer.

3. John's Vocabulary of Revelation

For St. John, Christ is the Word of God: this new approach echoes even in the language he uses and gives rise to a new vocabulary. The terms which express this inner vision of St. John's are, for the most part, bound up with the idea of revelation: word, witness, light, truth, glory, sign, and, among the verbs: know, recognize, see, manifest, show, make known, teach, witness, say, speak, interpret.[57]

In the Synoptics, Christ teaches, preaches, announces the good news of the Kingdom. In St. John He *speaks* and *witnesses*: He is the Son who tells about the Father (Jn. 1:18), the Witness who declares what He has seen and heard in the bosom of the Father. Twice, in the Apocalypse, Christ is called *faithful* witness (Apoc. 1:5; 3:14). St. John's notion of revelation is thus bound up with that of witness.[58] The substantive *marturia* comes up thirteen times and the verb *marturein* appears thirty-three times. Witnessing means asserting the reality of the fact, giving this affirmation all the solemnity required by the circumstances. A legal setting, a lawsuit—these are the natural background for witness. Witness implies two aspects that can be more or less dissociated. First of all, it means a communication concerning the events of which the witness possesses a knowledge based upon experience. Secondly, this declaration is generally made with reference to a particular person: the witness, by his deposition, takes a stand for or against a person. In St. John, the concept of witness unites both these aspects. To be a witness, for Christ, means to declare the existence of realities and facts of which only He has experience (primarily, the intimate life of Father and Son), and this declaration has a solemn and juridic character.[59] Christ is the perfect Witness and His testimony is presented as a public deposition in a vast trial in which He stands up against the world. In favor of Christ, there is the testimony of John the Baptist (Jn. 1:7), the Apostles (Jn. 19:35; 21:24), Scripture (Jn. 5:39), the Father (Jn. 5:32. 37; 8:18), and the Holy Spirit (Jn. 15:26). But men prefer darkness to truth. Confronted by Christ, the Jews, who represent the whole hostile world, reject His testimony and judge themselves. The testimony of Christ effects the discernment of men (Jn. 9:39).

Speaking, in St. John, also has the intensive force of bearing witness and is a special characteristic of authority in the words of the Son of God: "I tell you the truth that I have heard from God" (Jn. 8:40. 26. 38). This means that Christ proclaims revealed truth; His word is, in the absolute sense, the word of God which saves and judges (Jn. 12:48-49).[60]

4. Christ, Witness to the Father

Christ speaks as a qualified witness, for He is the Word of God (Jn. 1:1-2) and the Son of the Father (Jn. 1:18); He alone knows the Father, because He comes from Him (Jn. 6:46; 7:29; 8:55; 16:27; 17:8); He knows the Father (Jn. 7:29) just as the Father knows Him (Jn. 10:15), for He is in the Father and the Father is in Him (Jn. 10:30; 17:21. 23); He is in His own Person the Light (Jn. 1:8; 9:5) and the Truth (Jn. 14:6). He can also testify to the Father and to the mission of salvation He has received from Him. His word is the assertion of a man who has seen and heard personally: "We speak of what we know and we testify to what we have seen, but you do not receive our testimony" (Jn. 3:11). "I tell you what I have seen with the Father" (Jn. 8:38). "He who has sent me is truthful; and what I have heard from him that I speak in the word" (Jn. 8:26. 40). "He who comes from heaven testifies to what He has seen and heard" (Jn. 3:32). At the moment of His passion, Christ declares before Pilate: "I have come into the world only to give witness to the truth" (Jn. 18:37), that is, to proclaim the definitive revelation received from the Father.[61] St. Paul speaks of the testimony that Christ gave before Pontius Pilate (1 Tim. 6:13), but man did not receive His witness (Jn. 3:32; 1:11). The object of the testimony, essentially, is that Christ is the Son of the Father, sent from the Father, Savior of the World, and that, through faith in Him, man can acquire ever-lasting life (Jn. 3:16; 17:3; 1 Jn. 5:10-11). The testimony thus bears upon Christ Himself, upon the mysterious nature of His Person, upon His mission of salvation.[62]

The Apostles, in their turn, having lived intimately with Christ, having been with Him "since the beginning," testify to Christ (Jn. 15:27). John, who saw water and blood flow from His side, testifies to the salvation which He accomplished (Jn. 19:35-37). Because he has seen, heard, touched Christ, he testifies to the Word of life (1 Jn. 1:1-5); he "testifies that the Father has sent His Son, the Savior of the world" (1 Jn. 4:14; Jn. 20:30-31).

5. The Testimony of the Father

The Son testifies to the Father who has sent Him: He speaks the words that the Father has given Him (Jn. 3:34; 17:8; 14:24), and His witness is good (Jn. 8:13-14). The Father also testifies in behalf of the Son (Jn. 5:36; 8:18) and the mission that the Son has received from Him (Jn. 5:36). The Father testifies for His Son in two ways. First, through His works.[63] The Father "loves the Son" and "has given everything into His hands" (Jn. 3:35); particularly, He has given the Son all power, so that Christ will accomplish the works that the Father performs and thus be recognized as the envoy of the Father: "The works which the Father has *given* Me to accomplish, these very works that I do bear witness to me, that the Father has sent me" (Jn. 5:36; 10:25). The *works* of Christ are at once His works (Jn. 5:36; 7:21; 10:25) and the works of the Father (Jn. 9:3-4; 14:10); for the Father is in Him and He in the Father (Jn. 10-11), and what the Father has, the Son also has (Jn. 17:10). The Son, just like the Father, disposes of life, judges, and awakens the dead (Jn. 5:25-30). That the Father thus *gives* to the Son, who can do nothing of Himself (Jn. 5:30), both His power and His works (Jn. 5:36), is evidence of the perfect unity of will between Father and Son, a further witness of the Father in behalf of His Son: it is the Father who, through the works of Jesus, testifies in behalf of His Son.

Secondly, the Father testifies in behalf of the Son by producing an attraction in the souls of men which makes them give free consent to the testimony of Christ: "No one can come to Me unless the Father who has sent Me draw him. . . . Everyone who has listened

to the Father and has learned comes to Me" (Jn. 6:44-45). Isaiah and
Jeremiah spoke prophetically of the day on which all men would be
taught by God Himself (Is. 54:13; Jer. 31:33 ff); this time has come.
God speaks through His Son. But in order for anyone to hold fast to
the word of the Son, the Father has to *draw* Him and lead Him to
His Son. Faith is a "gift" of the Father (Jn. 6:65). Christ too can
assert that the Father *gives* Him those who believe in His word (Jn.
6:39; 10:29; 17:9-11). In his first letter, St. John speaks of "the
Spirit who testifies" and thereby gives rise to faith (1 Jn. 5:6).

Thus, testimony, whether it is interior or exterior, is aimed at
faith; it is essentially an invitation to believe. Receiving the testimony
and believing are practically synonymous (Jn. 3:11-12. 33-36).[64]
What is more, this testimony is an activity which involves the entire
Trinity. It is for the Son, as sent by the Father, to make the Father
known (Jn. 1:18), to give witness to His love (I Jn. 4:8-10); for He
is Witness and Word. The Father sends His Son and gives Him all
His power (Jn. 3:35; 10:28-29; 13:3); through the works which
He gives Him, He testifies that the Son is His envoy, and, by the
attraction He produces in the souls of men, He moves men towards
Christ. The Holy Spirit, finally, not only gives the gift of adhering to
the truth (1 Jn. 5:5-12), but also acts in the hearts of men to keep
alive the word received in faith (1 Jn. 2:20-27); it is the Spirit who
applies both word and testimony and makes them interior.

6. Christ, God Revealing and God Revealed

The position of Christ, with reference to revelation and to faith,
is entirely unique. Because He is, in His person, the Word of God, the
Son of the Father, Christ is at once God revealing and God revealed.
His doctrine is that of God, but in a different manner from that of
the prophet who receives revelation and announces it. Here, revelation
has its point of departure in Christ at the same time as in the Father.
Christ teaches the only religion that is pleasing to the Father (Jn.
4:23), but at the same time He is the object of that revelation, God
revealed. What does Christ actually reveal if not the plan of God, that
is, Christ Himself, the Son sent by the Father (Jn. 5:38), He who is
announced and recognized as true God (Jn. 17:3)? Christ is at once
the God who speaks and the God who is spoken of, He who reveals
the mystery and the mystery itself. He does not only communicate
word and truth: He *is* Word and Truth (Jn. 1:1; 14:5-6), He is in
person what He teaches and proclaims. That is why St. John can say
equivalently of the teaching of Christ what he asserts of the person

of Christ. We must believe in Christ (Jn. 1:12; 10:26), receive Christ (Jn. 5:43), come to Christ (Jn. 5:40; 6:35. 37. 44. 65; 7:37), abide in Christ (Jn. 15:4. 7) and, at the same time, we must believe in His word (Jn. 5:24), receive His word (Jn. 12:48; 17:8), receive His testimony (Jn. 3:11), abide in His word (Jn. 8:31. 51).[65] Just like the person of Christ, the word of Christ is life and truth (Jn. 6:63; 17:17). Faith in Christ is at the same time adhering to Christ and His word. Believing means receiving Christ (Jn. 5:43), and at the same time recognizing that God is truthful (Jn. 3:33), and believing everything His envoy says (Jn. 3:36; 14:10; 16:27. 30; 20:31; 1 Jn. 5:10); it means accepting as true the divine sonship of Christ and His mission of salvation.[66]

7. Characteristics of Revelation

Revelation, in St. John, presents very definite characteristics. It appears first of all as a scandal, for it is accomplished in an unheard-of and unexpected manner: for the Word to become flesh and for the event of salvation to be brought to us by a visible and tangible man whose words we can hear (Jn. 1:14; 1 Jn. 1:1-3; 4:2-3)—this is disconcerting; this is a scandal for human logic; this is grounds for an objection (Jn. 3:9; 6:42; 7:15. 26. 52; 8:33. 52; 12:34).

The word of Christ confronts man with his decisive choice: for or against life. Christ is come, not to judge (Jn. 3:17; 12:47), but to save (Jn. 3:16-21) and to give life (Jn. 10:10). But His word, being the word of salvation, is necessarily bound up with judgment and condemnation for the man who refuses it: "If anyone hear my words and do not keep them, it is not I who judge him; for I have not come to judge the world, but to save the world. He who rejects me, and does not accept my words, has one to condemn him. The word that I have spoken will condemn him on the last day" (Jn. 12:47-48). Judgment is thus only the other side of the salvation which is offered. It is less a divine sentence than a revealing of the secret of human hearts; it is men themselves who, in choosing for or against Christ, are their own judges (Jn. 9:39).[67] But the man who receives Christ and believes in His word is saved (Jn. 3:16-18); he becomes a new creature (Jn. 3:3), a child of God (Jn. 1:12), vivified, enlightened, sanctified, called to eternal life (Jn. 3:16), to vision (1 Jn. 3:1-2).

Revelation is light and life. In the Old Testament the terms Law, wisdom, word are intimately associated with the idea of light and life; for these realities permit a man to guide himself along the road of life without stumbling, and thus to arrive at God, who is the life of

78   THEOLOGY OF REVELATION

men (Wis. 2:13; 14:18-19; 6:12; 7:10. 30; 3:38; 4:3). In the prologue of St. John, the Logos is the light and the life of men. Christ, who is Incarnate Word, is presented as the Light of the world (Jn. 9:5), who keeps men from faltering along their path towards God. "I am the light of the world; he who follows Me will not walk in darkness, but he will have light and life" (Jn. 8:12; 12:46). Christ is the *light* which leads to life. The man who walks in darkness is on his way to death; but the man who receives the word of Christ and patterns his life after that word walks in light and possesses life: "He who hears My words and believes in Him who sent Me has life everlasting and is not subject to judgment, but he has passed from death to life" (Jn. 5:24). The Son of the Father has come "so that every man who believes in Him will not perish, but will have life everlasting" (Jn. 3:16). Christ is the Good Shepherd, who comes so that His sheep will have life and have it in abundance (Jn. 10:10). There is life only in Him (Jn. 6:53). "Life everlasting is for them to know You, the one true God, and Him whom You have sent, Jesus Christ" (Jn. 17:3). What is tragic about revelation is the fact that man can close his eyes to the light, refuse to accept the testimony and thereby run headlong to his own damnation (Jn. 1:11).

8. Conclusion

St. John conceives of revelation as the Word of God made flesh and, through this flesh, turning into word and testimony formulated in a human way, addressed immediately to the Apostles and, through them, to all humanity, to give witness to the charity of the Father who sends His Son among men, so that they might believe in Him and have life everlasting. Faith is man's answer to the external testimony of Christ, and at the same time to the interior attraction of the Father and the testimony of the Spirit. This is the twofold dimension of God's one single word of love.

Having completed this investigation of the Synoptic tradition, Acts, St. Paul, Epistle to the Hebrews, and St. John, we may now attempt to describe revelation such as it appears in the writings of the Fathers. Revelation is the eminently loving and free activity through which God, through the economy of the Incarnation, inaugurated in some way in the Old Testament (through the instrumentality of the prophetic word), makes himself known, in His intimate life, as well as the plan of love which He has conceived eternally for saving all humanity and leading them back to Himself through Christ. This activity is accomplished by the external testimony of Christ and the apostles and the interior testimony of the Spirit who cooperates in the conversion of all men through Christ. The testimony of Christ and the apostles is extended and confirmed by their signs of power. Thus, through the joint action of Son and Spirit, the Father *declares* and *accomplishes* His plan for salvation.

1. H. SCHULTE, *Der Begriff der Offenbarung im Neuen Testament* (Munich, 1949).

2. On the principal words for revelation used in the Synoptics, see primarily: G. Friedrich, "Kèrussô, Kèrugma," *Theol. Worterbuch*, 3:701-317; Id., "*Euangelizomai, Euangelion*," *ibid.*, 2:705-735; K. H. RENGSTORF, "*Didaskô, Didaskalos*," *ibid.*, 2:138-168; G. KITTEL, "Akouô," *ibid.*, 1:216-223; A. OEPKE, "*Apokaluptô, Apokalupsis*," *Wesen und Wirkirlichkeit der ubernaturlichen Offenbarung* (Fribourg, 1940).

3. V. TAYLOR, *The Names of Jesus* (London, 1954), pp. 12-17.

4. P. A. LIEGE, art. "Evangélisation," *Catholicisme*, 4:756.

5. A. RETIF, *Foi au Christ et Mission* (Paris, 1953), pp. 57-60.

6. O. CULLMANN, *Christologie du Nouveau Testament* (Paris, 1958), pp. 18-38, 42-47; F. GILS, *Jésus Prophète d'après les Synoptiques* (Louvain, 1957), pp. 9-47.

7. On this important logion of the Synoptics, see J. DUPONT, *Gnosis* (Paris-Louvain, 1949), pp. 58-62; A. FEUILLET, "Jésus et la Sagesse divine d'après les Evangiles Synoptiques," *Revue biblique*, 62 (1955): 161-196; L. CERFAUX, "L'Evangile de Jean et le logion johannique des Synoptiques," in *L'Evangile de Jean* (Coll. "Recherches bibliques," Louvain, 1958), pp. 147-159; ID., "Les sources scripturaires de Mt. 11:25-30," *Eph. th. lov.*, 30 (1954): 740-746; 31 (1955): 331-342; L. CHARLIER, "L'action de graces de Jésus (Mt. 11:25-30)," *Bible et vie chrétienne*, 1957, pp. 87-99.

8. J. SCHMID, *Das Evangelium nach Matthaus* (Regensburg, 1956), pp. 201-203.

9. D. MOLLAT, art. "Evangile," *Dictionnaire de spiritualité*, 4:1748.

10. For the words used, in addition to the articles in *Theologisches Worterbuch* already quoted in the preceding paragraph, see: H. Strathmann, "*Martus, Martureô, Marturia.*" TW 4:492-514. On the role of the apostles in revelation, see particularly: R. ASTING, *Die Verkundigung des Wortes Gottes im Urchristentum* (Stuttgart, 1939); L. CERFAUX, "Témoins du Christ d'après le Livre des Actes," *Recueil Cerfaux* (2 vol., Gembloux, 1954), 2:157-174; A. RETIF, *Foi au Christ et Mission* (Paris, 1953); N. BROX, *Zeuge und Martyrer* (Munich, 1961); PH. H. MENOUD, "Jésus et ses témoines," *Eglise et Théologie*, juin 1960, pp. 1-14; A. M. HUNTER, *Un Seigneur, une Eglise, un salut* (Paris ,1950); J. SCHMITT, *Jésus ressuscité dans la prédication apostolique* (Paris, 1949); C. H. DODD, *The Apostolic Preaching and its Developments* (London, 1936).

11. L. CERFAUX, "Témoins du Christ d'après le Livre des Actes," *Recueil Cerfaux*, 2:157.

12. A. RETIF, *Foi au Christ et mission*, pp. 40-47.

13. N. BROX, *Zeuge und Martyrer*, p. 46.

14. For Matthias, election by lots expresses the will of God.

15. N. BROX, *Zeuge und Martyrer*, pp. 44-45.

16. P. H. MENOUD, "Jésus et ses témoins," *Eglise, et Théologie*, June 1960, pp. 5-6.

17. N. BROX, *Zeuge und Martyrer*, p. 46.

18. *Ibid.*, p. 46.

19. PH. H. MENOUD, "Jésus et ses témoins," *Eglise et Théologie*, June 1960, pp. 8-9.

20. L. CERFAUX, "Témoins du Christ d'après le livre des Actes," *Recueil Cerfaux*, 2:159.

21. *Ibid.*, 2:164.

22. *Ibid.*, 171-172.

23. The official teaching or catechesis implies more elaborate instruction addressed to new converts, an explanation drawn up with some pedagogical skill on the subject of the Scriptures in the light of the Christian fact. Thus, the first Christians "continue steadfastly in the teaching of the Apostles" (Acts 2:42). The apostles "are standing in the Temple and teaching the people" (Acts 5:25. 28). They name seven deacons in order to devote themselves exclusively to "prayer and the service of the word" (Acts 6:4). Paul remains one year and six months at Corinth "teaching the people the word of God" (Acts 18:11). The first impact of the good news is quickly followed by the systematic statement and explanation of Christian doctrine.

24. D. MOLLAT, "Evangile," *Dictionnaire de spiritualité*, 4:1751; A. RETIF, *Foi au Christ et mission*, pp. 61-76.

25. J. DUPONT, "Repentir et conversion d'après les Actes des apotres," *Sciences Ecclésiastiques*, 12 (1960): 160-161.

26. J. Schmitt, *Jésus ressuscité dans la prédication apostolique* (Paris, 1949), pp. 218-222.
27. "*Pisteuein*" is used 39 times and "*pistis*" 15 times.
28. A. Retif, *Foi au Christ et mission*, pp. 112-114.
29. On this notion of mystery, see more particularly: G. Bornkamm, "*Mustèrion*," *Theologisches Worterbuch*, 4:809-834; D. Deden, "Le mystère paulinien," *Eph. theol. lov.*, 13 (1936): 403-442; K. Prumm, "Mysterion von Paulus bis Origenes," *Zeitschrift fur Katholische Theologie*, 61 (1937): 391-425; Id., "Zur Phanomenologie des paulinischen Mysterion," *Biblica*, 37 (1956): 135-161; Id., "Mystères," *Suppl. au Dict. de la Bible*, 6:10-225; C. Spicq, *Les Epitres pastorales* (Paris, 1947), pp. 116-125; R. E. Brown, "The pre-Christian Semitic Concept of Mystery," *Catholic Biblical Quarterly Review*, 20 (1958): 417-443; Id., "The Semitic Background of the New Testament Mysterion." *Biblica*, 39 (1958): 426-448; 40 (1959): 70-87; L. Cerfaux, *Le Christ dans la théologie de S. Paul* (Paris, 1954), pp. 229-242, 303-328; *Le chrétien dans la théologie paulinienne* (Paris, 1962), pp. 431-469; J. Dupont, *Gnosis, La connaissance religieuse dans les épitres de S. Paul* (Louvain, Paris, 1949), pp. 187-194, 493-498; J. Coppen:, "Le mystère dans la théologie paulinienne et ses parallèles qumraniens," in: *Littérature et théologie pauliniennes* (Coll. "Recherches bibliques," V. Bruges, 1960), pp. 142-165; B. Rigaux, "Révélation des mystères et perfection a Qumran et dans le Nouveau Testament," *New Testament Studies*, 4 (1958): 237-262. On the theme of the Gospel, see: D. Mollat, art. "Evangile," *Dictionnaire de spritualité*, 4:1747-1751; G. Friedrich, "*Euangelizomai, Euangelion*," *Theologisches Worterbuch*, 2:705-735.
30. M. Meinertz, *Theologie des Neuen Testaments* (2 vol., Bonn, 1950), 59-60; H. Schulte, *Der Begriff der Offenbarung im Neuen Testament*, pp. 21-22.
31. This notion, in St. Paul, underwent a progressive *development* in depth. Cf. J. Coppens, "Le mystère dans la théologie paulinienne et ses parallèles qumraniens," in: *Littérature et théologie pauliniennes*, p. 142; R. E. Brown, "The Semitic Background of the New Testament Mysterion," *Biblica*, 39 (1958): 440.
32. L. Cerfaux, *Le Christ dans la théologie de S. Paul*, pp. 304-305.
33. K. Prumm, "Mystères," *Suppl. Dict. de la Bible*, 6:193-194.
34. L. Cerfaux, *Le Christ dans la théologie de S. Paul*, p. 305.
35. J. Coppens, "Le mystère dans la théologie paulinienne et ses parallèles qumraniens," *Littèrature et théologie paulìniennes*, p. 143. In I Tim. 3:16, the stages of Christ's history coincide with the successive phases of the mystery. Just as, in the mystery, God decides upon a plan of salvation, makes it known to men, and leads them to glory, so also Christ, pre-existing as God, is manifested in the flesh, preached among men and believed by them; finally, He rises gloriously back into heaven. See: C. Spicq, *Les Épitres pastorales*, p. 119.
36. D. Deden, "Le mystère paulinien," *Eph. theol. lov.*, 13 (1936): 420-421; L. Cerfaux, *Le Christ dans la théologie de S. Paul*, pp. 310-311; *Le chrétien dans la thèologie paulinienne*, pp. 444-447; C. Spicq, *Les Épitres pastorales*, pp. 116-117.
37. D. Deden. "Le mystère paulinien," *Eph. theol. lov.*, 13 (1936): 422-423. There are numerous texts describing the Gospel as message, good news of salvation proclaimed to men through the preaching of the Apostles (1 *Cor.* 15:1-2; *Rom.* 2:16; 16:25; 2 *Cor.* 11:4; *Gal.* 1:6-7; *Eph.* 1:13; 6:15; *Col.* 1:5. 23; 1 *Tim.* 1:11; 2 *Tim.* 2:8).
38. L. Cerfaux, *Le Christ dans la théologie de S. Paui*, p. 304.
39. The Gospel is the revelation of God our Father (1 *Thess.* 1:3; 2 *Thess.* 1:1; *Rom.* 1:7), rich in mercy (*Eph.* 2:4), who calls us to His Kingdom and His glory (1 *Thess.* 2:12). This is the Gospel of the love of God (1 *Thess.* 1:4). In this Gospel, God reveals to men the free election of grace of which they are the object and invites them to turn towards Him (2 *Thess.* 2:13-16). See: D. Mollat, "Évangile," *Dict. de Spir.*, 4:1756.
40. B. Rigaux, *Les Épitres aux Thessaloniciens* (Paris, 1956), pp. 158-159.
41. H. Schlier, "La notion paulinienne de la parole de Dieu," in: *Littérature et théologie pauliniennes*, pp. 129-130; J. Dupont, "La parole de Dieu suivant S. Paul," *La Parole de Dieu en Jésus-Christ* (Casterman, 1960), pp. 68-70; B. Rigaux, *Les Épitres aux Thessaloniciens*, p. 160.
42. J. Dupont, "La parole de Dieu suivant S. Paul," in: *Le Parole de Dieu in Jésus-Christ*, pp. 72-73; H. Schlier, "La notion paulinienne de la parole de Dieu," in *Littérature et théologie pauliniennes*, pp. 134-135.
43. H. Schlier, *ibid.*, 127.
44. C. Spicq, *Les Épitres pastorales*, pp. 120-121.
45. L. Cerfaux, *Le chrétien dans la théologie paulinienne*, pp. 132-134.
46. I. de la Potterie, "L'onction du chrétien par la foi," *Biblica*, 40 (1959): 24-25.
47. J. Dupont, "La parole de Dieu suivant S. Paul," dans: *La Parole de Dieu en Jésus-Christ*, pp. 78-80; D. Mollat, "Évangile," *Dict. de Spir.*, 4:1760-1761.

48. D. DEDEN, "Le mystère paulinien," *Eph. theol. lov.*, 13 (1936): 418-419, 421; L. CERFAUX, *Le chrétien dans la théologie paulinienne*, pp. 461-468.

49. L. CERFAUX, *Le Christ dans la théologie de S. Paul*, pp. 59 et 330-331.

50. See particularly: C. SPICQ, *L'Épitre aux Hébreux* (2 vol., Paris, 1953); H. CLAVIER, "O logos tou Theou dans l'Épitre aux Hébreux," *New Testament Essays* (Studies in Memory of Thomas Walter Manson, ed. by A. J. B. HIGGINS, Manchester, 1959), pp. 81-93; R. SCHNACKENBURG, "Zum Offenbarungsgedanken in der Bibel," *Biblische Zeitschrift*, 7 (1963): 2-22; A. VANHOYE, *La structure littéraire de l'Épitre aux Hébreux* (Bruges-Bruxelles-Paris, 1963).

51. Is it necessary to go further in the personification of the word and understand at the same time "the eternal Logos who fills this message and inspires it?" This is not forbidden, believes H. CLAVIER, "O Logos tou Theou dans l'Épitre aux Hébreux," *New Testament Essays* (Manchester, 1959), p. 86.

52. On this role of Christ, Logos and Son of the Father, as Revealer, see: H. NIEBECKER, *Wesen und Wirklichkeit der ubernaturlichen Offenbarung* (Freibourg, 1940); H. HUBER, *Der Begriff der Offenbarung im Johannes-Evangelium* (Gottingen, 1934); M. E. BOISMARD, *Le Prologue de S. Jean* (Paris, 1953); J. GIBLET, "La théologie johannique du Logos," in: *La Parole de Dieu en Jésus-Christ*, pp. 85-119; G. KITTEL, "Wort und Reden im NT," *Theol. Worterbuch*, 4:100-140.

53. S. LYONNET, "Hellénisme et christianisme," *Biblica*, 26 (1945). 115-132; M. E. BOISMARD, *Le Prologue de S. Jean*, p. 110.

54. This interpretation is the one proposed by M. E. BOISMARD in *Le Prologue de Saint Jean* (Paris, 1953), p. 114. Other exegetes are of the opinion that this verse is concerned with the historic ministry of the Incarnate Word. According to Spitta, Zahn, Loisy, the historical perspective begins already in verse 4 of the Prologue; according to B. Weiss, in verse 5; according to Heitmuller, Bernard, Buchsel, Holzmann, Harnack, W. Bauer, Lagrange, in verse 9. On this subject see: R. Schnackenburg, "Logos-Hymnus und johanneischer Prolog," *Bibl. Zeitschrift*, I (1957): 69-109.

55. M. E. BOISMARD, *Le Prologue de S. Jean*, pp. 109-123.

56. J. ALFARO, "Cristo glorioso, Revelador del Padre," *Gregorianum*, 39 (1958): 225-226.

57. *Apokaluptein* does not belong to the vocabulary of St. John. The word appears only once, in a quotation from Isaiah (Jn. 12:38). In its place, St. John uses phaneroyn. (H. SCHULTE, *Der Begriff der Offenbarung im Neuen Testament*, p. 67). Likewise, the notion of witness replaces that of Gospel (D. Mollat, art. "Evangile," *Dict. de spir.*, 4:1761). The words *kèrussein* and *euangelizesthai*, characteristic of the Synoptic tradition, are also absent.

58. On the notion of witness in St. John, consult especially: I. DE LA POTTERIE, "La notion de témoignage dans S. Jean," *Sacra Pagina* (2 vol., Paris-Gembloux, 1959), 2:192-208; B. TREPANIER, "L'idée de témoin dans les écrits johanniques," *Rev. de l'Université d'Ottawa*, 15 (1945): 27°-63°; N. BROX, *Zeuge und Martyrer*, pp. 70-106; M. R. SCHIPPERS, *Getuigen van Jesus Christus in het Nieuwe Testament* (Franeker, 1938); E. BURNIER, *La notion de témoignage dans le Nouveau Testament* (Lausanne, 1939); CH. MASSON, "Le témoignage de Jean," *Rev. de th. et de ph.*, 1950, pp. 120-127; A. VANHOYE, "Témoignage et vie en Dieu selon le quatrième Évangile," *Christus*, n 6 (April 1955), pp. 150-171; J. GUITTON, *Le problème de Jésus et les fondements du témoignage chrétien* (Paris, 1950), pp. 153-178.

59. There is, in St. John, a whole vocabulary borrowed from legal procedure: convict, accuse, defender, judge, judgment, witness. The work of Jesus proceeds against the background of the court room; it is a defense (I. De La Potterie, "La notion de témoignage dans S. Jean," *Sacra Pagina*, pp. 195-196).

60. I. DE LA POTTERIE, "L'arrière-fond du thème johannique de la vérité," in: *Studia Evangelica* (Berlin, 1959), pp. 289-290.

61. *Ibid.*, 287; N. BROX, *Zeuge und Martyrer*, p. 76; B. TREPANIER, "L'idée de témoin dans les écrits johanniques," *Rev. de l'Univ. d'Ottawa*, 15 (1945): 45°-48°.

62. I. DE LA POTTERIE, "La notion de témoignage dans S. Jean," *Sacra Pagina*, p. 199.

63. On the witness of God through His works: A. VANHOYE, "Opera Jesu donum Patris," *Verbum Domini*, 36 (1958): 83-92; ID., "L'oeuvre du Christ, don du Père," *Rech. de sc. rel.*, 48 (1960): 377-420; H. VAN DEN BUSSCHE, "La Structure de Jean I-XII," in *L'Évangile de Jean* (Coll. "Recherches bibliques," Louvain, 1958), pp. 88-97; L. CERFAUX, "Les miracles, signes messianiques de Jésus et oeuvres de Dieu," in: *L'Attente du Messie* (Coll. "Recherches bibliques," Louvain, 1958), pp. 131-138.

64. I. DE LA POTTERIE, "La notion de témoignage dans S. Jean," *Sacra Pagina*, p. 202.

65. A. DECOURTRAY, "La notion johannique de la foi," *Nouvelle Revue théologique*, 81 (1959): 563.

66. J. ALFARO, "Fides in terminologia biblica," *Gregorianum*, 42 (1961): 497-504.

67. D. MOLLAT, art. "Jugement," *Suppl. Dict. de la Bible*, 4:1380.

part 2
the theme of revelation in the writings of the fathers of the church

In a recent study on Origen and the function of the Incarnate Word,[1] Marguerite Harl notes that the subject treated "not only was never the object of an investigation in Origen, but has not even been clearly enunciated in the history of dogma for the first three centuries. In order to put Origen in his proper frame of reference for this study," she continues, "it would be necessary to write at least the broader outlines of a history of the Incarnate Word as Revealer before Origen." She laments the fact that no preliminary work has been done in the area.[2]

The historians of dogma, completely absorbed in problems other than revelation (trinity, Christology, soteriology, sacramental theology, etc.), have not paid sufficient attention to the immense place occupied by the theme of revelation in the Fathers of the first three centuries. Yet anyone who reads the Fathers of the Church attentively and objectively cannot avoid the impression that the theme of Christ as source of knowledge is present on every page.

Taking up this theme of revelation in the Fathers, we must admit from the outset that it would be presumptuous to call this an exhaustive study. Our intention here is only to make a simple reconnaissance of the general area. A research of this nature, though it does not show up all the details, still puts us in a position to grasp the overall, to appreciate the outline, to make the approach easier. Neither is it possible to examine all the Fathers of the Church who have written on the theme of revelation. What is important however is to grasp the broader orientations of their thinking, to mark their continuity or discontinuity, their opposition and points of departure, in a word, to examine the leaders. This is what we have chosen to do. Our research bears upon some twenty authors, from the apostolic age to the time of St. Augustine.[3]

It is obvious that no one of the Fathers of the Church ever intended to write a *treatise* on revelation, even though we might frequently discover in their writings, scattered and uncoordinated, most of the elements necessary for a doctrinal synthesis on this subject. In grouping these elements, we must never lose sight of the theological context in which they are inserted. That is why we have let ourselves be guided by the writers themselves, by the themes and words we find them using, rather than by the categories of present-day theology, without, however, neglecting to examine each author on a certain number of points essential for our purpose. In order to find our way more clearly through the stages of patristic thinking, we have followed each monograph with a brief summary.

1. M. HARL, *Origène et la fonction révélatrice du Verbe incarné* (Paris, 1958).

2. *Ibid.*, p. 24. See also p. 84: "It was necessary to run rapidly through the three great works—those of Irenaeus, Clement, and Hippolytus—in order to discover the doctrine of Christ as Revealer of the Father. Unfortunately, there is no one work that gives a synthesis of this subject."

3. In addition to the classical works of A. VON HARNACK, *Lehrbuch der Dogmengeschichte* (Giessen, 1885; 5 éd., Tubingen, 1931), de J. TIXERONT, *Histoire des dogmes dans l'antiquité chrétienne* (Paris, 1930), de R. SEEBERG, *Lehrbuch der Dogmengeschichte* (Leipzig, 4 éd., 1930-1933) and the works on patrology by F. CAYRE, de J. QUASTEN et B. ALTANER, we here call attention, among the general works, to the following titles: D. VAN DEN EYNDE, *Les normes de l'enseignement chrétien dans la littérature patristique des trois premiers siècles* (Gembloux, 1933); E. MOLLAND, *The Conception of the Gospel in the Alexandrian Theology* (Oslo, 1938); M. SPANNEUT, *Le stoïcisme des Pères de l'Église* (Paris, 1957); J. DANIELOU, *Message évangélique et culture hellénistique aux II et III siècles* (Paris-Tournai-New York-Rome, 1961); G. L. PRESTIGE, *Dieu dans la pensée patristique* (Paris, 1955); J. LEBRETON, *Histoire du dogme de la Trinité* (Paris, 1928).

CHAPTER I

FIRST WITNESSES

I. THE APOSTOLIC FATHERS

Direct echo of the good news, the apostolic fathers[1] express their thinking in terms of the primitive preaching.

1. The author of the *Didache* advises us not to depart from the "commandments of the Lord" (4:12), but to follow "the rule of the Gospel" (11:3) and to act accordingly (15:3-4).

2. *Clement of Rome* testifies to the faith he has received. One of the characteristics of his letter is its fidelity to the heritage he has from the apostles, which he transmits in all its integrity. Christ is represented as a Master whose teaching leads to salvation (36:1), the apostles being the messengers of the good news preached by Him: "The apostles are sent to us as messengers of the good news through the Lord Jesus Christ. Now Christ comes from God, and the apostles come from the Christ: these two points proceed in perfect order from the will of God. Strengthened with the instruction of our Lord Jesus Christ and fully convinced by His resurrection, the apostles, strengthened by the Word of God, went out, with the assurance of the Holy Spirit, to announce the good news, the approach of the Kingdom of God" (42:1-3). The object of faith Clement calls the good news, the instructions of Christ, the Word of God preached in the power of the Spirit.

3. *Polycarp*, writing to the Philippians, recommends that they walk in the way of truth traced out by the Lord (5:2; 4:1) and be "docile to the word of justice" (9:1). Let us serve the Lord, he insists, "according as he has commanded, just like the apostles who have preached the Gospel to us and the prophets who have announced the coming of the Savior" (6:3). Let us say farewell "to the false doctrines in order to come back to the teaching which has been handed down to us from the beginning" (7:2).

4. *Papias*, for his part, contrasts the "strange commandments" to

the "commandments given through the Lord for our faith and born from truth itself" (Eusebeius, HE, 3, 19:3-4).

5. *Ignatius of Antioch* is steeped in the New Testament, particularly Paul and John. He sees Christ as the fullness of truth and life, the mediator of revelation and salvation.

Christ is the Son whom the Father sends into the world to make Him known: "There is only one God who manifests Himself through Jesus Christ His Son, who is His Word come out of silence" (Magn. 8:2; 6:1-2). Christ is "the unlying mouth through which the Father has spoken in truth" (Rom. 8:2).

Before the Incarnation, the Word was first of all manifested by the creation of the world (Eph. 15:1), then throughout the whole Old Testament: "the prophets, being His disciples through the Spirit, waited for Him as their Master" (Magn. 9:1-2: Philad. 5:2). These manifestations were all aimed at the definitive manifestation of the Incarnation: "God appearing under human form to inaugurate eternal life" (Eph. 19:3). "The Gospel is the consummation of eternal life" (Philad. 9:2). Very precisely, Ignatius declares that "the knowledge of God is Jesus Christ" (Eph. 17:2), meaning that Christ is the one sole Master (Eph. 15:1; Magn. 9:1) through whom God makes Himself known.

A leitmotif runs through all the letters of Ignatius. We must flee heretics and perverse doctrine (Philad. 2-3; Polyc. 3:1; Smyrn. 4:1). On the positive side, we must be firmly attached to the "teachings of our Lord and the Apostles" (Magn. 13:1). The Ephesians must not have any other ornament than the "commandments of Jesus Christ" (Eph. 9:2). In this movement of fidelity, there are three terms: Christ, apostles, Church, represented by its bishop and its presbytery. We must remain "inseparable from Jesus Christ our God and the bishop and the precepts of the apostles" (Tr. 7:1; 13:2). "Follow your bishop, all of you, as Jesus Christ followed His Father, and follow the presbytery like the apostles" (Smyrn. 8:1).

Ignatius uses the Old Testament very little. Still, he is aware of the profound unity between Gospel and prophets. In his prison, he finds refuge "in the *Gospel* as in the flesh of Jesus Christ and in the *Apostles* as the prebytery of the Church. And we also love the *prophets*, for they too announce the Gospel, they hoped in Jesus Christ and waited for Him; believing in Him, they have been saved, and, abiding in the unity of Jesus Christ, they are saints worthy of love and admiration, they have received the testimony of Jesus Christ and have been admitted in the Gospel of our common hope" (Philad.

5:1-2). Revelation embraces the whole *"economy*... concerning the new man, Jesus Christ" (Eph. 20:1), source of salvation for all men.

To the judaizers who oppose the prophets to the Gospel and subordinate the Gospel to the books of the Old Testament, Ignatius opposes the person of Jesus Christ in whom all things are reduced to unity, hope, and accomplishment: "For me, my archives is Jesus Christ; my inviolable archives is His Cross and death and Resurrection, and the faith which comes from Him" (Philad. 8:1-2). It is Christ alone to whom "the secrets of God have been entrusted. He is the *gate of the Father* through whom Abraham, Isaac, Jacob, and the prophets and the Apostles of the Church all enter. All this leads to unity with God" (Philad. 9:1). For everyone, Christ is the one Savior and Revealer.

The apostolic Fathers are convinced that the teaching of the Church is of divine origin. The object of faith is the Word of God, the whole list of commandments and instructions which were given to humanity through Christ, the prophets, and the Apostles. For everyone, Christ is the streaming fountainhead of Christianity, the one and only Teacher; the Church receives and transmits their teaching. More than any other, it is Ignatius of Antioch who sees in Christ the *whole* of revelation and the *whole* of salvation. In Him, truth and life are inseparably united. In the Incarnation of the Son, He finds the culmination of the economy of revelation. The knowledge of the Father is Christ.

II. THE APOLOGISTS

What makes the unity of the apologists[2] is not so much their theological tradition as their literary genre. They search through the philosophical systems of the second century for every opening they can find in order to present the Gospel to the Hellenistic world and to define it by reference to that line of thought. Thus, in their thinking, the Christian mystery can approach these souls without frightening them. Now one of the main points of the philosophy of that era, the stoic system primarily, is that God, spread throughout the universe, is *Logos* and *Pneuma*. On the other hand, the doctrine of God as Logos is already at the heart of the Johannine theology. As a result, it is from the theology of the Logos that the theology of the apologists takes its beginning. This theology will be a theology of the manifestations of a transcendent God through His Logos who is Creator, Revealer, and Savior.

1. Saint Justin

In the thinking of St. Justin, the Father, transcendent, unknowable, invisible, acts through the intermediary of the Logos: through Him He creates the world; through Him He makes Himself known; through Him He effects salvation in the world.

It is through His Logos that God created and organized the cosmos, and it is for this work that God conceived the Logos: "the Son of God, the only one who is properly Son, the Logos existing with Him and begotten before all creatures, when, at the beginning, He made and ordered all things" (II Apol. 6:3). This generation is bound up with creation, it took place in view of this creation. Still, in many texts, Justin insists on the absolute priority of the Logos to the whole of creation: "as principle before all creatures, God begot of Himself, before all creatures, a certain verbal power" (Dial. 61:1). Once again: "this offshoot really proceeding from the Father before all creatures, was with the Father and it is with Him that the Father speaks" (Dial. 62:4). For Justin, the generation of the Logos appears as an activity through which God, before creation, by His power and His will, emits the Word as the agent of creation.[3]

The Logos also exercises a religious activity as Revealer and Savior (II Apol. 6:1-5). His activity as Revealer is spread throughout humanity (I Apol. 46:2-5), is more manifest among the Jews and the prophets, total only in the person of Jesus Christ (II Apol. 10:8; I Apol. 5:4).

All truth, acording to Justin, draws its origin from the Logos or divine Word. In every man, there is a seed, "a germ of the Logos," permitting Him to come to a *partial* knowledge of the truth (*kata meros*) and express it (II Apol. 13:5; 8:1). Justin also says that all men *share* in the divine Logos (I Apol. 46:2). According to R. Holte, we must distinguish, in Justin, between the *spermatikos Logos* and the *spermata tou Logou*. The seeds are a participation of the Logos in the human mind. They depend on the activity of the Logos which sows them in the intellect: they are the seeds of the lowest order of knowledge; only Christ, incarnate Logos, will give perfection.[4] In virtue of the fact that these seeds have a participation in the Logos, the pagan thinkers were able to conceive some rays of truth and deserve the title of Christians (I Apol. 46:2-3). Still, Justin is not precise on how he conceives of the activity of the *Logos spermatikos* stirring up these germs within the mind. This first explanation is followed by a second, of the historical order: the elements of truth that can be found among the pagan philosophers and poets are all the result of borrowing from the Old Testament (I Apol. 44:8-9; 59:1). There is thus a twofold source for the same truths.

The revealing activity of the Logos is manifest still more in the patriarchs and prophets. Justin recognizes the Logos in the person who appeard to the patriarchs and spoke with them.[5] It is the Logos who appeared to Abraham near the oak of Mambre (Dial. 56:1-2); it is the Logos who wrestled with Jacob (Dial. 125:3). "Jesus is the one who appeared and spoke to Moses, Abraham, and, in a word, to all the patriarchs" (Dial. 113:4; 37:4; 58:3). Justin calls him the "angel" of God (Dial. 56:4; 127:4; 128:1) in order to stress his role as servant (Dial. 56:22), executing the plans of the Father (Dial. 127:1-4; 58:3), and "apostle" for "He *announces* everything that must be known and He is *sent* to signify everything that is announced" (I Apol. 63:4-5; Dial. 56:1; 67:6; 128:2). The Father, on the contrary, is invisible; He can neither appear nor speak, for He is a transcendent God who lives beyond the world (Dial. 127:1-4).

The prophets are the *witnesses* of God: they have "seen and announced the truth to men"; they have spoken of what they "heard and saw, filled with the Holy Spirit. It is not in terms of human reasoning that they spoke: far beyond all human reasoning, they were the worthy witnesses of the truth" (Dial. 7:1-2). What they announce is first of all Christ, His life on earth, the mystery of salvation. For Justin, there is only one group of announcers, the prophets (I Apol. 40:1; 52:3; 53:2; 54:2) and only one object of their announcing: Christ and His mystery (Dial. 14:8; 24:2; 34:2; 43:1; 48:4; 63:5; 71:2; 88:8).

Without saying that the theophanies of the Logos, in the Old Testament, *prepare* the theophany of the Incarnation, Justin, in order to stress the unity of God's plan, loves to speak of the one single economy of salvation which groups together the apparitions of the Logos in the Old and New Testaments. "The Father of the universe has a Son, who is Logos, First Born of God and God Himself. He showed Himself first of all under the form of fire and under an incorporeal form to Moses and the other prophets; and now ... He has become man, He is born of a virgin, following the will of the Father, for the salvation of those who believe in Him" (I Apol. 63:15-16). The pagan philosophers possessed some truth, but not the fullness of truth "thanks to the seed of the Logos sown in them by nature, they were able to see the truth obscurely. But it is one thing to have a seed and likeness which are proportioned to one's faculties, and another thing to behold the reality itself, whose participation and imitation proceed from the grace which comes from

Him" (II Apol. 13:3-6). St. Justin distinguishes the *full* knowledge that the Word has given through grace in revealing himself in Christ, and the *partial* knowledge which the pagans could have, according to the participation of the Logos which they received. Only the Christian lives "according to the entire knowledge and contemplation of the Logos who is Christ" (II Apol. 8:3; 10:2-3). Justin thus stresses the continuity and universality of action in the Logos: the Logos acts *spermatically* (like a seed) before Christ, in the whole of humanity, then in His fullness in Christ. Partial and obscure reality at first, it finally becomes clear and total.

It is through the Incarnate Logos that the knowledge of the Father comes to us (I Apol. 63:13). Through Christ, it has been given to us "to learn and know all the things of the Father" (Dial. 121:4; I Apol. 13:3). The Christian doctrine outweighs every human doctrine: "We have the whole Logos in Christ who has appeared to us, body, Logos, soul. All the true principles that the philosophers and legislators have discovered and expressed they owe to what they have found and contemplated in their partial knowledge of the Logos. It is because they did not know the whole Logos, who is Christ, that they so frequently contradict themselves" (II Apol. 10:1-3). In Christ, the Christian possesses eminently the truth of all philosophy, because philosophy is never more than a participation of the Logos. All truth is thus Christian.

Christ is thus our "teacher" (I Apol. 12:9; 21:1), He whom we must prefer to all other teachers (Dial. 142:2). He "illuminates" the nations (Dial. 122:4), by His "lessons," His "precepts," His "teaching," His "maxims" (I Apol. 14:3-4). His doctrine is the doctrine of salvation: the Logos became man "to bring us a doctrine distined to renew and regenerate the human race" (I Apol. 23:1-2). This doctrine, contained in the memories of the Apostles "which are called Gospels" (I Apol. 66:3; Dial. 102:5; 103:6-8; 104:1), we are invited to receive in faith and make our lives conform with them (I Apol. 61:2; 67:3-4). This adherence is worked out in grace, "for no one can either see or understand, if God and His Christ do not give him the gift of understanding" (Dial. 7:3).

2. *Athenagoras*

Athenagoras stresses the fact that God is invisible and incomprehensible: only God can teach us of God (Leg. VII). What Athenagoras teaches is not a human doctrine but a doctrine "taught by God" (Leg. XXXII). The precepts to which the Christians are bound "are not human precepts, but those that have been spoken and taught by God" (Leg. XI). Not that God could not be known in a certain measure outside His revelation. Athenagoras recognizes that the invisible God can be grasped by reason through the works of nature (Leg. V). The order of the world reveals the Creator, the Artisan and Architect of the invisible beauty and harmony (Leg. IV. XV. XVI). Side by side with this ascent towards God from the contemplation of creation, by the way of demonstration, Athenagoras also admits a sort of intuitive and popular knowledge of God: the way of conscience (Leg. V. XXII). Still, with regard to revelation, this knowledge of God remains faint, incomplete, and subject to error. The philosophers "managed to conceive, not to discover the truth; for they were not willing to learn from God what concerns God, but each of them learned from himself. That is why each of them produced a different opinion about God, about His nature, about His forms, and about the world" (Leg. VII).

3. Saint Theophilus of Antioch

Theophilus of Antioch also thinks that reason is capable of furnishing a certain demonstration of the existence of God: "Through His providence and through His works, He lets Himself be seen and understood" (Autol. I:5-6). Still, this requires a pure soul, untroubled by human passion (Autol. I:2). Here below, the human eye cannot see God unveiled: to enter into vision, we must pass along in faith and experience death (Autol. I:7).

Like Justin, and for the same reasons, Theophilus attributes theophanies to the Logos of the Father: "God, Father of the universe, cannot be contained in any place; for there is no place where He retires to take His rest. But His Word, through whom He has made everything, and who is the power of His wisdom, takes the role of the Father and Lord of the universe, and it is He whom we discover in paradise, playing the role of God and speaking with Adam" (Autol. II:22). Theophanies cannot be attributed to the Father, for the Father transcends all space and all time. It is the Logos, the Word of God, who serves as intermediary between God and the world. It is through Him that God has created everything and it is He who appears to men, taking the role of the Father. Theophilus conceives of the theophanies of the Logos as a mission which has its source in the generation of the Son. It is the Father who sends this Son when He wills, because it is He who has begotten Him when He willed.[6] "Thus, the Word being God and born of God, the Father of all things sends

Him when He wills into a determined place, and when He appears there we can hear Him, see Him, since He is sent from God and is present in a place" (Autol. II:22).

In the economy of revelation, Theophilus insists also on the role of prophets. "The prophets . . . have been taught by God," they have been "the organs of God" (Autol. II:). Thus they communicate "the teaching of the holy will of God" (Autol. II:14). Only Christians truly possess the truth, for they are "taught by the Holy Spirit speaking through the holy prophets and foretelling all things" (Autol. II:33). It is in order to assist our understanding that "God has given us a holy law and holy commandments" (Autol. II:27) and that He has sent us "to the school of His holy prophets" (Autol. III:17). We can also hear "the voice of the Gospel" which "gives us an instruction" (Autol. III:13) Let us then go "to the school of the divine precepts" rather than to the school of the "profane authors" (Autol. III:17).

4. The Letter to Diognetus

According to the author of the letter to Diognetus, Christians are not the "champions of a human doctrine," of earthly origin (V:3): their faith comes from God Himself who "has established in men His truth, His Holy and incomprehensible Logos" (VII:1-2). This is a gracious and condescending step on God's part: "It is He Himself who shows Himself" (VIII:5-6). This knowledge of God is opposed by the impotence of human reason, incapable of rising to an adequate knowledge of the divine nature. The author does not deny the possibility of a certain knowledge of God acquired by the natural powers of reason: He is speaking here rather of our inability to know by experience; as a matter of fact, our human ways of thinking cannot arrive at God. Only revelation can give us an authentic knowledge of God.

The Revealer is Logos, Son (IX:4), Son of God (IX:2), Only Begotten, Logos and truth (VII:2), His mission among men is to reveal to them the authentic and full knowledge of God (VIII:1-5). This letter concentrates on the Logos in His activity as Revealer, to the point of obscuring the role of the prophets and natural knowledge. The Logos teaches the truth to all those who hear Him (XI:2). He has come into the world in order to communicate to men "the knowledge of the mysteries of the Father." Rejected by His people, "He has been preached by the apostles and believed by the nations" (XI:2-4). He has come to unveil the plan of salvation conceived in the secret depths of God (VIII:9-11), the fruit of His love and mercy

(VII:3-5). With His coming, an era of justice begins for all humanity (IX:1). Through faith, we know God in a full and efficacious way (VIII:6; IX:6; X:1). To those who are astonished at the fact that revelation has come so late, the author answers that revelation is realized *in time*, but that it is the realization of an *eternal* plan in the heart of God (VIII:9). Above all, it was necessary for humanity, sinking deeper and deeper into evil, to have the experience of its own inability to rise by itself to a salvation which it would recognize as being at once urgent and the free gift of God (IX:1-2, 6).

The epistle stresses the continuity between the mission of the Logos and the mission of the Church. The teaching of the Logos received by the apostles, abides forever in the bosom of the Church. Thanks to this revelation, the Church grows, and thanks to the Church, "the grace of the prophets is recognized, the faith of the Gospels is strengthened, the tradition of the apostles is preserved" (XI:6). The Church is the privileged place where the activity of the Logos as Savior and Revealer is prolonged among men. Her norms are the Law, the prophets, the Gospels, the tradition of the apostles (XI:6).

While still recognizing that human reason has power to arrive at a certain knowledge of God and grasp the elements of moral and religious truth, the apologists conclude the necessity of revelation to know the unknowable and transcendent God with an authentic knowledge. It is through the Logos that the Father is knowable and known. Rather than speak of Christ, the apologists, with the exception of Justin, speak of the Logos. His activity begins with creation. After being addressed to the patriarchs and the prophets and after having instructed them, the Logos is manifested in His fullness through the Incarnation, making known to men the mysteries and secrets of the Father, His plan of salvation, teaching them divine doctrine and precepts. Because they address their arguments to a world of intellectuals, the apologists are inclined to consider revelation as the communication of a higher philosophy, the gift of true doctrine, absolute truth. The Logos of the apologists is teacher, master par excellence; Christians are his disciples and follow His school. His teaching, however, the apologists insist, is a doctrine of salvation, the gift of the Father of mercies, a doctrine which leads those who receive it in faith to eternal life. The prophets and apostles have a variable position in the apologists. Most of the apologists give a place of honor to the prophets: Justin, Athenagoras, Tatian, Theophilus of Antioch. Not that they rank the prophets above the apostles, but in the very antiquity and accomplishment of the prophecies they see an important apologetic argument. The verb *kèrussein*, used with

almost technical force in the New Testament to designate the testimony given to Christ by His apostles, is used, in Justin, to describe
the prophets' proclamation of Christ. The apostles are not however
forgotten, Justin and the letter to Diognetus link them closely to
Christ and the prophets, attributing to them a role of their own. But
their activity is less frequently described. The Church receives and
preserves, and makes *present* the teaching of Christ, the prophets,
and the apostles.

1. J. B. Lightfoot, *The Apostolic Fathers* (London, 1889-1890); J. Lebreton, *Histoire
du dogme de la Trinité*, 2:249-394; H. Schlier, *Religionsgeschichtliche Untersuchungen zu
den Ignatius-Briefen* (Giessen, 1929); P. Th. Camelot, *Ignace d'Antioche et Polycarpe de
Smyrne* (" Sources chrétiennes i," Paris, 1951), pp. 7-59.

2. J. R. Laurin, *Orientations maitresses des apologistes chrétiens* (Rome, 1954); J. Lebre-
ton, *Histoire du dogme de la Trinité*, 2:395-516; A. Puech, *Les apologistes grecs* (Paris, 1912);
J. Barbel, *Christos Angelos* (Bonn, 1941); A. L. Feder, *Justins des Martyrers Lehre von
Jesus Christus* (Freiburg, 1906); J. Danielou, *Message évangélique et culture hellénistique aux
II et III siècles*, pp. 42-50 et 317-328; C. Andersen, *Logos und Nomos* (Berlin, 1955);
R. Holte, "Logos Spermatikos, Christianity and Ancient Philosophy according to St.
Apologies," *Studia theologica*, 12 (1958) : 109-168; G. Bardy, *Athénagore, Supplique au sujet
des chrétiens* ("Sources chrétiennes 3," Paris, 1943), pp. 7-69; Id., *Théophile d'Antioche, Trois
livres à Autolycus* ("Sources chétiennes 20," Paris, 1948), pp. 7-56; H. I. Marrou, A. *Diognéte*
("*Sources chrétiennes* 33," Paris, 1951), pp. 5-42; M. Spanneut, *Le stoicisme des Pères de
l'Église* (Paris, 1957); G. Aeby, *Les missions divines, de saint Justin à Origène* (Fribourg, 1958),
pp. 6-24; A. Orbe, *Hacia la primera Teología de la procesión del Verbo* (2 vol., Roma, 1958),
pp. 565-603.

3. G. Aeby, *Les missions divines*, p. 14; A. Orbe, *Hacia la primera Teología de la procesión
del Verbo*, pp. 568-574.

4. R. Holte, "Logos Spermatikos, Christianity and Ancient Philosophy according to St. Justin's
Apologies," *Studia thelogica*, 12 (1958) : 144.

5. G. Aeby, *Les missions divines*, pp. 6-10.

6. G. Aeby, *Les missions divines*, pp. 16-20.

CHAPTER II

SAINT IRENAEUS

The work of St. Irenaeus[1] stands out in the midst of an antignostic polemic. Ptolomeans and Marcionites make Christ the Revealer of the unknown God of the Old Testament: Christ, they say, revealed a God distinct from the God of the Law and the prophets. Irenaeus declares, on the contrary, that God is one, and that the economy of revelation is one; for there is one and the same Word of God presiding over the revelation of the Old Testament and New Testament. The theme of revelation, in St. Irenaeus, is bound up with the broader theme of the activity of the Word and the work of salvation. Irenaeus sees the Word at work from the dawn of humanity. Under His guidance, humanity is born, grows and matures up to the fullness of times; through the Incarnation of the Word and His redemptive work, humanity becomes the body of Christ and, together with Him, in Him, walks towards the vision of the Father (IV, 38, 3).[2]

Since it is impossible to know God without God, the Word of God teaches men to know God (IV, 5, 1; 6, 4). It is in His commentary on Mt. 11:25-27 that St. Irenaeus expresses His thinking on God's activity as Revealer and upon the trinitarian roots of this activity.[3] "No one can know the Father excepting the Word of God, that is, unless the Son reveals Him; nor the Son, excepting through the good pleasure of the Father. The Son accomplishes the good pleasure of the Father. The Father sends, the Son is sent and comes. And the Father, invisible and uncircumscribed with respect to us, is known by His own Word and, since He is ineffable, it is this Word which makes Him known to us. In His turn the Father knows only His Word. That is why, by the very act of making Him known, the Son reveals the knowledge of the Father. The manifestation of the Son is the knowledge of the Father, for everything is made manifest through the Word" (IV, 6, 3). The Father reveals Himself to men "by making His Word visible to all; and, in His turn, the Word, in being seen by all, shows the Father and the Son to all" (IV, 6, 5). Thus, the beginning of revelation is the activity of the Father who sends His Son. In coming, the Son reveals Himself; and in becoming visible, He manifests the Father. "Through the Word, become visible and palpable, the Father also appears. The Father is whatever is invisible in the Son and the Son is whatever is visible in the Father" (IV, 6, 6). The Son not only brings about the knowledge of the Father: He is the living manifestation of the Father. Not that the Son is naturally visible: He is invisible by nature, just as the Father Himself, but the Incarnation makes Him visible (Dem. 84), giving Him, in many different ways, the power to manifest the Father (IV, 6, 6). Revelation, in the eyes of Irenaeus, appears thus as an *epiphany* of the Father through the Incarnate Word. The Christ, or the Incarnate Word, is the visible, tangible Person who manifests the Father, whereas the Father is the invisible Person who manifests the Son made visible. St. Irenaeus, obviously, is extending the wording of Jn. 1:18 and 1 Jn. 1:1-3.

Irenaeus admires the marvelous *unity* and *progress* of the plan of revelation. Revelation through the Incarnate Word is the final stage of a process which has been going on since the beginning of the world: first through the work of creation, then through the Law and the prophets, finally through the Incarnation (IV, 6, 6; Dem. 6). Since the Word of God is eternally present with the Father, He is present to humanity from the very beginning, continuously dispensing the graces and mysteries of the Father (III, 11, 1). "The Son, who is from the beginning with the Father, reveals from the beginning" (IV, 20, 7). This revelation of the Father through the Word takes place *progressively*. God wants to make Himself known, because He is good and because man needs this knowledge in order to live. But man is too weak to support the vision of God (IV, 20, 5). Like a good teacher, God *educates* humanity. Irenaeus compares the activity of the Word with a nursing process, which makes man used to eating and drinking the Word of God, and prepares him to assimilate the bread of immortality which is the Spirit of the Father. "Someone will say: could not God, from the very beginning, make a perfect man? Let Him understand that God is always the same, that He is uncreated, and that in what concerns God, all things are possible. . . . Just as a mother cannot give a perfect nourishment to her child because the child is not yet capable of supporting this solid nourishment, the same thing is true of God; He could have offered perfection to man from the very beginning, but man would have been incapable of supporting it: he was after all an infant. That is why our Savior came in these last times, recapitulating all things in Himself, not in accordance with His own power, but in accordance with our power to see Him. He could actually have come in an ineffable glory, but we would not have been able to bear the grandeur of His glory .... First man had to be made, and once he was made he had to arrive at a mature age, and once he had arrived at a mature age, he had to be strengthened, and once he had been strengthened, to grow in strength, and once he had grown in strength, to be glorified and once he had been glorified, he was able to see his Lord" (IV, 38, 1). God prepares man for the vision of Himself by a constant increase in the activity and presence of His Word among men (IV, 20, 5). The two testaments represent two different times in the education of humanity. First of all the Word forms humanity through an external discipline: it is the Law; then, once humanity is formed and capable of acting freely, the Word frees humanity from slavery and adopts it is as Son: this is the Gospel (IV, 9, 1; 11, 1; 20, 10; 36, 4).[4] The relationship between the two Testaments is itself to be found in the perspective of the *economy* or plan of salvation conceived and realized by God in a history which ends in Christ. From Abraham to Christ and the apostles, it is the same God who is acting, making promises and keeping them (IV, 7, 3), following a plan that is both one and manifold (III, 12, 11)). Revelation is pursued "according to a close connection, harmony, at propitious times"; it unfolds "in a thousand providential economies" (IV, 6, 7). The general economy of salvation is actually split into many partial economies which outline its accomplishment, but these manifold economies all hark back to the one universal economy. "There is only one and the same God who, from the beginning to the end, through these various economies, comes to aid the human race" (III, 12, 13). The one God, through His one Word, realizes one single plan of salvation, from creation to the end of the world (III, 16, 6). The history of salvation is one.

Creation constitutes the first stage of revelation. When Christ affirms that no one knows the Father excepting the Son and those to whom the Son has revealed Him (Mt. 11:27), this word holds good for all times, before as well as after the Incarnation. "He does not say this in the future, as if the Word had begun to manifest the Father when He was born of the Virgin Mary, but He is present in the whole of time. From the beginning the Word, present to creation, reveals the Father to everyone, to whom He wills, when He wills, and as He wills" (IV, 6, 7). "Through creation itself, the Word reveals God the Creator; through the world, it reveals the Creator as builder of the world; through its work, it reveals the Workman; through the Son, it reveals the Father" (IV, 6, 6; II, 6, 1; 27, 2; III, 25, 1; V, 18, 3). Irenaeus does not say whether this testimony that the created world gives to God can be grasped by the light of reason. In the order of fact, where He takes His stand, it is knowledge of a religious character that is in question, a manifestation that involves salvation or judgment (IV, 65, 5-6; 20:7).

"Through the Law and prophets as well, the Word proclaimed Himself and proclaimed His Father" (IV, 6, 6; 9,3). Just like Justin and Theophilus of Antioch, Irenaeus attributes theophanies to the Word of God. Man is hardly created when the Word begins to appear to him and to instruct him (Dem. 12). It is through the Word that Abraham knew the Father (IV, 7, 1. 3); it is the Word that spoke to Moses (IV, 5, 2). All those who, from the beginning, have known God and have prophesied the coming of Christ, received this revelation of the Son (IV, 7, 2). The Son of God "speaks now with Abraham, now with Noah, ... now He seeks out Adam, now He comes to judge the Sodomites; once again He appears leading Jacob on his journey, or in the bush speaking to Moses" (IV, 10, 1). It is the Son who appears, and not the Father: "All the visions of this type mean that the Son of God is speaking with men and conversing with them, for it is not the Father of all and the Creator of the universe ... who has come to this corner of the earth to speak with Abraham, but the Word of God who is always with the human race and who foretells future events and teaches the things of God to men" (Dem. 45). In Justin, theophanies tended to prove the distinction between Father and Word; in Irenaeus, they are meant to establish, against the Marcionites, the unicity (oneness) of God and the unity of the divine plan from one Testament to the other. God reveals Himself, not only since the days of Tiberius, but since the dawn of humanity. Through theophanies, God is used to living among men: "From the beginning, the Word of God is used to rising and descending for the salvation of those who are sick" (IV, 12, 4; Dem. 45). This habit finds its completion in the Incarnation, which is the habitual presence of God to man and man to God: "The Word became Son of Man in order to make man accustomed to receiving God and to accustom God to dwelling in man according to the good pleasure of the Father" (III, 20, 2). On the one hand, there is a descent on the part of God through the theophanies and the Incarnation and, on the other hand, there is an ascent on the part of man towards God through his education under the guidance of the Word. The Old Testament prepares divine nature to unite with human nature, and it prepares human nature to be united with divine nature. The theophanies are real anticipations of the Incarnation, but they remain only the first outlines of the supreme revelation, sketches of the future (IV, 20, 10-11), partial visions of the Word of God, who becomes visible only in the Incarnation, while still veiling His glory.[5] What is true of the patriarchs is also true of the prophets: Ezekiel, Elijah, Moses did not see the face of God, but only the figurative signs of His presence and the signs that announced a greater presence still (IV, 20, 9-10), namely, the human presence of the Word. Prophecy itself is an *announcing* of realities to come (IV, 20, 5) and at the same time a *preparation* of humanity for the time when the Word of God will come in human flesh (IV, 20, 8).

This manifestation of God through His Word throughout history effects the unity of the two Testaments. "The two Testaments have been established by one and the same great Father, our Lord Jesus Christ, who spoke with Abraham and Moses, and who, in these last days, has given us freedom" (IV, 9, 1). The prophets announce the Christ and the Gospel to come (IV, 34, 1); the apostles preached Him (IV, 36, 5). "It is not one God who inspired the prophets and another God who inspired the apostles, ... but one and the same God gave to some the power to preach the Lord, to others the power to make the Father known, to others the power to proclaim in advance the coming of the Son of God, to others finally the power to announce His presence to those who were distant" (IV, 36, 5).

There is unity between the two Testaments, but what a difference still between the Christ announced by the prophets and the Christ present in humanity! The Old Testament is only a promise, an announcing; the New Testament is realization, accomplishment, the gift of the Incarnate Word. In answer to the question: "If the Old Testament already knew the Word, in what does the novelty of the New Testament consist?" Irenaeus answers: the Son in His coming "has given us everything new in giving us Himself, He ... who came to renew and vivify humanity. The servants who are sent before the king announce His coming, so that His subjects will be prepared to receive their Lord. But when the King is come, when His subjects ... have received their freedom from Him, when they have looked upon His face, when they have heard His words, when they have enjoyed His gifts, we no longer ask what this King has given more than what His precursors had proclaimed. He has given Himself" (IV, 34, 1). The Incarnation is the culminating point of the constant intervention of the Word. "The Word, who is with God from the beginning (Jn. 1:1), by whom all things have been made (Jn. 1:13), and who constantly assists the human race, the same Word, in these last times, at the moment foreordained by the Father, has united Himself to the work that He modeled, has made Himself capable of suffering" (III, 18, 1; IV, 41, 4). The Incarnation is a new theophany of the Word of God, and the progress realized consists in the human and carnal presence of the Word, in flesh and blood, visible and tangible among men, in order to manifest the Father who remains invisible (IV, 24, 2). What is new about Christianity is the human life of the Word: there is no new God, but there is a new manifestation of God in Jesus Christ. Before the Incarnation, men knew the Incarnate Word only obscurely, in a veiled fashion, perceiving only images of His human presence; the Old Testament was ruled by the Word, but the Word was to become visible and tangible only through the Incarnation.[6] This is the first point that is new about the Incarnation; and it is the source of all the others, for the presence of the Incarnate Word is the source of new graces (III, 10, 2; IV, 36, 4). It is the same God "who has always something more to give to those of His household, and, in the measure that they progress in the love of God, always gives them more" (IV, 9, 2). The Incarnation inaugurates a new stage in our approach towards the divine likeness. The Word, who had made man in His own image, comes to repair His work now disfigured by sin; He shows "the image in all truth, by becoming Himself that which was His image, that is, man," and He stamps a deep "likeness, making man like to His invisible Father, through the visible Word" (V, 16, 2). With the gift of Christ, all humanity (and not only Israel) now passes from the law of slavery into the law of freedom (IV, 13, 2; 9, 1).

The terminus of this activity of revelation is the doctrine *taught* by Christ, *preached and transmitted* through the apostles, *preserved* in the Church. The terms: revelation, preaching, tradition, Church, present throughout the work of Irenaeus, are all closely bound together and need to be defined.

The Word of God, the one and only Revealer, is also our one and only Teacher. This title insists on the veracity and authority of the Word. "We should have been unable to know the things of God, if our Teacher had not become man, while still remaining the Word. For no one could reveal to us the things that are the Father's excepting His Word.... And, on the other hand we would be able to *learn* only by *seeing* our teacher and by actually *hearing* the sound of His voice" (I, 1, 1; III, 18, 7). Thus, through all the channels of the Incarnation, through word and through activity, Christ reveals the Father.

But Christ did not leave any writings: He lived and taught. The apostles are the intermediaries between Christ and the Church, for it is to them that Christ officially entrusted His message (I, 27, 2; IV, 37, 7). "The apostles transmitted purely and simply what they themselves had learned from the Lord" (III, 14, 2). They handed down to us, first of all, a living Gospel, later entrusted to writing in the form of a fourfold Gospel, "sustained by one single Spirit" (III, 11, 8). "The teacher of all things has given His apostles the power to *preach* the Gospel. It is through them that we know the truth, that is, the teaching of the Son of God.... This Gospel they first of all *preached*. Then, through the will of God, they *handed it down* in the Scriptures, so that it became the basis and support of our *Faith*" (III, 1, 1). The role of the apostles, witnesses to the word, is thus a role of *preaching* and *handing down* the doctrine of Christ, or the Gospel (III, 1, 1; II, 35, 4). The object of this preaching is not a different God from that of the Old Testament, but the Son of God who became man and suffered (III, 12, 3; IV, 23, 2).

The faith of the Church is based on this doctrine, received from the apostles (II, 9, 1), which she "faithfully *guards, teaches* without defect, and, in her turn, *hands down* to her children" (I, 10, 2). Thus, the apostles and the Church each *hands down*, but with different titles: the apostles communicate the very revelation of the New Testament (I, 8, 1), whereas the Church hands down the revealed truth, without changing anything (I, 10, 2). Such is the rule of salvation and the norm of life: "the prophets *announced* it, Christ *established* it, the apostles *handed it down*, the Church *offers* it to her children" (Dem. 98). Thus, if anyone is looking for the truth, he will find it in the faith preached by the apostles, handed down by them to the Church and preserved to our times (III, 2, 2; 3, 3). Irenaeus never tires of repeating this fact: the tradition of the apostles is preserved in the Church: "The apostles, laid away in her, like a rich storehouse, all truth, in its fullness" (III, 4, 1). What guarantees the fidelity of the Church to Christ and His doctrine is the activity of the Holy Spirit: the Holy Spirit is first of all sent to the apostles to remind them of the teaching of the Word in its true meaning and to strengthen them in their possession of the truth (III, 1, 1); the Spirit is also at work in the Church to guarantee the preservation of the faith, which "like a choice wine preserved in a cask of fine quality, retains its freshness and vigor, and gives new freshness to the cask in which it is stored.... For where the Church is, there also is the Spirit of God" (III, 24, 1). Thus, the unity which springs from God springs up once again, through Christ and the apostles, in the Church and the Church makes it known throughout the entire world (III, 3, 3). "The Church, spread over all the earth up to the very ends of the world, has received, from the apostles and their disciples, her faith in one single God ... and in one single Christ Jesus ... and in the Holy Spirit .... The Church, spread throughout the whole world, carefully guards this kerygma she has received, together with the faith. She guards them as if she had only one house; she believes them as if she had only one heart and one soul, and in the same way she preaches and teaches and passes them on as if she had only one mouth.... Just as the sun, a creature of God, is one and the same over the whole earth, thus the preaching of the truth appears everywhere and enlightens all who want to come to a knowledge of the truth" (I, 10, 2).

Revelation has charateristics which distinguish it from all human doctrine. It is first of all, essentially, a work of *grace*. No speculative effort can give access to the mystery of the intimate life of God. God alone can open Himself to man through a gracious gesture which is the work of love. Thus, every claim of human pride is abolished; knowledge of God appears as His gift to those who love Him: "Because of His *grandeur* and His admirable glory, no one will ever see God without dying. The Father cannot actually be known. But because of His *love* and His humanity, and because everything is possible for Him, He has granted even this, to those who love Him: the power of seeing God, as the prophets announced, because things which are impossible to men are possible to God" (IV, 20, 5). Second, revelation is the work of *salvation*. For those who do not believe, it is judgment, but for those who believe it is salvation and life; it tends to make man enter into vision and immortality (Dem. 31). "It is impossible to live, if we do not have life; we possess life only by sharing in God; now sharing in God means seeing God and enjoying His goodness. Men will see God in order to live, becoming immortal through this vision and arriving at the very presence of God" (IV, 20, 5-6). "Those who see God are in God and share in His light" (IV, 20, 5). Finally, revelation is at once an *unveiling* and a *veiling* of God: God reveals Himself to stir up human progress, but at the same time that He reveals He hides something so that man will not lose his sense of mystery and respect. The Word of God "has been made the Dispenser of the Father's glory in view of man's best interests. That is why He accomplished this whole economy, showing God to man, presenting man to God, preserving the invisibility of the Father, for fear that man should come to despise God and so that there will always be room for progress, but on the other hand making God visible to man through numerous theophanies, for fear that man, totally lacking the vision of his God, might cease to exist. For the glory of God is man alive, and the life of man is the vision of God" (IV, 20, 6-7).

Irenaeus is aware of the dynamic and historical aspect of revelation. He stresses the movement, the progress, the profound unity. He sees the Word of God at work from the very beginning: creation, the theophanies of the patriarchs, the Law, the prophets, Christ, the apostles, the Church—these are all distinct moments in the activity of the Word, in the economy of the progressive manifestation of the Father through the Word. Underlying this is one single movement, one single palpitation of love which has its origin in the Trinity and is felt throughout all time, culminating in vision. Hence, the indivisible unity of the two Testaments. As regards the Old Testament—this was the big problem of the second century—two attitudes might exist: one might fail to grasp the newness of the Gospel (this was the temptation in traditional Jewish circles) or one might underestimate the Old Testament and completely break with it, as did Marcion. Irenaeus, together with Clement of Alexandria and Tertullian, take their place in a current of thought which stresses the unity of the two Testaments. Irenaeus sees in the two Testaments two successive stages in the education of humanity by the one single Word of God. Still, between the two, there is the difference between Christ as announced and Christ as present and given. Irenaeus sees a close bond between revelation and the Person of Christ, as did Ignatius of Antioch. Revelation is the epiphany of God in Christ and through Christ; it is the manifestation of the Father through the Son and through all the manners of expression made possible by the Incarnation. Through His Word and through His activity, through His example and through His teaching, Christ makes known the Father and His plan for salvation. Witnesses to the Word, the apostles, enlightened by the Spirit, preach and hand down whatever they have learned from the Lord: it is through them that Christ delivers His message. The Church, for her part, receives the teaching handed down by the apostolic witnesses: she preserves it faithfully, she sees it grow in depth, without proving false to it, until the time of the second coming. Hence the essentially apostolic character of Church tradition. In its actual form, revelation, or the things handed down, is the teaching of the Son of God, the Gospel message, the tradition or teaching of the apostles, the faith of the Church, the Christian mystery, truth, the rule of salvation, the norm of life, Christ Himself. Revelation is thus not a human doctrine, but a gift of Love, a doctrine which stirs up faith, gives rise to life in those who believe and leads them towards vision and immortality. Irenaeus describes revelation like someone who is still under the impact of the event, someone who can still experience the excitement and communicate the freshness to those who read him.

1. On Irenaeus and the theme of revelation, we have consulted the following books and articles F. SAGNARD, *Irénée de Lyon, Contre les heresies, L. III* ("Sources chretiennes 34," Paris, 1952), pp. 9-85; L. M. FROIDEVAUX, *Irénée de Lyon, Demonstration de la predication apostolique* ("Sources chrétiennes 62," Paris, 1959); J. LEBRETON, *Histoire du dogme de la Trinité,* 2:517-617; ID., "La connaissance de Dieu chez S. Irénee," *Rech. de sc. rel.,* 16 (1926) : 385-406; A. BENOIT, *Saint Irénée, Introduction à l'etude de theologie* (Paris, 1960); A. HOUSSIAU, *La christologie de S. Irénée* (Louvain, 1955); ID., "L'exegèse de Mt. II, 27b selon S. Irenee," *Eph. theol. lov.* 29 (1953) : 328-354; J. FORD, *St. Irenaeus and Revelation, A Theological Perspective* (Dissertatio ad lauream, Romae, 1961); G. AEBY, *Les missions divines, de Saint Justin à Origène* (Fribourg, 1958); J. DANIELOU, *Message évangélique et culture hellénistique aux II et III siècles* (Paris-Tournai-New York-Rome, 1961); F. HITCHCOCK, *Irenaeus of Lugdunum, A Study of his Theology* (Cambridge, 1914); L. ESCOULA, "Le Verbe sauveur et illuminateur chez S. Irénée," *Nouvelle Revue theologique,* 66 (1939) : 385-400, 551-567; ID., "Saint Irénée et la connaissance naturelle de Dieu," *Revue des sc. rel.,* 20 (1940) :252-271; R. D. LUCKHART, "Matthew 11, 27 in the Contra Haereses of St. Irenaeus," *Rev. de l'Université d'Ottawa,* 23 (1953) : 65°-79°; B. REYNDERS, "Paradosis, Le progrès de l'idée de tradition jusqu'à S. Irénée," *Rech. de théol. anc. et méd.,* 5 (1933) : 155-191; H. HOLSTEIN, "La tradition des apotres chez S. Irénée," *Recherches de sc. rel.,* 36 (1949) : 229-270; ID., "Les témoins de la révélation d'après S. Irénée," *Rech. de sc. rel.,* 41 (1953) : 410-420; D. E. LANNE, "Le ministère apostolique dans l'oeuvre de S. Irénée," *Irenikon,* 25 (1952) : 113-141; J. DANIELOU, "S. Irénée et les origines de la théologie de l'histoire," *Rech. de sc. rel.* 34 (1947 : 227-231; K. PRUMM, "Gottliche Planung und menschliche Entwicklung nach Irenaus Adversus Haereses," *Scholastik,* 13 (1938): 206-224, 342-366; A. VERRIELE, "Le plan du salut d'après S. Irénée," *Rev. des sc. rel.,* 14 (1934) : 493-524; TH. A. AUDET, "Orientations théologiques chez S. Irénée," *Traditio,* 1943, pp. 15-54; H. DE LUBAC, *Catholicisme* (Paris, 1938); R. WILSON, *The Gnostic Problem* (London, 1958); A. ORBE, *Hacia la primera Teologia de la Procesión del Verbo,* (Roma, 1958).

2. References without contrary indication are the *Adversus Haereses.* The abbreviation *Dem.* is used for *Demonstration of the Apostolic Preaching.*

3. On this text see primarily: A. HOUSSIAU, *La christologie de S. Irénée,* pp. 72-73, 109-114, 127-128; ID., "L'exégèse de Mt. 11, 27b selon S. Irénée," *Eph. theol. lov.,* 29 (1953): 328-354; G. AEBY, *Les missions divines, de Saint Justin à Origène,* pp. 51-53.

4. J. DANIELOU, *Message évangélique et culture hellénistique aux II et III siécles,* p. 159.

5. G. AEBY, *Les missions divines, de Saint Justin à Origène,* p. 56.

6 A. HOUSSIAU, *La christologie de S. Irénée,* pp. 127-128.

CHAPTER III

TESTIMONY OF THE GREEK CHURCH

1. Clement of Alexandria

Other Fathers see primarily redemption in Christianity, salvation, deliverance from sin. Clement of Alexandria[1] looks primarily for the revelation of God: "If, for example, someone were to offer the gnostic a choice between the knowledge of God and eternal salvation, if these two things were really separate and distinct (whereas, on the contrary, they are one and the same) the gnostic would not hesitate for a moment to choose the knowledge of God" (Str. IV, 136, 5). This is an attitude inspired by Clement's intellectual temperament, and also by the atmosphere at Alexandria, oriented towards a religion based on revelation.

In the center of human history, as in the center of his theology, Clement locates the Incarnate Logos, Christ, source of all knowledge and Savior of all men. The Logos[2] is the Creator and Organizer of the world. He is the one sole Author of the manifestation of God in the Law, the prophets, the philosophy of the Greeks, the Incarnation. He is the teacher who instructs humanity, the Savior and Creator of new life. Life that begins with faith, progresses with the gnosis, and is consummated in eternal vision. In His relationship with humanity, Clement assigns Him a threefold role: He converts, educates, instructs. Still, the most comprehensive of His titles, the one which gathers together all the different attributes of the Logos with regard to humanity, seems to be that of Light (Str. VII, 5, 5).

The Logos is designed by nature to reveal the Father, for He is the Face and Image of the Father. "The Son is called the Face of the Father (Ps. 23:6), because He, the Word, revealer of the innermost nature of the Father, has put on human flesh." (Str. V, 34, 1). "The Face of the Father, that is the Logos through whom God is made known and revealed" (Paed. I, 57, 2; Str. VII, 58, 3-4). Insofar as He is Logos, the Son "is, before all ages, the first Image of the invisible God" (Str. V, 38, 7). He is the begotten Image who, through His mission among men, becomes the Incarnate Image; it is because the Logos is already begotten as the Image of the Father in the bosom of the Trinity that He is sent as Revealer of the Father. It is He, the Logos, ontologically qualified to reveal, who enlightens humanity and directs it towards the fullness of truth; it is He who effects the unity of revelation throughout human history.

The manifestation of the truth is accomplished by degrees, following a constant progress (Str. VI, 44, 1; 166, 4-167, 1). We can follow the activity of the Logos throughout the course of the ages. Like Justin and Irenaeus, Clement attributes theophanies to the Logos. It is the Logos who speaks to Abraham (Paed. I, 56, 2-3), who makes the promises to Jacob (Paed. I, 56, 3-4) and wrestles with him (Paed. I, 57, 1); again, it is the Logos who brings Israel out of Egypt, leads her across the desert, protects her as His child, becomes the guide of His people through Moses (Paed. I, 58, 1). In certain passages of the *Stromata*, Clement does not present theophanies as personal apparitions, affecting the external senses, but rather as an inner illumination, a sort of divine touch in which the soul recognizes God (Str. VI, 34, 2-3). It is once again the Logos who gives the Law (Str. I, 167, 3), who, through the prophets, sings, fortells, threatens (Prot. 8, 3). It is the Logos, finally, who is incarnate to instruct us in God (Prot. 8, 3-4) and teach us what we are ourselves (Str. I, 178, 2). Before this time, God needed some borrowed form (angel, prophet); with the Incarnation, He Himself becomes man (Paed. I, 58, 1) and "speaks to us in all clarity" (Prot. 8, 3-4; Str. I, 29, 5). In revealing, the Logos pursues one single goal, to save humanity: "God also sent the good shepherd. The Logos unfolded all truth to men in order to show them the grandeur of their salvation" (Prot. 116, 1). Logos of truth and incorruptibility, He "makes man divine by a heavenly teaching" (Prot. 114, 4) and regenerates him for eternal life (Prot. 117:4).

Clement lays great stress on the organic unity between the Old and New Testament. The Law, the prophets, the Gospel, are the work of one and the same God through His Logos; they are aimed at one and the same knowledge (Str. II, 29, 3; III, 70, 3). In the last analysis, there is only one history of salvation, throughout all time and space.

The divine law cannot be reduced to the Law of Moses—the law of nature, the law of the Greeks and barbarians have the same

God for their author—but in Moses and the prophets we have the true Law (Str. I, 165-167). The same Logos who instructed the people through Moses (Paed. I, 60, 1) has given us the Gospel. The precepts of the Sermon on the Mount complete the precepts given to Moses (Prot. 108, 4-5; Str. VI, 94, 6). From Law to Gospel there is progress: the Gospel demands are greater and reach down into the most intimate thoughts; the Gospel inspires, no longer fear, but freedom and love. "Before, the people of old had an Old Testament, a Law which educated the people with fear, and the Logos was an angel: but now, to the new and younger people a New and younger Testament has been offered, and the Logos is made flesh and fear is changed to love" (Paed. I, 59, 1). Still there is no opposition between the two: the Law prepares the Gospel (Str. II, 37, 2-3), and the Gospel accomplishes the Law (Str. VI, 94, 6). Christ is the terminus and accomplishment of the Law (Str. II, 42, 5). The Law is only an image of the truth; Christ *is* the truth (Str. VI, 58, 1 ff). He is Himself the Law (Prot. 2, 3). In the last analysis, the difference between Law and Gospel is to be found in the Incarnation of the Logos: the Law comes through Moses, the Gospel through Christ (Paed. I, 60, 1). But since it is the same Logos who makes Himself heard in the Law and in the Gospel, we must never look down on the Law, as do the heretics Valentin, Basilides, and Marcion (Paed. II, 29, 1).

Closer still is the relationship between prophecy and Gospel. In the oracles of the prophets, Clement sees riddles and symbols to which Christ is the solution. He distinguishes two phases of revelation: prophecy and explanation of prophecy. Prophecy is a figurative teaching, full of mystery, which remains obscure until its accomplishment. Christ offers Himself as the explanation of prophecy: "The light of truth, the Logos, once He has become Gospel, must loosen the mysterious silence of the prophetic secrets" (Prot. 10, 1; Str. VI, 68, 3). Clement sees in the silence of Zachary the mysterious silence of the prophecies, broken finally by the Incarnation of the Logos (Prot. 10, 1). The figure of the past thus becomes a call aimed at the future which enlightens it. Christ is the door and the key to the mysteries of the Father: "No one knows the Father excepting the Son and him to whom the Son has revealed. This door has been closed up till now, and the one who opens it ... reveals what is on the inside and shows what we could not know before, but only when we had passed through Christ, the only Intermediary who confers the initiation of revelation" (Prot. 10, 3). There are two consequences to this way of looking at things: the first is that the coming of Christ as key to the Old Testament testifies to the truth of His mission and

His Person. Revelation, at the same time that it is accomplished in history, is a demonstration of its own truth. The second is that the rule of faith is precisely the harmony of the two Testaments realized in the Person of Christ: "The canon of the Church is the accord and harmony of the Law and the prophets with the Testament given through the presence of the Lord" (Str. VI, 125, 3).

Clement's theology also locates philosophy within this same economy of revelation. He considers it as a "gift of God to the Greeks" (Str. I, 20, 1), as a particular economy willed by him to lead them to Christ: "Just as the kerygma has come today in its own time, even so the Law and the prophets were given in their time to the barbarians, and philosophy to the Greeks, to tune their ears for the kerygma" (Str. VI, 44, 1). Philosophy, for the Greeks, is what the Law was to the Jews; it is a preparation for Christ, just as the Law is for the Hebrews. "God is the source of all good things, some in a primary way, like the two Testaments, others in a subordinate way, like philosophy. But we might also say that it is by primary title that philosophy was given to the Greeks before the Lord called them: actually, it effected the education of Hellenism towards Christ, just as the law educated the Hebrews" (Str. I, 28, 1-3; VI, 41, 7-42, 1). Philosophy was given to the Greeks in view of their salvation: "Philosophy was necessary for the Greeks for their justification before the coming of the Lord" (Str. I, 28, 1). "Just as in giving them the prophets, God willed that the Jews should be saved, even so he stirs up, as it were, their own prophets among the Greeks, in their language, the most gifted minds among them, in the measure in which they were capable of receiving the gift of God" (Str. VI, 42, 3; 110, 3; 153, 1). Clement also sees the philosophy of the Greeks as a covenant, as a special testament: "If, in a general way, all the things necessary and useful for life come to us from God, then philosophy is all the more given to the Greeks as a covenant of their own, since it is a stage in the philosophy of Christ" (Str. VI, 67, 1). This gift of God to the Greeks was communicated to them through the angels set in charge over the nations, who are the ministers of the Logos (Str. VI, 57, 2-4). Thus, Jew, Greek, and Christian, philosophy, Law, and Gospel are of one and the same salvific order: they are three dispositions or Testaments with one and the same Logos for their Author.[3] These three peoples, in different economies, all received the divine teaching through the voice of one and the same Lord. There is only one truth, but it is like a river into which smaller currents empty from many sources (Str. I, 29, 1-4; 7, 38).

It is important to distinguish philosophy as an economy or historical disposition guiding the Greeks towards Christ and philosophy as an instrument in the service of revealed truth. Now it serves as a propaedeutic, preparing the way for faith and, in the inner workings of faith, a means of deepening and defending the faith. It prepares for revelation, "insofar as it is a search for truth" (Str. I, 97-100), insofar as it "stirs up an eager spirit of careful searching for the true philosophy," that is, Christianity (Str. I, 32, 4), and "prepares to let itself be steeped in truth" (Str. I, 80, 6). In the bosom of faith, it is a precious dialectic, serving to make that faith rich in fruit (Str. I, 35, 2-4), to demonstrate that faith solidly (Str. I, 20, 2) and to defend revealed truth (Str. I, 99-100).

Thus, finally, philosophy has only one right: to lead towards the Gospel and discover there a truth that is more perfect and more sound. It yields before the Testament of Christ. The truth that the philosophers could only glimpse, the faithful now possess in fullness: "For we are the *students* of God, it is His very Son who gives us a truly holy instruction" (Str. I, 98, 4); we are "disciples of God, depositaries of the only true wisdom" (Prot. 112, 2). The incomparable superiority of Christianity comes from the fact that it has the "Logos for Teacher" (Str. II, 9, 4-6), the Logos who teaches the way of eternal life (Prot. 7, 3. 6). The Incarnate Logos fills the universe with his truth and makes a new Athens of the whole earth: "This teacher now teaches us everything" (Prot. 112, 1); the "Word of our teacher ... has gone out over all the earth" (Str. VI, 167, 3-5). The stars all go out, in the morning, when the sun rises upon the horizon. The object of our faith is the teaching of our Master (Str. I, 38, 5), His divine doctrine (Str. VI, 122, 1-2; II, 21, 5).

Christ is the full light, the sun which dispels all night. This symbol of light, harking back to John and Plato, is Clement's favorite figure for revelation, natural as well as supernatural. The illuminating activity of the Logos is from the beginning of creation. Clement compares his activity to that of the sun rising: the sun of the soul "who alone, rising deep down within the innermost depths of the mind, illuminates the eye of the soul" (Prot. 68:4). This is an intimate activity which appears as a continued creation of light and intelligence. Through his Gospel particularly, the Logos is the light of the human race. He has "enlightened us" by His teaching (Prot. 110, 3). He has "enlightened our mind buried in darkness" (Prot. 113, 2). If we had not "known the Logos and had not been illuminated by His rays of light," we would be in a shadow, like birds that they are fattening for the slaughter (Prot. 113, 3). Men were wandering about in search of God: Christ instructs them in His Gospel and illuminates their whole life (Prot. 114:1). "Let us receive the light and let us become disciples of the Lord" (Prot. 113:4; 114). When Clement says that Christ is the light, this term extends to the whole salvific activity of the Logos: He tears us away from the darkness of ignorance, sin, and death, and leads us to the kingdom of truth, light, and life (Prot. 114-116). The apologists insisted on the activity of the Logos in the world; in saying that Christ is the light, Clement insists on his individual activity, in the intimacy of the human soul.

With the gift of revelation received in faith, a whole new movement is inaugurated, the fructification of the gnosis. The gnosis is not a new revelation, nor some occult knowledge, but the growth of faith. Clement conceives of the order of salvation as a passing from darkness to faith, and from faith to gnosis. At the interior of each stage, there is room for growth. The gnosis can be the work of philosopher, Jew, or believer. But the true gnosis is the property of the believer. At baptism, the believer receives the germ of faith. This germ demands a development. Gnosis is the growth of faith: not only adhering to the truth, but understanding of the faith which takes place in love (Str. VII, 1, 1; 57, 4; 68, 1), understanding acquired by study and practice of the commandments (Str. III, 44, 2). The perfect gnostic tries to live his life in accord with the will of God for, in the last analysis, love alone gives understanding of faith: "God is charity, making Himself known to those who love Him; likewise, God is deserving of faith, giving Himself through His teaching to those who believe" (Str. V, 13, 1-2). The gnostic has "complete faith which bears upon his actions, praising the Gospel both by his acts and by his contemplation" (Str. VII, 78, 2). By his faith, always searching and longing for the divine will, he turns little by little into a living image of Christ Himself, working in turn to form perfect gnostics, making himself a teacher like Christ (Str. VII, 52). Three things, actually, make up this Christian gnostic: contemplation, fulfillment of the precepts of the Lord, the formation of perfect Christians (Str. II, 46, 1). Finally, the end product of this gnosis is vision: "Then you will contemplate God, you will be initiated into the holy mysteries, you will enjoy the secret blessings of heaven" (Prot. 118, 4).

Clement's system rests upon his theology of the Logos, as Revealer and Savior. This idea certainly existed before him, in Justin and Irenaeus, but in Clement it is much more comprehensive and much more concrete. The Logos is the only source from which all truth derives. It is the same Logos who is revealed by gradual degrees through the Law, the prophets, and the Gospel. From the Logos once again derives the truth of Greek philosophy. Because he sees in Greek philosophy a gift of the Logos, source of all truth, Clement does not hesitate to consider it as a third Testament, as a special covenant between God and the Greeks, to lead them to Christ. This esteem for Greek philosophy distinguishes Clement from his contemporaries. The same esteem can be found somewhat in Justin, but in Clement it is a dominant factor in his thinking. Jews, Greeks, and Christians are all ruled by one and the same Lord who reunites them in one single people for one single faith. In the background of his thinking, there are always the marcionite and gnostic adversaries: thus he also insists on the unity, harmony, and development of revelation. The peak of this activity of revelation is the Incarnation of the Logos. It is the Incarnation which separates Gospel from Greek philosophy and from the Old Testament; it is also the Incarnation which gives them a meaning, for Christ is the fulfillment of the desires and longing of philosophy, Christ is the fulfillment of the Law, the explanation of prophecy, the exegesis of Scripture. The Incarnation continues, perfects, and consummates the history of revelation. For Clement, the quest for man is first of all the quest for truth; he sees in Christ primarily the Teacher, the great Master who brings the true philosophy, the truth. Christ is Sun and Light of souls. This truth, however, is not abstract, for the gnosis, which is the full appropriation of revelation, can be had only through charity.

2. Origen

Origen's system[4] is built up with God as a starting point (De Princ. I, 1, 1). Pure spirit, God generates the Word or Son. The Word proceeds from the Father as an invisible Image, equal to the Father, a filial Image, faithfully reproducing the characteristics of its model, an eternal Image, constantly begotten by the Father.[5] Since the Word is begotten by the Father as His Image, He is designed to manifest the Father. "We see, in the Word, who is God and Image of God invisible, the Father who has begotten Him; when we look at the Image of the invisible God, we can also see the Father, the Prototype of the Image" (Com. Jo. 32, 29). "When we see someone's image, we see the person whose image it is: in the same way, through the Word of God, His Image, we see God" (Hom. Gen., I, 13). Throughout the whole of the history of salvation, it is the Word which reveals the Father's secrets: "The Word can be called Son in so far as He announces the Father's secrets, the Father being Intelligence, just as the Son is called Word. Just as a human word reveals the visions of human intelligence, even so the Word of God knows the Father, and since no creature can approach the Father without a guide, He reveals the Father whom He knows" (Com. Jo. I, 38). Origen expresses himself in very nearly the same terms as Clement. The Word proceeds from the Father, and He is the born Revealer of the Father insofar as He is His Image and His Word. Since the Word already exists in the bosom of the Trinity even before being sent among men, as the revealing Image of God, the Word is naturally qualified to fill His mission as Revealer.

God is unknowable. He becomes something close to us only through Jesus Christ and His Spirit. "The Word was made flesh in order to dwell among us, and we can begin to understand Him only in this way" (Com. Jo. 1, 18). We come close to this Word only through His Incarnation. Still, this Incarnation of the Word is not the epiphany of an invisible God, but rather an instrument of His manifestation. Christ manfests the Father in the sense that the man who has understood Christ "understands the Father by that very fact, according to the words of Christ: He who sees me sees the Father" (De Princ. 1, 2, 6). There could be no question here of perceiving the Father in some visible way in Christ, but rather conceiving and understanding the Father as invisible and spiritual, on the basis of the sign and image that is Jesus (C. Cels. 7, 43). Whoever does not arrive at the Word by means of his human flesh, that is, whoever does not get beyond the humanity of Christ and glimpse His divinity, does not even understand the flesh itself, just as the man who stops at the literal meaning of Scripture, without going on to its spiritual meaning, does not really understand even the letter of Scripture. The Word became Flesh to lead us to His vision, so that we who are flesh might see Him as He was before taking flesh (C. Cels. 6, 68; 4, 15). Material vision is not enough to give us a knowledge of the Word of God (Com. Jo. 19, 2; 20, 30). Pilate, Judas, the Pharisees, the Jews all saw Jesus with their bodily eyes, but without approaching the "knowledge of the Word." Only he has really *seen* who has *known* Christ as the Word of God and, through this Word, has known the Father (Com. Cant. 3; Hom. Lc. 1). Thus, the apostles saw the body of Jesus and also know the Word of God (Hom. Lc. 3); the same is true of Peter who confessed Christ, and Paul the apostle of the Lord. Believing in Christ and recognizing in Him the glory of the Word, is a gift of the Spirit who illuminates human hearts (Hom. Jer. 10, 1).

The Word put on the form of a slave in order to instruct man "through His example and teachings" (De Princ. IV, 4, 5). The flesh is the privileged instrument which makes the Word understood as our Teacher and seen as our Model (De Princ. III, 5, 5; C. Cels. 2, 11. 16. 40. 44). As a Savior, Christ is the envoy from the Father who comes "to take the hand of those who were far away from God and lead them back upon the path of God" (Com. Jo. 32, 3): He shows the way of salvation. He comes "to instruct and educate man" (De Princ. I, 3, 8). The education of the Old Testament gives way to "the superior teachings of Christ" (De Princ. III, 6, 8), who has given "dogmas of salvation" (De Princ. IV, 1). Christ is the Light of the world through His doctrine (Hom. Lev. 13, 2; Hom. Gen. I, 5; C. Cels. 8, 5; 6:79). He is the one Master, the "Teacher of divine mysteries" (C. Cels. 3, 62. 81). He reveals the Father through His teaching, which is the source of all religious truth: "Those who believe and are convinced that grace and truth come through Jesus Christ, and that Christ is Truth itself, do not look for the knowledge of virtue and happiness anywhere but in the words and doctrine of Christ." But Christ "also spoke in Moses and the prophets" and, after His ascension, "He continues to speak in the apostles" (De Princ., praef. I). On the other hand, just as Christ is present to men only through the Church, the Church is also an authentic manifestation of the Word. Christ, the apostles, the Church—these are the "great lights" of the world (Hom. Gen. 1, 5-6). The doctrine of Christ comes to us through the preaching of the apostles and the teaching of the Church. The rule of faith is thus the preaching of the Church, which passes down the living teaching of the apostles in all its integrity (De Princ., praef. 2); it is the "word of the Church" (Com. Jo. 5, 8), the "doctrine of the Church" (Hom. Num. 9, 1). Scripture too contains His teaching (Com. Mtt. ser. 46). "Whoever perfectly understands the sense of an apostolic writing, without deforming it, receives, at the same time as he receives the apostle, the Christ who speaks and lives in the apostle, and he possesses as well the teachings of Christ" (Fragm. Mtt. 218). In Origen's thinking these terms are co-extensive. The Word of God becomes Flesh in Jesus and spreads throughout the Scripture. Scripture and Incarnation are two incorporations of the Word which aim at revealing Him to us (Hom. Jer. 9, 1; Com. Jo. 2, 1-9). But the voice of Christ in Scripture is addressed to the Church and echoes throughout the Church.

The teaching of Christ which the Church preaches is divine: it is accompanied by grace, for only grace lets us understand and grasp the meaning of the mysteries (Com. Jo. 20, 18). Man would not ever turn towards God if God Himself did not touch the human soul (C. Cels. I, 9). The words of Christ are "spoken with a divine

virtue" (C. Cels. 7, 54), and the preacher is incapable of touching
human hearts if "grace is not joined to what He says" (C. Cels. 6, 2).
But more than the objective manifestation of truth, Origen is concerned with the soul's ability to grasp and assimilate this truth. Those
who, illuminated by the divine Logos, have grasped the splendor of
the Father, no longer need anyone to instruct them (Com. Jo. 1, 24).
This inner illumination is bound up with our docility. God takes the
first step in drawing close to man, but man must also turn towards
the Lord and approach Him: there must be something reciprocal
about this approach. Origen insists on this, "Christ sends His light
into our minds, but the illumination will not take place if our blindness
presents an obstacle" (Hom. Gen. 1, 7). The closer one comes to
Christ, the more light he receives. To those who are open to the
Logos, He makes known the secret of the Father, and His word, in
the inner depth of human hearts, takes on a variety of forms, according
to the capacity and needs of each man (Hom. Gen. 1, 8). Christ
becomes at once Doctor, Shepherd, King, Vine, Bread, Lamb, Prophet.
His self-revelation as Wisdom and Life is reserved for the perfect
(Com. Jo. 1, 22-23), who are specially enlightened (C. Cels. 3, 60).

In the background of Origen's thinking, as with his predecessors,
always looms the Marcionite heresy, which digs a pit between Law
and Gospel, opposing the God of the New Testament to the God of
the Old. Origen too stresses the unity of the two Testaments. Old
and New have the same God for author. Apostles and prophets have
been inspired by one and the same Spirit (De Princ. I, praef. 4).
All Scripture has a bearing on Christ, who is Logos of truth from
the very beginning (Com. Mtt. ser. 47) and present in the world,
even before His Incarnation (Hom. Jer. 9, 1). In the theophanies
of the Old Testament, it is He who is manifest, directly or through
the intermediary of an angel (Hom. Jer. 16, 4; Com. Cant. 2).[6] To
stress this unity of the two Testaments, Origen claims that the
patriarchs, Moses, and the prophets saw the glory of Christ (Com.
Jo. 1, 17). On the plane of knowledge, the most perfect of the prophets
are not inferior to the apostles (Com. Jo. 6, 3). The saints of the
Old Testament received their knowledge from Christ for "the Word
instructed them even before He became Flesh" (Com. Jo. 6, 4). The
prophets, like the apostles, bore witness to Christ, for they understood
Christ and they announced Him (Com. Jo. 2, 34). Moses, Isaiah,
Ezekiel were conscious of the mysteries expressed in their writings
(Com. Jo. 6, 4). In a word, "the apostles were no more enlightened
than the fathers or Moses or the prophets" (Com. Jo. 6, 5). The
coming of Christ thus brought no new truth, but only the *manifestation*

of truths already known (Com. Jo. 6, 4). The mysteries that the prophets knew, the apostles saw realized and accomplished.

These statements, inspired by the anti-Marcionite attitude of Origen, must be interpreted in the light of other statements which stress the progress of revelation, both on the level of preparation and on the level of knowledge.

Origen recognizes that revelation had humble beginnings: it is inaugurated through the manifestation of God in the work of creation (De Princ. I, 1, 6) and the conscience of each man (De Princ. I, 3, 1), progressing with the Law and prophets (Com. Mtt. 13, 2) to find its fullness in Jesus (Hom. Lev. I, 4). God made Himself known "at opportune times" and "according to a certain order" (De princ. IV, 4, 8), for man could not from the outset receive "the precepts of freedom" (Hom. Ex. 8, 1). If Christ has come rather late in history, it is because His coming needed a preparation (C. Cels. 4, 8). The events of the history of Israel are intended to prepare a people that is incapable of bearing these mysteries, to receive them someday (C. Cels. 2, 2); to stir up, by announcing the coming of Christ, a desire for His arrival (Com. Cant. I). The Law and the prophets prepared the way for the Gospel; they were like "rudiments which led to the perfect understanding of the Gospel" (Com. Mtt. 10, 10).

From one Testament to the other there is progress, not only in the order of preparations, but also in the order of *knowledge*. "Since a reasonable man, when he hears some prudent statement, approves of it and adds something to it, it is evident that the apostles, making use of the seeds of the most secret and profound revelations that Moses and the prophets understood, have passed on to more numerous contemplations of the truth, under the activity of Jesus who elevated their minds and enlightened their intelligence .... It is not because they were in any way inferior that the prophets and Moses did not, from the outset, see what the apostles saw at the moment of Jesus's coming, but because they were still waiting for the fullness of time: since the coming of Jesus had been reserved for this particular time, now too must be revealed the truths which had been reserved for this time, truths different from those which had been already spoken and written in the world, and this revelation must be made through Him who did not think it a robbery to make Himelf equal to God, but who still emptied Himself to take the form of a slave" (Com. Jo. 13, 48). Origen asserts that Christ revealed mysteries which the prophets had not known, although they desired this revelation. What is more, the realization of the prophecies and the possession of the realities announced in the Old Testament have become the source of a higher and clearer knowledge. Thus, the ancients did not have a complete notion of the Trinity. The Second Person of the Trinity was *fully* known only through the Incarnation of the Son of God. The Holy Spirit was truly known only through His coming into the souls of men and His life in the Church (Hom. Jos. 3, 2). The apostles thus made their way further into the mysteries of Christ than did the prophets. Their knowledge, compared to that of the prophets, is like the plant compared to the seed. The Gospel surpasses the Law.[7]

Christ Himself, in the New Testament, manifests Himself only progressively and partially, for if the Word had manifested all His glory, the whole world would not be able to contain it (Com. Jo. 19, 10). Christ diversified His gift and adapted Himself to the capacity and needs of men (Com. Jo. 1, 20; Com. Mtt. 15, 24). He spoke in a different way, according to His audience. To the crowd, He speaks in parables; to His disciples, He gives some explanation. To some privileged few He reveals His glory: to Peter, for example, who confesses His divinity (Com. Mtt. 12, 10; Com. Jo. 32, 24); to the three apostles who are witnesses to His transfiguration, "example of the future glory of the Savior" (Fragm. Lc. 22). To the "beginners" whom He must lead to the faith, He presents Himself as the Word made flesh; to the perfect, as the glorious Word at the end of time: two levels of teaching, corresponding to two levels of soul and to two distinct comings of Christ, in the form of the slave and in the form of final glory. He offers each man a chance to increase his spiritual capacity, to constantly expand the interior room of his spirit, to approach the ranks of the perfect (Fragm. Jo. 7).

Although he is interested in the stages and preparations of revelation, Origen is still more taken up with the passage from flesh to spirit, from history to spirit, from letter to spirit. The world appears to him as one vast image of the truth, which it unveils and veils at the same time. The events of history are signs, symbols, types, images, in respect to the realities which are true, spiritual, invisible, divine, eternal. Man must go beyond the shadows and the images which are flesh, letter, and history, to arrive at full reality.

The coming of Christ constitutes a promotion of the Old Testament. "The light which the law of Moses contained, hidden under a veil, shone brightly at the moment of Jesus's coming; He took away the veil and quickly gave us an understanding of the blessings hidden in the letter of the Old Testament" (De Princ. IV, 1, 6). "Christ did away with every shadow and every image" (Fragm. Jo. 9. 12). Jesus Christ, in coming, gives us the Gospel for the Law, and, all of a sudden, "the Law of Moses appears spiritual in our eyes" (Sel. Ps.

118, 102). Through His presence, He makes the letter ring under the influence of the spirit. The Gospel "has done away with the oldness of the letter" and has given us "the newness of the Spirit which never grows old" (Com. Jo. 1, 6). "When the Savior had come and had given a body to the Gospel, then, through the Gospel, He made everything similar to the Gospel'" (Com. Jo. 1, 8). From that time onward, He lets us read the Old Testament "in a Gospel way, spiritually" (Hom. Lev. 6, 1). The glory of Christ transfigures the whole Old Testament; it brings Elijah and Moses out of the shadow, absorbing them in its own light.

But the Gospel too, as well as the Old Testament, must be understood in the Spirit. The truth of the Gospel is known only to those who know how to "transform the sense Gospel into a spirit Gospel" (Com. Jo. 1, 8). The Old and New Testament must be read in the same way: in order to have the spirit of the Scriptures, which is the spirit of Christ, we must have "the Spirit of Christ" (De Princ. IV, 2, 3). All the Gospel accounts, all the words of Christ shelter a mystery which we must penetrate: "the texts of the Gospel are not to be taken simply in their immediate sense; they are offered, pedagogically, to the simple as simple, but for those who can and will understand in a more penetrating fashion, wise instructions, worthy of the Logos, are hidden there" (Com. Mtt. 10, 1). The obscurity of the Gospel must stimulate the reader to discover its true meaning (De Princ. IV, 2). None of the words of Christ must be taken in its common meaning: "We must take great care in examining even those (words) which appear very clear and simple and we must not give up the prospect of finding, even in the simple and apparently unmysterious words, if we look carefully and wisely, something worthy of this Sacred Mouth" (Com. Jo. 20, 36). In the same way, all the activity of Christ, in addition to its sense reality, also has a spirit meaning which lives on in us. "The acts accomplished then were the symbols of acts always accomplished by the power of Jesus; there is no time in which, through the power of Jesus, each of His actions recorded in Scripture is not being actually produced" (Com. Mt. 11:17). Christ does not cease to cure the leper from his sin and give sight to the blind (C. Cels. I, 48; Hom. Lc. 17). All the facts of His life are historical, but, at the same time, they are the model of things to come (Com. Mtt. ser. 78). The spiritual understanding of the New Testament must thus be just as extensive as that of the Old Testament: a vertical progress which touches all of revelation.

The New Testament and the whole Christian economy are themselves a sign of the definitive reality of "the eternal Gospel" (De

Princ. IV, 2-3). We are invited to see, in the coming of the Incarnate Logos, an image of the economy of vision (Hom. II, 2 in Ps. 38). "A great many things have been sketched in outline by this first coming ... their accomplishment and perfection will be consummated by the second coming .... What we now have only a foretaste of, in faith and hope, we shall then grasp effectively in its substance" (Hom. Jos. 8, 4). The eternal Gospel will be revealed "when the shadow has passed and truth has arrived, when death is destroyed and eternity restored" (Com. Rom. 1, 4). The eternal Gospel is not a different Gospel from the Gospel of time, but a different state of the same Gospel, sign and symbol giving way before reality. The Gospel of the present time shows us the reality only in a mirror, darkly, whereas the eternal Gospel makes us contemplate it directly. The two Gospels are identical *quoad se,* but different *quoad nos.* To the Gospel of time corresponds Christ's coming in the form of a slave; to the Gospel of eternity, His coming in glory. The eternal Gospel is Christ in Person, unveiled in the glory of Divine Word (Com. Mtt. 17, 19). We draw near to this eternal Gospel in the measure that we progress in perfection. The perfect, that is, the Christians whose spiritual needs are greater, by the very fact that they make an effort to come to the divinity of the Word through the symbol of flesh, also make an effort, through the Spirit, to rise to the divine realities of which Christ's human acts are only figures, without, however, claiming to penetrate fully into the mystery of the Word which only the Father understands (De Princ., II, 6, 1; C. Cels. 2, 67). After the parousia, the Gospel of time will give way to the Gospel of eternity: those who have lived the Gospel of the present time spiritually "will live in the Kingdom of Heaven according to the laws of this eternal Gospel" (De Princ. IV, 3, 12-13).

The task of the theologian, according to Origen, is to examine the Scriptures, for every truth is contained there. Regarding natural revelation and philosophy, Origen is much more temperate than Clement. No doubt the Gentiles were never without the blessings and favors of God, but Origen does not go so far as to speak of a Testament for the Gentiles. The revelation of Grace takes place because the Word of God, who proceeds from the Father as His most faithful Image, becomes incarnate and, through the way of the Incarnation, "flesh of His body and flesh of the Scriptures," makes known the Father and His mysteries. This revelation achieves its full effect when man, through the sign and symbol of the flesh and the Gospel, recognizes in Christ the Word of God, the Image of the Father, and, in that Image, the Father Himself. This recognition takes place under the activity of grace. Origen, much more than Clement, stresses the subjectivity of revelation. What is important is not only that God comes out of His mystery, but also that man recognizes this coming of God. Thus he speaks of an illumination. This illumination, inaugurated by faith, is always capable of progess, in the simple and in the perfect. The problems which interest Origen are those which bear on the relationship between Law and Gospel, between letter and spirit. In him, as in his predecessors, we can discover an evolution in revelation. Origen recognizes a development and progress in revelation, a divine pedagogy directing the maturing of humanity up to the fullness of times. He stresses the unity and harmony of the two Testaments. The Incarnation, in his eyes, is less an abrupt transition in history than an advance of all things towards the Spirit. More than the passage from preparation to accomplishment, he stresses the passage from figure and sign to reality, the passage from history and letter to Spirit which the presence of Christ creates, the transfiguration of the Law effected by the light of the Gospel. Origen stresses also the tension of the Gospel of time towards the Gospel of eternity, reality of the mysteries outlined in the Gospel of time.

3. Saint Athanasius

In addition to the teaching of Christ, Athanasius[8] distinguishes two sources for our knowledge of God: the one direct and interior; the other through the testimony of creation.

The world bears the stamp of the Word which is its Author and Organizer. God "organized creation in such a way that, naturally invisible, He could still be known through His works" (C. Gent. 35). This knowledge of God, it seems, can be got through a simple inference, starting with the cosmos: "Looking at the heavens, seeing their order and beauty, ... it is possible to form some idea of the Word who is Author of this order; likewise, when we think of the Word of God, we necessarily think of God His Father ... ; seeing the power of the Word, we conceive an idea of His good Father" (C. Gent. 45). Athanasius, obviously, interprets the knowledge man has of God on the basis of creation, in terms of his Trinitarian faith. The Logos of which Athanasius speaks is not the "Seminal Logos" of the Stoics, but the Wisdom of the Father (C. Gen. 40-41). Everything the infidel sees exists and subsists only through this Wisdom of God. If "creation is capable of subsisting solidly," that is because the Word gives it a consistency through the exercise of His power (C. Gent. 41. 42. 46). The Word of God is Jesus Christ the Savior (C. Gent. 40).

Athanasius also speaks of the knowledge we have of God through an interior way. By the very fact that man is the image of God, he has the power to recognize this image in the Word of God and, in the Word, the Father, even before the image is manifest in the Incarnation: "When the soul puts off all the squalor of sin that clings to it and, in her new purity, retains only her likeness to the Image, it is only right that, when this Image is illuminated, she should contemplate there as in a mirror, the Word, Image of God the Father, and in Him the Father whose Image the Savior is" (C. Gent. 34). Athanasius is not precise on how this purification permits the soul, looking back upon herself, to perceive the Word, the Image of the Father.

Actually, these two ways of approaching the knowledge of God did not lead man to God. Man has disturbed this image of God in Himself and in creation. God, then, "provided for their weakness by giving them the Law, by sending them the prophets, men whom they could recognize"; thus they could be instructed by "teachers close to them" (De Inc. 12). This merciful favor of the Law and prophets, Athanasius points out, was addressed not only to the Jews, but to all men. It was, for the whole earth, a sort of "holy school of the knowledge of God and the spiritual life" (De Inc. 12).

Despite the Law and the prophets, man turned away from truth. "They forgot God ... and they fashioned other gods in His place" (De Inc. 11). They ended up by forgetting that they were "in the image of God" (C. Gent. 8): the work of God fell in ruins (De Inc. 6). The soul needed to be re-created according to His image. "And how could this take place excepting through the presence of the Image of God Himself, ... so that, being the Image of the Father, He could re-create man according to that Image" (De Inc. 13). The work of restoring man, being a work of creation, can belong only to the Word. By His "condescension," by his "philanthropy," the Word of God became incarnate (De Inc. 8): "a divine epiphany for men" (De Inc. 1). After He had shown Himself through creation, the Law, and the prophets, God speaks to us through His Son (1 C. Ar. 55; 2 C. Ar. 81). Re-creating man according to the Image, means restoring the true knowledge of God in him, in order to make him divine. Revelation is condition and means with respect to this goal which is divinisation. This restoration of man takes place through the knowledge of God which Christ brings into the world (De Inc. 20. 16).

In the manifestation of the Word through his Incarnation, Athanasius distinguishes two different aspects: the manifestation of Christ as a Divine Person, Image of the Father, and His communication of the doctrine of salvation.

Through sin, men had dragged God down to the rank of flesh and blood. God meets men at their own level: He becomes incarnate. Thus they are able to recognize "through the works done by the body, the Word of God who is in the body, and through Him the Father" (De Inc. 14). Miracles are much less signs of truthfulness than manifestations of the divine presence. Seeing the works of the all-power of Christ (healing, exorcism, resurrection), men must recognize in Him the Lord of the universe. Just as the invisible Word manifests Himself through the work of creation, so the Incarnate Word makes Himself recognized as "Head and King of the universe" by His works of power (De Inc. 16). Recognizing divine power in Him, men have some idea of the power of the Father; for everything in Christ is also in the Father, Christ being the perfect Image of His Father, His exact Copy (1 C. Ar. 16; 28), possessing, like the Father, all power (1 C. Ar. 33), lordship (2 C. Ar. 13), eternity (1 C. Ar. 33). Athanasius, like Origen, maintains that "the Word . . . made Himself visible in His body so that we could have some idea of His invisible Father" (De Inc. 54).

The way of the Incarnation also allows Christ to make known to men His doctrine of salvation. "The Savior came to bear witness (2 C. Ar. 55); He came to make Himself and His Father known (2 C. Ar. 81; De Inc. 20), to bring to men "a divine teaching," object of faith (De Inc. 3). Christ is also the Master whose doctrine rules the world (De Inc. 48), illuminates the universe (De Inc. 55), transforms souls (De Inc. 52). The whole earth is filled with the knowledge of the Father, which comes to us through the Son (2 C. Ar. 81; 82). This teaching is also the teaching of the apostles (1 C. Ar. 4), the teaching of the Church (C. Gent. 33), the faith of baptism (1 C. Ar. 8; 2 C. Ar. 34).

Man could have risen to the knowledge of the invisible God on the basis of visible creation; he could also contemplate, in his purified and illuminated soul, as in a mirror, the Word of God, Image of the Father. When these two means of knowledge ran aground, God instructed man through the Law and the prophets. Finally, the Word of God Himself, the Image of the Father, took flesh in order to re-create man according to His Image, that is, in order to make him divine by restoring in him the true knowledge of God. Through His works of power, Christ manifests Himself as Lord of the world.

Through His teaching, He fills the universe with the knowledge of the Son and the Father; He communicates a divine teaching to men which they are invited to receive in faith.

4. Saint Cyril of Alexandria

Following Scripture, Cyril[9] repeats that no one has seen God and that the knowledge of the Father comes to us through the Son (Jo. Ev. 1, 10: 73, 178).[10] Christ, Incarnate Word, is the door and way which leads to the knowledge of the Father (Jo. Ev. 5, 4: 73, 823).

Through Christ, the truth is proposed to us, no longer in figures as in the Old Testament, but in clear precepts (Jo. Ev. 1. 9: 73, 174). "Our Lord Jesus Christ no longer shows us the images of things, He shows us openly the truth of things . . . . The teaching of Christ's words was the transformation and conversion of figure into truth" (Jo. Ev. 10: 74, 298). From His mouth, we have heard the ineffable teaching (Com. Lc. 10: 72, 675). Before, God had spoken through the prophets; now, it is the Son Himself who has become our "Teacher and Master." "Only Christ, insofar as He is Master and Wisdom of the Father, can teach" (Com. Lc. 5: 72, 563). Thus His word is properly called the "preaching of the good news" (Jo. Ev. 5, 5: 73, 855).

Cyril's favorite word for the revealing activity of Christ is that of Light. "The nations have been illuminated by Christ, through the Gospel teaching" (Jo. Ev. 6: 73, 994), by the "doctrine of salvation" (Jo. Ev. 6: 73, 1050). "He who follows Me, says Christ, that is, follows the path of my teaching, will never be in darkness, but will have the light of life, that is, the revelation of the mysteries that lead to life everlasting" (Jo. Ev. 5, 2: 73, 778).

The apostles, in their turn, receive from Christ the mission of teaching and enlightening the earth. Pillars of the Church, they must preach the Gospel (Glaph. Ex. III: 69, 519). "They have been chosen for apostolic work and they have received the mission of dispensing sacred things over all the earth, through their apostolic preaching, that is, through the Gospel of Christ. He who told them: go, teach all the nations, set them up as illustrious and renowned masters. That is why in prompt and generous obedience to the divine precepts, they have enlightened the earth" (Glaph. Lev.: 69, 547).

Revealed truth Cyril calls: the good news, doctrine of salvation, Gospel doctrine, Gospel preaching, ineffable teaching, teaching of Christ, divine Gospel teaching, Gospel preaching of salvation, the words of Christ, the precepts of Christ, the word or message of salvation through Jesus Christ, the doctrine of faith, the doctrine handed down by the apostles. To the monks in Egypt, Cyril recommends that they "always keep, as a precious stone set deep in their souls, the faith that has been handed down to the Church by the holy apostles" (Ep. 1: 77, 14). In order to remain united with Christ, they must "keep as a divine and spiritual deposit the pure doctrine of the Gospel teaching and the true doctrine of faith" (Jo. Ev. 10: 74, 366). This deposit must neither be added to nor subtracted from. Every addition, every innovation, every subtraction would be heretical. Cyril repeats emphatically that they must not abandon "the very ancient tradition of the faith which, beginning with the holy apostles, has come down even to our day" (De recta fide, 17: 76, 1159).

The response which is proper to the teaching of Christ, to His word, His doctrine, is faith. But in order to confess Christ and His message, we need the gift of the Father of lights (Jo. Ev. 4, 3: 73, 606). Peter confessed Christ, but under the impulse of the Father who had "revealed" his Son. The Father reveals the Son by giving a call to faith. The Spirit reveals Christ by an inner teaching, by an anointing, by an illumination which takes place deep within (Jo. Ev. 4, 1: 73, 554-558). And the Son, in His turn, reveals the Father by giving each man "an illumination of the Spirit" (Jo. Ev. 11, 12: 74, 575).

It is through the Incarnate Word that we have access to the knowledge of the Father. Like Origen, Cyril maintains that the coming of Christ has made us pass from image, figure, type, to truth. From the mouth of Christ, Wisdom of the Father and Teacher of humanity, we have heard a teaching that is properly divine. Christ has enlightened us through His doctrine of salvation. He has revealed the mysteries which lead to eternal life. The apostles, in their turn, sharing the teaching office of Christ, have illuminated the universe through their Gospel preaching. They hand down to the Church the deposit of faith which must be kept intact. The word of the Gospel, to be efficacious and remain in the soul through faith, must be accompanied by an inner activity of grace which Cyril, following Scripture, calls revelation or illumination.

II. THE CAPPADOCIANS

The problem of revelation is not the problem of the Cappadocians. What occupies first rank in their thinking is the Trinity and Christology. Still, the heresy of Eunomius offers an occasion for stating the traditional doctrine. The first Christian writers—Justin, Irenaeus, Clement of Alexandria, Origen,—taught that the knowledge of the divine essence is beyond the natural powers of man. Eunomius, at the end of the fourth century, claimed on the contrary that the divine essence, once revealed, no longer presents any mystery. Faced with this error, Gregory of Nazianzen, Basil, and Gregory of Nyssa stress the incomprehensible character of the divine essence, which remains a mystery even for the intelligence that is enlightened by revelation. Man can arrive at a knowledge of God, his existence and his attributes, on the basis of the visible world, but the very essence of God remains a darkness that we can never entirely penetrate.

1. Saint Basil

Only the Son and the Spirit, says St. Basil,[11] know the Father entirely (De Sp. S. 16: 32, 139). Even the witnesses of God who have received communication of His secrets, such as David, Isaiah, and Paul, admit that the essence of God is inaccessible (Adv. Eunom. 1, 13: 29, 542). What we know of the secrets of God comes to us through Christ who makes us know the Father (De Sp. S. 8: 32, 104). "Those whom the darkness of ignorance hold captive, he enlightens: that is why He is the true Light" (De Sp. S. 8: 32, 101). He is Truth. From Him, the Master, we have received a "necessary and salutary doctrine" which we must keep intact, to which we must hold fast (De Sp. S. 10: 32, 11-113). This doctrine we find in Scripture, which is the word of truth (De Sp. S. 4: 32, 77), and in the oral tradition, which is authorized and guaranteed by the Church (De Sp. S. 27: 32, 188. 193).

Still, St. Basil is less interested in the gifts of revealed doctrine than in its full assimilation and fructification in the soul, thanks to the "enlightenment of the gnosis" (De Sp. S. 8: 32, 100). The gnosis is an essential element of the progressive assimilation towards God, of Christian divinisation (De Sp. S. 8: 32, 97). It is a higher knowledge of God under the enlightening influence of the Spirit (De Sp. S. 18. 32, 153).

St. Basil conceives of the sanctifying activity of the Holy Spirit in an intellectual way. The Holy Spirit deifies by *illuminating*, through *revelation*, giving the soul a share in His own light (De Sp. S. 24: 32, 172). He spreads the ray of His light in the soul which, under the influence of this radiation, becomes more and more transparent and spiritual. The sharpness of the soul's spiritual vision increases, giving it a higher intelligence of the things of God (De Sp. S. 30: 32, 217).

This gnosis, however, is not the privilege of some few initiates; it is addressed to all the baptized. Little .by little, the Spirit of truth, the Spirit of wisdom, reveals to them, in Christ, the glory of the Son issued from the Father (De Sp. S. 18: 32, 153). The intelligence, under the stream of light from the Spirit, rises, through the Son, up to the Father, penetrating deeper and deeper into the mysteries of God. The Spirit "knows the depths of God and from the Spirit the creature receives the *revelation* of the mysteries" (De Sp. S. 24: 32, 172).

2. Saint Gregory of Nyssa

Like St. Basil, Gregory of Nyssa[12] stresses, against Eunomius, the inaccessibility of the divine essence. But we must distinguish between the knowledge of God as Author of the World and the knowledge of His essence (De Beatit. Or. 6: 44, 1270). Gregory of Nyssa compares the universe to a work which lets us know, not the nature, but the existence and art of the workman: "Looking upon the order of creation, we get some idea, not of the essence, but of the wisdom of Him who made all things wisely ... ; what is invisible by nature becomes visible through His activity" (De Beatit. Or. 6: 44, 1270. 1050). This is an analogical knowledge of God, on the basis of the visible perfections of His creation (C. Cant. Hom. II: 44, 1010).

Not only does God let Himself be known through the silent preaching of the universe; He also comes down to man and enters into personal communication with him. For Gregory of Nyssa, the prime example of Old Testament witness to the revelation of God is Moses. Moses was "instructed ... through the ineffable teaching of God" (De Vita Moysis I: 44, 319). He was initiated in the divine secrets. He received "knowledge of the hidden mysteries," "the divine ordinances" (De Vita Moysis I: 44, 318). On the holy mountain, Gregory of Nyssa points out, Moses received "through the word the same teaching which had been given before through the shadow, in order, in my opinion, to strengthen our faith in this doctrine by the testimony of the divine word" (De Vita Moysis II: 44, 378) ; he then communicated to his people "the teachings ... received from the heavenly Master" (De Vita Moysis II: 44, 375). Gregory also notes, and properly so, that the revealed doctrine of creation and the fall has been communicated in the form of a *history*: "Moses tells this story more like an historian ... presenting doctrines under the form of a narrative" (Or. cat. 5: 45, 23; 8: 45, 34).

With time, the word of God became more and more distinct. Still faint under the Law and prophets, it sounds and echoes throughout the

Gospel preaching, borne along by the breath of the Spirit to the very ends of the earth (De Vita Moysis II: 44, 375). Revelation reaches its peak in Christ and His apostles. Gregory describes this divine activity very precisely. He insists upon the fact that our faith is sure, for we have been instructed, taught by the Lord Himself. "The faith of Christians ... does not come from man, nor through man, but through our Lord Jesus Christ who is the Word of God, Life, Light, and Truth, God and Wisdom, and all this by nature." The Word became incarnate so that men would stop relying on their own opinions as the truth. "Persuaded that God has appeared in the flesh, let us believe this one true mystery of piety, which has been handed down to us through the Word Himself who, through Himself, has spoken to the apostles." If "the Word in Person gives testimony in His Gospel" then we must believe in Him, for "what witness more worthy of faith could we find than the Lord Himself" (C. Eunom. II: 45, 466-467)?

Gregory of Nyssa frequently expresses the idea of revelation in the Pauline term *mystery*, that is, the secret hidden in God from all eternity and manifest through Christ. Here, as in St. Paul, it is a "mystery of piety" (C. Eunom. II: 45, 466-467), a mystery of "the economy of the Incarnation" (C. Eunom. II: 45, 582). This mystery is designed essentially to be *promulgated*, unlike the pagan mysteries. Thus, Peter clearly reveals the hidden economy of this mystery. John is the herald of the mystery of the knowledge of God. The mystery, as revealed, is essentially the "good news," the "Gospel mystery" (In Ps. c. 8: 44, 516). It is brought to the knowledge of men through the word of God, the word of mystery, and the apostles are "servants of the mystery." The truth brought to men by Christ, Gregory also calls the teaching of religion, the new doctrine, the Gospel, the doctrine of God, the grace of the Gospel, the doctrine of the mystery, the revealed teachings.

The Cappadocians, while fighting against the claims of Eunomius, recognize a double way of approach to the knowledge of God: through visible creation and through the teaching of the Faith. The knowledge of the divine mysteries comes to us through Christ. Basil sees in Christ and His teaching the Light of men. Like Clement of Alexandria, he insists on the movement of fructification which is inaugurated in the soul by adherence to faith. Under the enlightening activity of the Spirit, the soul penetrates more and more deeply into the mysteries of the Son and the Father. Gregory sees in revelation a beneficent step on God's part, taking His human witnesses, prophets and apostles into His confidence and, through them, all humanity. Revelation culminates in Christ and the Gospel. In Him, it is the

Word in Person who gives witness and instructs us in the divine secrets. The apostles have as their mission to proclaim the mystery of piety as a good news.

III. SAINT JOHN CHRYSOSTOM

Together with Basil, Gregory of Nyssa, and Cyril of Jerusalem, John Chrysostom[13] insists, against the Anomeans, on the fact that God, even revealed, remains a hidden, incomprehensible God. But there is a pastoral tone to his teaching.

God is invisible, ineffable, inscrutable, inaccessible, incomprehensible, "uncircumscribable, unrepresentable": he always remains the abyss, darkness. This incomprehensibility is radical. It affects all creatures: the psalmist, Isaiah, Abraham, Moses, the angels. The inaccessibility of God affects not only His essence, but also His presence in the world, that is, the mystery of His ways, His plans and accomplishments; these are as impenetrable as is His transcendence. When the prophets claim that they have seen God, this can be understood only in a figurative sense, a sign, accommodated to human weakness. Before the incomprehensible God, man must recognize that he does not know, at very least that he could not claim a complete knowledge of the divine essence (De incompr. Dei Nat. I-III: 48, 701-728).

Perfect knowledge of God is the exclusive privilege of Son and Spirit (Jo. Hom. 15, I: 59, 98). They alone can penetrate God in Himself; the Spirit of truth "who searches the depths of God" (1 Cor. 2, 10) and the only Son of God who lives in the bosom of the Father: "As Son, as Only Begotten, as living in the bosom of the Father, He knows perfectly all the secrets of the Father" (De incompr. Dei Nat. IV: 48, 732). He knows Him with an exact knowledge, full and entire (Jo. Hom. 15, 2: 59, 98-100).

Still, we do know something of God, for He has spoken to men "Himself from the very beginning" (Gen. c. I, Hom. 2, 2: 53, 27-28), then "through the prophets"; finally "through the Son" who "spoke to the apostles, and, through them, to a great number" (Heb. c. I, Hom. 1, 1: 63, 15-16). In Jesus Christ we are given the knowledge of the mystery hidden from the nations and from the angels. What God alone could know He has revealed to us through His Son Jesus Christ (Col. Hom. 5, 1-2: 62, 331-333). Thus it is not a man, but a God who has taught us our Christian faith (Rom. Hom. 27, 1: 60, 643-644). The doctrine preached by Christ contains a complex of truths that human intelligence could neither attain to nor suspect. Even after revelation, these mysteries remain impenetrable (Rom. Hom. 27, 1: 60, 644-645). The prophets and the apostles, who have had a revelation of the secrets of God, still proclaim an incomprehensible wisdom.

Before the immensity of God, man is seized with admiration, stupor, like Zachary; the angels are struck with trembling, with sacred horror. Before the holiness of God, all creation kneels to adore, to glorify, in utter silence. Before God who speaks and reveals Himself, creation gives her homage of faith (De incompr. Dei Nat. I-III: 48, 705-720). Thus Abraham: in his example, whenever God speaks, man must offer God a docile mind, swept clear of every profane knowledge; he must welcome the divine words in faith. "God, whether He speaks or whether He performs miracles, must be equally believed and obeyed" (Rom. Hom. 18, 1-2: 60, 574). Saint John Chrysostom does not forbid the Christian to deepen his faith, but he is opposed to the constant questioning of an over-curious mind (Ep. ad Tim. Hom. I, 3: 62, 507). If God speaks, man must also mold his life in accordance with the divine teachings. And since God speaks to us through His Son, "let us live in a manner worthy of so great an honor. It would be ridiculous for Jesus Christ to have condescended to the point where he no longer willed to speak to us through His servants, but by Himself, and for us to do nothing more in response than those who have come before us. They had Moses for their teacher, and we have for our Teacher the Master of Moses.... Jesus has brought His teaching from heaven only to elevate our thoughts, so that we might imitate our Teacher with all our strength and capacity" (Jo. Hom. 15, 3: 59, 100). The prophets, who knew Jesus Christ even before the Incarnation, who knew and announced that He was to come among men (Jo. Hom. 8, 1: 59, 66), have testified to Him and Scripture has preserved their testimony. Likewise, the apostles are the witnesses of Christ, but of Christ among men. They saw and heard Christ from the beginning, they ate and drank with Him, and thus they give witness of what they have seen and heard. Christ has instructed them, confided His secrets to them, communicated His teaching (Act. Ap. Hom. I, 2-3: 60, 16-17). Their mission is to spread over the whole universe the doctrine they have received from Christ. What they announce is the living word of Christ, the Gospel, the good news, "that is, deliverance from suffering, pardon from sin, justice, sanctification, redemption, the adoption of the sons of God, the heritage of His Kingdom and the glory of becoming brothers to His only begotten Son" (Mtt. Hom. I, 2: 57, 15). Just as all the acts of this Son have man's salvation as their goal, we might say that the subject matter of the Gospel is Christ and His economy of salvation through the cross. In a word, it is sacred history or "the word of the cross" (Mtt. Hom. 1, 2: 57, 16). The apostles, simple ministers of the Gospel, have transmitted it in all its purity. Their teaching is preserved without alteration in Scripture and in the tradition of the Church.

St. John Chrysostom presents nothing systematic on the subject of revelation. The reputation of the Anomeans, however, and his homilies on Scripture provide him with the occasion, if not to explain, at least to state the existence of revelation and describe it briefly. He insists, against the Anomeans, on the incomprehensibility and inaccessibility of God. Only the Son and the Spirit have a perfect knowledge of God. What we know of God comes to us through the prophets and primarily through Christ, the Son of the Father who has come to bring to men the knowledge of the economy of salvation hidden from the angels and the nations. The good news of salvation made public through Christ is entrusted to the apostles, His witnesses, whose mission is to preach and hand it down to the Church. Men, all men, are invited to make a response to this message of Christ through faith, and by conforming their life to the doctrine they have heard.

1. The quotations here are made from the edition of O. STAEHLIN. The first number indicates the book; the second, the paragraph; the third, the paragraph section. On Clement of Alexandria: E. MOLLAND, The Conception of the Gospel in the Alexandrian Theology (Oslo, 1938); E. F. OSBORN, The Philosophy of Clement of Alexandria (Cambridge, 1957); J. MOINGT, "La gnose de Clément d'Alexandrie dans ses rapports avec la foi et la philosophie," Rech. de sc. rel., 37 (1950) : 195-251, 398-421, 537-564; 38 (1951) : 82-118; W. VOELKER, Der wahre Gnostiker nach Clemens Alexandrinus (Berlin-Leipzig, 1952); C. MONDESERT, Clément d'Alexandrie (Paris, 1944); J. DANIÉLOU, Message évangélique et culture hellénistique II et III siècles, pp. 50-67, 334-344; G. AEBY, Les missions divines, de Saint Justin à Origène, pp. 120-146; C. MONDESERT, Clément d'Alexandrie, le Protreptique ("Sources chrétiennes 2," Paris, 1949), pp. 5-50; ID., Clément d'Alexandrie, Sromate I ("Sources chrétiennes 30," Paris, 1951), pp. 5-41; P. TH. CAMELOT, Clément d'Alexandrie, Stromate II ("Sources chrétiennee 38," Paris, 1954), pp. 7-29; H. I. MARROU et M. HARL, Clément d'Alexandrie, le Pédagogue ("Sources chrétiennes 70," Paris, 1960); P. TH. CAMELOT, Foi et gnose (Paris, 1945); M. SPANNEUT, Le Stoicisme des Pères de l'Église (Paris, 1957).

2. Whereas the apologists speak rather of the Son, Clement speaks primarily of the Logos. Under the influence of Philo of Alexandria, Logos becomes a favorite term in his theology.

3. If Clement justifies the value of philosophy, he still demonstrates its limitations. a. Philosophy is inferior to faith by its elementary character as compared with the perfect knowledge revealed through Christ (Str. VI, 68, 1). b. Philosophy possesses only a partial truth (Str. VI, 82, 1). c. Not only do the Greeks borrow from the Hebrews (Str. V, 29, 4), but they also partly deform what they borrow (Str. I, 87, 2; VI, 55, 4). d. Philosophy retains a conjectural character and does not have the certitude of Faith (Str. I, 100, 5). Even the greatest philosophers did not know God with certitude, but only approximately (Str. V, 39, 1). Thus, philosophy contains values which come from reason, or from the revelation of angels to wise men, or the borrowings from Scripture. But these values are mixed together and frequently falsified. Whole and perfect truth exists only in Christ. Thus it would be a mistake to accept philosophy as a whole. Care must be taken to distinguish what is good and what is bad in it. See J. Daniélou, Message évangelique et culture hellénistique aux II et III siècles, pp. 67-72.

4. The references are from the Berlin edition. On Origen: M. HARL, *Origène et la fonction révélatrice du Verbe incarné* (Paris, 1958); H. CROUZEL, *Théologie de l'image de Dieu chez Origène* (Paris, 1956); ID., *Origene et la connaissance mystique* (Bruges, 1961); H. DE LUBAC, *Histoire et Esprit* (Paris, 1950); ID., *Origène, Homélies sur l'Exode* ("Sources chrétiennes 16," Paris, 1947), pp. 1-62; E. MOLLAND, *The Conception of the Gospel in the Alexandrian Theology* (Oslo, 1938); G. AEBY, *Les missions divines, de Saint Justin à Origène*, pp. 146-183; J. DANIELOU, *Origène* (Paris, 1948); R. P. C. HANSON, *Origen's Doctrine of Tradition* (London, 1953); F. BERTRAND, *Mystique de Jésus chez Origène* (Paris, 1951); P. NEMESHEGYI, *La Paternité de Dieu chez Origène* (Paris-Tournai-New York-Rome, 1960); H. U. VON BALTHASAR, "Le mysterion d'Origène," *Rech. de sc. rel.*, 26 (1936) : 513-562; 27 (1937) : 38-64; A. ORBE, "La excelencia de los profetas según Orígenes," *Estudios Bíblicos*, 14 (1955) : 191-221; E. HASLER, *Gesetz und Evangelium in der Alten Kirche bis Origenes* (Zurich-Frankfurt, 1953), pp. 74-102; A. LIESKE, *Die Theologie der Logosmystik bei Origenes* (Munster, 1938); W. VOELKER, *Das Vollkommenheitsideal des Origenes* (Tubingen, 1931); G. BARDY, "La règle de foi d'Origène," *Rech. de sc. rel.*, 9 (1919) : 162-196; R. CADIOU, *Introduction au système d'Origène* (Paris, 1932); H. KOCH, *Pronoia und Paideusis* (Berlin, 1932); E. R. REDEPENNING, *Origenes, Eine Darstellung seines Lebens und seiner Lehre* (2 vol., Bonn, 1841-1846); E. FITZGERALD, *Christ and the Prophets, A Study in Origen's Teaching on the Economy of the Old Testament* (Dissertatio ad lauream, PUG, Romae, 1961).

5. H. CROUZEL, *Théologie de l'image de Dieu chez Origène*, pp. 87-88.

6. Origen attributes the theophanies of the Old Testament to the Word, but with more discretion than the apologists, Irenaeus, or even Clement. He appeals to the ministry of angels both to safeguard the transcendency of the Word and to play down the external character of the theophanies. In Origen there is a very marked tendency to make the theophanies something interior and spiritual.

7. H. CROUZEL, *Origène et la connaissance mystique*, pp. 301-311.

8. L. ATZBERGER, *Die Logoslehre des Hl. Athanasius* (Munchen, 1880); P. TH. CAMELOT, *Athanase d'Alexandrie*, I : *Contre les Paiens*; II : *Sur l'Incarnation du Verbe* ("Sources chrétiennes 18," Paris, 1946), pp. 7-104; R. BERNARD, *L'Image de Dieu d'après Athanase* (Paris, 1952); K. PRUMM, "Mysterion bei Athanasius," *Zeit. Kath. Theol.* (1939), pp. 350 ss.

9. H. DU MANOIR DE JUAYE, *Dogme et spritualité dans S. Cyrille d'Alexandrie* (Paris, 1944); J. LIEBAERT, *La doctrine christologique de S. Cyrille d'Alexandrie* (Lille, 1951); W. J. BURGHARDT, *The Image of God in Man according to Cyril of Alexandria* (Woodstock, (1957).

10. For Cyril of Alexandria, Basil, Gregory of Nyssa, and John Chrysostom, the references to the divisions of their writings, in present editions, are too general. The references in this text are to the edition of Migne: the first number after the colon indicates the volume, the second

11. B. PRUCHE, *Saint Basile, Traité du Saint-Esprit* ("Sources chrétiennes 17," Paris, 1946), pp. 1-100; H. DOERRIES, *De Spiritu Sancto, Der Beitrag des Basilius zum Abschluss des trinitarischen Dogmas* (Gottingen, 1956); S. GIET, *Basile de Césarée, Homelies sur l'Hexaéron* ("Sources chrétiennes 26," Paris, 1949), pp. 1-84.

12. F. DIEKAMP, *Die Gottleslehre des Hl. Gregor von Nyssa* (Munster, 1896); H. U. VON BALTHASAR, *Présence et pensée, Essai sur la philosophie religieuse de Grégoire de Nysse* (Paris, 1942); J. DANIELOU, *Platonisme et théologie mystique* (Paris, 1944); ID., *Grégoire de Nysse, La vie de Moise* ("Sources chrétiennes 1 bis," Paris, 1955), pp. x-xxxv; R. LEYS, *L'Image de Dieu chez Grégoire de Nysse* (Paris, 1951).

13. E. BOULARAND, *La venue de l'homme à la foi d'après S. Jean Chrysostome* (Rome, 1939); J. DANIELOU et F. CAVALLERA, *Saint Jean Chrysostome, Discours sur l'incompréhensibilité de Dieu* ("Sources chrétiennes 28," Paris, 1951), pp. 7-45; C. BAUR, *Der Heilige Joannes Chrysostomus und seine Zeit* (2 vol., Munchen, 1929-1930).

CHAPTER IV

TESTIMONY OF THE LATIN CHURCH

Versed in Roman law, Tertullian[1] is a passionate lover of truth. The problem of Christianity, for him, is the problem of truth faced with error (paganism, various heresies). Christ founded a religion in order to lead men to the knowledge of truth (Apolog. 21, 30). The only problem after that is to know who possesses this truth and who has a right to use it.

Justin had looked to philosophy for points of departure in his argument with the pagans. Clement saw philosophy as the counterpart to the Jewish Law. Tertullian is unwilling to admit any communication between philosophy and faith: "After the possession of Jesus Christ, we do not mean to open any inquisitive discussions" (De Pr. 7, 13). The analogies discovered between the teachings of the Church and the philosophers are the fruit of borrowings from the Old Testament or the Gospel (Apolog. 47, 2. 13-14). What is more, the philosophers have adulterated and corrupted revealed truth (Apolog. 47, 9), degrading the "doctrine of salvation" to the rank of human opinion (Apolog. 47, 11), comparing "divine revelation" to a "sort of philosophy" (Apolog. 46, 2). Still, we must not conclude that God can be known only through revelation. Tertullian reduces the natural ways of knowing God to two: the argument from the basis of creation, which he uses against Marcion: "There is no more evident sign of the existence of our God than this work which he has created" (Adv. Marc. I, 11; V, 16); then, the spontaneous testimony of the soul, an argument he uses to good advantage against the pagans (Apolog. 17, 5-6; Test. an. 2). This knowledge is indeed imperfect compared to that which comes from revelation (De anima I). Still, there is unity, and unity of object, between one knowledge and the other. The same God is known in two ways: "We maintain that God first of all must be known through nature, and then recognized through teaching; through nature, in His works; through teaching, in His preaching" (Adv. Marc. I, 18). God makes Himself our Teacher through creation as well as through revelation; but faith supplies the deficiencies of what nature offers. "In order for us to acquire a more complete and profound knowledge of Himself, His decrees, and His will," God sent His prophets, whose words are contained in Scripture (Apolog. 18, 1-5). What is more, He has sent us His Son, "the Light and Guide of our human race," who brought us all truth (Apolog. 21, 7).

Christ preached His doctrine (Apolog. 21, 17-18), He instructed His apostles and entrusted to them His mission of preaching over the whole earth (Apolog. 21, 23). Our *masters* are thus the apostles of the Lord who "have faithfully passed on to the nations the doctrine received from Christ" (De Pr. 6, 4). The truth comes to us from Christ, the source of revelation, through the apostles, its privileged mediators: "No one knows the Father, excepting the Son and He to whom the Son has revealed Him. Now we do not see Christ revealing Him to anyone except the apostles whom He sent out to preach—to preach, and this is an important point, everything He had revealed to them" (De Pr. 21, 1-2). The apostles, in their turn, entrusted the doctrine they received to the Churches "they founded in person, and they themselves instructed, both with their living voice, as we say, and, later, through letters" (De Pr. 21, 3). It follows that any teaching that is in harmony with these Churches is true, for "it obviously contains whatever the Churches received from the apostles, the apostles from Christ, and Christ from God" (De Pr. 21, 4; 20, 4-8; 37, 1). Tertullian never tires of repeating that the Church has received the truth from the apostles. The channel for this authentic revelation is the apostles and only the apostles (De Pr. 6, 4), especially instructed by Christ (De Pr. 20, 3; 21, 3; 22, 3), sent by Him as teachers and masters of nations (De Pr. 8, 14-15; 6, 4). The Holy Spirit, who was their teacher (De Pr. 8, 14-15), the "vicar of Christ" in them, led them to the fullness of truth (De Pr. 28, 1-2).

The answer to the objections of heretics leads Tertullian to greater precision on the unique position of the apostles in the economy of revelation. The objection was made that the apostles did not know everything, or, knowing everything, they did not teach everything to everyone (De Pr. 22, 2). Tertullian answers first of all that the apostles had full knowledge of revelation: "What reasonable man could believe that they were ignorant of something, these men whom

Christ set up as teachers, who were His companions, His disciples, His familiars, those to whom in private He explained all the obscurities of His teaching, saying that to them it was given to know the secrets that the people did not have a right to know?" (De Pr. 22, 3). What is more, Christ sent them His Spirit and promised them "the possession of all truth" (De Pr. 22, 9). The apostles did not reserve this fullness of knowledge they possessed for some few initiates. The idea of an occult Gospel is foreign to the thinking of Christ and the apostles. "Christ spoke publicly and never alludes to a secret doctrine. He Himself ordered (His disiciples) to preach in the open (and on the rooftops) what they had heard in privacy and secret" (De Pr. 26, 2-5). Thus we must conclude that "it is incredible that the apostles should not have possessed the fullness of the doctrine they announced, or should not have handed down the rule of faith whole and entire" (De Pr. 27, 1).

If Christ "entrusted once and for all" to His apostles "the Gospel and a teaching of like content" (De Pr. 44, 9), and if there are no other mediators of revelation besides the apostles, it follows that with them the action of revelation is terminated. The deposit of truths entrusted to the Church must be preserved intact. Every doctrine that dates from *after* the apostolic preaching, that is, every doctrinal novelty, can only be error. What is first is apostolic; what is later is heretical (De Pr. 35, 3-4). History moreover, shows that the doctrines of Valentin, Marcion, and Apelles are recent phenomena (De Pr. 29-30). None of these heretics can trace the list of his bishops all the way back to the apostles (De Pr. 32, 1). The Churches, on the contrary, have received their teaching from the apostles, as a direct heritage (De Pr. 37, 5). It is, in the last analysis, the *apostolicity* of a doctrine which is the criterion for its truth (Apolog. 47, 10; Adv. Marc. I, 1). And apostolicity is established by continuity of succession from the time of the apostles. The two arguments mutually reinforce each other.

The names Tertullian uses for objective revelation explain its nature. In its actual form, revelation is first of all "the unique and precise teaching" taught by Christ, which we are invited to receive in faith (De Pr. 9, 3). To stress the *normative* character of this doctrine, Tertullian calls it "the rule" given by Christ to His apostles, once and for all (De Pr. 44, 9), and communicated by them to all Christians (De Pr. 27, 1), the "rule of faith" (De Pr. 12, 5), the "rule of truth" (Apolog. 47, 10). He also calls it "discipline" (in the sense of doctrine, teaching) received from Christ (De Pr. 6, 4), "Gospel" (De Pr. 7, 12), *the* "doctrine" par excellence, in opposition to heresies (De Pr. 8, 15), the "doctrine of Christ" (De Pr. 8, 3; 26, 5), the "Catholic doctrine" (De Pr. 20, 2), the "truth" (De Pr. 12, 1), the "mystery," in so far as it is a sacred and mysterious truth (De Pr. 20, 9), the "light" (De Pr. 26, 5), the "word of God" (De Pr. 26, 5), the "preaching" (De Pr. 23, 10), the "deposit" (De Pr. 25, 3), the "faith" or "Christian faith" (De Pr. 19, 3), the "true faith" (De Pr. 44, 12). Revelation is thus conceived as a doctrine, a teaching of Christ to His apostles, transmitted by them to the Churches as absolute truth, to be kept intact as a deposit.

This brings us down into the heart of Tertullian's main preoccupation. What is important for him, actually, is not to know whether there is a revelation, but rather to know where it is to be found and how it is to be got at. Hence his interest in the idea of tradition, or the transmission of revealed doctrine. Tradition, in Tertullian as in Irenaeus, is revealed doctrine, but considered in its passage through the course of generations. Tertullian says that Christ "hands down" (De Pr. 37, 1); the apostles "hand down the doctrine of Christ" (De Pr. 22, 2; 32, 1), the Churches "hand down" (De Pr. 28, 4; 37, 2). Still there is an obvious difference from one term to the other. Christ hands down as a source of truth; the apostles, as mediators; the Church, as a depositary. The apostles received the doctrine handed down by Christ (De Pr. 21, 4), with the exclusive privilege of handing it on to the Churches founded by them, in their capacity as teacher and doctor. The Churches have no other right than that of handing down the apostolic teaching in its full integrity, throughout the centuries, as a heritage, a family heirloom which passes from father to son intact (De Pr. 36, 4-5). The "apostolic" Churches are the receptacle of this tradition. They alone have received the heritage. To learn the truth, we need only ask them (Adv. Marc. I, 21).

For Tertullian, the doctrine which is revealed and handed down is practically identical with Scripture. The apostles had as their mission, after the ascension, to teach the Churches, either by their living voice or by their writings (De Pr. 21, 3). There are two *forms* of teaching in question here, not two different teachings. Tertullian constantly stresses the essential harmony between their teaching and Scripture: a change in one necessarily implies a change in the other. And "the integrity of doctrine" cannot be conceived "without integrity in the means by which it is taught," that is, Scripture (De Pr. 38, 3). Thus it would be wrong to oppose Scripture and doctrine. Their content is identical. But the material possession of Scripture is not enough. We must learn its authentic meaning from the apostles. Scripture has only one meaning: that which the apostles have given it and which they have taught to the apostolic Churches. Scripture must be read in the Church.

While admitting that man can arrive at a knowledge of God by the demonstrative way, starting with creation, and by the spontaneous testimony of the soul "naturally Christian," Tertullian looks to authentic revelation for the knowledge of God. As a jurist, He is less concerned with the historical dimensions and progress of revelation than with its possession. Revelation being truth, the essential element is to possess it. And the idea of tradition, or transmission of the truth, finds greater stress in His writings than manifestation of truth. What guarantees the possession of truth is the *continuity* that exists between Christ and the apostles, and between the apostles and the Churches they established. Christ is the source of truth; the apostles, privileged witnesses of Christ, are its only mediators, instructed by Christ, given their mandate by Him, assisted by the Holy Spirit to enter into possession of all truth. The Churches founded by them and assisted by the Spirit are the only depositaries of apostolic truth, which they preserve intact, as their heritage. The apostolicity of doctrine, concretely expressed in the uninterrupted succession of bishops since the time of the apostles, is the criterion of truth. More than Irenaeus, Tertullian insists on the concrete character of the apostolic succession, on the assistance of the Spirit in the transmission of the apostolic teaching, and on the normative character of revealed doctrine. The doctrine of truth is entrusted to Scripture, as read and understood by the apostolic Churches.

II. SAINT CYPRIAN

Cyprian[2] uses the term *tradition* to designate the activity of revelation. At the origin, at the source of Christianity, is the tradition of God, Christ, and the apostles (Ep. 67, 5; 74, 2. 10; De Unit. 3. 12). . Refuting the error of certain bishops on the eucharistic rite, he opposes the authentic and primitive "tradition" of the Lord (Ep. 63, 2-10). The true disciple must not depart from the teachings of the Master: "Not even the apostle himself, nor an angel from heaven, could announce or teach anything other than what Christ has taught and the apostles have announced" (Ep. 63, 11). There is only one Master who must be heard, Christ (Ep. 63, 14), who is the Son Himself speaking to us and opening for us the path of life (Dom. Orat. 1). We must "observe and hold fast to what the Lord has taught us" (Ep. 63, 17) and "keep the truth of the tradition of the Lord" (Ep. 63, 19). "We must obey His precepts, His admonitions"

(De Unit. 15; Dom. Orat. 1), His "teaching office" (De Unit. 15);
for His Gospel is light, truth, teaching of God (De Unit. 22. 10. 8).
Heretics and schismatics are such because they depart from Christ,
because they do not go back to the "origin of truth," to the "source"
who is the Divine Master (De Unit. 3).

The same must be said for the apostolic tradition. A tradition has
no value unless it is based on "the Gospel and apostolic tradition"
that is, the tradition which "proceeds from the authority of the Lord
and the Gospel, from the precepts and the letters of the apostles"
(Ep. 74, 2). If truth begins to waver on a certain point, Cyprian
points out in the baptismal controversy, we must go back to the *origin*,
to the tradition of the Gospel and the apostles. This tradition is
deposited in Scripture (Ep. 63, 2-10). Cyprian takes pride in the
"authority," the "faith," the "truth" of Scripture (Ep. 73, 8; 64, 3;
69, 1). And Scripture is to be found in the Church. Thus we must
be faithful to the Church without fail: "A man cannot have God for
his Father if he does not have the Church for his Mother" (De
Unit. 6).

Cyprian gives the term tradition the strong active sense of the
first communication of truth, that is, revelation. The source, the
origin of Christian truth is the Gospel and apostolic tradition, or the
teaching of Christ and the preaching of the apostles.

III. SAINT AUGUSTINE

It is from St. John that Augustine borrows the words in which he
expresses the idea of revelation. The central point about which his
thinking crystallizes is Christ, Way and Mediator.

Despite a passage in his works which seems to assert the contrary
(De Gen. ad. litt. XII, 28-34), Augustine teaches that no one has
seen God here below (Ep. Jo. tr. 3, 17). Moses saw, not the essence
of God, but figurative signs, "creatures bearing the stamp of their
Lord." When the Old Testament says that God appeared to our
fathers, it must be understood that the bodily appearance under
which he showed himself to them was produced by angels speaking
and acting as if they were God in person, or borrowing from creatures
what they would not be by themselves (De Trin. III, 11, 27). What
we know of the intimate life of God comes to us through the testimony
of Christ. Even the knowledge of God, Author of the universe, a
knowledge at which man can arrive by a consideration of the created
world, is incomparably easier along the path of faith (De Util, cred.
10, 24). It is in order to allow man, whose inner eye is frequently

blinded by sin, to walk with assurance in the path of truth that the Son of God took human flesh, becoming thus our Way and our Goal (De Civ. Dei XI, 2).

The Son, who is in the bosom of the Father, makes the Father known to men (De Trin. VIII, 3; Jo. tr. 47, 3). He is the "Wisdom begotten by God the Father," who makes known to man the "secrets of the Father" (De fide et symb. 3, 3). To reveal, for God, means to "speak" to his creation (Jo. tr. 21, 7). The Son of God came down from heaven among men to announce His Gospel: we must believe the truths which he has condescended to reveal (Jo. tr. 22, 1). In making His Father known to the nations, Christ glorifies His Father (Jo. tr. 105, 1).

Revelation is not the communication of an abstract truth; it is bound up with time and takes the form of a history: "In this religion, the essential point to be admitted is the *history and prophecy* of the way in which Divine Providence will realize in time the salvation of the human race, restoring and renewing it for everlasting life" (De vera rel. 7, 13). The *City of God* describes the development of this revelation in time, the holy history of salvation announced in the Old Testament and accomplished in the New Testament.

Realized in an economy of incarnation, revelation makes use of all the ways of flesh. Christ proclaimed His Gospel by action as well as by word: "teaching, sometimes direct and sometimes figurative, using the word, gesture, sacred sign" (De vera rel. 17, 33). "Jesus Christ is the Word of God; every action of this Word is thus a word for us" (Jo. tr. 24, 2). In the context, Augustine is speaking of the miracle of the multiplication of the loaves. Commenting on the cure of the paralytic: "This power and this goodness were far more concerned in making known to souls, through these actions, the teachings which have eternal salvation for their object, than giving to sick bodies the passing health which they might need" (Jo. tr. 17, 1).

The word of Christ is not a human word: it is endowed with a double dimension, external and internal, by reason of the grace which accompanies and vivifies the doctrine He announces. St. Augustine develops this thinking in his commentary on Jn. 6, 44: "No one can come to me, unless my Father draw him," and in his *De Gratia Christi*, directed against Pelagius. "Coming to Christ" means experiencing an attraction from the Father, believing (Jo. tr. 26, 5). Thus Peter confessed Christ in virtue of a "revelation" of the Father: this "revelation is nothing more than that attraction." And it is a gift (Jn. 6, 65). Christ says again: "Whoever has heard the Father and *learned* from Him, comes to Me" (Jn. 6, 45). Is it not Christ who speaks and is thus the Master? Augustine answers: "The Son *spoke,* but it was the Father who *taught,*" for he who is *heard* is the one who teaches: "The Father teaches him who hears His Word" (Jo. tr. 26, 8). He who hears the Word is taught by the Father, drawn by Him: "Learn then how to be drawn to the Son by the Father, let yourselves be taught by the Father, and to that end, *hear* His Word." Christ makes His Word heard, but it is the Father who gives man the power to receive it in virtue of the attraction towards His Son which He produces in the human soul. *Receiving* the words of Christ, points out St. Augustine, means not only hearing them externally, "with the ears of the body, but in the depth of the heart," like the apostles (Jo. tr. 106, 6). Hearing with the inner ear, obeying the voice of Christ, believing: it is all one and the same thing (Jo. tr. 115, 4). Whoever does not consent to Christ, even if he has heard the external voice of Christ, has not heard the voice of the Father; he has not learned from the Father (De Gr. Christi I, 14, 15). Augustine insists upon this: the word that echoes externally is nothing if the Spirit of Christ is not at work within to make us recognize the truth of the word we hear: "Jesus Christ is our Master and His anointing is our instruction. If this inspiration and this anointing are lacking, the outer words strike against our ear in vain" (Ep. Jo. tr. 3, 13). This grace of faith Augustine conceives of as an inspiration and an illumination (Ep. Jo. tr. 4, 8; De Gr. Christi I, 14, 15). It is at once attraction and light. Attraction which stirs up the power of desire, light which makes us see Christ as the living truth. The council of Orange, expressing itself according to the views of Augustine, will say that no one can cling to the teaching of the Gospel and posit a salutary act, without "an illumination and inspiration of the Holy Spirit, which gives to all men the sweetness of belonging and believing in the truth" (D 180). Man receives a twofold gift from God: doctrine, and grace by which he consents in faith (De Gr. Christi I, 10, 11; 26, 27; 31, 34).

Augustine applies to Christ the Revealer the titles consecrated by the Synoptics and St. John. Following the prophecy of Moses, Christ is *prophet:* "The times which have preceded us deserved to hear the prophet inspired and filled with the Word of God; as for us, we have deserved to have for our prophet the very Word of God. Now Christ is Prophet and Lord of the prophets" (Jo. tr. 24, 7). One title of which Augustine is particularly fond is that of *Master.* Christ is the Master of the Old as well as the New Testament. The prophets heard His voice (Jo. tr. 45, 9), and there is no other Gospel than that which He has taught, Himself or through His apostles (Ep. ad Gal. exp. 4). Like the Master whose light shines in our eyes, Christ teaches the truths of salvation (Jo. tr. 17, 15; 21, 7). We must therefore cling "firmly to the teaching which He has determined Himself" (Jo. tr. 7, 7). In a more universal way still, Christ, as Word of God, is the one sole light of souls, the principle of all knowledge, natural as well as supernatural. He is the interior Master.

St. Augustine loves to define Christ in the Johannine terms of Way, Truth, Light, and Life. Not only does Christ teach the truth, but He *is* Truth (Jo. tr. 37, 7). He *is* Light. Here the Augustinian metaphor of illumination has a scriptural foundation. True Light, Christ is source of light. Enlightened by Him, man, in his turn, can become witness to the light and announce the day: thus John the Baptist, the prophets, the apostles. Christ, finally, is Life and source of life (Jn. 14, 6). The titles of truth and life designate Christ's divinity. It is through the Incarnation that the Word of God became *Way* for us: the way which leads to the truth and the life (Jo. tr. 34). Truth and Way: these two titles sum up for Augustine the whole mystery of Christ. Christ is the path towards the truth and the life. Truth and Life, He has taken human flesh in order to become our Way (Serm. 141, 4).

Christ is thus at once Goal and Way: God revealed and He through whom God is revealed. What He teaches us is His doctrine, but this doctrine has Christ Himself for its object: "Jesus Christ preaches Jesus Christ, because He Himself is the object of His preaching" (Jo. tr. 47, 3). He is in person the "doctrine of the Father, if He is the Word of the Father" (Jo. tr. 29, 3; 30, 6). His doctrine, taken in view of His statements, means His doctrine taken in view of reality. And the reality is the Word of God, Doctrine of the Father, Wisdom of God, Son of God. "Apply yourselves to the doctrine of Jesus Christ and you will arrive at the Word of God" (Jo. tr. 29, 4). From revelation-doctrine to revelation-mystery, from sign to reality, that is the movement of revelation.

Christ reveals not only Himself, but also the Father: "It is through His Son Himself that the Father reveals His Son, it is through His Son that He reveals Himself" (Jo. tr. 23, 4). The Father, in revealing Himself, wanted to express only one essential thing: His love. Christ "came above all to teach men how much God loves them and to make them realize that their heart should burn with love for God who has loved them first" (De cat. rud. 4, 8; De Gr. Christi I, 26, 27).

Christ is the light; the apostles and prophets are witnesses to this light. It is upon their *testimony* that we believe the invisible realities (De Civ. Dei XI, 3). The prophets are called "*prophets*, because of the future events which they have predicted or prefigured in a certain manner, events which have a bearing on the City of God and the Kingdom of Heaven" (De Civ. Dei XVII, 1). The past too was manifest to them. Thus, the prophet was not present at creation, but "the wisdom of God was present" through Whom all things were made, and this wisdom "tells the story of His works within, without any sound of words" (De Civ. Dei XI, 4). In the *De Gen. ad litt.* 12, 6-27, St. Augustine explains summarily how God acts in the soul of the prophet. He distinguishes three types of vision: corporal, spiritual or imaginary, and intellectual, according as whether the object of the vision is perceived by the senses, the imagination, or the intellect. He distinguishes further, in prophecy, between the *acceptio* of the signs and their interpretation. What makes the true prophet is the faculty of interpreting signs, thanks to a light he has received. The prophet is he "whose soul is enlightened in order to understand." Not only does he perceive figures and signs, but he also has the "interpretation of the images." Thus Daniel: "The bodily images were produced in his mind, and the meaning was revealed to his soul" (De Gen. ad litt. XXII, 9). St. Thomas will insist upon this in turn: what is primary in prophecy is not the mere representations perceived, but rather the light to judge them properly, grasp the sense intended by God.

The Word of God, "after having spoken first of all through the prophets, spoke through Himself, then through His apostles, as much as He thought necessary" (De Civ. Dei XI, 3). The apostles are witnesses of Christ, for they "saw the Savior present in the flesh, they received the words from His mouth and announced to us what they had seen and heard" (Ep. Jo. tr. 1, 3-4). They received from Christ Himself the mission to preach to the human race "His actions and His words" (De Cons. Evang. I, 16; Ep. Jo. tr. 4, 2). The word of the Apostles is thus the Word of God and we must believe it (Jo. tr. 109, 5). This word was preached first of all (Jo. tr. 109, 1), then faithfully set down in writing. We must receive the Gospel account as if the hand of the Savior Himself had written it (De Cons. Evang. I, 35. 54). Thus, the doctrine to be believed is found in the apostolic word "come down to our own time, wherever the Church extends her sway" (Jo. tr. 109, 1; De Fide et symb. 1, 1), and in Scripture which contains the apostolic teaching (Enchir. 1, 4). The apostles, the Church, Scripture: these are the links which bind us to Christ and guarantee the authenticity of the Catholic Faith. Those who are in search of the truth Augustine advises to follow "the Catholic rule which, from Christ in Person, through the apostles, has come down even to us and from us will pass on to our posterity" (De Util. cred. 8, 20).

The preaching of the Gospel by the Church has its response in personal faith: "We have heard the Gospel, we have consented; through the Gospel in Jesus Christ, we have believed" (Jo. tr. 16, 3). Faith, under the activity of charity and by its own dynamism, develops in a more and more penetrating knowledge of the mysteries. The immediate reward of faith is understanding. Faith, however, is not vision. By faith "the soul tries to arrive at the point of vision where holy and perfect hearts know the ineffable beauty whose very first intuition constitutes supreme happiness. . . . At the outset faith; at the end vision. This is our whole teaching in its briefest form" (Enchir. 1, 5). We walk in the economy of testimony and faith, looking to the vision. At that moment, the prophets, the apostles, the Gospel will all be silent. "We shall no longer have any need for their light, when the men of God who have dispensed it to us will share, together with us, the view of this true and brilliant light" of the Word Himself (Jo. tr. 35, 9).

St. Augustine does not treat the idea of revelation *ex professo* any more than the other fathers. The idea, however, is present throughout his work. In Johannine terminology, St. Augustine claims that the vision of God is impossible here below. The Mediator of all revelation is Jesus Christ, Word of God, Son of God, come to manifest through His Words and through His actions, the Gospel of salvation. Still, His message does not achieve its full effect unless man, drawn by the Father, opens His heart to the Word he hears externally. The external Word of Christ and the illumination and inspiration of the Spirit compose the one single Word of God. In respect to His role as Revealer, Christ is called Prophet, Lord of the prophets, and primarily Master. He teaches the truth and at the same time He *is* Truth, God revealing and God revealed, God and Way. His doctrine bears upon Himself, for He is in Person the doctrine of the Father, mystery revealed. What He reveals is Himself and, through Himself, the love of the Father. The prophets and the apostles share in His light: the light they announce or the light they bear witness to because they have seen and heard. The Word of Christ, object of our faith, we can arrive at through the apostolic word, set down in Scripture and proclaimed by the Church. Here below, we walk in faith, but our faith looks to a vision, when the light of the Word will absorb the lesser lights of faith.

1. L. FUETSCHER, "Die naturliche Gotteserkenntnis bei Tertullian," *Zeit. Kath. Theol.*, 51 (1927) : 1-35, 217-251; A. VELLICO, *La Rivelazione e le sue fonti nel "De Praescriptione haereticorum" di Tertulliano* (Roma, 1935); R. F. REFOULE, *Tertullien, Traité de la prescription contre les hérétiques* ("Sources chrétiennes 46," Paris, 1957), pp. 11-84; A. D'ALES, *La théologie de Tertullien* (Paris, 1905); M. SPANNEUT, *Le stoicisme des Pères de l'Église* (Paris, 1957).
2. A. D'ALES, *La théologie de Saint Cyprien* (Paris, 1922).

CONCLUSION

1. *The theme of revelation is to be found everywhere.*—There is no contesting the fact that the theme of revelation is in the foreground of all Christian awareness in the first three centuries. Christians are those who know God. The Unknowable has come out of his mystery and shown himself to man: to the Jewish people first of all, through the Law and the prophets, then to all of humanity through Christ, the Incarnate Word come in person to tell the mysteries of the Father. This interest for the theme of revelation has several causes:

A. The first Christian generations are still under the impact of the great epiphany of God in Christ. The witnesses of this overwhelming fact, or their disciples, are still living and preaching the Gospel of salvation. It is impossible for the impact of such an event not to have had its repercussions on the writing as well as the institutions of that age.

B. Their desire to reach the pagan generations leads the Christian thinkers to look for some common ground between Christianity and contemporary thinking. The apologists take up the idea of Logos, a common concept in all the religions of the empire and all the philosophical systems of the second century, fashioning a theology of the real Logos, of His life in the bosom of the Trinity and of His manifestations throughout creation: the Law and the Gospel. In this way they could make themselves heard in the cultivated circles and bring new apostles to Christ.

C. The first heretics also draw Christian thinkers on to the grounds of revelation. The Gnostics, in one sense, bring the idea of revelation to its climax, but at the same time they deform it. For them, salvation is reduced to a gnosis, instead of being *also* a knowledge. Christian writers will show that Christianity offers the true gnosis, but by pointing out that it is at once both life and knowledge, indissolubly.

Among the Gnostics, the Marcionites make Christ the Revealer of an absolutely new God, unknown in the Jewish world. They postulate a radical difference between the God of the Old Testament and the God of the New. This gives the fathers an oppurtunity to stress the unity, harmony, and progress of revelation, the work of one and the same God through His Logos.

In the fourth century, finally, the heresy of Eunomius leads the Cappadocians and St. John Chrysostom to a more precise statement of the traditional thinking on the knowledge of God.

2. *Natural knowledge and supernatural knowledge.*—It is a constant assertion among the fathers of the Church that God is beyond all definition and all comprehension: ineffable and incomprehensible. They see even in this unknowable character of God the necessity for revelation. The knowledge of God, in its intimate nature, can be had only through grace. God alone can instruct us about God, they claim, following Athenagoras.

On the other hand, they maintain, though less consistently, that God is knowable to a certain measure, even outside revelation, and this in two different ways. Beginning with the visible world, a man can conclude to the existence of its author and conceive some idea of His attributes: power, wisdom, beauty, providence. The second way is that of conscience, the spontaneous testimony of the human soul. The fathers insist, however, upon the weakness and imperfection of this natural knowledge compared with the knowledge had through revelation. Finally, they stress that there is no opposition between these two forms of knowledge but rather continuity, for it is the same Logos who manifests Himself in both.

3. *The two Testaments: unity and progress.*—One of the major problems, from the very outset of Christianity, is that of the relationship between the Old and New Testaments. The Judaizers want to keep the first place for the prophetic revelation, whereas the Marcionites oppose the two Testaments. The fathers are thus led to a more precise statement of the relationship between the Law and the Gospel. On the one hand, they stress the profound *unity* of the two Testaments. One and the same God is the Author of revelation through His word or Logos: creation, theophanies, Law, prophets, Incarnation, are all stages in this single and continuous manifestation of God throughout the course of human history.

On the other hand, they are equally insistent on the *progress* realized from one economy to the other. This progress is conceived of in a somewhat different fashion in each father. According to *Justin*, there is partial and obscure manifestation of the Logos in the Old Testament, fullness in the New Testament. According to *Irenaeus*: preparation, education of humanity, vague outlines and promises of the Incarnation in the Old Testament; then, accomplishment, presence, and gift in the New Testament; external discipline first, and then of adoption. According to *Clement* of Alexandria: puzzle and mystery in the Old Testament; explanation of prophecy in the New Testament. According to *Origen*: knowledge of mysteries in the Old Testament; realization and possession in the New Testament; passage from shadow and image to truth, from letter and history to spirit.

4. *Economy and pedagogy.*—The fathers, particularly Justin, Irenaeus, Clement, Origen, Basil, Gregory of Nyssa, and Augustine, insist on the element of *economy* in revelation. This economy is presented as a plan of salvation, infinitely wise, which God conceives of from all eternity and accomplishes patiently, following the ways foreseen by Him, preparing humanity, making it mature and progressively revealing what it could bear of God's plans. The fathers like to draw up the history of these steps on the part of God to accustom man to His presence, to the impregnation of human nature by grace.

This idea is closely connected with that of the delays in Christ's coming. The letter to Diognetus claims that men needed to have an experience of their own impotence before knowing the fullness of salvation (dramatic perspective). Irenaeus, Clement, Origen (in certain passages), develop the thesis of divine pedagogy. God educates humanity and prepares it to receive the fullness of divine gifts in the Incarnation (optimist vision). For Augustine and Origen (in other passages), the problem hardly comes up, for the Church is coextensive with humanity. The Church began with the patriarchs. The truth of Christ was already known to the prophets of the Old Testament.

5. *The stages of revelation.*—The fathers constantly hark back to the great stages of revelation and thereby stress its profoundly historical character. In this way of looking at revelation, the peaks of the history are always the same: on the one hand, the Law and the prophets; on the other hand, the apostles and the Church; in the center and at the very summit is Christ. In other words: preparation for Christ, coming of the Word Incarnate, sending of the apostles, the extension of salvation to the world and time through the Church.

This schema has several variants. The apologists find a very special place for the prophets. Ignatius of Antioch, Irenaeus, Tertullian, Cyril of Alexandria, John Chrysostom insist on the role of the apostles. Ignatius of Antioch, Irenaeus, Tertullian, Cyprian, Origen,

and Augustine definitely find the Church at work in the whole movement of revelation. Clement of Alexandria considers the philosophy
of the Greeks as a special testament, like the equivalent of the Law
for the Jews. For all of them, revelation culminates in Christ, the
Son of the Father, the perfect Revealer, the Word or Logos of God
incarnate.

6. *Christ and revelation.*—In a general way, the fathers understood
revelation to mean that Christ, the Word of God, the Image of the
Father, makes known the Father and His plan of salvation, and in
order to communicate this knowledge to men, uses all the ways of the
Incarnation—both word and action. Most of the time, however, it is
the human word of Christ to which they attribute the primary role.
Within this general conception we might distinguish different points
of emphasis, provided we do not push the difference

A. Ignatius of Antioch, Athanasius, and above all Irenaeus speak
of revelation in terms of a very biblical realism. According to Isaiah
40, 5, man in the Messianic era must see God. Irenaeus sees in Christ
the realization of this promise. Jesus Christ is the existential epiphany
of God. In the Son, visible and tangible, the Father also appears to
us and manifests Himself to us.

B. Opposed to this is the peculiarly Greek theology, less attentive
to the role of the flesh. This is the position represented by Justin and,
in large measure, by Clement of Alexandria, who see in Christ
primarily the Master, source of all truth, and in revelation, the
communication of absolute truth, true philosophy.

C. Where these two theologies come together Origen might be
located. According to Him, Christ reveals in the sense that, through
the instrumentality of his flesh, we *understand*, we *conceive, we form
some idea* of the word, and through the Word, Image of the Father,
we form an idea of the Father Himself.

7. *Mediators of revelation.*—The titles given to Christ, to the
prophets, and to the apostles, as well as the words used to designate
their activity, give us an insight into how the fathers conceived of
revelation.

A. The prophets, beside their habitual title of prophets, are called
the instruments of God, the witnesses of God, the witnesses of truth,
the witnesses of Christ, the witnesses of light, the disciples in the
Spirit of Christ, the announcers of Christ, the masters of men. Their
function is to announce Christ, to announce the mysteries of salvation,
to announce the truth, to bear witness, to teach the will of God.

B. The apologists use some terms in referring to Christ which
later disappear from literature. They call him *angel* and *apostle*

(Justin). The favorite and most frequent title to designate Christ's role of revealer is that of *Master*, universally used, particularly after Clement. Christ is the Word of God, the Incarnate Son, come to teach men the way of salvation. He is the Way, the Guide, the Shepherd, the good news in person. The doctrine He brings is light and life for men.

Christ *announces* the plans of God (Justin), the mysteries of God (Origen). He *manifests* God (Ignatius of Antioch, Athanasius), the Father (Irenaeus), the secrets of God (Ignatius of Antioch), the mysteries of the Father (Augustine). He *reveals* the Father (Tertullian, Irenaeus, Origen). He *speaks* (Origen, Gregory of Nyssa, Chrysostom, Augustine). He *makes known* the Father (Origen). He *testifies* (Athanasius, Gregory of Nyssa). He *preaches* (Tertullian, Augustine). He *hands down* the truth of the Gospel (Tertullian, Cyprian). Above all He *teaches* (Clement of Rome, Justin, Athenagoras, letter to Diognetus, Irenaeus, Tertullian, Cyprian, Clement of Alexandria, Origen, Athanasius, Chrysostom, Gregory of Nyssa, Augustine). He *enlightens* (Justin, Clement of Alexandria, Origen, Athanasius, Cyril of Alexandria, Basil, Augustine).

The Alexandrians see revelation primarily in terms of an *enlightening*. For them, Christ is He who brings light to the intelligence which is plunged in darkness. There is a Platonic nostalgia for the world of light and its contemplation by the intelligence.

C. The *apostles* are the messengers of good news, the preachers of the Gospel, the doctors and masters of nations, the witnesses of Christ. They *preach* (Polycarp, Letter to Diognetus, Irenaeus, Tertullian, Cyril of Alexandria, Origen, Augustine). They *preach* and *hand down* (Irenaeus). They *hand down* (Cyprian, Tertullian). They *testify* (Augustine). They *teach* (Ignatius of Antioch, Athanasius, Cyril of Alexandria, Tertullian). They *enlighten* (Cyril of Alexandria).

D. The *Church* faithfully *keeps, preserves, teaches* without defect, and *hands down* the truth. The idea of tradition is everywhere prevalent.

8. *Objective revelation and its names.*—Revelation, in its accomplished form, has many different names: true *wisdom* (Clement of Alexandria), the *word of God* (Clement of Rome, Tertullian), divine *revelation* (Tertullian), the *word of justice* (Polycarp), the *word of Christ* (Cyril of Alexandria), the *word of the cross* (Chrysostom), the *good news* or the *Gospel* (Clement of Rome, Ignatius of Antioch, Tertullian, Cyril of Alexandria), the *Gospel preaching*, or *apostolic preaching* (Cyril of Alexandria), the *mystery* (Tertullian, Gregory of Nyssa), the *prescriptions*, the *precepts*, the *commandment*, the *will*,

the *ordinance* of God or Christ (*passim*), the *teachings*, the *instructions*, the *doctrines*, the *doctrine*, the doctrine of faith, the doctrine of salvation, the Gospel doctrine (*passim*), the *teachings* of the apostles (Ignatius of Antioch), *faith*, or Christian faith (Ignatius of Antioch, Irenaeus, Tertullian), the *rule of faith*, the rule of truth (Tertullian), the *rule of the Gospel* (Didache), the *Catholic rule* (Augustine), *tradition* (Irenaeus, Tertullian, Cyprian), *deposit*, (Tertullian, Cyril of Alexandria).

9. *Twofold dimension of revelation.*—Most of the fathers of the Church insist on the fact that the word of revelation is not a human word, but a divine word: it is accompanied by grace. The external activity of Christ who speaks, communicating the doctrine of salvation, has a corresponding interior activity which the fathers, following Scripture, call a revelation, an attraction, an inner hearing, an illumination, an anointing, a testimony. At the same time that the Church proclaims the good news of salvation, the Spirit is at work within in order to make the word that is heard without both fruitful and salutary. Origen, Augustine, Cyril of Alexandria insist on this second dimension of revelation. It is the activity of this grace of faith to which we must attribute adherence to the Gospel message.

10. *Fertility of revelation.*—The apologists are particularly aware of the communication of the message of truth to men. The Alexandrians and the Cappadocians are more concerned with the subjective appropriation of this truth and its fructification in the soul through faith and the gifts of the Spirit. Faith is the point of departure for a growing penetration of the truth received, a more and more intense and ardent search on the part of intelligence. The Christian gnosis, however, is not a pure knowledge, as it could be for the Greeks; it is wisdom and life. It is intelligence of the mysteries oriented towards spiritual perfection, under the unfluence of the Spirit and His gifts, who enlightens the believer, transfigures him, makes him like Christ, and makes him, in his turn, capable of begetting perfect gnostics.

part 3
the notion of revelation in the
theological tradition

The purpose of this third part of the book is to show how the theologians, on the basis of the Scriptural data, tradition, and the teaching of the Church, describe and conceive the notion of revelation. Our investigation begins with the thirteenth century: not because the centuries before that offer nothing of interest, but because scholastic theology, at this moment of its full maturity, gathers all the riches of the past, organizing them and submitting them to a rigorous and methodic analysis. Our plan has not been to make our way through all the centuries, and all the theologians—an exhaustive research. We have simply meant to indicate the main lines of the theology of revelation, as they are to be found in the different schools, and primarily in the works of the leading thinkers.

We shall thus investigate: 1. the tradition of the thirteenth century, represented by St. Bonaventure and St. Thomas; 2. the post-Tridentine theologians, primarily the Dominicans Cano and Bañez, the Jesuits Suarez and De Lugo, the Carmelites of Salamanca; 3. some representatives of the theological renewal of the nineteenth century: Mohler, Denzinger, Franzelin, Newman, Scheeben. From the contemporary period, following the crisis of Modernism, we shall examine what constitutes the common teaching of the theologians beginning with the twentieth century; then we shall show how, for almost a quarter century, there has been evidence of an important renewal in the theology of the revelation.

We shall insist particularly on the contribution of the thirteenth and twentieth centuries (chapters one and four), because they appear richer in the elements that are essential to a theology of revelation. In the second and third chapters, we shall be content with staking out the path that leads from the medieval era to the contemporary.

CHAPTER I

SCHOLASTICS OF THE THIRTEENTH CENTURY

A special investigation into the nature and properties of Christian revelation is not among the preoccupations of Scholasticism in the thirteenth century, nor in the theological frameworks sketched out before their time. St. Thomas, for example, outside his commentaries on Scripture where the sacred text dictated his subject matter, has only brief mention of the revelation through Christ and the apostles. What takes up most of the attention of the schoolmen is the immediate revelation addressed to the prophets: charism of knowledge, conceived as an illumination of the mind. They also speak of objective revelation (the Gospel), but only in passing.

I. SAINT BONAVENTURE

Saint Bonaventure speaks occasionally of revelation in his Commentary on the Sentences of Peter Lombard and in his biblical commentaries; he is more explicit in his treatise on prophecy.[1]

1. Revelation and Economy of Revelation

The use of the word "revelation" in the foreword to the Commentary on the Sentences shows us his line of thinking: revelation is light to the mind. There are four abysses, he says, open before the theologian, four secrets or mysteries: the mystery of God and His intimate life, the mystery of creation and sin, the mystery of Incarnation and redemption, the mystery of the sacraments and the glory to which they lead. It is properly the Holy Spirit (1 Cor. 2, 10) who scrutinizes these mysteries, the Revealer of the secrets and abysses of the Trinity. Analogically, however, says Saint Bonaventure, the role of the theologian approaches that of the Holy Spirit. He scrutinizes the divine mysteries in order *to discover, to make known, to manifest* their depths.[2] "Reveal" means thus to *illuminate the mind* on a subject which was darkness, secret, mystery. A second element, essential to the idea of revelation, is the certitude it engenders. "I call revelation the fact of giving a *certain* inner illumination" concerning an event to come.[3] In this respect, revelation is distinct from prediction,[4] conjecture, and opinion.[5]

For God, revealing something to humanity means speaking to man, that is, enlightening his mind.[6] Revelation, word, illumination are interchangeable terms. The word of God is both eternal and temporal: eternal as the word by which, in the bosom of the Trinity, the Father begets a Son like to Himself in all things; temporal as the word which God projects outside Himself through creation and His Self-revelation to humanity.[7] God speaks to man in three ways: either by signs which affect his external senses, or by signs which affect his internal senses and imagination, or finally by a word which he inspires or breathes directly into his mind. In the first two cases, the angels can serve as instrumental causes; the third way is proper to God alone.[8]

Man needed revelation; human activity, which meets with success when it is aimed at the realities of the natural world, must admit it is strangely impotent in the things of salvation: man regresses more than he advances, unless he is "directed by the teaching of divine revelation"; that is why "we have been given Scripture, divinely revealed by the Holy Spirit," to instruct us in matters of faith and morals.[9]

Revelation is an activity common to the whole Trinity, but it is appropriated especially to the Son and the Spirit.[10] Still, the Son and the Spirit have not revealed everything, only what was necessary for our salvation.[11] The hour of final judgment, for example, is hidden from us, because it is not important for our salvation that we know it.[12]

The activity of revelation unfolds in time and history, according to the rhythm willed by God, who prepares humanity to receive greater gifts; that is why the sacramental economy has been kept until the "sixth age of the world".[13] Revelation, begun with the prophets, casts its full light only in the teaching of Christ and the apostles.[14] The prophetic revelation itself, in the course of the centuries, underwent development, always understood in a fuller and more living light.[15] The fullness of revelation comes to us through Christ, who exists among men "as the infinitely wise Teacher who enlightens them through the word of His teaching".[16] Only He has the right to the title of Teacher, for He alone possesses all knowledge and from Him all truth derives as from its only source. He preaches the true way which leads to God. We must listen to His word and welcome it with faith.[17]

2. Prophetic Revelation

Saint Bonaventure, like the whole of the Middle Ages, is primarily interested in prophetic revelation.[18] His doctrine depends on that of Saint Augustine and, more directly, on his teacher, Alexander of Halès. His thinking can be summed up in the following points. We must distinguish first of all between prophecy and the gift of prophecy. The gift of prophecy is a *habitus* which, in order to be actuated, demands an actual divine illumination.[19] Prophecy, in itself, is a transitory act. It implies a *receptio* of the matter which takes place in the senses, in the imagination, or in the mind,[20] and, on the other hand, a *judicium*, the result of an illumination of the mind. If a person is favored with sense or imagination images, without, however, receiving the special light needed to grasp their meaning (such was the case of the Pharaoh, Balthazar, and Nabuchadnezzar), the revelation is called imperfect; it is perfect if the person also receives an understanding of the signs.[21] What makes the true prophet is the enlightenment he has to understand what is represented.[22] This illumination is called infused because through it, the mind rises to a knowledge of what, by its own unaided powers, it would be unable to perceive.[23] The judgment of the prophet rests, not on an evidence which comes from the object, but on the "Truth which enlightens and instructs him".[24] The position of the prophet, in this respect, is similar to that of the believer, each of them supported by the inner light which enlightens them.[25] Insofar as it is a revelation or illumination of the mind, prophecy, unlike the gifts of wisdom and charity, does not of itself imply sanctifying grace. It is ordered to the advantage of someone else, and not the personal advantage of the one who receives it: as a result, it can exist in prophets whose conduct is deserving of blame.[26] The light received determines the position of the prophet. Elijah received a more abundant light; David a more penetrating light, for his prophecy is of the intellectual order. We can distinguish three kinds of prophetic revelation: sense, imagination, intellect. This last mode is superior and always implies a revelation; the same is not always true of the sense or imagination.[27] In prophetic revelation, the subject is more passive than active. We can also see that God often reveals Himself in a dream; no doubt because the soul is then most fully at the disposition of the divine activity.[28]

3. Faith and Revelation

Faith is born of the combined activity of the external word and internal word, the teaching and preaching which strikes the ear of the body and the teaching of the Holy Spirit who speaks to the heart in secret. Saint Bonaventure explains that there are two ways of learning: one through discovery, the other through teaching. The sense of sight is conditioned towards the first method; the sense of hearing is proper to the second. Knowledge of faith is a knowledge through teaching. But, as Saint Bonaventure points out, faith comes primarily from the inner hearing, for the preacher works in vain if there is no "illumination of the inner Teacher" within the soul.[29]

This inner illumination which does not show a new object, but enables the mind to grasp this object as it should be, Saint Bonaventure calls, in the words of Scripture, "revelation," "testimony," "inner inspiration." Commenting on John 5, 37, he observes that Christ was believed not only through the witness of John the Baptist and the testimony of his own miracles, but also through the inner testimony of the Father. The Father, who had sent His Son and made Him visible through the Incarnation, testifies to Him through an "inner inspiration" and "reveals Him in an intelligible voice." The Jews, caught up in the things of the flesh, could not hear this voice, but to Simon Peter, who listened to it, was given the power to confess Christ.[30]

What is communicated through revelation, that is, the object of faith, Saint Bonaventure calls: "the teaching of divine revelation," "the Gospel, apostolic, or prophetic teaching," the "truth of salvation," the "truth of the faith and of Holy Scripture," for this teaching, this truth is all contained in Scripture. "Every truth of salvation is in Scripture, or comes from Scripture, or is connected with Scripture".[31] Saint Bonaventure also speaks equivalently of the "truth of the Faith and the Holy Scripture",[32] for, according to him, all Scripture comes "through the divine revelation of the Father of lights".[33] This origin is the foundation of its authority and of the incomparable certitude to which it gives rise.[34]

4. Conclusion

Revelation, according to Saint Bonaventure, designates in the first place the *illuminating activity* of God or the *subjective illumination* which results from this activity. Such is primarily the revelation made to the prophets. The teaching of Christ is also conceived as an illumination of humanity. Saint Bonaventure makes no clear distinction between the two notions of revelation and inspiration. He frequently uses revelation where we would be inclined to speak of inspiration today. Following the usage of Scripture, he also uses the word revelation to describe the inner illumination of the grace of faith. He stresses the Trinitarian character of the activity of revelation, just as he stresses its aspect of economy. In his constant preoccupation with illumination we recognize the trademark of Augustine's thinking. Between the illumination of natural knowledge, revelation, faith, contemplation and vision, Saint Bonaventure finds a continuity and progressively increasing depth in the gifts of God. From shadow, slowly, light springs forth until it becomes full vision.[35]

II. SAINT THOMAS AQUINAS

Saint Thomas speaks of revelation under many aspects.[36] He considers it sometimes as an operation of salvation, proceeding from the free love of God and furnishing man with all the lights that are indispensable or simply useful for the pursuit of his salvation; sometimes as an historical event, unrolling in time and touching men of all centuries through a complex economy of intermediaries, stages, and modalities; sometimes as a divine activity penetrating into the psychological life of the prophet and, as a consequence, into the whole fabric of humanity; sometimes as a sacred doctrine communicated through Christ to His apostles and handed down by them, a doctrine contained in Scripture and proposed, through the preaching of the Church, for the belief of the faithful; sometimes, finally, as a degree of knowledge which he lines up in relation to the other types of knowledge: natural knowledge, knowledge of faith, knowledge of vision. These manifold aspects only mirror the richness of the reality.

1. Revelation as a Salvific Operation

In the beginning of the Summa, as a starting point for theology and Christian faith, Saint Thomas posits the fundamental fact of revelation. Inspired by the free love of God, revelation is aimed at the salvation of man. Now the salvation of man is God Himself, in His intimate life, that is, an object which absolutely surpasses the powers and exigencies of human nature. Thus it was necessary for God to reveal Himself, to make Himself known to man in order to show him his final goal and the way which leads to that goal.[37]

Without being *absolutely* necessary, the revelation of truths of the natural order, concerning God and our relationship with Him, was *morally* necessary. There would have been three disadvantages, actually, if this area of truths had been left simply to the efforts of human reason: few men would have managed to know these truths, by reason of the lack of intellectual power in the majority of men, their absorption in the work of everyday living, or simply the innate laziness of their minds. Then those who did arrive at these truths would do so only after long and painful searching, while the rest of mankind would remain condemned to the darkness of ignorance. Such an investigation, finally, would be fraught with doubt, error, and inaccuracy in its demonstration. "That is why the divine clemency wisely disposed that even those things which human reason can arrive at should be imposed upon us as objects of faith, so that all men would be able to share in the divine knowledge, easily, without either doubt or error".[38]

Saint Thomas thus conceives of revelation as the activity of the God of salvation who freely and gratuitously furnishes man with all the truths necessary and useful to the pursuit of his supernatural end.

The revealed truth or *revelatum* is primarily and essentially the knowledge of God, which is inaccessible to reason and consequently can be known only by way of revelation. The *revelabile* extends further to all knowledge which does not surpass the innate capacity of natural reason, but which God has revealed because it is useful to the work of salvation, and because the majority of men, left to themselves, would never come to a knowledge of these truths; thus they are part of the bloc of revelation.[39] The *revelatum must* be revealed, whereas the *revelabile can* be revealed.

2. *Revelation as an Event in History*

As a temporary event, revelation, for Saint Thomas, stands out as an operation which is hierarchical, successive, progressive, and polymorphous.

Hierarchical first of all. Supernatural truth comes to us like a torrent whose mighty waters, coming from God who is their source and fountainhead, come down to the plain only after they have formed successive basins. The angels were the first to receive it, following the order of the celestial hierarchies,[40] then men and, among men, the greatest first of all, that is, the prophets and the apostles. Truth extends through the multitudes of those who receive it in faith, following on analogous operation: those who possess a broader knowledge are bound to pass it on and explain it to the simple faithful, who in their turn are bound to adhere explicitly only to the articles of faith.[41] This movement of revelation in its genesis sets the pattern for its application. To some it is given to receive and preach revelation; to others, only to preach it. Still, all are true mediators between God and men: "with respect to God they are only men, but with respect to men they are gods, insofar as they share the thinking of God," either through revelations which are addressed directly to them, or through more advanced knowledge they have of revelation.[42]

Secondly, revelation is characterized by *succession*: it does not take place all at once, but by following steps which each constitute a partial realization of the divine plan. God intervenes several times to make His secrets known: such was the richness of its content that it took men many long centuries of preparation to gradually master and assimilate it.[43] It is possible to distinguish three ages or principal "moments" in the history of revelation, and, at the head of each age there stands a higher revelation from which all the others flow: the revelation made to Abraham, inaugurated by the revelation of the one God; the Mosaic revelation, inaugurated by the revelation of the divine essence; the revelation of Christ, inaugurated by the revelation of the mystery of the Trinity. The first revelation is the foundation of the patriarchal era, and is addressed to only certain families; the second is the foundation of the prophetic era and is addressed to a whole people; the third is the basis for the Christian era and is addressed to all humanity.[44] Like a master who does not pass on the whole knowledge of his trade, all at once but "hands it down little by little, adapting himself to the capacity of his disciple," God bends to the weakness of humanity, showing us just as much light as we are able to receive in any age.[45]

A double movement runs through the economy of revelation and makes up the dynamism of its *progress*. On the one hand, there is a movement which, little by little, augments the deposit of revelation. The prophets of the last times knew more of the truth than those of the patriarchal age, and the apostles knew many things that were unknown to the prophets.[46] On the other hand, there is a movement which brings humanity, little by little, to a clearer and clearer vision of the Incarnation to come: "The vision of Moses . . . was more excellent with respect to the knowledge of divinity: but David had a fuller knowledge and better expressed the mysteries of Christ's Incarnation."[47]

The closer one comes to Christ, the closer one comes to the fullness of revelation. With Christ, there is the springtime of grace, the hour of youth, the time of perfection. "The ultimate consummation of grace took place through Christ; thus the time of Christ is called the time of fullness (Gal. 4, 4). And thus those who were closer to Christ either before, like John the Baptist, or after, like the Apostles, had a fuller knowledge of the mysteries of faith. We find that the same thing is true in the case of man: perfection is to be found in youth, and his state is more perfect the closer he is to his youth, either before or after".[48] The closer the relationship with Christ, the more alive this light. John the Baptist has an advantage over Moses, for he pointed out Christ in His human presence.[49] The apostles also surpass Moses, for they witness a fuller unveiling of the mysteries of Christ.[50]

Revelation is *polymorphous*. In order to make himself known, God did not overlook any form of communication. Saint Thomas, in his commentary on the Epistle to the Hebrews,[51] notes the extraordinary richness and variety of God's ways: the multiplicity and variety of the persons whom he addresses; the diversity of the psychological processes (bodily vision, imagination vision, intellectual vision); revelations bearing upon the future, the present, the past; addressed to men, either to instruct or to punish; finally a diversity in the degree of clarity or obscurity. At times, revelation is something brilliant and striking, but more often than not the element of divinity is "veiled in the novelty and obscurity of words and things".[52] This very veil invites us to a humility before the presence of God.

With Christ and His apostles, the salutary event of revelation is accomplished. The Spirit of revelation has not, however, withdrawn. He still operates under the more modest form of particular revelation. "No time in history has been lacking in men endowed with the prophetic spirit; not with a view towards proposing a new doctrine, but for the direction of human acts."[53] For the Catholic Faith "rests upon the revelation made to the apostles and prophets . . . , and not on a revelation which might have been made to any other teachers".[54]

3. *Prophetic Revelation as a Charism of Knowledge*

Saint Thomas, too, is primarily interested in prophetic revelation.[55] A too exclusive attention to the content of revelation might result in a lack of consideration for the concrete process of revelation. Thus, modernism saw the rise of the legend that Catholic revelation is taken up only with truths that "dropped down from heaven." Saint Thomas, however, considers revelation in its psychological phase, insofar as it is a divine activity at work in the human psyche. His *De Prophetia* is characterized by a constant reference to the statements of the prophets and by an astonishing respect for the complex data of prophetic experience.[56]

By prophecy, Saint Thomas understands "the knowledge, given to men supernaturally, of truths which actually surpass the scope of the human mind, truths in which the mind is instructed by God for the good of the human community".[57] A social charism, prophecy instructs humanity in "everything that is necessary for salvation".[58] Together with this predominant usage, Saint Thomas sometimes adopts a more restricted sense which limits the gift of prophecy to the knowledge of future things; he then considers it as a charism which "confirms" revelation (or prophecy in the broad sense of the word), just like miracles.[59]

He distinguishes (in prophecy) the prophetic *knowledge* from its *usage*, that is, the *denuntiatio* or proclamation of the prophecy. Prophecy, he says, is primarily and principally an act of knowledge; only secondarily is it a discourse.[60] In the first case, the prophet receives: he is more passive,[61] like the atmosphere under the radiation of the sun;[62] he experiences the activity of the light and the divine contact.[63] In the *denuntiatio*, however, his will plays a greater role: the prophet chooses his images according to his temperament and personal experience.

Prophecy opens the eyes of the prophet to a knowledge which was far removed from his mind.[64] "The prophets know many things which are *far removed* from the ordinary knowledge of men".[65] Thus Scripture is right in calling them *seers*. They "see what escapes other men, they perceive what is shrouded in mystery".[66] They see what is *opaque* and *distant*: in particular, they see the future, which is especially distant and obscure with relation to the present.[67] But they also see things that are removed because they surpass the scope of natural reason, that is, mystery.[68] The distance prophecy passes through is a distance of the order of knowledge. God is not distant from us; it is our mind that is far from God and will remain so until the time of vision.[69] Prophetic revelation takes away the veil which darkens our mind and thus reduces the distance which separates us from God.[70]

In the concrete, how does this *unveiling* take place, how does the prophet come into the possession of divine truth?[71] Prophecy is defined on the basis of the two elements which are implied in all human knowledge: *representations* (*acceptio rerum*), which furnish the material for judgment, and *judgment*, taking place in the natural light of the mind. These two elements come up again in prophetic knowledge, but there they are elevated by the gift of prophecy. The *acceptio rerum* can be effected in different ways: either by God Himself producing sense forms (visible, tangible) on the exterior (as in the case of Daniel, who saw the writing on the wall); or by making use

of figures in the imagination, deriving from objects which fall under
the scope of the senses, but giving them an unexpected orientation, or
by directly imposing entirely new forms (as in the case of a man
born blind, in whose imagination the images of various colors would
be impressed); or finally by God acting directly on the human
intelligence, imprinting an "intelligible species" (species intelligibilis)
on the mind.[72]

The speculative judgment is effected under the influence of a
special light granted to the prophet. "The formal element in prophetic
knowledge is the divine light; the unity of this light gives prophecy its
specific unity, despite the diversity of the objects which this light
makes known to the prophets".[73] This light, actually, enlightens a
specific object with an astonishing historical and psychological richness: the events of history, human conduct, the objects of nature,
inner visions, images, dreams, etc. The essence of prophecy, however,
does not reside in this representative element, but in the divine light
which is communicated to the seer. Under this aspect, the activity of
God defies all comparison with that of the human teacher: the human
teacher can "present his disciple with realities by means of the signs
and symbols of language, but he cannot enlighten him from within, as
God does. Now, in prophecy, it is superelevation of the judgment that
is most important; it is in the judgment that knowledge has its final
completion".[74] The essence of prophecy thus does not reside in the
representative element, but in the divine light granted to the prophet
so that he will discern, judge, and express the intentions and activities
of God. Even in the case where the divine activity, drawing on the
psychological endowment of the prophet, makes use of images or
pre-existing ideas, the human person of the prophet would have been
unable by himself to associate these images in such a way as to make
them yield truths as yet unknown, which constitute the object of his
message; he needs divine enlightening.[75] Thanks to the illumination
he receives, the prophet judges the elements present to his consciousness, with certitude and without error, and thus takes possession of
the truth that God means to communicate. It is through this illumination
and this judgment, in the prophet, that the unveiling of the divine
thought really takes place. The prophetic light really perfects and
strengthens the natural light of intelligence, allowing it to perceive
what it would be incapable of discovering of itself. Once he receives
this gift, the prophet reacts in a vital way. Under the inspiration
which lifts him above the human he was passive; now he perceives
actively in the revelation.[76] Above and beyond the plane of images,
he arrives at the deeper truth to which they point.[77]

This light is so much the essential element of prophecy that it alone is enough to characterize the true prophet: thus Joseph, explaining the dream of Pharaoh,[78] or Daniel, interpreting the vision of Balthazar. Pharaoh and Balthazar, however, who are only favored with the representations, without the light for interpreting them, cannot be called prophets except in a very relative way, or for that matter in any way at all.[79] The type of the true prophet is the seer who receives from God both the representations and the light to judge them.[80] This revelation par excellence implies degrees of dignity, according to the nature of the representations: sense visions are less elevated than those of the imagination, and the imagination itself gives way to a vision of the intellect. It is obvious, says Saint Thomas, "that the manifestation of divine truth resulting from pure contemplation of this truth is superior to the manifestation which makes use of the symbolism of corporal realities: it comes closer to the vision of heaven where truth is contemplated in the essence of God".[81]

If the prophet, finally, is favored only with the supernatural light for judging not some supernatural object, but merely truths which he might have arrived at himself through purely human activity, this is a degree that is inferior to prophecy properly so called, for the prophet does not arrive at supernatural truth.[82] Saint Thomas still finds a place for him in the chapter on revelation, since the light granted to him allows him to judge according to divine truth[83] and with a certitude which comes from on high.[84] Such is the condition of the hagiographers who "most often spoke ..., in their own name, of truths which human reason could know, though only with the help of divine light".[85] This limited case of prophetic charism corresponds to what we call inspiration in the modern sense of the word.[86]

The prophet is not always conscious of the charism with which he is favored. It can happen, as Saint Thomas observes, that he is not "fully able to decide whether his words and thinking are the result of a divine inspiration or of his own mind." Such a case would be an "imperfect degree of prophecy".[87] On the contrary, in genuine revelation, "the prophet possesses the greatest certainty regarding the realities he knows through his gift of prophecy, and he holds it for certain that they have been divinely revealed".[88] Just as we recognize the incontestable presence of the sun in the light which shines in a room, so the prophet, in the light which he receives, recognizes the divine origin of the revealed truth. "We have indication of the certitude attaching to prophecy in the fact that Abraham was prepared to sacrifice his only son after he had been advised by a prophetic vision; this he would never have done, had he not been completely sure of the divine revelation".[89] In the brightness of the light received, and without explicit reasoning (just as our thinking arrives at the cause in its effect) the prophet realizes that God is the Author of this light and the Author of the truth which this light makes known to him.

Enlightened by the divine light, the prophet's field of vision is unlimited. Prophetic knowledge, being a reflection of divine knowledge, can extend to any object that is subject to this knowledge, human or divine, corporal or spiritual;[90] to whatever object can be necessary or useful for salvation, present, past or future, little or big.[91] Jeremiah sees divine meaning in an almond tree (Jer. 1, 11-12), Amos in a basket of fruit (Am. 8, 1-2): the only important thing is the meaning which God attaches to these humble realities.

4. Revelation as Word

The activity through which God shares man's human thinking process Saint Thomas calls *word of God*, because of its analogy with the type of relations men establish among themselves through the spoken word. In his commentary on Saint John, he notes that God reveals in three ways: either through a voice heard by the senses (the voice of the baptism and the transfiguration), or by the manifestation of His Essence (the vision of the blessed), or by an inner word (in the case of the prophets).[92] This inner word is merely the illumination of the mind.[93]

Speaking, according to Saint Thomas, means making known one's thinking to someone else.[94] A man manifests his thinking by sensible signs (imitation, sound, writing), but the word, understood in its formal sense, is a category which embraces at once human, angelic, and divine communication.[95] Between the human word and the divine word there is an *analogy*. Insofar as it is sound or gesture, word can be attributed to God only by way of metaphor; but insofar as it is a spiritual entity and a manifestation of thought, it implies no imperfection and can be attributed to God.

We can distinguish, Saint Thomas continues, two different ways of hearing and two different words: "one word is external, God speaking through his preachers, and the other is interior, when He speaks through an inner inspiration. Inner inspiration is called word by reason of its analogy with external words. Just as, in the external word, we present our hearers, not with the actual thing we mean to make known to them but rather a sign or symbol of this thing, a word that bears a meaning, even so God, inspiring man from within, does not give a vision of His essence but rather a sign of His essence, a spiritual likeness of his wisdom." It is thus that God makes Himself known from within to the prophets; in a similar way too, he addressed Himself to Adam and taught him directly.[96] The signs or likenesses received in the mind are inadequate representations of the divine object, but through them, and thanks to the light which enlightens them, God truly communicates His thinking to us, initiates us into His mysteries: God speaks to us.[97]

5. Revelation through Christ and the Apostles

On the subject of Christ's revelation and that of the apostles, Saint Thomas, in the *Summa*, has brief but meaningful references. The third part, which treats of Christ the Savior, begins with these words: *viam veritatis nobis in seipso demonstravit* (Prologue: "The way of truth He demonstrated for us in Himself"). In order for man to walk with greater confidence towards the truth, Truth itself, the Son of God, became man, established and gave foundation to faith: thus, supported by the word of Christ, man is also supported by the word of God.[98] All the activities of Christ's life (birth, baptism, transfiguration, miracles, passion, death, resurrection) unveil one or another aspect of the mystery of salvation.[99] Through His whole incarnate Person, Christ shows us the way of salvation. The seventh question presents Christ as "the first and principal Teacher of faith".[100] Question 42 points out that Christ has become the Light and Salvation of nations by instructing His apostles first, and then entrusting to them His mission of handing down His teaching to all peoples, beginning with the Jews.[101] Question 40, finally, points out that Christ preferred to "converse" with men rather than lead a solitary life, for He came into the world to make known the truth.[102]

There is more to be found in the Commentary on Saint John: "Before this, the Son had made known the knowledge of God through the prophets who announced Him, insofar as they were sharers in the eternal Word . . . . But now the only Son Himself tells the faithful about their God. Consequently, this teaching surpasses all other teachings in authority, usefulness; for it has been handed down to us immediately by the only Son of God who is First Wisdom."[103] To make known His thinking, a man makes it incarnate in sounds or letters: in the same way, "God, wanting to make Himself known to men, clothed His Word, conceived from all eternity, in flesh and time"[104] Through the flesh which He has taken, the Word speaks to us and we hear Him.[105] Christ, through His humanity, is thus the *way* for us to draw near to the knowledge of the truth; on the other hand, as God,

He is this truth in Person.[106] He bears testimony to the truth, to this
truth which is Himself.[107] No one can make known the truth better
than He; He is Light and Truth.[108] Insofar as He is Wisdom and
Word of God, He is the beginning and principle of our wisdom,[109]
the root and source of all knowledge of God.[110]

Christ is the Teacher par excellence, whose word reveals the
secrets of the Father. Saint Thomas sees in this ministry one of the
two principal roles of Christ, the other being that of "opening the
gate to heaven through His passion".[111] Christ preaches by His actions
as well as by His words.[112] But, unlike human teachers, He teaches
both from without and from within.[113] Saint Thomas sometimes
identifies this role of teacher with that of prophet. Like the prophets,
Christ had, in His imagination, the reflection of divine things;[114] but
already as man he surpasses the prophets through His intellectual
vision of God.[115] As God He is more than a prophet: He is the inspirer
of the prophets and the angels; He announces the truth about God,
but at the same time He is this truth.[116] He instructed His apostles
through His preaching and through His Spirit[117] which made known
to them the meaning of His doctrine.[118] But the apostles, in their
turn, can, by their preaching, illuminate all men,[119] bear witness to
the Christ whom they have seen and heard,[120] hand down His teaching.

6. Revelation, Scripture, Church

The complex of truths that God has revealed to the prophets and
the apostles Saint Thomas calls "sacred doctrine," "the teaching
according to revelation," which is contained in Scripture.[121] "All faith
rests upon the revelations made to the apostles and the prophets
which are written in the canonical books".[122] Revelation being
contained in Scripture, we must believe both the one and the other:
"quidquid scriptura continet" (whatever is contained in Scripture).[123]
The object of our faith is the first truth proposed to us in Scripture,
but Scripture understood according to the proper teaching of the
Church. To the prophets and to the apostles, God proposed His truth
directly; to us, He proposes it through the Church. The Church is
thus the infallible rule in whatever concerns the proposition of revealed
truth.[124] God stands revealed through a multiplicity of writings and
under the most diverse literary forms, and as a result, His teaching is
often difficult to grasp; thus the Church has received the mission of
pointing out what in Scripture is properly called divine testimony.
The creeds represent the activity of the Church, asserting and proposing what is revealed and thus what must be believed.[125] The

Apostles' Creed is the assemblage of the whole Church in the unity of faith: it is the meeting place of the multitude of the believers, the apostles who are its authors and the preachers who have announced it. It is the harvest of the Scriptures, a resumé of the greatest mysteries and favors of God.[126] The different creeds are "different from each other only in the fact that one explains more fully what the other contains implicitly, according to the changing times and the shifting emphasis of what the heretics attack".[127] "In the teaching of Christ and the apostles, the truths of faith are all sufficiently explained: but since there are perverse men who ... pervert the apostolic teaching and the rest of Scripture, some explanation of faith has become necessary in the course of the centuries, as a protection against the errors which arise".[128]

7. From Revelation to Faith

Unlike God's great witnesses, the apostles and the prophets, most men have no immediate access to revelation: it is through a human intermediary that they receive the truths of faith.[129] This external word is also word of God, because it derives from first revelation;[130] still, before clinging to it, before risking the whole of his life on its truth, it is only proper for man to verify the credentials which make up the authority of the messenger.

What gives credence to the preacher of faith and qualifies his teaching as divine are the miracles which God lets him work:[131] this is the divine seal which attests the divine origin of the doctrine he preaches,[132] the proof which shows that the word of the prophet is in reality the word of God.[133] The persuasive activity of the preacher and the contagion of his own conviction also figure as elements which bolster up certitude from without.[134]

Joined with this external activity of the preaching authorized by God Himself, grace is at work from within, inviting the listener to believe in the message proposed to him. God draws us, not only through the message of salvation and through signs of power (miracles), but also through the attraction He produces within.[135] A double call resounds: "one, external, through the voice of the preacher; the other, internal, which is nothing more than inspiration of mind through which the heart of man is drawn to give its assent to the object of faith. ... This call is necessary, for our heart would never turn towards God if God Himself did not draw it to Him".[136] Elsewhere, Saint Thomas observes that God helps us believe by a threefold aid: through an inner call, through the outer teaching and preaching, through miracles.[137] The inner call of grace is the "witness" of "first Truth which illuminates and instructs man within".[138] If the help of God and His inner preaching are lacking, the preacher does his work in vain.[139] Thus, God offers man a twofold gift: the gift of His teaching and the gift of grace to confess the doctrine proposed.[140] This activity of grace Saint Thomas does not, usually, call revelation,[141] but vocation, call, attraction or a drawing on the part of the Father, a motion, a succor, a testimony, and above all, inner instinct and inspiration.[142]

8. *Revelation as a Degree of the Knowledge of God*

Revelation and faith are not ordered towards their own end, but towards vision; for the end of man is to some day enter face to face into the contemplation of God. In this sense, revelation is an imperfect knowledge, a step or "moment" in our initiation to that vision. "Man can know of divine things in three ways," observes St. Thomas. "In the first way, man, thanks to the natural light of human reason, *rises* to the knowledge of God from the world of creation. In the second, divine truth, which surpasses the limits of our intelligence, *comes down* to us by way of revelation, not like a proof to be analyzed, but like a truth to be believed. In the third way, the mind *is raised* to a perfect vision of what has been revealed".[143] In the first degree, man turns towards God; in the second, God bends down towards man, revealing Himself and leading man gradually through faith towards vision. Revelation, says Saint Thomas, "is like a genus, in which prophecy constitutes an imperfect degree.... The perfection of divine revelation will be realized in heaven".[144] Meantime, in our waiting, we walk in faith. "The contemplation which does away with all need for having faith is the contemplation of our heavenly fatherland, in which supernatural truth is seen in its essence".[145] Only then "will first Truth be known, not in faith, but in vision; ... not only shall we then perceive something of the divine mysteries, but divine majesty itself, with all the perfection of its total essence.... Truth will then be proposed to man, no longer hidden under any veils, but fully and completely revealed".[146] This manifestation will be like a thunderbolt. God is truth in His being and in His speaking. Through the truth of His word, He makes us enter little by little into the truth of His being.

9. *Conclusion*

As the principle of theology and Christian faith, Saint Thomas posits the primary fact of revelation: the salvific operation through which God, in order not to leave man to the simple resources of his human reason, furnishes him with all the truths necessary and useful to work out his salvation. This operation takes place in time, through successive stages, marking out a progress in the number as well as the understanding of the truths revealed. Beginning with the patriarchs and the prophets, and down to the time of the apostles, the sacred deposit of revealed truth grows little by little. The Incarnation of Christ marks the fullness and consummation of revelation. The Old Testament, up to the time of the last prophet, is turned towards Christ. But once Christ has come, revelation has no other role than to make Him known and to appreciate His gift of salvation. Ever after, just as there is no new redeemer to be awaited, neither is there any revelation towards which the faith of the Church need turn.

Saint Thomas is primarily interested in *immediate* revelation, and principally *prophetic* revelation. He speaks of this essentially as a cognitive act: thanks to a special illumination, the prophet judges with certitude and without error, in conformity with the divine intention, regarding an object present to his consciousness, and thus takes possession of the truth which God means to communicate to him. Through this enlightening and this judgment, the unveiling of the divine thought really takes place in the prophet. This activity through which God communicates His thought to men by means of likenesses and created signs, Saint Thomas calls word of God to man, by reason of the analogy it offers with the human word which is also a communication of thought through signs. Regarding the immediate revelation of Christ to the apostles, Saint Thomas has less to say. He sees in Christ primarily the Master par excellence, the Teacher of faith, the Word in Person, Truth and Wisdom of God, assuming human nature in order to teach man, in human action and in human terms, the road to salvation.

The majority of men have no immediate access to revelation, that is, they need the preaching of the doctrine of salvation. This is preaching authorized as the word of God through miracles which attest to its divine origin. God leads us to believe through external preaching and through miracles, but also through the interior activity of His grace, inviting us to adhere to the message heard. This activity of grace Saint Thomas does not, usually, call revelation, but vocation, attraction, succor, motion, testimony and, primarily, interior instinct.

The complex of truths which God makes known to us, Saint Thomas does not call directly revelation, but the teaching which proceeds from revelation, sacred doctrine, the truth of faith. This truth is contained in Scripture as it is properly understood and interpreted by the Church which proposes it to us in the creeds of our faith.

Since man is ordered towards vision, revelation represents only a transitory stage toward the definitive economy of our heavenly fatherland. It is a level of knowing God superior to that of natural knowledge, arrived at from considering the works of creation, but still it remains imperfect compared to the face-to-face of the beatific vision.

What needs to be stressed is the perfect coherence of Saint Thomas' teaching. According to his constant thinking, all knowledge is accomplished only in judgment. Revelation, being knowledge to the highest degree, implies, like every other knowledge, an acceptance of the material and a light which permits the enunciation of judgment. This is the case in natural knowledge. And thus it is also the case in the knowledge of faith, conceived as following the same plan. Two things are required in faith: on the one hand, an object to believe, the truths which are proposed; and on the other hand, assent to these truths. The proposition of truths is effected through external preaching attested to by miracles, whereas the supernatural assent is made possible by the light of faith. The same will one day be true of the knowledge of glory, where the object (divine essence) will be seen in conformity with Truth only in the light of glory. The ascending movement of faith is possible only through this light. Everything comes from God: both revelation and the faith which is its response. In the theologians who follow, we shall not find, on this theme of revelation, any more sweeping perspective than that which lies at the basis of Saint Thomas' thinking. The terminology will be more precise, more technical, but the underlying reflection will have no greater depth.

---

1. Saint Bonaventure studies prophecy in a treatise which has remained unedited, currently the property of the municipal library of Assisi, cod. 186. Cf. F. M. HENQUINET, "Un brouillon autographe de S. Bonaventure sur le Commentaire des Sentences," *Études franciscaines*, 44 (1932) : 633-655; 45 (1933) : 59-81.

2. 1 *Sent.*, proemium. We quote from: *Doctoris Seraphici S. Bonaventurae Opera omnia edita studio et cura Patrum Collegii a S. Bonaventura* (Quaracchi, 1882-1902).

3. *II Sent.*, d. 4, a. 3, q. 2, c.

4. "differt praedicere et revelare... ; quia quod revelatur, certitudinaliter scitur; quod vero praedicitur, non; quia aliquando creditur ex comminatione dictum, aliquando vero sub conditione" (*In Jo.*, c. XIII, 55).

5. Assisi, cod. 186, 31va.

6. "In Deo enim loqui ad alterum supra intellectum notat effectum, videlicet revelationem. Non enim dicitur Deus nobis loqui solum quia intelligit, sed etiam quia revelando aliquam illustrationem in nobis efficit. Unde Gregorius in Moralibus : Dei locutio, ad nos intrinsecus

facta, videtur potius quam auditur; quia, dum semetipsum sine mora sermonis insinuat, repentina luce tenebras nostrae ignorantiae illustrat" (*II Sent.*, d. 10, a. 3, q. 1, c.).

7. *II Sent.*, d. 13, dub. 3; *I Sent.*, d. 27, p. 2, a. un., q. 1, c.

8. *II Sent.*, d. 10, a. 3, q. 2, c.

9. "Ad cognitionem naturalem rerum multum potest proficere proprio studio atque ingenio, sed in cognitione modi perveniendi ad vitam per se ipsum plus deficit quam proficit, nisi divinae revelationis instructione dirigatur. Et propterea magis data est nobis Scriptura, divinitus et per Spiritum Sanctum revelata, in cognitione fidei et morum, quam in cognitione rerum naturalium, licet omnis veritas aliquo modo a Spiritu Sancto esse dicatur" (*II Sent.*, d. 23, dub. 3).

10. *In Jo.*, c. VI, 79, arg. 3; c. XIII, 71; *IV Sent.*, d. 48, a. 1, q. 4, ad 2 et 3.

11. *IV Sent.*, d. 48, a. 1, q. 4, ad 2 et 3.

12. *IV Sent.*, d. 48, a. 1, q. 4, ad 4.

13. *IV Sent.*, d. 2, a. 1, q. 2, c.

14. "Lumen plenum est in doctrina evangelica, scilicet doctrina Christi... ; lumen subsequens in doctrina apostolica... ; lumen praecedens in prophetica" (*IV Sent.*, d. 24,p. 2, a. 2, q. 4, c.).

15. *III Sent.*, d. 25, a. 2, q. 2,f. 2.

16. Dom. III Adv., sermo 1.

17. Dom. XXII post Pent., sermo 1.

18. On Saint Bonaventure and prophecy: B. DECKER, "Die Analyse des Offenbarungs-vorganges beim hl. Thomas im Lichte vorthomistischer Prophetietraktate," *Angelicum*, 16 (1939) : 195-244; ID., *Die Entwicklung der Lehre von der prophetischen Offenbarung von Wilhelm von Auxerre bis zu Thomas von Aquin* (Breslau, 1940), pp. 134-164; F. M. HENQUINET, "Un brouillon autographe de S. Bonaventure sur le Commentaire des sentences," *Études franciscaines*, 44 (1932) :633-655; 45 (1933) : 59-81; J. G. BOUGEROL, *Introduction à l'étude de saint Bonaventure* (Paris-Tournai-New York-Rome, 1961), pp. 246-247.

19. "Dicendum est quod differt dicere prophetiam et donum prophetiae; nam donum prophetiae est habilitatio naturalium ad intelligendum quod ostenditur; prophetia autem est actualis illustratio ad intelligendum actu quod ostensum est; ... et dicitur ergo donum prophetiae habitus primus, prophetia vero habitus secundus, quia facit habilem actu intelligere quotiuscumque vult, et ideo ordinat ad denuntiandum" (Assisi, cod. 186, ɪɪra).

20. *II Sent.*, d. 10, a. 3, q. 2, c.

21. "Revelatio autem quaedam est imperfecta, quaedam perfecta... Imperfectam revelationem voco, in qua fit ostensio alicujus signi, non tamen per illud signum directe et certe ducitur intellectus in signatum, sicut fuit in Pharaone et Baltassar et Nabuchodonosor; et talis potest esse sine habitu superinfuso et mediante ministerio angelico. Revelatio autem perfecta (est), in qua non solum est speciei signantis impressio, sed signati manifesta declaratio" (Assisi, cod. 186, 10vb).

22. "Nullus dicendus est propheta nisi illustratus fuerit ad intelligendum quod sibi ostende-batur" (Assisi, cod. 186, 30ra).

23. "Illuminationem ad futura praecognoscenda dicimus esse infusam propter hoc quod in ipsa elevatur anima supra ea quae sunt ei naturalia" (*III Sent.*, d. 23, a 2, q. 2, c.).

24. "Propheta non assentit ei quod praenuntiat, propter se, sed propter Veritatem ipsum illuminantem et erudientem" (*III Sent.*, d. 24, a. 1, q. 2, ad 5).

25. "Cognitio fidei et prophetiae et cujuslibet revelationis divinae... non pendet ab eo quod creditur vel quod revelatur, sed ab illo lumine, per quod ad hoc cognoscendum illuminatur" *III Sent.*, d. 24, a. 1, q. 1, ad 2).

26. *I Sent.*, d. 18, a. un., q. 1, c.; *III Sent.*, d. 34, p. 2, a. 1, ad 1.

27. "Dicendum quod ad esse prophetiae duo concurrunt : similitudinis repraesentatio et revelatio significationis illius similitudinis. Ista revelatio semper est intellectiva; sed impressio similitudinis potest esse in vi intellectiva per se et primo, non mediante sensu vel imaginatione, vel in ipsa imaginativa primo, non mediate sensu, et sic dicitur visio imaginaria; vel in ipso sensu et tunc visio corporalis. Impressio similitudinis intellectiva primo per se semper habet revelationem conjunctam; sed similitudo imaginaria aliquando habet, ut in prophetis veris, aliquando non, ut in Pharaone. Similiter dicendum est de impressione in sensu. Ad hoc ergo quod sit propheta, requiritur revelatio in parte intellectiva" (Assisi, cod. 186, 12vb). Cf. *I Sent.*, d. 16, a. un. q. 2, arg. 4.

28. "...quia in somnis magis agitur homo quam agat, et in revelatione divina plus se habet homo per modum suscipientis quam agentis... " (*II Sent.*, d. 25, p. 2, a. un., q. 6, ad 5).

29. "Dicendum quod, sicut dicit Philosophus, dupliciter contingit aliquid addiscere, videlicet per inventionem et per doctrinam. Et sensus quidem visus maxime deservit illi modo addiscendi, qui est per inventionem; sensus vero auditus illi modo, qui est per doctrinam. Quoniam igitur ea quae fide novimus, non cognoscimus per inventionem, sed magis per doctrinam, per doctrinam, inquam, non solum praedicatoris loquentis per aurem corporis, sed etiam Spiritus Sancti loquentis

per aurem cordis; hinc est quod in Littera dicitur, quod fides non tantum est ex auditu exteriori, sed etiam interiori. Et quamvis Apostoli multa didicerint videndo Christum, multo tamen plura didicerunt audiendo ipsum qui loqueretur exterius et qui loqueretur eis interius per Spiritum Sanctum... Ad illud quod objicitur quod fides est per infusionem, non per auditum, dicendum quod fides, quantum ad suum formale per infusionem est, sed quantum ad materiale, videlicet quoad notitiam illam qua cognoscitur... est per auditum, ita quod unum est per auditum cordis, et aliud per auditum corporis. Ideo generaliter dicit Apostolus, fidem ex auditu esse, magis principaliter ratione auditus interioris quam exterioris. Et sic dicit Gregorius quod in vanum laborat sermo praedicatoris, nisi adsit illustratio doctoris interioris" (*III Sent.*, d. 24, dub. 2). q. 5, c.; d. 25, a. 2, q. 2, f. 4.

30. "Et qui misit me Pater, etc. Tangitur hic tertium testimonium, scilicet divinum, quod et paternum dicit; propter quod ait: et qui misit me Pater, per incarnationem, testimonium perhibuit de me per internam inspirationem; quia, sicut dicitur infra sexto (v. 44), nemo venit ad me, nisi Pater traxerit eum. Unde voce intelligibili revelat et testificatur, quam Judaei carnales nec audire poterant, nec ipsum loquentem videre. Ideo dicit: neque vocem ejus unquam audistis, per mentis revelationem; sicut Petrus audivit, Matthaei decimo sexto (v. 17) : Beatus es, Simon Bar Jona, quia caro et sanguis non revelavit tibi, sed Pater meus qui in coelis est" (*In Jo.*, c. V, 65; c. VI, 68).

31. "Omnis veritas salutaris vel in Scriptura est, vel ab ipsa emanat, vel ad eam reducitur" (In circumcisione Domini, sermo 1). "Veritas enim fidei et vitae sanctitas non aliunde quam ex scripturarum fonte hauritur" (Opusc. 13, *Determinationes quaestionum circa regulam fratrum minorum*, p. 1, q. 3).

32. *III Sent.*, d. 23, a. 1, q. 4, ad 4.

33. "Ortus namque non set per humanam investigationem, sed per divinam revelationem quae fluit a Patre luminum" (*Prol. in Breviloq.*, V).

34. "Nullus autem est, qui falli non possit et fallere nesciat, nisi Deus et Spiritus Sanctus; hinc est, quod ad hoc, quod Scriptura sacra modo sibi debito esset perfecte authentica, non per humanam investigationem est tradita, sed per revelationem divinam" (*Prol. in Breviloq.*, V).

35. "Sicut sacramenta dicunt quoddam velamen gratiae interioris, quod tamen aliquo modo illuminat ad cognoscendum; sic fides velamen dicit futurae contemplationis et visionis, et tamen hoc velamen potius est illuminans quam obscurans" (*IV Sent.*, d. 3, p. 1, a. 1, q. 3, c.).

36. S. *Th.*, 1a, q. 1; 2a 2ae, q. 1-7, 171-174; S. *Contra Gentiles*, L. III, c. 154; *De Verit.* q. 12; *Expos. in Jo.*, passim.

37. 1a, q. 1, a. 1, c.

38. "Salubriter ergo divina providit clementia ut ea etiam quae investigare potest, fide tenenda praeciperet; ut sic omnes de facili possent divinae cognitionis participes esse, et absque dubitatione et errore" (*C. G.*, L. 1, c. 4). Cf. 1a, q. 1, a. 1, c.

39. 1a, q. 1, a. 3, ad 2um; E. Gilson, *Le thomisme, introduction à la philosophie de saint Thomas* (Paris, 1948), pp. 20ff.

40. 2a 2ae, q. 172, a. 2, 3.

41. On many occasions, Saint Thomas describes this descending and hierarchical economy of revelation. For example: 2a 2ae, q. 2, a. 6, 6.

42. "Illi quibus incumbit officium docendi fidem sunt medii inter Deum et homines; unde respectu Dei sunt homines, et respectu hominum, sunt dii, in quantum divinae cognitionis participes sunt" (*III Sent.*, d. 25, q. 2, a. 1, qla 4, sol. 4).

43. "Tam magna erant quae de Christo dicebantur, quod non poterant credi, nisi cum incremento temporum prius didicissent. Unde dicit beatus Gregorius : per successiones temporum crevit divinae cognitionis augmentum" (*Ad Heb.*, c. 1, lect. 1).

44. 2a 2ae, q. 174, a. 6, c.

45. "Sicut magister qui novit totam artem non statim a principio tradit eam discipulo, quia capere non posset, sed paulatim, condescendens ejus capacitati. Et hac ratione profecerunt homines in cognitione fidei per temporum successionem. Unde Apostolus, ad *Gal.* 3, 24 ss., comparat statum Veteris Testamenti pueritiae" (2a 2ae, q. 1, a. 7, ad 2). "Et ideo tantum dabatur Patribus qui erant instructores fidei de cognitione fidei, quantum oportebat pro tempore illo populo tradi vel nude vel in figura" (2a 2ae, q. 1, a. 7, ad 3).

46. 2a 2ae, q. 1, a. 7.

47. "Visio... Moysi fuit excellentior quantum ad cognitionem divinitatis: sed David plenius cognovit et expressit mysteria Incarnationis Christi" (2a 2ae, q. 174, a. 4, ad 1).

48. "Ultima consummatio gratiae facta est per Christum: unde et tempus ejus dicitur tempus plenitudinis, ad *Gal.* 4:4. Et ideo illi qui fuerunt propinquiores Christo vel ante, sicut Joannes Baptista, vel post, sicut Apostoli, plenius mysteria fidei cognoverunt. Quia et circa statum hominis hoc videmus, quod perfectio est in juventute, et tanto habet homo perfectiorem statum vel ante post, quanto juventuti propinquior" (2a 2ae, q. 1, a. 7, ad 4). Cf. 2a 2ae, q. 174, a. 6, c.; *De*

Verit., q. 12, ad 1. On the development of revelation according to St. Thomas, see: A. HAYEN, "Le thomisme et l'histoire," *Revue thomiste*, 62 (1962): 51-82.

49. 2a 2ae, q. 174, a. 6, ad 3.

50. 2a 2ae, q. 174, a. 4, ad 3.

51. *In ep. ad Heb.*, c. 1, lect. 1.

52. *In Boet. de Trin.*, pr., q. 2, a. 4.

53. "Et singulis temporibus non defuerunt aliqui prophetiae spiritum habentes, non quidem ad novam doctrinam fidei depromendam, sed ad humanorum actuum directionem" (2a 2ae, q. 174, a. 6, ad 3).

54. "Innititur enim fides nostra revelationi Apostolis et Prophetis factae, qui canonicos libros scripserunt; non autem revelationi, si qua fuit aliis doctoribus facta" (1a, q. 1, a. 8, ad 2).

55. Saint Thomas speaks of prophecy in the following places: *De Verit.*, q. 12; 2a 2ae, q. 171-174; C. G., L. Ill, c. 154; *In primam ad Cor.*, c. 14, lect. 1; *In Is.*, 1, 1; 6, 1. For supplementary, reading, cf. S. THOMAS D'AQUIN, *La prophétie* (trans. P. SYNAVE and P. BENOIT, Paris, 1947); B. DECKER Die Analyse des Offenbarungsvorganges beim hl. Thomas im Lichte vorthomistischer Prophetietraktate," *Angelicum*, 16 (1939): 195-244; ID., *Die Entwicklung der Lehre von der prophetischen Offenbarung von Wilhelm von Auxerre bis zu Thomas von Aquin* (Breslau, 1940); V. WHITE, "Le concept de révélation chez S. Thomas," *L'année théologique*, 11 (1950): 1-17, 109-132; S. M. ZARB, "Le fonti agostiniane del trattato sulla profezia di S. Tommaso," *Angelicum*, 15 (1938): 169-200; A. GARDEIL, *Le donné révélé et la théologie* (Paris, 1932); A. LEONARD, "Vers une théologie de la parole de Dieu," in *La parole de Dieu en Jésus-Christ* (Paris, 1961), pp. 13-18. In this question of prophecy, Saint Thomas depends in particular upon the Arabs, Avicenna, Algazel, and Averroes, who were interested in the psychological problems of prophetic revelation; on the Jew Maimonides, whom he corrects and improves; on the scholastics who were his predecessors and teachers; on Saint Augustine, particularly in his *De Genesi ad litteram*.

56. See in particular: *De Verit.*, q. 12. F. White stressed this aspect of Saint Thomas' treatise: "Le concept de révélation chez S. Thomas," *L'année théologique*, 11 (1950): 6-8.

57. S. THOMAS, *La Prophétie* (trad. P. BENOIT), p. 270.

58. *De Verit.*, q. 12, a. 2, c.

59. *C. G.*, L. III, c. 154; *In primam ad Cor.*, c. 12, lect. 2; 2a 2ae, q. 172, a. 5, ad 3.

60. "Prophetia primo et principaliter consistit in cognitione... ; prophetia secundario consistit in locutione, prout prophetae ea quae divinitus edocit cognoscunt, ad aedificationem aliorum annuntiant" (2a 2ae, q. 171. a. 1, c.).

61. At least when he receives light and assistance; but he is active in the subjective process of prophetic knowledge.

62. "Oportet quod lumen propheticum non sit habitus, sed magis sit in anima prophetae per modum cujusdam passionis ut lumen solis in aere" (*De Verit.*, q. 12, a. 1, c.).

63. *Ibid.*, c.

64. Saint Thomas has sound considerations but he starts from a false etymology. The word prophecy is taken to come from *phanos* and *procul*.

65. "Cognoscunt quaedam quae sunt procul remota ab hominum cognitione" (2a 2ae, q. 171, a. 1, c.).

66. "In Vetere Testamento appellabantur Videntes: quia videbant ea quae ceteri non videbant, et prospiciebant quae in mysterio abscondita erant" (2a 2ae, q. 171, a. 1, c.).

67. 2a 2ae, q. 171, a. 3, *De Verit.*, q. 12, a. 2.

68. 2a 2ae, q. 171, a. 2, c.

69. 2a 2ae, q. 171, a. 4, ad 2.

70. 2a 2ae, q. 171, a. 1, ad 4.

71. 2a 2ae, q. 171, a. 6, c.

72. 2a 2ae, q. 173, a. 2, c. This article, which we have only summed up here, is the heart of Saint Thomas's explanation of prophetic knowledge. See also *C. G.*, L. III, c. 154.

73. "Formale in cognitione prophetica est lumen divinum, a cujus unitate prophetia habet unitatem speciei, licet sint diversa quae per lumen divinum prophetice manifestantur" (2a 2ae, q. 171, a. 3, ad 3).

74. "Per donum autem prophetiae confertur aliquid humanae menti supra id quod pertinet ad naturalem facultatem, quantum ad utrumque: scilicet et quantum ad judicium, per influxum intellectualis luminis; et quantum ad acceptionem seu repraesentationem rerum, quae fit per aliquas species. Et quantum ad hoc secundum, potest assimilari doctrina humana revelationi propheticae, non autem quantum ad primum: homo enim suo discipulo repraesentat aliquas res per signa locutionum, non autem potest interius illuminare, sicut facit Deus. Horum autem duorum primum principalius est in prophetia: quia judicium est completivum cognitionis" (2a 2ae, q. 173, a. 2, c.).

75. "Dicendum quod quascumque formas imaginatas naturali virtute homo potest formare, absolute hujusmodi formas considerando: non tamen ut sint ordinatae ad repraesentandas intelligibiles veritates quae hominis intellectum excedunt, sed ad hoc necessarium est auxilium supernaturalis luminis" (2a 2ae, q. 173, a. 2, ad 3).

76. 2a 2ae, q. 171, a. 1, ad 4.

77. "Ex eisdem formis imaginatis subtilior conspicitur veritas secundum illustrationem altioris luminis" (2a 2ae, q. 173, a. 2, ad 2) Cf. la, q. 1, a. 9, ad 2. St. Thomas states that the prophet sees in speculo aeternitatis. This expression can mean two things: either the objects offered to the conscience of the prophet have the character of presentiality that they have in God, the future, for Him, coinciding with the present and the past (De Verit., q. 12, a. 6, c.); or it may be also that the prophet perceives reality as offered to him with the eternal sense that it has in God and for God.

78. "Erit autem propheta si solummodo intellectus ejus illuminetur ad dijudicandum etiam ea quae ab illis imaginarie visa sunt: ut patet de Joseph, qui exposuit somnium Pharaonis" (2a 2ae, q. 173, a. 2, c.).

79. De Verit., q. 12, a. 7, c.; 2a 2ae, q. 173, a. 2, c.

80. "Sed sicut Augustinus dicit... maxime propheta est qui utroque praecellit: ut videat in spiritu corporalium rerum significativas similitudines et eas vivacitate mentis intelligat" (2a 2ae, q. 173, a. 2, c.).

81 "Manifestum est autem quod manifestatio veritatis divinae quae fit secundum nudam contemplationem ipsius veritatis, potior est quam illa quae fit sub similitudine corporalium rerum; magis enim appropinquat ad visionem patriae, secundum quam in essentia Dei veritas conspicitur. Et inde est quod prophetia per quam aliqua supernaturalis veritas conspicitur nude secundum intellectualem veritatem, est dignior quam illa in qua veritas supernaturalis manifestatur per similitudinem corporalium rerum secundum imaginariam visionem" (2a 2ae, q. 174, a.2, c,).

82. 2a 2ae, q. 174, a. 3, c.

83. 2a 2ae, q. 173, a. 2, c.

84. 2a 2ae, q. 174, a. 2, ad 3.

85. "Plures loquebantur frequentius de his quae humana ratione cognosci possunt, non quasi ex persona Dei, sed ex persona propria, cum adjutorio tamen divini luminis" (2a 2ae, q. 174, a. 2, ad 3).

86. But Saint Thomas does not give it this name. Inspiration and revelation, in the only passage where he joins the two words (2a 2ae, q. 171, a. 1, ad 4), are counterdistinguished as species with respect to the genus "prophecy": inspiration being the motion of the intellectual order which gives the mind an increased vigor; and revelation being the perception of the truth which lowers the veil of mystery and ignorance which hid the unknown. There is no revelation without inspiration, at least in the case of prophecy properly so called. Speaking of a prophetic charism in general, Saint Thomas uses the word revelation or prophetic revelation rather than inspiration; for this is the word which better expresses the essential element of prophecy. The proportion of the two terms, according to P. Benoit, is 106 to 17, the word revelation coming up thirty times in the expression prophetica revelatio. And, just as Saint Thomas speaks of prophecy in the broad sense of the term as including cases outside that of prophecy so called, he also uses the term revelation when he is speaking only of light without new representations (2a 2ae, q. 173, a. 2, c.). Revelation according to Saint Thomas, does not thus imply the technical and limited meaning of light accompanied by a species, as opposed to inspiration: a lumen without a species. Revelation embraces at once inspiration and revelation in the limited sense. Since, however, Saint Thomas recognizes the two cases of light with species and light without infused representation, it is a legitimate conclusion to find a basis for the actual distinction between revelation and inspiration in his thinking. See P. Benoit: S. Thomas, La Prophétie, pp. 278-282.

87. "Sed ad ea quae cognoscit per instinctum, aliquando sic se habet ut non plene discernere possit utrum hoc cogitaverit aliquo divino instinctu, vel per spiritum proprium. Non autem omnia quae cognoscimus divino instinctu, sub certitudine prophetica nobis manifestantur: talis enim instinctus est quiddam imperfectum in genere prophetiae" (2a 2ae, q. 171, a. 5, c.).

88. "De his ergo quae expresse per spiritum prophetiae propheta cognoscit, maximam certitudinem habet, et pro certo habet quod haec sibi sunt divinitus revelata. Unde dicitur Jer. 26, 15: in veritate misit me Dominus ad vos, ut loquerer in aures vestras omnia verba haec" (2a 2ae, q. 171, a. 5, c.).

89. "Et signum propheticae certitudinis accipere possumus ex hoc quod Abraham, admonitus in prophetica visione, se praparavit ad filium unigenitum immolandum: quod nullatenus fecisset nisi de divina revelatione fuisset certissimus" (2a 2ae, q. 171, a. 5, c.). Saint Theresa of Avila says the same thing regarding her visions.

90. "Cognitio autem prophetica est per lumen divinum, quo possunt omnia cognosci, tam divina quam humana, tam spiritualia quam corporalia" (2a 2ae, q. 171, a. 3, c.).

91. *In Rom.*, c. 11, lect. 1.

92. "Ostenditur triplex modus quo a Deo aliquid revelatur alicui. Quia vel per vocem sensibilem et sic testificatus est Christo in Jordane et in monte,... vel per visionem suae essentiae, et hanc revelat beatis,... vel per interius verbum inspirando" (*In Jo.*, c. 5, lect. 6).

93. "Perceptio divinae locutionis, qua prophetam alloquitur interius, quae nihil est quam mentis illustratio" (*De Verit.*, q 12. a. 1, ad 3).

94. "Nihil aliud est loqui ad alterum quam conceptum mentis alteri manifestare" (1a, q. 107, a. 1, c.).

95. 1a, q. 107, a. 2; *De Verit.*, q. 18, a. 3.

96. "Est etiam quadam locutio exterior, qua Deus nobis per praedicatores loquitur; quadam interior, qua loquitur nobis per inspirationem interam. Dicitur autem ipsa interior inspiratio locutio quaedam ad similitudinem exterioris locutionis: sicut enim in exteriori locutione proferimus ad ipsum audientem non ipsam rem quam notificare cupimus, sed signum illius rei, scilicet vocem significativam; ita Deus interius inspirando, non exhibet essentiam suam ad videndum, sed aliquod suae essentiae signum, quod est aliqua spiritualis similitudo suae sapientiae. Ab utroque fides in cordibus fidelium oritur. Per auditum interiorem in his quae fidem primo acceperunt et docuerunt, sicut in apostolis et in prophetis; unde in *Ps.* 84, 9: Audiam quid loquatur in me Deus. Per secundum vero auditum fides oritur in cordibus aliorum fidelium, qui per alios homines cognitionem fidei accipiunt. Adam autem primo fidem habuit, et primo est fidem edoctus a Deo; et ideo per interam locutionem fidem habere debuit" (*De Verit.*, q. 18, a. 3, c.). "In statu primae conditionis non erat auditus ab homine exterius loquente, sed a Deo interius inspirante: sicut et prophetae audiebant" (2a 2ae, q. 5, a. 1, ad 3). "Ita igitur in homine duplex cognitio erat: una qua cognoscebat Deum conformiter angelis per inspirationem interam; alia qua cognoscebat Deum conformiter nobis per sensibiles creaturas" (*De Verit.*, q. 18, a. 2, c.).

97. 1a, q. 107, a. 1.

98. 3a, q. 1, a. 2, c.

99. Birth (3a, q. 36, a. 3, ad 1); baptism (3a, q. 39, a. 8, ad 2 et 3); miracles (3a, q. 44, a. 3, ad 1); transfiguration (3a, q. 45, a. 4, ad 2); resurrection (3a, q. 53, a. 1 et 3).

100. "Manifestum est quod in Christo fuerunt excellentissime omnes gratiae gratis datae, sicut in primo et principali Doctore fidei" (3a, q. 7, a. 7, c.).

101. 3a, q. 42, a. 1, ad 1.

102. 3a, q. 40, a. 1; *In Jo.*, c. 3, lect. 5.

103. "Olim enim unigenitus Filius manifestavit Dei cognitionem per Prophetas, qui eum in tantum annuntiaverunt in quantum aeterni Verbi fuerunt participes... Sed nunc ipse unigenitus, Filius, enarravit fidelibus... Et haec doctrina ideo omnibus aliis doctrinis supereminet dignitate, auctoritate et utilitate, quia ab unigenito Filio, qui est prima sapientia, immediate est tradita" (*In Jo.*, c. 1, lect. 11).

104. "Et sicut homo volens revelare se verbo cordis, quod profert ore, induit quodammodo ipsum verbum litteris vel voce, ita Deus, volens se manifestare hominibus, Verbum suum conceptum ab aeterno, carne induit in tempore" (*In Jo.*, c. 14, lect. 2).

105. *In Jo.*, c. 8, lect. 3.

106. *In Jo.*, c. 14, lect. 2; c. 1, lect. 8.

107. *In Jo.*, c. 3, lect. 5.

108. *In Jo.*, c. 18, lect. 6. Cf. A. NYSSENS, *La plénitude de vérité dans le Verbe incarné. Doctrine de Saint Thomas d'Aquin* (Baudouinville, 1961).

109. *In Jo.*, c. 1, lect. 1.

110. *In Jo.*, c. 17, lect. 6.

111. *In Jo.*, c. 4, lect. 4.

112. *In Jo.*, c. 11, lect. 6.

113. *In Jo.*, c. 13, lect. 3; c. 3, lect. 1.

114. 3a, q. 7, a. 8, ad 1; 2a 2ae, q. 174, a. 5, ad 3.

115. *In. Jo.*, c. 4, lect. 8.

116. *In Jo.*, c. 4, lect. 6; c. 6, lect. 2.

117. *In Jo.*, c. 17, lect 6.

118. *In Jo.*, c. 14, lect. 4.

119. *In Jo.*, c. 12, lect. 8.

120. *In Jo.*, c. 15, lect. 5.

121. 1a, q. 1, a. 1, c.

122. "Innititur enim fides nostra revelationi apostolis et prophetis factae, qui canonicos libros scripserunt" (1a, q. 1, a. 8, ad 2).

123. 2a 2ae, q. 2, a. 5, c.

124. "Formale objectum fidei est veritas prima, secundum quod manifestatur in Scripturis sacris et in doctrina Ecclesiae. Unde quicumque non inhaeret sicut infallibili et divinae regulae,

doctrinae Ecclesiae, quae procedit ex veritate prima in Scripturis sacris manifestata, ille non habet habitum fidei" (2a 2ae, q. 5, a. 3, c.). "Omnibus articulis fidei inhaeret fides propter unum medium, scilicet propter veritatem primam propositam nobis in Scripturis secundum doctrinam Ecclesiae intelligentis sane" (2a 2ae, q. 5, a. 3, ad 2).

125. "Veritas fidei in Sacra Scriptura diffuse continetur et variis modis, et in quibusdam obscure; ita quod ad eliciendum fidei vertatem ex sacra scriptura requiritur longum studium et exercitium, ad quod non possunt pervenire omnes illi quibus necessarium est cognoscere fidei veritatem... Et ideo fuit necessarium ut ex sententiis sacrae scripturae aliquid manifestum summarie colligeretur quod proponeretur omnibus ad credendum. Quod quidem non est additum sacrae scripturae, sed potius ex sacra scriptura assumptum" (2a 2ae, q. 1, a. 9, ad 1).

126. *III Sent.*, d. 25, q. 1, a. 1, qla 3.

127. "Quae in nullo alio different nisi quod in uno plenius explicantur quae in alio continentur implicite, secundum quod exigebat haereticorum instantia" (2a 2ae, q. 1, a. 9, ad 2).

128. "In doctrina Christi et apostolorum veritas fidei est sufficienter explicita. Sed quia perversi homines apostolicam doctrinam et ceteras scripturas pervertunt, ...necessaria est, temporibus procedentibus, explanatio fidei contra insurgentes errores" (2a 2ae, q. 1, a. 10, ad 1).

129. 2a 2ae, q. 6, a. 1, c. See: B. DUROUX, *La psychologie de la foi chez Saint Thomas d'Aquin* (Fribourg, 1956), pp. 28-30.

130. *De Verit.*, q. 18, a. 3, ad 2.

131. "Fides non habet inquisitionem rationis naturalis demonstrantis id quod creditur, habet tamen inquisitionem quamdam eorum per quae inducitur homo ad credendum, puta quia sunt dicta a Deo et miraculis confirmata" (2a 2ae, q. 2, a. 1, ad 1). Cf. *C. G.*, L. III, c. 154.

132. "Ut, dum aliquis facit opera quae solus Deus facere potest, credantur ea quae dicuntur esse a Deo, sicut cum aliquis defert litteras annulo regis signatas, creditur ex voluntate regis processisse, quod in illis continetur" (3a, q. 43, a, 1, c.). "Hoc contingere non potest quod aliquis falsam doctrinam annuntians, vera miracula faciat, quae nisi virtute divina fieri non possunt; sic enim Deus esset falsitatis testis, quod est impossibile" (*Quodl.* 2, q. 4, a. 6, ad 4). Cf. 2a 2ae, q. 178, a. 1.

133. "Ad hoc datum est hominibus facere miracula ut ostendatur quod Deus per illos loquitur" (*III Sent.*, d. 25, q. 2, a. 1, qla 4, ad 4). Cf. A. VAN HOVE, *La doctrine du miracle chez S. Thomas et son accord avec les principes de la recherche scientifique* (Louvain, 1927); B. DUROUX, *La psychologie de la foi chez Saint Thomas d'Aquin*, pp. 38-44.

134. 2a 2ae, q. 6, a. 1, c.; q. 171, a. 5, c.

135. "Quia non solum revelatio exterior, vel objectum, virtutem attrahendi habet, sed etiam interior instinctus impellens et movens ad credendum; ideo trahit multos Pater ad Filium per instinctum divinae operationis moventis interius cor hominis ad credendum" (*In Jo.*, c. 6, lect. 5). Cf. 2a 2ae, q. 2, a. 9, ad 3.

136. "Primum in quo incipit praedestinatio hominis impleri est vocatio hominis, quae quidem est duplex: una exterior, quae fit ore praedicatoris... ; alia vero vocatio est interior quae nihil aliud est quam quidam mentis instinctus quo cor hominis movetur a Deo ad assentiendum his quae sunt fidei et virtutis... Et haec vocatio necessaria est quia cor nostrum non se converteret ad Dominum, nisi ipse Deus nos se traheret" (*In Rom.*, c. 8, lect. 6).

137. "Adjuvatur autem a Deo aliquis ad credendum tripliciter. Primo quidem per interiorem vocationem, de qua dicitur *Jo.* 6, 45: omnis qui audivit a Patre, et didicit, venit ad me; et ad *Rom.* 8, 30; quos praedestinavit, hos et vocavit. Secundo, per doctrinam et praedicationem exteriorem, secundum illud Apostoli ad *Rom.* c. 10, 17: Fides ex auditu, auditus autem per verbum Christi. Tertio, per exteriora miracula; unde dicitur 1 *Cor.* 14, quod signa data sunt infidelibus ut scilicet per ea provocentur ad fidem" (*Quodl.*, 2, q. 4, a. 6). "Ille qui credit habet sufficiens inductivum ad credendum: inducitur enim auctoritate divinae doctrinae miraculis confirmatae, et, quod plus est, interiori instinctu Dei invitantis" (2a 2ae, q. 2, a. 9, ad 3).

138. "Deus testificatur alicui dupliciter, scilicet sensibiliter et intelligibiliter ... Intelligibiliter autem testificatur inspirando in cordibus aliquorum quod credere debeant" (*In Jo.*, c. 5, lect. 6). "Dicendum quod interior instinctus quo Christus poterat se manifestare sine miraculis exterioribus pertinet ad virtutem Primae Veritatis quae interius hominem illuminat et docet" (*Quodl.* 2, q. 4, a. 6, ad 3).

139. *In Jo*, 21, lect. 1; *In Mt.* 4, 18.

140. "Fides ex duabus partibus est a Deo, scilicet ex parte interioris luminis quod inducit ad assensum, et ex parte eorum quae exterius proponuntur, quae ex divina revelatione initium sumpserunt; et haec se habent ad cognitionem fidei sicut accepta per sensum ad cognitionem principiorum, quia utrisque fit aliqua cognitionis determinatio. Unde sicut cognitio principiorum accipitur a sensu, et tamen lumen quo principia cognoscuntur est innatum, ita fides est ex auditu, et tamen auditus fidei est infusus" (*In Boet. de Trin.*, lect. 1, q. 1, a. 1, ad 4). Cf. 2a 2ae, q. 6, a. 1, c.

141. *In Jo.*, c. 6, lect. 5.

142. 2a 2ae, q. 2, a. 9, ad 3; q. 10, a. 1, ad 1, *In Jo.*, c. 6, lect. 5; 2a 2ae, q. 1, a. 4, ad 3; *In Rom.*, c. 8, lect. 6; *Quodl.* 2, q. 4, a. 6, ad 3. Cf. B. Duroux, *La psychologie de la foi chez Saint Thomas d'Aquin*, pp. 32-38. The following work studies the texts of Saint Thomas on this inner instinct: M.-L. Guerard des Lauriers, *Dimensions de la foi* (2 vol., Paris, 1952), excursus VI: "Instinct intérieur, grace actuelle et grace sanctifiante," 2:253-269; see also the authors cited under footnote 11, chapter 5, part V.

143. "Est igitur triplex cognitio hominis de divinis. Quarum prima est, secundum quod homo naturali lumine rationis, per creaturas in Dei cognitionem ascendit; secunda est, prout divina veritas intellectum humanum excedens, per modum revelationis in nos decsendit, non tamen quasi demonstrata ad videndum, sed quasi sermone prolata ad credendum; tertia est secundum quod mens humana elevabitur ad ea quae sunt revelata, perfecte intuenda" (*C. G.*, L. IV, c. 1.).

144. "Prophetia est sicut quiddam imperfectum in genere divinae revelationis... Perfectio autem divinae revelationis erit in patria" (2a 2ae, q. 171, a. 4, ad 2). Cf. 2a 2ae, q. 173, a. 1,c.

145. "Contemplatio quae tollit necessitatem fidei est contemplatio patriae, qua supernaturalis veritas per essentiam videtur" (2a 2ae, q. 5, a. 1, ad 1). Cf. *De Verit.*, q. 14, a. 9, ad 2.

146. "Ad tertiam cognitionem pertinet, quia prima Veritas cognoscetur, non sicut credita, sed sicut visa; videbimus enim sicuti est, ut dicitur (1*Jo.* 3, 2.); nec aliquid modicum de divinis mysteriis percipietur, sed ipsa majestas divina videbitur, et omnis bonorum perfectio; ...non autem proponetur veritas homini aliquibus velaminibus occultata, sed omnino manifestata" (*C. G.*, L. IV, c. 1).

CHAPTER II

SCHOLASTICS AFTER TRENT

In the sixteenth century, the humanist movement on the one hand, and the demands of the anti-Protestant controversy on the other hand, stir up a whole complex of new questions in the Church and give rise to an intense effort towards the creation of a new theology in which the sources of revelation are studied with greater attention, and for their own sake. In the *De Locis*, in particular, drawn up by Melchior Cano, and in the *De Fide*, theologians generally find some paragraphs where they are at pains to define revelation.

The period which extends from the sixteenth to the eighteenth centuries is characterized by an effort at definitions of terms. There is always an interest in prophetic revelation, but the center of attention rests more securely on the free favor of Christ's revelation and that of the apostles. As a reaction against the over-zealousness of the Protestant Illumination, which flatters each individual faithful with an immediate revelation of the Holy Spirit, there is great effort to demonstrate the sufficiency of *mediate* revelation. The essential which is always stressed is the fact that God's testimony in His own behalf is communicated to us and solidly guaranteed as divine. What is more, our faith is based on this mediate revelation.

Lengthy discussions on the formal aspect of faith also lead theologians to a more precise definition of what must be understood by revelation, to a better distinction, primarily, between the inner illumination of the grace of faith and the objective manifestation of mysteries hidden heretofore.

I. MELCHIOR CANO AND DOMINIC BANEZ

1. In Melchior Cano, the notion of revelation comes up only indirectly, on the occasion of his analysis of faith. In the road that

leads towards faith, he writes in his *De Locis theologicis* (1563), external elements are required (persuasive preaching, miracles), which tempt a person to believe, but they themselves do not yet constitute the light which opens the mind to the brightness of the spiritual world. "All the external and human forms of persuasion are not enough to engender faith . . . ; there must also be an interior cause, that is, a divine light which inclines to belief, inner eyes given by God which make us see. . . . This is clearly confirmed by the word of Christ to Peter, when he tells him: 'Blessed art thou, Simon Bar Jona, because flesh and blood have not revealed to you, but My Father who is in heaven.' Indeed, Peter had heard the witness of John the Baptist who had proclaimed the Son of God; he had also seen many of Christ's miracles; and still, after all that, Christ attributes his confession of faith, not to the testimony or authority of John, not to the miracles he had observed, but to divine revelation".[1]

The ultimate foundation of our faith, says Cano once again, is not the authority of the Church, nor that of Scripture, but the authority of God who reveals. "I give my assent to all the principles of Christian doctrine through infused faith, not because John or some other man has spoken, but because God has revealed them; and the very fact of revelation I believe in immediately under the motion of the special divine instinct".[2] The authority of the Church is not the final reason for faith, but rather the *"causa sine qua non"*.[3] The external proposition of the truth of faith, the persuasiveness of the preacher, miracles—these are conditions of faith: the formal reason for the assent of faith is the interior light which God infuses in the believer.[4]

Melchior Cano thus reserves the term revelation for uncreated revelation, existing in God, or rather the interior illumination of the grace of faith which leads to belief. He does not give the name of revelation to the doctrine of salvation as proposed by the preaching of the Church.[5]

2. Dominic Bañez, disciple of Cano, conceives of revelation in the same manner. If it is proper, he says, to understand by revelation the divine activity as existing in God, it is even more proper to speak of revelation as "the effect which God, in His revealing, produces in us, and through which something is formally manifested or revealed to us." This effect is the light of faith or the illumination resulting from it.[6] Just as God, Author of nature, reveals truths of the natural order by favoring us with the light of the mind, in the same way He reveals truths of the supernatural world "by infusing in us the light through which certain truths are revealed to us".[7] It is God who produces this light and His activity results in illumination which gives

rise to a new knowledge.[8] In Bañez as in Cano, attention is centered on the illumination of the *subject* rather than on the unveiling of the *object*.

II. FRANCIS SUAREZ

Suarez insists on *mediate* revelation. God reveals Himself to the majority of men not immediately, but by His envoys. In the Old Testament, God spoke immediately to Moses, to the prophets and, through them, to all the people. The economy of the New Testament is not different: "John was sent first, so that all might believe through him; then, God Himself, through the humanity which He assumed, instructed those who were able to hear Him immediately. To the others, He sent His apostles, telling them to preach the Gospel to every creature.... Such is, therefore, the sufficient, and even the ordinary way of proposing and conceiving faith. This is why Paul tells the Romans that faith is from hearing, but hearing is through the Word of Christ".[9] Since Christ has taught the apostolic Church, it is through the Church that He instructs each of the faithful, so that "the definition of the Church has the force of revelation about it".[10] He who hears the Church hears God Himself speaking.[11] Still, if it is not necessary that the proposition of truth be made immediately by God Himself, it is necessary that this proposition be presented under circumstances and with guarantees that manifest it as "believable," that is, vouched for by the divine power.[12]

1. *Revelation in the Strict Sense*

By revelation, Suarez understands "the simple and sufficient proposition of the revealed objects, whether or not this object be believed on the part of him to whom this revelation is made, and whether this revelation be effected interiorly and directly by God Himself or through His angels, or again whether this revelation be made externally through human preaching".[13] He thus envisages revelation from the viewpoint of the *object* and represents it as a proposition of the revealed object which is to be believed on divine authority (*sub divina auctoritate*). Suarez explains this thinking by distinguishing the component elements of faith: "Two things are necessary for the knowledge of faith: one is the learning of the things to be believed, in so far as they are proposed to man as spoken by God and thus believable in virtue of the divine testimony; the other is assent to the things proposed, in which faith properly consists".[14] The object is *believable* and, as a result, its proposition is called *sufficient*, when the truth proposed is covered by the authority of God, solidly attested by Him.

In the historical proposition of faith Suarez sees two steps or "moments." Faith was proposed "first of all through the general preaching which took place when it was first introduced, with the preaching of Christ and the apostles; and then it was most necessary for the teaching to be confirmed by evident signs of the divine power, which are miracles." As a matter of fact, God has always respected this economy, both in the promulgation of the prophetic doctrine as well as in the Gospel message. But now that the faith is spread and applied to everyone, miracles are no longer necessary, but "it is still necessary for the divine power to aid and work within so that each person sufficiently perceive the proposition of faith and judge of it as he ought; for this work is wholly supernatural and cannot be effected without the aid of grace".[15]

Since the adherence of faith is not possible without the help of grace, "Scripture sometimes calls revelation inspiration and the infusion of interior light which efficaciously gives rise to faith. It is thus that Christ tells Peter (Mt. 16): Flesh and blood have not revealed to you, but my Father, and (Mt. 11): No one knows the Son except the Father, nor does anyone know the Father except the Son, and He to whom the Son willed to reveal Him. This revelation takes place, not only on the part of the object, but also on the part of the power and, as a result, includes the proposition of the object as well as the inspiration and help to believe".[16]

By revelation in the strict sense, Suarez thus understands this sufficient proposition of faith which the judgment of faith presupposes: "Faith is after all revealed to many who do not believe, even though, without a preliminary revelation, no one could believe".[17]

2. *Illumination or Revelation of the Object and the Power*

Faith comes from God, considered in its object as well as in the help or supernatural virtue given to increase our strength.[18] The teaching is from God and the grace is from God. From both sides, we are justified in speaking of an *illumination*. On the one hand, proposing an object and demonstrating its truth, the reasons for adhering to it, like a professor who directs his students, is the work of illumination. In a pre-eminent sense, Christ, through the preaching of His doctrine, enlightens the world: His teaching is Light. On the other hand too, the infusion of faith is light: Saint Paul says that the baptized who receive faith are enlightened or illuminated.[19] Still, there is one important difference between these two illuminations: whereas illumination, *ex parte objecti* (from the viewpoint of the object), can be produced by God or by His angels, illumination, *ex parte potentiae*, (from the viewpoint of the power), is always made immediately by God, for the infusion of supernatural light is an activity which belongs properly to Him.

In these two cases too, we may speak of *revelation*, not however with equal rigor of terminology. To *reveal* means to lift the veil which hides an object from view; but the veil can cover the object or the faculty of vision. In the order of faith, the object as well as our power to see are both veiled: the object, as totally unknown and unsuspected; the power as disproportionate to this object. God lifts both veils: the first by the revelation of the object of faith; the second, by the infusion of faith, but "properly speaking and according to the most frequent usage of Scripture, revelation is viewed under the aspect of the object. . . . In the same sense, Saint Thomas teaches frequently that revelation takes place through the medium of angels . . . , a statement which can be true only in speaking of objective revelation; in the same way too, in current usage, we speak of 'revealing secrets.' As a result, theologians distinguish between the revelation necessary for faith and the infusion of the *habitus*, revelation properly so called and the divine instinct. . . . Moreover, there is one clear difference between them: revelation properly so called is something perceived by the intelligence, . . . whereas the infusion of faith is not perceived by the mind, but is effected by God Himself in an invisible manner".[20]

Revelation, according to Suarez, has thus to be defined from the point of view of the object rather than the power. It is defined as being a sufficient proposition (that is, one guaranteed by God) of the divine mysteries, of the divine truth, of the doctrine of salvation. In a *broader* sense, we speak of revelation as designating the light or the illumination of the grace of faith.

III. JOHN DE LUGO

1. *Revelation as word*

Scripture speaks of revelation, mediate or immediate, as the *word of God*. De Lugo studies the analogy of this word.[21] It is not enough, he says, to justify the concept of word, or one man to present an object to another; it is also necessary to show him what we mean by this object. The heavens declare the glory of God, but they do not speak to us in the strict sense of the word. The word "is ordered, of itself and immediately, towards making someone else understand the thinking of the one who speaks. Speaking *to* someone is thus not the same thing as speaking *before* someone".[22] Word is thus distinguished from every other activity which can give rise to knowledge, in the sense that it is aimed immediately at communicating knowledge to someone else, and in the sense that it signifies the will to be heard and understood.[23]

In *immediate* revelation (to the prophets, for example), God can make use of tangible signs, just as in the human word, and thus manifest His thought; or, acting within, he can immediately give rise to the knowledge of the object He means to communicate, making it known as the true object of His thinking.[24]

The same statement, in due proportion, can be made regarding the *mediate* word through which God actually proposes the mystery of faith. This word is the proposition of the mystery, but in such a way that "I can understand—as in the mediate voice of God—that God is the Author of this doctrine and through this intermediary He wants to communicate his thinking to me: it is in this that the concept of word is verified".[25]

The Protestants, vindicating the claim of interior inspiration from the Holy Spirit for each of the faithful, have no adequate appreciation of mediate revelation. We, on the contrary, claim that God has spoken immediately only to the prophets and apostles; for the multitude, revelation remains mediate. Still this revelation, just like first revelation, deserves the title of *word of God*.[26] "God speaks in a human way when speaking to men who perceive objects through their material senses, that is, by proposing His mysteries and working miracles, so that we can perceive, not only through our ear, but through our eye, the voice of God who speaks to us".[27] Thus, when I read a friend's letter, I know that my friend is speaking to me; and if I doubt it, the examination of his writing would assure me that it is really his letter.[28] In the same way, the proposition of the mysteries of God which is made to me, together with the signs that accompany it, gives me the assurance that this doctrine proposed as coming from God is truly God's message. The certitude is no less great than in the case of immediate revelation.[29] It is truly word and word of God.

Mediate revelation is presented thus as the complex of *doctrine* and the *signs* which authenticate this doctrine as divine. The signs are an integral part of this word which is presented to us *hic et nunc* as the word of God. He who believes in the prophet's preaching believes not in the prophet, abstracting for the moment from his authority; likewise he who believes in the proposition of the Church, does not believe in the Church, abstracting again from her authority; he believes in a word authorized as divine by the signs which accompany it.[30]

2. Revelation and Habitus or Assistance of Faith

If revelation properly so called is word of God, communication of the divine thinking, it must not be confused with the *habitus* of faith or with the assistance of the grace of faith. "God," according to De Lugo, "does not speak in so far as he gives the habitus of faith, but in so far as he 'speaks' the Incarnation or the Trinity: likewise we do not say that God speaks to us by the fact that he gives us the understanding to believe and to know other objects.... God, in giving us understanding and the habitus of faith, gives us the faculty which makes us capable of hearing His voice and believing; but we do not say that He speaks, for speaking is the production of words with a view towards expressing the thinking of the one who speaks...; the understanding, or habitus of faith, is not the word of God; that is why its production is in no sense the word or revelation of God".[31] The interior instinct is neither wholly or partially a word of God.[32]

Saint Thomas himself, De Lugo continues, distinguishes precisely between the interior motion which predisposes and inclines towards the assent of faith and the divine teaching: "God, interiorly proposing revelation, moves men to give their assent; that is why this interior invitation of God is not a new word of God, excepting in some allegorical way, in the sense that God, through His grace, disposes the inner understanding of the mind to better perceive the force and authority of the divine testimony that is being proposed".[33] Interior grace only restates the word proposed from without, in order to make its truth better understood.

Revelation, in the strict sense, is thus the word of God to men, that is, the communication of the divine thought. Through this communication, man knows the truth as proposed by God and knows it as being truly His thought. This notion applies to mediate revelation as well as to immediate revelation: both are word of God. In mediate revelation, the *whole* word is presented as being the complex of message and the signs which authenticate the message understood as word of God.

IV. THE CARMELITES OF SALAMANCA

The *De Fide* of the theologians of Salamanca contains some very precise paragraphs on the notion of revelation.[34] By revelation, they say, we must understand the activity of God who lifts the veil that hides the understanding of some thing: a veil which can conceal the object from the knowing subject. This object can be veiled from the mind by reason of its excellence (the mysteries of the supernatural order), its indeterminacy (the future free acts), its way of proposition (enigmas and figures in the Old Testament). The veil can also cover the mind, by reason of the evil dispositions of the soul, as in the case of the unfaithful Jews. Every activity which takes away one of these veils and produces an understanding of the object is properly called divine revelation.[35]

We must distinguish two sides in this revelation: active and passive. Under its active form, revelation is "the activity or speaking of God who testifies to a truth through word or fact, immediately in itself or immediately through his ministers: the angels, the apostles, and prophets".[36] Under its passive form, revelation "consists in the actual or habitual knowledge of that which God has said and attested." Thus it can designate the habitus as well as the assent of faith. This is justified for several reasons: first of all because the habitus or act of faith is the effect of active revelation; second, because the assent of faith excludes the veil of infidelity on the part of the subject; finally, because it communicates the proper understanding of the things revealed. Beyond the mere vision of the object, such as Pharaoh and Nabuchadnezzar were privileged to see, it gives also the understanding of the object revealed.[37]

The theologians of Salamanca thus apply the notion of revelation both to the testimony of God making known the mysteries of His intimate life, through Himself or through His ministers, as well as the illumination of the grace of faith (act or habitus).

---

1. "Externae igitur omnes et humanae persuasiones non sunt satis ad credendum..., sed necessaria est insuper causa interior, hoc est divinum quoddam lumen incitans ad credèndum, et oculi quidam interni Dei beneficio ad videndum dati... Hoc quoque sua voce dilucide confirmavit Christus Petro inquiens: Beatus es Simon Bar Jona, quia caro et sanguis non revelavit tibi, sed Pater meus qui in coelis est. Certe Petrus audierat Joannis Baptistae testimonium, quo aperta voce clamaverat Christum esse Filium Dei; multa insupèr Christi miracula viderat: et tamen post haec omnia, non aut testimonio, aut auctoritati Joannis, non miraculis visi fidei confessionem Christus assignat, sed divinae revelationi" (De Locis theologicis, L. 2, c. 8, ad 4).

2. "Coèteris universis doctrinae christianae principiis assentio per infusam fidem, non quod Joannes dixerit, aut quivis alius homo, sed quod Deus revelaverit; huic autem: Deus revelavit, immediate credo, a Deo motus per instinctum specialem" (Ibid.).

3. "Non est enim Ecclesiae auctoritas ratio per se movens ad credendum, sed causa sine qua non crederemus" (De Locis, L. 2, c. 8).

4. "Proponere credenda, suadere, miracula facere, determinant intellectum ut credat, quasi conditiones, sine quibus vix unquam intellectus determinatur; at ratio formalis assentiendi lumen fidei est, quod Deus infundit credendi" (Ibid.).

5. "Ex parte objecti ratio formalis movens est divina veritas revelans; sed illa tamen non sufficit ad movencum, nisi adsit causa interior, hoc est Deus etiam movens per gratuitum specialemque concursum" (De Locis, L. 2, c. 8).

6. "Divina revelatio potest considerari ut est actio Dei in ipso Deo existens. Et isto modo non est ratio formalis nostrae theologiae aut fidei, sub qua objectum fidei vel theologiae attingitur. Quoniam illa nobis extrinsece tenens se ex parte causae efficientis et superioris. Altero modo, divina revelatio sumitur pro ipso effectu, quem Deus revelans efficit in nobis, quo formaliter fit nobis aliquid manifestum seu revelatum. Et isto modo nihil aliud est ratio formalis sub qua objecti theologiae vel fidei, quam ipsum lumen, aut effectus formalis luminis, quod Deus infundit in nobis, ut per illud immediate assentiamus principiis, mediate vero conclusionibus deductis" (*In primam Partem*, q. 1, a. 3, B and C). Next text cited: *Scholastica commentaria in primam partem angelici Doctoris D. Thomae usque ad sexagesimam quartam quaestionem complectentia*, auctore Fratre Dominico BANES Mondragonensi (Romae, 1584).

7. "Quemadmodum... dicitur Deus manifestare, seu revelare, ut auctor naturae, aliqua quae de Deo naturaliter cognoscibilia sunt non alia ratione nisi quia confert hominibus lumen naturale: ita etiam dicitur revelare ea quae ad supernaturalem cognitionem pertinent quatenus infundit lumen, quo talia revelentur" (*Ibid.*, E).

8. *Ibid.*, D.

9. "Praeter haec autem saepe Deus per Prophetas loquebatur, et novas revelationes proponebat... Denique in lege gratiae, idem modus providentiae et praedicationis fidei servatus est. Nam imprimis missus est Joannes, ut omnes crederent per illum; postea vero Deus ipse per humanitatem assumptam docuit eos qui illum immediate audire potuerunt. Ad reliquos autem misit apostolos dicens, *Mt.* ultimo: praedicate Evangelium omni creaturae... Ergo hic est modus sufficiens, imo et ordinarius, ad proponendam et concipiendam fidem. Et ideo dixit Paulus ad *Rom.* 10: fides ex auditu, auditus autem per verbum Christi. Loquitur autem de verbo sensibili, nam subdit: quomodo audient sine praedicante?" (*De Fide*, disput. 4, sect. 1, n. 2: t. 12, 112).

10. "Verbo suo Christus fidem tradidit, et apostolicam ecclesiam docuit, et per Ecclesiam singulos fideles instruit, et Ecclesiae definitio virtutem habet cujusdam revelationis" (Proleg. V, *De variis erroribus divinae gratiae contrariis*, c. 3, no. 16: t. 7, 233).

11. "Ecclesia... est sensibilis regula, quam facilius audiunt et percipiunt; in illa tamen auctoritatem divinam quasi loquentem supponunt, et ita implicite saltem suam fidem in Deum resolvunt" (*De Fide*, disput. 3, sect. 10, no. 10: t. 12, 94).

12. "Statuendum est ad sufficientem objecti fidei propositionem non satis esse objectum utcumque proponi tamquam dictum seu revelatum a Deo, sed necessarium saltem esse cum talibus circumstantiis proponi ut prudenter appareat credibile, eo modo quo proponitur" (*De Fide*, disput. 4, sect. 2, n. 3: t. 12, 116). "Quamvis necessarium non sit ut sufficiens propositio fidei a Deo immediate fiat, necessarium saltem est ut divina virtus in ea proxime intercedat" (*De Fide*, disput. 4., sect. 1, no. 5: t. 12, 112).

13. "...solam objecti revelati sufficientem propositionem, sive credatur ab eo cui fit talis revelatio, sive non, et sive revelatio fiat mere interius ab ipso Deo per se ipsum, vel per angelos, sive fiat exterius per hominum praedicationem" (*De Trinitate*, L. I. c. 12, nos.. 4-5: t. 1, 571).

14. "Sed quaeret aliquis primo quid nomine revelationis intelligamus. Respondeo breviter intelligi omnem sufficientem fidei propositionem, sive interius tantum fiat, sive per exteriorem praedicationem. Ut hoc autem magis intelligatur, adverto ad cognitionem fidei duo esse necessaria: unum est apprehensio rerum credendarum, quatenus homini proponuntur ut dicta a Deo, et consequenter ut credibilia ex testimonio divino; aliud est assensio ad res propositas, in quo proprie fides ipsa consistit" (*De necessitate gratiae*, L. II, c. 1, no. 8: t. 7, 588).

15. "Haec fides dupliciter potest proponi: primo per generalem praedicationem quae fit quando primum incipit introduci, sicut praedicata est per Christum et per apostolos, et tunc profecto necessarium fuit doctrinam confirmari signis propriis divinae virtutis, ut sunt miracula, ... et ideo semper hunc ordinem Deus observavit, ut constat in promulgatione Evangelii, et in promulgatione Veteris Testamenti, et fere in singulis prophetis; ac denique de seipso dixit Christus: si non venissem et locutus eis fuissem, et si opera non fecissem in eis quae nullus alius fecit, peccatum non haberent. Alio modo contingit fidem jam sufficienter praedicatam et introductam, singulis praedicari et quasi applicari, et tunc non sunt necessaria exteriora signa divinae virtutis; necessarium autem est ut divina virtus interius adjuvet et cooperetur, ut unusquisque sufficienter percipiat propositionem fidei et de illa convenienter judicet; nam totum hoc est opus valde supernaturale, quod sine auxilio gratiae praestari non potest" (*De Fide*, disput. 4, sect. 1, no. 6: t. 12, 114).

16. "Haec assensio per fidem supernaturalis est in se, et ideo praeter objecti propositionem sufficientem, indiget supernaturali principio, a quo fiat. Atque hinc ortum est ut nomine revelationis interdum in Scriptura significetur ipsamet interna inspiratio et infusio interioris luminis, quae efficaciter generat fidem, quomodo dixit Christus Petro *Mt.* 16: caro et sanguis non revelavit tibi, sed Pater meus, et *Mt.* 11, generaliter dixit: nemo novit Filium nisi Pater, neque Patrem quis novit, nisi Filius et cui voluerit Filius revelare. Haec enim revelatio non solum ex parte

objecti, sed etiam ex parte potentiae fit, et ideo objecti propositionem et inspirationem, ac adjutorium ad credendum includit" (*De Trinitate*, L. I, c. 12, nos. 4-5: t. 1, 571).

17. "Non ita loquimur de revelatione, sed priori modo quatenus ad judicium fidei praesupponitur; sic enim contingit multis revelari fidem qui non credunt, quamvis sine praevia revelatione nemo credat" (*De Necessitate gratiae*, L. II, c. 1, n. 8: t. 7, 588). Cf. *De Fide*, disput. 8, sect. 4, no. 24: t. 12, 157.

18. *De Fide*, disput. 3, sect. 3, no. 5: t. 12, 47.

19. "Primo modo fit manifestando in objecto veritatem ejus, vel rationem assentiendi illi; sic enim praeceptor illuminat auditores... Sic ergo Deus revelans et testificans res fidei, merito dicitur illuminare illas, et sic dicitur illuminare prophetas, et Christus Dominus dicitur illuminasse mundum praedicatione sua. Denique, ait Paulus, omne quod manifestatur, lumen esse, atque etiam manifestatio objecti est quaedam illuminatio. Deinde ipsa etiam infusio fidei divinae illuminatio est, nam fides est quoddam lumen, et ideo Paulus, ad *Heb.* 6, baptizatos vocat illuminatos quia lumen fidei recipiunt" (*Ibid.*, no. 6).

20. "Primum ergo velamen tollitur per revelationem objecti fidei; nam per illam fit aliquo modo cognoscibile sub testimonio divino: per infusionem autem fidei tollitur ignorantia mentis, et ideo utraque dici potest revelatio. Proprie tamen, et juxta frequentiorem modum loquendi Scripturae, revelatio dicitur illa quae est ex parte objecti, juxta illud ad *Rom.* 1: Justitia Dei in eo, id est in Evangelio, revelatur ex fide in fidem; in Evangelio enim objectum fidei aperitur... Sic etiam D. Thomas saepe docet revelationem fieri mediantibus angelis (2a 2ae, q. 2, a. 6; q. 172, a. 5; 1a, q. 96, a 3), quod non est verum nisi de revelatione objectiva; et sic etiam in communi sermone dicimus revelari secreta: hoc ergo modo distinguunt theologi revelationem necessariam ad fidem ab infusione habitus; ita etiam distingui solet propria revelatio ab instinctu Dei... Estque valde notanda differentia quod revelatio propria percipitur ab intellectu, et per eam concipitur aliquo modo objectum revelatum, et ratio quae ostenditur ad assentiendum illi; infusio autem habitus non ita percipitur ab intellectu, sed invisibili modo ab ipso Deo fit, ut per se constat" (*Ibid.*, *no.* 7: t. 12, 48).

21. *De Fide*, *disput.* 1, sect. 10, no. 193. Cited next: J. DE LUGO, *Disputationes scholasticae et morales* (8 vol., Paris, Vivès, 1891-1894).

22. "Requiritur ergo ad locutionem quod ordinetur per se et immediate ad manifestandum alicui mentem loquentis. Ex quo fit ut non sit idem loqui aliqui et loqui coram altero" (*Ibid.*, no. 197).

23. *Ibid.*, no. 210.

24. *Ibid.*, no. 203.

25. "Idem cum proportione dicendum esse de locutione mediata, qua Deus mihi hic et nunc proponit mysterium fidei credendum: haec enim locutio est ipsa mysterii propositio mihi facta a praelatis et magistris cum talibus circumstantiis, etc.; haec enim propositio talis mihi apparet, ut in ipsa tanquam in Dei voce mediata possim cognoscere Deum esse auctorem huius doctrinae, et Deum per hoc medium velle mihi suam mentem communicare: in quo consistit ratio locutionis" (*Ibid.*, no. 204).

26. "Adverte revelationem Dei aliam esse immediatam, qua Deus immediate aliquid revelat; aliam esse mediatam, seu notitiam quae ad nos venit ex revelatione immediata aliis facta. Priorem revelationem videntur exigere in singulis ad assensum fidei haeretici nostri temporis, dum dicunt regulam fidei esse instinctum et Spiritum internum uniuscuiusque. Posteriorem nemo catholicus negat: necessarium enim omnino est nobis ad credendum fide christiana, quod mysterium nobis proponatur tanquam a Deo alicui immediate revelatum, et licet Deus non loquatur nobis immediate, loquitur tamen aliquo modo per os illorum qui mysteria sibi revelata proponunt, nam multifariam multisque modis Deus loquitur, ut dixit Paulus. Nec novum est appellare locutionem Dei hanc locutionem mediatam; sic enim appellatur saepissime in Scriptura" (*De Fide*, disput. 1, sect. 7, no. 122).

27. "Loquitur autem, sicut expedit Deum loqui cum hominibus percipientibus objecta per sensus materiales: nimirum taliter proponendo mysteria, talia miracula operando, ut non solum auribus, sed visu etiam percipiamus vocem Dei loquentis nobiscum. Ideo enim Paulus ad *Heb.* 2, miracula dixit esse quamdam Dei locutionem... Sunt ergo miracula ipsa aliquo modo vox Dei; unde Augustinus... absolute dixit: Deus mirabilibus loquitur" (*De Fide*, disput. 1, sect. 7, no. 122).

28. *Ibid.*, no. 122.

29. *Ibid.*, no. 123.

30. *De Fide*, disput. 1, sect. 8, no. 130.

31. "Revelatio enim propria Dei est locutio Dei, qui certe non loquitur quatenus dat habitum fidei, sed quatenus dicit Incarnationem vel Trinitatem; sicut non dicitur Deus loqui nobis, quatenus dedit nobis intellectum, quo possimus ei credere et cognoscere etiam alia objecta... Deus dans intellectum, vel habitum fidei, dicitur dare nobis potentiam, qua ejus vocem audire et credere possimus; non tamen dicitur loqui, quia locutio est productio verborum ad exprimendam

mentem loquentis... ; intellectus autem, vel habitus, non est verbum Dei, quare ejus productio non est ullo modo locutio vel revelatio Dei" (*De Fide*, disput. 1, sect. 2, no. 9). Cf. *De Fide*, disput. 1, sect. 10, no. 194.

32. *De Fide*, disput. 1, sect. 2, no. 22.

33. "Per auctoritatem divinae doctrinae intelligi a Sancto Thoma totum quod se tenet ex parte objecti... ; motionem adaequate distinguit a tota doctrina et auctoritate divina, solumque vult inducere ad credendum; quatenus Deus proponendo interius eamdem revelationem, movet homines ad praebendum assensum; quare illa invitatio Dei interna non est nova locutio Dei nisi allegorica, quatenus Deus accommodat sua gratia aures internas mentis ut melius percipiat vim et veritatem divini testimonii propositi" (*Ibid.*, no. 26).

34. Tractatus XVII, *De Fide*, disput. 1, dub. 3. Next to be cited: *Collegii Salmanticensis FF. Discalceatorum B. Mariae de Monte Carmeli primitivae observantiae Cursus theologicus, juxta miram Divi Thomae Praeceptoris angelici Doctrinam* (Lyon, 1779).

35. *De Fide*, disput. 1, dub. 3. para. 1, no. 81.

36. "Est actio, vel locutio Dei testificantis nobis verbo vel facto aliquam veritatem, sive immediate per se ipsam, sive mediate per suos ministros, quales sunt angeli, apostoli et prophetae" (*Ibid.*, no. 82).

37. "Consistit in actuali vel etiam habituali cognitione eorum quae nobis Deus loquitur et testificatur; sic enim interiorem illi adhibemus auditum. Quo pacto, tam habitus quam assensus fidei dicitur divina revelatio. Nec immerito, tum quia generaliter loquendo, actio divina passive accepta supponit pro illius effectu; constat autem tam habitum quam actum fidei esse effectum revelationis activae Dei; tum etiam quia praedictus assensus fidei excludit in genere causae formalis in fidelitatem, quae est velamen ex parte subjecti se tenens; tum denique, quia communicat formaliter suo subjecto rectam intelligentiam eorum quae divinitus revelantur, sive ex parte objecti proponuntur; haec enim est differentia essentialis constitutiva revelationis passivae... " (*Ibid.*, no. 83).

CHAPTER III

THE SCHOLASTIC RENEWAL OF THE XIX CENTURY

From 1760 to 1840, theology, instead of seeking its inspiration in the great Christian tradition of Saint Augustine, Saint Thomas, Saint Bonaventure, looks for its ferment in the constantly changing philosophies of the age. Bit by bit, it turns into something cheap, and finally into the emaciated shadow of philosophism.

After this period of contempt for medieval scholasticism, a revival gradually begins, in the sense of tradition, heralded already in Spain and Italy, where scholasticism had always continued, but promoted and stimulated primarily by the Church herself, in her leaders and thinkers. Pius IX, in particular, reaffirms the rights of the supernatural in the face of rationalism and restores theology to her true status. In this renewal many familiar names come up: Möhler, Kleutgen, Denzinger, Franzelin, Scheeben. In re-emphasizing the value of the supernatural, they are all drawn to a discussion of revelation, if not always to study the notion, at least to assert the possibility and reality. In Möhler, Kleutgen, Denzinger, we find nothing more elaborate than the notion itself. Towards the end of the century, however, at the time of the first Vatican Council, we begin to find more, especially in Franzelin and Scheeben. Newman, in England, supports a very firm and at the same time profoundly religious position.

I. JOHN MOHLER

More than anyone else, Möhler was, in Germany, the head of the theological renewal. His *Unity in the Church* is a reaction of life against the impoverishment of the Age of Enlightenment. Möhler there represents the Church as a living, active, and creative reality, which the Spirit of Christ never ceases to fill with life. He does not forget the fact of the Church's foundation, but what he wants to stress most of all is the fact that the Spirit is the dispenser of life, principle of unity and growth, within as well as without, continual source of dynamism: "So that whoever penetrates into the complex of our faith, sees that the life of the Spirit holds priority over the teaching of formulated faith, even though," as he later adds, "in time, the act of preaching precedes our adherence in faith".[1] Still, the vigorous affirmation, in his *Unity*, of the primacy of the Spirit and the representation of our awareness of faith in terms which sound like Schleiermacher —this was enough to frighten the minds of his age. Thus Möhler himself retrenched his position. Just as, in *Unity*, he insists that what is first is the Spirit, in his *Symbolic* he repeats that what is first is the visible Church. And when he speaks of revelation, it is only to stress its objectivity and exteriority.

To the principle of Protestantism which makes the visible Church derive from the invisible, he opposes the very different idea of the visible Church existing first, and then the invisible Church. "When Christ began announcing the Kingdom of God, this Kingdom existed only in Him and in the divine idea; it came to man, and first of all to the apostles, in whom the Kingdom of God was established by the Word of God speaking to them from without, in human terms, so that the Kingdom penetrated deep within them, but always coming from without".[2] What Christ did, the apostles in their turn also did, forming apostles of their own. It is thus that, through the course of the centuries, the invisible Church has always proceeded from the visible Church: "This order demanded the idea of an exterior and historical revelation, whose whole genuine essence demanded a permanent, determined, and exterior Magisterium, to which every man must be attached if he means to know this revelation".[3]

Luther, on the contrary, reasons "as if revelation in Christ Jesus were an interior revelation, as if God had not become man, as if consequently revelation did not end in an exterior testimony, as if it made no difference for what Christ taught to have been vouched for by an external authority.... The external authority of the Church is transformed in Luther into an interior authority, and the exterior word recognized as divine becomes the interior voice of Christ and His Spirit".[4] In strict logic, according to Luther, "we could very well get along without an exterior Christ and without an exterior revelation".[5]

Also "Luther never clearly understood what is meant by: The Word was made Flesh, became Man".[6] "His error ... was to have never basically considered what is meant by the fact that immediate revelation in Christ was an exterior revelation".[7] For want of this, he rejected the visibility of the Church, he rejected the external testimony.

Finally, he proclaims this revelation of inner awareness to be the interpreter of written revelation.[8] The Protestant position, which bases the whole of religious life on the immediate communication of the Spirit in the inner awareness of each man, forgets "that to this interior revelation there corresponds an exterior revelation and that the understanding of the interior word has as its condition the exterior word which is addressed to man".[9] It also forgets that the "voice of inner awareness" frequently changes the testimony of God. "That is why, together with Holy Scripture, which is without error, we have been given the living authority of the Church, to keep the divine word just as it is".[10]

Thus, according to Möhler, the revelation made to the apostles is the communication, through the human word of Christ, the Incarnate Word, of the good news of the kingdom, which was hidden in Him and in the Father. After having received the mission to preach, the apostles, in their turn, proposed this doctrine of salvation. The revelation of Christ and the apostles is thus a teaching proposed from without and destined for the mind which assimilates it. This teaching comes to us from the visible Church which proposes it with authority. This word received from without has a corresponding interior light, the word of the Spirit, interior revelation. If Möhler appears to overstress the objective and exterior character of this revelation, it is because he is writing against the Protestants who sacrifice everything before the concept of subjectivity and interiority. The real depth of his thinking is certainly to be discovered by a discreet comparison with the earlier positions of his *Unity*.

II. H. J. DENZINGER

In any discussion of the Enlightenment, as well as the effort at scholastic renewal, Denzinger must be mentioned. He did not, like Möhler, offer any innovation, but he pushed on further in the sense of a more positive theology. His principal work, *Vier Bücher von der religiösen Erkenntniss* (Four Books on Religious Knowledge), published in 1856-1857, is remarkable for its wealth of documentation and critical analysis.[11]

Denzinger maintains that we must define revelation beginning with its object, as a communication of truth; truth known immediately as truth, and not on the basis of any other object from which it might be deduced. Otherwise, he says, the term revelation is proper to the works of creation as well as to the events of history. In the same way, some outstanding fact, in so far as it manifests divine activity and expresses one of the divine properties, can just as well claim the name of revelation. In strict rigor of terms, we must not consider as revelation the gift of the faculty or the means for knowing the object. In a word, the immediate object of revelation is truth itself as truth, and revelation is the communication of this object by words, or by some adequate sign, or by direct contemplation.[12]

III. J. B. FRANZELIN

Franzelin, like Möhler and Denzinger, orients his teaching in the sense of positive investigation.[13] Papal theologian at the first Vatican Council, he took an active part in the preparation of the schemas of the dogmatic constitution: his testimony deserves to be studied. It is in his *Tractatus de divina traditione et scriptura* (Treatise on Divine Tradition and Scripture), which appeared in 1870, that he explains his conception of revelation.[14] For the most part, he borrows his elements from Suarez and De Lugo, but the use he makes of them gives them a consistency which is wholly new.

When God speaks to men, says Franzelin, either immediately, as in the prophets and in the apostles, or mediately through His envoys, he makes His word known by signs which identify it as being truly His. These signs are the miracles and supernatural charisms: "the Divine message is composed of *words* which announce the truth, and *facts* which manifest these words as the divine message".[15] "God actually speaks, not by words alone, but by the whole complex of his words and deeds".[16]

These deeds or *real words* which, together with the *formal words*, make up the divine message, are, in the New Testament, the whole life of Christ, particularly His miracles, His death, His Resurrection, the sending of the Spirit, with all its marvelous effects; in the Old Testament, the whole of human history, and primarily the history of Israel with the great divine manifestations which accompany it; and, after the coming of Christ, the preaching of the Gospel and its admirable spread, the revolution of ideas and morals which it effected, its preservation through the course of centuries, despite persecution, its fruits of holiness, the miracles and charisms which have never ceased to make it shine. "All these facts, taken together, are like so many rays all emanating from the word proposed as divine word; they manifest its divine origin".[17] The word proposed, says Franzelin, restating the words of Suarez, is "*proposed sufficiently* as word of God".[18] The word of revelation is thus the complex of formal words and divine deeds: the words announce the truth, the deeds authenticate this word as *divine* and *revealed*. Thus, when a king speaks to his envoy, through his letters patent, the royal seal and external trappings all enter in as component elements of the royal word which they make recognizable as such.[19]

For us, the word of God comes to us through the Church. Franzelin shows how, following the same economy, God, through His Church, that is to say, through the intimate union of real words (divine deeds) and formal words, addresses Himself to the men of all ages. Christ first of all made the apostles known as his envoys through His divine deeds, that is, through the signs which accompanied their preaching. These deeds, accomplished by Christ and His apostles, belong now to the Church and constitute her heritage. What is more, the Church, in her turn, has been blessed, in the course of centuries, with new deeds that are "like divine seals demonstrating her divine institution and her union with Christ and the apostles".[20]

Franzelin, pursuing this explanation, shows how the Church, through the course of the centuries, appears as one great divine deed, a component element herself of the *divine word*. "The preaching and first promulgation of revelation accomplished by Christ and his apostles was composed of *words* and *things*, and through these things the word was recognizable as divine . . . ; likewise, the revelation now proposed by the Church as a revelation deriving from Christ and His apostles is composed not only of words, but also of the whole complex of things and deeds through which the Church appears as divinely founded and entrusted by Christ with the mandate to preserve and preach His doctrine. Thus, not only in the personal preaching of Christ and the apostles, but also and always in the Church, *these things and these facts,*—and I mean the union of the Church with Christ and the apostles, its admirable spread, its unity of doctrine, the supernatural charisms which are evident in her, the constancy of the faith she has received, her martyrs, the whole spiritual vitality she always manifests, everything which is the Church, under this relationship of *things and deeds,* is an integral element of the divine word itself, in so far as it is made up of words and things".[21]

The *sufficient* promulgation of revelation, with the whole complex of words and deeds which make it up, could not however replace the role of grace. The role of grace is threefold: to help recognize the value of the facts which demonstrate the existence of revelation and the credibility of its content; to help man surmount the resistance of his nature in the face of truths which contradict the inclinations of the flesh; finally to enlighten his mind, to fortify and move his will, in order to give him the gift of adhering to God, with the humility and reverence of a child, on the sole testimony of His word, recognized as such.[22]

This, briefly, is how Franzelin conceives of revelation. All salutary truth has been revealed to the apostles through Christ, visibly or invisibly teaching through the sending of His Spirit. This truth is the Gospel which the apostles must preach to every creature and hand down to the Church.[23] This Church, in her turn, preserves and preaches the whole definitive truth as received from the apostles.[24] By revelation, Franzelin understands the sufficient promulgation[25] by Christ to the apostles, or by the apostles to the Church, or by the Church to all men, of the divine word, that is, the complex of words and divine deeds which authenticate these words as divine truths and revealed truths. We have already met this concept in De Lugo. Grace comes in to guide the soul in her search, to enlighten the mind and move the will to give allegiance to God on the basis of His word. This conception takes into account the external activity of revelation. Signs and propositions are both based on one single reality which makes up the actual message of God. Still, it seems to be a less happy integration of the interior activity of the Spirit.

IV. JOHN HENRY NEWMAN

In the passages where, incidentally, he speaks of revelation, Newman recognizes the following characteristic traits.[26] Its first and essential quality is to be *religious* knowledge. It is not given to increase our profane knowledge, but to make us better and more holy, to lead us along the path of salvation. Scripture too, which contains revelation, is a *religious* book.[27]

In the second place, revelation is a *mystery*. It makes God known to us, but does not take away the mystery which surrounds him.[28] "When you knew nothing of the revealed light, you knew not revealed darkness. Religious truth requires you should be told something, your imperfect nature prevents your knowing all".[29] Imperfect creatures that we are, we shall never manage to pierce the shadow of mystery.

In the third place, revelation is presented as an *economy*. It is made up of three successive stages, following a progress in quality and in quantity, up to the fullness of Christ.[30] God, in His condescension, has adapted Himself to human conditions and to the weakness of His people.[31] The Incarnation is the type par excellence of this divine economy.

In the fourth place, revelation has a *doctrinal* character. It communicates a teaching, a message.[32] "The Gospel faith is a definite deposit, a treasure, common to all, one and the same in every age, conceived in set words, and such as admits of being received, preserved, transmitted.... The deposit certainly was a series of truths and rules".[33] That is why faith is not a sentiment or feeling or emotion, but an assent of the mind.

Finally, revelation has a *dogmatic* character: it is imposed with *authority*. Christianity is a *"revelatio revelata*: it is a definite message from God to man distinctly conveyed by his chosen instruments, and to be received as such a message, and therefore to be positively acknowledged, embraced, and maintained as true ... because it comes from Him (God) who neither can deceive nor be deceived.... The matter of Revelation is not a mere collection of truths, not a philosophical view, not a religious sentiment or spirit, not a special morality, ... but an authoritative teaching, which bears witness to itself and keeps itself together as one, in contrast to the assemblage of opinions on all sides of it, and speaks to all men, as being ever and everywhere one and the same, and claiming to be received intelligently, by all whom it addresses, as one doctrine, discipline, and devotion directly given from above".[34] If we admit the existence of a revelation, this revelation demands our faith, precisely because it is *revealed*.[35] Its dogmatic character derives from its character of revealed religion. The same is true of its *immutability*. If God, in the course of time, has revealed a supernatural truth, in order to work out the salvation of men by this truth, such a truth can neither disappear nor be substantially altered. On the other hand, this revelation, being called to live and develop in the human mind, being exposed consequently to all the fluctuations of human reason, a living and infallible authority was necessary to assure at once the immutability and the development of the revealed deposit. The Church is this infallible authority.[36] "Revelation is all in doctrine; the Apostles its sole depository, the inferential method its sole instrument, and ecclesiastical authority its sole sanction. The divine Voice has spoken once for all, and the only question is about its meaning".[37]

Newman thus lays great stress upon the doctrinal and imperative character of revelation. If God has spoken, man must obey this word which comes from the world above him. Newman is equally careful to stress the religious, salvific, and mysterious character of this supernatural knowledge. Finally, he shows how revelation has been given to us in accordance with an economy and pedagogy that are full of wisdom.

V. M. J. SCHEEBEN

In his *Dogmatik*, Scheeben has some pages on the notion of revelation. Following one of his favorite methods of approach, namely, developing the bond that exists between mysteries and studying them as one vast complex whose various parts shed mutual light on each other, Scheeben likes to compare the different forms of revelation in order to mark out their resemblances and their differences, in order to find the correct place for this type of revelation which is at the beginning of faith and theology. We can distinguish, he says, three forms of revelation.

In the *broad* sense, God reveals Himself to man through the works of creation which reflect His power and perfections, and also through the communication of the inner light of reason, which makes us capable of knowing the works of God and God Himself in His works. This activity deserves the title of divine message; still, it does not give rise to faith, but only to an imperfect and indirect knowledge of God.[38]

"In a more restricted and elevated sense, we speak of revelation as the act through which one mind presents to another mind the object of its own knowledge and enables him, without seeing the object himself, to make the content of that knowledge his own, basing himself upon the lights of the one who reveals to him. The vehicle of this revelation is the word properly so called (*locutio formalis*—formal speaking). Corresponding to this word, there is, on the part of him who receives the revelation, that form of knowledge which we call faith".[39] In the same way as God has joined his revelation through His works with the gift of the intellectual light that permits Him to be known, in that way, the objective promulgation of revelation which is made to us has a corresponding inner illumination, making us capable of taking for our own the content of divine knowledge. This illumination is also called revelation or word of God. Scripture, in very expressive terms, calls it the revelation and the word of the Father (Mt. 16:17; Jn. 6:45), to distinguish it from the external revelation and from the word of the Son who, in His quality as Envoy of the Father, announces what He has received from the Father. The term also shows that the inner illumination leads us to the source of truth from which the external revelation proceeds.

"In a still more restricted and more elevated sense, we speak of divine revelation as a manifestation through which God makes our knowledge in complete conformity with His own, such that we know

Him as He knows Himself: this is vision face to face".[40] In this revelation, the objective manifestation, real or verbal, is replaced by the unveiled contemplation of the intimate nature of God. In place of the subjective light which is given for us to grasp and understand the content of God's revelation, it is the fullness of divine light which makes His creature contemplate the essence of God.

These three forms of revelation represent three degrees or depths according to which the general notion of revelation is realized more and more perfectly. Each degree implies, on the part of God, a measure of grace and a communication of himself which are more and more abundant, more and more elevated; it also implies in return, on the part of His creatures, homage and submission which are more and more perfect. At the supreme degree, the highest measure of grace coincides with the supreme interior homage of the creature and the highest external glorification of God. These three forms of revelation have this in common that, not only do they communicate an objective content proposed by works, by words, or by direct vision, but they also produce the subjective knowledge itself by an interior illumination, a constantly growing source of light, which comes from reason, grace, and glory.

These three degrees have God Himself as their common Principle and, more precisely, the Word of God, His Logos. The principle of the first is the Logos as Creator, through Whom all things have been made, and particularly the light of reason which He has put in man as in His own image; the principle of the second is Christ, Incarnate Logos, sent by the Father, who has spoken through the prophets and through the humanity He has put on; the principle of the third is once again Christ, by reason of the divine glory which shines out in Him.

The revelation of grace appears as a middle term between the revelation of nature and the revelation of glory: presupposing and completing the first, preparing the way for the last, aspiring to it, sharing in the imperfection of the first and the perfection of the last. This twofold relationship gives it its place and proper meaning.

The definition of Scheeben is thus characterized primarily by its care to integrate the exterior and interior elements of revelation, by its respect for the necessary proportion between the object proposed and the light offered. By revelation in the strict sense, Scheeben understands the communication of divine thought through the human word of Christ, Incarnate Logos. This external speaking has a corresponding inner illumination which also bears the name of revelation: it is this that permits a man to make external revelation his own. The definition is also richer for the comparison he establishes between the two other types of revelation: that of nature and that of glory. In each of these he notes the conjunction of an objective element and an inner light. His claims are based on Scripture, which says that the Christian faith demands, along with the external revelation, an inner revelation (Mt. 16:17), together with the hearing of the external word, the teaching of the Master who speaks within (Jn. 6:44). In his analysis of the act of faith, Scheeben is very precise on the nature of this interior revelation. "This inner illumination has the character of an inner revelation, insofar as it renews and gives new life to the invitation to faith which has been made to us through external revelation. That is why it is commonly called a voice, God drawing us (Jn. 6:44). Saint Thomas calls it a divine instinct: *interior instinctus Dei moventis* (2a 2ae, q. 2, a. 9, ad 3) which invites us interiorly to believe; Saint Paul calls it an openness of heart (Acts 16:14) or ear to the word of God".[41]

Another of Scheeben's merits is that he has brought out what is at once the supernatural and historical character of revelation. The supernatural character of revelation appears in the *end* of revelation, which is to help man realize his supernatural destiny, that is, the vision of God;[42] in the *new relations* of Father and son, friend to friend, established by revelation;[43] in its *specific content*, that is, the mysteries of God's bosom (life of the Trinity) and the heart of God (God's salvific plan);[44] finally, in the *response* which revelation demands, namely, faith.[45]

The historical character of revelation appears in the successive phases of its temporal realization. In public revelation, Scheeben distinguishes two phases: the revelation made to humanity in its original state, or the revelation of paradise, and the revelation made to humanity in a state of sin, or the evangelical or redemptive revelation. This last, in its turn is divided into two periods: the preparatory revelation of the Old Testament and the consummation of revelation in the New Testament. The progress of revelation is *extensive*: patriarchal revelation is addressed to one family, Mosaic revelation to one people, Christian revelation to all of humanity. It is *quantitative* and *qualitative*: the field of revelation is constantly growing and the light it sheds is always more abundant.[46] In Jesus Christ there is fullness of light and truth. In Jesus Christ and through Jesus Christ, the eternal Word of God is addressed to the apostles and, through His spirit, accomplishes, within, the work begun by preaching. The destination of this revelation is universal, for the envoys of Christ, the apostles, are to announce it over all the earth, in order to reunite all men in one single Kingdom. "This revelation is not only higher and more complete than the preparatory revelation; it is also, in many respects, higher and more complete than the revelation of paradise, and it will, by that very fact, be the last and constitutive public revelation of the divine word that will ever take place".[47]

1. J. A. MOHLER, *L'Unité dans l'Église ou le principe du catholicisme d'après l'esprit des Pères des trois premiers siècles de l'Église* (trans. by DOM ANDRE DE LILIENFELD, Paris, 1938), pp. 22-23.

2. "Als Christus das Reich Gottes zu verkunden begann, war es nirgends vorhanden, als in ihm und der gottlichen Idee; es kam von aussen zu den Menschen, und zwar zuerst zu den Aposteln, in welchen also das Reich Gottes durch das von aussender, menschlich zu ihen sprechende Wort Gottes ausgerichtet ward, so dass es von aussen in sie hineindrang" (J. A. MOHLER, *Symbolik oder Darstellung der dogmatischen Gegensatze der Katholiken und Protestanten nach ihren offentlichen Bekenntnisschriften* (Mainz, 1838(5)), L. I, ch. 5, par. 48, p. 426).

3. "Diese Ordnung forderte der Begriff einer ausseren historischen Offenbarung, deren ganzes, eigenthumliches Wesen ein fortwahrendes, bestimmtes ausseres Lehramt erheischt, an welches ein Jeder such zu halten hat, der dieselbe will kennen lernen" (*Ibid.*, p. 426).

4. "Und worin hat nach Luther Jemand in letzter Instanz die Gewissheit zu finden, dass er in der Wahrheit steche? In einem lediglich inneren Acte, in dem Zeugnisse des heiligen Geistes; gleich als war die Offenbarung in Christo Jesu eine innere, gleich als ware er nicht Mensch geworden, als kame es mithin nicht auf ein ausseres Zeugniss, als kame es nicht darauf an, durch eine aussere Auctoritat gewiss zu werden, was er gelernt hat... Die aussere Auctoritat der Kirche verwandelte sich bei Luther in eine innere, und das ausserliche als gottlich beglaubigte Wort in die innere Stimme Christi und seines Geistes" (*Ibid.*, 427).

5. "Hatte er einen ausseren, historischen Christus, eine aussere Offenbarung wohl recht missen konnen" (*Ibid.*, 427).

6. "Was es heisst: das Wort ist Fleisch, ist Mensch geworden, wurde Luther'n niemals klar" (*Ibid.*, 430).

7. "Sein Fehler... war, dass er nicht grundlich erwog, was es heisst, die unmittelbare Offenbarung in Christo sei eine aussere" (*Ibid.*, section 49, p. 431).

8. *Ibid.*, 432.

9. "Der inneren Offenbarung entspricht die aussere, und das inneren Einsprachte hat die aussere Ansprache zur Bedingung" (L. II, ch. 2, section 71, p. 531).

10. "Daher ist der heiligen Schrift, der irrthumslosen, die lebendige Auctoritat der Kirche zur Seite gegeben, damit wir das gottliche Wort, wie es an sich ist, fur uns erhalten" (L. II. ch. 5, section 44, p. 403).

11. H. DENZINGER, *Vier Bucher von der Religiosen Erkenntniss* (Wurzburg, 1856).

12. "Die Offenbarung ist eine Bekanntmachung von Wahrheiten, welche unmittelbar ist a parte objecti, d. h. welche die zu offenbarende Wahrheit in sich bekanntmacht, nicht aber bloss darin besteht, dass ein Anderes als Objekt der Offenbarung gesetzt wird, aus dem man durch Schluss auf eine Wahrheit kommen kann, in welchem Sinne auch die Werke Gottes in der Natur und in der Geschichte eine Offenbarung genannt werden; oder eine besondere Tatsache als Offenbarung angesehen und bezeichnet werden kann, weil sie irgend eine Eigenschaft Gottes als Wirkung derselben manifestiert. Ferner kann die Offenbarung nicht bloss in der Verleihung des Vermogens oder der Mittel oder Anleitung zum Erkennen bestehen, sondern ihr unmittelbares Objekt muss die zu offenbarende Wahrheit sein. Kurz, sie ist die Bekanntmachung durch das Wort oder durch dem Worte gleichkommende Zeichen oder durch unmittelbares Schaulassen des zu offenbarenden Gegenstandes selbst. Wir werden allerdings finden, dass viele das Wort ganz anders fassen: allein der hergebrachte Sprachgebrauch beweist, dass der aufgestellte Begriff der allein eigntliche und stricte ist" (*Ibid.*, vol. 1, L. 2, pp. 116-117).

13. About Franzelin, cf. DTC 6: 765-767; E. HOCEDEZ, *Histoire de la théologie au XIX siècle*, 2: 356-358.

14. Our quotation is taken from the fourth edition (1896).

15. "Animadvertendum est locutionem divinam esse complexam ex verbis enuntiantibus veritatem, et ex factis quibus verba exhibentur ut locutio divina" (J. B. FRANZELIN, *Tractatus de divina traditione et scriptura*, p. 618).

16. "Non enim solis verbis sed una cum verbis etiam factis illis omnibus loquitur ipse Deus" (p. 626).

17. "Si consideretur fastigium divinae revelationis in Christo, imprimis tota vita Jesus Christi, miracula, mors et prae ceteris resurrectio, electio paucorum rudium hominum ad conversionem generis humani, missio Spiritus Sancti spectata in evidentibus effectibus; tum tota historia generis humani, et maxime historia populi Israel cum omnibus suis manifestationibus supernaturalibus ut praeparatio et paedagogia ad Christum, atque tota historia humana subsequens ut effectus promanans ab ipso Christo; apostolica praedicatio, mirabilis religionis propagatio, media ad finem propositum, omnia contraria iis quibus homines utuntur, et quae humanitas spectata non tam ad obtinendum quam ad impediendum effectum viderentur idonea; effectus autem ex nulla humana causa ingens et universalis in humano genere, inter ferrum et ignem, inter tormentorum omnia genera quibus per tria saecula et amplius saevitum est, conversio omnium idearum ordinis theologici et moralis, commutatio totius vitae publicae et privatae; non minus mirabilis totius institutionis conservatio per saeculorum decursum, omnibus aetatibus moraliter perpetua sanctitas et virtutum nuspiam extra hanc religionem cognitarum, constans exercitium heroicum in multis, aestimatio in omnibus, charismata supernaturalia effectibus externis etiam sese manifestantia; postremo totus hic rerum divinarum complexus tum universim tum in factis singulis diu antea promissus et praenuntiatus; haec inquam omnia simul spectata sunt totidem radii, quibus verbum propositum ut divinum resplendet, et suam originem divinam manifestat" (Ibid., 618).

18. Ibid., 624.

19. Ibid., 641.

20. "Deus rebus et factis cognoscibiles reddidit primum apostolos tamquam suos legatos in promulganda revelatione... Successores serie perpetua immediate nectuntur cum ipsis apostolis, et in mundo universo communione et doctrina inter se conjuncti, velut unum corpus ad nos usque pertingunt. Ex connexione cum apostolis et cum Christo ipso res illae et facta Christi et apostolorum pertinent ad totam Ecclesiam subsequentem, quae et ipsa insuper novis rebus et factis quavis aetate insignitur, tamquam sigillis demonstrantibus ejus institutionem divinam et connexionem cum Christo et apostolis" (Ibid., p. 639).

21. "Praedicatio et prima promulgatio revelationis, ... peracta a Christo et ab apostolis, componebatur verbis et rebus, et per res locutio erat cognoscibilis ut divina... Pari modo, revelatio, quae nunc ab Ecclesia proponitur tamquam revelatio derivata inde a Christo et ab apostolis, non tantum verbis constat, sed etiam tota serie rerum et factorum, quibus Ecclesia exibetur ut divinitus instituta, et pro Christo legatione fungens ad conservationem et praedicationem doctrinae. Ergo non solum in personali praedicatione Christi et apostolorum, sed etiam perpetuo in Ecclesia res illae et facta, connexio inquam Ecclesiae cum Christo et apostolis, mirabilis propagatio et conservatio, consensio, supernaturalia charismata sese manifestantia, constantia in fide accepta, martyria, tota spiritualis vita Ecclesiae manifestata, omnia scilicet illa quae diximus Ecclesiam spectatam secundum res et facta, componunt ipsam divinam locutionem, quatenus constat duplici elemento verborum et rerum" (Ibid., 640-641).

22. Ibid., 648-649.

23. Ibid., 247-249.

24. Ibid., 250-251.

25. That is a proposition confirmed by signs attesting the Divine origin of the message.

26. On this subject, see in particular: J. SEYNAEVE, Cardinal Newman's Doctrine on Holy Scripture (Louvain, Oxford et Tielt, 1953), pp. 30-37; 205-214.

27. "That knowledge which God has given... is religious knowledge" (J. H. NEWMAN, Parochial and Plain Sermons [8 vol., London, 1834-1843], 7:246). "What is the knowledge which God has not thought fit to reveal us? Knowledge connected merely with this present world... No divinely authenticated directions... have been given to the world at large, on subjects relating merely to this our temporal state of being" (Ibid., 244).

28. "God has promised us light and knowledge..., but in His way, not in our way" (Parochial and Plain Sermons, 7: 221). "The Divine Scheme is larger and deeper than our own capacities" (Ibid., 3: 358).

29. Ibid., 1: 211.

30. Ibid., 2: 123.

31. J. SEYNAEVE, Cardinal Newman's Doctrine on Holy Scripture, pp. 33-34 et 209-211; J. H. NEWMAN, The Idea of a University (London, 1886), p. 223; ID., Discussions and Arguments on various Subjects (London, 1872), p. 135.

32. J. H. NEWMAN, The Idea of a University (London, 1886), p. 223; ID., Discussions and Arguments on Various Subjects (London, 1872), p. 135.

33. H. NEWMAN, Parochial and Plain Sermons, 2: 265

34. J. H. NEWMAN, An Essay in Aid of a Grammar of Assent (London, 1885), pp. 386-387.

35. "Revelation implies a something revealed, and what is revealed is imperative on our faith, because it is revealed. Revelation implies imperativeness" (J. H. NEWMAN, Discussions and Arguments on various Subjects, p. 132).

36. J. H. Walgrave, *Newman, Le développement du dogme* (Paris-Tournai, 1957), pp. 261-280.

37. J. H. Newman, *The Idea of a University*, p. 223.

38. M. J. Scheeben, *Handbuch der Katholischen Dogmatik* (Freiburg, 1948), 1:10.

39. "*Im engeren und hoheren Sinne* heisst Offenbarung diejenige Kundgebung eines Geistes an den andern, wodurch jener diesem den Inhalt seiner eigenen Erkenntnis als solchen vorlegt und so ihn befahigt und veranlasst, ohne eigene Anschauung auf Grund der Einsicht des Offenbarenden des Inhaltes derselben sich zu bemachtigen. Das Vehikel dieser Offenbarung ist das Wort im eigentlichen Sinne (locutio formalis), und ihm entspricht vonseiten des Empfangers der Offenbarung als die Form der durch dieselbe ermoglichten Erkenntnis der Glaube" (*Ibid.*, 10).

40. "*Im engsten und zugleich hochsten Sinne* heisst gottliche Offenbarung diejenige Kundgebung vonseiten Gottes, durch welche er unsere Erkenntnis der seinigen vollkommen gleichformig macht und bewirkt, dass wir ihn ahnlich erkennen, wie er sich selbst erkennt, durch die Anschauung von Angesicht zu Angesicht" (*Ibid.*, no. 11).

41. "Auch diese Erleuchtung hat insofern ebenfalls den Charakter einer innern Offenbarung, als sie die Aufforderung zum Glauben, die in der aussern Offenbarung an uns herantritt, innerlich wiederholt und belebt. Sie wird daher gewohnlich als der Ruf oder Zug Gottes (*Jo.* 6, 44; Thomas nennt ihm 2a 2ae, q. 2, a. 9, ad 3: interior instinctus Dei moventis), der uns innerlich zum Glauben einladet, resp. als Offnung unseres Herzens (*Act.* 16, 14) oder unseres Ohres fur die Aufnahme des Wortes Gottes... bezeichnet" (*Ibid.*, 356-357).

42. *Ibid.*, 19.

43. *Ibid.*, 22-23.

44. *Ibid.*, 26.

45. *Ibid.*, 27.

46. *Ibid.*, 35-41.

47. *Ibid.*, 38.

CHAPTER IV

THE THEOLOGY OF REVELATION IN THE XX CENTURY

I. THE COMMON TEACHING AT THE BEGINNING OF THE XX CENTURY

Fundamental theology, in the twentieth century, is built upon the outline of the first Vatican Council and the anti-Modernist documents; it defines revelation in the perspective of these documents. What was needed was to protect the concept of revelation against the denials of rationalism and from the contamination of liberal Protestantism. Despite a certain diversity of emphasis, we generally discover a fundamental agreement among our authors.

They all insist on the transcendent character of the activity of revelation, as well as the doctrinal character of the object revealed: what is communicated to man is a complex of truths necessary for salvation. "When we say that God has revealed, we understand that God has spoken to man to make known some truth, and that man has recognized His voice".[1] "Revelation is the communication of religious truth".[2] "Divine revelation is the manifestation of truths, made by God to a rational creature, so that he may attain his final goal".[3] In this object, there is sometimes made a distinction between the *teachings* and the *will* or *decrees* of God.[4]

The analogy of word serves to represent the activity through which God communicates His thinking to men. "Direct supernatural revelation is the manfestation of God through the divine word, that is, through an act of God directly and immediately ordered to make known to man His own knowledge".[5] Obviously, this word must not be conceived of in an anthropomorphic way, but defined in terms of knowledge: what is under discussion here is the supernatural *illumination* of the intelligence by God. "Revelation is nothing more than the manifestation of a truth which God effects in man through a supernatural illumination of his intelligence".[6]

What corresponds to this word is not knowledge but faith. "Divine revelation strictly so-called is the word of God through which He communicates certain things which He knows, so that men believe these things by reason of the authority of God who speaks".[7] Thus, to express the formal element of this word, we speak of *testimony*: revelation is the word of witness, the word of God who testifies.[8] On the other hand, just as this word enriches the mind with new and superior knowledge, it also takes on the character of an authoritative *teaching*.[9] Still, there are very few theologians who elaborate these notions of word and testimony by making a comparison to the philosophy of language.

Among the authors who devote a fuller treatment to the notion of revelation, we might mention Gardeil, Garrigou-Lagrange, Dieckmann.

1. Father A. Gardeil, in *Le Donné révélé et la théologie* (Revelation and Theology), devotes an entire chapter, the second, to the notion of revelation. He laments the fact that teaching, through an extreme process of oversimplification, "is not always sufficiently taken up with the psychological approach" through which revelation comes to us, thus giving "the impression of a veneer of formulas without spirit, which is, however, in no way an adequate expression of the realities".[10] Faithful to Saint Thomas, Father Gardeil describes revelation in terms of the *De Prophetia*. But where Saint Thomas is more interested in the first revelation, in itself, Father Gardeil is taken up primarily with defending the homogeneity of revealed truth through the medium of dogma and theology.

After having passed judgment on the Modernist concept of revelation, as represented by Loisy and Tyrrell, Father Gardeil insists upon the social finality of the prophetic charism and on the *denuntiatio* of the revealed truth.[11] Prophetic knowledge being essentially a social charism, it must necessarily "communicate an object that has meaning for us, expressed with enough precision to serve as a meeting place for all those who are in search of the divine . . . . Without this fixed and sufficiently precise meaning of the object of prophetic knowledge, we should never have a socialized participation in the very light that God has spread in the mind of the prophet".[12] The revealed truth must be communicated under a form which guarantees its determined, absolute, and immutable value, capable of being handed down indefinitely throughout space and time. This communicability, with all its characteristic traits, is assured, according to Father Gardeil: 1. thanks to its thought content, sufficiently precise, as proposed by God; 2. thanks to the activity of the Spirit who maintains an absolute fidelity between the *denuntiatio* and the inner truth;[13] 3. thanks, finally, to the absolute character of which certain human statements are capable. Hence, "once God's activity as Revealer dawns in the affirmative faculty of man, humanity is in possession of a determined truth which can be handed down indefinitely. What is directly acted upon in revelation is not the prophet's heart, but rather his intelligence, which is capable of the absolute".[14] Revelation, according to Father Gardeil, is thus presented as a divine activity, a social finality, which sets in motion and directs the prophet's faculty of expression, so that his judgments, pronounced in the divine light, are communicable to the whole of human society.

In the analysis of the very process of prophetic knowledge, Father Gardeil stays with the teaching of Saint Thomas on all essential points. Prophetic knowledge, like all knowledge, presupposes *acceptio rerum* and *judicium*, that is to say, an awareness of images or ideas and a judgment which joins them in truth. Under the divine activity, first of all, the consciousness is flooded with images and notions (acquired or infused or reorganized), corresponding analogically with the aspect of divine reality that God means to reveal. The divine light calls attention to the expressive power of these mental signs; then the prophet, "reacting under the divine enlightenment of the object called to his attention," conceives, asserts, and announces the very thing that God wanted to be announced.[15] God does not force the prophet's judgment: it is the prophet who complies with this light. Light in its fountainhead, God reinforces the light of the human mind, without modifying human nature or hampering the free play of its activities. The light received begets a twofold certitude: the knowledge that the truth is precisely what the signs and light make it out to be, and also that the truth and the light are not from the prophet, but from God.[16] The prophet asserts what he sees, to himself first of all, then to other men whose enlightenment in these matters is his mission from God. Prophecy being a social charism, "the prophet must express on the outside what he judges in his inner self to be the truth revealed by God, and this in such a way that it can be handed down to other men and thus indefinitely become the object of social exchange among men".[17]

2. Father Garrigou-Lagrange devotes thirty pages of his *De Revelatione* to the concept of revelation.[18] First he defines this notion on the basis of the documents of the Church, then offers a theological explanation. "Revelation," he says, "is the free and essentially supernatural activity through which God, in order to lead the human race to its supernatural end, which consists in the vision of the Divine

Essence, speaking to us through the prophets and in these last times through Christ, has made known to us in a certain obscurity some supernatural mysteries and also truths of natural religion, so that they might thereafter be infallibly proposed by the Church, without any change in meaning, down to the end of the world."[19] He takes up this definition once again, based primarily on the first Vatican Council, and arranges its elements in accordance with the four classic causes: final, efficient, formal, material. The activity of revelation, he stresses, is a free and essentially supernatural activity: by reason of its end and its proper object, that is the mysteries of the inmost life of God. It is not activity of revelation enjoying the ordinary divine concourse, nor a supernatural activity only *quoad modum*, as in a miracle, but an essentially supernatural activity, proceeding from God and His inmost life. And since this activity is a word, it is different from the infusion of the light of faith.

When he comes to a theological explanation, Father Garrigou-Lagrange formally defines revelation as "the word of God in the form of teaching".[20] This statement he bases primarily on Heb. 1:1; Is. 50:4; Hos. 2:4; Ps. 84:9, and on the passages of Scripture where it is said that the crowds give Christ the title of teacher and that Christ claimed this title for Himself (Mt. 8:28; Jn. 8:13); then on the decree *Lamentabili*, condemning the following proposition of the Modernists: "Christ did not teach a body of doctrine applicable to all times and all men, but rather He began a religious movement adapted, or capable of being adapted, to different times and places;"[21] finally, on an analysis of the notion of revelation conceived as the word of a very wise superior making known sublime truths to an inferior. On the basis of this idea of revelation, *word of teaching*, it is easy to deduce the conditions required before we can be instructed by a teacher, either divine or human. There must be, according to Saint Thomas,[22] an objective proposition of the truth and an inner light to judge the truth proposed or, at least, to judge the authority of the teacher. The human teacher obviously, is unable to give this inner light of intelligence; still, he does produce an objective light, in the sense, that through his demonstration, he methodically guides his student from the known to the unknown and lets him see by himself what he could never have seen without the assistance of a teacher. The divine teacher can propose the truth in two ways: either in the evidence of vision or in the obscurity of faith. In this second case, two conditions are required for man to make the divine thinking his own. *Objectively*, there must be a supernatural proposition of the truth: something, which was heretofore hidden, is now made known by God, brought to man's knowledge and proposed as emanating from God. Under this aspect, revelation is similar to the word of the human teacher. *Subjectively*, a supernatural light is required, to enlighten the terms of the proposition and to permit a man to unite them in an infallible way in a judgment which is in conformity with the truth; this light also lets him discover with certitude the divine origin of the truth communicated. Under this last aspect, revelation differs from human teaching, for God alone can act immediately on the mind and thus infuse His light.[23]

Thus, revelation, according to Father Garrigou-Lagrange, is described primarily in terms of teaching, in terms of the relationship between master and student. In this analysis, whose elements are furnished by the *De Magistro*[24] and the *De Prophetia*[25] of Saint Thomas, the very rich concept of *testimony*, present throughout Scripture, hardly comes into discussion. It is true that revelation teaches us something that must be handed down as a body of doctrine. Still, what makes it specific as word is not knowledge but faith. In the genus of word, it belongs to the species of testimony rather than to the species of teaching. Father Garrigou-Lagrange is more inspired when he stresses, on all degrees of revelation, the collaboration of an object and a light proportioned to that object: to the prophetic light must correspond proportionally, in the believer, the light of faith and, in the blessed, the light of glory. This proposition is simply stated in the chapter on revelation; it is developed at great length in the chapter on faith.[26] In the same way he insists on the free and supernatural character of revelation,[27] just as on the intimate relationship between Church and revelation.[28]

3. H. Dieckmann[29] precedes his definition of revelation with a brief paragraph which sums up the principal names for revelation in the New Testament;[30] then he defines revelation as being *locutio Dei attestans* (God's word of testimony). "The word" he says, "is the act through which someone directly manifests his thinking to another".[31] This notion of word includes three elements: 1. A manifestation of thinking; 2. A *direct* manifestation of thinking: thus the knowledge we have of God on the basis of His works does not strictly verify the notion of word; 3. A *duality* of person grasped as such: God must be conceived as a Person addressing man as a person.

The word of revelation is in the order of *testimony*: this means that it demands an assent based on the authority of the one speaking. Dieckmann distinguishes theoretical authority and the juridic authority of a witness. The first is based on the knowledge and truthfulness of the witness; the second also implies, in the witness, a right to be heard and believed. The authority of God is at once theoretic and juridic: it rests not only on His infinite knowledge and truthfulness, but also on His quality of absolute Teacher of the human creation, whose author and final end He is. Since revelation is a word of witness it demands the homage of faith.[32]

There is no denying the fact that these essays contain precious elements which must be retained. But they also present many serious gaps. Following Saint Thomas, they insist on prophetic revelation, but almost completely ignore revelation through Christ. In a general way, moreover, their biblical approaches to revelation remain hesitant, not to say non-existent. Revelation is defined on the basis of etymology or on the basis of the documents from the Church magisterium, which, moreover, are merely summed up rapidly; then the authors pass on quickly to the problem of the possibility of revelation, without sufficiently realizing that what is under question is not any revelation at all, but one very specific revelation which comes to us through history and the Incarnation. They insist much more on the revealed truths than on God who both reveals and is revealed. They preserve an astonishing reserve on the interpersonal relationship which revelation establishes between God and men. These deficiencies, to all appearances, arise for the most part from an inadequate consideration of the data of Scripture. A preoccupation with apologetics can only obscure the wealth of the reality under discussion.

II. FACTORS OF RENEWAL AND PRESENT-DAY ORIENTATION

For almost a quarter of a century, there has been, among Catholic theologians, a newly regained interest in this first Christian reality which is revelation. Here, briefly, are the reasons for this renewal and the orientation it has taken today.

1. Point of Departure: Dissatisfaction and Complaint

At the beginning of this renewal, we are aware of a state of dissatisfaction which is expressed in a number of complaints, frequently rather vehement. Since 1911, Father Lebreton has been deploring the classical theologians, who were strong on systematising certain parts of dogma but wholly neglected the fundamental categories of revelation and faith.[33] Father Charlier finds fault with Father Gardeil for having insisted too much on the conceptual aspect of the revealed data and not enough on the real aspect.[34] Father Chenu asks whether the transition from Scripture to theology does not frequently result in a real impoverishment.[35] Father de Lubac notes that the majority of theologians are content to treat revelation with a quick, superficial view, frequently reducing it to a series of detached propositions.[36] A good number of authors (such as H. Rondet, G. Thils, H. Delesty, J. Bonsirven, P. Benoit) remark that there are many precious indications in Scripture which are too often forgotten. Father V. White, following Father Gardeil[37] thinks that traditional theology frequently deprives revelation of its temporal aspect and its view towards Incarnation: it is not sufficiently concerned with its historical character, nor with the psychological way in which it is accomplished.[38] Fathers de Lubac, Danielou, Fessard, Bouillard, Von Balthasar, take a stand against a certain intellectualism which tends to make Christian revelation a communication of a system of ideas rather than the manifestation of a Person who is Truth in Person.[39] "Revelation," says R. Aubert, "has too frequently been conceived as a communication by God of a certain number of disconcerting statements which men must hold for true in order to understand them. Actually, revelation is presented by Scripture in a much less notional and much more personal manner: it is primarily the manifestation of God Himself who, through a sacred history, culminating in the death and resurrection of Christ, gives a brief glimpse of the mystery of His love".[40] G. Thils blames this inadequate presentation of so many Catholic manuals for the imprecise idea which Protestants have of the Catholic notion of revelation, quite wrongly opposing a revelation as "knowledge of supernatural truths" to a revelation "of salvific events," the gift of God Himself, presenting Himself to man in time. Actually, he says, for Catholics, revelation is also the revelation of the real mystery which is God Himself, but it obviously includes a doctrinal revelation.[41] The representatives of kerygmatic theology (primarily J. Jungmann and H. Rahner) stress, in their turn, the inadequacy of the traditional presentation of the idea of revelation and feel the need for substituting a realist-historical conception, closer to the biblical mentality. Only revelation, says Guardini, can tell us what revelation is, and it would be pointless to attempt to sum up in one short formula all the wealth of content of the biblical reality.[42] In a word, the complaints of theologians can be grouped about the two following points: *negatively*, fear of reducing Christianity to an exaggerated intellectualism; *positively*, the desire for a greater fidelity to the sources of Scripture and tradition.

2. Protestant Theology

Protestant theological production, by its very abundance and quality, has acted as a stimulus for Catholic thinking. The majority

of contemporary Protestant theologians devote not only important
chapters, but even entire works to the theme of revelation. It is enough
to mention, among the more recent names, those of K. Barth, R.
Bultmann, E. Brunner, H. W. Robinson, W. Temple, E. F. Scott, G.
E. Wright, H. H. Schrey, J. Wolff, H. Huber, H. Schulte, J. de Saussure, P. Tillich, H. R. Niebuhr, L. S. Thornton, A. Neher, A. Oepke,
O. Procksch, G. Kittel, J. Baillie, H. D. McDonald, James G. S. S.
Thomson, W. J. Martin, P. K. Jewett, etc. Revelation is the central
point of theology in Bultmann. "Bultmann," writes Father Malevez,
"offers us a theology of revelation. Valid or not, at least it has the
merit of leading the Christian's attention to the very heart of a central
problem, the theme of revelation and the word of God, and its place
in history . . . . It invites us to give new depth to the Christian theology
of revelation".[43] The same must be said about K. Barth and E.
Brunner.

One might say, that, taken as a whole, present-day Protestant
thinking resists the idea of a revelation conceived as a manifestation
and making known of truths about God or truths spoken by God. It
sees primarily in revelation the personal manifestation of the living
God who makes Himself actively present to man in order to save
him and enter into communion of life with him. P. Althaus reproaches
Catholic theology for having depersonalized revelation. Revelation is
not, he says, a communication of truths, a teaching, but the personal
meeting of God with man, "not a sum total of *credenda* (things to
be believed), but a *credendus* (a person to be believed)".[44] "Revelation,"
stresses Oepke, "is not the communication of a supernatural knowledge
. . . , but properly speaking the activity of Yahweh, an unveiling of his
essential ministry, His offering of Himself in friendship".[45] It is the
activity of God who comes out of His mystery and addresses man.
For Bultmann, revelation is actually reduced to being no more than
an activity, a speaking, to the practical exclusion of every message.[46]
What is important, for Bultmann, is not the message of the Word, its
intelligible content, but the *very fact* that it echoes throughout time
like a call to final decision; it is the *very event* of the Word and the
event of faith that it stirs up.[47]

Protestant biblical theology lays great stress on the event-and-
history character of revelation. Revelation is an event and bound up
with events, that is, with the salvific acts of God. Not only is it
intruded into the woof of human history, but it is history itself. The
God who speaks, says G. E. Wright, is above all the God who acts.[48]
Finally, all insist on the salvific and existential character of revelation:
meeting between God and man, in the bosom of a choice which

commits the whole of human existence and stirs up a new understanding of the human condition.

Activity, event, encounter: these are the aspects that present-day Protestant theology puts in the foreground of revelation. The doctrinal aspect is carefully played down.[49]

3. Biblical and Patristic Renewal

Interest for the theology of revelation, in our Catholic world, is due to many different factors, quite unequal in importance. Whereas the currents of thinking in the twentieth century (existentialism, personalism) unroll like a constant background, and Protestant activity acts as a restless ferment, as a stimulus for Catholic reflection, other factors exercise a more direct and definite activity.

The first and most important of these factors is the biblical and patristic renewal. The attention centered on revealed data cannot go far without attention on the God who reveals; biblical research has had a corollary in the primacy of the word and the activity of revelation.

Semantic investigation, more exhaustive than ever, gives us a better understanding of the notion of revelation and lets us draw up a whole body of texts which exhibit the themes and structures of revelation. Such study as was attempted by H. Schulte,[50] or such as can be pursued on the basis of the biblical dictionaries, affords an approach which gets much closer to reality. The articles in *Theologisches Wörterbuch* on hearing, knowing, evangelizing, preaching, revealing, speaking, teaching, witnessing;[51] those in the *Supplément* to the *Dictionnaire de la Bible* on word, mystery, oracle;[52] also those in the *Lexikon für Theologie und Kirche* and the *Dictionnaire de spiritualité*,[53] frequently, in their breadth and wealth of information, are veritable monographs. Outside of those dictionaries, there are numerous works on these fundamental themes, all of them necessary to an understanding of revelation: for example the studies of J. Dupont on *gnosis*;[54] of D. Deden, K. Prümm, R. E. Brown, C. Spicq, J. Coppens, on the pauline *mystery*,[55] of E. Pax on *epiphaneia*,[56] of B. Trépanier, I. de la Potterie, N. Brox, on *witness* and *testimony*;[57] of H. Schlier J. Giblet, J. Dupont, C. Larcher, on *word of God*;[58] of I. de la Potterie on *truth*;[59] of T. Crisan on *glory*.[60] In this inventory of scriptural data, there is certainly much more to be done. "Important concepts," remarks Schnackenburg, "... are still waiting for a Catholic study which will take into account the most recent results of research ... ; this is the case for such themes as conversion, peace, hope, ... and even word of God or Holy Spirit".[61] The biblical theologies, however, are already gathering the results of these partial studies and preparing a synthesis; this will always be difficult work, for revelation is a primary category of Christianity, present throughout Scripture and manifold in its expression.[62]

The points that exegesis and biblical theology appear to insist on most are the following: A. the progressive education of Israel: revelation is a slow progression from darkness to light (the idea of God, covenant, Messiah, Kingdom, salvation, grace, etc.) which must be understood with proper attention to each term and not in the sense of a false and premature effort at concordance; B. the historical character of revelation: God makes Himself known only in history and through history by means of His activity of salvation; C. the infinite diversity of the modes of revelation and the modes of expression or literary genres; D. the unity and continuity of the divine plan, however allowing for tentative experiment and even setbacks; E. the essentially interpersonal and dynamic character of the divine word.

Even though patristic research on the theme of revelation is not progressing with the same speed, the theology of revelation is already beginning to benefit from the general renewal of patristic studies. Among the monographs which treat revelation directly, we must point out the work of Marguerite Harl on Origen,[63] the study of J. Ford on Saint Irenaeus,[64] the work of E. Molland on the theme of the Gospel in the school of Alexandria.[65] To these studies must be joined the great number of others which devote one or several chapters to the theme of revelation.[66] The authors of these researches on the fathers of the Church are taken up principally with defining the role of Christ as Revealer of the Father in an economy of Incarnation, putting prophet and apostle into their proper relationship with Christ, and thus determining the points of comparison and distinction between apostle and prophet. The themes of the unity of the two Testaments, the progress of revelation, divine pedagogy, the historical and salvific character of revelation, are everywhere in evidence.

4. Reflections on Theology

Between the years 1936-1939, there is much discussion among theologians on the nature and method of theology. The source of this debate is to be found in two conferences by R. Draguet[67] which served as inspiration for L. Charlier in his *Essai sur le problème théologique* (Essay on the Problem of Theology).[68] At the same time, Father Chenu published a work in which he explained how the problem of the theological research was conceived of at Le Saulchoir.[69] Finally, in the *Ephemerides* of Louvain, J. Bonnefoy published a series of articles on theology as a science.[70] These publications, especially those of Chenu, Draguet, and Charlier, set loose a chain reaction. Y. M. Congar,[71] M. R. Gagnebet,[72] W. Goossens,[73] C. Boyer,[74] T. Zapelena,[75] and many others entered the debate in their turn. It is not our intention here to reopen this debate, but merely to report what was said on the subject of revelation. Revelation is the object of faith, and since it is also the object to which the understanding of theology is applied, we cannot speak of one without speaking of the other. It is thus, primarily, that Fathers M. D. Chenu and L. Charlier were led to explain what must be understood by revelation and revealed truth.

The Catholic world is well aware of Father Chenu's laments regarding a certain type of theology, exaggerated in its intellectualist and conceptualist approach,[76] more interested in the conclusions to be drawn from revealed truth than in the reality of the mystery itself, too little attentive to the role of faith on the work of theology,[77] thus giving rise to a sort of practical divorce between theology and spiritual life.[78] In a vigorous reaction against this type of theology, Father Chenu set out to re-establish the realist, historical, and religious character of revelation and faith.

With theology as the point of departure, there is faith in revelation, which is the testimony of God on Himself, but this "testimony here is only the vehicle of a real knowledge, giving us, even in mystery, as object of our perception and love, a *reality*, divine reality".[79] The object of this divine testimony, "delivered in a confidence that calls for trust",[80] is God Himself, "He in whom I now recognize the whole of my life, the perfect object of my happiness".[81] We can thus distinguish two "faces" in the object of faith: on the one hand, concepts, propositions, through which the divine testimony is expressed; on the other hand, the very reality expressed in the propositions. Faith, no doubt, is an assent to the propositions which express this mystery, but, what it aims at through this process is the very reality of the mystery, that is, the God of vision and beatitude.[82] Faith is "the realist perception of God in a conceptual proposition".[83]

Father Chenu also stresses, as a reaction against abstract intellectualism, indifferent with respect to history, that the revealed truth comes to us under the form of history, and not under the form of abstract ideas. What theological understanding needs to grasp is an *economy* whose realization is bound up with time; a series of initiatives of free love on the part of God who directs history according to His own good pleasure.[84] The data of theological science is not "an *inventum philosophicum* (D 1800) to be treated unceremoniously as a set of metaphysical or physical principles, from which clear conclusions can be logically deduced. These are the works of God, the God of Abraham, Isaac, and Jacob, not of Pure Act; and his central work, the Incarnation of his Son, is not intruded into any cosmic order where we can make out so much as a shadow of determining reason".[85] Theology must remain centered in the history of salvation, on the "unforeseeable histories of the gratuitous love of God".[86] Theology is thus *realist*, in second place, because it is the understanding of an order of salvation in its historical realization.[87]

A faithful description of revelation must stress one more element. The object of faith (propositions and reality) is formally attained only by a light which is proportioned to it: the light of faith. This inner light is the word of God in men: "a personal grace, putting me into conversation and direct intercourse with Him, mysterious presence, to whom the new man has access, not because his reason leads him there, but because God reveals Himself, *sibi ipsi testis*. He who believes in the Son of God has the testimony of God in him (1 Jo. 5:10)".[88] Without this light, there can be no true communion with the divine thinking. The knowledge of faith is an obscure, imperfect, and far from obvious possession of its object, but at the same time it is a perception of the reality expressed by the proposition which is "savory",[89] "religious",[90] "contemplative",[91] "mystic",[92] "a vital knowledge, a harbinger of further penetration until vision".[93]

Thus, in the face of a theology which he considers unfaithful to its object, too intellectual and not religious enough, not "theological" enough, Father Chenu stresses the realist, historic, and mystic aspect of revelation. The testimony of God is expressed through concepts and propositions which are its vehicle, but, in the last analysis, what is communicated to man is the reality of the mystery. Father Chenu does not deny the conceptual and propositional aspect of revelation, but he is opposed to a unilateral consideration of this aspect, to the detriment of the reality of revelation, and primarily to the detriment of the inner word, the inner testimony, the inner illumination which accompanies the external teaching and lets it be appropriated. In revelation and in faith, we can insist on the message heard and accepted, on the *fides ex auditu*, or rather on the reality of the mystery and on the inner testimony, the inner light. Father Chenu is well aware of the fact that our encounter with God will normally take place by our adherence to the message of salvation, the Gospel, under the activity of His grace which invites and elevates us; but he reacts against a certain form of intellectualism which would see in revelation only a series of propositions about God. That is why he insists on the realist aspect of revelation and on the inner word which precedes and sustains adherence to the external testimony.[94]

The exposition of Father Charlier in his *Essai sur le problème théologique*,[95] in addition to views similar to those of Father Chenu, contains some new and quite different considerations. It is in the fourth chapter of the first part of his work[96] that he expresses the conception of revelation which is peculiar to him. Like Father Chenu, Father Charlier notes, first of all, that there is too much insistence on the conceptual side of revelation and not enough insistence on the real side: "Revealed truth is above all a given reality".[97] And divine faith "is not simple adherence to any divine external testimony," adherence to God Himself in His mystery, to God who reveals Himself to us in His light. "Faith presupposes that through the concept and the formula, we touch upon the *res*, here the divine reality itself".[98] "What is first in revelation is . . . , in the concrete, God in Person telling Himself to us, revealing Himself to our soul in His own light . . . ; transcendent testimony, truth testifying to herself through the direct contact she establishes between herself and us. No matter what mystery truth is surrounded by in the face of our human intelligence, the reality, in order simply to be revealed, envelops us with its presence".[99] Father Charlier sees, as the foreground of revelation, not the communication of a *message* concerning God and our salvation, but rather the *revealed reality itself*, that is, God Himself in Person giving Himself and showing Himself to the faithful in His own light. But, in the Christian economy, the gift of God consists in the mystery of the whole Christ, that is, Christ and the Church, and therefore the revealed-datum-as-reality is the whole Christ, and with Christ, the entire Trinity.[100] Thus when Christ is given to us and the Church is founded, all the revealed-datum-as-reality is acquired in its fullness, as also the external revelation which brings it to our knowledge.[101] This revealed datum is present in the Church, and in the Church it develops "in proportion as the Church assimilates it into herself and lets it grow in her".[102]

After having stressed the revealed-datum-as-reality and its complexity, Father Charlier makes it the basis of his theory for dogmatic development. In its nascent stage, the revealed reality is given at the same time it is officially notified in the first place. All further development stems organically from this beginning. Growth takes place on the level of *reality* as well as on the level of *knowledge*: "In the concrete, there is a growth of the Church and, in the Church, a growth of the whole mystery of God: the whole divine reality grows in so far as it is given and lived, in so far as there is a growth of Christ in His Church, to the measure in which the Church identifies herself with Him . . . . This development of the revealed-datum-as-reality in the Church, is followed, by way of consequence, by the development of the revealed-datum-as-knowledge".[103] The magisterium defines "in precise and rigorous but always analogous terms, and under the seal of infallibility, the exact bearing of this inner growth of the revealed datum".[104]

Father Charlier also insists on the *historical* character that revelation presents. It "is not a system of abstract ideas," but the "narration of divine realizations stemming from a grandiose plan which has God for its center and man for the beneficiary".[105] History also affects the progress of dogma: "the progress of revealed truth is not (far from it) only the fruit of the abstract study of a doctrine; it is first and primarily the progress of the whole divine reality included in the mystery of the Church, giving rise, by way of consequence, to a progress in the profound knowledge of the faith and the decisive interventions of the magisterium".[106]

Thus, for Father Charlier, revelation is first of all the communication of the divine reality itself: a mysterious presence offered to the experience of faith. Revelation-as-doctrine (message of salvation communicated to humanity) clearly falls into the background. For him once again, the revealed-datum-as-reality (God Himself in the mystery of Christ and the Church) is in a perpetual labor of growth. It is the whole mystery which grows and, as a consequence, the knowledge we have of it. Such a conception of revelation, apart from being in contradiction with the data of Scripture and the pronouncements of the Church magisterium which represent the object of faith as a message, that is, the good news of salvation, compromises the true notion of dogmatic progress. This progress, actually, is not to be conceived, acording to Father Charlier, as a deeper and deeper, more and more explicit knowledge of a deposit of faith, historically and objectively constituted (it being understood of course that the Church, in this work, thanks to the positive assistance of the Holy Spirit, enjoys a power of penetration which transcends that of reason left to itself), but as an assimilation of the divine reality itself, possessed mystically, by a supraconceptual contact, in the experience of faith: the formulas of the magisterium come in to express, in an analogical and provisional way, the steps or "moments" of this *growth* and this experimental *grasp* of revelation-reality. On the other hand, if the revealed datum itself is always in a state of growth, it is hard to see how it is possible to hold, excepting in words, that revelation is closed with the apostolic age.

These essays of Fathers Chenu and Charlier on the status of theology, despite certain excesses in Father Charlier, contain precious elements that certainly have their place in a theology of revelation. These elements concern: A. the *realist* character, not merely the conceptual and propositional character of revelation; B. the *historical* character of revelation as opposed to a revelation of an abstract and purely philosophical type; C. the *supernatural* character of revelation, which is not only a divine message addressed externally, but also the inner testimony of the uncreated Word; D. the *interpersonal* and *vital* character of revelation: God's confidence of love, inviting man to a return of trust and love, in view of a community of life and happiness; E. the *free* and *gratuitous* character of revelation: the initiative comes from Love.

5. Kerygmatic Theology

In this same era, that is, around the years 1936 to 1940, another current of thinking, this time springing up in Austria and Germany, the current of kerygmatic theology, made powerful contribution to revitalizing the theology of revelation which had lost much of its brilliance.[107]

The context in which kerygmatic theology appeared is well known. Moved by the laments of pastors of souls who deplored the ignorance and mediocrity of Christian living in the souls committed to their care, a certain number of theologians (J. A. Jungmann, F. Lackner, H. Rahner, J. B. Lotz, F. Dander) thought they might discover the reason for this state of things in the inadequate presentation of Christianity and, more profoundly, in the inadequate teaching of theology. Preaching, they point out, is frequently no more than a diluted form of theological instruction, with its proper terminology, arguments, and objections. At school, catechism resembles nothing so much as a digest of the treatises of theology.[108] Theology itself, too much taken up with demonstrations and refutations, comes very close to forgetting that it is a science of salvation and that each of its Christian dogmas is supposed to echo in personal religious living. There is too much distance between the theology of the seminary course and pastoral activity.[109] Faced with this problem, Jungmann suggests a precise distinction between the proclamation of the Christian message and scientific theology, and he hoped that preaching would be inspired more by the presentation of Scripture and the Fathers, that it would be grounded, consequently, on Christ and the history of salvation.[110]

F. Lackner and J. B. Lotz[111] claimed that the needs of the apostolate demanded more: they proposed to draw up, side by side with the traditional theology, a so-called kerygmatic theology. The first (the theology of the universities) scientific, systematic, theocentric, preoccupied primarily with research; second (theology of the seminaries), organized with a view towards preaching and, consequently, historical, Christocentric, attentive to the progress and economy of revelation, concerned with psychology and pedagogy in the presentation of the Christian message, in the example of Christ Himself and the Fathers of the Church in their homilies. Whereas the theology of the universities envisages revealed truth under the aspect of *true*, kerygmatic theology looks upon it under the aspect of *good, value*. Whereas the first expresses itself in technical language, in conformity with the demands of science, the second needs a simple, suggestive expression, rich in images; it means to be a theology of the heart, a profound and moving presentation of the fundamental themes of revelation. H. Rahner and F. Dander have drawn up preliminary samples of such a theology.[112]

Quick to meet opposition (primarily from M. Schmaus, A. Stolz, C. Fabro, H. Weisweiler), the idea of a double theology was finally rejected, and rightly. As Schmaus pointed out, if a theology wants to be simply faithful to its object, that is, to the word of salvation of God the Savior, it must make this value of salvation stand out in every mystery, and demonstrate its aptitude to give life to Christian existence. Failing this, it is no more than a sterile metaphysics. On the other hand, a theology which would renounce the rigor of demonstration and systematisation, would no longer be a science.[113] That theology should be more attentive to the economy of revelation, more Christocentric, more pastoral in its slant, more conscious of its social function in the Church—theologians as a whole were glad to admit this. But, while still admitting that the state of things as described by the kerygmatic advocates demanded urgent attention, the majority of theologians thought it would be superfluous to draw up a special theology in place of the classic theology: the task should be assumed by scientific theology itself.[114]

Actually, the argument had changed grounds. "The primary question," as Jungmann so opportunely pointed out, "is not that of a theology of preaching which would be independent of the scientific theology, but rather the rule proper to preaching in connection with theology".[115] F. X. Arnold pointed out on his side: "It is not the *kerygmatic theology* but the *kerygma* which claims a character of its own. It is proper to the kerygma, to preaching, to be aware that it must above all else conceive, organize, concentrate the Christian message in a properly kerygmatic manner, but also using a method and language which are its own".[116] Preaching, catechesis, and theology all work on revealed truth, but on different levels, but with different goals, and, consequently, in accordance with different laws. Thus there is room, side by side with theology, for a science of preaching under its different forms: evangelization, catechesis, homily.[117] The most concrete result of this controversy was the creation of a "pastoral year" in the preparation of clerics, and the more precise determinations of the status of homiletics and catechetics.[118]

Kerygmatic theology, without presenting a new concept of revelation, has still cast light on a certain number of aspects which have contributed to the renewal of the theology of revelation:

1. The *historical* character of revelation. The essential content of revelation, as the kerygmatic school stresses, is the Gospel, that is, the good news of salvation. The object of this good news is not primarily a system of propositions, speculative and practical, but Christ in His life and in His work of salvation. The apostles testify to the whole work of salvation announced and begun in the Old Testament, then accomplished and completed by the death and resurrection of Christ. Kerygmatic theology does not deny the doctrinal character of revelation, but it is opposed to a too abstract, too conceptual presentation of the revealed truth, which tends to conceal the fact that revelation is given to us under the form of history: *history of salvation.* It casts light on the realist-historical character of revelation.[119]

2. The character of *economy* in revelation. Christianity is based on events, not isolated, but organically bound together, according to the harmonious unity of the divine plan. Revelation is presented as an economy: it has been dispensed to humanity according to an order, which is that of the wisdom of God. It is important then to have in the foreground of revelation those truths which God Himself, in revealing, has put in the foreground: the unheard-of fact of His word, history as a pedagogy preparing the way for Christ, Incarnation, Christ's death and resurrection, the gift of the Spirit, the leading of all humanity towards God through the Church and in the Church.[210]

3. The Christocentric character of revelation. Revelation in its entirety is focused on Christ. The Old Testament is the announcing and preparation for Christ: a prophecy and a pedagogy of Christ.

The center and object of the Gospel, in the New Testament, is Christ. In the order of revelation and in the accomplishment of salvation, Christ has everywhere the primacy. Thus kerygmatic theology is closely connected with the revelation of the Person of Christ.[121]

4. The *salvific* character of revelation. The idea which dominates and directs the whole progress of revelation, from beginning to end, and which gives it its basic unity, is the salvation announced and finally given in Christ and through Christ. Revelation is the revelation of a God who saves through Christ. The Gospel is a message of salvation: it tells us of the salvation put within our grasp by Christ and the Church. Revelation is taken up with the whole of existence.[122]

5. The *interpersonal* character of revelation. Revelation is the word of the living and personal God addressing Himself to man in order to invite him to faith and obedience. Further, it is an initiation into the personal mysteries of God. It proceeds from His absolutely free and infinite love.[123]

Kerygmatic theology is thus aware of the progress, the pedagogy, and the economy of revelation. It is attentive to its historical character, as a sequence of meaningful events. It is careful to stress the place of Christ as Author, Center, and Object of revelation. It stresses the interpersonal and salvific character of the word of God.

6. *The Theological Problem of Preaching*

The theological problem of preaching and that of kerygmatic theology, though they both rise from the same historical situation, are still two quite different problems. There is no question here of contrasting two theologies (the one kerygmatic and the other scientific), but determining, in the light of revelation, the *sense* of the ministry of preaching in the Church: nature, necessity, efficacy. This dogmatic reflection on preaching is a rather recent phenomenon: beginning around 1936, it is only now on its way to full development. The long controversy set off by Jungmann has not obscured the essential truth of his claims, mainly, that we are faced with a crisis in the field of preaching and that it can be surmounted only by theological reflection on the content and function of teaching.[124]

This urgency has been keenly felt throughout France and Germany, where the awareness has been accelerated by the sad conditions of parish ministry: the mediocre yield of preaching in Germany and de-Christianisation in France. Theological reflection, already promoted by recent philosophical currents (philosophy of values, phenomenology of encounter) and stimulated by Protestant theology which is particularly active in this field, has furthermore benefited from the results of the liturgical renewal, which has stressed the cultual value of preaching,[125] as well as from the rapid progress of the biblical and liturgical sciences. All of a sudden, theology finds herself in possession of a great number of indications which could serve to draw up a treatise on preaching as well as one on the sacraments. The study of sources has given fresh understanding of the great importance of preaching in Christian living: an importance comparable to that of prayer and the sacraments.[126] The time of the Church is the time of the word;[127] thus it is only proper to give the prophetic mission of the Church the same attention as its priestly mission and its power of jurisdiction.

The actual preaching of the Church being the prolongation of the apostolic preaching, it is to this first preaching we must look to discover the meaning of preaching. The study of the Acts is the favorite source for theological reflection on the subject of preaching.[128] The primitive kerygma, notes Father Grasso, such as it appears in the Book of the Acts, must be the norm which defines our present-day preaching; the Gospels themselves are only the development of the primitive kerygma, and the whole preaching of the Church does no more than apply the essential data of the kerygma to the following generations. In the primitive kerygma, the essence of preaching is manifest in its pure state, in its essential preoccupation with announcing the salvific plan of God, accomplished in Christ and through Christ.[129] "Preaching," notes Father Liégé, "must reproduce as closely as possible the very forms in which God revealed Himself".[130]

On the basis of this rapprochement between our present preaching and the apostolic preaching it is obvious that preaching must have the following characteristics: A. It must be *historical-biblical*, that is to say, focused on the history of salvation and on Scripture which contains this history; for the primitive kerygma is not presented as a higher metaphysics which has an answer for the questions of human intelligence, but rather as a sacred history. Preaching, being the announcing of the salvation historically effected through Christ, must respect the organic structure of this history. B. It must be *Christocentric*, like the plan of salvation itself. Preaching must follow a concentric rather than a linear order, each mystery leading back to Christ or proceeding from Him. C. It must be *paschal*, for in the complex of Christ's mysteries, the most important is that of the resurrection. It is, properly speaking, the resurrection which makes the Gospel a good news. D. It must be *ecclesial*, not only because the ministry of preaching has been entrusted to the Church, but also because the history of salvation continues in the Church which works to build up the body of Christ. E. It must be *liturgical*, for the salvation which the kerygma announces and which the catechesis details, is accomplished in the liturgy, in the sacraments, especially in Baptism and Eucharist. It is in the Mass above all that preaching fully lives up to its definition of sacred, living, active word: the whole first part of the Mass is a liturgy of the word, the Church's solemn proclamation of the message of salvation.[131] F. It must be *eschatological*, that is to say, it must present the word as the living word of God which calls men to a decisive choice, bound up with the final destiny of man. G. Finally, it must be a *testimony*, that is, it must show, in the life of the preacher, the Gospel's aptitude to transform human existence.[132]

Three problems in particular catch the attention of the theologians who are concerned with preaching. The *first* is that of the respective causalities of God and the preacher. The majority claim that God is the principal cause of preaching, whereas the preacher is the instrumental cause, the preaching establishing a dialogue between God and man through the instrumentality of the Church.[133] The *second* problem concerns the forms of preaching. Some, like Father Liégé, are in favor of a bipartite division, mainly, kerygma and catechesis;[134] others, like Father Grasso, are in favor of a tripartite division, that is, kerygma or missionary preaching, catechesis or Christian initiation, homily or liturgical preaching in the Christian assembly.[135] The *third* problem, still much under discussion, is the problem of the efficacy of Church preaching, which is a prolongation of the apostolic preaching.[136] For some, preaching is the *occasion* for the infusion of grace, just like the infusion of the soul is infallibly united with the procreation of the human body.[137] For others, preaching, like the sacramentals, produces grace *ex opere operantis*.[138] Others think that it acts *ex opere operato*, but in the order of actual graces.[139] A certain number, finally, speak openly of the sacramentality of preaching, while still obviously maintaining the difference between sacraments and preaching.[140] E. Schillebeeckx points out that, the word of the Church being the word of Christ, in its ecclesial expression, just as the sacraments are the ecclesial form of the salvific acts of Christ, this is intrinsically efficacious: "Grace is not given *on the occasion* of this ministry, but *through* this very ministry".[141] In the word of the Church, Christ is present and active according to the fashion of the word which *invites to faith*, and consequently according to a mode which is "quite different from the efficacy of the ritual sacrament which *presupposes* this faith, although on both sides ... there is the same sacramental structure".[142] The invitation to faith, because it is incarnate in the ecclesial word, does not lose its efficacy. The word of preaching is thus bound up with the sacramental structure of the Church.

It appears then that preaching, in an effort at definition, must find new depth in the theme of word of God. If preaching actually is the transmission of the word of God, it would be impossible to reflect on preaching without having reference to this first promulgation of the plan of salvation which was revelation. The elaboration of a theology of preaching has thus, predictably enough, brought about a renewal of the theology of revelation. The preoccupations of this theology, in its essential elements, are equivalent to those of kerygmatic theology. It insists on the historical, Christocentric, salvific, and dynamic character of revelation. The efficacy of God's word is a primary object of attention.

7. Development of Dogma

In its turn, the problem of the development of dogma has led theologians to inquire into the notion of revelation. In the understanding and elaboration of a theory of this deepening of the object of faith which the Church describes as a passage from explicit to implicit, from obscure to clear, the task is made more or less easy depending upon the fundamental idea of revelation. This aspect of the problem has not escaped the notice of Catholic scholars. Father Hugueny already notes that, to understand the laws and character of dogmatic development, it is essential "to have an exact idea of the fact of revelation which gave the world a supernatural truth whose passing down preserves and fecundates its treasure".[143] Father de Lubac also stresses the urgency of new depth in the notion of revelation.[144] As a matter of fact, the majority of authors who treat dogma and its development (C. Dillenschneider, C. Journet, H. Delesty, E. Dhanis, C. Pozo, G. Thils, C. Boyer, H. de Lubac, L. Charlier, F. Marin-Sola, H. Simonin, R. Draguet, F. Taymans, J. Lebreton, L. De Grandmaison, A. Gardeil, etc.) also speak of revelation, but sometimes in different terms.

This, for example, is how Father de Lubac expresses himself.[145] On this question of dogmatic development, he points out, the core of the problem is to be found in a proper idea of revelation which is the point of departure for this development. Now "the content of revelation, taking revelation under its first form and its subsistent integrity, is neither exactly nor sufficiently described as a series of statements".[146] It "would not be legitimate to believe that revelation has been made without an intrinsic bond joining it to the one total reality of Christ, that has been committed to us like a simple formula, in a series of propositions which are detached from this unique mystery and thus separated from each other, like ready-made majors for our future syllogisms".[147] "The case of revealed Truth is unique".[148]

After these very fitting remarks, Father de Lubac explains how he conceives of revelation. What is primary in the Christian economy, he says, "is the activity of redemption; it is the gift God makes of Himself in His Son; it is the final and definitive realization of this great plan hidden in Himself from the origin of the world and now revealed",[149] namely, the call of all men to eternal life through Christ and in Christ. What is equally primary, at the same time as this activity of redemption, is the revelation of redemption, that is, the manifestation of this activity, in its *reality*, and with its *meaning* of gift of salvation realizing a plan of salvation. In Jesus Christ, revealed reality and activity of revelation, gift and revelation of the gift coincide. Christ is at once mystery and revelation of mystery, the whole of revelation and the whole of dogma.[150] We can introduce divisons into this whole and distinguish "particular truths and detached propositions, concerning respectively the Trinity, the Incarnate Word, baptism, grace, etc.... This is a legitimate and necessary abstraction..., but only on condition that one is always aware of its being an abstraction and never under-evaluates the concrete Whole whose content it can never exhaust".[151] Father de Lubac goes on to a more precise statement, based on a text from Father Lebreton, saying that at the beginning, adherence to Christ must be presented as a "very concrete and very living perception," and that a number of dogmas at first remained "latent in the wealth of this first perception".[152] "In Jesus Christ, everything has been given and revealed to us all at once...; consequently, all the explanations to come, whatever their tenor and their mode, will be nothing more than the recoining in fractional currency of a treasure already possessed in its entirety;... everything was really, actually contained, in a higher state of knowledge, and not only in principles and premises".[153] Father de Lubac presents these ideas, not as a theory for a definitive solution, but rather as suggestions which might cast light on the difficult problem of dogmatic development.

If we understand him correctly, Father de Lubac puts the very reality of the mystery of Christ in the foreground of revelation. This concrete Whole, in faith, is the object of a total, overall, intuitive, living grasp: a superior state of knowledge, it contains in advance "really, actually" all of dogma with all the richness of its later development. The necessary conceptual expression, with its notions and propositions, would be a sort of second stage to revelation, compared with this first perception. Dogmatic development, therefore is to be conceived, not as an "infinite construction of conclusion on the basis of first premises",[154] but rather as the passage from the phase of intuition to that of conceptualisation: the first perception still global, but growing more detailed in particular truths and more and more precise formulas, always with reference to the normative truth of the mystery itself,[155] arrived at according to a higher mode of knowledge. It is possible to extend this role of dogmatic development to great lengths.[156]

It is true that the whole of revelation, in the terminology of Saint Paul primarily, is the *mystery*, that is, the whole plan of salvation as conceived and willed by God; concretely, in the order of execution of this design, it is Christ. But the mystery, in so far as *revealed*, that is, brought to the knowledge of men, Saint Paul calls Gospel, that is, good news, message of salvation (Rom. 16:25; Col. 1:25-26; Eph. 1:25-26; Eph. 1:9-13; 3:5-6) or once more *word* (Col. 1:25-26; 1 Thess. 1:6). Access to this mystery is effected by accepting the word (Rom. 10:16; 1 Cor. 15:11; Eph. 1:13) and by obedience to the Gospel (Rom. 1:5; 16:26), under the illuminating activity of grace (2 Cor. 4:5-6). Christ, or the mystery, is the object of faith, but in so far as He is presented to the awareness of the faithful through the apostolic testimony and preaching of the Church. The mystery (reality) is certainly first in the ontological order, but in the order of knowledge, which is that of revelation, the apostolic testimony is first. It is the Gospel (concerning Christ and His mystery) which is preached and which is believed (Rom. 10:14-17). By faith, we adhere to the testimony and, through the testimony, to the *reality* which it portrays.

It seems important to make a clear distinction between the condition of the apostles and that of the Church. The condition of the apostles is unique and privileged. Only they saw and heard Christ, before and after His resurrection, and only they received the mission to testify to the reality of the facts and the meaning of those facts, whose sense and bearing had been patiently explained by Christ, then understood in the light of the Holy Spirit. Christian revelation necessarily implies two things: on the one hand, the reality of the preaching and the salvation accomplished through Christ; on the other hand, the testimony rendered to Christ by the apostles. We have access to the reality of Christ only through the apostolic testimony (1 Jn. 1:1-3). We know no other Christ than Him who was preached and witnessed to by the apostles. We have communion in their experience of the Word of life only through testimony and through faith in this testimony. Our knowledge of Christ is thus *mediated* and *normalized* by the deposition of these privileged witnesses. In this testimony, certainly, not everything has the same clarity, nor the same precision, nor the same emphasis. There is, in the deposition of the apostles, in addition to the more explicit teaching, a whole complex of intuitive perceptions, ideas not yet clearly produced in them through their meeting with Christ and still handed down by them to the Church, in what we might call a germ stage, orally or written, or under the form of practices. It still remains true that we have access to Christ in His reality only through the mediation of the signs and judgments bound up in the word of the apostles, and deposited by them in the memory of the Church. This is the apostolic testimony, this deposition of witnesses, considered *concretely*, which makes up the point of departure for dogmatic development; it is the testimony which the Church, thanks to her power of penetration which depends not only on logic and dialectics, but also on the illuminating activity of the Spirit, assimilates, understands better and better, according to all its implications, and expresses in terms that are always clearer and more precise. If these distinctions are not made, there is some danger of ambiguity, from the very outset.

Father de Lubac has indeed seen that dogma must be able to develop beyond the limits of a purely logical and dialectical operation. Basing his thinking upon a vigorous tradition, represented by Newman, Gardeil, Bainvel, De Grandmaison, Lebreton, he clearly demonstrates that we must also take into account a supra-conceptual element, situated beyond the realm of purely logical deduction. But when he comes to treat the theory of this development, his explanation does not, to our way of thinking, entirely do away with the ambiguity of which we have warned.

8. *Theology of Revelation and Faith*

If it is true that the theology of revelation, among Catholics, has been plagued with some tardy development, we must not exaggerate the seriousness of this fault. This theology does exist in the Church, but its presence is not so readily felt in that its various elements are dispersed among a variety of treatises: *De Trinitate, De Verbo Incarnato, De Deo uno, De Ecclesia, De Fide, De Traditione*, without forgetting the *De Revelatione*. There also exists, among Catholics, a certain number of monographs, explicitly treating the subject of revelation, primarily those of H. Niebecker,[157] R. Guardini,[158] L. M. Dewailly,[159] W. Bulst,[160] Karl Rahner,[161] D.

Barsotti[162] To these essays must be joined the collective works on the general theme of the Word of God.[163]

This theology insists first of all on the specificity of Christian revelation. What is under question here is not any given revelation, the Greek gnosis or the hermetic knowledge of the mystery religions, but a revelation of a type which is absolutely unique, quite beyond the realm of human expectation or deduction. To know what revelation is, we must go to the school of revelation. A theology of revelation must be based on the data of Scripture.[164] And just as Scripture does not possess a technical term for expressing the idea of revelation, but rather makes use of different words, the only access to the reality of revelation is that of phenomenology. This is the way followed by H. Niebecker and W. Bulst. H. Niebecker describes the theophanies with which the patriarchs of the Old Testament were favored, then the prophetic visions whose objectivity and modalities he studies at great length.[165] Passing on the writings of the New Testament, he tries to separate the distinctive traits of the notion of revelation in the synoptic Gospels, in Saint Paul, in Saint John, in the Acts of the Apostles.[166] W. Bulst and R. Guardini, in their concern with being faithful to Scripture, speak of a triple form of divine manifestation:[167] A. the manifestations of divine activity (*Tatoffenbarung*), which are expressed by creation, by the great salvific acts of the Old Testament and Christ's acts of power which are his miracles; B. the manifestation of God under visible form (*Schauoffenbarung*), such as the theophanies, the angel of Yahweh, the glory of Yahweh, prophetic visions, the Incarnation of the Son; C. the manifestations of God through his word (*Wortoffenbarung*), which is the principal form of divine manifestation, that which gives the manifestations of power and visions their full meaning.[168] It is also through the word of witnesses that revelation as action and revelation as vision escape the limits of space and time and continue to be active. Bulst concludes his phenomenological research by proposing the following definition of revelation: "Supernatural revelation is God who, through His grace and through His personal initiative, in a plan of salvation, opens to man the intimacy of His Person, and this in the framework of history, in an activity which is supernatural and divine in character, in a visible manifestation, but above all—interpreting and summing up this activity and this visible manifestation, in the testimony of His word; an event which, outlined in Israel and definitively realized in Jesus Christ, is presented to us in the word and activity of the Church; still veiled here below, under many aspects (and for this reason received in faith), but ordered towards the immediate vision of God in eternity."[169] In a word, he concludes, revelation is Christ.[170]

Christ is established among us as revelation in person; in Him, everything is given and revealed. Such is the statement taken up and stressed by so many theologians, primarily H. de Lubac, K. Rahner, L. M. Dewailly, J. Mouroux, R. Guardini, H. Niebecker, G. Söhngen, H. U. von Balthasar.[171] They all insist on the necessity of attaching revelation to the Person of Christ. If God, in order to work out revelation, has chosen an economy of Incarnation, then He has taken up all the dimensions of mankind to serve as the expression for the Person of the Son: gestures, actions, conduct, as well as words. Consequently, for the theology of revelation, these theologians call for a greater fidelity to the realism of the Incarnation, a fidelity which is pushed to its ultimate consequences. Still, very few of them are taken up with demonstrating how Christ, concretely, in order to reveal Himself and in order to reveal His Father, has made use of all the ways and all the resources of the Incarnation;[172] there are also very few who study the serious problems posed by the choice of such an economy, particularly the "incarceration" of divine truth in a human proposition; the mystery of Incarnation is here complicated by the problem of natural analogy and revealed analogy.[173]

The theologians of revelation, unanimously, stress the historical character of revelation. God intervenes in human history through a series of events which culminate in the central event of Incarnation. It is at the inner heart of our history that God means to speak to us. These interventions themselves make up a history, the history of salvation, and this history gives all other history its meaning.[174] Finally, not only is history the place of revelation, not only does revelation make history, not only does revelation have its own history, but history, divinely interpreted, is the medium of revelation. Revelation progresses, grows in depth, but always in relation with the events of history. Here again, with regard to the historicisation of revelation as well as the economy of the Incarnation, we must say that theology is frequently content with general statements.[175] What is still needed is to define, in a more precise fashion, the manifold relationships between history and revelation; what is needed is to consider the implications of a revelation so completely incorporated in history, implications which affect both its nature and its progress; what is needed in particular is to examine the difficult and dramatic situation of a revelation which claims to be immutable and which still is steeped in history and must meet the men of all times.

Another characteristic stressed by the theology of revelation, and this time better studied, is the *interpersonal* character of revelation. Revelation is a personal step on the part of the living God, the manifestation of His personal mystery. God enters into a person-to-person relationship with man: the divine *ego* opens a conversation with the human *ego*.[176] Revelation is personalised and personalising.[177] Before revealing something, God reveals Himself in His mystery: God has a Name, He speaks, man can call upon God and God will answer; He makes known His will, His demands, but also His inmost life; He makes a covenant with man and offers him His friendship, His love, His life.[178] In Christ, this living God is in our midst: He speaks, He preaches, He teaches, He testifies. Moses heard the voice of Yahweh; John testifies to what he has seen, heard, and touched of the word of life (1 Jn. 1, 1 ff). Man, on his side, hears the word of God, gives himself to God through faith, or resists God and hardens his heart. Revelation thus takes on the nature of a long and pathetic dialogue between God and creature. The unheard-of element about this dialogue is that one of the parties is the All-powerful, the Thrice Holy; and the other, His creature, the work of His hands. And the tragic element is that the creature can close his heart to the word of infinite Love which is offered to him.[179]

The numerous recent works on the philosophy and psychology of *word*[180] and *testimony*[181] have contributed much to the understanding of revelation as conceived in Scripture in the categories of word and testimony. In the analysis of word, it is not only the interpersonal and conversational aspect which is highlighted, but also the free and gratuitous character of the word; it is a gift when, in its most noble form, it becomes the unveiling of the mystery of awareness. The analogy of the human word, however, must not obscure what is unique about the word of God: the divine *Dabar* is animated by the power of God. The word of God effects what it signifies; it announces and realizes salvation, reconciliation.[182] Supple and subtle, it makes its way deep into the mind and heart of man: at the same time that He stirs us to motion through the testimony of the prophets, Christ, the apostles, the Church, God by His grace, is at work deep within, making the message heard without, soluble in the human soul. This inner activity of grace and the external proposition of the message make up the two dimensions of the one single word of God: a word endowed with unique efficacy, precisely because it is word of God.[183]

Finally we must note the important contribution of the *theology of faith* to the theology of revelation. Revelation and faith are correlative notions; any effort towards a better grasp of one of the components has always involved a more attentive study of the other, as a sort of natural consequence. Of all the theologians of faith, Father Alfaro is beyond doubt the one who has given most study to the bonds that unite faith and revelation. Just as revelation is the first and free step of God towards man, faith is the first and free step of man towards God. Father Alfaro insists on the element of grace involved, the interpersonal, salvific, and supernatural character of revelation. The ultimate reason for the supernaturality of revelation is to be found, he says, in the fact that God, in revealing, bridges the infinite distance between His transcendence and humanity, enters into a relationship of friendship with His creature, initiates him into the mysteries of His own inmost life, particularly the mystery of the Trinity, and inaugurates here below a communication of His divinity which is one day destined to be fulfilled in full vision. Such a step on the part of God is pure gratuity.[184] Father Demann[185] and Father Alfaro[186] show how faith, in the Old and New Testaments, is emphasized in a different fashion, precisely because of this different emphasis in revelation itself.

The return to Scripture and the Fathers of the Church has revitalized the theology of revelation. This theology distinguishes and gives better equilibrium to the presentation of the manifold aspects of revelation: revelation as divine activity, as historical event, and as history, as knowledge and as message, as encounter with the living God. This theology is in tune with progress, with pedagogy and the economy of revelation, with the different and manifold ways through which it is accomplished. It insists on the singular efficacy of God's word and on the intimate communion it inaugurates with the living God. In the revealed truth, it insists on the revealed reality, on the mystery itself, on the Person who reveals Himself, and not only on the signs, concepts, statements, propositions which make it possible for the mind to grasp something of the mystery or the Person. Finally, it is careful to stress the place of Christ as Author, Center, and Object of revelation. Theology is working towards a better integration of all these elements, known or rediscovered.

1. J. LEBRETON, L'encyclique et la théologie moderniste, DAFC, 3: col. 675, 677.

2. "Offenbarung im theol. Sinne ist die Mitteilung religioser Wahrheiten an die Menschen durch Gott, sei es personlich oder durch einen Engel" (H. STRAUBINGER, art. "Offenbarung," Lexikon fur Theologie und Kirche (Freiburg, 1935), 7: col. 682).

3. "Revelatio divina est manifestatio veritatum per Deum creaturae rationali facta, ut haec ad debitum suum finem perveniat" (W. POHL, De vera religione, quaestiones selectae (Freiburg, 1927), p. 269).

4. J. DIDIOT, art. "Révélation divine," DAFC, 4: col. 1005; I. OTTIGER, Theologia fundamentalis (2 vol., Fribourg, 1897), 1: 45.

5. "Revelatio supernaturalis directa est manifestatio Dei per locutionem divinam, i.e. per actum Dei directe et immediate ordinatum ad hoc ut cognitionem propriam homini manifestet" (L. LERCHER, Institutiones theologiae dogmaticae (4 vol., Barcelone, 1945), 1: 11); A. DORSCH, Institutiones theologiae fundamentalis (2 vol., Innsbruck, 1930), 1: 300; G. LAHOUSSE, De vera religione (Louvain, 1897), p. 87; J. V. BAINVEL, De vera religione et apologetica Paris, 1914, p. 152.

6. E. ROLLAND dans M. BRILLANT et M. NEDONCELLE, Apologétique (Paris, 1939), p. 199; J. LEBRETON, "L'encyclique et la théologie moderniste," DAFC, 3: col. 675; H. FELDER, Apologetica seu theologia fundamentalis Paderborn, 1932), p. 28; A. TANQUEREY, Synopsis theologiae dogmaticae fundamentalis (Paris-Tournai-Rome, 1929(22)), pp. 110-111; J. MAUSBACH, Grundzuge der kath. Apologetik (Munster, 1933), p. 9.

7. "Revelatio divina stricte dicta est locutio Dei, qua Deus ex iis quae cognoscit, quaedam cum hominibus communicat, ita ut homines ea propter auctoritatem Dei loquentis credant" (C. PESCH, Compendium theologiae dogmaticae (Fribourg, 1935(5)), 1: 29).

8. Dieckmann, Pesch, Tromp, Gobel, Lercher, Dorsch, Mors, Vizmanos, Nicolau.

9. R. Garrigou-Lagrange, J. Rivière, I. L. Gondal.

10. A. GARDEIL, Le donné révélé et la théologie (Paris, 1909), p. 71.

11. Ibid., 49.

12. Ibid., 53.

13. Ibid., 63-64.

14. Ibid., 54-55.

15. Ibid., 75.

16. Ibid., 66-67.

17. Ibid., 70.

18. R. GARRIGOU-LAGRANGE, De Revelatione per Ecclesiam catholicam proposita (2 vol., Romae, 1950), 1: 130-160. At the same time, we present the thought of J. BRINKTRINE, Offenbarung und Kirche (2 vol., Paderborn, 1947), pp. 33-53.

19. "Actio divina libera et essenealiter supernaturalis qua Deus, ad perducendum humanum genus ad finem supernaturalem qui in visione essentiae divinae consistit, nobis loquens per prophetas et novissime per Christum, sub quadam obscuritate manifestavit mysteria supernaturalia naturalesque veritates, ita ut deinceps infallibiliter proponi possint ab Ecclesia sine ulla significationis mutatione, usque ad finem mundi" (R. GARRIGOU-LAGRANGE, De Revelatione, 1: 132).

20. Ibid., 1: 143 .

21. "Christus determinatum doctrinae corpus omnibus temporibus cunctisque hominibus applicabile non docuit, sed potius inchoavit motum quemdam religiosum diversis temporibus ac locis adaptatum vel adaptandum" (D 2059).

22. De Verit., q. 11,; S. th., 1a, q. 117, a. 1.

23. R. GARRIGOU-LAGRANGE, De Revelatione, pp. 143-153.

24. De Verit., q. 11, a. 1; S. Th., 1a, q. 117, a. 1.

25. S. Th., 2a 2ae, q. 171-178.

26. R. GARRIGOU-LAGRANGE, De Revelatione, 1: 150, 427 ss.

27. Ibid., 1: 135-136.

28. Ibid., 1: 134-135.

29. H. DIECKMANN, De Revelatione christiana (Fribourg, 1930).

30. Ibid., 135-136.

31. Ibid., 138.

32. Ibid., 138-141.

33. J. LEBRETON, "Son Éminence le cardinal Billot," Études, 129 (1911) : 521-522.

34. L. CHARLIER, Essai sur le problème théologique (Thuillies, 1938), p. 66.

35. D. CHENU, "Vocabulaire théologique et vocabulaire biblique," Nouvelle Revue Théologique, 74 (1952): 1029-1041.

36. H. DE LUBAC, "Le problèmee du développement du dogme," Rech. de sc. rel., 35 (1948): 153-155.

37. A GARDEIL, Le donné révélé et la théologie (Paris, 1910), p. 30.

38. V. WHITE, "Le concept de revélation chez S. Thomas d'Aquin," L'année théologique, 11 (1950): 2-6.

39. Dialogue théologique (Saint-Maximin, 1947), p. 90.

40. "La rivelazione è stata troppo spesso concepita come la communicazione da parte di Dio di un certo numero di sconcertanti affermazioni che gli uomini dovrebbero considerare come vere senza comprenderle. In realtà, la rivelazione si presenta nella Bibbia in una maniera molto meno nozionale e molto più personale: essa è sopratutto la manifestazione di Dio stesso, il quale, attraverso una storia sacra, culminante nella morte e risurrezione di Christo, ci fa intravedere il mistero del suo amore" (R. AUBERT, "Questioni attuali intorno all'atto di Fede," dans: Problemi

e Orientamenti di Teologia dommatica (Milano, 1957, 2 vol.), 2: 671). Meme idée dans R. Aubert, *Le Problème de l'acte de foi* (Louvain, 1958(3)), p. 3. Father Bonsirven, on his part, notes that the word revelation, in theology and the documents of the magisterium, always has a very intellectual ring and is used to designate a teaching, communicating well defined notions. The biblical notion is much broader: "Revelation, in its profound essence, appears as the total grace through which the Creator introduces creation into the community of his divinity" (J. Bonsirven, *Théologie du Nouveau Testament* (Paris, 1951), p. 9).

41. G. Thils, "L'évolution du dogme dans la théologie catholique," *Eph. theol. lov.*, 28 (1952): 680.

42. R. Guardini, *Die Offenbarung, ihr Wesen und ihre Formen* (Wurzburg, 1940), pp. 118-119.

43. L. Malevez, *Le message chrétien et le mythe* (Bruxelles-Bruges-Paris, 1954), pp. 115-116.

44. P. Althaus, *Die christliche Wahrheit* (Gutersloh, 1947), 1: 285-286.

45. "Offenbarung ist nicht Mitteilung ubernaturlichen Wissens...sondern recht eigentlich *Handeln Jahwes*, Aufhebung seiner wesenhaften Verborgenheit, Selbstdarbietung zur Gemeinschaft" (A. Oepke, art. *"Apokaluptô,"* in TW 3: 575).

46. R. Bultmann, *Der Begriff der Offenbarung im Neuen Testament* (Tubingen, 1929), pp. 40 ss.

47. R. Marle, "La théologie bultmannienne de la Parole de Dieu," dans: *La Parole de Dieu en Jésus-Christ* (Paris, 1961), pp. 268-280.

48. G. E. Wright, *God who acts* (London, 1952).

49. J. Baillie, *The Idea of Revelation in Recent Thought* (London, 1956), pp. 49-50.

50. H. Schulte *Der Begriff der Offenbarung im Neuen Testament* (Munchen, 1949).

51. G. Kittel, *"Akouo,"* 1: 217-225; R. Bultmann, *"Ginôskô,"* 1: 688-715; G. Friedrich, *"euangelion,"* 2: 714-718, 724-733; G. Friedrich, *"kèrussô,"* 3: 701-717; A. Oepke, *"Apokaluptô,"* 3: 565-597; O. Procksch, *"Legô, Logos"* in l'A.T. 4: 89-100; G. Kittel, *"Lego, Logos,* in le N.T., 4: 100-140; K. H. Rengstorf, *"Didaskô,"* 2: 138-168; H. Strathmann, *"Martus," "Martureô," "Marturomai,"* 4: 492-520. See also corresponding articles in *Vocabulaire de théologie biblique* (Paris, 1962).

52. A. Barucq, "Oracle et divination," 6: 752-787; A. Robert, J. Starcky, et al., "La Parole divine dans l'A. et le N. Testament," 5: 425-497; R. Follet et K. Prumm, "Mystères," 6: 1-225.

53. Par exemple l'article de D. Mollat, "Evangile," 4: col. 1745-1772.

54. J. Dupont, *Gnosis, La connaissance religieuse dans les épitres de S. Paul* (Louvain-Paris, 1949).

55. D. Deden, "Le mystère paulinien," *Eph. th. lov.*, 13 (1936): 403-442; K. Prumm, "Mystères," DBS 6: 1-225; R. E. Brown, "The pre-Christian Semitic Concept of Mystery," CBQ 20 (1958): 417-443; "The Semitic Background of the N. T. Mysterion," *Biblica*, 39 (1958): 426-448; 40 (1959): 70-87; C. Spicq. *Les Épitres pastorales* (Paris, 1947), excursus V: "Le mystère chrétien," pp. 116-125; J. Coppens, "Le mystère dans la théologie paulinienne et ses parallèles qumraniens," dans: *Littérature et théologie pauliniennes* (Coll. "Recherches bibliques," V, Louvain, 1960), pp. 142-165.

56. E. Pax, *Epiphaneia. Ein religionsgeschichtlicher Beitrag zur biblischen Theologie* ("Munchener Theologische Studien," I, 10, Munchen, 1955).

57. B. Trepanier, "L'idée de témoin dans les écrits johanniques," *Rev. de l'Université d'Ottawa*, 15 (1945): 5-63, section étoilée; I. de la Potterie, "La notion de témoignage dans S. Jean," dans: *Sacra Pagina* (2 vol., Paris-Gembloux, 1959), 2: 192-208; N. Brox, *Zeuge und Martyrer* (Munchen, 1961).

58. H. Schlier, *Wort Gottes* (Wurzburg, 1958); Id., "La notion paulinienne de la Parole de Dieu," dans: *Littérature et théologie pauliniennes* (Coll. "Recherches bibliques," V, Louvain, 1960), pp. 127-141; C. Larcher, "La parole de Dieu entant que révélation dans l'Ancien Testament," dans: *La Parole de Dieu en Jésus-Christ*, pp. 35-67; J. Dupont, "La parole de Dieu suivant S. Paul," *ibid.*, 68-84; J. Giblet, "La théologie johannique du Logos," *ibid.*, 85-119.

59. I. de la Potterie, "L'arrière-plan du thème johannique de la vérité," dans: *Studia evangelica* (Berlin, 1959), pp. 277-294.

60. T. Crisan, *De notione Doxa in Evangelio S. Joannis in luce Veteris Testamenti* (Dissertatio, Romae, 1953).

61. R. Schnackenburg, *I a théologie du Nouveau Testament* (Bruges, 1961), pp. 38-39.

62. There are some thirty words used to express the idea of revelation.

63. M. Harl, *Origène et la fonction révélatrice du Verbe incarne'* (Paris, 1958).

14. J. Ford, *St. Irenaeus and Revelation, A Theological Perspective* (Dissertatio, Romae, 1961).

65. E. Molland, *The Conception of the Gospel in the Alexandrian Theology* (Oslo, 1938).

66. Cf. par exemple les ouvrages de H. Crouzel, *Origène et la "connaissance mystique"* (Bruges, 1961); J. Danielou, *Message évangélique et culture hellénistique* (Paris - Tournai-Rome, 1961); A. Houssiau, *La christologie de S. Irénée* (Louvain-Gembloux, 1955); J. Lebreton, *Histoire du dogme de la Trinité* (2 vol., Paris, 1928); D. Van Den Eynde, *Les normes de l'enseignement chrétien dans la littérature patristique des trois premiers siècles* (Gembloux, 1933); H. De Lubac, *Histoire et Esprit* (Paris, 1950); G. Aeby, *Les missions divines, de Saint Justin à Origène* (Fribourg, 1958).

67. R. Draguet, "Méthodes théologiques d'hier et d'aujourd'hui," *Revue catholique des idées et des faits*, 15 (1936), January 10, pp. 1-7; February 7, pp. 4-7; February 14, pp. 13-17.

68. L. Charlier, *Essai sur le problème théologique* (Thuillies, 1938).

69. M. D. Chenu, *Une École de théologie, le Saulchoir* (Le Saulchoir, Kain-lez-Tournai, Belgique, et Étiolles, France, 1937).

70. J. F. Bonnefoy, "La théologie comme science et l'explication de la foi chez S. Thomas d'Aquin," *Eph. th. lov.*, 14 (1937): 421-446 et 600-631; 15 (1938): 491-516.

71. Y. M. Congar, "Recensions," *Bulletin thomiste*, 1938, pp. 490-505.

72. M. R. Gagnebet, " Un Essai sur le problème théologique," *Revue thomiste*, 45 (1939): 108-145.

73. W. Goossens, "Notion et méthode de la théologie," *Coll. Gand.*, 26 (1939): 115-134.

74. C. Boyer, "Qu'est-ce que la théologie?" *Gregorianum*, 21 (1940): 255-266.

75. T. Zapelena, "Problema theologicum," *Gregorianum*, 24 (1943): 23-47 et 287-326; 25 (1944): 38-73 et 247-282.

76. M. D. Chenu, *Une École de théologie, le Saulchoir*, p. 72.

77. M. D. Chenu, "Position de la théologie," *Rev. des Sc. ph. et th.*, 24 (1935): 254.

78. M. D. Chenu, *Une École de théologie, le Saulchoir*, p. 71.

79. M. D. Chenu, "Position de la théologie," *Rev. des Sc. ph. et th.*, 24 (1935): 233.

80. *Ibid.*, 234.

81. *Ibid.*, 234.

82. *Ibid.*, 234.

83. *Ibid.*, 253, 239.

84. *Ibid.*, 246-247.

85. *Ibid.*, 247.

86. *Ibid.*, 248.

87. *Ibid.*, 249.

88. M.-D. Chenu, *Une École de théologie, le Sauchoir*, p. 59.

89. M.-D. Chenu, "Position de la théologie," *Rev. des Sc. ph. et th.*, 24 (1935): 235-236.

90. *Ibid.*, 239.

91. M.-D. Chenu, *Une École de théologie, le Saulchoir*, p. 76.

92. *Ibid.*, 70.

93. M.-D. Chenu, "Position de la théologie," *Rev. des Sc. ph. et th.*, 24 (1935): 233.

94. Still, to qualify the knowledge of faith, as does Father Chenu, with the terms "savory and mystical perception," appears to be imprecise on two counts. First of all, because, in strict rigor of terminology, God is not *perceived*, even obscurely, in faith, but rather *believed*; and in the second place, because the experimental character of faith (faith as experienced) is the result of a *privileged faith* rather than a *common faith*.

95. L. Charlier, *Essai sur le problème théologique* (Thuillies, 1938).

96. *Ibid.*, 66-80.

97. *Ibid.*, 50.

98. *Ibid.*, 66.

99. L. Charlier, *ibid.*, 67.

100. *Ibid.*, 68-69.

101. *Ibid.*, 69.

102. *Ibid.*, 65.

103. *Ibid.*, 70.

104. *Ibid.*, 71.

105. L. Charlier, *Essai sur le problème théologique*, p. 74.

106. *Ibid.*, 74.

107. The literature relating to this movement has been listed by G. B. Guzzetti, "Saggio bibliografico sulla teologia della predicazione," *La Scuola Cattolica*, 78 (1950): 350-356; and by E. Kappler, *Die Verkundigungstheologie* (Fribourg, 1949), pp. 7-110.

108. F. Lackner, "Das Zentralobjekt der Theologie," *Zeitschrift fur katholische Theologie*, 62 (1938): 1-36.

109. G. B. GUZZETTI, "La controversia sulla teologia della prèdicazione," *La Scuola Cattolica,* 78 (1950): 260-266; H. RAHNER, *Eine Theologie der Verkundigung* (Freiburg i. Br., (1939), p. 7.

110. J. A. JUNGMANN, *Die Frohbotschaft und unsere Glaubensverkundigung* (Regensburg, 1936). This fundamental work is at the head of the whole controversy. See also JUNGMANN, *Catéchèse* (Bruxelles, 1955); the third appendix, "Kerygmatic theology," constitutes a retrospective judgment on the whole of the debate; see primarily pages 275-280.

111. F. LACKNER, "Das Zentralobjekt der Theologie," *Zeitschrift fur katholische Theologie,* 62 (1938): 1-36; J. B. LOTZ, "Wissenschaft und Verkundigung," *Zeitschrift fur katholische Theologie,* 62 (1938): 465-501.

112. H. RAHNER, *Eine Theologie der Verkundigung* (Freiburg i. Br., 1939); F. DANDER, *Christus Alles und in Allen* (Innsbruck-Leipzig, 1939).

113. M. SCHMAUS, "Brauchen wir eine Theologie der Verkundigung?" in: *Die Seelsorge,* 16 (1938-1939): 1-12. Voir aussi la préface du second volume de sa *Katholische Dogmatik* (Munchen, 1949), II: VII-XI.

114. A. STOLZ, "De theologia kerygmatica," *Angelicum,* 17 (1940): 337-351.

115. J. A. JUNGMANN, "Le probléme du messagè à transmettre ou le problème kérygmatique," *Lumen Vitae,* 5 (1950): 276.

116. F. X. ARNOLD, "Renouveau de la prédication dogmatique et de la catéchèse," *Lumen Vitae,* 3 (1948): 504.

117. D. GRASSO, "Evangelizzazione, Catechesi, Omilia," *Gregorianum,* 42 (1961): 242-268. Dès le début de la controverse, cette distinction fut proposée par T. SOIRON, "Das Wort Gottes," *Wissenschaft und Weisceit,* 9 (1942): 24.

118. J. A. JUNGMANN, *Catéchèse* (Bruxelles, 1955), p. 278; F. X. ARNOLD, "La catéchèse en partant du mystère central de l'histoire du salut," *Évangéliser,* 15 (1960): 212.

119. G. CORTI, "Alla radice della controversia kerigmatica," *La Scuola Cattolica,* 78 (1950): 284-291. The numerous works on the theology of history that appeared shortly after the war also contributed much to stressing this historical character of revelation. See primarily the works of Daniélou, Cullmann, Féret, Thils, Von Balthasar, Malevez, H. Rahner, Mouroux, etc. The theologians of history insist on the incorporation of the word in the event of history. Revelation is bound up with the history of a hidden community chosen by God, directed by Him, and it is through the history of this community that God makes Himself known. "God acts in history, God reveals Himself in history," points out Father de Lubac (*Catholicisme* Paris, 1947, p. 133). Consequently, Christian faith is not simply adherence to a doctrinal complex on the relationship which joins man to God, but the recognition of a series of supernatural and irreversible interventions on the part of God in the course of human history, with a view towards leading humanity to its final and definitive state, which is that of the heavenly Jerusalem (M. Flick and Z. Alszeghy, "Conspectus, Teologia della storia," *Gregorianum,* 35 (1954): 292).

120. H. RAHNER, *Eine Theologie der Verkundigung;* p. 11.

121. J. A. JUNGMANN, *Die Frohbotschaft und unsere Glaubensverkundigung,* pp. 61 ff. All kerygmatists stress this christic character of revelation.

122. E. KAPPLER, *Die Verkundigungstheologie* (Fribourg, 1949), pp. 22-28.

123. H. RAHNER, *Eine Theologie der Verkundigung,* p. 15.

124. J. A. JUNGMANN, *Die Frohbotschaft und unsere Glaubensverkundigung* (Regensburg, 1936). More than twenty years later Father J. Hamer declared once again to a group of priests that the crisis of preaching is a "theological crisis" which will not be resolved until we have a clear view of the place of the word of God in the divine plan (*La Revue Nouvelle,* 29 [1959]: 137-147). In the same sense, see C. MOELLER, "Théologie de la parole et ecuménisme," *Irénikon,* 24 (1951): 330-331.

125. See, for example: *Parole de Dieu et liturgie* ("Lèx Orandi," Paris, 1958); *La Parole de Dieu en Jésus-Christ* ("Cahiers de l'actualité religieuse," Paris, 1961).

126. Z. ALSZEGHY et M. FLICK, "Il problèma teologico della predicazione," *Gregorianum,* 40 (1959): 672-676.

127. J. MOUROUX, *Le Mystère du temps* (Paris, 1962), pp. 196-204.

128. For exåmple: A. RETIF, *Foi au Christ et mission* (Paris, 1953); J. R. GEISELMANN, *Jesus der Christus, Die Urform des apostolischen Kerygmas als Norm unserer Verkundigung und Theologie von Jesus Christus* (Stuttgart, 1951); R. ASTING, *Die Verkundigung des Wortes Gottes im Urchristentum dargestellt an den Begriffen 'Wort Gottes,' 'Evangelium,' und Zeugnis'* (Stuttgart, 1939); R. KOCH, "Die Verkundigung des Wortes Gottes in der Urkirche," *Anima* (1955), pp. 256-265; ID., "Témoignage d'après les Actes," *Masses ouvrières* (April 1957), pp. 16-35; (juin 1957), pp. 4-23; J. GEWIESS, *Die Urapostolische Heilsverkundigung nach der Apostelgeschichte* (Brèslau, 1939); H. TRAUB, *Botschaft und Geschichte* (Zurich, 1954); N. BROX, *Zeuge und Martyrer, Untersuchungen zur fruchristlichen Zeugnis-Terminologie* (Munchen, 1961).

129. D. Grasso, "Il kerigma e la predicazione," *Gregorianum*, 41 (1960): 439-444.

130. A. Liege, "Le ministère de la parole: du kérygme à la catéchèse," dans: *La Parole de Dieu en Jésus-Christ* (Casterman, 1961), p. 170.

131. *Parole de Dieu et liturgie*, p. 381; J. Gelineau, "L'annonce de la parole de Dieu dans le mystère du culte," dans: *La Parole de Dieu en Jésus-Christ*, pp. 202-209.

132. D. Grasso, "Il kerigma e la predicazione," *Gregorianum*, 41 (1960): 445.

133. They base this statement on Scripture.

134. A. Liege, "Le ministère de la parole: du kérygme à la catéchèse," dans: *La Parole de Dieu en Jésus-Christ*, pp. 170-184.

135. D. Grasso, "Evangelizzazione, Catechesi, Omilia," *Gregorianum*, 42 (1961): 242-268.

136. On this problem in general see: Z. Alszeghy et M. Flick, "Il problema teologico della predicazione," *Gregorianum*, 40 (1959): 671-744; C. Davis, "The Theology of Preaching," *The Clergy Review*, 45 (1960): 524-545.

137. V. Schurr, *Wie heute predigen* (Stuttgart, 1949).

138. L. Agustoni, "Das Wort Gottes als kultisches Wort," *Anima*, 10 (1955): 272-284.

139. J. Betz, "Wort und Sakrament. ersuch einer dogmatischer Verhaltnisbestimmung," *Verkundigung und Glaube* (Freiburg i. Br., 1958), pp. 76-99.

140. O. Semmelroth, "Christliche Existenz und Gottes Wort," *Geist und Leben*, 31 (1958): 245-256; Id., *Wirkendes Wort* (Frankfurt, 1962); E. Schillebeeckx, "Parole et sacrement dans l'Église," *Lumiére et Vie*, 9 (janvier-mars 1960): 32-39.

141. E. Schillebeeckx, "Parole et sacrement dans l'Église," *Lumiére et Vie*, 9 (janvier-mars 1960): 33.

142. *Ibid.*, 36.

143. E. Hugueny, *Critique et Catholique*, vol. II, *Apologie des dogmes* (Paris, 1924), p. 37.

144. H. De Lubac, "Bulletin de théologie fondamentale. Le problème du développement du dogme," *Recherches de science religieuse*, 35 (1948): 153.

145. Fr. de Lubac wrote this essay on revelation in reference to the following article of Fr. Boyer, in *Gregorianum*, 21 (1940): 255-266, under the title: "Qu'est-ce que la théologie? Réflexions sur une controverse récente."

146. H. de Lubac, "Bulletin de théologie fondamentale. Le problème du développement du dogme," *Rech. de sc. rel.* 35 (1948): 154.

147. *Ibid.*, 155.

148. *Ibid.*, 156.

149. *Ibid.*, 156.

150. *Ibid.*, 156-157.

151. *Ibid.*, 157.

152. *Ibid.*, 155.

153. *Ibid.*, 157-158.

154. H. De Lubac, *ibid.*, 139.

155. *Ibid.*, 148.

156. *Ibid.*, 157.

157. H. Niebecker, *Wesen und Wirklichkeit der ubernaturalichen Offenbarung* (Fribourg, 1940).

158. R. Guardini, *Die Offenbarung, ihr Wesen und ihre Formen* (Wurzburg, 1940).

159. L. M. Dewailly, *Jésus-Christ, Parole de Dieu* (Paris, 1945).

160. W. Bulst, *Offenbarung, Biblischer und Theologischer Begriff* (Dusseldorf, 1960).

161. K. Rahner, *Horer des Wortes*, Munchen, 1941.

162. D. Barsotti, *Il Mistero cristiano e la Parola di Dio* (Florence, 1954).

163. *Parole dc Dieu et liturgie* ("Lex Orandi," 25, Paris, 1958); *La Parole de Dieu en Jésus-Christ* (Cahiers de l'actualité religieuse," 15, Paris, 1961). This last work contains many articles of excellent quality on the theme of the Word of God understood as revelation: primarily those of A. Léonard on the urgency of a theology of revelation (pp. 11-32), of C. Larcher on revelation of the Old Testament (pp. 35-67), of J. Dupont on the word of God in Saint Paul (pp. 68-84), of J. Giblet on the Johannine theology of the Logos (pp. 85-119), of L. Charlier on Christ, Word of God (pp. 122-139). The second part of the work studies more directly the problem of preaching the word of God. For an analysis of these different articles see: D. Grasso, "Nuovi apporti alla teologia della predicazione," *Gregorianum*, 44 (1963): 92-95; E. Fortin, in: *Sciences Ecclésiastiques*, 15 (1963): 141-144.

164. W. Bulst, *Offenbarung*, pp. 15-16; R. Guardini, *Die Offenbarung*, pp. 118 ss.

165. H. Niebecker, *Wesen und Wirklichkeit der ubernaturlichen Offenbarung*, pp. 59-90.

166. *Ibid.*, 112-172.

167. W. Bulst, *Offenbarung*, pp. 70-86.

168. *Ibid.*, 90-91.

169. "Die ubernaturliche Offenbarung ist die gnadenhafte, personale, heilschaffende Selbster-schliessung Gottes an den Menschen im Raun seiner Geschichte; und zwar in unbernaturlichem gottlichem Tun, in sichtbarer Erscheinung und vor allem, jene interpretierend und umfassend, in seinem bezeugenden Wort; vorbereitend geschehen in Israel, endgultig in Christus Jesus, uns gegenwartig im Wort und Wirken der Kirche; hienieden noch in vielfaltiger Verhullung (darum vom Menschen aufzunehmen im Glauben), aber hingeordnet auf die unmittelbare Gottesschau der Ewigkeit" (W. Bulst, *Offenbarung*, p. 111).

170. *Ibid.*, 113.

171. H. de Lubac, "Le problème du développement du dogme," *Rech. de sc. rel.*, 35 (1948): 157-158; K. Rahner, *Écrits théologiques*, t. 1 (trans. J. Y. Calvez et M. Rondet Bruges, 1959), p. 164; L. M. Dewailly, *Jésus-Christ, Parole de Dieu*, p. 28; J. Mouroux, *L'expérience chrétienne* (Paris, 1952), p. 193; R. Guardini, *Essence du christianisme* (trans. Lorson, Paris, 1947), p. 74; H. Niebecker, *Wesen und Wirklichkeit der ubernaturlicher Offenbarung*, p. 155; G. Soehngen, *Die Einheit in der Theologie* (Munich, 1952), pp. 316, 354 s., 359; H. Urs von Balthasar, *La théologie de l'histoire* (Paris, 1955), p. 193.

172. The problem is opened by: L. M. Dewailly, *Jésus-Christ, Parole de Dieu*; H. Urs von Balthasar, "Dieu a parlé un langage d'homme," dans: *Parole de Dieu et Liturgie*, pp. 71-103.

173. This subject is studied by: C. De More-Pontgibaud, *Du fini à l'infini* (Paris, 1957); H. Bouillard, *Karl Barth* (3 vol., Paris, 1957), t. 3: 190-217; Y. Congar, art. "Théologie," DTC 15 (1): 473-474.

174. W. Bulst, *Offenbarung*, pp. 59-62; M. Schmaus, *Dommatica Cattolica* (Rome, 1959), pp. 18-24.

175. The Protestant reflection on this point is very strong. See for example: O. Cullmann, *Christ et le Temps* (Neuchatel, 1957); W. Pannenberg, R. Rendtorff, T. Rendtorff, U. Wilkens, *Offenbarung als Geschichte* (Gottingen, 1961); W. Eichrodt, "Offenbarung und Geschichte im A. T.," *Theol. Zeitschrift*, 4 (1948): 321-331; G. von Rad, "Grund-probleme einer biblischen Theologie des A. T.," *Theol. Lit. Zeitung*, 68 (1943): 225-234; Id., "Theologische Geschichte im A. T.," *Theol. Zeitschrift*, 4 (1948): 161 ss.

176. J. Alfaro, "Persona y gracia," *Gregorianum*, 41 (1960): 11; R. Aubert, "Questioni attuali intorno all'atto di Fede," *Problemi e Orientamenti di Teologia dommatica* (2 vol., Milan, 1957), t. 2: 672.

177. W. Bulst, *Offenbarung*, pp. 63-65; A. Lang, *Die Sendung Christi* (Munich, 1957), pp. 40-41.

178. W. Bulst, *Offenbarung*, pp. 63-68.

179. K. Rahner, *Écrits théologiques*, t. 1: 59-60.

180. For example the works of K. Buhler, H. Noack, H. Heidegger, G. Sieworth, M. Merleau-Ponty, M. Nédoncelle, L. Lavelle, G. Gusdorf, E. Verdonc, etc.

181. J. Guitton, *Le problème de Jésus et les fondements du témoignage chrétien* (Paris, 1950), pp. 147-187.

182. W. Bulst, *Offenbarung*, pp. 18-19; J. L. McKenzie, "The Word of God in the Old Testament," *Theological Studies*, 21 (1960): 183-206.

183. Other aspects of this question, though they are mentioned, receive a much briefer treatment: for example, the ecclesial aspect, the eschatological aspect. Cf. W. Bulst, *Offenbarung*, pp. 97-101 et 105-106.

184. J. Alfaro, *Adnotationes in tractatum de Virtutibus* (Romae, 1959).

185. P. Demann, "Foi juive et foi chrétienne," *Cahiers Sioniens*, 6 (1952): 89-103.

186. J. Alfaro, "Fides in terminologia biblica," *Gregorianum*, 42 1961): 504-505.

CONCLUSION

1. *Problematic.*—The theologian's center of attention changes over the centuries, according to the peculiar problems of his age.

In the thirteenth century, theology was interested primarily in prophetic revelation. The term "revelation" conjures up a phenomenon of the interior order, an intimate and supernatural communication of God to the soul. Prophetic revelation belongs to the world of charism: it is a grace *gratis data,* for the benefit of all humanity. Little is said of revelation through Christ and His apostles. The questions raised by the coming of Christ concern mostly Incarnation and Redemption.

After the Council of Trent, while still speaking of prophecy, which they later integrate in the treatise on faith, theologians begin to speak more of mediate revelation.

The problem now is to demonstrate that this external word is truly the word of God, guaranteed by the undeniable signs which testify to its divine origin. This is a new emphasis brought out by the errors of Protestantism, which is more and more exclusively interested in Scripture and the inner word of the Spirit, tending to make the encounter with the Bible the only place for immediate and individual revelation, as well as to exclude the magisterium of the Church from her right to propose and interpret the word of God.

Religious thinking, before the Renaissance, was at first very much attentive to the demands of God. In the modern world, on the contrary, the demands of the thinking subject pass over into the foreground. According to Spinoza and Kant, revelation can be a type of natural knowledge, since man has no other principle of knowledge than his natural faculties. According to the liberal Protestants, Schleiermacher, Ritschl, Sabatier, and then according to the Modernists, revelation is as universal a category as religion, a common and immanent experience. The theologians of the nineteenth century, therefore, are led to distinguish between two orders of revelation (natural and supernatural), to assert the existence and possibility of a supernatural revelation, to insist on the objective and doctrinal character of revelation.

In the twentieth century, under the influence of the currents of contemporary thought (existentialism, personalism), it is the personal encounter with the living and personal God that occupies the center of attention both for theologian and simple believer. God reveals, but primarily he reveals Himself; God speaks, but primarily He speaks to me. There is great effort here to make revelation something interior, to safeguard its personal and personalising character. What follows is a sort of *valorization* of the subjective elements and a *reification* of the objective elements. There is insistence on the revealed truth, not only as proposed, but also as grasped and possessed. And in this revealed truth itself, there is less insistence on the signs, concepts, and propositions that express the mystery than on the mystery itself and the Person who reveals. There is open suspicion over a certain tendency, excessively conceptualistic, which sees revelation only as a system of propositions about God.

The theologian of the twentieth century, aware of the historical dimension, is particularly interested in the implications of a revelation which goes through the course of history, using and transforming it. It is not enough to know the result of the activity of revelation, that is, the *depositum fidei,* he also wants to understand its genesis; he wants to grasp revelation in its historical development, in its progress through the course of centuries, in its economy and its pedagogy. He feels that the theology of revelation must rest on phenomenology and the history of revelation.

2. *Points of contact.*—From St. Bonaventure until the 20th century the whole scholastic tradition represents revelation as a supernatural and supremely free activity in which God graciously furnishes humanity with the truths necessary for salvation. There is frequent stress, in this activity, on the loving initiative on the part of the Father, and the combined roles of Son and Spirit in the concrete economy of revelation. This activity is described as an unveiling and communication of God's thinking, manifestation of His plan for salvation to humanity. With Scripture, this activity is called the word of God to man. It is, after all, through this activity that God addresses Himself to man, speaks to him, communicates His thought, inviting him to the response of faith. More precisely, to mark the formal element of this word, theologians speak of divine testimony; sometimes too, in order to

highlight the new wealth of experience it affords the human mind, they call it word of teaching.

This word, which comes from God, is received in man. The scholastics of the thirteenth century conceive of *immediate* revelation as an illumination of the mind which gives rise to a certain knowledge of the truth. It is a cognitive act, of the intellectual order, enabling the prophet to judge the elements present to his awareness with certitude and without error. Apostolic revelation is also effected under the illuminating influence of the Holy Spirit, who gives the apostles the power to grasp Christ's message in its true meaning.

Mediate revelation is the proposition of divine truths through envoys, whose word is authorized as word of God, by the signs which attest its divine origin. All the theologians repeat that mediate revelation is sufficient and that it fully deserves the title word of God. In a quite consistent way, too, theologians note the cooperation between the external proposition of truth and the interior light, an external word and an inner word, a preaching without and an illumination within, an external witness and an inner witness. The word of God is present on every side; it surrounds man in some way, through the external pressure of the spoken word and the miracle, through the interior attraction of supernatural grace.

3. *Oscillations.*—In the 13th century theology had a synthetic view of revelation. By revelation theology understood the complex of phenomena which put man in possession of a properly divine knowledge. New object, special light proportioned to this object: together, the two phenomena are called illumination, word, revelation. The word "revelation" does not yet have its technical sense. It is used to designate the object revealed as well as the subjective illumination. After this indeterminacy of the thirteenth century, there is evidence of a movement inclining theologians towards a definition of revelation, a definition which proceeds sometimes *ex parte objecti*, sometimes *ex parte potentiae*, sometimes *ex parte objecti et potentiae*. One of the first currents of thought sees revelation, properly so-called, in the phenomenon of interior illumination which opens the soul to the brilliancy of the supernatural world: thus Bañez and Cano. The Jesuits Suarez and De Lugo, on the contrary, reacting against the excesses of the Protestant Enlightenment, reserve the term revelation for the manifestation of the object, the light of faith deserving the name revelation only in a broad sense. The Carmelites of Salamanca think that revelation *ex parte objecti* and revelation *ex parte potentiae* both deserve the title of revelation. In the first case, it is the object which is

unveiled; in the second, it is the human faculty. In the nineteenth century, the prevailing usage was to define revelation *ex parte objecti*, as being the manifestation of the truths of salvation, the secrets of God, God's plan. This complex of truths makes up revealed doctrine or revelation or object of faith. However, theologians always recognize the need for an inner help, an inner light by which man makes this object his own.

The twentieth century, more conscious of the complexity of the activity of revelation and the multiplicity of the aspects of revelation, oscillates from one aspect to the other, always in danger of stressing one element to the detriment of the other. Revelation-reality or revelation-doctrine; revelation as event of salvation or revelation as knowledge; revelation as progressive history or revelation as immutable and definitive deposit of faith; revelation as act of God or revelation as human testimony; revelation as truth or revelation as personal encounter; revelation as the totality of Christ or revelation as the multiplicity of mysteries and propositions; revelation as a deposit to be preserved or revelation as a word to be understood and assimilated; revelation as external message or revelation as inner word. Present-day theology is unwilling to lose any of these aspects; it wants to harmonize them in unity, for revelation is at once activity, event, history, knowledge, testimony, encounter, doctrine, immutable deposit, inner word. In this work of organizing and harmonizing, it can happen that theology stresses one or another aspect too vigorously, underestimating another aspect, as a reaction against the excesses of the past. This is a final proof of the fact that the reality of revelation will always be much richer than the constructions of the human mind, and that theology must vary her approaches in order not to be too unfaithful to this reality.

part 4
notion of revelation and church magisterium

Anyone who studies the documents of the Church is immediately struck by the fact that errors concerning the notion of revelation are a recent phenomenon. During the first centuries and throughout the whole of the Middle Ages, the notion seems not to have been attacked at all. There is no evidence of any anathema or condemnation attesting to a denial of the fact or a contamination of the concept. The controversies which call for the attention of the Church, echoed by the decrees of the councils, are related primarily to the Trinity, the Incarnation, the mystery of Christ (natures and person), the sacraments, the authority of the Roman Pontiff. That God spoke to men through Moses and the prophets, and then through Christ and the apostles, is a truth no one dreamed of denying or doubting. The Law, the prophets, the Gospel, which contain this word, are thus also equally the word of God. The Church, which preaches the divine word, knows how to preserve the integrity of the faith entrusted to the apostles, free from all contamination and innovation (D 159-160),[1] free from every seed of error which could stir up the evil spirit who never stops mixing the cockles with the wheat (D 246). "We confess," says the second Council of Constantinople in 553, "that we hold and preach the faith which has been given from the beginning by God the Father and our Lord and Savior Jesus Christ to the Holy Apostles and, through them, preached throughout the entire world; and that it is this faith which the holy Fathers, particularly those who were united in the four holy councils, confessed, explained, and handed down to the holy Churches" (D 212).

The most complete expression of the notion of revelation, in the medieval era, is no doubt that furnished by the Fourth Lateran Council in 1215: "This holy Trinity, ... first through Moses and the holy prophets and his other servants, according to a most wise disposition of circumstances, has given the human race a doctrine of salvation. And finally, the only Son of God, Jesus Christ ... showed us the path of life in a more clear manner" (D 428-429). According to the teaching of this council, revelation is common to the whole Trinity, who is its Author. The mediators of this revelation, for the Old Testament, are Moses and the prophets. What they bring to the human race, for whom revelation is destined, is a "doctrine of salvation." In the New Testament, the Second Person of the Trinity, the only Son of the Father, becomes incarnate to address Himself directly to humanity and point out the path of life in a more clear manner, in other words, the means of arriving at salvation. The goal of revelation is to lead to life everlasting. The important elements of the concept of revelation are already joined: the author (Trinity); the destinees (human race); the goal (salvation, everlasting life); the object (a doctrine concerning salvation and the means of obtaining it); the rapid progress realized from one economy to the other by the Incarnation of the Son of God.

Actually, it is only in the eighteenth and nineteenth centuries, in the name of the demands of the thinking subject, that the possibility of a supernatural revelation was first doubted, then, by slow degrees, reduced to one of the forms of universal religious experience. Still, the principles which led to the corruption and dissolution of the concept of revelation were already at work in the birth of Protestantism. Thus, it is from an analysis of protestantism that our study begins. We can distinguish five periods in this history: 1. The Council of Trent, which combats Protestantism; 2. The First Vatican Council, which combats rationalism; 3. The decree *Lamentabili*, the encyclical *Pascendi* and the motu proprio *Sacrorum antistitum*, which combat Modernism; 4. The contemporary period before the Second Vatican Council; 5. Finally, the Second Vatican Council.

CHAPTER I

THE COUNCIL OF TRENT AND PROTESTANTISM

Protestantism, in its first beginnings, even though it is not directly opposed, in principle, to the notion of revelation, still seriously threatens it. Saint Thomas, in the *Contra Gentiles*, points out that there are three ways of knowing divine things: "In the first way, man, thanks to the natural light of reason, rises to the knowledge of God through the means of creatures; in the second, the divine truth, which surpasses the limits of our understanding, comes down to us through the mode of revelation . . . ; in the third way, the mind rises to a perfect vision of what has been revealed."[1] The Reformers still subscribe to these statements; still their anthropology somewhat distorts this clear vision of things. In his *Institutes of the Christian Religion*, Calvin admits that God shows Himself to men through the works of creation,[2] but he adds that human reason has been so seriously wounded by Adam's fall that this objective manifestation of God remains without effect for us.[3] That is why God gives humanity not only "mute teachers," but also His divine word.[4] Our path towards God can now be accomplished only by the revelation attested to in Scripture. Thus, of two types of knowledge of God traditionally recognized—natural knowledge and knowledge through revelation—the first is played down in favor of the second, whereas scholastic theology, always eager to maintain the value of human reason in its approach towards God, is caught up in the repercussions of this breach of equilibrium and falls in disgrace. Protestantism quickly goes on to devaluate any knowledge of God which does not come from revelation through Jesus Christ.[5]

At the same time that it affirms the principle of salvation through grace, and through faith alone, Protestantism poses the principle of the sovereign authority of Scripture. The rule of faith is Scripture alone, with the individual guidance of the Holy Spirit permitting each reader to grasp what is revealed and thus what he needs to believe. The testimony of the Holy Spirit in souls and the word of God in Scripture are inseparable. Only the Holy Spirit can enlighten His word.

At first, Protestantism seems thus to exalt the transcendent character of revelation, since it does away with everything intermediary between the word of God and the soul which receives it. As a matter of fact, it compromises this character; for at the same time that it poses the principle of the sovereign authority of Scripture, it stands up against the authority of the Church (D 767), either in her tradition, or in the actual decisions of her magisterium. It keeps alive the notion of the word of God, but, by detaching this word from all objective forms it runs the risk of falling into an uncontrollable private inspiration: it leads to individualism or rationalism, either directly, or through the byways of illuminism and pneumatism.[6] This is a laicisation of the notion of revelation which will appear full grown in the day of liberal Protestantism, but whose evolutionary process is already in full swing beginning with the seventeenth century.

It will be the role of the First Vatican Council to reaffirm the existence and the validity of the two orders of knowledge of God, natural and supernatural (D 1785). For its part, the Council of Trent was taken up with turning away the more immediate danger posed by a too exclusive attention to Scripture, to the detriment of the teaching Church and her living tradition.

1. From the beginning, the Council was taken up with defining the means through which God communicates His revelation. On February 12, 1546, Cardinal del Monte made a statement to help orient the discussions; he pointed out that our faith comes from divine revelation, which is handed on by the Church, who receives it, partly from the Scriptures of the Old and New Testament, and partly also from tradition. As a result, the first point to be treated, he concludes, is Scripture and tradition.[7] A decree was then drawn up on this matter and published on April 8, 1546:

"The Holy, Ecumenical, General Council of Trent, legitimately assembled under the guidance of the Holy Spirit, the same three legates of the Apostolic See here presiding; having always before her eyes the task of preserving in the Church, by destroying all contrary errors, the purity of the Gospel, which after having been promised in advance by the prophets in the Holy Scriptures, was published first through the mouth of our Lord Jesus Christ, Son of God, then through His apostles to whom He gave the mission of announcing it to every creature as being the source of all truth of salvation and all discipline of morals;

and considering that this truth and this rule of morals are contained in written books and in non-written tradition, which, received from the very mouth of Christ by the apostles, or handed down by the apostles, to whom the Holy Spirit had dictated these truths, have, as it were, from hand to hand, come down to our own day; the Council then, following the example of the orthodox Fathers, receives all the books both of the Old and the New Testament, the same God being the Author of one and the other, as well as the traditions which concern both faith and morals, as coming from the very mouth of Christ or dictated by the Holy Spirit and preserved in the Catholic Church by a continual succession; the Council receives and venerates them with the same respect and filial devotion" (D 783).

It must be noted first of all, that throughout this whole paragraph the word *revelation* does not appear even once. The pivotal word in this decree is *Gospel*, more concrete, closer to the usage of the New Testament. It is the *Gospel* which the Church has received a mission to preserve in all its purity. The Gospel, that is, the good news of the message of salvation delivered and realized through Christ, and preached to every creature. Such is the meaning which the Council gives this word by referring explicitly to the closing words of Matthew and Mark: "Preach the Gospel to every creature. He who believes and is baptized, will be saved" (Mk. 16:15-16). The Fourth Lateran Council had called it: *doctrina salutaris* (doctrine of salvation). The Gospel, the doctrine of salvation: that is the object proposed for our faith.

There are three principal statements in the text: A. The Gospel was given to us in a progressive manner: *announced* first of all through the prophets, *promulgated* through Christ, finally *preached* by the apostles, on Christ's order, to every creature. The Gospel is the *one source* of all truth of salvation and all discipline of morals. In order to stress the historical character and continuity of this economy, an amendment proposed the introduction of the first verse of the Epistle to the Hebrews.[8]

The faith in question here is not the faith-trust, the *fides fiducialis* of the Protestants, but a faith which adheres to revealed truths, an act of intelligence which submits to God and recognizes the truth of what He reveals. The different redactions of this text testify to the Council's firm intention to clearly mark out the dogmatic character of the Catholic Faith.[9] Still, these truths can also be *promises* which stir up the light of trust and hope in man.[10] They are not merely to enrich the human mind; they are a message of salvation which orients man towards God.

Such is faith, and its object is presented by preaching. In referring to Rom. 10:17 (*fides ex auditu*—faith from hearing), the Council envisages faith as the response proper to the good news, the message of salvation. "This is what we preach, and this is what you have believed," writes Saint Paul to the Corinthians (1 Cor., 15:11). "After having heard the word of truth, the good news of salvation, and having believed in it," he says in speaking to the Ephesians (Eph. 1:13). This external preaching, however, in the thinking of the Council, is without efficacy unless it is accompanied by the inner *hearing* of grace. This is brought out clearly in the words of the text: *excitati divina gratia et adjuti* (stirred up and helped by divine grace).[11] This point of view is in perfect conformity with Scripture which frequently stresses the activity of grace which opens the heart of man to the word heard without and at the same time gives man the light to offer free consent.[12]

The teaching of the Council can be summed up in the following points: without explicitly using the term revelation, it represents revelation as being the content of a communication. Concretely, this content is the Gospel or message of salvation promised first of all through the prophets, made public through Christ, preached by the apostles, handed down to the Church, preserved and defended by the Church. This Gospel is also called a doctrine, taught and handed down; a doctrine of salvation, constituting a complex of truths and promises offered to Christian faith through preaching, and which are to be found in Scripture and in tradition. Correlatively, faith, which is man's reponse to the preaching of the Gospel, is assent to the truths and promises which it contains, under the activity of grace which sets the mind in motion and helps it. This assent has for its terminus, not the simple statements in themselves, but the very God of these truths and promises.

B. This truth of salvation and this law of our moral activity, of which the Gospel is the one and only source, are contained in the inspired books of Scripture and in non-written traditions.

C. The Council accepts with equal devotion and equal respect the Scripture (Old and New Testaments) as well as the traditions which come "from the mouth of Christ or dictated by the Holy Spirit and preserved in the Catholic Church by a continual succession."

The one and only Gospel message, the one and only good news of salvation is thus expressed in two distinct forms: written and oral. That is why we must believe everything that is contained in the word of God, written and handed down (D 1792). The current of revelation passed through one highly privileged moment, when it was put in writing under the inspiration of the Holy Spirit. But it is no less true that the Church still possesses, in all its entirety, the living teaching which she received from the beginning. And thus when Scripture does not seem to be sufficiently clear and explicit on some point, the Church can always find, in the tradition which she preserves, the means to make it clear.

2. In the *proemium* of the decree on justification, the object of faith is once again presented as a doctrine, taught by Christ, handed on by the apostles, preserved by the Church, and defended by her against all error. The Council declares that "she means to explain to all the faithful of Christ the true and sound doctrine of this same justification which Jesus Christ ... , Author and Fulfiller of our faith, has taught, which the apostles have handed down and which the Catholic Church, under the activity of the Holy Spirit, has always preserved, severely forbidding anyone to dare believe, preach, or teach anything other than what is decided in the present decree" (D 792a).

3. In the fifth chapter, the Council opposes the Protestant doctrine of justification by faith alone with the Catholic teaching which declares the necessity of grace, source of divine initiative, and the free cooperation of man in the divine activity (D 797). The following chapter explains in what this collaboration between man and grace actually consists: "Men are disposed for the state of justice in the sense that stirred up and aided by divine grace, they conceive of faith through preaching (Rom. 10:17) and freely turn towards God; that they believe in the truths and promises revealed by God, and primarily in the truth that man the sinner is justified by the grace of God by means of the redemption which is in Christ Jesus" (D 798).

---

1. H. DENZINGER K. RAHNER, *Enchiridion symbolorum, definitionem et declarationum de rebus fidei et morum* (30th edition). Designated: D.

1. S. THOMAS, *Summa contra Gentiles*, L. IV, c. 1.

2. J. CALVINUS, *Institutio christianae religionis* (Geneva, 1618), L. I, c. 5, no. 2.

3. *Ibid.*, L. I, c. 2, no. 1; II, c. 6, no. 1.

4. *Ibid.*, L. I, c. 6, no. 1.

5. J. BAILLIE, *The Idea of Revelation in Recent Thought* (London, 1956), pp. 5-9; W. NIESEL, *The Theology of Calvin* (London, 1938, from the original German *Die Theologie Calvins*, Munich, 1938), pp. 39-53.

6. L. BOUYER, *Du Protestantisme à Église* (Paris, 1954), pp. 128-129; 151-152.

7. "Noverunt Paternitates Vestrae qualiter omnis fides de revelatione divina est et hanc nobis traditam ab Ecclesia *partim ex scripturis*, quae sunt in Veteri et Novo Testamento, *partim* etiam ex simplici traditione per manus. Ut itaque omnia a nobis ordine proficiscantur, post professionem fidei a nobis factam consequens est ut scripturas sacras probemus, deinde de traditionibus ecclesiasticis etiam disserendum" (Societas Goerresiana, ed., *Concilium Tridentinum. Diariorum, actorum, epistolarum, tractatuum nova collectio* [13 vol., Fribourg, 1901-1938], 5: 7-8). Instead of affirming, as does del Monte, that the Church receives revelation: *partim ex scripturis...*, *partim ... ex simplici traditione*, the text adopted by the Council states that revelation is contained: in libris scriptis *et* sine scripto traditionibus.

8. *Concilium Tridentinum*, 5: 51.

9. In September, 1546, the wording was: *"per fidem· qua credimus omnia quae nobis divinitus revelata et promissa sunt"* (Concilium Tridentinum,—through the faith by which we believe everything which has been divinely revealed and promised to us); on October 31: *"qua credimus vera esse quae divinitus revelata et promissa sunt"*—by which we believe those things which have been divinely revealed and promised to be true"; on December 10, finally, the phrase was added: *"ex auditu concipientes"*—hearing the faith *by preaching.*

10. R. AUBERT, *Le Problème de l'acte de foi* (Louvain, 1950), pp. 77-78.

11. Certain fathers of the Council also wanted to mention explicitly the *auditus interior* (the inner hearing) by inserting the words: *"ex dono Dei et auditu"* (Concilium Tridentinum, 5: 697—from the gift of God and from hearing). Seripando did not think this addition necessary, but pointed out: "The truth of the matter is that the hearing of the external word accomplishes nothing without the inner word. Thus it is written: The Lord has opened my ear" (Ibid., 5: 704-705).

12. For example: Acts 16, 16; Mt. 16, 17; 1 Jn. 2, 27; Mt. 11, 25-27; Jn. 6, 44-45.

CHAPTER II

THE FIRST VATICAN COUNCIL AND RATIONALISM

I. THE ACTIVITY OF THE CHURCH IN ITS CONTEXT

The First Vatican Council sees, in rationalism, the bitter fruits of Protestantism. Paragraphs II and III of the prologue to the constitution *Dei Filius* thus describe the fatal development of the principles which underly the Reformation:

"Everyone knows ... that after having rejected the divine teaching office of the Church and abandoned religious questions to the private judgment of each individual, the heresies proscribed by the fathers at Trent gradually broke down into an infinite number of sects, which divided and fought among each other, and that finally a considerable number of their members lost all faith in Jesus Christ. The Holy Books themselves, which Protestantism first claimed as the only source and sole rule of Christian doctrine, ceased to be regarded as divine; they even came to be ranked among the fictions of mythology. It is this that gave birth to and, unfortunately, spread so widely throughout the whole world this doctrine of rationalism and naturalism, which, in open opposition to Christian religion on every point, by reason of the supernatural character of this institution, applies itself with ever renewed efforts to exclude Jesus Christ, our one and only Lord and Savior, from the thinking of men, from the life and morals of peoples, in order to establish the reign of what is called pure reason or nature".[1]

If it is true that rationalism derives from Protestantism, it is equally certain that it was helped in its development by many important factors: by the Cartesian philosophy which broke with authority and tradition, by the moral philosophism and pantheism of Spinoza, which *a priori* excludes all revealed religion, by the German Kantian philosophy which confuses theology with philosophy and Christian morality with natural ethics, by the English experimental philosophy, finally, which claimed to be restricted solely to the laws and observations of reason and nature. Thus the Council can speak of a "reign of reason and nature." In its extreme forms, the Council adds, rationalism ends up in "pantheism, materialism, atheism".[2]

When the demands of the thinking subject came to occupy first place in Western consciousness, the problem of a divine intervention through revelation, effected in a transcendent manner, necessarily had to be posed. As a result, in addition to the Catholic position, it was possible, in theory, to conceive of three different responses which, actually, did exist. It is possible first to refuse the hypothesis of a transcendent revelation and activity on the part of God in human history: this is the answer of deism and progressism (D 1807-1808) which claim full autonomy and sufficiency for unaided human reason. It is also possible to deny the transcendent character of revelation and turn it into a purely immanent reality and something human, a particularly intensive form of a universal religious sentiment: this is the answer of liberal Protestantism and, more or less, of Modernism. Finally, it is possible to suppress one of the two terms, God: the proponents of absolute evolutionism, such as the Hegelians, keep the word revelation, but empty it of its traditional meaning. The universe and God being only one, human reason is not substantially distinct from the divine reason and can, as a result of this fact, know everything in its own natural evolution, Christianity representing only one "moment" in the evolution of reason towards its total development.

Faced with pantheism and deism, the First Vatican Council solemnly affirmed the fact of supernatural revelation, its possibility, its expediency, its finality, its discernibility, its object. In order to grasp the bearing of this intervention, we need to have in mind the names which, for two centuries, have dominated western thinking: Protestants for the most part, who shift little by little towards the varying forms of rationalism and materialism.[3] To keep our thinking within the immediate context of the Council, we must remember that the nineteenth century, except for a short period of romantic religious feeling, was almost entirely under the influence of the English deists and the French encyclopedists. The notions of supernatural, revelation, mystery, and miracle, in cultivated circles, were called into question, and the claims of Christianity were discussed in the name of historical criticism and philosophy. The entirely new science of comparative history of religions even questions the problem of transcendence. The Hegelian left, with Feuerbach, prepares the way for the atheism of Marx, whereas materialistic explanations of the world and life, the transformist interpretation of the universe, under the influence of Spencer and Darwin, rapidly gain the favor of the public.[4]

This growing ascendency of rationalism happens to coincide with a period of decadence in Catholic theology.[5] The whole effort of theologians, in line with the apologetics of the seventeenth century against the free-thinkers, consists in defending religion against its adversaries and rescuing it from the contempt into which it had fallen. Even dogmatic theology is taken up primarily with making her dogmas acceptable to the philosophers of her day, fighting on their own terrain. Unfortunately, the defenders of Church, themselves not untouched by the spirit of philosophism, and lacking a solid traditional philosophy, sometimes find themselves in dangerous positions. Some, in an effort to effect the passage from reason to religion through the unaided resources of human reason, fall into a semi-rationalism which the Council will condemn.[6] Theologians, such as Hermes, Günther and Frohschammer, under the unconscious influence of the philosophy of Kant and Descartes, are inclined to exaggerate the powers of human reason.[7] They do not deny revelation, but this revelation, in the last analysis, is no longer supernatural excepting in its mode: once he is in possession of the formulas of faith, man can penetrate their secret and scientifically demonstrate their truth. Others, on the contrary, as a reaction against the absolute reign of human reason, think that they must take refuge in faith and authority of tradition. The fideists, exaggerating the objections of rationalism, and believing that the fact of revelation cannot be established by solid demonstration, think that faith needs to be completely blind. The traditionalists, on their part, maintain that tradition, the result of a primitive revelation, is absolutely necessary to know the truths of natural religion as well as the mysteries of the supernatural order. Among these are Lamennais, Bautain, Bonnetty, Ventura, De Bonald.

Whereas semi-rationalism gives reason an unjustified preponderance, fideism, on the other hand, and traditionalism, excessively cheapen the role of reason. Up until the First Vatican Council, it is possible to note an oscillation between these two poles among Catholic theologians, evidence of the uneasy situation created by the difficult problem of the relationship between faith and reason. Throughout the whole of the pontificates of Gregory XVI and Pius IX, there is an echo of this uneasy spirit. Rome constantly has to intervene to condemn errors, point out deviations, reaffirm Catholic teaching.

Gregory XVI strikes at the absolute traditionalism of Lamennais (*Mirari vos arbitramur*, August 15, 1832; *Singulari nos affecerant gaudio*, June 25, 1834), supports reason against the mitigated traditionalism of Bautain, and repudiates the semi-rationalism of Hermes (*Dum acerbissimas,* Sept. 26, 1835). Pius IX, with the encyclical *Qui pluribus* (Nov. 9, 1846), explains the doctrine of the Church on the relationship between faith and reason. He condemns the mitigated traditionalism of Bonnetty, the semi-rationalism of Günther and the intellectual liberalism of Frohschammer. Finally, in the *Syllabus* of December 8, 1864, and in the encyclical *Quanta cura* which accompanies it, he denounces the errors and false principles of the nineteenth century: pantheism, naturalism and absolute rationalism, moderate rationalism, indifferentism, liberalism, socialism.

In this period which immediately precedes the First Vatican Council, the only text which touches upon our subject is the encyclical *Qui pluribus.* This document sees the positive statement of principles which, twenty-five years later, will be taken up once again by the Council. Pius IX states that there is no possible conflict between faith and reason, since both derive from the one and the same Source of eternal truth; on the contrary, they must lend each other mutual support (D 1635). Rationalism, "enemy of divine revelation," wants to reduce Christian religion to the conditions of a human work, or a "philosophical system," subject to the law of constant progress. The Pope takes a stand against this claim and declares that: A. our religion has been "*revealed* by God to humanity" and enjoys all the "power and authority of this same *God who speaks*";[8] B. the duty of human reason, as a consequence, is "to inquire diligently into the fact of *revelation* in order to obtain the certitude that *God has spoken* and to offer Him . . . a reasonable homage"; C. "we must give entire faith to *God who speaks* and that nothing is more in conformity with reason itself than to acquiesce and adhere firmly to everything that is established as *revealed* by God who can neither deceive nor be deceived".[9] The encyclical then lists the arguments which clearly prove the divine origin of Christianity and states, together with Saint John Chrysostom, "that the whole principle of our dogmas took root from the Lord of Heaven" (D 1638).

In three different contexts, the text of the encyclical compares the terms revelation, word, and faith, illustrating them by each other. The Council envisages revelation in turn under its objective, active and passive aspects. In the first case, it is speaking of *religion as revealed* (in the sense of *doctrine,* according to the interpretation of the Vatican Council, which takes up the same text, D 1800), as opposed to what would be only human doctrine, the fruit of philosophical reflection; in the second case, the text establishes an equivalence between the activity of revealing and the activity of speaking; the third case envisages man's reaction to a God who reveals: faith is the response to God who speaks, acquiescence to what is revealed. It is addressed properly to the Person revealing and adheres to what he says. The motive for this adherence and this homage is the word of God itself: word of authority from Him who can neither be deceived (which excludes all error) nor deceive us (which excludes all falsehood). Faith is thus a reasonable homage, based on the truthful and infallible word of God Himself. The word of God is of the order of testimony.

II. DOGMATIC CONSTITUTION ON CATHOLIC FAITH

In four chapters, the constitution *Dei Filius* explains the doctrine of the Church on God, revelation, faith, the relationship between faith and reason. Our analysis will bear upon the second, third, and fourth chapters. Once again it must be pointed out that what is directly treated in this document is less the nature of revelation—as in the case of the encyclical *Pascendi*—than the fact of its existence, its possibility, its object. The explanation of Catholic doctrine, however, provided the fathers with an occasion to define the traditional notion of revelation in simple and concrete terms.

1. In the first paragraph of the chapter on revelation, the Council distinguishes two ways by which man can arrive at a knowledge of God: the ascendant way of natural knowledge, and the descendant way of revelation. The first takes its point of departure in creation, with the innate light of human reason for its instrument, and arrives at God, not in His innermost life, but in His causal relationship with the world. The second has for its author God who speaks, Author of the supernatural order, who makes Himself known, together with the decrees of His will. These are two distinct and equally legitimate kinds of knowledge.

The first part of the paragraph claims that it is possible for man, by the natural light of his reason, through the medium of creatures (*per ea quae facta sunt*—through the things which have been made— according to the language of Scripture), to arrive at a certain knowledge of God, beginning and end of all things. The Council thus vindicates the value of natural theology against two errors which threaten the conditions of faith. These two errors are those of atheism and positivism, in which there is no way for man to know God; and that of advanced traditionalism, which concedes to human reason only the passive power of knowing God and, as a consequence, expects all knowledge of God to come either from revelation or from a positive teaching received through tradition.

The second part contrasts the natural knowledge of God with the "supernatural way" of revelation: "Still it pleased the wisdom and goodness of God to reveal to the human race, by another and supernatural way, both Himself and the eternal decrees of His will; as the apostle says: God, who at sundry times and in divers manners spoke in times past to the fathers by the prophets, last of all in these days has spoken to us by His Son".[10] Though only in summary, this text furnishes several important statements on the notion of revelation:

A. The text establishes the fact of supernatural and positive revelation, such as it is described in both the Old and New Testaments.

B. God is Author and Cause of this revelation. It is a free and gratuitous operation of His will, the result of His good pleasure: *placuisse* (He was pleased to). We might say that revelation, like the whole supernatural order, is essentially grace, pure gratuity, gift of love.

C. Divine initiative, revelation still is not without its motive; it was fitting both to the wisdom and goodness of God: *sapientiae et bonitati*. To God's wisdom, first of all, as Creator and Providence (D 1782 to 1784), so that the religious truths of the natural order might be known by all men, "without difficulty, with firm certitude, and without any admixture of error" (D 1786). To His wisdom as Author of the supernatural order, for if God raised man to this order, he was necessarily bound to make him know the end of that order and the means to it. Revelation was equally fitting to the goodness of God. Already the initiative with which God comes out of His mystery, addresses man, speaks to him, enters into personal communication of thought with him, is a sign of His infinite kindness. That this communication not only makes man's natural road towards God easier, but also makes him an associate of the secrets of divine life, the "sharing of divine blessings" (D 1786): this is the hallmark of infinite charity.

D. The material object of revelation is God Himself and the eternal decrees of His free will. The paragraphs which follow (D 1786, 1795) indicate that this object embraces truths accessible to reason as well as mysteries which surpass reason. By the word *God*, we must understand His existence, His attributes, as well as the intimate life of the three Persons. And by the word *decrees*, we must understand those which concern the creation and natural government of the world, as well as those which concern our elevation to the supernatural order, the Incarnation, Redemption, call of the elect.

E. The human race in its entirety is the beneficiary of this revelation; it is as universal as salvation itself.

F. The text of Scripture, according to Msgr. Gasser,[11] only confirms this doctrine of the fact of revelation and marks the progress from one covenant to the other. The quotation, closely bound up with the text, gives us to understand that revelation is conceived, by the fathers of the Council, as the word of God addressed to humanity. *Deus loquens ... locutus est*: this is what makes for the unity and continuity between the two covenants, the one and only word of God, the word of the Son being the continuation and fulfillment of the word for which the prophets were God's instruments of old. The revelation of the Old Testament was successive, fragmentary, polymorphous; that of the New Testament is unique, total, and definitive. On the one hand, there is a multiplicity of inspired prophets; on the other, the one and only Son of God.

2. The second paragraph enlarges these elements of definition with new determinations concerning the necessity, the finality, and the object of revelation.

If revelation is absolutely necessary, says the Council, it is "because God, in His infinite goodness, has ordered man towards a supernatural end, that is, the sharing of the divine good".[12] There was an amendment, recognized as being an exact expression of the fathers' thinking, even though it was not adopted; it proposed the addition: "God has ordered man towards a supernatural end, that is, to that admirable sharing of divinity to be begun by grace and consummated in glory, surpassing the comprehension of the human mind, of which the apostle says that eye has not seen ... "[13] Since God has assigned man a supernatural end, he must, if He means to respect the intelligence and free nature of man, make him know this end and the means which will assure its possession: He must reveal them to him. It is thus, in the last analysis, the salvific will of God which explains the necessary character of revelation of the truths of the supernatural order.

With respect to the religious truths of the natural order, revelation does not have this same character of absolute necessity. The Council, using the same words as Saint Thomas, describes this revelation in terms of moral necessity; this necessity bears upon neither the object nor the active power of human reason, but rather the actual condition of humanity; without such revelation, religious truths of the natural order could not be "known by all, without difficulty, with firm certitude, without admixture of error".[14]

At the same time that it determines the degree of necessity of revelation, the Council is led to distinguish, in the material object, on the one hand, those truths which are connatural to man and, on the other hand, those "which completely surpass the scope of the human mind." The Council is treating the same object as in the preceding paragraph, but this time considered under its aspect of proportion or disproportion with natural reason.

3. A word like *revelation* always calls to mind the activity as well as the objective terminus of this activity, that is, the gift received or the truth revealed. Thus the Council, having just spoken of the activity of revelation, distinguishing connatural truths and mysteries in the object of revelation, is necessarily led, by a normal process of transition, to consider revelation under its objective aspect as spoken or expressed word. The content or sources of this revelation, says the Council, taking up once again the words of the Council of Trent, are the written books and the traditions which, "having been received by the apostles from the mouth of Jesus Christ in person, or having been handed down, from hand to hand so to speak, by the apostles themselves, to whom the Holy Spirit had dictated them, have come down to our own day" (D 1787). But, with a precision that did not appear in the wording of the Council of Trent, the Vatican Council explicitly uses the word revelation to designate the content of the divine word: *haec porro supernaturalis revelatio*. This word spoken by God, the subject of Scripture and tradition, is the object of our faith. That is why the Council declares, in the third chapter, that we must believe "everything that is contained in the word of God written or handed down by tradition".[15]

4. Msgr. Martin connects the third chapter on faith with the preceding chapter, which treats of revelation, pointing out that "faith on the part of man corresponds to revelation on the part of God".[16] This chapter informs us particularly on the specific element of the word of revelation.

The first paragraph recalled first of all the foundation of our obligation to believe in God who reveals. The general foundation is to be found in the fact that "man depends entirely upon God as his Creator and Lord"; the special foundation is the fact that human reason, once created, is "completely subject to the uncreated truth" (D 1789). Creation is the basis for the homage of intelligence and will which man owes to God;[17] *created* reason must bow before *uncreated* Truth.[18] The first canon on faith states, against the rationalists, that reason is not autonomous and that God can command faith (D 1810). Man, in so far as he is a creature, must accept this indirect way of knowing, no matter how mortifying it is to his tendencies towards complete emancipation.[19]

The rest of the paragraph declares that the motive for faith is the *authority* of God who speaks; this motive distinguishes faith from science.[20] This statement is directed against the rationalists who understand religious faith as simply the philosophical science which is connected with God and religion.[21] Against the semi-rationalists too, such as Hermes, who think that "every firm conviction about God and divine things constitutes faith properly so called, even though the assent of such faith comes slowly from an appreciation of the inner bond between ideas".[22] In this sense, faith must be called the knowledge of God obtained from the consideration of the universe. Faith, says the Council, adheres to revealed things, "not by reason of their intrinsic truth as perceived by the natural light of reason, but because of the authority of God Himself who can neither deceive nor be deceived".[23] Such is the formal motive for faith.

The authority of God *in dicendo* proceeds from His infinite wisdom and truthfulness, excluding every error and every deception. The all-knowing God can neither be mistaken nor deceived; the all-truthful God cannot deceive us. He has the authority of an infinitely *qualified* witness, whose word deserves total and definitive assent. In thus contrasting faith and science, natural evidence and the assent of faith, the Council says equivalently (for the precise word does not appear) that the word of God comes under the species of *testimony*. A word which commands a reaction of faith, that is, a word which invites man to give credence on the sole authority of the one who speaks, as guarantee of truth, is, properly speaking, a testimony.

The Council, taking up in turn the essential elements of the description of the act of faith as given by the Council of Trent, states that faith is a supernatural virtue through which, under the action of grace which comes before and helps, we believe as true what God has revealed, precisely because of the authority of God who reveals. The Council of Trent spoke of the act of faith rather than the virtue and mentioned, in the object of faith, the promises made by God; the Council was speaking of faith which justifies, of a faith, consequently, which must stir up trust and confidence through the consideration of the divine promises.[24]

Faith, in itself, is a gift of God. Arguments of the rational order can prepare and sustain our adherence of faith; the real cause for this adherence, in the last analysis, is to be sought in a supernatural activity of God. It is not enough for the Gospel teaching to sound in our ear; there must also be an interior activity of grace which enlightens the intelligence and inclines the powers of our will. Taking up the text of the Council of Orange (D 180), the Council says that "no one can adhere to the Gospel teaching, in the way that is necessary to arrive at salvation, without an illumination and an inspiration of the Holy Spirit, who gives everyone sweetness in adhering to the word and believing in the truth".[25] Faith is religious adherence to the word of God under the combined activity of the external word and the inner activity of the Holy Spirit. At the same time that the preaching of Christ, the apostles, or the Church echoes without, proclaiming the Gospel and inviting to faith, the Spirit is at work within, making this activity fertile. God Himself takes the initiative in drawing man to himself; and in this interior activity of His grace there is already a first impulse of the return movement which is the response of faith. The assent of faith to the Gospel preaching is at the same time a free abandon to the motion of the Spirit.[26]

5. The fifth chapter, devoted to the problem of the relationship between faith and reason, contains a precise teaching on the object of revelation, and especially its privileged object, that is, the mysteries.

The first paragraph distinguishes two orders of knowledge: one natural, the other supernatural; the one having for its principle natural reason; the other, divine faith. Natural knowledge has for its object truths accessible to human reason. Supernatural knowledge of faith possesses a twofold object: first of all "truths at which natural reason can arrive" (D 1795). This statement is in keeping with what has already been said in the preceding chapters: the first chapter actually enumerates the attributes of God which play a part in our theodicy (D 1782); the second chapter speaks of those points which "in the divine affairs, are not inaccessible to our human reason" (D 1786); the third chapter indicates as the object of our faith "everything that is contained in the word of God as written or handed down by tradition" and which the Church proposes by a solemn judgment or by her ordinary and universal magisterium as being divinely revealed (D 1792). The present chapter, finally, indicates as the proper object of supernatural revelation "the mysteries hidden in God which cannot be known without divine revelation",[27] that is, mysteries properly so called (D 1816). These mysteries are the truths of which only God possesses a natural knowledge. The texts of Scripture quoted by the Council illustrate this fact well: we are speaking here of "the wisdom of God, mysterious and hidden" (1 Cor. 2:7 ff), the secrets of God which only the Spirit can reveal to us, who scrutinizes the depths of God (1 Cor. 2:10). A letter from Pius IX to the Bishop of Munich, on the same subject, in 1862, spoke of "the mystery hidden for centuries and generations past" (Col. 1:26) and harked back to the text in the prologue of Saint John: "No one has ever seen God; the only Son of God, who is in the Father, He has told of Him" (Jn.

1:18; D 1672). These mysteries "surpass created understanding" and, consequently, "even the natural intelligence of the angels" (D 1796, 1673). In the concrete, what are these mysteries? The letter of Pius IX to the Bishop of Munich stresses particularly those which regard man's supernatural elevation and his intercourse with God (D 1671), and primarily the Incarnation (D 1669). In other words, we might say that the principal mystery which God means to manifest is that of his salvific will, that is, the mystery of our participation in the divine life given by Christ ("*ordinavit hominem ad . . . participanda bona divina*"—He ordered man towards . . . sharing divine blessings, D 1786). The Council of Trent, for its part, asserts that, in faith, we believe in the truth which God has revealed and promised, first of all in the fact that man the sinner is justified by the grace of God, through redemption in Jesus Christ (D 798). This salvific character is essential to the concept of revelation.[28]

6. The fourth chapter ends with a paragraph which proposes the true notion of dogmatic development. "The *doctrine of faith* which God has revealed has not been proposed as a philosophical discovery to be developed and perfected by human intelligence; it has been entrusted to Christ's Bride, as a *divine deposit* to be faithfully preserved and infallibly proclaimed".[29] And in the dogmatic constitution on the Church: "The Holy Spirit has been promised to the successors of Peter . . . so that they will holily preserve and faithfully propose the *revelation* handed down to them by the apostles, or the *deposit of faith*".[30] These two passages explain each other and make it clear that the revealed doctrine, revelation and the deposit of faith, are one and the same reality. The Church must faithfully preserve (as a deposit) and infallibly proclaim that revealed doctrine. And in the second text: she must holily preserve (as a deposit) and faithfully explain (as a doctrine) the revelation handed down to her. Revelation is obviously here understood in the objective sense of doctrine. The content of the divine word is a religious doctrine, a complex of propositions which state and designate the mystery of our salvation.

The Church adds nothing to this deposit of faith received from the apostles. What can however be perfected is the understanding of the deposit, the assimilation on the part of the faithful of the revealed doctrine, whose sense always remains identical, and whose interpretation remains unchanging (D 1800). But for the doctrine of Christ to be taught without addition or corruption, the Church necessarily needs not only to preserve it, but also to denounce the errors which threaten it. Thus she has the right to proscribe opinions which are opposed to revealed doctrine (D 1817).

In summing up the teaching of the First Vatican Council, we have the following points. The Council envisages revelation either in the active or objective sense, as word addressed or as word spoken. But it is revelation in the objective sense which claims fullest attention.

The activity of revelation is the sovereignly gratuitous activity of the God of Salvation who, in His wisdom and goodness, makes Himself known to the human race: both Himself and the decrees of His will. This divine activity is conceived of as word of God to humanity, as distinguished from His manifestation as cause and end of His creatures, a word of authority, qualified by the knowledge and truthfulness of an infinitely wise and infinitely holy God. This activity is personal, from subject to subject, and not from object to subject; historical, progressive, culminating with the revelation of the Son; salvific, universal, desiring to associate all humanity with the blessings of divine life.

Faith, gift of God, response to His word, is not the assent of the philosopher or wise man before the evidence of truth, but rather a response to testimony. Faith is certainly homage to God, to His person, but to a God who speaks (Deus loquens); the homage proper to Him is faith in what He says. In the last analysis, faith is addressed to the person, but immediately to what He says; and the motive upon which this adherence is based is the authority of God Himself.

The material object of revelation can be viewed in itself: God and His secrets; or according to the proportion between this object and power of our human mind: then we distinguish between truths accessible to natural reason and mysteries which surpass the scope of our mind. These mysteries have to do with the intimate life of God and our sharing in this life through the Incarnation and redemption.

The truths revealed or spoken by God are contained in the holy books and in tradition. They constitute revelation in the objective sense of the word, revealed doctrine, entrusted to the Church by Christ as a deposit to be preserved, proclaimed, protected against error. This doctrine is offered to our faith through preaching. But to consent, we need an activity of grace or the Holy Spirit who accompanies the preaching of the divine message and gives man the power to abandon himself to the interior motion of God. The revealed doctrine is unchangeable and can produce fruit only by an unceasing process of assimilation.

1. Latin text to be found in L. Petit and J. B. Martin, ed., Collectio Conciliorum recentiorum Ecclesiae universae sive amplissimae collectionis conciliorum a Mansi et continuatoribus editae

(vols. 49-53 on the First Vatican Council, Paris, 1923-1927), 51: 429-430. This we shall designate: Mansi.

2. Mansi, 51: 430.

3. In *Germany* Wolf (1679-1754), Kant (1724-1804), Fichte (1672-1810), Schelling (1775-1843), Hegel (1770-1831), Schopenhauer (1788-1860), Schleiermacher (1768-1834), Strauss (1808-1874), Baur (1792-1860). *English* rationalism is bound up with the philosophy of Bacon (1561-1626), the materialism of Hobbes (1588-1679), the sensualism of Locke (1631-1704). This strain develops gradually and directly into the positivism of Stuart Mill (1773-1836), the evolutionism of Spencer (1820-1903) and Darwin (1809-1882). In *France,* Voltaire (1694-1778) and Rousseau (1712-1778), with the *Encyclopedia,* become the masters of modern laicism. Locke's materialistic theories made their way into France through Condillac (1715-1780), whereas English positivism, with Hume, Spencer, and Darwin, was introduced by Comte (1798-1857), Taine (1828-1893), and Littre (1801-1880).

4. R. Aubert, *Le Pontificat de Pie IX* (Paris, 1952), vol. 21 of *Histoire de l'Église,* edited by A. Fliche et E. Jarry, p. 219.

5. E. Hocedez, *Histoire de la théologie au XIX siècle* (3 vol., Brussels and Paris, 1949-1952), 1: 13-21; R. Aubert, *Le Pontificat de Pie IX,* p. 220.

6. In particular in paragragh V of the Prologue to the Constitution *Dei Filius* (Mansi, 51: 430).

7. On semi-rationalism in the 19th century: E. Hocedez, *Histoire de la théologie au XIX siècle,* 1: 161-205; J. M. A. Vacant, *Études théologiques,* 1: 119-138; R. Aubert, *Le Pontificat de Pie IX,* pp. 193-211; articles du *DTC* aux noms cités.

8. "Et sane cum sanctissima nostra religio non ab humana ratione fuerit inventa, sed a Deo hominibus clementissime patefacta, tum quisque vel facile intelligit religionem ipsam ex ejusdem Dei loquentis auctoritate omnem suam vim acquirere neque ab humana ratione deduci aut perfici unquam posse" (D 1636).

9. "Humana quidem ratio, ne in tanti momenti negotio decipiatur et erret, divinae revelationis factum diligenter inquirat oportet, ut certo sibi constet Deum esse locutum ac eidem, quemadmodum sapientissime docet Apostolus, rationabile obsequium exhibeat. Quis enim ignorat vel ignorare potest omnem Deo loquenti fidem esse habendam, nihilque rationi ipsi magis consentaneum esse quam iis acquiescere firmiterque adhaerere quae a Deo, qui nec falli nec fallere potest, revelata esse constiterit?" (D 1637).

10. "Eadem sancta mater Ecclesia tenet et docet, Deum, rerum omnium principium et finem, naturali humanae rationis lumine e rebus creatis certo cognosci posse; 'invisibilia enim ipsius, a creatura mundi, per ea quae facta sunt, intellecta, conspiciuntur' (*Rom.* 1, 20); attamen placuisse ejus sapientiae et bonitati, alia eaque supernaturali via seipsum ac aeterna voluntatis suae decreta humano generi revelare, dicente Apostolo: Multifariam multisque modis olim Deus loquens patribus in Prophetis: novissime diebus istis locutus est nobis in Filio (*Heb.* 1, 1)" (D 1785).

11. Mansi, 51: 272.

12. "Revelatio absolute necessaria dicenda est... quia Deus ex infinita bonitate sua ordinavit hominem ad finem supernaturalem, ad participanda scilicet bona divina, quae humanae mentis intelligentiam omnino superant" (D 1786).

13. "Deus ordinavit hominem ad finem supernaturalem, scilicet ad illud mirandum consortium divinitatis inchoandum per gratiam, consummandum per gloriam, rationis comprehensionem excedens, et de quo dicitur quod oculus non vidit... " (Mansi, 51: 280).

14. "Huic divinae revelationi tribuendum quidem est, ut ea, quae in rebus divinis humanae rationi per se impervia non sunt, in praesenti quoque generis humani conditione ab omnibus expedite, firma certitudine et nullo admixto errore cognosci possint" (D 1786). In S. Thomas: *Summa theol.,* 1a, q. 1, a. 1; 2a 2ae, q. 2, a. 4, c.; *Contra Gentiles,* L. I, c. 4. The encyclical *Humani Generis* will speak explicitly of "moral necessity": "divina revelatio *moraliter necessaria* dicenda est ut ea quae in rebus religionis et morum rationi per se impervia non sunt, in praesenti quoque humani generis conditione, ab omnibus, expedite, firma certitudine et nullo admixto errore cognosci possint" (D 2305).

15. "Fide divina et catholica ea omnia credenda sunt, quae in verbo Dei scripto vel tradito continentur et ab Ecclesia sive solemni judicio sive ordinario et universali magisterio tanquam divinitus revelata credenda proponuntur" (D 1792).

16. Mansi, 51: 313.

17. Msgr. Martin explains: "Haec autem radix, haec fundamentalis ratio obligationis humanae Deo fidem praestandi aperte posita est in eo quod Deus sit supremus auctor, quod Deus sit creator noster, quod Deus sit Dominus noster, a quo toti cum omnibus viribus nostris dependemus. Haec est intentio prima partis hujus primae paragraphi" (Mansi, 51: 313, 316).

18. The original text read: *increatae rationi.* An amendment suggested replacing the expression

by: *increatae rationi quae est ipsa Veritas* (the uncreated reason which is truth itself.) It was accepted by the fathers and became, in the definitive text: *increatae Veritati* (MANSI, 51: 315).

19. MANSI, 51: 329.

20. "Ut omnes scimus, dit Mgr. Martin, propria ratio fidei posita est in motivo seu in objecto suo formali, nempe in auctoritate Dei loquentis, quo quidem motivo fides a scientia naturali essentialitèr distinguitur" (MANSI, 51: 313).

21. "Rationalistae... nomine fidei generatim non aliud intelligunt quam rationalem scientiam rerum ad Deum et ad religionem pertinentium" (MANSI, 50: 85).

22. "Semi-rationalistaè... docent enim firmam persuasionem de Deo et de rebus divinis esse fidem illam proprie dictam, a qua fideles denominantur, etiamsi motivum amplectendi et tenendi veritatem non sit auctoritas Dei, sed vèritas teneatur et solummodo propter perspectum intrinsecum nexum idearum" (MANSI, 50: 85).

23. "Hanc vero fidem... virtutem esse supernaturalem qua... ab eo (Deo) revèlata vera esse credimus, non propter intrinsecam rerum veritatem naturali rationis luminè perspectam, sed propter auctoritatem ipsius Dei revelantis, qui nec falli nec fallere potest" (D 1789).

24. J. M. A. VACANT, *Études théologiques*, 2: 26.

25. "Nemo... evangelicae praedicationi consentire potest, sicut oportet ad salutem consequendam, absque illuminatione et inspirationè Spiritus Sancti, qui dat omnibus suavitatem in consentiendo et credendo veritati" (D 1791).

26. Saint Thomas frequently comes back to this idea; for examplè: "Not only external revelation, or the object, has the power of drawing us, but also the interior instinct which impels us and moves us to believè; thus the Father draws many towards the Son through the instinct of His divine activity which moves the heart of man from within to believe" (In JOAN., c. 6, lect. 5). And once again: "Now a man is helped by God to believe in three ways. First of all through the interior call which is described in John 6, 45: Everyone who heard from the Father and learned has come to me; and in Rom. 8, 30: Those whom he predestined, he also called. Secondly, through the external teaching and preaching, according to the words of the Apostle in Romans 10, 17: Faith is from hearing, but hearing is through the word of Christ. And thirdly, through external miracles...." (Quodl. 2, q. 4, a. 6). Sèe also: Summa theol. 2a 2ae, q. 2, a. 9, ad 3.

27. "Hoc quoque perpetuus Ecclesiae catholicae consensus tenuit et tenet, duplicem esse ordinem cognitions non solum principio, sed objecto etiam distinctum: principio quidem, quia in altero naturali ratione, in altero fide divina cognoscimus; objecto autem, quia praeter ea ad quae naturalis ratio pertingere potest, credènda nobis proponuntur mysteria in Deo abscondita, quae, nisi revelata divinitus, innotescere non possunt" (D 1795).

28. In Saint John: "This is life everlasting: that they know you the one true God and Him whom you have sent, Jesus Christ" (Jn. 17: 3). Saint Thomas insists on this salvific finality in revelation (Summa theol., 1a q. 1, a. 1, c.).

29. "Neque enim fidei doctrina, quam Deus revelavit, velut philosophicum inventum proposita est humanis ingèniis perficienda, sed tanquam divinum depositum Christi Sponsae tradita, fideliter custodienda et infallibiliter declaranda" (D 1800).

30. "Petri successoribus Spiritus Sanctus promissus est... ut, eo assistente, traditam per Apostolos revelationem seu fidei depositum sancte custodirent et fideliter exponerent" (D 1836).

CHAPTER III

THE MODERNIST CRISIS

Faced with the scope of Modernism and its many forms, Pius X was led to denounce it as "the rendezvous of all heresies" (D 2105). Its distinctive note, however, according to J. Rivière, "is to attack the notions of revelation, faith, and dogma, which are the foundations of traditional Christianity, and dissolve them in a pure subjectivism".[1] Modernism, actually, is really a reappearance of an old problem already envisaged by Vatican Council I, harmonizing the data of revelation with the discoveries of philosophy and science. Such a problem really embraces too many factors to be resolved at a single stroke. Inevitably, there were always new blows to be met, evidence of fresh unrest.

In their chapters on revelation, primarily, the Modernist theologians, under the pretext of reforming a pseudo-notion of revelation, conceived of in a monolithic manner as having fallen straight from heaven without any relationship to human consciousness, practically come to the point of denying the transcendent character of revelation, turning it into a purely immanent reality, a purely human experience. Some, such as Tyrrell, without falling into such a radical subjectivism, still seriously compromise the notion of objective revelation and dogmatic development.

I. SOURCES OF MODERNISM

Modernism is the offspring of liberal Protestantism, through the intermediary of Schleiermacher, Ritschl and Sabatier.

1. As a reaction against Kant, in religion, Schleiermacher re-establishes the value of sentiment and religious experience. For Kant, it will be recalled, the exercise of pure reason makes it impossible for us to have any knowledge of a suprasensible reality, of an absolute

situated outside the circle of phenomena: "I could not ... admit God, freedom, and immortality according to the need which my reason has for them in its necessary practical usages, without at the same time repudiating the claims of pure reason to transcendent views, for, in order to arrive at these views, it has to make use of principles which, in reality, extend only to the objects of possible experience and which, if they are applied to an object which cannot be the object of an experience, really and always transform this experience into a phenomenon, and thus declare every practical extension of pure reason impossible. I have thus suppressed knowledge in order to substitute faith for it".[2] But the faith in which Kant is interested is much different from the faith of Luther. It is *Vernunftglaube*, simple rational faith, exercise of the practical reason. Once purified from all the elements which are foreign to its nature—rites and creeds— religion is reduced to a moral will which is itself based on the categorical imperative, the *du musst*, imposing its imperative in a universal and absolute manner. A transcendent revelation, providing humanity with a supplementary knowledge, obviously has no place in the Kantian agnostic universe. If the concept, in itself, is not contradictory, we at very least have no way to verify its objectivity. A religion which claims to be historical and revealed must then itself be judged in function of moral and pure reason which alone are universals. "Historical faith ... has no particular value .... It can suffice for the creed of the Church, but only pure religious faith, based entirely upon reason, can be recognized as necessary".[3] Jesus Christ Himself is nothing more than a good example of obedience to this categorical imperative. Kant denies Christ's real divinity and transforms the biblical data and expressions of the Gospel into terms of moral philosophy.

2. Schleiermacher (1768-1834), pietist and romantic, reacting against the dead negations of Kant, set about re-evaluating prayer and religious sentiment. In his day, in the churches of Germany, there were two opposing currents: rationalism, tending to reduce religion to the limits of reason, and supernaturalism, at work to maintain the transcendence of Christianity as a revealed religion. The *father* of modern Protestant theology managed to find, between these two currents, a sort of middle ground. His theology is based no more on the doctrine *ex auditu* than on the truth *ex intellectu*, theologian of the heart, he bases his religion on a feeling of dependence, more or less pure, more or less profound, in accordance with the variety of actual religions. Revelation, thus, is not a privilege of Christianity, but a common possession of all religion. It is only the "spontaneous

and subjective fruit of the concept of God springing forth from the feeling of dependence or religious sentiment".[4] In Christ, this feeling of dependence is expressed by His awareness of His unity with God, by the sentimental certitude of His mission as Mediator between men, His brothers, and God the Father. What counts is not the fact that Christ is God, but His awareness of that fact. Faith itself is a certitude which accompanies a more vivid and profound awareness of our redemption in Christ. This is an anthropocentric theology, infected with subjectivism.[5]

3. Hegel, colleague and rival of Schleiermacher at Berlin, from 1818 to 1831, made no effort to conceal his contempt for this religion based on feeling, and claims to have reintroduced the speculative and theoretical element into religion (opposed thus to the moralism of Kant as well as the sentimentalism of Schleiermacher). There was a lively struggle between the followers of these two men; nonetheless, under the influence of A. Ritschl, it was the current initiated by Schleiermacher which ended up triumphant. Ritschl (1822-1889), like Schleiermacher, vindicates the autonomy of religious awareness and protests against the interference of philosophy in matters of religion; he shares Schleiermacher's metaphysical agnosticism, his anthropocentric conceptions, and, like him, reduces theology to Christology; he is interested only in value judgments (*Werturteile*), as opposed to speculative judgments (*Seinsurteile*, bearing upon the existence and nature of things). Ritschl, however, stands out as a reactionary, compared to Schleiermacher. He feels that Schleiermacher is seriously in error when he bases religion only on the subjective awareness of the community rather than on positive Christian revelation. Therefore he rests his argument upon the Gospel, upon the historical fact, as it is set down in the Bible. But how is it possible, in a Kantian conception of the universe, which makes a fundamental axiom of the opposition between the *noumenon* and the *phenomenon*, to preserve any meaning in the Bible's statements about God, revelation and salvation through the Word Incarnate? "We would do better simply to call God, revelation, salvation, *the entirely immanent religious experience of man*. Christ will reveal God and save man, simply in this sense that He will express and allow us to express, through the image that the Gospels have immortalized of Him, the highest awareness that humanity can have of itself".[6] This will preserve the word revelation, but deprive it of its traditional content. The Gospel is nothing more than a collection of religious experiences, and its only interest is to provoke a similar experience in us.

Ritschl and Schleiermacher conditioned Protestant thinking to give first place to religious experience rather than adherence to dogmatic truths. This did away with the notion of objective revelation, of doctrine effectively received from God. Religion, instead of being the result of a divine initiative, is quite simply an immanent elaboration, unfolding in the depths of human awareness. Faith is exalted, but faith is nothing more than an affective disposition of the soul, implying no particular creed. The religion which lives in the heart of the faithful is one thing, and that which proceeds from dogmas and formulas is another.

4. The spread of Protestant liberalism in France was the work of A. Sabatier, in his *Esquisse d'une philosophie de la religion d'après la psychologie et l'histoire*.[7] Sabatier establishes a close relationship between religion, prayer, and revelation. Religion is essentially the prayer of the heart, a movement of the soul which puts it into relationship "with the mysterious power which it feels it is dependent upon and upon which its destiny is dependent".[8] But what would devotion amount to if it did not imply some positive manifestations on the part of God? Revelation is God's response to prayer, "but always on the condition that this response is always, at least in germ, in the prayer itself",[9] for the God to whom prayer is addressed is also the God who inspires the prayer. Revelation is thus not a communication of unchanging doctrines made once and for all, but God Himself or rather the feeling of God's presence in us. Revelation is in prayer and progresses together with prayer. More precisely, says Sabatier, "revelation consists in the creation, purification, and progressive clarification of the awareness of God in the individual man and in humanity".[10] As a result, revelation exists for who ever submits to the divine activity, and revelation can be conceived of under a personal and immediate form. The fact of revelation has no need for proof, because it coincides with the fact of religious awareness, existing in all men and in all religions, although much more vividly in the prophets and in Christ. The essence of Christianity is to be found "in a religious experience, in an intimate revelation of God which took place for the first time in the soul of Jesus of Nazareth, but which is verified and repeated, in less luminous a manner no doubt, but still not unrecognizably, in the soul of all His true disciples".[11] The filial devotion towards the Father and the fraternal feeling towards all men which we observe in the consciousness of Jesus we also find in the experience of all Christians.

Religious emotion, which is at the basis of the experience of revelation, is expressed first of all under the form of images, then under the form of concepts and judgments which the Church, if she wishes, can approve and receive as dogmas. Still, the authentic and permanent element is always to be found in the religious experience (for example justice, divine fatherhood, Kingdom of God), for the dogmatic expressions are purely symbolic and subject to the law of evolution: they vary, as a consequence, with varying ages, philosophies, cultures in accordance with the progress of the human mind. Thus, dogmas can die (the existence of demons, the eternity of hell), change their meaning (Trinity, miracle, revelation, satisfaction, inspiration), revive after a period of oblivion, or even make their first appearance (justification by faith, universal priesthood).[12]

Sabatier is violently opposed to the notion of revelation, as revealed deposit, a hybrid product born, as he says, of the encounter between Greek rationalism and Hebrew supernaturalism:

"It is pointless to deduce this scholastic theory from Holy Scripture; it is only an unfaithful translation of the biblical notion. God's revelation is uprooted from the soil of religious life and turned into a body of supernatural truths subsisting by itself, to which we set up an obligation and reward for adhering, forcing our judgment and our conscience to be silent if necessary .... Basically, this idea of revelation is quite pagan .... Let us then bravely conclude, in the face of all traditional orthodoxies, that the object of God's revelation can only be God Himself, that is, the feeling of His presence in us, waking up our soul to the life of justice and love".[13]

Since revelation is only the manifestation of God in prayer, we find the following traits:

"It will be interior, because God, having no phenomenal existence, can only reveal Himself to the mind and in the filial devotion which He Himself inspires .... Secondly, this interior revelation will always be evident. The contrary would imply contradiction. Whoever speaks of revelation speaks of a veil taken away and a light uncovered .... Finally, this revelation will be progressive. That means it will develop with the progress of the moral and religious life which God brings to maturity in the bosom of humanity".[14]

The religious experiences of the men of God are naturally expressed in the words of Scripture, and are destined, after having illuminated their own awareness, to give light and life to other souls. But how can other souls recognize an authentic revelation in these books or in this word?

"Now observe that one single criterion is infallible and sufficient: all divine revelation, all religious experience that is truly good for nourishing and sustaining your soul, must be able to repeat and continue itself as actual revelation and individual experience in your own awareness .... Do not believe, my good brother, that the prophets and initiators have handed down their experiences in order to spare you the work of having your own, or that their revelation is given to you so that you have only to receive it passively like a sum of money, or if it happens that you borrow from them thus, you will not be the richer for it. The revelations of the past are never shown to be efficacious and real unless they make you capable of receiving the personal revelation that God reserves for you .... Divine revelation which is not realized in us and does not become immediate does not exist at all for us".[15]

The *Esquisse* of Sabatier was complemented by a more positive exposition, *Les Religions de l'autorité et la religion de l'Esprit* (in 1904), in which he tries to find support in the New Testament and the history of the primitive Church for this conception of a Christianity which is all interior, without dogmas or rites, without visible heads, set up against all the forms of orthodoxy (Catholic or Protestant). These two works are perhaps the best respresentatives of the type of religious subjectivism which characterizes modern Protestant theology.

II. SYMPTOMS OF THE CRISIS

In their daily and practically indispensable dealings with the Protestant world, the danger of succumbing to Protestant thought for Catholics has always been a reality. Actually, Catholic theological science, from the beginning of the twentieth century, counts, among those who remained entirely faithful to their religion (such as Duchesne, Battifol, Jacquier, Lagrange, Tixeront), minds which did not entirely resist the Modernist fever and in which we can discover, in a sort of chiaroscuro, the tendencies which appear in full light in liberal Protestantism.

1. A. Loisy, primarily, represents an advanced degree of exegetical and historical criticism. The publication of *l'Evangile et l'Eglise*, in 1902, as an answer to the claims of Harnack, was like a thunderbolt and soon became, in Catholic circles, a sign for contradiction. Looking back on this work, Loisy declares that he wanted to produce simply "an essential reform in biblical exegesis, in the whole of theology, and even in Catholicism in general".[16] At any rate, *Autour d'un petit livre*, appearing in 1903, did away with any ambiguity on his attitude and doctrinal positions.

In this work, where relativism is one of the major dogmas, the notion of revelation is directly challenged. From the outset, Loisy proposes a notion of truth which is very vague and disturbing: "It seems obvious to me by common experience that truth is something necessarily conditioned within us, something relative, always capable of being perfected, always susceptible of diminution ... that truth, as a human property, is no less changeable than man himself. It evolves with him, in him, through him; and this does not prevent it from being truth for him; in fact it could not be truth on any other condition".[17] He then denounces what he claims to be the Catholic concept of revelation:

"Even scientific theology retains an extremely anthropomorphic idea of revelation, which is quite disconcerting for our contemporary science and philosophy. Since we have not yet generally stopped taking the first chapters of Genesis literally, we find not the least difficulty in seeing God Himself, in the earthly Paradise, in the intimate conversations which preceded the Fall, and in the terrible sentence which followed it, having explained to the first man and the first woman all the fundamental dogmas of Christianity, the whole economy of redemption".[18]

For this anthropomorphic conception, he substitutes a psychological conception, imposed as he believes by his discoveries in the history of Israel's religion. "Revelation could only have been the awareness man acquired of his relationship with God. What is Christian revelation, in its principle and point of departure, if not the perception, in the soul of Christ, of the relationship which united Christ Himself to God, and of the relationship which unites all men to their heavenly Father ... ? What was the beginning of revelation at a given moment was the perception, no matter how rudimentary we suppose it to have been, of the relationship which must exist between man, conscious of himself, and God present behind the world of phenomena. ... The development of revealed religion is brought about by the perception of new relations, or rather by a more precise and distinct determination of the essential relationship, which was seen in the beginning, man thus coming to a better and better knowledge of both the grandeur of God and the character of his own duty".[19]

Thus, according to Loisy, revelation properly so called is only an awareness of the man-God relationship. This awareness, he adds, "unlike the perceptions of the rational and scientific order, ... is a work of the intelligence executed, so to speak, under the impulse of the heart, of the religious and moral sentiment, of real will for the good".[20] What results is an intuitive, experimental, and hearty perception of our relationships with God. What then is the object of revelation? Simply the ideas which take root in humanity and which describe the relationship which must exist between God and man: "Revelation has for its proper and direct object the simple truths contained in the statements of faith .... Their native form is a supernatural intuition and a religious experience".[21] Finally, according to Loisy, there can be no question of an unchanging deposit of revelation: "The Church proclaims that the truth of revelation is not found entirely in Scripture. This truth is not to be found entirely in the traditions of the past either, nor in the teaching of the present; insofar as all believers have a share in it, this truth is made over perpetually to them, in the Church, with the help of Scripture and tradition".[22] And in his *Simples réflexions*: "The idea of setting bounds to define revelation is a very mechanical and artificial one ..., foreign to the apostles; but it is closely bound up with the idea, which is no less mechanical and quite mythological, we might even say infantile in character, which we have of revelation itself".[23]

To sum up, for Loisy, revelation is not a doctrine offered to our faith, an unchanging deposit of truths, but rather an intuitive and experimental perception, always in development (always becoming), of our relationship with God. Revelation, like dogma and theology, always evolves; it is always happening.

2. Whereas Loisy bases his critique of the idea of revelation on history,[24] G. Tyrrell bases his on philosophy and theology. Modernistic tendencies found an enthusiastic follower in this intuitive and mystical temperament. A strange relationship of attitude, thinking, and expression, draws him very close to Sabatier and Loisy. Tyrrell recognizes the transcendence of revelation, but his conception of revelation-experience leads in a straight line to dogmatic relativism. In its final stage, the deviation is a flagrant one.

Like Loisy, Tyrrell finds fault with an anthropomorphic and "extrinsecist" conception of revelation: "To conceive revelation as necessarily trumpeted from the clouds is surely to be led astray by the naive symbolism of Christian art".[25] And consequently, he feels the same about a faith which is presented as the mind's assent to a system of propositions,[26] instead of being "in the adhesion of the whole man, heart, mind and soul, to the divine spirit within—primarily a spirit of life and love".[27] The Gospel is a power, not a science; Christianity is not a body of definitions and affirmations divinely guaranteed, but a life.[28]

The source of the actual conflict, according to Tyrrell, is to be found in a confusion between *revelation* and *theology* and the heterogeneous modes of knowledge which they represent.[29]

Revelation properly so called, which, he points out, must be distinguished from its transcription and communication,[30] "belongs rather to the category of impressions than to that of expression".[31]

It is emotion, impulse, touching the heart, a commotion in the whole soul.[32] "Revelation is not statement but experience".[33] Tyrrell is more precise: "It is very important to remember that, strictly speaking, revelation consists in the total religious experience and not simply in the mental element of that experience".[34] When God reveals Himself, the experience is total, pre-emptive. God acts rather than speaks, and man's reaction is comparable to the reaction he experiences at thunder. The shock effects his whole person: but whereas the experiential element is something almost identical in every man, the mental reaction which follows is different with each subject, according to the culture of each individual.[35] Tyrrell is taken up with stressing the totality of the experience of revelation, as well as the emotional elements it sets in motion; still, this insistence does not entirely hide a certain mistrust regarding its properly mental elements.

By nature, revelation remains individual, incommunicable: it is an experience which each prophet translates as he can, following his own mental endowment and formation, with the help of images and concepts: "That which is communicated is a certain experience of God's presence or providence or fatherhood, of Christ's saving and atoning power over the soul, of communion with the Saints, of the forgiveness of sins, of the hope of immortality, which fills and inspires the spirit of the prophet, and spontaneously utters and expresses itself through the categories and images with which his mind happens to be instructed".[36] But this transposition is no longer revelation-experience, that is, the original and only authentic vital data, but a shadow, a very relative representation, an object that needs interpreting; one thing is certain, in no way can it be called a judgment that needs developing or a doctrinal absolute. Prophecy is experience and vision: experience of the power, the majesty, and the transcendence of God. In the same way, the apostles had a revelation of Christ in a living, intuitive and total experience. This experience they expressed first of all in the form of images (for Peter, Christ is Messiah; for John, Logos; for Paul, second Adam), then, and later on in the Church, under the more elaborate conceptual form of Word, consubstantial with the Father. No one of these conceptions is, properly speaking, revelation.[37]

The images which rise from the apostolic experience have a special sacred character in so far as they are "the vestiges, the imaginative impressions made by Christ on the mentality of an age which knew, saw, and touched him".[38] They prolong the experience and help us call it to mind, but they are obviously incapable of equalling or exhausting it. Images and concepts, born spontaneously or reflexively in the soul of the prophet or apostle, are only the human reaction, spontaneous or reflex, of the human mind "to God's touch, felt deep within the heart," just like the dreams of a man asleep are created or formed by some external cause.[39] These elements have value as suggestions, but they remain a human product, fallible and subject to change. Our mistake in this area is to treat them as truths, as certain affirmations.

Can revelation itself, as experience, vindicate some title of truth? Yes, Tyrrell answers; but this truth is directly practical, preferential, and only indirectly speculative. "What is immediately approved, as it were experientially, is a way of living, feeling, and acting with reference to the other world. The explanatory and justificatory conceptions subsequently sought out by the mind, as postulated by this 'way of life,' have no direct divine approval".[40] As a result, only revelation has a sacred character; dogma and theology have a profane character. The truth of revelation is prophetic, visionary; that of theology and dogma is intellectual and scientific.[41]

Since revelation is "a spiritual and massive experience," it is wrong, Tyrrell explains, "to speak of a development of revelation as though it were a body of statements or theological propositions".[42] To speak thus is evidence of a confusion between revelation and theology. Their truths being of a different order, it is impossible to have any homogeneity between one and the other. The dogmatic formulas have as their goal to allow each individual to call to mind and make his own, under the activity of the Spirit, the initial religious experience. But between dogmas and primary revealed truth, the relationship is not one of formula to objective and intellectual data defined, but one of interpretation of prophetic or apostolic experience; the conceptual elaboration which is the fruit of community reflection on the memory left behind by the inspired writers; provisory formulas, pointing towards the experience, born of the needs of the time and adapted to the spirit of the age.[43]

But if, on the one hand, revelation is a vital and ineffable experience, and if, on the other hand, the dogmatic statements are only its provisory interpretation on the basis of the rudimentary and incomplete experience of the prophet, is it still possible to have access to revelation? And how is revelation to be handed down? According to Tyrrell, we must postulate in each individual a capacity for religious experience similar to that of the prophet or apostle. Revelation is an experience which is repeated analogically in the soul of each individual. Our mind responds to the Spirit and the experience of the prophet becomes our experience. The assimilation of revelation "is precisely an act of inward recognition—a response of spirit to spirit, and not only the mental apprehension and acceptance of statements and meanings. ... The teaching from outside must evoke a revelation in ourselves; the experience of the prophet must become experience for us. It is to this revelation evoked within us that we answer by the act of faith, recognizing it as God's word in us and to us .... Revelation cannot come from the outside; it can be occasioned, but it cannot be caused by instruction".[44]

The ideal for the Christian is thus to see Scripture and the formulas of faith as the vehicle of direct revelation, the breath of the Spirit, just as the disciples of Jesus welcomed it within themselves. The only infallible teacher is the Spirit of God who reveals Himself to each of the faithful, but more clearly to a choice group of spiritual men, who form a sort of vanguard before the mass of Christians. The Christian makes use of formulas which unite Christians to each other, in the measure in which they nourish his religious feeling. Every dogma which does not stir up some echo in the soul is no longer necessary for salvation. "If you can live on the undeveloped germ, you may dispense with the developments, especially if they but puzzle and hinder you".[45] Thus if the formulas become a burden, because they are barren and give rise to barrenness, it would be better to be free of them and lead the Church to free her souls from expressions which have passed out of date.[46]

This Protestant attitude is the consequence of Tyrrell's whole system. If revelation is communicated directly to each soul, if it is essentially an experience, if dogma is only a human conception, a fallible and provisory interpretation, more or less bound up with this experience and only more or less satisfying, there is no longer any room for a dogmatic authority, and we must choose with Sabatier for a religion of the mind against a religion of authority. The Church still remains a respectable institution, uniting Christians in their profession of the same formulas, but it is no longer the Bride of Christ through whom all grace and all truth are communicated.[47]

Side by side with these obviously erroneous expressions, such as we have just encountered, we find in Tyrrell many ambiguous expressions which tend to mislead us as regards his real thinking.[48] Still, his work, taken as a whole, with the conclusions he draws from it, clearly shows that, for him, revelation is not, as it is for the Church, the word spoken by God, a divinely guaranteed doctrine; nor is faith an adherence of the mind to the teachings of the apostles and the Church. For Tyrrell, revelation is only an experience, given from above, of supernatural realities. Not only, according to Father de Grandmaison, does it not rest upon a communication of defined truths and certain judgments, but it is not even compatible with them.[49] And dogma (which Tyrrell confuses with theology) is only the "natural, tentative, fallible analysis of that experience".[50] Revelation-experience is something unchanging and can receive no further development; it is only dogma and theology, a necessary superstructure, but alway heterogeneous with regard to the experience, which constantly evolve and change. It is in the name of this dissociation between revelation-experience and theology that Tyrrell finds authority for all his freedom in doctrinal matters. For Loisy, on the contrary, revelation, dogma, and theology are subject to a perpetual and unlimited development (becoming). In these two cases, the very concepts of revelation and dogmatic development are at stake.

III. ANTI-MODERNIST DOCUMENTS

1. Faced with such a serious danger, and particularly because of the illusions that abounded on every side, Rome was forced to intervene: first of all in sentences passed through the Index; then, through decisions of the Biblical Commission (in 1905, 1906, 1907); finally, by the Decree of the Holy Office *Lamentabili* (July 3, 1907). A brief preface indicates the intention of the Holy See: to counteract the excesses committed by modern criticism in the area of Bible studies and dogma. The Congregation gathered together and condemned sixty-five propositions.

Three of them (XX, XXI, XXII) directly concern our subject. Though separated, these propositions are connected with each other by an internal bond, the system of Loisy to which they refer.[51] It is not our intention here to repeat an explanation already made, but to show how, under a negative form, this decree reaffirms the earlier positions, primarily those of the First Vatican Council. This harking to doctrinal decisions long since opposed by the Church to Protestant free examination or modern rationalism shows her resolution to react against an offensive of the same tendencies. The decree maintains the notion of objective revelation in all its rigor, as doctrine received from God, with inspired Scripture constituting the principal deposit and the Church having a mission to assure its integrity. Propositions LVII to LXV condemn the very principles of religious, absolute, unlimited evolutionism; in other words, the whole religious philosophy which, through Sabatier, issues from Schleiermacher and Ritschl.

Proposition XX condems Loisy's definition of revelation: "Revelation can have been nothing more than the awareness man acquires of his relation to God".[52] For the historian of Israel's religion (Loisy), we must remember that revelation is something progressive, and its evolution depends on political, social, and cultural circumstances. Revelation appears to him as the human activity through which man becomes aware of his relationship with God. The object of this revelation is constituted by the ideas which spring up in humanity and which describe the relationship which should exist between God and man. These ideas are worked out little by little, as the awareness of the man-God relationship becomes more distinct. As a result, "the dogmas which the Church proposes as revealed are not truths which have come down from heaven, but a certain interpretation of religious facts which the human mind has acquired by laborious effort".[53] Finally, in logical consequence, revelation is never something finished, for humanity's total self-awareness is never finished: "The revelation which constitutes the object of Catholic faith was not closed with the apostles".[54]

Negative as it is, this exposition clearly calls for the positive teaching of the Church. The Church does not deny the fact that revealed truth, destined for man, is received *in* man, but she refuses to see revelation as the product of a simply human and natural activity. In the Modernist perspective, revelation, in the last analysis, is attributable to man, and the truths known through revelation do not surpass the immanent content of the religious consciousness of humanity. From something transcendent it becomes something immanent. It ceases to be the word spoken by God, the expression of His thinking, having God for its Author, personal and transcendent agent, communicating to man, by a free and gratuitous activity, truths which can even surpass the scope of human intelligence (D 1785, 1786, 1787). In revelation such as the Church conceives it, it is God Himself who comes before man, illuminating the prophet's mind or making public the Gospel of salvation through Christ, Incarnate Word (D 783, 1785). Man, it is true, actively receives this divine message, but the doctrine proceeds from an Other. The religious history of humanity rests on a divine gift: on the "doctrine of faith which God has revealed" and which has been entrusted to the Church "as a deposit" to be faithfully preserved and infallibly declared (D 1800). In one sense, the revealed truths are "truths which have come down from heaven," because the human lips of Christ, Incarnate Word, communicate to us with an authority and without any possible error the very "doctrine" of the Father (Jn. 7:16), His plan of salvation for humanity (Rom. 16:25-27; Col. 1, 25-28).

Revelation is thus not a reality always in becoming, bound up with the development of human consciousness, but a deposit of supernatural truths, entrusted to the guardianship of the Church and completed from the times of the apostles. "Revelation, constituting the object of Catholic faith, . . . was completed with the apostles" (D 2021). The text of the decree implies the following points of Catholic teaching: first of all, that the sum total of the truths offered to our faith is already complete in the apostolic doctrine and, as a result, can undergo neither real accretion nor real diminution; next, that the object of our faith has been constituted by a divine-apostolic revelation and by that revelation alone; finally, that the deposit of revelation, which has been constituted the object of our faith, is completed with the times of the apostles. Since the apostolic era, the object of our faith has been constituted in its entirety, that is, realized in its essential perfection as object of belief for all men: brought into existence, in its totality, as the object of a divine invitation to faith.[55] Revelation, in this context, can thus designate the whole activity of revelation as well as the doctrine or deposit of faith: of the one and the other it is true to state that they are both completed with the apostles. The decree does not deny, for all that, that the completion of revelation can be the point of departure for a real movement of subjective assimilation on the part of the Church, who penetrates more and more deeply into the deposit which God has entrusted to her, not like an inert block of precious metal, but like a living and fertile word. The fountainhead is there; we must never cease drinking from it.

This doctrine is perfectly coherent with the other propositions of the decree, as well as with the earlier teaching of the Church. Revelation has been communicated to men through Moses, through the prophets, and finally through Christ, through the Lateran Council, the Council of Trent, and the Vatican Council (D 428, 429, 783, 1785). It is not a human work resulting from a philosophical elaboration (D 1636, 1656, 1800); it is not subject, either, to the indefinite progress of human reason (D 1705): it is a deposit to be preserved and explained (D 1800). The decree makes it clear that Christianity has not been a religious movement without doctrinal basis; quite the contrary, Christ "taught a determined body of doctrine applicable to all times and all men".[56] It is impossible to admit the evolutionist principle according to which "Christian doctrine, from its very outset, was Jewish, but, by a series of successive evolutions, became first Pauline, then Johannine, finally Hellenistic and universal".[57] Far from having undergone successive and heterogeneous forms, Christian doctrine preserves the same meaning for the Christians of our times as it did for those of the first centuries (D 2062). Revelation is thus unchanging (D 125, 148, 160, 212, 293, 300). This immutability of doctrine, however, is not an obstacle to the true progress of modern sciences (D 2063); this progress does not demand "that the concepts of Christianity be reformed on the subject of ... revelation".[58]

2. Two months after the decree *Lamentabili*, on September 8, 1907, the Encyclical *Pascendi* appeared. Whereas the decree was content with calling attention to the errors, the encyclical uncovers the philosophical roots of the evil. No Modernist, it goes without saying, had ever professed as such the well-structured body of doctrines presented by the encyclical. The encyclical meant simply to correct the tendencies and principles scattered among the different authors and to show how these authors were on common grounds in their conscious or unconscious avowal of the same principles and tendencies. It was an easy matter, in grouping these principles, to show many serious examples in the domains of philosophy, theology, history, criticism, and apologetics.

At the basis of their religious *philosophy*, the modernists "place the doctrine commonly called agnosticism." In virtue of this doctrine, whatever surpasses the range of human phenomena is beyond our knowledge. That is why God could not be the object of knowledge (science) nor be recognized as the Author of certain historical interventions; as a consequence too, natural theology, the motives of credibility, and external revelation all belong to the outmoded and antiquated system of intellectualism (D 2072).

Agnosticism represents the negative aspect of Modernism. The doctrine of vital immanence constitutes the positive aspect. It comes in to explain religion: "Once natural theology is repudiated, all access to revelation closed by the rejection of the motives of credibility, and, what is more, all external revelation entirely abolished, it is clear that this explanation must not be sought for outside man himself".[59] In the depths of the sub-conscious, there exists a *need* for the divine, whose pressure "stirs up within the soul which is prone to religion a peculiar feeling. This feeling has the peculiar faculty of enveloping God both as object and as innermost cause, and in some manner uniting man with God".[60] This is the origin of religious faith, for which revelation is only another name:

"In a feeling of this kind the Modernists discover not only faith but also, with faith and in faith, revelation. And for revelation, actually, what more could one want? Is not this sentiment which appears in the consciousness and this God who, in this sentiment, even though still in a confused manner, manifests Himself to the soul, after all a revelation or at very least a beginning of revelation? What is more, if we look at the matter clearly, from the moment that God is both cause and object of our faith, in faith, we find revelation both as coming from God and as bearing upon God, that is, that God is at the same time revealer and revealed. This, venerable brothers, explains the absurd doctrine of the Modernists that all religion is at once natural and supernatural, according to the point of view. This also explains the equivalence between consciousness and revelation. And finally it explains the law which makes religious consciousness into a universal rule, perfectly on a par with revelation, a law to which everything must be subject, even supreme Church authority, in its threefold manifestation as pertaining to doctrine, cult, and discipline".[61]

Thus, religious sentiment, under the impulse of the universal need for the divine, is actuated, blossoms out in the consciousness, and becomes experience of the divine reality. Such is the germ of religion, of all religions, Christianity included: they are all nothing more than a blossoming of religious sentiment and, on this ground, they can all be called revealed (D 2077).

God, or rather the feeling for God has risen from the depths of the sub-conscious, but still confusedly. The intelligence then, coming to the assistance of this sentiment or feeling, "works there like a painter who, on an old canvas, rediscovers and brings back to life the all but obliterated lines of the original design".[62] This work of the intelligence, spontaneous at first, ends up in formulas or simple and popular statements which represent in a still somewhat awkward manner the phenomena of life for which the soul was the show place; finally, a further reflection interprets the primitive formula by means of derived formulas, richer in depth and more distinct. These formulas, sanctioned by the Church, make up the body of dogma.[63]

The formulas of dogma have no other purpose than to "furnish the believer with the means for taking stock of his faith" (D 2079). Elaborated by the intelligence, their only value is that of inadequate signs, symbols, with reference to their object; and, with reference to the believer, they have an instrument value. They do not contain the absolute truth: "As symbols, they are images of the truth which must be adapted to the religious feeling ... ; as instruments, they are vehicles of the truth and, reciprocally, they must accommodate to man in his relation with religious feeling".[64] Now, as the absolute, which is the object of religious sentiment, presents infinite aspects, and since, on the other hand, the believer can face the most dis- similar conditions, it follows that these formulas are subject to continual variations. Dogma can and must change: it must live just as religious feeling lives. Modernism exalts religious experience and has no use for formulas (D 2079-2080).

Modernist theology does nothing more than adapt the philosophical principles of immanence, symbolism and evolution to faith.[65]

In conformity with the principle of vital evolution, revelation develops with religious feeling, in the measure that religious feeling frees itself from foreign elements (family and national feeling) and penetrates the consciousness of humanity (D 2094). This evolution is generally parallel to the cultural and moral development of society, but it can be aided and promoted by the activity of certain extraordinary men, such as the prophets and Christ (D 2094). Religious experience can thus be communicated to others through the organ of preaching or Scripture. By virtue of their power of suggestion, formulas can re-awaken religious sentiment, which has perhaps become deadened, or enable the believer to revive experiences long past (D 2083). When, through the suggestive power of preaching or Scripture, religious feeling emerges to the consciousness of the hearer or reader, he then experiences revelation. On the other hand, dogmas being only the inadequate approaches to religious experience, instruments whose role is to evoke this experience, "the believer must use these formulas in the measure that they can help him, for it is as a support to his faith that they have been given, and not as a stumbling block".[66]

It is hardly necessary to point out how faithfully this picture reproduces the various statements encountered in Sabatier, Loisy and Tyrrell. They do not have the fixed outline in these authors that the encyclical gives them. But it is still true that, taken as a whole, the descriptions are exact. The pontifical document assembles them and puts them side by side in order to discover their common basic elements. On Loisy's own admission, the Pope wanted to maintain "what many whom he calls Modernists are contesting, mainly, that there is an immutable deposit of revealed truth, and the Sovereign Pontiff is its one and infallible guardian".[67] The encyclical, Loisy once again admits, "is only the total, inescapably logical expression of the teaching commonly accepted in the Church since the end of the thirteenth century".[68]

Throughout the whole encyclical, there are many expressions which show that Modernism is only a renewal of ancient errors, already denounced, but taken up once again in the spirit of the new sciences. The text calls to mind the teaching of the Vatican Council against agnosticism, as regards the knowledge of God, the motives of credibility, the possibility of revelation (D 1806, 1807, 1812, 2072); immanentism is opposed by the dogma of the supernatural (D 1808, 2075); rationalism is opposed by the teaching of Pius IX and Gregory XVI on the subordination of philosophy (D 1634, 1635,

1636, 2085); relativism is opposed by the censure of Gregory XVI against those who lose sight of the notion of truth (D 1617, 2080); religious evolutionism, finally, is opposed by the immutability of revelation and dogmas, vindicated by Pius IX and by the First Vatican Council (D 1705, 1800).

3. The anti-Modernist activity of Pius X is crowned by the motu proprio *Sacrorum antistitum* of September 1, 1910, and the oath it imposed. This oath, without adding anything essential to preceding acts, is a sort of solemn resumé. It also offers the precious advantage of being not only, like the Syllabus, a condemnation of errors, or, like *Pascendi*, the exposition of a series of doctrinal deviations, but a re-affirmation of the Church's positive teaching. It constitutes directly a profession of the Catholic doctrines to which the Modernist heresies are opposed.

This oath contains two parts, the first of which is of interest to us. After a general declaration of fidelity to all the teachings of the Church, five points are the object of special mention. Only the first three of these are directly concerned with our subject.

The third article speaks of the foundation of the Church, "guardian and mistress of the revealed word," by the historical Christ (D 1800, 1836). In the same sense, the following article states the immutable character of the "doctrine of faith," a divine deposit entrusted to the Bride of Christ and her vigilant guard, and it rejects the claim that would reduce this deposit to a discovery of philosophy (D 1800) or a creation of human consciousness, subject to indefinite progress:

"I sincerely receive the doctrine of faith such as it has been handed down by the apostles and the orthodox fathers, and I receive it in the same sense and the same interpretation as they. That is why I absolutely reject the heretical supposition of the evolution of dogmas, according to which these dogmas would change their meaning and receive a different sense from that which was given them by the Church at the beginning. And in like manner I reprove every error which consists in substituting for the divine deposit of faith, entrusted to the Bride of Christ and her vigilant guard, a philosophical fiction or creation of human consciousness, which, formed little by little, through human effort, would be susceptible, in the future, of an indefinite progress".[69]

In this twofold statement, the article has little to add to the declarations of the First Vatican Council. The Council, actually, had already taught that "the doctrine of faith, revealed by God ... has been entrusted to the Bride of Christ as a divine deposit, to be faithfully preserved and infallibly proclaimed," but always in the same sense, according to the same interpretation.[70] It also rejected as heretical the evolution of dogmas which would consist in attributing to them, under the pretext or appearance of a "higher understanding" or a "progress of science," a "different sense from that which, once and for all, has been declared by the Church".[71] The last part of the paragraph rejects the rationalist conception of revelation already condemned by the Vatican Council (D 1789) and denounces further the Modernist conception which sees Christian doctrine as a "creation of human consciousness" gradually formed by human effort and subject to indefinite progress and perfection. The Church repeats for the Modernists what she has already said for the rationalists and semi-rationalists: that "the doctrine of faith" was "handed down by the apostles and orthodox fathers" as a "divine deposit," and not as a human product, the fruit of human thinking or awareness.

The fifth article, finally, combining the teaching of the First Vatican Council (D 1789) and then the encyclical *Pascendi* (D 2074), recalls that faith is not a blind feeling, but an adherence of the intelligence to the truth revealed by God:

"I hold in all certitude and I sincerely profess that faith is not a blind religious feeling, rising from the shadowy depths of the sub-conscious under the impulse of the heart and the inclination of a will which is morally educated, but rather that it is a real assent of the intelligence to the truth extrinsically acquired by the teaching received; an assent through which we believe as true, because of the authority of God whose truthfulness is absolute, everything that has been said, testified, and revealed by the personal God, our Creator and Teacher".[72]

The text defines faith first negatively, then positively. Whereas the First Vatican Council was opposed to rationalism, for which faith is only a science which has God for its object, the oath censures the Modernists for conceiving of faith in the manner of the liberal Protestants, reducing it to pure non-rational feeling, rising from the depths of the sub-conscious under the impulse of the heart and will, cut off from every dependence on an external revelation.

In a positive way, and as opposing the exclusivity of the Modernist position, the oath stresses the intellectual character of faith: true assent of the mind to the truth extrinsically acquired by the teaching received (Rom. 10:17). Obviously, it does not deny that revelation, as addressed to man, is received in man; it simply means that, mediate or immediate, the revealed truth does not proceed *totally* from man, but from an *Other*, from God as a personal agent distinct from man, Creator and Lord. The prophets, the apostles, Christians: all receive revealed truth through an inner or an outer hearing.

Through faith, we recognize as true "what has been said, testified, and revealed" by God. The oath does away with every possible ambiguity: revelation is not the result of a religious emotion rising to the full consciousness, completely human and subjective in character, but the *content* of a word, of a testimony: the word and testimony of God. This content, elsewhere called doctrine, Gospel, is proposed to the intelligence and claims the assent of faith.

For the first time, in an official document, we find three pertinent terms joined together: word (*dicta*), testimony (*testata*), revelation (*revelata*). Each of these terms embraces the preceding one and makes it more precise. Revelation belongs to the genus of word and the species of testimony. As word, it is addressed to man and manifests divine thinking to him; as testimony it calls for a specific reaction, that of faith. We can discover, in these documents of Pius IX and Pius X, a movement of growing precision relative to the general notion of revelation. The encyclical *Qui pluribus* of Pius IX explains that we owe faith to God who speaks and who can neither deceive nor be deceived; in other words, revelation is the word of authority (D 1637). The First Vatican Council points out that the assent of faith rests, not on the internal evidence of the truth presented, as in the case of science, but on the very authority of God who reveals (D 1789). Finally, the anti-Modernist oath makes it clear that the word of authority of God who reveals is a divine testimony, to which faith is the proper response (D 2145). At the end, we are furnished with the elements for a formal notion: the God who reveals is the God with authority of witness sovereignly true and deserving the specific response of faith. Revelation is the word of testimony (*locutio Dei attestans*).

Thus, against the Modernists, who went counter to the Catholic notion of revelation as divine deposit, opposing to it their conception of revelation as a human creation, issuing from the depths of the subconscious, gradually elaborated from obscurity to clarity, from unformulated to formulated, the oath asserts that revelation, which is the object of faith, has a doctrinal character. What God has said, testified, revealed, the Church calls: revealed word, doctrine of faith, divine deposit committed to the guardianship of the Church, to be preserved without addition, without alteration, without change in sense or interpretation. This doctrine is not the teaching of man, but of God. In the Modernist perspective, revelation tends to become pure immanence. For the Church, it remains a transcendent divine activity, whose objective and created terminus is a doctrine, a teaching, communicated to man, made for him, received in him actively, but not coming from him. If the Church, in the age of Modernism, has stressed the transcendence of revelation (without however denying its character of immanence) and also the doctrinal character of the object of faith (without denying its other values), this is because Modernism was interested precisely in replacing the notions of supernatural revelation and immutable dogma by a religious development for which individual or collective religious awareness is the only rule. The Church, which is never bound to say everything in each one of her interventions, did away with the equivocations and reaffirmed the traditional positions.

1. J. Rivière, *Le Modernisme dans l'Église* (Paris, 1929), p. 11; R. Marle, *Au coeur de la crise moderniste* (Paris, 1960), p. 349; E. Poulat, *Histoire dogme et critique dans la crise moderniste* (Paris, 1962).

2. E. Kant, *Critique de la raison pure* (trans. J. Barni, revised by A. Archambault), preface to the second edition, 1: 28.

3. E. Kant, *La Religion dans les limites de la simple raison* (trans. J. Gibelin, Paris, 1943), pp. 152-153. And again: "La pure foi morale... seule constitue en toute foi d'Église ce que celle-ci contient de religion proprement dite" (*Ibid.*, p. 159). "La pure foi religieuse est assurément celle qui seule peut fonder une Église universelle, parce que c'est une simple foi rationnelle qui peut se communiquer à chacun pour le convaincre" (*Ibid.*, p. 138).

4. L. Cristiani, article "Schleiermacher" in DTC, 14: col. 1500.

5. D. C. Macintosh, *The Problem of religious Knowledge* (New York, 1940), pp. 236-242.

6. L. Bouyer, *Du Protestantisme à l'Église*, p. 239. On Ritschl, see also: D. C. Macintosh, *The Problem of religious Knowledge*, pp. 243-250; article "Réforme" in DAFC, 4: col. 677-680.

7. The work was published in Paris, in 1897. Sabatier explains his ideas on religion and revelation in the first two chapters of the first book: "The psychological origin and nature of religion" (pages 3-31) and "Religion and revelation" (pages 32-61).

8. A. Sabatier, *Esquisse d'une philosophie de la religion*, p. 24.

9. *Ibid.*, p. 32.

10. *Ibid.*, p. 35.

11. *Ibid.*, pp. 187-188.

12. A. Sabatier, *Esquisse d'une philosophie de la religion*, pp. 305-312, 390-400.

13. *Ibid.*, pp. 43-44.

14. *Ibid.*, pp. 52-54.

15. A. Sabatier, *ibid.*, pp. 58-59. We have presented these texts because they show to what point Loisy and Tyrrell are contributors of Sabatier in doctrine and even in expression. The originality of Catholic Modernists appears very reduced if their works are read after those of their liberal superiors.

16. A. Loisy, *Choses passées* (Paris, 1913), p. 246. In 1906, he claimed that he wanted to present: "First of all, a sketch and historical explanation of Christian development; secondly, a general philosophy of religion and an essay at interpreting dogmatic formulas, official symbols, and conciliar definitions, with a view towards adapting them, by sacrificing the letter for the spirit, to the data of history, and the mentality of our contemporaries" (*Revue d'histoire et de littérature*, II (1906): 570).

17. A. Loisy, *Autour d'un petit livre* (Paris, 1903), pp. 191-192. The decree *Lamentabili* condemned the following proposition drawn from Loisy's work: "Truth is not unchangeable, any more than man himself, since it evolves with him, in him, and through him" (4 2058).

18. *Ibid.*, pp. 192-193. Loisy no doubt never studied how Saint Thomas conceives of this primitive revelation: "In the state of their first condition, there was no hearing of a man speaking without, but from God inspiring within: just as the prophets heard, according to the words of the Psalm (Ps. 84, 9): I shall hear what the Lord God speaks in me" (2a 2ae, q. 5, a. 1, ad 3; De Verit., q. 18, a. 2, c.).

19. A. Loisy, *Autour d'un petit livre*, pp. 195-197. Comparer avec Sabatier, *Esquisse d'une philosophie de la religion*, pp. 34-35, 176-177, 183-184, 394-395.

20. A. Loisy, *Autour d'un petit livre*, p. 197.

21. A. Loisy, *Autour d'un petit livre*, p. 200.

22. *Ibid.*, p. 207.

23. A. Loisy, *Simples Réflexions* (Ceffonds, 1908), p. 58.

24. A. Loisy, *Autour d'un petit livre*, p. 154.

25. G. Tyrrell, *Through Scylla and Charybdis* (London, 1907, p. 314). The essential element of Tyrrell's thinking on revelation is found in chapters 11 and 12 of this work: "Revelation" (pp. 264-307), "Theologism, A reply" (pp. 308-354).

26. G. Tyrrell, *A Much-abused Letter* (London, 1907), pp. 39, 51, 52.

27. G. Tyrrell, *Through Scylla and Charybdis*, p. 213.

28. G. Tyrrell, *A Much-abused Letter*, pp. 51-52; *Medievalism* (London, 1908), pp. 217-218.

29. In this term of *theology,* Tyrrell comprises and often confuses dogma and theology.

30. G. Tyrrell, *Through Scylla and Charybdis*, p. 268.

31. "Revelation belongs rather to the category of impressions than to that of expression" (*Ibid.*, p. 280).

32. *Ibid.*, pp. 282-283.

33. "Revelation is not statement, but experience" (*Ibid.*, p. 285).

34. "It is very important to remember that, strictly speaking, Revelation consists in the total religious experience and not simply in the mental element of that experience" (*Ibid.*, p. 285).

35. *Ibid.*, pp. 287-288. Compare with Sabatier, *Esquisse d'une philosophie de la religion*, pp. 304-305.

36. G. Tyrrell, *Through Scylla and Charybdis*, p. 314.

37. *Ibid.*, pp. 280-289.

38. *Ibid.*, p. 291.

39. *Ibid.*, pp. 208-209.

40. *Ibid.*, p. 210.

41. *Ibid.*, pp. 209, 238.

42. *Ibid.*, p. 292.

43. *Ibid.*, pp. 237, 303-305.

44. *Ibid.*, pp. 305-306.

45. G. Tyrrell, *A Much-abused Letter*, p. 86.

46. *Ibid.*, p. 87. And in *Through Scylla and Charybdis*: "Deferential within the limits of conscience and sincerity to the official interpreters of her mind (of the Church), they must, nevertheless interpret such interpretations in accordance with the still higher and highest canon of Catholic truth: with the mind of Christ. It is He who sends us to them; not they who send us to Him. He is our first and highest authority. Were they to forbid the appeal, their own dependent authority would be at an end" (p. 19).

47. J. Lebreton, article "Modernisme" in DAFC, 3: 683.

48. For example: "Can revelation be communicated? Can I believe on the strength of God's word to another? Can such belief be (in defiance of logic) stronger than my purely human faith in the veracity of that other? Must not God speak to me directly? Must He not, at least from within, illuminate the revelation thus verbally communicated to me by another, and bring it home to me with a super-rational intuitive certitude?" (*Through Scylla and Charybdis*, p. 268).

49. L. de Grandmaison, "Le Développement du dogme," *Revue pratique d'apologétique*, 6 (1908): 97-98.

50. "Revelation is a supernaturally imparted experience of realities—an experience that utters itself spontaneously in imaginative popular non-scientific form; theology is the natural, tentative, fallible analysis of that experience. The Church's divine commission is to teach and propagate a new life, a new love, a new hope, a new spirit, and not the analysis of these experiences" (G. Tyrrell, *Medievalism*, p. 129). Cf. *Through Scylla and Charybdis*, p. 277.

51. The intention of the Holy See, however, was not to single out any particular author, but to group propositions of a clearly heterodox bearing. That is why, according to Father de Grandmaison, "several propositions were deliberately defined in a very judicious way, more tightly developed, perhaps even overstrssed, in order to make their meaning, and their heterodox bearing, clearly visible without any possible excuse." (DAFC, 3: col. 605). On the origins of the decree *Lamentabili* see: P. Dudon, "Origines francaises du décret *Lamentabili* (1903-1907)," *Bulletin de littérature ecclésiastique*, 32 (1931): 73-96; R. Aubert, "Aux origines de la réaction anti-moderniste. Deux documents inédits," *Eph. theol. lov.*, 37 (May-Sept. 1961): 557-579.

52. "Revelatio nihil aliud esse potuit quam acquisita ab homine suae ad Deum relationis conscientia" (D 2020). Proposition drawn from *Autour d'un petit livre*, p. 195. Commentary by Loisy himself in *Simples réflexions*, p. 57.

53. "Dogmata, quae Ecclesia perhíbet tanquam revelata, non sunt veritates e coelo delapsae, sed sunt interpretatio quaedam factorum religiosorum, quam humana mens laborioso conatu sibi comparavit" (D 2022). See: *L'Évangile et l'Eglise*, pp. 202-203; *Autour d'un petit livre*, p. 189; *Simples Réflexions*, p. 59.

54. "Revelatio, objectum fidei catholicae constituens, non fuit cum Apostolis completa" (D 2021). See *Autour d'un petit livre*, p. 207; *Simples Réflexions*, p. 58.

55. E. Dhanis, "Révélation explicite et implicite," *Gregorianum*, 34 (1953): 214-215.

56. "Christus determinatum doctrinae corpus omnibus temporibus cunctisque hominibus applicabile non docuit, sed potius inchoavit motum quemdam religiosum diversis temporibus ac locis adaptatum vel adaptandum" (D 2059).

57. "Doctrina christiana in suis exordiis fuit judaica, sed facta est per successivas evolutiones primum paulina, tum joannica, demum hellenica et universalis" (D 2060).

58. "Progressus scientiarum postulat ut reformentur conceptus doctrinae christianae de Deo, de creatione, de revelatione, de persona Verbi incarnati, de redemptione" (D 2064).

59. "Explicatio autem, naturali theologia deleta adituque ad revelationem ob rejecta credibilitatis argumenta intercluso, immo etiam revelatione qualibet externa penitus sublata, extra hominem inquiritur frustra. Est igitur in homine quaerenda... Ex hoc immanentiae religiosae principium asseritur" (D 2074).

60. "Indigentia divini in animo ad religionem prono... peculiarum quendam commovet sensum: hic vero divinam ipsam realitatem, tum tanquam objectum, tum tanquam sui causam intimam, in se implicatam habet atque hominem quodammodo cum Deo conjungit" (D 2074).

61. "In ejusmodi enim sensu modernistae non fidem tantum reperiunt; sed, cum fide inque ipsa fide, prout illam intelligunt, revelationi locum esse affirmant. Enimvero ecquid amplius ad revelationem quis postulet? An non revelationem dicemus, aut saltem revelationis exordium, sensum illum religiosum in conscientia apparentem; quin et Deum ipsum, etsi confusius, sese in eodem religioso sensu animis manifestantem? Subdunt vero: cum fidei Deus objectum sit aeque et causa, revelatio illa et de Deo pariter et a Deo est; habet Deum videlicet revelantem simul ac revelatum. Hinc autem, Venerabiles Fratres, affirmatio illa modernistarum perabsurda, qua religio quaelibet pro diverso aspectu naturalis una ac supernaturalis dicenda est. Hinc conscientiae ac revelationis promiscua significatio. Hinc lex, qua conscientia religiosa ut regula universalis traditur, cum revelatione penitus aequanda, cui subesse omnes oporteat, supremam etiam in Ecclesia potestatem, sive haec doceat, sive de sacris disciplinave statuat" (D 2075).

62. "Mens ergo, illi sensui adveniens, in eundem se inflectit inque eo elaborat pictoris instar, qui obsoletam tabulae cujusdam diagraphen collustret, ut nitidius efferat" (D 2078).

63. D 2078. The same terms come up again in the exposition of the theological principles of Modernism (D 2089).

64. "Mediae illae sunt inter credentem ejusque fidem: ad fidem quod attinet, sunt inadaequatae ejus objecti notae, vulgo symbola vocitant; ad credentem quod spectat, sunt mera instrumenta. Quocirca nulla confici ratione potest, eas veritatem absolute continere: nam qua symbola imagines sunt veritatis atque idcirco sensui religioso accommodandae, prout hic ad hominem refertur; qua instrumenta sunt veritatis vehicula atque ideo accommodanda vicissim homini, prout refertur ad religiosum sensum" (D 2079).

65. D. 2087 to 2096.

66. "Addunt praeterea formulas ejusmodi esse a credente adhibendas quatenus ipsum juverint; ad commodum enim datae sunt, non ad impedimentum" (D 2087).

67. A. Loisy, *Simples Réflexions*, p. 139.

68. *Ibid.*, p. 23.

69. In following text we underline the words which are identical or almost identical in the First Vatican Council: "Quarto: *fidei doctrinam* ab Apostolis per orthodoxos Patres *eodem sensu eademque* semper *sententia* ad nos usque transmissam, sincere recipio; ideoque prorsus rejicio haereticum commentum evolutionis dogmatum, ab uno ad *alium sensum* transeuntium, diversum *ab eo, quem* prius *habuit Ecclesia*, pariterque damno errorem omnem, quo, *divino deposito, Christi Sponsae* tradito ab eaque *fideliter custodiendo*, sufficitur *philosophicum inventum*, vel cretio humanae conscientiae, hominum conatu sensim efformatae et in posterum indefinito progressu perficiendae" (D 2145).

70. "Neque enim fidei doctrina quam Deus revelavit, velut philosophicum inventum proposita est humanis ingeniis perficienda, sed tanquam divinum depositum Christi Sponsae tradita, fideliter custodienda et infallibilite declaranda" (D 1800).

71. "Hinc sacrorum quoque dogmatum is sensus perpetuo est retinendus, quem semel declaravit sancta Mater Ecclesia, nec unquam ab eo sensu altioris intelligentiae specie et nomine recedendum" (D 1800). Et dans le canon correspondant: "Si quis dixerit fieri posse ut dogmatibus ab Ecclesia propositis aliquando secundum progressum scientiae sensus tribuendus sit alius ab eo quem intelligit Ecclesia: A. S." (D 1818).

72. "Quinto: certissime teneo ac sincere profiteor, fidem non esse caecum sensum religionis e latebris subconscientiae erumpentem, sub pressione cordis et inflexionis voluntatis moraliter informatae, sed verum assensum intellectus veritati extrinsecus acceptae ex auditu, quo nempe quae a Deo personali, creatore ac Domino nostro dicta, testata et revelata sunt, vera esse credimus, propter Dei auctoritatem summe veracis" (D 2145).

CHAPTER IV

CONTEMPORARY PERIOD

The interesting feature of this period is the somewhat new character of the interventions on the part of the Church magisterium. Not only are these interventions more frequent, particularly in the form of the encyclical, which becomes the favorite instrument of the more recent popes, but they also tend to turn into lengthy dogmatic expositions. We need mention only *Mystici corporis* (1943), *Mediator Dei* (1948), *Sacra Virginitas* (1954), *Haurietis aquas* (1956): each of these encyclicals is a lengthy exposition of the Catholic doctrine on a given point; the encyclical is interested less in condemning and reforming or putting on guard, than in enlightening, teaching, making clear, for the Christian people, the unfathomable riches of the mystery of Christ. Thus even if no one of these documents bears directly on the theme of revelation, we might still look for occasional explanations which are better developed, better founded, and also, for that matter, closer to Scripture. There can be no question here, obviously, of examining each of the contemporary pontifical documents for all the allusions made to revelation; these allusions are innumerable. The term is used most of the time for revelation in the objective sense, that is, doctrine itself, the Gospel of Christ, the message of salvation, the Gospel faith, the complex of truths and precepts taught by the Master, the deposit, the sum of revealed truths. Sometimes too, it is used to designate the activity of revelation itself. It will be enough here to study only those documents which offer a particular interest or more abundant material for our subject.

I. UNDER THE PONTIFICATE OF PIUS XI

Two contrary tendencies mark the history of the first half of the twentieth century: one towards a human brotherhood embracing the whole world, a sort of planetary collectivism, heralded by great international movements, such as Communism, labor unions, ecumenical activities of every kind; the other, inspired by Nietzsche, towards the glorification of the superman, individual or collective, the expansion of the superior races by violence, heralded by the birth of great dictatorships and by the cult of race. The encyclical *Mortalium animos*, directed against pan-Christianism, and *Mit brennender Sorge*, directed against the racism of the German Nazis, proclaimed the doctrine of the Church against the excesses of both these tendencies.

1. In *Mortalium animos* (January 6, 1928), Pius XI puts the Christian world on guard against a *pan-Christianism* which would be accomplished at the price of doctrinal concessions unacceptable to the Church: "Some non-Catholics," he says, "nourish the hope that they could easily lead all peoples, despite their religious differences, to unite in the profession of certain doctrines admitted as a common foundation for spiritual life".[1] Towards this end, they hold congresses which assemble men of all denominations, with the most divergent religious ideas. These efforts "are based on the erroneous opinion that all religions are more or less good and praiseworthy, in the sense that they all equally reveal and express, although in a different manner, the natural and innate sentiment which leads man towards God and inclines him to respect before God's presence. Aside from the fact that they are obviously caught up in error, the proponents of this opinion at the same time reject the true religion; they falsify the notion of religion and gradually turn it into naturalism and atheism. It is thus perfectly evident that joining the followers and propagators of such doctrines is tantamount to abandoning divinely revealed religion entirely".[2]

This idea of a pan-Christianity, continues the encyclical, has found favor with certain Catholics; thus it is most important to recall the thinking of the Church on the one and only possible religious unity. True religion is a revealed religion, and it is in an economy of revelation that humanity must work out its salvation:

"God could have imposed upon man, as his rule, only the natural law which he had engraved upon his heart in creation, and forever after regulated human history according to his ordinary providence; however he judged it preferable to add certain precepts for man to observe and, in the course of the ages, that is to say, since the origin of the world up until the coming and preaching of Christ Jesus, He Himself instructed man in the duties which are proper to every rational being with respect to his Creator: 'After having spoken in sundry times and in divers manners to our fathers through the prophets, God, in these last times, has spoken to us through His Son.' As a result, there is no true religion outside the religion which rests on divine revelation; this revelation, begun at the beginning of the world, pursued under the Old Law, Jesus Christ Himself has completed and accomplished in the New Law. But from the very moment that God has spoken—and history is witness to the fact that He has—it is evident that man has an absolute obligation to believe God when He speaks and to obey Him fully and absolutely when He gives a command".[3]

The teaching of the Church presents revelation as an historical fact: an intervention of God in history, under the form of a word spoken to humanity. This activity is carried on throughout the whole Old Testament, to end with Christ. But the historical fact goes side by side with a social fact, the fact of the Church.

In order to aid humanity along the road to salvation, Christ founded His Church, the only true Church. The "pan-Christians," on the contrary, think that all churches have equal value and would like to set up a "sort of universal federation" of all churches by a process of mutual compromise in doctrinal areas: "Can we possibly tolerate anything like this," asks the encyclical, "can we allow truth, and particularly revealed truth, to become the object of such a discussion? What is really at stake here is the defense of revealed truth".[4]

Since revealed truth is found only in the Church of Christ, which has a mission to teach the truths of the Gospel to all the nations of the earth and, toward this end, has received the special assistance of the Holy Spirit, how is it possible to conceive of a Christian federation built upon the coexistence and fusion of the most contradictory opinions? The "double precept of Christ—that of teaching and that of believing—can be observed and, for that matter, even understood, only if the Church publicly and integrally expounds the Gospel teaching, and if, in this exposition, she is sheltered from every danger of error".[5] A union of churches could be accomplished only at the expense of the faith. The Church cannot maintain that "dogmatic truth is not absolute but relative, that is, that it must adapt to the varying demands of times and places and different needs of souls, since it is not the content of an immutable revelation, but must, of its very nature, accommodate itself to the life of men".[6] Among the dogmas of faith, the Church can neither accept nor distinguish between fundamental articles and non-fundamental articles: "The supernatural virtue of faith has for its formal object the authority of

God the Revealer, an authority which admits of no distinction of this kind".[7]

The encyclical then describes the role of the Church with respect to revealed truth. The magisterium of the Church "has been established here below in accordance with the plan of God to guard perpetually intact the deposit of revealed truths and to assure their knowledge for men".[8] In addition to its ordinary and daily exercise, this magisterium "also implies, as often as it is necessary to oppose more effectively error and the attacks of heretics or to develop certain points of *sacred doctrine* with greater clarity or more detail, in order to make them enter further into the minds of the faithful, the mission of proceeding to opportune and solemn definitions. This usage of the extraordinary magisterium does not involve anything new; neither does it add anything to the sum of truths contained, at least implicitly, in the *revelation* which God has entrusted as a *deposit* to His Church; either it proclaims what could have been obscure to some minds up to that point, or it establishes an obligation of faith on some point which, otherwise, could, for some people, have been the object of some discussion".[9] Once again, we find the equivalent terms of sacred doctrine, revelation, and deposit of truths all joined together.

In the last analysis, concludes the encyclical, the only means to effect religious unity is to promote the return of all dissidents to the true Church of Christ. But no one can have any part with this Church, "pillar and support of truth," if he does not accept the whole of her doctrine.

2. The doctrine inspired by the thinkers of German Nazism in their racial pride were also the occasion for Pius XI to define a good many concepts—among them that of revelation—which Nazism made use of, after submitting them to a sacriligious transubstantiation. On March 14, 1937, Pius XI published the encyclical *Mit brennender Sorge.*

This encyclical points out "that no faith can maintain itself pure and undefiled over a long period of time if it is not sustained by faith in Christ," for it is the Son who reveals the Father and, following the plan of God, it is the knowledge of Christ which must lead to the knowledge of the Father:

"No one knows the Son excepting the Father, and no one knows the Father excepting the Son and him to whom the Son wills to reveal Him" (Mt. 11:27). "This is life everlasting, that they know you, the one true God, and Him whom you have sent, Jesus Christ" (Jn. 17:3). Thus no one can say: I believe in God, that is enough religion for me. The work of the Savior leaves no room for subterfuges of this sort: "Whoever denies the Son, does not possess the Father, and whoever confesses the Son, also possesses the Father (1 Jn. 2:23). In Jesus Christ, the Son of God made Man, the fullness of divine revelation has appeared. 'God, who at sundry times and in divers manners spoke to our fathers through the prophets, in these last days, has spoken to us through His Son' (Heb. 1:1)".[10]

In Jesus Christ the fullness of divine revelation has appeared, says the encyclical. This statement can be understood in three ways, all of them authorized by the text: A. In this sense first of all (indicated by the immediaté context), that the knowledge of the true God comes to us through Christ who has shown us who God is, no longer in a successive and partial manner, as did the prophets of the Old Testament, but all at once and completely. Christ is the perfect Revealer, for he is the Son, sharing the knowledge of divine secrets with the Father and ontologically qualified, as a result, to reveal. Christ has told us fully, at least as to essentials, what the Father is and what is His plan of salvation for humanity; for the apostles, in a subsidiary way, are also revealers, instructed by the Holy Spirit. B. Christ is also the fullness of revelation in this sense that He is Himself, in person, the Word of the Father, "radiation of His glory, imprint of His substance" (Heb. 1:3), "the image of the invisible God" (Col. 1:15; 2 Cor. 4:4), God revealing and God revealed, He who speaks and He who is spoken of. C. Finally, in this sense (suggested by the verb *erscheinen* and the preposition *in*) that the Word, in becoming Incarnate, has enrolled in the service of His mission of revelation all the human ways of expression, *facere* as well as *docere* (Acts 1:1): facts as well as actions (life, passion, death, resurrection) were all subject to the Word of Christ, who interprets them, explains their bearing on salvation and presents them as the object of divine testimony.

All purely human revelation, added to the good news brought by Christ, can only be a pseudo-revelation: "The culminating point of revelation, arrived at in the Gospel and in Jesus Christ, is definitive. Its obligations are for all time. This revelation will never undergo any further completion from a human hand; neither does it admit of being rejected and replaced by arbitrary revelations that spokesmen of the present time claim to derive from what they call the myth of blood and race".[11]

Faith in Christ itself, adds the encyclical, cannot be maintained unless it is protected and sustained by the faith of the Church. Since Christ has given the Church a mission to preserve the purity of the divine word, it is through the Church that the Gospel of

Christ comes to us. "The order Christ gave to listen to the Church (Mt. 18:17), to accept His own words and His own commandments in the words and commandments of the Church (Lk. 10:16), holds for all men of all times and all countries".[12]

Pius XI, finally, recommends that we be on guard lest "the fundamental concepts of religion be emptied of their essential content and turn toward a profane meaning. Revelation, in the Christian sense of the word, means the word spoken by God to men. To use this word to support the claims of blood and race, to bolster up the history of a people, is certainly to make it equivocal. A false coin of this sort does not deserve to circulate among the faithful of Christ".[13] Correlatively, the faith which is a response to Christian revelation "consists in holding for true whatever God has revealed and proposes, through His Church, for the belief of mankind".[14]

The teaching of Pius XI on revelation can be reduced to the following points. The existing economy is an economy of revelation. God has spoken: this is a fact attested by history. He has spoken first of all through the prophets, then through Christ, Word Incarnate, come to bring men to a knowledge of the true God. In Christ, only Son of the Father, divine revelation reaches its peak, as activity, as message, and as economy. As a result, there exists only one religion: revealed religion. There exists also only one Church, founded by Christ and assisted by the Holy Spirit, through which the divine word comes down to us, immutable and absolute. The role of the Church is to preserve revealed doctrine forever intact, as a deposit, without adding or changing anything, bringing it to the knowledge of men as a good news, defending it against error and, if necessary, defining certain points by making explicit what was implicit and clarifying what was obscure. The duty of man is to accept this revelation, that is, the word spoken by God, and to submit to it. Faith consists in holding for true whatever God has said and revealed and whatever He proposes through His Church. In adhering thus to the truth proposed, with all his soul and in the spirit of the truth, the Christian inaugurates, in his heart, this knowledge of God which Christ foretold would have its completion in everlasting life.

II. UNDER THE PONTIFICATE OF PIUS XII

Among the documents published by Pius XII, we shall examine *Humani Generis* (August 12, 1950), *Munificentissimus Deus* (November 1, 1950), and *Ad Sinarum Gentem* (October 7, 1954), which contain passages relative to our subject.

1. *Humani Generis*, without explicitly treating the very notion of revelation, still touches upon points which are connected with it: dogmatic development, the motives of credibility, the role of the Church magisterium with respect to revealed truth. Speaking of revelation in the objective sense, the encyclical gives it the name of: "revealed truth" (D 2310) "divinely revealed truth" (D 2307, 2308, 2311), "doctrine of faith" (D 2325), "divinely revealed doctrine" (D 2314) which contains "the treasures of truth" (D 2314), the "revealed deposit" (D 2314), the "deposit of faith" (D 2313-2314). Christ has entrusted to the Church "the whole deposit of faith, Holy Scripture and tradition, to preserve, defend, and interpret".[15] To these sacred sources of revelation, the document continues, "God also added a living magisterium to enlighten and explain whatever existed only obscurely or as it were implicitly in the deposit of faith".[16] This means that all dogmas are contained in revealed doctrine, some explicitly, others implicitly; and it is the theologian's task to show how the Church teaching "is found explicitly or implicitly in the holy books or in divine tradition".[17]

2. In the dogmatic bull *Munificentissimus Deus*, of November 1, 1950, Pius XII expresses himself in an identical fashion. The bull declares that the bodily assumption of the Blessed Virgin into heaven "is a truth revealed by God and contained in the divine deposit, entrusted by Christ to His Bride the Church, for her to preserve it faithfully and make it known in an infallible way. The magisterium of the Church, not with the aid of purely human instruments, but with the assistance of the Spirit of truth (Jn. 14:26), and, because of this assistance, freed from every possible danger of error, fulfills the mission which has been entrusted to her: preserving the revealed truths throughout the course of the centuries, in all their original purity and integrity; that is why she hands them down without change, without adding anything, without suppressing anything".[18]

Revelation, in the objective sense, is thus presented as a complex of truths, a sacred deposit which the Church preserves with vigilance. But this deposit lives in the heart of the Church, divinely assisted to preserve it pure and free from every alteration, to come to a fuller and fuller awareness, not by adding new truths, but by explaining and investigating truths already implicitly contained in a deposit which human reflection cannot ever exhaust. The Church is led to offering such explanation, either by the necessity of defending revealed truth, or by the impulse of piety or theological reflection. It is from this always living Church that we receive the object of our faith; the sources of revelation are in her hands together with the explanations she has received, and we go back to the original sources, the encyclical says, not to judge the Church's explanation on the basis of their study, but rather to enlighten these sources in the light of the Church teaching, which tells us infallibly what they contain. To proceed in any other way would be to "explain what is clear by what is obscure," to prefer what is indistinct to the explicit truth.[19]

3. The encyclical *Ad Sinarum Gentem* (October 7, 1954), warning the faithful in China against a false conception of autonomy (in matters of government, economy, preaching), explains, with regard to this autonomy in the field of preaching, that a proper and sound freedom in the methods of preaching could never go so far as to call the doctrine itself, or its interpretation, into question: "With what right could men interpret, according to their own will, and differently according to their nationality, this one Gospel that our Lord and Savior Jesus Christ has divinely revealed?" The bishops, successors to the apostles, and the priests, collaborators of the bishops, are charged with "announcing and teaching this Gospel which our Lord Himself and His apostles announced and taught." They "preserved it entire and handed it down through the course of centuries, in its integrity." They are not its authors, but "only its guardians and heralds," and this they are "by divine right." Thus they can repeat the words of Christ: "My teaching is not Mine but His who sent Me" (Jn. 7:16). The bishops of all times repeat the exhortation of Paul: "Oh Timothy, guard the deposit. Avoid all empty and frivolous discussion, and the contradictions of a pseudoscience." And also the words of the same apostle: "Preserve the good deposit, with the aid of the Holy Spirit who dwells in us." Since the doctrine whose integrity the Church must defend "has been divinely revealed," anathema on him who announces a Gospel different from that which the Church preaches.[20]

---

1. "Eam in spem ingressi videntur, haud difficulter eventurum ut populi, etsi de rebus divinis alii aliud tenent, in nonnullarum tamen professione doctrinarum, quasi in communi quodam spiritualis vitae fundamento fraterne consentiant" (AAS, 20 (1928): 6).

2. "Ejusmodi sane molimenta probari nullo pacto catholicis possunt, quandoquidem falsa eorum opinione nituntur, qui censent religiones quaslibet plus minus bonas ac laudabiles esse, utpote quae etsi non uno modo, aeque tamen aperiant ac significent nativum illum ingenitumque nobis sensum, quo erga Deum ferimur ejusque imperium obsequenter agnoscimus. Quam quidem opinionem qui habent, non modo ii errant ac falluntur, sed etiam, cum veram religionem, ejus notionem depravando repudient, tum ad naturalismum et atheismum, ut aiunt, gradatim deflectunt: unde manifesto consequitur ut ab revelata divinitus religione omnino recedat quisquis talia sentientibus molientibusque adstipulatur" (AAS, 20 (1928): 6).

3. "Potuit quidem Deus regendo homini unam tantummodo praestituere naturae legem, quam, scilicet, creando, in ejus animo insculpsit, ejusque ipsius legis ordinaria deinceps providentia temperare incrementa; at vero praecepta ferre maluit, quibus pareremus, et decursu aetatum,

scilicet ab humani generis primordiis ad Christi Jesu adventum et praedicationem, hominem ipsemet officia docuit, quae a natura rationis participe sibi Creatori deberentur: Multifariam multisque modis olim Deus loquens patribus in prophetis, novissime diebus istis locutus est nobis in Filio.,, Liquet inde, veram religionem esse posse nullam praeter eam quae verbo Dei revelato nititur: quam quidem revelationem, fieri ab initio coeptam et sub Vetere Dei revelato nititur: quam quidem revelationem, fieri ab initio coeptam et sub Vetere Lege continuatam, Christus upse Jesus sub Nova perfecit. Jamvero si locutus est Deus — quem reapse locutum, historiae fide comprobatur —, nemo non videt hominis esse Deo et revelanti absolute credere et omnino oboedir imperanti" (*Ibid.*, p. 8).

4. "Num nos patiemur — quod prorsus iniquum foret — veritatem, eamque divinitus revelatam, in pactiones deduc? Etenim de veritate revelata tuenda in praesenti agitur" (*Ibid.*, p. 11).

5. "Utrumque Christi praeceptum, ...alterum scilicet docendi, alterum credendi ad aeternae adeptionem salutis, ne intelligi quidem potest, nisi Ecclesia evangelicam doctrinam proponat integram ac perspicuam sitque in ea proponenda a quovis errandi periculo immunis" (*Ibid.*, pp. 11-12).

6. "Tenent iidem, veritatem dogmaticam non esse absolutam, sed relativam, id est variis temporum locorumque necessitatibus variisque animorum inclinationibus congruentem, cum ea ipsa non immutabili revelatione contineatur, sed talis sit, quae hominum vitae accommodetur" (*Ibid.*, p. 13).

7. "Supernaturalem enim virtus fidei causam formalem habet Dei revelantis auctoritatem, quae nullam distinctionem ejusmodi patitur" (*Ibid.*, p. 13).

8. "Etenim Ecclesiae magisterium — quod divino consilio in terris constitutum est ut revelatae doctrinae cum incolumes ad perpetuitatem consisterent, tum ad cognitionem hominum facile tutoque traducerentur... " (*Ibid.*, p. 14).

9. "Ecclesiae magisterium... quanquam per Romanum Pontificem et Episcopos cum eo communionem habentes quotidie exercetur, id tamen complectitur muneris, ut, si quando aut haereticorum erroribus atque oppugnationibus obsisto efficacius aut clarius subtiliusque explicata sacrae doctrinae capita in fidelium mentibus imprimi oporteat, ad aliquid tum solemnibus ritibus decretisque definiendum opportune procedat. Quo quidem extraordinario magisterii usu nullum sane inventum inducitur nec quidquam additur novi ad earum summam veritatum, quae in deposito Revelationis, Ecclesiae divinitus tradito, saltem implicite continentur, verum aut ea declarantur quae forte adhuc obscura compluribus videri possint aut ea tenenda de fide statuuntur quae a nonnullis ante in controversiam vocabantur" (*Ibid.*, p. 14).

10. "Kein Gottesglaube wird sich aur die Dauer rein und unverfalscht erhalten, wenn er nicht gestutzt wird vom Glauben an Christus. "Niemand kennt den Sohn ausser dem Vater, und niemand kennt den Vater ausser dem Sohn, und wem es der Sohn offenbaren will" (*Mt.* 11, 27). "Das ist das ewige Leben, dass sie Dich erkennen, den allein wahren Gott, und den Du gesandt hast, Jesus Christus" (*Jo.* 17, 3). Es darf also niemand sagen: Ich bin gottglaubig, das ist mir Religion genug. Des Heilands Wort hat fur Ausfluchte dieser Art keinen Platz. "Wer den Sohn leugnet, hat auch nicht den Vater; wer den Sohn bekennt, hat auch den Vater" (1 *Jo.* 2, 23). In Jesus Christus, dem menschgewordenen Gottessohn, ist die Fulle der gottlichen Offenbarung erschienen" (AAS, 29 (1937): 150).

11. "Der im Evangelium Christi erreichte Hohepunkt der Offenbarung ist endgultig, ist verpflichtend fur immer. Diese Offenbarung kennt keine Nachtrage durch Menschenhand, kennt erst recht keinen Ersatz und keine Ablosung durch die willkurlichen "Offenbarungen," die gewisse Wortfuhrer der Gegenwart aus dem sogenannten Mythus und Rasse herleiten wollen" (*Ibid.*, p. 151).

12. "Eein Gebot, die Kirche zu horen (*Mt.* 18, 17), aus den Worten und Geboten der Kirche Seine eigenen Worte und Gebote herauszuhorem (*Lk.* 10, 16), gilt fur die Menschen aller Zeitn und Zonen" (*Ibid.*, p. 152).

13. "Ein besonders wachsames Auge, Ehrwurdige Bruder, werdet Ihr haben mussen, wenn religiose Grundbegriffe ihres Wesensinhaltes beraubt und in einem profanen Sinne umgedeutet werden. Offenbarung im christlichen Sinn ist das Wort Gottes an die Menschen. Dieses gleiche Wort zu gebrauchen fur die Ausstrahlungen der Geschichte eines Volkes ist in jedem Fall verwirrend. Solch falsche Munze verdient nicht in den Sprachschatz eines glaubigen Christen uberzugehen" (*Ibid.*, p. 156).

14. "Glaube ist das sichere Furwahrhalten dessen, was Gott geoffenbart hat und durch die Kirche zu glauben vorstellt" (*Ibid.*, p. 156).

15. "Christus Dominus totum depositum fidei — Sacras nempe Litteras ac divinam traditionem — et custodiendum et tuendum et interpretandum concredidit" (D 2313). Meme affirmation reprise dans divers passages de l'encyclique: D 2307, 2315, 2325, 2327.

16. "Una enim cum sacris ejusmodi fontibus Deus Ecclesiae suae Magisterium vivum dedit, ad ea quoque illustranda et enucleanda, quae in fidei deposito nonnisi obscure ac velut implicite continentur" (D 2314).

17. "Eorum... est indicare qua ratione ea quae a vivo Magisterio docentur, in Sacris Litteris et in divina traditione, sive explicite, sive implicite inveniantur" (D 2314).

18. "Ejusmodi privilegium veritatem esse a Deo revelatam in eoque contentam divino deposito, quod Christus tradidit Sponsae suae fideliter custodiendum et infallibiliter declarandum. Quod profecto Ecclesiae magisterium non quidem industria mere humana, sed praesidio Spiritus veritatis, atque adeo sine prorsus ullo errore, demandata sibi munere fungitur revelatas adservandi veritates omne per aevum puras et integras; quamobrem eas intaminatas tradit, eisdem adjiciens nihil ab iisdem detrahens" (AAS, 42 (1950): 756-757).

19. "Si autem hoc suum munus Ecclesia exercet, ...patet omnino falsam esse methodum, qua ex obscuris clara explicentur, quin immo contrarium omnes sequi ordinem necesse est" (AAS, 42 (1950): 569).

20. "Evangelium, divinitus a Jesu Christo traditum, quonam jure possunt homines, alio in aliis Nationibus modo, pro arbitrio suo interpretari? Sacrorum Antistitibus, qui Apostolorum successores sunt, ...munus demandatum est Evangelium illud annuntiandi ac docendi, quod Christus ipse ejusque Apostoli annuntiavere ac docuere primi, et quod haec Apostolica Sedes omnesque Episcopi, eidem adhaerentes, per saeculorum decursum illibatum inviolatumque servarunt ac tradiderunt. Sacri igitur Pastores hujus Evangelii non inventores auctoresve sunt, sed solummodo custodes ex auctoritate, ac praecones divinitus constituti. Quamobrem Nosmet ipsi et Episcopi una Nobiscum hanc Jesu Christi sententiam iterare possumus ac debemus: "Mea doctrina non est mea, sed ejus qui misit me" (Jn. 7, 16). Atque omnibus cujusvis temporis sacrorum Antistitibus hoc Apostoli Pauli hortamentum tribui potest: "O Timothee, depositum custodi, devitans profanas vocum novitates et oppositiones falsi nominis scientiae"; itemque haec ejusdem Apostoli sententia: "Bonum depositum custodi per Spiritum sanctum, qui habitat in nobis" (2 Tim. 1, 14)... Cum certissimum Nobis sit hanc doctrinam quam, Sancti Spiritus ope innixi, tueri integram debemus, divinitus fuisse traditam, haec Apostoli gentium iteramus verba: "Sed licet nos, aut angelus de coelo evangelizet vobis praeterquam quod evangelizavimus vobis, anathema sit" (AAS, 47 (1955): 10-11).

SCHOLASTICS AFTER TRENT   191

mentem loquentis... ; intellectus autem, vel habitus, non est verbum Dei, quare ejus productio non est ullo modo locutio vel revelatio Dei" (De Fide, disput. 1, sect. 2, no. 9). Cf. De Fide, disput. 1, sect. 10, no. 194.

32. De Fide, disput. 1, sect. 2, no. 22.

33. "Per auctoritatem divinae doctrinae intelligi a Sancto Thoma totum quod se tenet ex parte objecti... ; motionem adaequate distinguit a tota doctrina et auctoritate divina, solumque vult inducere ad credendum; quatenus Deus proponendo interius eamdem revelationem, movet homines ad praehendum assensum; quare illa invitatio Dei interna non est nova locutio Dei nisi allegorica, quatenus Deus accommodat sua gratia aures internas mentis ut melius percipiat vim et veritatem divini testimonii proposui" (Ibid., no. 26).

34. Tractatus XVII, De Fide, disput. 1, dub. 3. Next to be cited: Collegii Salmanticensis FF. Discalceatorum B. Mariae de Monte Carmeli primitivae observantiae Cursus theologicus, juxta miram Divi Thomae Praeceptoris angelici Doctrinam (Lyon, 1779).

35. De Fide, disput. 1, dub. 3. para. 1, no. 81.

36. "Est actio, vel locutio Dei testificantis nobis verbo vel facto aliquam veritatem, sive immediate per se ipsam, sive mediate per suos ministros, quales sunt angeli, apostoli et prophetae" (Ibid., no. 82).

37. "Consistit in actuali vel etiam habituali cognitione eorum quae nobis Deus loquitur et testificatur; sic enim interiorem illi adhibemus auditum. Quo pacto, tam habitus quam assensus fidei dicitur divina revelatio. Nec immerito, tum quia generaliter loquendo, actio divina passive accepta supponit pro illius effectu; constat autem tam habitum quam actum fidei esse effectum revelationis activae Dei; tum etiam quia praedictus assensus fidei excludit in genere causae formalis in fidelitatem, quae est velamen ex parte subjecti se tenens; tum denique, quia communicat formaliter suo subjecto rectam intelligentiam eorum quae divinitus revelantur, sive ex parte objecti proponuntur; haec enim est differentia essentialis constitutiva revelationis passivae... " (Ibid., no. 83).

CONCLUSION

Before collecting the data of our investigation on the Catholic notion of revelation, one observation is in order. The Church, in all the special interventions of her magisterium, does not claim to declare everything she possesses on a given subject. An important part of her knowledge, known and recognized by her, elaborated and spread by her doctors and theologians, who are constantly exploring Scripture and tradition, does not appear in the official text. Each document pursues a very precise and quite limited purpose. This circumstantial aspect of the interventions of the Church magisterium must never be lost sight of. Each document is the result of an historical context, from which it draws its perspective, from which it borrows its special tone. Frequently directed against a very definite error, it implies, even in its exposition of Catholic doctrine, a proper and individual tone of emphasis which must be grasped. In no way does it claim to exhaust the doctrine living in the heart of the Church. Also it is necessary, in order to penetrate this doctrine, even in its broader essential traits, to consider not one single document, but the whole complex of Church documents.

1. *Author and finality of revelation.*—Under its active aspect, revelation appears as the activity of the whole Trinity (D 428, 429): the Father reveals (D 1795), the Son reveals (D 1672), the Spirit reveals (D 1795). God could have refused to reveal Himself, and, while still providing man with the help of his ordinary providence, limited him to the sole light of human reason (MA).[1] He could have made Himself known only by the natural way of creation (D 1785). But it pleased His wisdom and His goodness to make Himself known also by the way of supernatural revelation (D 1785). Revelation is thus the gratuitous initiative of God's good will towards humanity (D 1636, 1785), the pure gift of His love, like the whole of the super-

natural economy: Incarnation, Redemption, election. If God has revealed, it is because he wanted to raise man to a supernatural end, make us share His own happiness, associate us with His divine life: that is why He has furnished us with the means for knowing and attaining something that completely surpasses our intelligence and all its natural resources (D 1786).

2. *Economy and formal element of revelation.*—Humanity, in its present state, is living under an economy of revelation; God has entered into relation with man, made known His thinking, instructed man in His divine will (D 1785, MA). This communication between a personal and transcendent God (D 2145) and His creature is represented by the Church in the terms used by Scripture, as the word of one person to another: God has spoken to man (Heb. 1:1; D 1636, 1785, MBS, MA). This is the primary fact which dominates all of history. The religion of the two Testaments is the result of this word spoken to men. In the Old Testament, God spoke to the patriarchs and prophets and, through them, to His chosen people. In the New Testament, God addresses humanity through His own Son, the Word Incarnate: in Jesus Christ the fullness of revelation is accomplished: in Him and through Him we have the knowledge of the true God and His mysteries, the truth which leads to life (D 429, 792a, 2202, MBS). The Gospel, first preached by Christ, the apostles also preached at His command and in their turn handed it on to the Church (D 212, 783, 792a, 1785). With the apostles, the constitutive phase of revelation is completed, the object of faith is constituted (D 2021). Revelation, in its formal element, is a word (communication) or species of testimony, that is, a word of authority, qualified by the infinite wisdom and holiness of uncreated Truth, all-knowing, infallible, and most truthful. *This* word of testimony deserves, not the adherence of knowledge, but the full homage of faith (D 1637, 1639, 1789, 2145).

3. *Object of revelation.*—The material object of revelation can be considered either in itself—namely God and the eternal decrees of His will (D 1785), such as they are made known through Christ and in Christ (MBS),—or with respect to the natural capacity of created intelligence (D 1786, 1795). Thus we distinguish between truths accessible to human reason and mysteries hidden in God, which can be known only through positive revelation (D 1795), for they surpass not only human intelligence (D 1642, 1645, 1646, 1671, 1795), but the capacity of all created intelligence (D 1673, 1796). Still, these mysteries, if they surpass human reason, do not contradict it (D 1649, 1797). We can even, by the way of analogy, arrive at a certain and very fruitful knowledge of these mysteries (D 1796),

but never, even once they are revealed, can we penetrate them as we can the truths which make up the object of our natural knowledge (D 1795, 1797); up until the day of full vision, they will remain veiled (D 1673, 1796). These mysteries are primarily those which concern our elevation to supernatural life and our intercourse with God (D 1671, 1786); these are properly the secrets which only the Spirit can know, because it is He who scrutinizes the depths of God, and which the Son, who has the Spirit of the Father, reveals to those to whom He will (D 1644, 1795, MBS). In addition to these mysteries, the object of revelation also includes truths of religion which, of themselves, are not inaccessible to reason, but which God, in His goodness, has willed to reveal in order to assure that all men would arrive at a knowledge that is certain, rapid, and free from all error (D 1786, 1795). In the last analysis, the object of revelation is God Himself and His plan of love for humanity, such as it is manifest in Christ and through Christ.

4. *Revelation and its names.*—Revelation, in its accomplished form, has many different names in the documents of the Church, which leave no doubt as to its nature. It is called equivalently: word of God (D 1781, 1792), divine word (D 48), revealed word (D 1793), the word spoken by God (MBS), the word testified (D 2145), revelation (D 1787), unchangeable revelation (MA), the revelation or deposit of faith (D 1836), the deposit of faith (D 1836, 1967, 2204, 2313, 2314), revealed deposit (D 2314), apostolic doctrine (D 300), doctrine of the faith (D 1800, 2145), revealed doctrine (D 2314), revealed doctrines (MA), sacred doctrine (MA), doctrine of faith (D 2325), revealed truth (D 2310, 2145), truth divinely revealed (D 2308, 2311), the Gospel promised, published, and preached (D 783), the Gospel divinely revealed (ASG), faith entrusted to the apostles (D 93), faith given by Christ to the apostles (D 212), absolute and immutable truth preached by the apostles (D 2147), revelation handed down by the apostles or the deposit of faith (D 1836), the deposit of faith entrusted to the Church (D 2204), the divine deposit entrusted to the Church (D 1800), the true and sound doctrine of Christ (D 792a), the doctrine of salvation (D 428-429). This divine word, good news brought to the knowledge of men, doctrine, message of truth, this revelation is, however, distinct from purely speculative truth; it is a doctrine of salvation (D 428-429), which leads to life everlasting in the vision of the Father (D 429, 1786), a message containing the promises which give substance to our hope of eternal salvation (D 798).

5. *Church and revelation.*—The role of the Church with respect to revealed truth is threefold. With the assistance of the Spirit, she must first of all safeguard and faithfully and holily preserve the deposit of faith which has been entrusted to her care (D 792a, 1781, 1800, 2145); preserve it in its integrity and inviolate, free from all contamination and all innovation (D 93, 159, 1679, 2204, MD). She must also explain it, according to its true sense, and infallibly declare the revealed doctrine (D 1781, 1800, 1836, HG, MD). Finally, she must proscribe all errors which threaten this truth (D 792a, 1817, HG). Revelation is complete with the end of the apostolic age (D 2021). As such, the deposit of revealed doctrine which is found in Scripture and tradition (D 783, 1787) can receive nothing which will augment it: "No new discovery is introduced and nothing new is added to the sum of truths contained at least implicitly in the deposit of revelation entrusted to the Church" (MA). What is perfected is the understanding of the revealed deposit (D 1800, MA, HG). The Holy Spirit "directs the universal Church towards a more perfect knowledge of the revealed truths" (MD); thus the Church can make explicit what is implicit, cast light on what is obscure, "enlighten and elucidate what had existed only obscurely and as it were implicitly in the deposit of faith" (D 2314). It is through the preaching of the Church, who has received the mission to teach all nations (ASG, MA, D 2204), that revelation is made living and actual. Only the Church, in the living tradition which she has received from Christ and the apostles, knows how to interpret the revealed truth, assisted by the Spirit. When she says that she is "guardian" of revelation (D 1793), this is not a question of human conservatism, pure material respect for the letter. The word which she safeguards is a living word of Christ and the apostles, which she assimilates by an unceasing meditation and which she constantly explains to the Christian people.

6. *Characteristics of revelation.*—Though they are not always explicitly formulated, these characteristics are still very real; in her manner of speaking, it is clear that the Church presupposes and understands them:

A. Revelation is *interpersonal*: quite different from natural revelation in which God shows Himself to the human mind as an *object* and lets Himself be reasoned to as beginning and end of all things, supernatural revelation is the word of God, the manifestation of His thinking (D 1785). God Himself takes the initiative, comes to man, enters into personal communication with man, subject to subject, in a relationship of the spiritual order. Personal in its initiatives on

God's part, revelation also demands a personal response: revelation and faith are interpersonal.

B. Revelation is *gratuitous*: a free step on the part of God's kindness which inclines Him towards man, a free initiative bound up with the plans of His salvific love (D 1636, 1785, MA). Revelation is grace, even in the welcome it receives; for God, who communicates the gift, also furnishes the power to receive it in faith (D 180, 798, 1789, 1791). His thinking is a thinking of love; it is accompanied by the power of the Spirit. The culminating point of this initiative is the Incarnation of the Word of God, the Son, coming in person to reveal the Father and the secrets of His love (D 783, 792a, 1785, MBS).

C. Revelation is *social*: the man whom God has created is not only an individual, but a society. Thus revelation, which we have called interpersonal, is also social, destined for all humanity, addressed to individuals, not as isolated unities, shut up from each other, but as belonging to a collectivity, so that all will be aware of their community in revelation, in faith, in love, in salvation (D 428, 429, 1785). Still there is a hierarchy: revelation is not addressed to all immediately, but through the medium of those whom God has chosen to be His witnesses: the prophets and the apostles.

D. Revelation is *historical*: addressed to a nature which is not purely spiritual (and thus incapable of possessing its whole perfection in one instant), but to a creature subject to the conditions of matter (space and time), revelation is subject to progress in its duration. Beginning with the origins of the world, it develops in quality and quantity, throughout the whole Old Testament, and is finally complete with Christ and the apostles (D 428-429, 783, 1785, 2021, MBS). Partial first of all, successive and polymorphous, it attains its fullness in Christ (D 792a, MBS). It is presented as an economy, that is, as a plan conceived and realized by God over the course of centuries.

E. Revelation is *doctrinal* and *"realist"*: in its accomplished form, revelation is not the simple activity of God offering Himself to human friendship, the pure contact of the Spirit in us, the simple experience of our consciousness without content and without doctrinal absolute, but rather a complex of truths which are offered to us through the grouping of concepts which are bound together by Christ, the prophets, and the apostles. The propositions which state and designate this certainly do not exhaust the mystery, although they do sketch its true aspect. That is why the Church always speaks of revelation, in the objective sense, as a religious teaching, a doctrine, a deposit of truths (D 428-429, 783, 792a, 1787, 1800, 2059). It goes without saying, however, that faith is not terminated with the simple conceptual or verbal statement, but rather with the reality, the mystery itself. Doctrine, as conceptual signs, is the means for the believer to give assent to doctrine understood as the realities signified by the signs. What is revealed, in the last analysis, is God Himself, His eternal decrees (D 1785), His mysteries (D 1795), but in a human way of signs and judgments which lead us to the reality.

F. Revelation is *salvific*: universal in its destination, revelation pursues a salvific end. It is an order of knowledge finalized by an order of life. It is not a human wisdom, a philosophical discovery, nor a product of the sub-conscious, but a divine wisdom, essentially ordered towards salvation (D 1786, 2074, 2075, 2145). If God speaks to us, it is to make us associates in His life. Revelation is aimed towards vision (D 1786) and seeks to ensure encounter, our communion, with the true God: "This is life everlasting, that they know you, the one true God, and Him whom you have sent, Jesus Christ" (Jn. 17:3). Thus, revelation is called doctrine of salvation (D 429), Gospel of salvation (D 783).

7. *Faith, response to revelation.*—The faith which corresponds to revelation is "an assent of the mind to the truth acquired extrinsically by the teaching received" (D 2145). It consists in holding for true all that God has said, testified, revealed, and proposed through His Church (D 2145, MBS). The believer does not give his assent because of the intrinsic evidence of the truth, but because of the authority of God who speaks: this authority is based on the infinite knowledge and the truthfulness of God (D 1789, 2145). In adhering to the statements immediately proposed by the Church, it is to the mysteries, that is, to God Himself and His word that the believer adheres. Faith is his answer to the uncreated testimony: total homage, firm adherence which unites the human mind to the infinite Truth, affording him absolute certitude, participation in the light and infallibility of Truth itself. This adherence, free and meritorious, could not be salutary and of the theological order without an activity of grace which gives the power to will and consent; faith remains a gift of God (D 180, 798, 1791).

In a word, we can describe revelation, as the teaching office of the Church understands it, as being the salvific activity, sovereignly wise and free, through which God, in order to lead man to his supernatural end, which consists in the vision of the divine essence, makes Himself known to man, together with the plan for salvation which He has conceived for humanity. This activity is the word of testimony of uncreated Truth, divine testimony demanding the homage of faith. Christian revelation, the effect of this divine eternal activity, is the word of salvation announced through the prophets, and primarily through Christ and the apostles, handed down to the Church to be safeguarded faithfully and proposed infallibly to men of all times. This word is contained in Scripture and tradition. In its accomplished form, revelation is presented as a religious doctrine or a deposit of truths which the Church has a mission of preserving, defending, and explaining. The preaching of the divine message takes place through signs which confirm the divine origin (miracles) and an activity of grace which works together with the message of the Church and moves the soul to the adherence of faith. External word, interior grace: this is the twofold dimension of the word of God.

1. In these conclusions, we use the following abbreviations to indicate these recent pontifical documents: *Mortalium animos* (MA), *Mit brennender Sorge* (MBS), *Ad Sinarum Gentem* (ASG), *Humani Generis* (HG), *Munificentissimus Deus* (MD).

part 5
theological reflection

Theology is the understanding of faith, the mind's search for understanding. The mystery it possesses through faith theology seeks to penetrate, to acquire an understanding that is always more living and more satisfying. This is a work that is never finished, for the mystery uncovers new depths in the measure that the mind delves into it. If theology is the science of the object of faith, it must first of all, on its own level which is that of science, take possession of its object and then, in a complementary process, work at understanding it. The reflexive function of theology is thus not merely juxtaposed to its positive function: it is rather the homogeneous fructification of the positive. It is understanding, but understanding of a *revealed truth*.

The object of this fifth part of the book is primarily to sum up the reflections which spring from the very contemplation of the object of faith, collected and systematized; a reflection faithful to revealed truth, taking account of the theological activity of past centuries, in all its best elements, and also taking account of the aspirations and orientations of present-day research, with the Church magisterium furnishing a norm to direct theological investigation along the proper direction.

The study of the biblical and patristic material on revelation brings up numerous problems, for the most part bound up with the very complexity of the reality under consideration. This reality, actually, is closely bound up with many other realities, such as history, Incarnation, Church, light of faith, the economy of signs (miracles) which accompany or constitute revelation. This intimate relationship is evident already in the language itself. Thus, we can say that history is revelation, that Christ is revelation in person, that the light of faith is inner revelation, that the Church is concrete revelation, that miracles are a revelation of accomplished salvation. On the other hand, the creation and parousia are a framework for the revelation of grace, like two types of divine manifestation, and closely bound up with it.

This multiplicity of realities is further complicated by the multiplicity of aspects under which they can be viewed, giving rise to contrasts, even oppositions, sometimes apparently even to contradictions. How, for example, can we reconcile such varied aspects as mystery, history, person, doctrine, deposit? In stressing one of these aspects, we always run the risk of selling another short. This is a phenomenon of frequent occurrence among the Protestants, and a constant danger for Catholic theologians.

Finally, the analogies which serve to represent the experience of revelation cannot be treated without great precaution. Scripture speaks of word and testimony. When we use these terms, are we certain that we do not cheapen them, that we preserve their whole religious vitality? When we speak of Christ and His doctrine, are we certain that the intellectual overtones this word takes on through its association with philosophical systems does not affect the specific character of the Master's teaching?

These then are the problems posed by revealed truth itself which we mean to study in this last part of the book. The chapters are arranged according to the three approaches suggested by the First Vatican Council for arriving at a certain understanding of the mysteries: the way of analogy (chapter 1), the bonds existing between the mysteries themselves (chapters 2-8), the approach of finality (chapter 9). The last chapters (chapters 10 and 11) will serve as a conclusion to the whole study.

CHAPTER I

REVELATION AS WORD, TESTIMONY, ENCOUNTER

On the basis of the concept of word with respect to human relationship, Israel first understood this manifestation of God to man that we call *revelation*. Seen in its totality, revelation is a phenomenon of *word* (speaking), obviously including great diversity in forms and means of communication.[1] In the Old Testament, the prophets are presented as witnesses and heralds of the word of God.[2] This analogy of the word receives its full and strict accomplishment in Jesus Christ. In Jesus Christ, the Son in Person speaks to us,[3] preaches,[4] teaches,[5] testifies to what He has seen and heard in the bosom of the Father.[6] "Eyewitnesses and servants of the Word" (Lk. 1:2), the apostles, in their turn, preach,[7] teach,[8] testify to everything Christ did and said.[9] This word and this testimony have a content, which is the message of salvation, the good news *par excellence*: the Gospel.[10] By faith in this message of the word we achieve an encounter with the living God, prelude to the face-to-face of final vision. *Word, testimony, encounter*—these are the analogies that theological reflection must examine and purify, indicating how and in what measure they give access to the mystery of revelation (D 1796).

I. REVELATION AS WORD

1. *Human Word*

We shall begin with the generic element of revelation: word. On this notion of word, the analysis of the scholastics is very brief. Following Saint Thomas, they teach that speaking means manifesting one's thinking to someone through the medium of signs.[11] The accent here is on the *unveiling* of the thought which is effected through the word and on the *sharing* of knowledge which is thus realized. This is a rather static conception. De Lugo is one of the few to stress the dynamic character of the word and note its essential orientation towards another person. The word does not consist only in *proposing* an object of thought, but of its nature it tends to the communication of this object; it implies a will to be heard and understood.[12] Contemporary theology, attentive to the data of philosophy and the psychology of language,[13] insists with good reason on the interpersonal, existential, dynamic, and out-going character of the word.

Karl Bühler distinguishes a threefold aspect in word: 1. The word has a *content*. It signifies or represents something: it names an object, it formulates a thought, a judgment, it recounts a fact (*Darstellung*). 2. The word is *interpellation*. It is addressed to someone and tends to provoke a response in him, a reaction. It acts like a call, a provocation (*Appell, Auslösung*). 3. Finally, the word is the *unveiling* of the person, the manifestation of his interior attitude, of his dispositions (*Ausdruck, Kundgabe*).[14] To sum up, we might define word as being the activity through which one person *addresses* and *expresses* himself to another person with a view towards *communication*.[15]

Word is primarily an *interpersonal* encounter. Man speaks *of* the world, but he does not speak *to* the world. With objects, man can enter into a relationship of *me* to *it*, but conversation (word) is established only between *me* and *you*. Every word (conversation) is aimed at another man. Even in the "professionals of silence" (Montaigne, Descartes, Vigny, Proust), the word is always an attempt towards personal authentic presence.

To speak means to *address* someone. Before it is an expression, word is an *interpellation*. "To address one's thinking to someone means to make it manifest in the form of address, it means to make it the subject matter about which one converses with someone else".[16] Every word is a call, a demand for reaction. By its dynamic character, it tends to establish a circle of address and response, to become conversation, dialogue. Generally understood and presupposed, this element of interpellation sometimes blossoms forth in the conversation, particularly when there is a marked increase in the emotional content. It is expressed then in forms of syntax which range from the simple use of the personal pronoun to open question and dissociation of the members of a sentence.[17] The interpellation, just like its reaction, can take on a variety of forms: corresponding to a command there is obedience; to prayer, the granting of the prayer; to promise, trust; to explanation, attention; to testimony, faith.[18]

If every word is a demand for reaction, this is because word tends towards *communication*, even if it does not always produce communication. The goals of this communication can vary. The destination of the word can be purely *utilitarian*: a means for action at the service of the *homo faber*. This pragmatic language is the language of exchange of information, orders, messages; it is the language of newspaper, radio, television; it is the language of everyday life, family life, technical, juridic, professional activity; it is the language which is extended and amplified in the scientific terminology of doctors, chemists, mathematicians. This utilitarian aspect represents the lowest degree of human expression and intent. In this level, the word is impersonal. The ego remains neutral, outside the process of communication.[19]

On a somewhat higher plane, word is not only simple information or instruction: it becomes *expression* (in the sense that we say an act can express ourselves), revelation of person, testimony regarding self. To the extent that we *express* ourselves *in our speaking*, or that we put ourselves into our speaking, and in the measure that we truly communicate ourselves to someone else, or *see him in himself* as a person, our human word achieves its fullness of meaning. The authentic word is that of the person as such, in his individuality, expressing himself to another person, seeing him as a person too. As expression of personal mystery, this word is addressed to the personal mystery of the other man. The word accomplishes its mission of conversation all the better according as man (in the image of God who speaks of Himself in His Word) puts himself into his word, to communicate the profound meaning of his person.[20] For communication and dialogue to become a reciprocal exchange, revelation, each party must have a respect for the other in his personal mystery, complete readiness to accept and give, mutual trust, a friendship existing or at least beginning.[21]

Word, in its higher essence, is thus the means through which two interiorities unveil themselves to each other with a view towards reciprocal exchange. When word attains this level, it is the sign of friendship and love; it is the welling up and expression of a freedom which opens to another person and thus *gives itself*. Speaking turns into a form of giving from one person to the other. Each opens to the other, offering him hospitality in everything that is best within himself. Each gives and gives himself in a communion of love.

But the articulate word cannot express everything: there is a place for gesture to support and give depth to human words. When the gift of person made through words is not sufficient to express *everything* about the profound being of the person, the word ends up as the gift of the person through the commitment of his living: that is what happens in married love, and in the apostolate. Sometimes, a series of words and actions culminates in a gesture which, in some way, plastically sums up the fundamental intention of the person speaking: for example, in martyrdom, where the sacrifice of one's life is a seal upon what he professes in his words.

2. *Divine Word*

In revelation, it is God Himself who addresses man: not the God of philosophic abstraction, but the living God, all-powerful, thrice holy. He wants to be a *Me* addressing *You*, in an interpersonal and living relationship, with a view towards communication, dialogue, sharing. This word which springs up from the transcendent world of divine life, *calls* to man and invites him to the obedience of faith, with a view towards communion of life. It is teeming with the unheard-of news of salvation offered to humanity: man is saved, the Kingdom of heaven is among us, the plan of love pursued by God from all eternity is accomplished. For the word of God does more than speak and inform: it effects what it signifies, it changes the situation of humanity, it gives life. The word of God is an active, efficacious, creative word.

If God, through His word, enters into interpersonal relationship with man, this is not, this cannot be, for a purely utilitarian intention. The word of God is a word of friendship and love. The Word of God is a Word of Love. This intention of love stands out in many ways.

It appears first of all in the *very fact of the word*. Through revelation, God, Uncreated Person, addresses man, simple creature. In some way He bridges the infinite distance between man and God and stands before man. The Most High, the Transcendent, makes Himself a *God near at hand*, God with us, Emmanuel. This gesture, through which God comes out of his mystery, *condescends*, makes himself present to man, can only mean salvation and friendship for man. At the very root of the fact of this word, there is God's gratuitous will to establish bonds of friendship with man. If God means to reveal Himself, this can, after all, only be in order to establish bonds of friendship and love with man and associate us in His own divine life; and, on the other hand, if He means to enter into a relationship of friendship with man and make us associates of His divine life, that can only mean that he wants to reveal Himself. The fact of revelation and the fact of our supernatural call coincide in God.[22]

The intention of love in the divine word is even more obvious if the creature thus addressed and called, here below, to enter into a relation of friendship with God, is an *enemy creature*, having turned away from God. God, in friendship and love, approaches a creature who has rebelled against Him. What is more, He pushes his condescension to the point of assuming the very condition of this creature. God puts Himself completely on a human level, to the point of being incarnate, meeting man on his own level. God expresses Himself and expresses His plan of salvation by using all the resources of the Incarnation: action, gesture, conduct, and primarily word. Christ declares the mystery of His Person and His mission in human discourse, which the ear can hear and the intelligence can assimilate.

The intention of love in the divine word appears not only in the *fact* and *economy* of revelation, but also in its *object*. The communication of God has for its object not only religious truths of the natural order, but also, and principally, secrets of the divine life itself. The mystery of the Trinity, primarily, is the divine secret par excellence, the secret of divine intimacy, known only to the three Divine Persons, for only they make up this secret: "No one knows the Son excepting the Father, just as no one knows the Father excepting the Son" (Mt. 11:27; Jn. 1:18). "No one knows the secrets of God except the Spirit of God" (1 Cor. 2:11). In revealing this secret, God initiates man into what is most intimate in God: the mystery of His own life, the heart of His personal subsistence. God cannot thus reveal the secret of His life except to a person who is joined to Him by friendship or whom He wants to join to Himself by friendship. The revelation of the Trinity, in inviting us to an astonishing degree of intimacy with God, thus appears as the beginning of our sharing in the divine life and constitutes a free gift of God to man. Revelation is a self-gift.[23]

God has pursued this gift to man through His word with an excess of love. Christ, after having exercised His prophetic mission, that is, after having made known the name of the Father (Jn. 17:6. 26), the doctrine of the Father (Jn. 7:16; 12:50), consummates, through the sacrifice of His life, the gift made by His word. Through His passion He accomplishes the charity that He came to signify: "Jesus, knowing that his hour was to come to pass out of this world and go to the Father, having loved his own who were in the world, loved them up to the limit (of love)" (Jn. 13:1). This is the completion of the mystery of the word as self-gift. The *articulated* word becomes the *immolated* word. Christ on the cross *tells* (Jn. 1:18) the charity of the Father up to the last inarticulate cry in which everything is said and witnessed to. The word of God is exhausted, to the point of silence. "The time of death and silence becomes the supreme expression of the love offered to humanity".[24] Everything which was incommunicable in the divine communication is expressed in the outstretched arms and the body drained of its blood, and in the heart pierced with the centurion's lance (Jn. 19:34). The Word of Love delivered Himself entirely to men. Revelation through the word is consummated and sealed by revelation-action.

II. REVELATION AS TESTIMONY

Revelation is a specific word: *testimony*. It invites to a specific reaction: *faith*. In its active form, as in its actuated form, revelation is testimony: it is an action or deposition of witnesses.

Scripture describes revelation as an economy of testimony. In the Old Testament, God chose privileged persons, who were neither truth nor light themselves, but came to give testimony to the truth. These men speak in the name of God and say: "This is what God told me to say. You are invited to accept my word in faith; for my word is His word." These men make themselves heard by the tone of authority in their words, by their example, by their works of power or mercy, by their patience in persecution, and even by their martyrdom, which is the supreme testimony. In the New Testament, Christ presents Himself as the Witness par excellence. He tells what He has seen and heard in the bosom of the Father, and we are invited to the obedience of faith. He Himself sets up a body of witnesses, the apostles. They testify to the life and teaching of Christ. They invite all men to believe what they have seen and heard and experienced of the Word of life. Those who believe are introduced, through baptism, into a new society, the Church; they share in the Body and Blood of Christ; they live from His life. What the apostles hand down to the Church is a *testimony*, a *deposition* of witnesses. This testimony the Church receives, preserves, and protects, but also proposes, explains, interprets, assimilates, and grows to *understand* more and more.

Just as testimony binds souls together, over the course of history, it also binds time to eternity. The idea of testimony projects its light on the Incarnation and on the Trinity itself. Scripture describes the Trinity's activity of revelation under the form of mutual testimony. The Son appears as Witness to the Father, and it is thus that He makes Himself known to the apostles. But the Father, in His turn, testifies that Christ is the Son, through the attraction which he produces in human souls, through the works which He enables His Son to accomplish, and primarily through the resurrection, which is the decisive testimony of the Father in behalf of His Son. The Son testifies to the Spirit, for He promises to send him as educator, consoler, sanctifier. And the Spirit comes, testifying to the Son, for He recalls and manifests and teaches the fullness of Christ's words, and instills them in human hearts. Thus in the intercourse of the three Divine Persons with humanity, we see an exchange of testimony which is intended to propose revelation and nourish faith. There are three who reveal or give testimony and these three are one. The testimony is a secret bond between eternity and time, between heaven and earth. And just as the Word rests in the bosom of the Father, the Apostle John reposed on the bosom of Christ.[25]

The documents of the magisterium also describe revelation in terms of testimony (implicitly most of the time), representing revelation as a word of authority: the word of uncreated Truth, infallible and most truthful, to which must correspond, not the adherence of knowledge, but the homage of faith (D 1637, 1639, 1789). Only the anti-Modernist oath explicitly says that revelation is a word of testimony (D 2145). God who reveals is God who speaks with the authority of a witness whose infallibility and truthfulness are absolute.

Theologians, on their part, generally define revelation as *locutio Dei attestans* (God's speech as testimony). In order to cast fuller light on the notion of testimony, they oppose the word of teaching to the word of testimony. In the word of teaching, the hearer acquiesces to the teacher's explanation because of arguments whose intrinsic value he himself perceives. In the word of testimony, on the contrary, the hearer gives his assent because of the authority of the one who speaks; he believes on this person's word, because of the knowledge and truthfulness of the one who speaks. In both cases, the human mind is enriched with new truths. The essential element is to be found in the motive which inspires the mind's assent: in the one, there is evidence based on demonstration; in the other, the mere authority of the teacher who speaks. These basic statements are true enough, but they can be carried further.

1. Human Testimony

In its essence, testimony is a word by which a person invites another to admit something as true by trusting in his invitation as the immediate guarantee of truth, and in his authority as its remote guarantee. This *invitation to believe*, as guarantee of truth, is the specific element of testimony. Very often, it is explicit in the language itself: "I tell you.... Believe me.... I have seen, with my own eyes".[26] The object in which belief is demanded is the object witnessed to, the object of testimony. Faith, which is the response demanded by testimony, is "a judgment which holds the object testified to for true, relying on the testimony as the immediate guarantee of truth".[27]

The testimony is the immediate guarantee of truth, for the witness, by the very fact that he invites belief, makes an appeal to trust, and binds himself to speak the truth; he binds himself not to betray this confidence and trust, he promises to be sincere and truthful. The testimony is thus something more than a mental fact; it is a moral fact. Testifying means more than simply recounting: testimony commits the witness. His word must become the substitute for the experience itself, for the one who has not had the experience. Faith in testimony thus calls for a certain resignation in the area of reason; this is a legitimate resignation, however, for its motive is based on the mental (knowledge, perspicacity, critical spirit) and primarily the moral qualifications of the witness.

It is important to note that, if human faith is based on the actual testimony of a witness and on his authority, this authority, however, is not in itself the ultimate guarantee of truth. Fallible by nature, it always needs to be accompanied by objective signs which proclaim its true value. This appreciation of the witness and his authority is a complex operation, like all personal knowledge, and, as a result, open to error and deception. Thus, even though the mind, through an attentive examination of the claims of the witness, has provided itself with every possible guarantee, it can never completely sound the ultimate depths of human testimony, for human knowledge and human fidelity are always suspect. Man is an identity who always needs to reconquer himself. Only God can give an absolute guarantee to His word, by reason of its eternal and absolute identity with God Himself. Human faith can never be a faith of pure and simple authority.[28]

Inferior, in this respect, to the way of evidence, the way of testimony is, however, superior in the values it sets in motion. Whereas demonstration makes its primary appeal to the intelligence, testimony, since it calls for an intensity of trust which is measured by the values that are risked on its behalf, enlists not only the intelligence, but also, in different degrees, the will and love. The possibility of any communication between men rests, in the last analysis, on the trust which is called for by human testimony and upon the promise which it tacitly makes not ever to betray. Thus, on the one hand, there is the moral commitment of the witness and, on the other hand, trust, which is already a first beginning of love, on the part of the man who adheres to the testimony.

As soon as we leave behind the universe of material things, to approach the level of human persons, we leave the plane of evidence and enter into that of testimony. On the level of intersubjectivity, which is that of persons, we rub shoulders with mystery. Persons are not problems which can be enclosed within a formula and solved in an equation. Persons can be known only by revelation. We have access to personal intimacy only through the free testimony of the person. And persons testify to themselves only under the inspiration of love. Knowledge by testimony is thus an inferior knowledge only where, because of the nature of the object, we are capable of arriving at a direct and immediate evidence of the reality; but it is in no way inferior when there is question of realities which are persons, or where testimony is the only way of entering into union with a person and sharing in his personal mystery.[29]

2. Divine Testimony

Revelation is precisely the revelation of the personal mystery of God. God is interiority *par excellence,* the personal and sovereign Being whose mystery can be known only through *testimony*, that is, through a spontaneous confidence that we are invited to receive in faith. Christianity is a religion of testimony, for it is the manifestation of persons, and it is testimony which assures this interpersonal communication. Christ speaks, teaches, legislates, like the other founders of religion. But what He says, teaches, communicates, is, in the last analysis, the mystery of His Person. He establishes a religion which is an initiation to the personal mystery which is He Himself. The apostles testify to their intimacy with Christ, the Word of life, the Son, who is Himself in relation with the Father and the Spirit, but in a communication so special that it admits no sharing. The whole Gospel appears as a confidence of love, in which Christ progressively unfolds the mystery of His Person, the mystery of the life of the Divine Persons, and the mystery of our new status as sons. The apostles are witnesses to all that Christ said and did, but primarily they are witnesses to His Person: this is the element which bears the whole weight of their testimony.

Divine testimony is unique in species, as distinct from human testimony, on the objective plane as well as on the subjective plane. It has one particular characteristic about it first of all; not only does it affirm the truth of what it proposes for belief, but at the same time it affirms the absolute infallibility of its own testimony. When God testifies to a thing, He testifies at the same time to His own infallibility, for He is subsistent Testimony, pure Testimony, whose activity as witness is identified with pure Being. God who attests is in Himself the absolute and ultimate foundation of the infallible truth of His testimony. He is in Himself His own guarantee. In Christian revelation, the signs which accompany it are intended to assure the identification of the witness, to make known in the human voice and in the human words of Christ the testimony of the living God and, in the deposition of the apostles, the authentic message of God. But faith itself is based on uncreated divine testimony, the ultimate foundation of truth. Man rests the whole burden of his faith on a Word which bears its own guarantee.[30]

Divine testimony is also distinguished from human testimony in that the invitation to believe, on the part of God, takes place in two ways: exteriorly and interiorly. Through the prophets, Christ, and the apostles, God, in distinct terms, makes known His plan of salvation and invites to faith: "Repent and believe in the good news (Mk. 1:15; 16:15). But divine testimony is not limited to this external manifestation which takes place through human language and the signs of power. Its most profound dimension is a completely interior activity. Different from man who can only harness the psychological efficacy of the human word and its power of expression, God can act directly in the soul. To describe this activity, Scripture speaks of a revelation (Mt. 11:25; 16:17), an illumination (2 Cor. 4:4-6; Act. 16:14), an anointing (2 Cor. 1:21-22); an attraction (Jn. 6:44), an inner testimony (Jn. 5:37; 1 Jn. 5:6). As divine witness, God can infuse a light into the human mind through which He draws this mind to conform its knowledge with the divine knowledge, by subordinating itself to the first Truth through homage to His infinite authority, and to admit the divine testimony by reason of its unique excellence which makes God the ultimate and absolute guarantee of truth. Illuminated and moved by the divine light which fills his mind and becomes his own light, the mind of the believer can adhere simply and totally to the divine testimony in itself and for itself. Supernatural faith is the only pure faith, based on simple authority.

III. REVELATION AS ENCOUNTER

Every word presupposes a *me* and a *you*. Every word implies the intention of being understood by a *you*. The word is an existential delegation: a *me* goes out in search of a *you*, entrusted with the existence of the *me* who utters it. The word becomes reality only in an *encounter* with the *you*. This encounter can attain different degrees of depth. In its weakest degree, it tends to establish a contact. Failing this, the persons miss each other. But its innate objective is for word and response to become authentic dialogue, reciprocity, communion, mutual commitment. This reciprocity is the condition for an effective encounter. There are encounters in which reciprocity is understood as an exchange, in pure equality, but only in a loving encounter can reciprocity be complete. This reciprocity is the fruit of a revelation and a gift.[31]

This encounter which tends to be a dialogue in love we also discover on the infinitely more elevated plane of revelation and faith.

In revelation, God addresses man, speaks with him, communicates the good news of salvation. But there is really and fully an encounter between God and man only in faith. Only then does the word of the living God find acceptance and recognition in man. Faith is the first and free step of man towards God. Through His word, God invites man to an intercourse of friendship; through faith, man responds to God's invitation. The first encounter between God and man, faith is the equivalent of that smile of friendship which begins a human conversation. When man opens his heart to God who speaks, shares in his thinking, lets himself be filled and directed by it, God and man meet each other, and this encounter develops into a communion of life.

Revelation and faith are thus essentially *interpersonal.* "What appears as the principal element," Saint Thomas points out, "and has final value in every act of belief, is the person to whose word we give our adherence".[32] Faith is the encounter with the personal God in His word. It always presupposes the adherence of the mind to God's message, for if God manifests Himself as a God who *speaks,* faith must be assent to what He *says.* But this adherence itself is finalized by the encounter with the living and personal God. Faith, in this *conversation,* inaugurates an encounter which will be completed in final *vision.* But it is already a mysterious presence of God, a living relation between man and God, person to person.[33] It is thus that faith is frequently described by Saint Paul and Saint John: a total attitude of the whole man responding to God's advances, as an indivisible totality, where knowledge and love are only one in the spiritual impulse of the whole person. The faith which works through charity (Gal. 5:6) is knowledge and commitment of the whole person:

it accepts the whole truth of God and gives God the whole human heart.

It is important to note some particular traits of this encounter effected through faith. A first characteristic of this encounter is the fact that God always takes the *initiative*. His infinite transcendence is also infinite condescension. Every salutary encounter always finds Him coming first. "It is not we who have loved God, but He who has loved us" (1 Jn. 4:10). In revelation and faith, everything is God coming first, everything is grace: the activity of God coming out of His mystery, the economy of word, the message of salvation, the capacity of responding to this message and meeting God in faith. It is God, finally, who initiates in us the movement of a return towards Him; it is God who stamps upon our intelligence a tendency, a supernatural impulse which inclines us towards him, first Truth, as towards its supreme Good; it is God who creates the ontological foundation on the basis of which, while remaining human, we can still posit the act of theological faith. This activity of God, however, does not encroach upon human freedom. Our wills remain free to accept or not accept this other freedom which is open to us. But we are invited to put ourselves more and more at the disposition of His word, making it our own in order to live in it (Mt. 13:23).

A second characteristic of this encounter with the word is the seriousness of the *choice* it presents. For the word of God puts the meaning of our personal existence at stake as well as the meaning of all human existence. There is no question here of modifying our system of values in one or another detail: it is our whole person which needs a different orientation. If Christ is God, who is truth in person, then His word becomes the basis, norm, criterion for everything. Human thinking and conduct are subject to the judgment of this word. It is a question of choosing either for God or for the world, for the word of God or for the word of man. This is a question of venturing everything for everything, including life and death, including violent martyrdom or the humble and patient martyrdom that lasts a lifetime; in the strict sense of the word, this is a question of being or not being. Faith is thus a decision for God, and all one's life must revolve upon this dramatic decision which commits man down to his most intimate desires. A commitment of this nature is an uprooting of the human ego, sinking new roots in Christ (Eph. 3:17). This death to self can never be brought about by the mere intellectual contemplation of the revealed message: there has to be the allure of love. Thus the word of God, in Christ, has a human countenance and a human heart in order to entice the heart of men. What God tells us is His love (1 Jn. 4:8. 16). But if this word of God succeeds in getting man's consent, that is because it is a word of love revealed and manifested to the point of the greatest sacrifice. Revelation as encounter can succeed in being acceptance, dialogue, and reciprocity only through this enticement of love expressed in Christ and effected through His Spirit, which transforms the indocile heart of man into the heart of a son.

One final trait of this encounter is the *depth of communion* it establishes between God and man. Whoever receives the word of Christ and abides in this word passes from the condition of servant to that of son and friend (Gal. 4:4-6; Rom. 8:15; Jn. 15:15); he enters into a share of knowledge and love with the Father, the Son, and the Spirit. By faith in Christ, man is initiated into the secrets of the Father which the Son, who is in the bosom of the Father (Jn. 1:18; Mt. 11:25-27), and the Spirit, who scrutinizes the depths of God (1 Cor. 1:10), alone know. The very love with which the Father loves the Son and the Son loves the Father has now taken root in the heart of man: "I have revealed your name to them ... so that the love with which you have loved me will be *in them*, and *I in them*" (Jn. 17:26). Christ who says: "The Father and I are one" (Jn. 10:30), also says: "That all might be one. As you, Father, in me and I in you, that they may be *one in us* ... that they may be one as we are one, *I in them* and *you in me*, so that they may be perfectly one" (Jn. 17:21-23). As a result of their union with Christ and the union of Father and Son, the faithful are united among each other and united to the Father, just as the Father is united to the Son. The Spirit of love, which unites Father and Son, makes them live the same life as the Divine Persons. Thus the first epistle of Saint John can repeat that we are "in communion with God" (1 Jn. 1:3. 6), that we are "in God" (1 Jn. 2:5; 5:20), that we "abide in God" (1 Jn. 2:6. 24; 3:24; 4:13. 15. 16). No human encounter, no matter how perfect, can ever attain to this degree of intimacy and communion, which is inaugurated by the encounter of faith acting through charity.

Thus, whether we envisage it as word, as testimony, or as encounter, revelation always strikes the same fundamental note: God is love (1 Jn. 4:8-10) and His word is the word of love. Faith is thus not submission to the arbitrary will of a God who is pleased to claim the homage of the human mind, but rather man's recognition of God's plan of love and his free entry into that plan; it is an overture to divine friendship, inviting us to a share in God's own life. Revelation and faith are a work of love.

1. Revelation as communication designates both the phenomenon of interior illumination which puts the prophet in possession of divine thinking, as well as the testimony given in the behavior of the living Christ.

2. *Ex.* 4, 15-16; 7, 1-2; *Jer.* 1, 9; 18, 18.

3. *Heb,* 1, 1; *Jo.* 1, 18; 8, 26. 38. 40.

4. *Mk.* 1, 14. 39; *Mt.* 4, 17.23; 9, 35; *Lk.* 8, 1.

5. *Mk.* 1, 21-22; 6, 6; 14, 49; *Mt.* 4, 23; 5, 1-2; 7, 28-29; 9, 35; 26, 55; *Lk.* 4, 31-32; 19, 17; 20, 1; 23, 5.

6. *Jn.* 3, 11. 32; 8, 26. 38; 18, 37; *Apoc.* 1, 5; 3, 14.

7. *Mk.* 16, 20; *Act.* 5, 42; 8, 25; 9, 20; 20, 25; 28, 31.

8. *Act* 2, 42; 4, 2. 18; 5, 25.. 42; 11, 26; 18, 11.

9. *Act.* 1, 21-22; 2, 32; 3, 15; 5, 32; 10, 39; 13, 31.

10. *Mk.* 16, 15; *Eph.* 1, 13; *Rom.* 16, 25.

11. *S. th.,* 1a, q. 107, a. 1.

12. *De Fide,* disp. 1, sect. 10, n. 197 et n. 210.

13. See, for example, the works of K. Buhler, H. Noack, M. Heidegger, G. Siewerth, M. Merleau-Ponty, M. Nédoncelle, L. Lavelle, G. Gusdorf, H. Delacroix, G. Parain, A. G. Robledo, etc.

14. K. BUEHLER, *Sprachtheorie* (Jena 1934), pp. 2, 28-33. Corresponding to this threefold aspect of the word are the three persons of the verb: the word expresses (first person), addresses (second person), recounts (third person).

15. In order to express himself, a man can use more than one means: mimicry, gestures with the hand and body, his whole bearing. But the *word* remains the most perfect expression of his person; the *living* word primarily, where intonation, accent, rhythm, expression, gesture, all come together to give the expression a richness, variety, precision and fullness that are available in no other means of communication.

16. E. DHANIS, "Révélation explicite et implicite," *Gregorianum,* 34 (1953): 209-210.

17. For example: *I tell you... Isn't it true?... Remember?... You saw this, you say?... Imagine that! Let's see! Seriously, what do you think about it?*

18. E. DHANIS, "Révélation explicite et implicite," *Gregorianum,* 34 (1953): 210.

19. J. DELANGLADE, "Essai sur la signification de la parole," *Signe et Symbole* (Neuchatel, 1946), pp. 22-24; G. GUSDORF, *La parole* (Paris, 1956), pp. 74-75; R. MEHL, *La rencontre d'autrui* (Neuchatel, 1955), pp. 21-23.

20. G. GUSDORF, *La parole,* p. 55; H. NOACK, *Sprache und Offenbarung* (Gutersloh, 1960); C. LE CHEVALIER, *La confidence et la personne humaine* (Paris, 1960), p. 66.

21. R. MEHL, *La rencontre d'autrui,* pp. 13-17; A. BRUNNER, *La personne incarnée* (Paris, 1947), p. 266; C. LE CHEVALIER, *La confidence et la personne humaine,* pp. 40, 85-88, 179; G. MARTELET, "L'homme comme parole et Dieu comme révélation," *Cahiers d'études biologiques,* n. 6-7 (1960): 167-168; G. AUZOU, *La parole de Dieu* (Paris, 1960), p. 415.

22. J. ALFARO, *Adnotationes in tractatum de virtutibus* (ad usum auditorum, Romae, PUG, 1959), 99-100.

23. J. ALFARO, "Persona y gracia," *Gregorianum,* 41 (1960): 11.

24. H. ZRS VON BALTHASAR, "Dieu a parlé un langage d'homme," *Parole de Dieu et liturgie* (Paris, 1958), p. 90.

25. J. GUITTON, *Le problème de Jésus et les fondements du témoignage chrétien* (Paris,

26. E. DHANIS, "Révélation explicite et implicite," *Gregorianum,* 34 (1953): 210-211.

27. *Ibid.,* 211.

28. J. ALFARO, *Adnotationes in tractatum de virtutibus,* pp. 310-314; A. BRUNNER, *La personne incarnée,* pp. 257, 271, 279-281; R. LUQUET, "'L'acte de foi," *Lumière et vie,* sept. 1955, pp. 25-31.

29. A. BRUNNER, *La personne incarnée* pp. 255, 256, 268.

30. J. ALFARO, *Adnotationes in tractatum de virtutibus,* pp. 315-319.

31. M. NEDONCELLE, *La réciprocité des consciences* (Paris, 1942), pp. 16-17; F. J. J. BUYTEN-DIJK, *Phénoménologie de la rencontre* (Paris, 1953), p. 42; T. SOIRON, *La condition du théologien* (Paris, 1953), pp. 82-87.

32. *S. th.,* 2a 2ae, q. 11, a. 1, c.

33. J. ALFARO, "Persona y gracia," *Gregorianum,* 41 (1960): 11-12; J. MOUROUX, *Je crois en toi* (Paris, 1949), pp. 15-21; R. AUBERT, *Le problème de l'acte de foi* (Louvain, 1958(3)), pp. 696-703; R. GUARDINI, *Vom Leben des Glaubens* (Mainz, 1935); C. CIRNE-LIMA, *Der personale Glaube* (Innsbruck, 1959). W. BULST, *Offenbarung* (Dusseldorf, 1960), p. 125.

CHAPTER II

REVELATION AND CREATION

Revelation and creation are realities which are frequently joined together in Scripture, in the Church fathers, and in the documents of the magisterium. Creation is presented as a type of the divine manifestation and even as a word of God. What, then, makes this manifestation and this word different from revelation properly so called or supernatural? In the study of the relationship between creation and revelation there are three questions to be considered. First of all, in what way did the Hebrew people know God as Creator: through the works of creation or through the events of history? Second, how are the works of creation a manifestation of God, and what is the nature of this manifestation? Finally, what are the points of similarity and the divergences between natural revelation and supernatural revelation.

I. FROM THE GOD OF HISTORY TO THE GOD OF CREATION

In theodicy, human reflection, beginning with the world, rises to the ultimate principle of the explanation of the universe. It discovers that this principle is spirit, that it is transcendent to the world, that it is personal. Then it can ask whether this personal God, principle of the world, has not perhaps intervened in some original manner, that is, not only through the silent activity of original creation, but also by means of conversation or word.

In the Old Testament, the knowledge of God, as we have seen, followed an inverse order. Chronologically the God of the covenant was known before the God of creation. Israel did not discover God through a process of metaphysical reflection, beginning with the universe, but by means of God's interventions in her history. Israel rose from the God of history to the God of creation, from God as Savior to God as Creator.[1] Yahweh, actually, did not at first reveal Himself as God the Creator of heaven and earth, but as God the Savior who delivered His people from bondage to make a covenant with them. The faith of Israel was born of her first experience of exodus and covenant which revealed a God of salvation, present to His people, with all His power; thus the idea of creation will always be associated with this idea of salvation and power. Creation will appear as a projection towards the past of the power of God already at work in history, and thus as the first act in the history of salvation.

After exodus and covenant, Israel knows that she is in the powerful hand of Yahweh. Little by little, throughout the history of her relation with God, Israel discovers the dimensions of this power; Israel passes from the experience of this power to the knowledge of its absolute character. The deliverance from Egypt and the establishment of Israel in the land of Canaan presuppose that God is master of nature and the peoples of earth: the miracles of exodus presuppose that God can mobilize nature according to His will, to effect the salvation of His people. The cosmic power of Yahweh, however, does not necessarily postulate the affirmation of His power of creation. Only in a second "moment" did inspired reflection understand that, if God is master of all and disposes of all according to His good pleasure, this is true precisely because He has called everything from nothingness into being. The creation of the world is thus the basis for His sovereignty over the powers of nature as well as nations.

Towards the end of the exile, the all-power of Yahweh as Creator becomes a central theme of the prophetic message. In Deutero-Isaiah, first creation is called upon to give substance to the great promises of salvation. The new exodus from Babylon to Jerusalem will be a triumph, for the same power of Yahweh, who laid the foundations of earth and heaven, will now be enlisted to save His people (Is. 41:4; 45:11-12; 48:14-15; 50:2); it will effect a new historical creation: "This deliverance which I, Yahweh, am about to *create*" (Is. 45:8). It is because Yahweh is the *Creator* of all things that He is continually at work in nature and that He directs the history of Israel. The historical perspective is thus primary; the cosmic perspective is invoked only to guarantee the efficacy of the historical manifestation. The prayer of the psalms and the prayer of the mother of the Maccabees correspond to this awareness of Deutero-Isaiah: He who has made heaven and earth and who has saved Israel from her enemies, can do it once again and always (Ps. 18; 104; 102; 136; 2 Macc. 7:22-29).[2]

Since creation was understood on the basis of history and salvation, it will aways remain associated with this history, explained in the light of this history, particularly in the light of exodus and covenant.

Just as the salvation to come is announced and described as a new exodus, the origin of the world is conceived of as a sort of prehistoric exodus, first manifestation of God's power and a pledge of His future victories. Creation, exodus, eschatological salvation: these are three "moments" of one and the same triumph of Yahweh, and these three "moments" all cast light upon each other (Is. 44:24-28; 42:5-9; 45:6-8). Exodus, seen in the framework of creation, takes on a more universal bearing; and, inversely, creation appears already as an intervention of God the Savior (Is. 51:9-10; Ps. 77:17-20; Hab. 3:8-13). God the Creator appears in the same light as the God of exodus: the miracles of creation, just like those of exodus, reveal Yahweh in His power and His love. And just as the covenant is inseparable from exodus, covenant and creation are also closely linked together. Creation is the framework, the temple of the covenant, the road that leads to the covenant, just as exodus is finalized in the covenant. In creating the world, God was already thinking of the covenant, that is, of a plan of love and salvation for humanity through the medium of His people Israel.[3] In thus extending the theology of the covenant to the origins of the world, the Old Testament universalized the covenant; it is not only Israel, but the entire world which is the scene of Yahweh's activity. This theology of creation develops in the exilic era, in precisely those surroundings in which Israel came to a clear awareness of her universal vocation. If Yahweh is the Yahweh of the nations, it is because, from the very beginning, He is absolute Lord over the nations (Is. 45:18-24; 51:5).[4]

Creation, for Israel, is thus the first chapter in the history of salvation. At the beginning, that is to say, before Moses, before Abraham, before Noah, God created and, through creation, inaugurated the work of salvation. Creation is the first of the mighty deeds of God. The psalms, which evoke the wonders of God, place creation at their head (Ps. 136:5-15). In Deutero-Isaiah, creation really appears as the beginning of salvation, the introduction to the work of salvation. For the same reason, Genesis, whose account presupposes a lengthy meditation on the most ancient elements of popular history, opens with a vision of the work of creation. Finally, for the whole Christian tradition, there is a perfect continuity from the word of creation to the Incarnate Word. Creation, election, Law, prophets, Incarnation— these are the stages of salvation. The history of salvation does not begin with Abraham, but with the fiat of creation.[5]

Thus it is easy to understand how Israel, contemplating the work of creation through her faith in the living God, her Savior, finds primarily His presence and His activity. Creatures recount God's mystery, His wisdom, His power, His love, like the voice on Sinai and the prophets (Ps. 192). The heavenly hosts call to mind the power of Yahweh who has conquered Egypt and the monsters of the deep. All things, even the chosen people, owe their existence to Yahweh's free initiative which has raised them up from nothingness. Israel's view of the world is that of a believer who reads and interprets the universe on the basis of faith. It is the God of history which Israel contemplates in the God of creation. The same is true for the Christian who contemplates, in the universe, the work of Christ, Incarnate Word, in whom all things have being and subsistence (Jn. 1:13; Col. 1:16). Our faith in creation is part of our faith in God, one and triune.

II. CREATION AS MANIFESTATION OF GOD

In addition to this knowledge of God as Creator arrived at by contemplating the God of history and faith, the magisterium of the Church, once again based on Scripture, speaks of a manifestation of God and an authentic knowledge of God outside all positive revelation. Before comparing this manifestation with positive revelation, it would be well to investigate its nature. Let us consider first of all the teaching of the Church.

The First Vatican Council distinguishes two types of divine manifestation and, as a result, two ways of access to the knowledge of God. The prosynodal schema, drawn up by Franzelin and submitted to the fathers of the council, speaks of the *"natural manifestation"* of God, "through creatures" (T, 416, n. 1) and of God *"manifesting* Himself through the light of human reason" (T, 416, n. 2). A note attached to this schema opposes this "objective manifestation of God, through the intermediary of creatures" to "revelation".[6] Whereas the primary draft of the constitution thus contrasts *natural manifestation* and *revelation,* the definitive text distinguishes between *knowledge* of God through a *natural way* and *revelation* of God through a *supernatural way:* "Our Mother the Holy Church believes and teaches that God, beginning and end of all things, can be known with certainty in the natural light of human reason by means of creatures; in fact, what cannot be seen of Him can, since the creation of the world, be contemplated through His works (Rom. 1:20). Still it pleased God, in His wisdom and goodness, to *reveal* to the human race, by some *other way,* supernatural this time, His own nature and the eternal decrees of His will".[7] We might conclude that the knowledge of God through the objective medium of creation and human reason is a certain revelation or manifestation of God, but in a natural way.

The text of the council is directed against two errors: traditionalism, which admits of no other means of knowing God than the positive teaching received by revelation and handed down by tradition; and agnosticism, either under the Kantian form of critique or under the positivist form, which judges human reason incapable of arriving at a certain knowledge of God.[8]

It is important to have a precise notion of the full scope of the conciliar text:

A. The council states the *possibility*, not the fact, of knowing God by the light of human reason.

B. The possibility of such knowledge is rooted in the very nature of man. It belongs to man independently of revelation and his call to supernatural light. This possibility never ceases, even when man has sinned.

C. This is a knowledge distinct from every form of personal revelation of God to man, either by means of interior illumination or external and historical revelation.

D. There is no question here of a purely irrational experience, of the order of feeling and sentiment, which cannot be expressed in a conceptual and verbal manner, but rather a process of the rational order, in the way of causality, as the anti-Modernist oath makes clear (D 2145).

E. The council does not claim that the natural knowledge of God must precede the knowledge of faith either in origin or in time, but that it is at least logically implied.

F. The means which permit human reason to know God with certainty are creatures, not only material and visible, but every contingent being which leads us to God.

G. In speaking of God as beginning and end of all things, the council does not mean to define that creation in the strict sense can be demonstrated by reason.

H. The council does not say whether this knowledge is *actually* achieved in virtue of human nature alone. It does not say whether other causes, such as supernatural grace, might not be at work. It does not say what, in this process, is the role of rational discursive thinking and what is the role of moral decision.

I. The council also speaks of supernatural revelation as a free and loving intervention on the part of God which introduces man into the intimacy of God and His plan: if man already has a relationship with God, by his very nature and by the nature of things, it is easier to understand how revelation is truly a grace, that is, a manifestation which is not to be taken for granted, an event which is not interior to this world, nor a constitutive element of human nature. It is addressed to a person already in possession of his nature, independently of this intervention.

J. The God of natural knowledge must be a free, personal, and transcendent God, in relation to man; otherwise, man could not expect God's silence as logically as God's intervention through history, and His word; otherwise too, man cannot be accused of having refused to hear the word which is personally addressed to him.

K. The fathers of the council declare that human reason is capable of arriving at a natural knowledge of God, because denial of this truth leads to religious skepticism, but primarily because they see this truth in Scripture and the whole of the patristic tradition. Msgr. Gasser, explaining why we must condemn traditionalism, refers to the *Adversus Marcionem* of Tertullian and adds: "On this point, Tertullian is certainly in accord with Holy Scripture; this can be readily checked by anyone who reads chapter 13 of the Book of Wisdom, chapter one of the Epistle to the Romans, and chapters fourteen to sixteen of the Acts of the Apostles; he is equally in accord, in my opinion, with the other fathers of the Church" (T, 417, n. 4). Whereas Franzelin, in his proposed text, harks back to Wisdom as well as Saint Paul, the definitive text of the council refers to the Epistle to the Romans, and the knowledge of God which the pagans could have had through the works of creation.[9]

Thus the distinction which the magisterium establishes between the historical revelation of God and His cosmic manifestation, outside of all positive revelation, is authorized on the basis of Scripture itself, which distinguishes between these two forms of divine manifestation. Although the habitual direction of Scripture towards God the Creator takes place in the interior of faith in the living God, certain texts do outline a rational approach of the mind towards God, beginning with nature.

In the Book of Wisdom, this approach, elsewhere merely suggested (Is. 40:12-26), becomes explicit. The author of the book, in the section consecrated to idolatry (Wis. 13:1-9), refers to the learned men who make divinities of the forces of nature. These pagans, cultivated as they are, do not know God, because they have not followed the clear evidence of nature (13:1). Nature should have led them to recognize the existence of a transcendent God, Author of the universe. These men are called "vain" (13:1) and "unpardonable" (13:8); for, even though they were wise men and experts in the knowledge of nature (13:9), they did not succeed in discovering the Master of the universe. Looking at created things, and struck particularly by their beauty, their grandeur, their power, they should have been able to rise, by way of analogy, towards the Author of all this beauty and this power. Reflecting on the marvels of creation, they should have concluded to the existence of a Supreme Being which is its unique source. *Wisdom*, however, only indicates this method of knowledge by analogy without applying it. It simply states that, struck by the beauty and grandeur of created nature, man *can* arrive at the concept of One God, Author and Lord of all things. The human mind is capable of coming to this knowledge by an intellectual approach, which if not spontaneous, is at least relatively simple; for the world speaks invincibly of its Author. All this, of course, presupposes that the soul is sufficiently sensitive to the beautiful and the good.[10]

In many contexts, Saint Paul refers to this manifestation of God through creation: before the pagans of Lystra, in order to make them understand the goodness of their Creator (Acts 14:15-17); before the pagans of Athens, to make them understand His spiritual character (Acts 17:22-29); in his Letter to the Romans, in order to stress His "eternal power and divinity" (Rom. 1:20).

In the Epistle to the Romans, Saint Paul is considering the religious state of humanity, in order to demonstrate the need of salvation for all mankind: Jew and Gentile. Outside the Gospel, there is room only for the wrath of God (Rom. 1:18-3, 20). All men have a need for Christ and His redemption, for all are subject to the slavery of sin.[11] But how can the wrath of God be unleashed against the Gentiles if it is not first of all an established fact that the Gentiles are really guilty? Their guilt consists, according to Saint Paul, in the fact that, having had a real knowledge of God through the medium of creation, they still did not recognize Him. Such is the primordial sin of the Gentiles, the sin which runs through all the others (Rom. 1:24-32). Thus, when Saint Paul speaks of the manifestation of the Creator through His creatures and the knowledge that the pagans had of His law, that is His testimony that they are without excuse, just as the Jews are without excuse for having transgressed the written law which they knew. Both Jew and Gentile are guilty. [12]

The pagans Saint Paul reproaches first of all for having failed to recognize the Creator who stood revealed before them. God took the initiative himself, manifested (*ephanerôsen*)[13] everything that could be known of himself (*gnôstos*); for, since creation, the world is like an open book in which we can constantly read the perfections of God. Since the act of creation, the invisible perfections of God (*aorata*) are made visible in some respect (*kathoratai*) through His works (including His work *par excellence* which is man): not by a direct intuition, but by a reflex activity of the human mind which, on the basis of what it sees with its human eyes, conceives of the realities it does not see. The word *nooumena*, joined with a verb of perceiving, makes the nature of this knowledge more precise:[14] the invisible attributes of God are "visible to the eye of the intelligence." Thus both the intellectual character of this knowledge and the full certainty it affords are both equally asserted.[15] What God thus manifests of Himself is primarily His power (*dunamis*) and His divinity, that is, His transcendence over the world, His divine majesty which man must adore. Creation constitutes a permanent manifestation of God and His perfections to humanity. In looking at the world, men should have been able to recognize the power and majesty of its Author: if they do not find Him, they are inexcusable. After having expressed this general principle, which holds for all times, St. Paul passes on to the historical fact. We are free to hold, with A. Feuillet, that Saint Paul is here describing the original fall of humanity, its historical passage from monotheism to idolatry. Primitively, men, as a collectivity, knew God; but their pride made them lose this sense of God, blinding them and making them incapable of understanding the language of creation. "Only the simple, only the humble know how to read the glory of God in the mirror of creation".[16] Saint Paul thus not only states the possibility (like *Wisdom, 13*, or the First Vatican Council) of knowing God, but also the concrete fact: the Gentiles did know God. The pagans had this knowledge of God which implies an obligation to recognize and venerate the God they know: they *knew* God but they did not *recognize* Him as such. They did not glorify Him (*ouk edoksasan*: they did not recognize His excellence), they did not thank Him (*ouk èucharistèsan*: they did not give him the cult which he deserved).[17] Saint Paul does not only blame the pagans for not having guided their moral conduct by their knowledge of God (religion and moral), but also for not having brought their religion (glory and thanksgiving) into accord with their knowledge of God. Then, like the Book of *Wisdom*, he shows that all moral disorders are a consequence of this failure to recognize God.[18]

The knowledge of God of which Saint Paul speaks is thus not a fruit of revelation, Judaic or Christian, nor of the revelation made to Adam and handed down to his descendants; it is rather a knowledge acquired by the light of reason reflecting on the works of creation. This knowledge, in its operation, can very well be sustained by grace, and Saint Paul, more than anyone else, knows that both Jew and pagan are under the influence of the grace of Christ. But this in no way changes the fact that the knowledge which the pagan has of God and of the need for recognizing Him is a knowledge drawn from visible creation by the light of human reason. In indicating the source (created world), and the force (reason) from which this knowledge proceeds, Saint Paul, *implicitly*, shows that what he has in mind is a natural knowledge of God, outside of Christ and his Gospel. He *explicitly* asserts that creation is a permanent manifestation of God and His perfections. God thus enters into communication with man in a twofold way: through the work of creation and events of history.[19]

III. NATURAL REVELATION AND SUPERNATURAL REVELATION

On the basis of Scripture and the Church magisterium, theologians generally distinguish two forms of revelation: one natural and improperly so called; the other supernatural and properly so called.

1. The knowledge of God through the contemplation of the created world is revelation in a certain sense; for it is a gift of God and a manifestation of God which calls for religious homage on the part of man.

It is first of all a *gift of God*. In this knowledge everything is free gift: God is the Author of the world, the Author of human nature, the Author of the light which allows us to interpret the world. It is not our mind that rises up towards God; it is God who, through creation, descends towards us. The initiative in this manifestation comes from Him, as Saint Paul remarks: "God manifests himself to men so that they can know Him" (Rom. 1:19). The demonstration is ours, but the sign which invites and permits the demonstration, the light which authorizes it, all come from God. God makes the sign. What is more, this forward step of reason is normally accompanied by actual graces which help to undo the mystery and make God's presence seen.[20]

It is a *certain manifestation* of an unknown God. The universe, actually, is not only a thing, but a *creature*. It is a sign that points towards its Author: not an artificial sign, set up as an after-thought, by convention, but rather a natural, necessary sign, based on the objective relationship between Creator and creature. It is no arbitrary decree on God's part when He invites man to discover His invisible perfections in the visible works of creation, but rather the ontological bonds that join Him with the world. If God is the Creator of all things, it is impossible that there should be no resemblance between creature and Creator, for the creature owes his whole existence and his being to the First Cause which brought him into being. If God is the fullness of being and perfection, every creature must have received something of this fullness and this perfection. In material creation, the spiritual God shines through, although only obscurely. By its power, immensity, order, and beauty, the universe points to its Author, clearly demonstrating His presence and letting us see some of the attributes of His person, source of all perfection. Man primarily, mind and will, far more than the physical world, reflects the perfection of his Author: he bears the traits of God in himself, he is in God's image. What is more, since God has created this image of Himself according to a determined nature, and according to a determined relationship with God, in the very fact of creation He reveals His will regarding man. And man, a spiritual and conscious being, must discern, in the particular character of his being, the expression of God's will for this rational creature composed of body and soul. The will of God, expressed in the physical laws of the inanimate world, is expressed for man in the natural law. Man, like the whole universe about him, is a revelation of God *in action*.[21] But, in the interior of this revelation *in action*, which is an implicit language, God addresses humanity with an explicit and personal word, to sanction, explain, and complete this first form of divine manifestation.

Finally, the manifestation of God through creation implies, for man, the obligation of rendering the *religious homage* which is due to God through glorification and thanksgiving. "Inexcusable" are those who have not recognized God and have not given him this homage (Rom. 1:20; 2:14-16; Wis. 13:1. 8).

2. There are, however, profound differences between natural revelation and supernatural revelation.

Natural revelation is so called because it is inscribed in the order of things, because it exists by the very fact of creation. It has creatures as its point of departure; for its light it has the innate light of human reason. It arrives at God as Author of the world, in His causal relationship with the world. It arrives at God in creation, through creation, as the foundation of creation. It discovers His will, not as the object of a personal address, but as implied in an established order. It discovers a present and personal God, but the mystery of this Person escapes it. It arrives at the threshold of the mystery, but cannot go in. God's presence through creation is like a presence through the medium of a manufactured object, as opposed to presence to the living body. This presence always remains pale and indetermined on many points. For man in the present order of things, this knowledge frequently remains obscure, difficult, full of puzzles. By reason of

man's sin, his pride, the weakness of his heart, there is always a
tendency to confuse the Author of nature with nature itself.

Supernatural revelation, on the other hand, has for its principle
the benevolent and gratuitous approach of God, one and triune,
Author of the supernatural order. For its immediate goal it has faith,
but, through faith, it tends towards encounter, towards the vision of
the living God. Its light is the prophetic light of the light of faith. For
object, it has the very mysteries of the intimate life of God. This
revelation inaugurates a dialogue, a friendship, a communion, a sharing
of goods between God and his creature.[22]

3. In the last analysis, what distinguishes the two forms of
revelation is the fact that in the revelation of pure grace, the notions
of word and testimony are verified in the strict sense. The world
exists as the terminus of a free act of God, as thought and willed by
God and, as such, it is *said* (*spoken*) by God. Then too, in natural
revelation, the object (creation) and the subject (human reason) are
willed by God with a view towards knowledge of God through
encounter. This will and this knowledge, however, are never enough
to constitute a word or a testimony properly so called. In contemplating
creation, man does not feel that he is addressed; he does not have to
answer a call, but to decipher an object placed before him. Creation
refers him to God as to its cause. Creation betrays the presence of
God, manifests His perfections. It speaks of God, but God Himself
does not speak; God does not enter into a dialogue. He is like a
person present but silent. And thus the encounter between man and
universe does not terminate in the assent of faith, but in an existential
attitude: that of homage and adoration. In supernatural revelation, on
the other hand, God intervenes in person, at a given point in time
and space; he enters into a *dialogue* of friendship with man, makes
known to him the mystery of His inmost life and plan for salvation,
invites him to a personal communion of life. Through faith, man,
directly called upon thus by God, freely responds to the personal call
of God and enters into a covenant with Him. Natural revelation
does not have this characteristic of word and testimony. Thus it
deserves the name of revelation improperly so called. There are two
forms of divine manifestation and two orders of knowledge: "The
Catholic Church" according to the First Vatican Council, "has always
unanimously held and still holds that there are two orders of knowledge,
distinct not only by reason of their principle, but also by reason of
their object. In their principle, because in the one it is natural reason,
and in the other it is divine faith which makes us know. By their
object because, outside the truths which natural reason can attain to,

mysteries hidden in God are proposed for our belief, mysteries which cannot be known if they are not revealed from above. That is why the apostle who testifies that God was known by the Gentiles through his works (Rom. 1:20), when he speaks of "the grace and truth given through Jesus Christ" (Jn. 1:17), declares: "We preach the wisdom of God, mysterious, hidden, which God fore-ordained before the world unto our glory, a wisdom which none of the rulers of this world has known.... God has revealed it to us through his Spirit, for the Spirit searches all things, even the deep things of God" (1 Cor. 2:7-8. 10; D 1795).

1. J. Mouroux, *Le Mystère du temps* (Paris, 1962), p. 36; K. Rahner, *Écrits théologiques* (Bruges, 1959), 1: 34-35; A. Feuillet, "La connaissance naturelle de Dieu par les hommes d'après Rom. 1, 18-23," *Lumière et Vie*, March, 1954, p. 69; E. Beaucamp, *La Bible et le sens religieux de l'univers* (Paris, 1959), pp. 53-54; P. Van Imschoot, *Théologie de l'Ancien Testament*, 1: 142.

2. P. Biard, *La puissance de Dieu* (Paris, 1960), pp. 63-69; G. Lambert, "La création dans la Bible," *Nouvelle Revue théologique*, 75 (1953): 274-277.

3. E. Jacob, *Théologie de l'Ancien Testament*, pp. 110-112; G. von Rad, "Das theologische Problem des Schopfungsglauben," *Beihefte zur A. T. Wissenschaft*, 66 (1936): 138-147; texte repris dans: *Gesammelte Studien zum A. T.* (1958), pp. 136-147.

4. L. Legrand, "La création, triomphe cosmique de Yahvé," *Nouvelle Revue théologique*, 83 (1961): 460-467.

5. This is the position of St. Augustine and St. Irenaeus. Cf. J. Danielou, *Essai sur le mystère de l'histoire* (Paris, 1953), pp. 34-35; E. Escoula, "Le Verbe sauveur et illuminateur chez S. Irénée," *Nouvelle Revue théologique*, 66 (1939): 551-556.

6. Mansi, 50: 76-77.

7. "Eadem sancta mater Ecclesia tenet et docet, Deum, rerum omnium principium et finem, naturali humanae rationis lumine e rebus creatis certo cognosci posse; invisibilia enim ipsius, a cratura mundi, per ea quae facta sunt, intellecta, conspiciuntur (*Rom.* 1, 20); attamen placuisse ejus sapientiae et bonitati, alia eaque supernaturali via seipsum ac aeterna voluntatis suae decreta humano generi revelare" (D 1785).

8. R. Aubert, "Le concile du Vatican et la connaissance naturelle de Dieu," *Lumière et Vie*, mars 1954, pp. 21, 41.

9. On the text of the Vatican Council and its exact bearing, see: R. Aubert, "Le concile du Vatican et la connaissance naturelle de Dieu," *Lumière et Vie*, mars 1954, pp. 41-44; K. Rahner, *Écrits théologiques*, 1: 17-23.

10. C. Larcher, "De la nature à son auteur d'après le Livre de la Sagesse," *Lumière et Vie* Mar. 1954, pp. 53-62.

11. Saint Paul, notes Feuillet, "always stands on the concrete plane of the history of salvation, and what he wants to make clear, what he wants to express in every possible way, is the great turning point of history effected by Jesus coming upon earth," (A. Feuillet, "La connaissance de Dieu par les hommes d'après *Rom.* 1, 18-23," *Lumière et Vie*, Mar. 1954, p. 63).

12. S. Lyonnet, *Exegesis epistulae ad Romanos cap. I ad IV* (Romae, 1960), pp. 118-119; J. Fuchs, *Le Droit naturel, essai théologique* (Paris-Tournai-New York-Rome, 1960), pp. 18-19.

13. This is the verb used to describe the theophanies of the Old Testament. This manifestation is not yet revelation properly so called, but it does correspond to an act of God. And such is the power of this act of God that His invisible attributes are made visible in full light. Since God has done everything, even made His own invisible being visible in some respect, men are without excuse. Cf. L. Ligier, *Péché d'Adam et péché du monde* (2 vol., Paris 1960-1961), 2: 174-175.

14. *Ibid.*, 2: 175.

15. *Ibid.*, 2: 175.

16. A. Feuillet, "La connaissance de Dieu par les hommes d'après Rom. 1, 18-23," *Lumière et Vie*, Mar. 1954, p. 75.

17. These are the two verbs which are habitually used in Scripture to express the duties of men towards God (*Lk.* 17: 16-18; *Acts* 12: 21f; *Jn.* 9: 24; *Rom.* 4: 21). Dom Dupont is right

in stressing that Saint Paul distinguishes two separate approaches among the pagans. The knowledge of God arrived at by inference, on the basis of the created world, should have been followed by a second approach: giving glory to God and thanking Him. The pagans did not follow the first with the second: they knew God, but they did not honor Him as such: hence the unnatural separation between the knowledge of God and the religious homage which is generally the obligatory result of such knowledge. This explains the guilt of the Gentiles (J. Dupont, *Gnosis, La connaissance religieuse dans les épitres de S. Paul*, pp. 29-30).

18. Sur *Rom.* 1, 18-23, voir: S. LYONNET, *Exegesis epistulae ad Romanos cap. I ad IV* (Romae, 1960), 118-122; ID., *Quaestiones in epistolam ad Romanos* (Romae, 1955), pp. 68-108; J. DUPONT, *Gnosis*, pp. 21-30; A. FEUILLET, "La connaissance naturelle de Dieu par les hommes d'après *Rom.* 1, 18-23," *Lumière et Vie*, mars 1954, pp. 63-80; L. LIGIER, *Péché d'Adam et péché du monde*, 2: 174-179.

19. J. FUCHS, *Le droit naturel, Essai théologique*, pp. 18-19.

20. H. DE LUBAC, *Sur les chemins de Dieu* (Paris, 1956), pp. 109-110.

21. J. FUCHS, *Le droit naturel, Essai théologique*, pp. 58-59.

22. In revelation through creation, everything is the work of God: the activity of God, as a result, disappears in some respect into the anonymity which is everywhere and always in evidence. In supernatural revelation, on the contrary, men have knowledge of a new and gratuitous initiative on God's part which is not implied by the mere existence of the world.

CHAPTER III

HISTORY AND REVELATION

A strong current of thinking, in contemporary Protestant theology, tends to oppose revelation-activity and revelation-doctrine, revelation-event of salvation and revelation-knowledge, and, as a result, a God who acts and a God who speaks. This current of thinking stresses the fact that Yahweh is a God who intervenes in the field of human history and that revelation is presented primarily as a series of events with God for their subject. Revelation is thus God's activity in human history.[1] The Bible, observes G. E. Wright, is not primarily the word of God, but the narrative of God's activity.[2]

It is true that the God of the Old and New Testament is a God who intrudes into the field of human history and there makes Himself manifest by the great works He accomplishes. The Old Testament recounts the wonderful deeds of God in behalf of His people. The prophets constantly refer to these deeds, the psalms praise them, and the liturgical feasts commemorate them. The New Testament is the good news which has arrived in Christ Jesus. This character of historicity is undeniable and Catholic theology also stresses it. But the disjunction between a God who acts and a God who speaks is not so obvious. Is it objectively based on Scripture? Or, to put the question in another way, what is the relationship between history and revelation? Is there an opposition between history and doctrine?

I. HISTORY, FRAMEWORK FOR REVELATION

It has become almost a commonplace to state that the Hebrews were the first to replace a cyclic conception of time with a linear conception; or that they were also the first to look upon history as a manifestation of God.[3] It is in Israel that, for the first time, we find an encounter between revelation and history. Outside Israel, there is no firmly established idea of a continuous succession of temporal events embracing past, present, and future, all unfolding according to a direction and towards a goal. Among the ancient polytheistic peoples, attention is directed first of all to *nature*. Attentive to the rhythm of the stars and the seasons (the rhythm of birth and death), man looks for security by integrating himself into this rhythm and its annual repetition. The religions of India, China, and Persia are centered on a wisdom rather than on a history. Indian time is cyclic time. More precisely, as M. Eliade distinguishes, in the Indian concept of time, there are three planes: *individual time* which is a continual flux of unreal instants; *cosmic time*, eternal repetition of the same rhythm (creation, destruction, re-creation), operating within a series of enormous cycles whose numerical terms are staggering; and finally, the *intemporal instant*, outside time, immobile, eternal present. What is really important is to be delivered from cosmic time by transcending it. Time is thus devaluated with respect to eternity; what is more, it is an obstacle which must be overcome in order to be freed from it. Time, for the Indians, is measured, but it has no center; it is barren.[4] Hellenism, in its general aspects, is trapped within a cyclic conception of things. The Greek concept of time is one of despair: without origin, without any privileged moment, without meaning, without any bond with freedom and human salvation. History, as it is conceived by Herodotus and Thucydides, has movement, but not *teleology*. In order to escape the fatal cyclism which holds even the gods captive, the individual must escape from time. Salvation, for the Greek, could never result from an historical event.[5]

Israel was the first to break this fatal circle of seasons and repetitions in which the ancient world was so enclosed; it broke with change that is only perpetual new beginning. For Israel, time is *linear*: it has a beginning and an end. Salvation is accomplished in temporal history: it is bound up with a succession of events unfolding according to a divine plan and leading towards one unique fact, the death and resurrection of Christ.[6] For Israel, life is framed in the cosmic context but the focus of its attention is *history*. What counts is not so much the annual cycle in which everything begins anew as what God *does*, what God *has done*, and what God *will do* according to His promises. Promise and accomplishment make up the dynamism of this time in a threefold dimension. The present heralds the future which is announced and promised in the past.[7] The annual feasts (Easter in spring, the feast of tabernacles in autumn) are not so much acts in the cyclic drama of nature as they are a reminder of the salvific work of God.

If Israel managed thus to break the cyclic conception of time, it is because she recognized God *in history*. Israel proclaims that God intervened in her history, that this encounter took place *on a given day* and that it turned her whole existence upside down. Her God is not submerged in nature: He is a personal, living God, with sovereign freedom, and .He manifests himself precisely where freedom can be shown, that is, in the history of events. The Old Testament revelation does not take place in any mythical time, "at the extra-temporal instant of the beginning" but in the framework of historical continuity.[8] Moses received the Law at a certain place and on a certain date; it is an irreversible event, which cannot happen again, just like the other manifestations of God.[9] *History is thus the framework for revelation.* Judaism, Christianity, and Islam are the only religions which thus claim a revelation on the basis of history.[10] In this conception of a living God who reveals Himself in history is to be found the essence of Israel's faith in God.[11]

This conception of revelation *in* history has two effects. First of all, it *gives value* to history. If God intervenes in history and manifests His will, historical events themselves acquire a new dimension: they become the bearers of God's intentions and give history a meaning, a sense of direction. Since the other peoples did not know the God of history, they had no way of interpreting history; they are unconscious of their role and, in periods of crisis, they do not know how to orient themselves.[12] The idea of a revelation *in* history thus gives revelation an intense character of *actualization*. God is He who, at every instant, can intervene and change the course of events: He is near, He is there, unforeseeable in His interventions as well as in His effects. Always, man must look to His coming.

II. HISTORY OF REVELATION

Regarding the interventions of God in history, we neither say nor predict anything. Everything depends on His free decision. Nothing, in God, demands an intervention at one given moment rather than another, more frequently or less frequently. Neither is there anything in man to demand that God converse with him. Revelation is a free and gratuitous event. The interventions of God stretch out over the course of many centuries. God did not say everything nor do everything all at once, He intervened at opportune moments, chosen by Him. The time of the Old Testament is a succession of meaningful moments. "It is not every part of the continuous line of time which forms the ·history of salvation properly so called, but rather the *kairoi*, those isolated points in the whole course of time".[13] Thus there is a *history of revelation* and this history does not coincide with universal history. Revelation is made up little by little, progressing in quantity and in quality, as the centuries unfold and God intervenes (Heb. 1:1). These interventions of God in universal history are, as it were, out-croppings of the divine in time. But they are not isolated points, without relationship: they present an intimate coherence. From Abraham to Jesus Christ, there is one single line, one single plan appearing little by little, the divine plan, the economy of salvation. In each of the interventions of God only one part of this economy is involved. This plan, restricted to Israel first of all, enlarges to the proportions of all humanity, then, in the Church, tends to incorporate all men of all times.[14]

If God has intervened at certain determined moments, we can then trace a *history of revelation*, that is, successive interventions of God. What is this history which is properly speaking the history of salvation?

At the beginning of Old Testament revelation, there are first of all events which mark the birth of Israel as a people and which reveal God as the God of history, at work in history.[15] These events are those of exodus, covenant, entry into the promised land. These events are not independent, but closely bound together. The primordial fact is the *deliverance* of Israel, snatched away from the bondage of Egypt. This deliverance is the work of Yahweh, for it is He who forced the Pharaoh, through the plagues of Egypt, to set Israel free (Ex. 12:31-32), and it is He who, by letting loose the waters of the Red Sea, completed the Egyptians' defeat (Ex. 14:27-28). At the very moment of Exodus, God manifests Himself as an all-powerful and saving God (Ex. 14:31). The experience of this first encounter with God left a profound mark upon the consciousness of Israel; and thus from the very outset she qualifies revelation as historical.[16] Never again will Israel cease to consider herself as the "people of *deliverance through Yahweh*."

This deliverance and this setting apart are in view of an overall plan. The traditions of Sinai (Ex. 19-25) show that the goal of this deliverance is covenant. Election, exodus, and even the gift of the promised land, are in view of covenant. It is covenant which gives exodus its meaning and turns the tribes delivered from Egypt into a religious and political community.[17] God associates with a people whom He has literally created (Ez. 16:1-9), just as He created Adam at the beginning, and the Church after the coming of Christ. Israel is saved *by grace* to become the people of Yahweh.[18] God makes a people for Himself and, in order to indicate the intimacy of this society, He reveals His *name*, that is, His personal being. God reveals Himself as a Person who can be called upon and who will respond to man's call. The covenant thus inaugurates an interpersonal relationship between God and His people. On the other hand, it also implies a relationship of *obligations* based on the fact of deliverance.[19] Israel commits herself to be faithful to the clauses of the covenant, that is, to obey the law of Yahweh (Ex. 19:3-6; Deut. 7:7-14). Fidelity to the law will make Israel a holy people, consecrated to Yahweh (Deut. 7:6; 26, 17-19), called to glorify His name among the nations.[20] The entry into the promised land will be the culmination of what God has begun in Egypt. It is the accomplishment of the promise made to Abraham (Gen. 17:3-8) and the first testimony of Yahweh's fidelity to His covenant. In this first encounter between Yahweh and his people, everything is *grace*: deliverance, covenant, the gift of the promised land.

If, in addition to these events which constitute the germ of Old Testament revelation, we add the concepts of kingdom and royal messianism, the Temple and the presence of Yahweh, the exile and restoration, we have the essential core of historical events which will never cease to nourish the religious reflection of Israel.[21] What remains is only its organic development, its homogeneous fructification. Prophetic revelation does no more than re-assert and apply the implications of the rule of the covenant to the whole unfolding of human history. It is in expressing the will of God on the events of their times, in the light of the covenant and the Holy Spirit, that the prophets make the knowledge of God grow in depth and extent. They are always calling to mind the first encounter between Yahweh and His people. At the time of exile primarily, Ezekiel and Deutero-Isaiah take up the theme of Exodus and promised land. There will be a new desert, a new shepherd, a new Moses. Deliverance will be a new Exodus, followed by a new covenant.[22]

This, obviously, is revelation of a very concrete type. As a result, Israel's professions of faith are also very concrete. The most ancient creeds of the Old Testament are nothing more than the succinct recital of the salvific acts of God.[23] The essential theme is always the same: God has chosen our fathers and promised them the land of Canaan; the descendants of Abraham have become a great people, but, after a long sojourn in Egypt, this people has been reduced to servitude. God had pity on His people and delivered them; through marvelous works of His power, He led them through the desert and made them enter into the promised land. Such are the facts confessed in Deut. 26:5-9; 6:20-24; Jos. 24:2-13. The psalms themselves, which are Israel's prayer, frequently take on a *narrative* form. Israel incorporates her own history into her prayer and finds in this recollection a further motive for contemplation, for confidence, for recognition, for contrition (Ps. 78; 105; 107; 77; 114; 136; 44).

III. REVELATION THROUGH HISTORY

God acts in history; He reveals himself *through history*. But, this statement demands a more precise explanation. In what sense can we speak of history *as revelation*? Let us say first of all that by history we understand not the simple course of human events and their material record, but only those events which, by reason of their importance for the Hebrew community, deserve to be preserved. But this first distinction is not enough. In order to speak of revelation *through* history, two realities must come together: event and word.

The events can be of a quite unequal nature. There can be real miracles, such as are necessary for the establishment of a supernatural religion; but it can also be events which result simply from the play of natural causes, according to ordinary divine operation. An historical event can be at the same time a miracle and a providential event, the two elements being inextricably joined: for example, in the case of exodus. In addition to this type of event of the physical order, we must also include events of the political, social, or moral order, such as victories or defeats of armies, crimes and the hard-heartedness of kings, collective unfaithfulness; all of these God can take as the occasion for making known His will.

It is true that there exists an objective divine activity in history (either providential or miraculous), and it is also true that Old Testament revelation is presented as the experience of this activity of a sovereign power directing the cause of human history and individual existence. This activity, however, does not become fully intelligible as revelation unless it is accompanied by the word which expresses the meaning of the divine activity. At one and the same time God establishes the fact of salvation and develops its meaning; God intervenes in history and explains the meaning of His intervention; God acts and comments on His own action.

From the beginning of her history, Israel lived through a certain number of events: deliverance from bondage, wandering through the desert, entry into Canaan. But what would these events be without the word God spoke to Moses, in secret (Ex. 3-4; 6:1), and without the word of Moses who, in the name of God, makes known to Israel the meaning of this history and explains its supernatural dimension? The deliverance from Egypt would no doubt be nothing more than a migration of peoples, one among many; it would not have become so fundamental a fact without Moses' interpretation (Ex. 14:31).[24] This interpretation itself has become an event which determined the course of future history. Through Moses' interpretation, God revealed Himself to Moses' contemporaries and to future generations.[25] The structure of revelation is sacramental: facts, events, enlightened by word.

The prophet is the qualified witness and interpreter of history, the man who explains its supernatural meaning. There are two complementary lines in the Old Testament: the line of events and the line of prophets who interpret events, proclaiming, in the name of God, what they mean. God reveals Himself through history, but through history as divinely interpreted by the prophets. History is not manifest as *history of salvation* unless it is commented on authoritatively by the word of the prophet who explains to Israel the presence and content of God's activity. This activity, hidden within the historical event, needs to be complemented by a word if it is to be *fully* grasped. Through the word of the prophet Israel becomes aware of the salvific activity of God in her history. The historical event, as revelation of God, must receive its meaning from the spoken word of the prophet (Am. 3:7; Is. 42:9).[26] We must distinguish, on the one hand, the *historical event* (real, objective) and on the other hand, the *event of the word* (real, objective) which accompanies the historical event, and we must stress that it is this event of the word which "consecrates" the historical event as an event of revelation, for it is the word of the prophet which explains the event and proposes it to Israel's faith as an event of salvation, attested by God.[27]

The process of revelation, in its totality, is thus made up of the following elements: A. Historical event. B. Interior revelation which provides the prophet with an understanding of the event, or at very least the reflection of the prophet directed and illuminated by God. C. The prophet's word, presenting the event and its meaning as objects of divine testimony. It is the complementary character of historical event and event of the word (God's word to the prophet, and the prophet's word to the people of Israel), that makes revelation grow. Thus the moments of revelation in the history of Israel are always marked by the appearance of one or several prophets. The presence of prophets always means that God is at work in history.[28]

The structure of revelation, in the New Testament, is not essentially different from that of the Old. Christ is He who has come, accomplished the work of the Father and who, for this reason, has been exalted to the Father's right hand. The first credos of christianity are the statement of these historical facts and their bearing on salvation. The most simple forms have to do with Christ's resurrection and exaltation as Lord and Son of God (1 Cor. 12:3; Rom. 10:9; Acts 8:37). The more elaborate forms tell how Christ lived, died, rose from the dead, in order to work out the salvation of the human race. The liturgical profession of 1 Tim. 3:16 sums up in one simple formula the principal phases of the history of salvation. Likewise, the discourse of Peter, in Acts, mentions all the principal facts on which Christianity is based, as well as their supernatural meaning (Acts 2:23-36; 3:12-26; 10:34-43). The first apostolic preaching, says J. Schmitt, has for its object a history viewed in the light of the Spirit.[29] The substance of this first kerygma is bound up with the following points: the time of the fullness announced by the prophets has been inaugurated with Christ: salvation has arrived through the death and resurrection of Christ, in full agreement with Scripture; Christ, by His resurrection, is lifted up to the right hand of the Father, as Christ and Lord, and the actual existence of the Church testifies to the coming of the Holy Spirit; as a result, each individual must repent, receive baptism and the Spirit in whom this new life is inaugurated. What is preached through the apostles is *the history of salvation* through the life, death, and resurrection of Christ. In Him, the history of salvation is completed and culminated. Ever after, Christ is the focal point of history: not only the history of salvation, but all history; for the coming of God in person into our history turns even profane history into something sacred.

The historical character of the revelation of the New Testament is thrown into relief by the use of Old Testament vocabulary to express the salvific work of Christ. Christ is the new Adam, the new Moses, the King according to the heart of Yahweh, the Suffering Servant, Daniel's Son of Man, the Priest according to the order of Melchisedech. His work is *deliverance* from the *bondage* of sin (Col. 1:13-14). The shedding of His blood seals the new *covenant* (Synoptics). His miracles recall the *marvels* of Exodus (Saint John). But whereas, in the Old Testament, revelation appears as something spread over the the course of the events of several centuries, here it is contracted and condensed in the life and activity of Christ. Everything takes place in the one unique event of Christ; everything is said in the word of the Son. Since the Old Testament did not have the human word of the Son, explaining the Father's plan of salvation in human words, the doctrinal character of revelation is less apparent; the historical character is predominant there. The Incarnation of the Son precipitates the rhythm of history: God expresses Himself once and for all, fully (Heb. 1:1).

Thus, in the New as well as in the Old Testament, revelation is presented under the form of history, but a history whose fullness of meaning can be grasped only through the event of the word. The event of the Cross, like that of Exodus, is not fully revelation unless the word *interprets* and *proposes* it to our *faith*. Without this *testimony*, bearing at once on the event and its meaning for salvation, there is no revelation in the full sense of the word.

IV. THE IMPLICATIONS OF A REVELATION IN AND THROUGH HISTORY

The admission that revelation comes to us primarily in history and through history also implies a certain number of consequences which we must now examine.

1. The first concerns the *nature* and *progress* of revelation. Revelation is not given as a system of abstract propositions concerning God, but it is incorporated in events of history. God, His attributes, His plan, are all known to us, but only through the events of history. We see thus in what sense we can speak of a history as well as a doctrine. Doctrine is viewed here under the form of the *meaningful events* of God and His plan; it does not derive from pure speculation on God. Scripture has not set up a philosophical system, but rather recounts the concrete facts to which a religious and supernatural meaning is attached. Reciting the creed means recapitulating what God has done to save humanity. The events of this history have such a *dimension*, such a *fullness of sense*, that explaining them means telling the whole *economy of salvation*, explaining the *doctrine of Christianity*, that is, what Christianity professes and what it teaches. It would be incorrect, however, to maintain that history and interpretation of history exhaust the whole content of revelation. If the historical character of one part of the object of faith is incontestable, it is equally certain that this object contains far-reaching explanations whose historical bonds are much less immediate: for example, the teaching of the poetic and wisdom literature, the moral teaching of Christ, as developed in the Sermon on the Mount. The revelation of the mystery of the Trinity is accomplished by the word rather than by history. Still, historicisation remains the characteristic and predominant trait of Christian revelation.

The *progress* of revelation is equally bound up with history. Consider, for example, the *attributes* of God: at the time of Exodus,

God revealed Himself as a personal God and Savior; at the time of entry into the promised land, as the all-powerful Warrior; the prophets insist on the spiritual and moral attributes of God (love, justice, holiness), in reaction against nationalism within and naturalism without. The exile puts Israel into contact with the nations: God, in Deutero-Isaiah, reveals Himself as the God of the nations, and Israel becomes aware of her missionary call. The knowledge of God grows deeper and more purified, but always through the medium of history.[30] The events of Exodus, covenant, conquest, royalty, all make up a sort of prototype of the relations of Yahweh with His people, which is a sort of key to the whole prophetic interpretation that will follow. Beginning with these facts, Israel never stops reflecting on her history, always discovering new dimensions. This reflection, always directed by the prophetic office, makes revelation progress both quantitatively and qualitatively. *Salvation* is primarily deliverance from Egypt, then from the enemy who is at the national frontier; but little by little, the punishments which strike Israel make her aware of another and deeper bondage: social injustice, the infidelity which is at the heart of man. The *covenant* is understood first of all as a pact which assures the protection of Yahweh, once the conditions He imposes have been fulfilled (Am. 5:14; Is. 28:15). Then, the multiplied infidelities of Israel, in contrast with the constant faithfulness of Yahweh, call attention to the gratuity of the covenant, show that God's whole activity has been dictated by His love for humanity; finally, under the pressure of national disaster, the conception of the covenant spiritualizes and becomes a covenant within the heart of man. The new covenant announced by Ezekiel will be a regeneration of hearts accompanied by the gift of the Spirit (Ex. 36:23-28). It will not be concluded with only one people, but with all nations.[31] We have already seen that Israel arrived at the idea of *creation* on the basis of history. He who showed Himself master over the lawless powers of nature (Red Sea, plagues of Egypt, trek through the desert); He who showed Himself as the Lord of the peoples, using them as His instrument, and then punishing them for their pride, must also be the Creator of peoples and of the cosmos. Only creation can explain so sovereign a domination. The notion of *remnant* is the fruit of reflection on history. Israel has lived through the bondage of Egypt, the desert, the wars of occupation, the exile, the dispersion. Israel has seen in this that divine activity which spares and saves a remnant of her nation. Finally, in the doctrine of *messianism*, it is noteworthy that each of the social structures of Israel's history has undergone a reidentification in terms of messianism: the king during the royal era; savior at the time of prophecy; priest in the times of the priestly theocracy, after the exile.[32] But always, and it is important to insist on this fact, this forward progress of revelation is realized only by the word which accompanies history and explains its bearing upon salvation.

2. A second implication concerns the *particularism* of revelation. It is repugnant to certain minds for God to have revealed Himself to one particular people: to the Jews rather than the Egyptians, Greeks, or Romans. Toynbee, for example, does not refuse the idea of revelation, but he does resist the idea of a revelation to one *privileged* people. The Incarnation of God, unique, definitive, in one people, seems to smack of something both arbitrary and unacceptable.[33]

This difficulty is not a new one. Celsus already had the Christians saying, in a mocking tone: "It is to us that God reveals and announces all things. He is not the least bit concerned with the rest of the world; we are the only persons with whom he speaks".[34] This difficulty can be answered first of all by pointing out that if the *facts* plead in favor of a revelation to one people rather than to another, we must, in faithfulness to history, write them down that way. It is not ours to decree *a priori* what God ought to do or what he ought not to do in the economy of salvation. Now the tradition of Israel puts us in contact with one absolutely unique fact in the history of nations: the fact of prophecy and of this particular prophecy. The continued religious progress of Israel, over the course of centuries, under the influence of prophets, remains without comparison in the religious annals of humanity; just as the fact of Christ and the Church, which in its way is a logical development of the fact of prophecy.[35]

Actually, the scandal of the particularism of revelation is inseparable from its historical character. If revelation is given to us in history and through history, as an event, it necessarily follows that this event is subject to the conditions of history: it must happen here rather than there, now rather than later, in one group rather than in another. In the Incarnation, revelation is even more *particularized*: it takes place not only in *this* given community, but also in *this* given person who lived in Palestine and died in the days of Pilate.[36] But for the event to take place in Israel rather than Egypt or Greece, this remains a *mystery of grace* which is explained neither by the religious genius of Israel nor her faithfulness to the conditions of the covenant (Is. 1:4). We might add that the election of the chosen people takes place primarily with a view towards *service*. Revelation is entrusted to Israel, but, through Israel, revelation is to come to the entire world. It comes through Jesus Christ, but Christ, through His death and resurrection, becomes the center of a community which bursts the boundaries of time and space. Revelation takes place in Israel, but with a view towards its extension to all nations; it is concentrated in Jesus Christ, but with a view towards *universalization*.[37] The Gospel must be preached to every creature. This economy of the *mediation* of individuals and peoples is a *constant* element of divine activity which wants men to be conscious of their community in revelation and in salvation. Finally we might point out that the election of Israel as mediator of revelation is primarily an election to a *responsibility*. On the material plane, the election offered Israel only a few advantages (excepting for one very brief period). Israel never knew the power of great empire, only persecution, deportation, exile, hate. The election of Israel as *depositary* and *witness* to the word means primarily obedience to that word. This is a privilege little sought after by a humanity bound to earth and flesh. Israel, for the most part, showed herself unfaithful to the word. The Bride of Yahweh turned adulteress. And the love of Yahweh, shining out in his choice of Israel, shone out further in His mercy towards His unfaithful bride. Election is not a scandal, but a mystery of grace.

3. A third implication concerns the *validity* of a revelation given in *time*. How can a revelation which is given to us through the way of history be valid for all men and for all times? How can it escape the *relativism* inherent in history? Even if we claim that it comes from God, it is necessarily received in the categories of a given era, a given mentality; consequently, how can it enter into history, without being mutilated, deformed, exposed to all the vicissitudes that history cannot escape? Such seem to be the necessary conditions of historical revelation.[38]

This is a serious difficulty, and would be practically unanswerable if we were speaking of a human doctrine. But, in this hypothesis, it is not a human doctrine at all we are discussing, but a divine doctrine. Still, it is true that a doctrine, even a divine doctrine, if it comes to us in history and through history, will be affected by the conditions of history. But here once again, revelation takes place in conditions such that it seems that God himself foresaw and resolved these difficulties.

Long in advance, God prepared the human mind into which His words must enter: by the election of a people which would be the depositary of revelation; by a long, patient, and progressive preparation of that people; by His continuous intervention throughout a long series of prophets; by a long elaboration and purification of the concepts which would serve to express His divine message. We need think only of the notions of kingdom, Messiah, covenant, salvation, justice, sin, law, etc. Centuries of history prepared the categories of revelation. And, most important of all, the fullness of revelation does not come to us through the relatively ordinary medium of a prophet, but through the extraordinary medium of the Word Incarnate. Christ is the Man-God, perfectly connatural to human language as well as divine thinking. As Creator, He dominates man and is familiar with all his psychological make-up and his every human resource; He dominates history and knows all its ins and outs. And it is He, the Man-God, who chooses the analogies which can serve as likenesses to the divine mystery. *What is more*, He does not leave His doctrine to the chance of history and individual interpretation. He protects it first of all by handing it down through a charism of *inspiration*, then He entrusts it to a Church which He fortifies with a charism of *infallibility* to preserve, defend, propose, and authentically interpret revelation. The Church, which is the Bride of Christ, possesses His word as a deposit which she meditates and assimilates unceasingly, in the light of the Spirit. Without this divinely established magisterium, and without the special assistance of the Spirit, we gladly concede that it is impossible to conceive of a doctrine, even though divine in its origin, which could escape the fluctuations of history.

The role of the Church, in particular, is to determine what, in concrete revelation, is properly revealed material and what are the relative elements which are the vehicle of every historical expression. Since doctrine is expressed by means of the conceptions of a given era, it is necessary to distinguish truth itself from its mode of presentation: such is the case with the doctrine of creation, proposed in terms of the sacred author's concept of cosmogony. We must also take into account the literary genre which is used: thus the doctrine of last judgment comes down to us under the description of an apocalyptic genre. An oratorical device of the prophets must not be treated as a strictly didactic expression. It is for the Church to *explain* and *interpret* revealed doctrine, according to its authentic meaning, and also to apply it to each generation, so as to keep it always identical, and still always up to date.

No doubt such a set of conditions is unheard of, unique. But Christianity and Christ are also unique in history. If it is true that a revelation, given in history and through history, cannot escape the vicissitudes of historical change, we must nonetheless carefully consider the very particular conditions of this revelation: in its preparation (election), its progress (prophecy), its definitive communication (Christ, Incarnate Word); in its transmission (inspiration) and in its preservation (Church, charism of infallibility). The *specificity* of Christian revelation keeps it from being treated like any ordinary human doctrine.

V. CONCLUSION

In conclusion, it would be well to list the various senses in which we can speak of *historical* revelation:

1. Revelation does not take place outside time, nor in a mythical time, the extra-temporal instant of beginning: it is an event which can be located in time. Through revelation God takes a role in human history, and His entry can be dated. Revelation makes history.

2. Revelation does not stand out as a unique point in the succession of time, but as a *succession* of discontinuous interventions. It is a progressive event: there is a *history of revelation*, that is, a history of the divine initiatives which make revelation progress quantitatively and qualitatively up to the death of the last apostle. In this history there is a *peak*, which is the coming of God in the person of Christ. This peak is an event which can be understood only in its *preparation* througout the course of centuries. The events follow each other, but also *prepare* for each other. Over the course of centuries, God comes close to man and draws man close to Him. The history of revelation is an *economy*, a disposition, a plan of divine wisdom. It is directed towards an end; it is a teleology.

3. Revelation is accomplished *through history*, but not without the interpretation of the word. It is presented as a complex of meaningful events proceeding from God and His plan for salvation. It follows that revelation is at once history and doctrine. It is doctrine about God, but a doctrine made up on the basis of God's activity in history. It is an essentially concrete type of knowledge.

In the last analysis, if revelation, in both the Old and New Testaments, comes to us through history and in history, it is because the word of God, by its essence, is an efficacious word, always active. It effects what it says; it accomplishes what it promises. When God reveals his plan of salvation to humanity, He puts this plan into effect at the same time. The noetic order is always accompanied by the order of activity and life. The word always comes in the power of the Spirit.

---

1. One may find texts typical of this school of thought in: J. BAILLIE, *The Idea of Revelation in Recent Thought* (New York and London, 1956), pp. 50, 62 ff.; K. S. KANTZER, "Revelation and Inspiration in Neo-Orthodox Theology," *Bibliotheca Sacra*, A Theological Quarterly, 115

HISTORY AND REVELATION   357

(1958): 120-127, 218-228. A number of Protestant authors, however, vigorously opposed this one-sided view of revelation as action. Thus, H. W. ROBINSON, *Inspiration and Revelation in the Old Testament* (Oxford, 1956), pp. 43, 45; A. RICHARDSON, *Christian Apologetics* (London, 1955), p. 145; D. B. KNOX, "Propositional Revelation the only Revelation," *The Reformed Theological Review*, 19 (1960): 1-9; C. H. DODD, *La Bible aujourd'hui* (Tournai-Paris, 1957), p. 58. For the Catholic viewpoint, see: R. SCHNACKENBURG, "Zum Offenbarungsdanken in der Bibel," *Biblische Zeitschrift*, 7 (1963): 2-13.

2. G. E. WRIGHT, *God Who Acts* (London, 1952), p. 107.

3. M. ELIADE, *Le mythe de l'éternel retour* (Paris, 1949), pp. 154-155; P. GRELOT, *Sens chrétien de l'Ancien Testament* (Paris-Tournai-New York-Rome, 1962), p. 114.

4. M. ELIADE, *Images et Symboles* (Paris, 1952), ch. 11; J. MONCHANIN, "Le temps selon l'hindouisme et le christianisme," *Dieu vivant*, n. 14 (1949), pp. 11 ff.

5. O. CULLMANN, *Christ et le temps* (Neuchatel, 1957), pp. 36-37; G. E. WRIGHT, *God who acts*, pp. 39-42; J. MOUROUX, *Le mystère du temps*, pp. 48-49; C. MUGLER, *Deux thèmes de la cosmologie grecque: devenir cyclique et pluralité des mondes* (Paris, 1953); J. MOREAU, *L'idée d'univers dans la pensée antique* (Turin, 1953); C. PUECH, "La gnose et le temps," dans: *Eranos Jahrbuch*, 20 (1951): 60-76; M. ELIADE, *Le mythe de l'éternel retour* (Paris, 1949).

6. O. CULLMANN, *Christ et le temps*, pp. 22-23. On time in the Bible, see: G. PIDOUX, "A propos de la notion biblique du temps," *Revue de théologie et de philosophie*, 3 série II (1952), pp. 120-125; R. MARTIN-ACHARD, "La signification du temps dans l'Ancien Testament," *Revue de théologie et de philosophie*, 3 série IV (1954), pp. 137-140.

7. E. DARDEL, "Magie, mythe et histoire," *Journal de psychologie*, 43 (1950): 217-221.

8. M. ELIADE, *Le mythe de l'éternel retour*, pp. 156-157.

9. There is no repeating the passover, or the covenant: they are celebrated. Christianity, as J. Mouroux notes, is the religion of the *ephapax* (once and for all), not of repetition. Redemption is actualized and applied, but never repeated (J. MOUROUX, *Le mystère du temps*, p. 219).

10. H. W. ROBINSON, *Redemption and Revelation* (London, 1947), p. 162.

11. J. DANIELOU, *Essai sur le mystère de l'histoire* (Paris, 1953), pp. 9 ff.; G. AUZOU, *La Parole de Dieu* (Paris, 1960), p. 169; TH. C. VRIEZEN, *An Outline of Old Testament Theology* (Oxford, 1958), pp. 29-30.

12. G. E. WRIGHT, *God who acts*, pp. 24-26; M. ELIADE, *Le mythe de l'éternel retour*, pp. 154-155.

13. O. CULLMANN, *Christ et le temps*, p. 28; K. RAHNER, *Écrits théologiques* (Bruges, 1959), 1: 25-26; J. MOUROUX, *Le mystère du temps*, p. 85; P. GRELOT, *Sens chrétien de l'Ancien Testament*, p. 112.

14. J. MOUROUX, *Le mystère du temps*, pp. 18-19; R. SCHNACKENBURG, "Zum Offenbarungsgedanken in der Bibel," *Biblische Zeitschrift*, 7 (1963): 3-7.

15. W. EICHRODT, "Offenbarung und Geschichte im Testament," *Theologische Zeitschrift*, 4 (1948): 321-322.

16. W. EICHRODT, *op. cit.*, p. 322; G. E. WRIGHT, *God who acts*, p. 44.

17. G. E. MENDENHALL, *Law and Covenant in Israel and the Ancient Near East* (Pennsylvania, 1955), p. 5.

18. *Ibid.*, p. 25.

19. *Ibid.*, pp. 37, 43. The Mosaic covenant owes its literary structure to the literary structure of the Hittite treaties. In these treaties, there is always a prologue with two aspects: *a.* an *ethical* aspect: the king recalls the favors he has performed in behalf of his client, with a view towards stirring up recognition and the desire to serve such a master; *b.* a *juridical* aspect: the favors authorize the king to impose obligations, which are the stipulations of the contract. The same structure can be found in the covenant of Yahweh with Israel: recall of God's favors (Jos. 24; Deut. 6: 10-19), the obligations of the covenant, the blessings of Yahweh. The historical and salvific event par excellence which establishes Yahweh's right to demand this service and leads Israel to make this covenant is the Exodus. Cf. W. MORAN, "De foederis mosaici traditione," *Verbum Domini*, 40 (1962): 3-17.

20. P. VAN IMSCHOOT, *Théologie de l'Ancien Testament*, 1: 237-259.

21. Let us add, among the secondary themes: *creation*, subordinate itself to election and covenant, and the *patriarchal age*, subordinate in turn to the Mosaic covenant.

22. E. JACOB, *Théologie de l'Ancien Testament*, pp. 156-157.

23. G. E. WRIGHT, *God who acts*, pp. 28, 70-72.

24. H. W. ROBINSON, *Inspiration and Revelation in the Old Testament*, pp. 43, 45; E. JACOB, *Théologie de l'Ancien Testament*, p. 167.

25. H. W. ROBINSON, *Redemption and Revelation*, pp. 182-183.

26. E. SCHILLEBEECKX, "Parole et sacrement," *Lumière et Vie*, 9 (1960): 27-28; H. M. FERET, *Connaissance biblique de Dieu* (Paris, 1955), pp. 36-40; A. LIEGE, "Le ministère de la parole:

du kérygme à la catéchèse," in *La Parole de Dieu en Jésus-Christ* (Paris, 1961), p. 171;
N. DUNAS, "Pour une proposition kérygmatique de l'Évangile aujourd'hui," dans: *L'annonce de
l'Évangile aujourd'hui* (Paris, 1962), p. 243.

27. K. RAHNER, *Écrits théologiques*, 1: 26.

28. Saint Thomas' explanation of prophetic knowledge is not essentially different from this
view of things. For Saint Thomas, prophetic knowledge has three elements: material, light,
judgment. The material judgment can be furnished by external facts, events of history, or the
prophet's own earlier experiences. Saint Thomas sees the essential of prophetic revelation in
the illumination which gives the prophet the power of pronouncing a judgment on historical
events (external or internal) that is in conformity with the divine intention. The almond tree of
Jeremias, the invasion of Sennacherib, the dream of Pharaoh can be called revelation only through
the *judgment* or *interpretation* of the prophet. The event in itself is not revelation; the perception
of the event is not revelation either. What *is* revelation is the manifestation of the divine meaning
behind this event. What is important in this event is the goal towards which it tends in the plan
of God; this all takes place in the enlightened judgment of the prophet who brings out the
intelligibility of events (*S. th.*, 2a 2ae, q. 173, a. 2, c.; *De Verit.*, q. 12, a. 1, ad 2; V. WHITE, "Le
concept de révélation chez S. Thomas," *L'Année théologique*, 11 [1950]: 123-125). The great
scholastics, we must remember, are less concerned than we with the historical and concrete
"envelope of revelation," less attentive to the material that history supplies it. They are interested
in the ultimate stage of revelation, rather than with its preparations. Revelation, for them, is
primarily an inner phenomenon, of the cognitive order: it is communication of divine truth by
means of illumination. In virtue of this increased light which he receives, the prophet judges
the objects present to his conscious with certitude and without error. This insistence, unilateral
as it may be, on the formal element of revelation is, when all is said and done, less serious in
consequence than the unilateral insistence of neo-protestantism of our day on revelation as event.
The totality of revelation is made up of history and word, event and interpretation; matter,
(facts, representations, events,) and judgment, according to the scholastics.

29. J. SCHMITT, *Jésus ressuscité dans la prédication apostolique* (Paris, 1949), pp. 5-22.

30. TH. C. VRIEZEN, *An Outline of Old Testament Theology*, pp. 31-34; W. EICHRODT,
"Offenbarung und Geschichte im Alten Testament," *Theologische Zeitschrift*, 4 1948): 322-
323; P. GRELOT, *Sens chrétien de l'Ancien Testament*, pp. 129-130, 259, 267, 273, 279.

31. P. VAN IMSCHOOT, *Théologie de l'Ancien Testament*, 1: 237-259; J. LEVIE, *La Bible,
parole humaine et message de Dieu* (Paris-Louvain, 1958), p. 285.

32. A. GELIN, art. " Messianisme," *Suppl. au Dict. de la Bible*, 5: col. 1168.

33. A. TOYNBEE, *An Historian's Approach to Religion* (New York and London, 1956),
pp. 135-144.

34. ORIGENES, *Contra Celsum*, IV, 23.

35. A. RICHARDSON, *Christian Apologetics* (London, 1955), pp. 139-145.

36. C. H. DODD, *La Bible aujourd'hui*, pp. 111-112.

37. *Ibid.*, pp. 111-114.

38. Here is Aubert's formulation of this contemporary objection: "In the idea of revealed
and immutable truth, once and for all defined, they see a danger for what constitutes the
grandeur and power of contemporary humanism, that is, for the almost tragic sense of the
complexity of truth, the imperfection of human thinking, the necessity of constantly recreating
the world of values, to adapt it to new possibilities always rising up from changes in situation
and in the world. The Christian appears as a reactionary and conservative by his very vocation.
What is more, since we Christians claim to be the only ones who possess the truth, and because
error has no right, they accuse us of intolerance and say that we favor dictatorship. Faith in
God, they say, annihilates our sense of historicity and leads naturally to inflexibility in thinking
and the death of open-mindedness." (R. AUBERT, "Questioni attuali intorno all'atto di Fede,"
dans: *Problemi e Orientamenti di Teologia Dommatica* (2 vol., Milano, 1957), 2: 675-676).

CHAPTER IV

INCARNATION AND REVELATION

Contemporary theology strongly insists on the necessity of joining revelation closely to the Person of Christ. *H. de Lubac*: "In Jesus Christ, everything has been at once given and revealed".[1] *L. M. Dewailly*: "Jesus Christ is the Word of God made flesh.... He is, in his very Person, the revelation of God, He does not simply bring this revelation to us".[2] *G. Söhngen*: "Jesus Christ... is quite simply revelation itself, God revealed in Himself".[3] *K. Rahner*: Christ is "the epiphany of God" in our history.[4] *J. Mouroux*: "He is the existential epiphany of God".[5] *R. Guardini*: "Christ is in the world as the epiphany of the Father".[6] Theology also calls for a more authentic fidelity to the realism of the Incarnation, a fidelity pushed to its ultimate consequences. If the human nature of Christ is not a travesty, but rather the "self-expression of God when His Word is uttered with love in the absolute and godless nothingness";[7] if, through the Incarnation, there is a veritable "in-humanization" of God,[8] then it is man as man who becomes the expression of God's mystery. And it follows that "all human dimensions, known and unknown, must be assumed and utilized to serve as the expression of Absolute Person".[9] It is by His activity, by His gestures, by His attitude, by His entire conduct, as well as by His words, that Christ is the perfect revelation of God.[10]

In the Old Testament, the central problem, for the understanding of revelation, is that of the relationship between revelation and history. In the New Testament, the problem is that of the relationship between *Incarnation* and *revelation*, between Christ and revelation. What then is the relationship between Christ and revelation? And, more precisely, how did Christ use the way of Incarnation to reveal God and His plan of salvation? What is the effect of this economy on the very nature of revelation? What bearing does it have on Christ, on the apostles, on the Church? Is there an opposition between the revelation of person and the revelation of truth?

I. INTELLIGIBILITY OF AN ECONOMY OF INCARNATION FOR REVELATION

Saint Thomas, speaking of the economy of Incarnation with respect to revelation, says quite simply: just as man, in order to communicate his thought, clothes it in some way with letters and sounds, "even so God, wanting to manifest Himself to men, clothes with human flesh, in time, His Word conceived from all eternity".[11] There is no simpler way of expressing the perfect fittingness of an economy of incarnation for revelation.

To demonstrate the fittingness of a mystery means to manifest its intelligibility, that is, its inner harmony and coherence. Now in the case of a revelation of God to man by way of incarnation, whether we consider the mystery from the point of view of God or from the point of view of man, this intelligibility is breath-taking.

God expresses Himself first of all, in Himself, and for Himself: he knows Himself in His Word. And when he expresses Himself *ad extra*, this expression is then the *expression* of the Immanent Word. He who is already the eternal Word of God, in the bosom of the Trinity, is also He who expresses that Word to men.[12] He who already, in the bosom of the Trinity, is the Son, that is, pure self-gift to the Father, is also He who has a mission of making men come to understand their condition as sons. How can any other person better reveal the Father than this Person who is the perfect Image of the Father, the Word which exhausts the knowledge that the Father has of Himself? And how could any other person than the Son reveal our condition of sonship and teach us to adore the Father? It was sovereignly fitting for the Word of God to be the Revealer, and for the Word of the Father, His *Amen*, to be He who initiates men into their life as sons of God. Thus, the Greek fathers, such as Justin, Irenaeus, Clement of Alexandria, and Origen, see in the Word not only the one and only Revealer of God, but also, in one sense the only possible revealer. What is more, revelation being the revelation of persons and not of problems, as we have stressed above, only a person could introduce us to the knowledge of the history of the Trinity.

On the other hand, man, a being of flesh and spirit, cannot communicate at his own level excepting through the way of bodily realities, and thus it is fitting for God to meet man at this level and address him with bodily signs. Through the Incarnation, God took upon Himself the means to make His presence accessible to us. In Christ, God becomes present to us in a human fashion, still manifesting Himself as God. What gesture and word accomplish in ordinary presence, the Incarnation accomplishes in the supernatural order of revelation. In Jesus Christ, and through Jesus Christ, He who, in God, is the truth and *Amen* of the Father, interprets the Father to us (Jn. 1:18) in human words and gestures: the *Eternal Word becomes Gospel.* What God wants to say about Himself Christ says in a human way. And just as, in gestures and above all in words, we grasp the person, even so, in the life, gestures, and teachings of Christ, we have access to the Person of the Word, and, through Him, to the Father and the Spirit. In Him we know the mysteries of the personal and intimate life of God.[13]

Finally, it was most fitting for God to *complete,* in the New Testament, this economy of incarnation which He had in some way inaugurated in the Old Testament, using, as instruments of his revelation, the word and psyche of the prophets. How could we understand that God did really speak through the prophets, if He did not intend to inaugurate an economy in which He meant to assume not only speech, but the whole being of man, who finds his most perfect expression in speech? If God really used the language of man, it is because the prophetic economy was the first stage of an economy of incarnation in which God was going to assume what is proper to man in His own Person. The mystery of God who uses the mouth and words of the prophets is the mystery of God beginning His apprenticeship as Word Incarnate among men.[14] Thus the Incarnation completes the economy of revelation from the Old Testament.[15]

II. FULLNESS AND REALISM OF THE INCARNATION

It is important to insist on the fullness and realism of the Incarnation. The humanity of Christ is not a simple appearance, a sort of personage whom Christ used to manifest His presence while still disguising Himself; Christ's human nature is the expression of God Himself: "the self-expression of God outside Himself".[16] Christ is Son of God even in His humanity. The second Person of the Trinity is *personally* man; and this man is *personally* God. Christ is God in a human manner, and Man in a divine manner. God is charity, but it is in man that He shows this fact. His human love is the human form of the redemptive love of God, "God's love becoming visible".[17] The words of Christ are the human words of God; the acts of Christ are the acts of God in the form of a human manifestation.

The Son of God, through His human word, addresses man, person to person.

Every spiritual encounter between men takes place through the mediation of the body. It is *through* the body and *in* the body that man makes himself present to other men. The body is the sign which both covers and uncovers the human person within. For the contemporaries of Jesus, personal meeting with Him was thus a meeting with a living God. The man they heard, and saw, through the sign of the body, was the Son of God in person. Christ is no one else but God. To establish contact with Christ through His humanity is to establish contact with the Word of God. Thus Saint John can testify to his *experience* of the Word of life (1 Jn. 1:1-3). The Word appeared, becoming incarnate, and, thanks to this sign of His humanity, John was able to hear, see, contemplate, touch the living God.

God Himself, *in person,* revealed Himself concretely in Christ: such is the unheard-of and decisive fact which the New Testament proclaims and which it tries to express in the fullness of formulas in which Christ and the knowledge of God are indissolubly bound together: "God, in these last days, has spoken to us through his Son" (Heb. 1:2). "No one has ever seen God; the only-begotten Son of God, who is in the bosom of the Father, he has made him known" (Jn. 1:18). "This is life everlasting, that they know you, the one true God, and him whom you have sent, Jesus Christ" (Jn. 17:3). The grace of God is manifest to us "by the enlightenment of our Savior Jesus Christ; who has destroyed death and brought to light life and incorruption by the Gospel" (2 Tim. 1:10). Salvation is accomplished through "the knowledge of God and Jesus our Lord" (2 Pet. 1:2; Tit. 2:11; 1 Tim. 3:16). In Christ also, the *Agape* of God (Rom. 5:8; 1 Jn. 4:9), that is, "the goodness of God our Savior and his love for men" appeared to us (Tit. 3:4). Christ's reality needed to be realized for this love to be effectively and properly present in our midst. In Christ, God Himself gives Himself to man without reserve, and through human ways: His divine love comes to us through a human heart. It is this fullness of Incarnation that the fathers of the Church express, in their concise and concrete way: "The knowledge of God is Jesus Christ," says St. Ignatius of Antioch.[18] And again: "There is only one God, manifest in Jesus Christ His Son, who is the Word come out of silence".[19] For Saint Irenaeus, revelation is the epiphany of the Father through the Word Incarnate: "Through the Son, visible and tangible, the Father appears".[20]

It does not, however, follow that revelation is identified only with the objective event of the Incarnation of the Word. The simple fact of God's appearance in human flesh in our world is not yet revelation. To reduce revelation thus to the event of the Incarnation would mean, actually, separating revelation and history and finding no purpose to an economy of revelation through the means of Incarnation. Such a revelation would be only an *activity*, without any bond to join it to our awareness: it would remain unknowable. More properly, the Incarnation is the *way* chosen by God to reveal and to reveal Himself. It is the foundation and condition for revelation, but not its complete accomplishment, for it does not make it an *object of faith*. Its purpose is to make possible, on the human level, a knowledge of God and His plan for salvation; it makes it possible for God, through all the dimensions of human experience, to express to man, in human terms and in human gestures, the knowledge and love of the only true God.

III. REVELATION THROUGH THE WAY OF INCARNATION

If the Son becomes incarnate in order to reveal, we must expect that all the resources of human nature will be used by Him to serve as the expression of His Person, the Son of God. The words of Christ, as a result, His teaching, but also His actions, His attitudes, His conduct, His whole human existence will be completely utilized to reveal the depths of the divine mystery.

Such indeed is Christ's concrete way of acting. The method adapted by our Master for the formation of His apostles was that of teachers in Palestine. The disciple never left his master; he attached himself to his master, observing him, learning all his attitudes by heart, his answers, his counsels. He did not miss a single gesture, a single one of the master's words. Christ made no innovations in this respect; He accepted the tradition of His people. What He preserved most of all was the contact, the common life of master and disciple. The apostles are always present: they follow Him in His journeyings, they are present at His miracles, they share in His activity. They hear His *word*, for it is the *Master* who speaks with authority: He explains the law to them, unveils the meanings of His parables, initiates them into the mystery of His Person and the knowledge of the Father. But activity and gesture, like a continuous commentary, accompany and stress this teaching. Christ teaches His apostles that they are sons of their Father and they must conduct themselves as such in prayer, fasting, trial, persecution, even in their fall and reparation; but at the same time, by His attitude when He prays, by His constant submission to the Father's will, He expresses the tangible and lived example for the conduct He teaches with His words. The mysterious bent of

God's love for children, for the poor, for sinners, is expressed by Christ in parables; but how much more concretely is it expressed in His acts of blessing, healing, pardon, in His condescending to sit with publicans and sinful women. The principles of this new morality (humility, meekness, patience, charity, forgiveness) all shine out in the example of the Master, meek and humble of heart, who serves His disciples and washes their feet, in the love that shines in His eyes when He looks at Peter and Judas, in His patience and meekness in the face of insult and indignity, and above all in His passion and in His death. "He went his way doing good" (Acts 10:38). "I have given you the example" (Jn. 13:15).

Revelation is thus accomplished according to a double line of manifestation: through words and activity, through words and gesture, the words explaining the gestures, the actions, and giving them their full meaning; the gestures and actions, in their turn, making the words incarnate and giving them the force of life. In this combined activity of *facere* and *docere* in the service of revelation, we must still admit that it is the word which has the primacy, just as in human expression. It is through the human word of Christ, speaking to us in explanation, that the event and meaning of the Incarnation are unveiled for us. Christ is at once the event and the interpretation of the event. The mystery of His Person and His mission Christ declares progressively, with great discretion, but the fact that He is God and sent by God is *testified* by His human word. What would the gestures of the last supper be without the words to explain their redemptive value? It is through His actions and through His gestures, but primarily through His words, that Christ testifies to the Father and to Himself. The actions of Christ are, in the New Testament, what the events of history are in the revelation of the prophets. They become *fully* the vehicle of revelation only through the word of Christ who declares their meaning and interprets them. The event of Incarnation, which we can call a revelation "in the first degree," must always be completed by the revelation-word which is its necessary commentary.[21] Revelation as event calls for revelation as word. Facts, actions, gestures, Christ's conduct, all these are subject to His word which expresses their salvific bearing and presents them to the apostles as the *object of divine testimony*.

The *word* of Christ is thus the necessary formal element of revelation. And it is so for many reasons. *First of all*, because God, taking on human nature, at the same time takes on the word as the privileged form of expression among men: the most spiritual and the most perfect. He tells us what He is accomplishing, in intelligible human discourse. *In the second place*, since truth is in the judgment, and not in the mere presentation of external events, it is through the word that judgment is expressed, uniting subject and attribute. *In the third place*, since the object of revelation is not only historical facts but also mysteries: the mystery of the Trinity, of the divine sonship of Christ, of our share in the life of the Trinity. All these mysteries can be *testified* to only through the word. *In the fourth place*, since activities, gestures, events, the mysteries of the life of Christ, *can be believed with divine faith only if they are presented as the object of divine testimony*. This attestation is the work of Christ's word.

IV. HUMAN PROPOSITION, DIVINE TRUTH

The Incarnation offers a solution to the most serious and apparently the only real difficulty posed by revelation, namely, that of an authentic communication of God's plan to the human mind. Actually, Christ is the qualified witness of the divine mysteries, for His revelation derives from the very vision with which the Son sees the Father. What is more, He who sees is at once God and man, connaturalized both to human discourse and divine thought. As the Word of God, He does not speak our human language, He speaks only to the Father; but as Word Incarnate, He speaks to us. And it is the same Person, living in the bosom of the Father, who expresses what He knows in human terms. The union of natures and the unity of person authorizes the transfer from the divine milieu, in all its inaccessibility, to the human milieu, and at the same time assures the fidelity of the transmission. Christ is the perfect seer of God, and He expresses what He sees in human language. The passage is thus effected from divine vision to human expression.

Actually, this answer only raises a further difficulty, a still more fundamental one. If revelation comes to us through the vehicle of human notions and human propositions, how can these notions and propositions give us access to the divine mystery? How can a human proposition, by its very nature made up of terms borrowed from the world of creatures, claim to contain and in some way "imprison" a divine truth, to pronounce it in human terms: this *is*, or this *is not*? To put it in other words, how can God make Himself the guarantee for the truth of a statement which is essentially made up of human ingredients?[22]

Karl Barth answers this difficulty by saying that the truth of the human affirmation, that is, the correspondence between human discourse and divine reality, is only assured through the *grace* of revelation. Our human concepts and our human terms, in so far as they are *ours* and human, are totally incapable of expressing God and His mysteries; their aptitude for adequate and correct expression comes only from revelation.[23] This answer does not solve the problem. "Whether they rest on revelation or not," as H. Bouillard correctly points out, "the concepts and terms which we relate to God are ours, they are human. It is a question rather of knowing by what right a human discourse, even based on the Bible, can correctly refer to God. To say that it refers adequately to God by virtue of revelation is merely to answer one question with another . . . . We might be tempted to say that the author substitutes a natural equivocation for an univocation of grace".[24]

Revelation, even Christ's revelation, is unthinkable apart from its basis in analogy, with its process of negation and pre-eminence. Whoever refuses this analogy must also refuse the concept of revelation. For revelation presupposes two terms, (God and man) which both meet each other and remain distinct. If a distinction between God and man is impossible, we are reduced to monism; if, on the other hand, an encounter between God and man is called impossible, we are reduced to absolute agnosticism or absolute transcendentism, which condemns God to silence. The concept of analogy denies both that the word of God is of the same nature as the word of man, and also that it is a word without any relation to human words, and thus completely incapable of setting up a true dialogue.

Since God has made all things and, particularly, human creation, as a reflection of His own perfection, and because all things have their source in God, a relationship is possible between God and man. Revelation *by word* presupposes God's *language of creation*, just as grace is based on the intellectual and spiritual nature of man. It is not simply because they have been chosen by Christ that our human concepts and our human terms are adaptable to the expression of mystery: it is rather because they are essentially *not unrelated* to the Divine Person that Christ can make use of them.

Of course, revelation by the way of incarnation does represent an *exceptional* case. In Jesus Christ, God Himself is manifest, living in our world, as a person whom we might meet and with whom we might communicate directly, just as with any other human person. This accounts for the character of direct vision, springing up from within, in the words of Christ (Jn. 1:18; Lk. 10:22; Jn. 5:20). For Christ, the knowledge of God is a "family possession," something He shares with Father and Spirit, something He communicates with those whom He will. Whereas, in natural knowledge of God, the point of departure is in the creature as such; in Christ, the knowledge of God proceeds from the very Person of God: "The Father and I are one" (Jn. 10:27-30; 14:6; 8:58). It is on the basis of this knowledge that Christ *condescends*, that is to say, descends to the level of man whom He means to reach, and that He chooses the realities in our world that have a force of likeness by their relationship to the divine mystery. Christ, for example, contemplating the richness of divine life, which communicates its whole reality, without reserving anything for its own, outside the communication itself, perceives a distant but real image, in creatures, in the organic communication which exists between Father and Son. Fatherhood and Sonship are revealed analogies, chosen by Christ; consequently they have the necessary power to serve as an analogy dictated by God Himself. These revealed analogies stimulate human reflection which then sets about the task of purifying them and transfiguring them in order to glimpse something of the depths of divine life. This work takes place under the direction of the Church who approves, corrects, rejects.[25]

It remains true that the notions chosen by Christ to introduce us to the divine mystery are still human notions. Christ borrowed them from human language, from the whole range of created realities. And it is on the basis of these realities, objects of human experience, that is effected a purification and development of meaning which are dictated by the necessities of revelation. If these realities, even though deficient, were without any relation to the mystery of the Divine Person, the dialogue between God and man would, as a matter of fact, be only two parallel monologues, with no possible point of contact. If Christ can utilize all the resources of the created universe to make us know God and the ways of God, it is because the word of creation has preceded and left a foundation for the word of revelation; it is because both one and the other have their principle in the same interior Word of God. The revelation of Christ presupposes the truth of analogy.[26]

The revelation of Christ is made up not only of revealed analogies; it also implies judgments which link these analogies together. For example: the Father and Son *are* one. The truth of this judgment entirely escapes the evidence or demonstration of human reason. Such a perfection is not shared by any creature, nor can it be shared. All that man can do is receive testimony to it through Him who manifests the glory of Yahweh in the brilliance of His signs.

Thus, in the last analysis, if the human affirmation of Christ can claim "to contain" divine truth, it is by reason of analogy which legitimates the use of human notions, and by reason of Christ's presence among us, His knowledge originating in a vision such that

He alone can say: *est* and *non est*. It is this analogy which makes it legitimate to use terms of a proposition; it is the quality of Son of the Father which makes it possible for Christ to unite these terms in judgments which are in conformity with the reality of the divine mystery.

V. CHRIST'S POSITION

The Incarnation establishes relationships between Christ, the apostles, and the Church, with respect to revelation. Christ is at once God the revealer and God revealed, way and sign of revelation, response to revelation.

He is *God the revealer*, for the Word of God, the Son, Jesus Christ—are all one. "He is the image of the invisible God" (Col. 1:15; 2 Cor. 4:4), "the radiance of His glory, the image of His substance" (Heb. 1:3), ontologically qualified to reveal the Father for whom He serves in some way as an eternal revelation. Christ is *cause* and *author* of revelation, for revelation originates in Christ as well as in the Father and the Spirit. He is the light which shines and makes us see (Jn. 8:12; 9:5; 1:9). As God, Word of God, only Son of the Father, He is born for revelation, for giving the world the fullness of revelation.[27]

Christ is God the revealer, but also *God revealed*. The true God whom He teaches is the God announced by Him and recognized in Him, so that in confessing the Son we confess also the Father. Christ is at once God who speaks and God who is spoken of, witness and object of testimony, author and object of revelation, He who reveals the mystery and the mystery itself in person. As Incarnate Word, He is the expression of revelation; as Word of God, He is in person the truth whom He preaches and teaches. He is the truth which keeps us from falsehood, and the love which keeps us from the loneliness of our self-seeking. "He is truth and life" (Jn. 14:6), the truth which teaches us (Tit. 2:12). "Hear him," says the Father (Mt. 17:5). In this respect, there is no possible comparison beween Christ and Buddha, Confucius, Mohammed, or the founder of any other religion. In the other religions, doctrine and the object of doctrine are distinct from the founder. Here, however, the doctrine of Christ has Christ for its object. Our faith is faith in Christ as God. Salvation is a choice for or against Christ. "Jesus Christ," according to Pascal, "is the object of everything, the center towards which everything tends".[28]

Christ is the *way* of revelation (Jn. 14:5-6; Mt. 11:27), that is, the means chosen by God to make known what He is (Father, Son,

Spirit) and what we are (sinners called to life). He is the way which reveals life and the way to life. In the Old Testament, God used the psyche of the prophets to make Himself known; this time, he unites hypostatically with human nature and makes known His plan of life through the words, actions, gestures, attitudes, the whole conduct of Christ. In Jesus Christ, the eternal and interior Word of God echoes without and makes Himself heard by man through the ways of flesh. Ever after, all knowledge of the true God, just like all true salvation, comes to us through Christ.

Christ is the *sign* of revelation: at once the confirmative sign (motive of credibility) and the figurative sign (symbol). The glory of the All-powerful and Thrice Holy God rests on Christ and sets Him apart as He who declares Himself the equal of the Father. By the sublimity of His doctrine, by the brilliance of His holiness and the power of His works, that is, by the radiance of His person and activity, Christ *shows* that he is truly what he claims to be, God among men, and that His witness is true. He is in person the motive of credibility par excellence. At the same time, He unfolds before our human eyes the transformation of humanity that is effected by the invasion of grace. He is in person this new man whom He announces, wholly vivified by the Holy Spirit.

Finally, Christ is the perfect *response* of humanity to revelation. The descending movement of revelation has a corresponding ascending movement, which goes from Christ to the Father. Christ is at once revelation of the Father's love and response to this love. He is the prototype, the supreme and perfect realization of the human response of love to the divine invitation of the Father. Christ begins this harmonious dialogue with the Father which is the norm of all response and all meeting with God. By His human conduct as Son, always doing the will of the Father, He is the prototype of the filial attitude of humanity adopted by the Father. He is the perfect adorer of the Father.

Christ is thus the *fullness* of revelation. He is the culmination of revelation as activity, as economy, as message, and as encounter.

VI. THE APOSTLES' POSITION

In the economy of revelation through incarnation, the apostles occupy a unique place with respect to Christ in the Church.[29]

They are privileged witnesses, "chosen beforehand" (Acts. 10:41) and "set aside" (Rom. 1:1) to be "servants of the Word" (Lk. 1:2) and the "foundation" of the Church (Eph. 2:20-21). There are twelve, like the twelve patriarchs and the twelve tribes of Israel. They constitute the germ of the new people whom Christ has acquired by His blood, and they will be the shepherds of this people (Jn. 21:15-17; Mt. 10:6; 1 Pet. 5:2-3; 1 Cor. 9:7). Christ called them, banded them together, so that they would be with Him: companions on His way, hearers of His words, witnesses to His actions. And the apostles followed Him (Mt. 19:29); they stayed with Him in the heart of temptations (Lk. 22:28), even when other men abandoned him (Jn. 6:66). Christ made them His intimate collaborators; to them He entrusted His powers and His mission. As Son of the Father, He made known to them what he had learned from His Father (Jn. 15:15). He manifested the name of the Father, He gave them the words and doctrine of the Father (Jn. 17:6. 8. 14). Just as He had been sent by the Father to preach, cast out devils, and heal every sickness, so He also sends his apostles to preach and cast out demons (Mk. 3:13-15), to heal all infirmities (Mt. 10:1). Whoever receives them, receives Christ and the Father who has sent Him (Mt. 10:40-41; Lk. 10:16). Their mission is a sharing in the very mission of Christ, which He received from the Father. This continuity between the mission of Christ and the mission of the apostles is expressed by Clement of Rome in these words: "Christ comes from God and the apostles come from Christ" (42; 1-4). Tertullian speaks of the doctrine which "the Church has received from the apostles, the apostles from Christ, and Christ from God".[30]

Christ did not come to write a book or create a new philosophical system; He came to found a religion in which He himself, in person, is center and object. Thus if revelation is effected by an encounter with the living God, in Jesus Christ, only those can be the authentic mediators of revelation who were then the witnesses of His life, who have been initiated into the mystery of His person. Without them, it is impossible to reach Christ; to separate from them means to lose contact with Christ.

Now the apostles were the only ones who had living and direct experience of Christ. If Christ had written a book, we could have dispensed with Christ and the apostles and taken only His book. But since the good news has the living Christ for Author and Object, it is essential to receive it from Christ Himself and from His living witnesses. The apostles are those who saw, heard, touched Christ (1 Jn. 1:1-3), who ate and drank with Christ, before and after His resurrection (Acts 10:41), who were with Him "from the beginning" (Jn. 15:27), from the baptism of John to the resurrection (Acts 1:22). This first experience gained new depth with the coming and gift of the Spirit. At the very beginning, the apostles, with their earthly and still not completely opened eyes, walked along beside Jesus of Nazareth without understanding Him very well. Then, later on, they *re-read*, in the Spirit, all the events which they had lived together with Him (Jn. 14:20. 26; 16:12-13). It was then that they understood what was incomprehensible before the passion, resurrection, and outpouring of the Holy Spirit. What they thus pass down to the Church are the words and actions of Christ, but with the intelligence and understanding which have come to them through the illuminating activity of the Spirit as well as the experience of the very life of the Church.[31] All this, the words and activities of Christ, together with the progress in the understanding which the apostles had of all these things, has the force of revelation for us and constitutes or realizes the object of our faith. From the beginning of our faith, we believe in what, for the apostles, was the end product of their reflection. We participate in the full knowledge at which the apostles arrived only in the Holy Spirit.

No one can rival the apostles in the knowledge of Christ. Theirs is a unique moment in the history of revelation, the fullness and freshness of the first morning in new creation.[32] No doubt the apostles did not have the *explicit* knowledge which the Church possesses now; but, in its intensity, depth, richness of intuition, and character of totality, their knowledge of Christ and revelation could surpass all the knowledge the Church now has or ever will have. They, according to C. Journet, had a "supreme, exceptional knowledge which assumed, but in a higher intuition, the explicit meaning, such as could be grasped immediately, of the deposit entrusted to the primitive Church" and which "surpassed all that the Church, assisted by the Spirit, could discover throughout the course of centuries, in making explicit and developing this first deposit".[33]

From this fullness of experience, the apostles did not hand down and could not hand down everything. Their preaching could not "exhaust" the ineffable element in every personal encounter. What is more, they did not mean to hand down everything (Jn. 20:30). At least they did hand down the essential in the words and actions of Christ: that which constitutes properly the economy of salvation (*res fidei et morum*). They reported the teaching of Christ with all the faithfulness that was humanly possible (this is not to say that they handed it down with stenographic fidelity) and in the context of a living Christian community, for whom the doctrine of Christ is a doctrine of life, capable of casting light on new situations, and resolving unexpected problems. They reported the actions of Christ with honesty and faithfulness (which is not to say photographic fidelity) and taking into account both their hearers and their circumstances.

The activity which posits in existence the object of our faith and *constitutes* it, that is, gives it *being* and the right to be *believed,* is the apostolic *testimony,* this *deposition* by those who have seen and heard Christ and who testify to what they have seen and heard of Him, that is, His death and resurrection (Acts 4:33), but also His whole career (Acts 10:39) and His whole work of salvation (Acts 5:31 ff; 10:42).

VII. THE CHURCH'S POSITION

There is thus a difference between the condition of the apostles and that of the Church. This difference in condition is expressed clearly in the first letter of Saint John. The Christians to whom he addresses this letter did not know Jesus; they have no other means of knowing Him than the testimony of John who lived with Him. Hence the solemn proclamation of the apostle: he is bearing testimony to make known to men his own personal experience of Christ, Son of the Father, and, through this experience, to the mystery of His eternal life: "I write of what was from the beginning, what we have heard, what we have seen with our eyes, what we have looked upon and our hands have handled: of the Word of life. And the life was made known and we have seen, and now testify and announce to you, the life eternal which was with the Father, and has appeared to us. What we have seen and have heard we announce to you, in order that you also may have fellowship with us, and that our fellowship may be with the Father, and with his Son Jesus Christ" (Jn. 1:1-3). Thanks to the sign of Christ's humanity, Saint John was able to hear, see, look upon the living God. How are Christians now to have a share in this experience? By means of the apostolic testimony and faith in this testimony (1 Jn. 1:3; 4:14-15; Jn. 19:35). It is through the objective preaching of the apostles, subjectively received in faith and practiced in the commandments, that the Christians also enter into communion with the word of life. The apostles, as Ph. H. Menoud points out, are "the necessary intermediaries between the living Christ and men who are destined to have a share in the salvation realized by the life, death, and resurrection of Jesus. Even when these witnesses inaugurated the time of the Church by preaching according to their vocation, they still belong to the time of revelation by a unique bond which joins them to Christ. Their ministry is the last act of the revelation announced by John the Baptist".[34]

The experience that the apostles had of Christ is brought to the knowledge of all men through the testimony and kerygma of the apostles. The content of this testimony is the good news, the message of salvation, the word of truth, the word, or quite simply, Christ. And the activity which responds to this testimony, preaching and evangelizing, is hearing with faith (Acts 18:8; Rom. 10:17). What is first proposed to the faith of the Church (revelation in its actual and accomplished form) is thus not the concrete, living, and intuitive experience of the person of Christ, such as the apostles could have it in the way of the Incarnation, but rather the *apostolic testimony* on the *facere* and *docere* of Christ: a testimony which is addressed, "by ear," to the intelligence assimilating what the ear has heard, thanks to the Spirit who enlightens within.[35] Mediate revelation, handed on to the Church, is contained in its entirety in this apostolic testimony, that is, in the word of the apostles inviting us to believe what Christ did and said, in a doctrine consequently, in a complex of notions and judgments which enunciate and designate the mystery. In this doctrine, Christ occupies the central place, but only in so far as it is proposed by means of signs which are held together by the apostolic word. The object of faith is Christ, words and gestures, manner of acting, person in its entirety, but only such as is proposed in the doctrine of the apostles regarding Christ. It is this doctrine, entrusted to the Church as a deposit, that Saint Paul wants to see preserved (1 Tim. 6:20; 2 Thess. 2:15).

The documents of the Church magisterium are in conformity with the data of scripture and tradition when they speak equivalently of apostolic doctrine (D 300), revealed doctrine (D 2314), revelation handed down by the the apostles as the deposit of faith (D 1836), the deposit of faith entrusted to the Church (D 2204). Revelation, in its actual, objective form, is a doctrinal testimony, the apostolic testimony deposited in the memory of the Church.

Present-day Protestant theology resists the idea of a revelation conceived as the dispensation of divinely guaranteed truths.[36] Protestant theology sees revelation primarily as a divine act, an event: the activity of the living God making an inroad into human existence and inviting man to a choice which can be his salvation. Correlatively, faith is primarily man's acceptance of the divine epiphany, existential encounter with God in the person of Jesus Christ. For Bultmann, revelation tends to be nothing more than *action*, to the practical exclusion of all doctrine; strictly speaking, it exists only in the existential encounter of faith.[37]

Catholic theology is the first to admit that revelation is an *activity*, an *event*, an *encounter* which upsets the whole existence of man and calls him to a decision, to a commitment of his whole person; but Catholic theology adds, faithful always to the realism of the Incarnation, that the encounter with Christ and His mystery is effected only through hearing the apostolic witness, handed down through the Church and consigned to Scripture. It is by adherence to the apostolic doctrine that we touch upon God and His mystery; it is through the fragility of conceptual and verbal signs that we have access to the very reality of Christ: not only through them alone, but with the aid and penetration of the light of faith. Adherence to the kerygma, to the message, is a means of encounter and communion with the person.[38] Revelation is an order of knowledge finalized by an order of life. If God speaks to us, it is in order to associate us with His life (D 1786). We pass from message to life, just as we pass from knowledge to love, from faith to charity. The *doctrine* does not tend to assure the fidelity of our thinking to an orthodoxy conceived for itself, but to assure an encounter, a *union in truth* with the true God. Our adherence to Christ is *mediated* and *normalized* by our adherence to the witness and doctrine of the apostles: a doctrine of *salvation*, a word of *life*.

This concept presents no obstacle to the human mind. If we admit that God could have chosen an economy of incarnation in order to reveal Himself, we must think that God has been logical to the very end of His plan: it is through the gestures and words of Christ, it is through the apostolic testimony expressed in human terms, that we have access to this mystery. The Word of God is wrapped up in Christ's flesh, in the flesh of words, in sacramental signs. It is both a veiling and an unveiling of God, the essential dialectics of a revelation which is not yet vision. Resistance to a revelation conceived as a doctrine proceeds, among many present-day Protestants, from their desire to lay greater stress on the personal, existential character of revelation and its character of event; but, in the case of others, it results from a deliberate and poorly veiled refusal to admit the Incarnation.

1. H. De Lubac, "Le problème du développement du dogme," *Recherches de science religieuse*, 35 (1948): 157-158.

2. L. M. Dewailly, *Jésus-Christ, Parole de Dieu* (Paris, 1945), p. 28.

3. G. Sohngen, *Die Einheit in der Theologie* (Munchen, 1952), pp. 316, 354 ff., 359.

4. K. Rahner, *Écrits théologiques*, 1: 164.

5. J. Mouroux, *L'expérience chrétienne* (Paris, 1952), p. 193.

6. R. Guardini, *Essence du christianisme* (trad. Lorson, Paris, 1947), p. 74.

7. K. Rahner, "Réflexions théologiques sur l'Incarnation," *Sciences Ecclésiastiques*, 12 (1960: 15.

8. H. Urs von Balthasar, "Dieu a parlé un langage d'homme," dans: *Parole de Dieu et liturgie* (Paris, 1958), p. 73.

9. *Ibid.*, p. 73.

10. H. Niebecker, *Wesen und Wirklichkeit der ubernaturlichen Offenbarung*, p. 155; H. Urs von Balthasar, *La théologie de l'histoire* (Paris, 1955), p. 193; R. Guardini, *Essence du christianisme*, p. 48; Id., *Die Offenbarung, ihr Wesen und ihre Formen* (Wurzburg, 1940), pp. 78-79; L. M. Dewailly, *Jésus-Christ, Parole de Dieu*, p. 28.

11. "Et sicut homo volens revelare se verbo cordis, quod profert ore, induit quodammodo ipsum verbum litteris vel voce, ita Deus, volens se manifestare hominibus, Verbum suum conceptum ab aeterno, carne induit in tempore" (*In Jo.*, c. 14, lect. 2).

12. K. Rahner, "Réflexions théologiques sur l'Incarnation," *Sciences Ecclésiastiques*, 12 (1960): 14-15.

13. A. Brunner, *La personne incarnée*, pp. 272-273; E. H. Schillebeeckx, *Le Christ, sacrement de la rencontre de Dieu* (Paris, 1960), pp. 40-41, 55; W. Temple, *Nature, Man and God* (London, 1956), p. 319.

14. Irenaeus, *Adversus Haereses*, IV, 12, 4.

15. G. Martelet, "L'homme comme parole et Dieu comme révélation," *Cahiers d'études biologiques*, nos. 6-7 (1960), pp. 177-180.

16. K. Rahner, "Réflexions théologiques sur l'Incarnation," *Sciences Ecclésiastiques*, 12 (1960): 15.

17. E. H. Schillebeeckx, *Le Christ, sacrement de la rencontre de Dieu*, p. 39.

18. *Eph.* 17, 2.

19. *Magn.* 7, 2.

20. *Adversus Haereses*, IV, 6, 6.

21. E. Schillebeeckx, "Parole et sacrement dans l'Église," *Lumière et Vie*, 9 Jan.-Mar. 1960): 28-29.

22. A. Durand, "Incarnation et christocentrisme," *Nouvelle Revue théologique*, 69 (1947): 482-483; P. Rousselot, art. "Intellectualisme," *Dictionnaire apologétique de la Foi catholique,* 2: 1075-1076.

23. H. Bouillard, *Karl Barth* (3 vol., Paris,1957),3: 210.

24. *Ibid.*, 3: 210.

25. C. De More-Pontgibaud, *Du fini à l'infini* (Paris, 1957), pp. 121-131; M. T. L. Penido, *Le role de l'analogie en théologie dogmatique* (Paris, 1931), pp. 244-247; Y. Congar, art. "Théologie," DTC 15: col. 473-474; Id., *La foi et la théologie* (Tournai, 1962).

26. It also presupposes, obviously, the aptitude of the human mind to understand and signify the objective reality of things, as well as the capacity of the human mind to be open to all that has the attributes of being and truth.

27. St. Thomas, *In Jo.*, c. 1, lect. 4.

28. Brunschvicg, fr. 556.

29. Ph. H. Menoud points out: "It is not enough, for the salvation of the world, for Jesus to die and rise again; it is also necessary for Jesus to have witnesses and for these witnesses to speak. If it were a question of spreading a philosophical religion like the wisdom of the stoics so well known in the hellenistic age, preachers and teachers would have been enough for the work. But to announce to mankind that men are saved, not by a doctrine outside time, but by an intervention of God in history, by facts that have taken place once and for all, at a given moment and a given place, there need to be witnesses, that is, men who were present when these facts took place and men whose preaching is based on these words: "We have seen." Christian revelation thus necessarily implies two aspects: on the one hand, the redemptive work accomplished by Jesus and, on the other hand, the testimony that the disciples render to the risen Lord.... This amounts to saying that the Church is founded at once on the work of Christ and the testimony of the apostles" (*Jésus et ses témoins*," *Église et Théologie*, June 1960, p. 1).

30. *De praescr.* 21, 4.

31. Thus, the apostles had the whole conceptual knowledge of revelation appropriate to their mission of communicating the deposit of faith in its totality. What is more, they had a privileged understanding of this deposit, thanks to the light of the Spirit who made them penetrate to the very depths of divinity (1 *Cor.* 2: 10).

32. This thought is expressed by the Fathers of the Church, such as Irenaeus (Adv. Haer., III, 1-2), Tertullian (De Praescr., 22), Epiphanius (Haer., 66, n. 61), and also by Saint Thomas: "Those who were closer to Christ, either before, like John the Baptist, or after, like

the apostles, had a fuller understanding of the mysteries of the faith" (1a 2ae, q. 106, a. 4; 2a 2ae, q. 1, a. 7, ad 4; q. 171, a. 1, ad 1).

33. C. JOURNET, *L'Église du Verbe incarné* (Bruges, 1955(2)), 1: 169-170.

34. PH. H. MENOUD, "Jésus et ses témoins," *Église et théologie*, June 1960, p. 9.

35. A *concrete* testimony, however, including also the manner of acting, the practices, the rites.

36. J. BAILLIE, *The Idea of Revelation in Recent Thought* (New York and London, 1956), pp. 29, 32; G. E. WRIGHT, *God who acts* (London, 1958), pp. 35-38, 57-58, 83, 107, 109.

37. R. BULTMANN, *L'interprétation du Nouveau Testament* (trad. O. Laffoucrière, Paris, 1955), pp. 203-214. The same orientation may be found in the article "*apokalypto*" by A. OEPKE, *Theol. Worterbuch zum N. T.*, 3: 575, 586.

38. Saint Thomas observes, quite properly, that the terminus of faith is not the concept, but the reality (2a 2ae, q. 1, a. 2, ad 2; q. 11, a. 1; De Verit., q. 14, a. 8).

CHAPTER V

REVELATION AND LIGHT OF FAITH

For a long time scholastic tradition used the term revelation both for the communication of divine thought made to man under the form of doctrine or message, as well as for the interior grace which moves man to give his free assent to this external word. This manner of speaking was based generally on the texts of scripture which mention, side by side with the external preaching of Christ and the apostles, a revelation, teaching, illumination, attraction, or testimony that comes from within. Saint Bonaventure, for example, attributes faith primarily to an inner hearing, to a revelation (Mt. 16:17), to a "drawing" by the Father (Jn. 6:44). Saint Thomas does not usually take the word revelation to designate this interior activity, but he speaks of an inner instinct,[1] an inner call,[2] an inner attraction.[3] What is really in question here is a grace which invites belief, which moves to faith. After the protestant crisis, a certain number of theologians, primarily Cano and Bañez, continue to use the word revelation to designate the inner illumination of the grace of faith. But, more generally, following Suarez and De Lugo, they reserve this term for the proposition of the object of faith made by Christ and the apostles. Still, theologians never fail to stress the combined activity of the external and internal word. Scheeben primarily, in the nineteenth century, speaks of an inner word and an inner hearing, of a teaching, of an opening of heart, which echoes the external word and gives it life. The theology of the twentieth century is particularly attentive to this inner dimension which gives the word of God its specific character. What then is the nature of this inner revelation, and what is its relationship to the external word? On what grounds does it enter into the notion of revelation? In all logic, what should it be called?

1. Two passages from the Synoptics are constantly brought up by the theologians and fathers of the Church, when they call revelation the inner illumination of the grace of faith. The first comes down in two traditions: "I bless you, Father, Lord of heaven and earth, for having hidden these things from the wise men and the prudent, and revealing them to little ones" (Mt. 11:25; Lk. 10:22). The text opposes the condition of the wise and prudent with that of the "little ones." The wise and prudent are described as Pharisees (Mt. 23:1-12) and all those who are like them, that is, those who claim self-sufficiency, not understanding that, in the order of the kingdom, everything is grace, everything is free gift. The little ones are those who, in all simplicity and humility, like the disciples, recognize their insufficiency in the face of God and are open to His word. Their wisdom comes to them, not from themselves, but from God. To them, God has revealed the mysteries of the kingdom, that is, all that Christ had a mission to make known to men, and especially the persons of the Father and the Son; all this, on the contrary, has been hidden from the wise and prudent of this world. The revelation spoken of here is the inner activity of the Father, and not the mere external proposition of the teaching, for this teaching took place before both the wise and prudent and the little ones. It refers then to a divine operation which is concerned with the acceptance of the doctrine rather than its communication. To recognize the mission of Christ and the truth of His message, there has to be an interior illumination which is the work of the Father. It is Christ, Son of the Father, whose work it is to make known the Father and His secrets; but it is the Father's work to make this external word fruitful so that man will adhere to it in faith.[4]

We find the same expression in Mt. 16:17. Christ, after Peter's confession at Caesarea, addresses these words to him: "Blessed are you, Simon, son of Jonah, for this revelation has come to you, not from flesh and blood, but from my Father who is in heaven" (Mt. 16:17). What are we to understand by this revelation? Obviously it is not a distinct and authentic expression on the part of the Father, added to the declaration of Christ, showing Peter who Christ is; this revelation, rather, is so indistinct that Christ Himself must call Peter's attention to the activity that has taken place in him, since Peter himself was not aware of having been spoken to within. The revelation of which Christ speaks is rather to be compared to that interior activity of the Father which is spoken of in Mt. 11:25, giving Peter, together with the lowly and little people, the power of being open to the external preaching of Christ and confessing Christ for what He is.[5] In confessing that Jesus is "Christ" (Mark), "the Christ, the Son of the living God" (Matthew), Peter is not following the messianic dreams of the Jews of his time, nor only his sentiments of admiration for his master, but he is adhering, in all docility, to the testimony of the Father who is in heaven: he is open to a light which comes from on high.

2. A text in the Acts of the apostles, frequently quoted, stresses how Christians are the product of faith in the apostolic word and the interior activity of God. Lydia, a seller of purple from the city of Thyatira, heard Paul's preaching. Then "the Lord touched her heart to give heed to what was being said by Paul" (Acts 16:14). "Opening the heart," in the Semitic mentality, means enlightening the understanding.[6] While Saint Paul was proposing the divine message, grace was secretly at work in Lydia to enlighten her and to dispose her properly.

3. In his letters to the Corinthians, Saint Paul speaks of divine enlightenment and anointing. In the first passage (2 Cor. 4:4-6), Saint Paul compares the enlightenment which he received with the faith at the moment of his conversion and his apostolic vocation (Gal. 1:15-16; Acts 26:18), to the creation of light on the first morning of the universe.[7] The glory of God, which then shone upon the face of Moses, now shines on the face of Christ; but for us to recognize this, God has to enlighten our hearts: "For God, who commanded light to shine out of darkness, has shone in our hearts, to give enlightenment concerning the knowledge of the glory of God, shining on the face of Christ Jesus" (2 Cor. 4:6).[8]

4. What Saint Paul calls enlightenment, anointing, to designate the activity of God in the genesis of our faith, Saint John calls attraction, testimony, teaching. "No one can come to me, unless the Father who has sent me draw him .... Everyone who has listened to the Father and has learned comes to me" (Jn. 6:44-45). Isaiah (54:13) and Jeremiah (31:33 ff) spoke of the day in which all men would be taught by God himself. This time has arrived. God speaks through his Son (Jn. 1:18). We must listen to Him who has seen God, who comes from God. But, in order to adhere to the word of Christ, it is not enough to have heard His preaching (Jn. 6:21-41), nor to have seen His miracles (Jn. 6:1-21): we also need an inner attraction, the gift of the Father (Jn. 6:66). The adherence of faith is the Father who establishes the beginning through the inclination He stirs up within us, through attraction, through the supernatural drawing which He makes us experience and to which we freely consent. Thus, Christ can say that the Father gives Him those who believe in

His word (Jn. 6:39; 17:9-11. 24; 10:29). In 2 Cor. 1:21-22, Saint Paul uses the term *anointing* to designate the divine activity which stirs up faith in the heart of those who hear the word: "Now it is God who is warrant for us and for you in Christ, who has anointed us, who also stamped us with his seal and gave us the Spirit as a pledge in our hearts." The God who strengthens Paul and all Christians in their faith is He who, through His anointing, has led them all to believe.[9]

The Father who *draws* men and gives them to Christ is also the Father who *testifies*. The Father testifies in favor of His Son by the works of power which He lets Him accomplish (Jn. 5:37), by the scriptures which announce His coming (Jn. 1:45; 5:47), but also by a more intimate and personal testimony (Jn. 5:37; 6:44). In his first letter, Saint John comes back to this same theme, but, this time, expressly mentioning the activity of the Spirit. In a passage that is completely dominated by the theme of faith (1 Jn. 5:5-12), he says: "It is the Spirit who *bears witness*, because the Spirit is the truth" (1 Jn. 5:6). The Spirit bears witness in this sense that He is at work within the soul so that the soul will recognize the truth of Christ and confess that the Son is God. He who believes has consented to the testimony of the Spirit who is at work within him to make him accept the word of Christ.[10] It is the Spirit once again who plants the word of Christ in the soul so that it will remain there as a living and active force; He is the principle of an indefinite assimilation of the word received in faith (1 Jn. 2:27).

In all the passages studied, there is question of an interior activity joined to the external word. This activity is described under the terms of attraction, illumination, testimony, teaching, revelation, anointing. There is someone who acts first in us: the sovereign initiative inviting us to believe in the word of Christ that we hear externally. Our response is free, but grafted on to this initiative of God. In the attraction of grace, the movement of return, that is, man's free response to God's word, is already foreshadowed. The whole Christian life begins with this first submission, this first passivity. The word does not come alone, but with the breath of the Holy Spirit, who works to plant His word, to establish it and make it stay.

The fathers of the Church, in their turn, re-emphasize these expressions of Scripture. We can even say that there is, among them, a real tradition of the interior teacher. The documents of the Church, speaking of the inner attraction which invites us to believe the Gospel message, do not use the term revelation. The Council of Orange speaks of an "illumination and inspiration of the Holy Spirit, which gives us a sweetness of adherence and belief in the truth" (D 180). This expression is taken up by the First Vatican Council (D 1791). The Council of Trent speaks of a grace which "stirs up" (D 798), of an "illumination" through which God "touches the human heart," "stirs it up," "calls it" (D 797, 814). The Vatican Council speaks of an inspiration of grace (D 1789), of an "aid" which comes from on high. God, through His grace, "stirs up" those who are looking for the truth (D 1794). This grace accompanies the preaching of the Gospel message (D 180), the external word (D 798).

II. NATURE AND FUNCTION OF THE INTERIOR ATTRACTION

Beginning with the indications of Scripture and the Church magisterium, let us try to determine the characteristics of this revelation or interior attraction.

1. In many different contexts, Saint Thomas notes that God *invites* men to believe, not only by an external teaching, but also by an *interior instinct*.[11] The Father *draws* men by the word of His Son and by an interior attraction.[12] This divine attraction produces an *inclination* in the soul *by way of nature*.[13] Instinct, inclination, attraction: these terms well describe the reality.

In the natural order, the faculty of knowledge, sense or spirit, tends towards its formal object as its own good, by an innate impulse, that is, by the very nature of its ontological structure, by its constitution and internal dynamism. Thus, before every actual exercise of its innate capacity, the eye is destined for color, the intelligence is destined to grasp being. The formal object thus exercises the function of final cause for the faculty: it *draws*. In the order of faith, man is the free recipient of a new principle of knowledge, of a new formal object. God imprints a tendency, a supernatural impulse in the superelevated intelligence which inclines it towards Him, first truth, as towards its supreme good. God draws the intelligence towards Himself, inviting it to conform its thinking to the thinking of God, its knowledge to the very knowledge of God, personal and subsistent Truth. To believe means voluntarily to abandon oneself to this divine invitation and lean on God Himself, as sovereignly infallible and truthful. This tendency, inscribed in the intellectual activity as a first and deep-seated instinct, like an inclination of nature as Saint Thomas puts it, is *necessary*, for, in faith, the intelligence must renounce its connatural way of knowing, based on evidence, and rely on the uncreated testimony of a God whom it does not see, as upon an absolute. This is a passage from autonomy to "theonomy." Such a surrender on the part of the intelligence is psychologically impossible without a connaturalization of the mind to this superior world to which it now has access. Thus the intelligence, under the control of God who inclines and draws it, can give a total assent to the mystery of His intimate life and His divine plan, such as it is presented in the Christian message.[14] The invitation to believe cannot be reduced to an external manifestation operating through language and signs of power; it necessarily implies also a more profound dimension, the work of the Spirit. Not only does God, through Christ, give us the Gospel, but He also gives us the strength to adhere to it. While the preaching of Christ and the apostles and the Church echoes on the outside and distinctly announces the salvific plan of God, God Himself is at work within our mind inviting it to ratify as true this new order of awareness proposed by the Church.[15]

2. The interior attraction and the external word are closely connected, but the attraction is not a revelation. To speak of revelation in the strict sense, there must be a distinct proposition of a thought content, a distinct invitation to believe this thought content, a distinct perception of this thought content and this invitation to believe as authentically coming from God. Now, in the present case, God is at work within, but His activity remains indistinct. We know the existence of this divine attraction through the sources of revelation rather than through any psychological reflection on the living experience of our own faith. The attraction of truth and the attraction of personal Truth are at this point bound together in the intellectual dynamism which, excepting for the case of extraordinary mystical life, cannot be distinguished by reflex awareness. The divine attraction shows God inviting us to believe, but only obscurely, like a tendency which, in its very exercise, designates the object or terminus of its inner impulse. This attraction acts by way of inspiration and not by way of expression. It needs a further determination which comes from the express word of God, that is, the message of salvation. Its influence, however, is real and decisive in the assent of faith, for it is faith that gives our intelligence the *capacity* to rely on the first Truth, in itself and for itself. It gives us the power to adhere to the Gospel and to the God of the Gospel. But it is not yet the Gospel, nor a new word. It is first in the order of efficient causality, just as the Gospel is first in the order of expression. Strictly speaking, we cannot call it by the name of revelation: it invites us to believe, but it remains anonymous. It is rather an inspiration or illumination of the Holy Spirit (D 180, 1791).[16]

3. Properly speaking, the interior attraction verifies the notion of *testimony*. This attraction, actually, designates "obscurely the God of truth as demanding assent..., relying upon God, who draws or invites, as upon the incomparable guarantee of truth".[17] Now we have already seen that this *invitation to believe*, as guarantee of truth, is the specific element of testimony. God, principle and terminus of the interior attraction of the grace of faith, can also be called in a *broad* but not improper sense a God who testifies. Still, this testimony is not a revelation in the strict sense, for it always remains *indistinct and obscure*. It is completely ordered towards the message of salvation, disposing us to receive and making it possible for the soul to assimilate.[18]

III. TWOFOLD DIMENSION OF THE WORD OF GOD

We cannot speak of the external and internal testimony without giving rise to the question of the connection between these two realities which Scripture, tradition, and the documents of the teaching Church constantly join together. How are the historical Christ, preaching the good news, and the Holy Spirit, at work within our souls, both joined together in the unity of our encounter with God? We are thinking here of two complementary realities, ordered towards each other, making up as it were two dimensions of the word of God.

1. God addresses the soul and invites it to faith in the message which Christ, the apostles, and the Church make heard from without and, complementarily, through the inclination and inner attraction which He produces in the soul. There is the combined activity of the external announcing and the interior attraction. This attraction adapts itself to the external testimony, subtending and subsuming it, giving it life and making it fruitful. Grace *inspires* what the external preaching *expresses* and *proclaims*. Christ and the apostles *declare* what the Holy Spirit *instills* and *implants* in human souls. God testifies by the way of conceptual signs and by the way of interior call. From without, the message of salvation reaches us through a distinct and solidly guaranteed manifestation, inviting us to believe, whereas within the activity of grace makes us perceive the external message and call as a living word, personally addressed to us. The interior attraction *moves* us to give an assent of faith to the first truth, but such as is signified by the concepts and external statements. In one and the same act, we say yes to the Church and to God. But the power to pronounce this assent or to surrender ourselves to God Himself and for Himself proceeds from the interior activity of His grace. Without this we should never be able to believe with a faith properly theological.

2. In one sense we might say that the interior attraction has a primacy over the objective presentation of the message, for in this supernatural inclination produced by God, the object of the tendency is already signified in advance. The attraction is waiting for its object. This is particularly striking in the case of peoples who have not yet heard the preaching of the Gospel. Even before the message comes to them, grace is at work. The attraction of grace obscurely designates the God of truth as the sovereign object capable of fulfilling the appetite of their human intelligence for truth. By this attraction, God already gives and communicates Himself inchoatively; He infuses an inclination towards Himself, supreme truth. Under the influence of this grace, men begin to search, groping at first, vaguely sensing the presence of a mystery of salvation.

This initiative of grace, however, in the actual economy, is ordered towards the Gospel which it prepares, and which is not only a confused suggestion of the mystery of salvation, but the distinct manifestation of God's salvific plan. The Spirit is waiting for the word in order to make it fertile and productive of fruit. In the order of knowledge, which is that of revelation, there is a primacy of message, that is the Gospel, over the interior attraction.

The attraction is given to dispose man to hear the message, to connaturalize man to the divine mystery and give him the power to ratify as true this new order of Kingdom of God. The interior revelation made to Peter bears on the declarations of Christ concerning His mission. The illumination given to Lydia opens her mind with respect to the message she has heard. The attraction of which Saint John speaks is in relation with the teaching of Christ on the bread of life (Jn. 6:21-41): it is destined to make Christ's words bear fruit. The inspiration to believe is in the service of the message. Even at the basis of contemplative and mystical experience, there is always this conformity to the word of God, such as is proposed by the Church. It is this which gives rectitude and authenticity to our impulse towards truth and our encounter with truth. The experience of faith remains subject to the doctrine which judges it. Grace always acts in full dependence upon the teaching. Hence, to put the ineffable experience of the word secretly addressed to the soul in the foreground of revelation is to falsify the perspective of Scripture and the Church teaching office. In the order of revelation, the mission of the Spirit completes and fulfills the mission of Christ. The attraction is in the service of the Gospel. Christ, the apostles, the Church all proclaim the message of salvation, whereas it is the Spirit who makes the hearing of the word fruitful by giving the soul the power to adhere

to it. The combined activity is in view of one single effect: faith. The
The manifestation of the divine plan comes from the Gospel; the
disposition to hear, the power to grasp comes from the attraction.

By reason of this dimension of grace, revelation constitutes a word
of a unique species. Its efficacy as external word is joined by a
particular efficacy which comes from the divine activity penetrating
the very heart of all of the activity of our intellect and will, predisposing
us for the response of faith. This grace is an actual help acting on the
mind: it moves, stirs up, calls, goes before, according to the documents
of the magisterium.

IV. REVELATION AND SACRAMENT

The word of revelation is thus not without analogy with the
sacraments. Like the sacraments, it can be called an efficacious word,
but in a sense which must be described more precisely.

In a general way, revelation and sacrament can be considered as
different and analogous forms of this vast divine economy through
which salvation is given to us by means of signs. In this economy,
sacramentality forms, as it were, concentric circles, following an order
of decreasing efficacy: A. Incarnation of the Word, source of all grace;
B. sacraments properly so called; C. revealed word.[19] Revelation, as
divine word, enjoys its own proper efficacy, superior to that of
human word, inferior to that of sacraments. Whereas human word
can work upon us only from without, the divine word, thanks to the
divine aid which accompanies it, acts at the very heart of our faculty.
Revelation and sacraments are ordered towards salvation, but each
in its own manner. Revelation *tends* to the obedience of faith, which
is "the beginning of salvation, the foundation and root of all justification" (D 801), but it does not produce faith *ex opere operato*, in the
manner of the sacrament. It is efficacious, in the sense that the actual
help which gives it an interior dimension, really stirs up, calls, draws
us towards receiving the message, and really develops in the soul a
power to grasp the new realities which can actually find its fulfillment
in the adherence of faith, if man freely surrenders himself to the
invitation of grace. Nothing is lacking on the part of God, provided
man does not fail the invitation of grace; but the efficacy of this word
is conditioned by the free response of man. In this first and dramatic
encounter between God and man, which is the choice of faith, God,
by His word which is made fruitful by the Spirit, invites man's free
adherence, but without doing violence to his free will. If revelation is
accepted in faith, it leads to the sacraments, which presuppose faith

as the condition necessary for their fruitful reception; for, without faith, the sacraments would be only empty signs, without efficacy.

What is announced by revelation is accomplished by sacrament. The salvation which is preached is at work in the sacrament. Revelation prompts the obedience of faith to salvation which the sacrament effects in us. Salvation, announced by revelation, recognized by faith, is present in the sacrament.[20] "Announce the good news (*kèrugma*) to every creature. He who believes (*faith*) and will be baptized (*sacrament*), will be saved" (Mk. 16:16). "After having heard the word of truth," says Saint Paul to the Ephesians (Eph. 1:13), "the good news of your salvation (*kèrugma*) and after having believed (*faith*), you have been marked with a seal by the Spirit of the promise" (*sacrament of baptism*).[21] Revelation, faith, sacrament are all closely joined together. Revelation is in view of faith, and faith, in turn, is necessary to receive the sacrament. This union makes us better understand that the sacrament is not a magic rite: man must first have faith in salvation announced by God. It is the same in the Old Testament, where the promise of Yahweh and the faith of Abraham are fulfilled in a rite of covenant (Gen. 17; Rom. 4:11), where a bloody rite comes in to ratify the revelation of Sinai and the obedience of Israel (Ex. 24). Thus, the sacrament completes what is begotten by revelation and faith. That is why Christ entrusted his Church with the twofold ministry of word and sacrament. The word is given first of all under the form of word and finally received under the form of Eucharist. Beyond the veil of words, beyond the veil of sacramental species: we advance, through these signs, towards the God of vision.

---

1. *III Sent.*, d. 23, q. 3, a. 3; *IV Sent.*, d. 17, q. 1, sol. 2; *Quodl.* 2, q. 4, a. 6; *In Jo.*, 3. 6, lect. 5; 2a 2ae, q. 2, a. 9, ad 3; a. 3, ad 2; q. 10, a. 1,ad 1; *In Rom.*, 3. 8,lect. 6.

2. *Quodl.* 2, q. 4, a. 6.

3. *In Jo.*, c. 6, lect. 5.

4. L. CERFAUX, "L'Évangile de Jean et le logion johannique des Synoptiques," in: *L'Évangile de Jean* (Louvain, 1958), pp. 147-159; ID., "Les sources scripturaires de *Mt.* 11, 25-30," *Eph. theol. lov.*, 31 (1955): 334 ff.; L. CHARLIER, "L'action de graces de Jésus (*Mt.* 11, 25-30)," *Bible et Vie chrétienne*, 1957, pp. 87-99; A. FEUILLET, "Jésus et la sagesse divine d'après les Évangiles synoptiques," *Revue biblique*, 1955, pp. 161-196.

5. Matthew seems to represent this confession of Peter as a confession of divinity: "You are the Christ, the Son of the living God" (*Mt.* 16:17). Mark however, in the parallel passage, says simply: "You are the Christ" (*Mk.* 8:29). If we consider that this confession takes place after the ministry in Galilee, focused upon the messianism of Christ, and if we also take into account the very human way in which the apostles, before the resurrection, conceived of the messianic role of Jesus, it is possible to consider the text of Matthew as representing a *re-reading* of the event "in terms of a more evolved faith" (P. Benoit, "La divinité de Jésus dans les Synoptiques," *Lumière et Vie*, n. 9 (April 1953), pp. 58-59, 53). The interpretation proposed by D. M. Stanley, even though it is less probable in our opinion, deserves to be reported. The progress of faith in the apostles, he says, is parallel to that of the revelation which Christ makes of the mystery of His person: Christ shows Himself first of all as rabbi and teacher (master), then as Messiah, finally, as glorious Son of the Father. In this continuous ascent on the part

of the apostles towards faith in Christ, we can conceive of special moments. Thus it could very well be that at Caesarea, at a time when the proclamation of Christ's mystery was not yet completed, Peter was as it were carried away by grace beyond his actual knowledge. "Profession of faith in the hidden divinity, not yet consciously grasped, but already accepted in advance" (D. M. Stanley, "Etudes matthéennes: la confession de Pierre à Césarée," *Sciences Ecclésiastiques*, 6 (1954): 51-61).

6. L. Cerfaux et J. Dupont, *Les Actes des apotres* (Paris, 1953), p. 146.

7. The letter to the Hebrews also says that those who have received faith have been "enlightened by the Holy Spirit (*Heb.* 6:4).

8. J. Dupont, *Gnosis, La connaissance religieuse dans les épitres de S. Paul* (Louvain et Paris, 1949), pp. 36-37; D. Mollat, "Nous avons vu sa gloire," *Christus, n.* 11 (1956), p. 316.

9. I. de la Potterie, "L'onction du chrétien par la foi," *Biblica*, 40 (1959): 24, 27.

10. I. de la Potterie, "La notion de témoignage dans S. Jean," in: *Sacra Pagina* (Paris, 1959), pp. 205-206.

11. 2a 2ae, q. 2, a. 9, ad 3; q. 10, a. 1, ad 1. On theology and psychology of faith in Saint Thomas, see in particular: B. Duroux, *La psychologie de la foi chez Saint Thomas d'Aquin* (Fribourg, Switzerland, 1956); J. de Wolf, *La justification de la foi chez Saint Thomas d'Aquin et le Père Rousselot* (Paris, 1946); A. Stolz, *Glaubensgnade und Glaubenslicht nach Thomas von Aquin* (Studia Anselmiana, 1, Romae, 1933); H. Lang, *Die Lehre des hl. Thomas von Aquin von der Gewissheit des ubernaturlichen Glaubens, historisch untersucht und systematisch dargestellt* (Augsburg, 1929); Id., *Die Entfaltung des apologetischen Problems in der Scholastik des Mittelalters* (Freiburg-Basel-Wien, 1962); M. D. Chenu, "Pro fidei supernaturalitate illustranda," *Xenia Thomistica*, III (Romae, 1925), pp. 297-307; Id., "La psychologie de la foi dans la théologie du xiii siècle," in *Études d'histoire littéraire et doctrinale du XIII siècle*, second series (Paris-Ottawa, 1932), pp. 163-191; R. Tucci, "La soprannaturalità della fede per rapporto al suo oggetto formale secondo S. Tommaso d'Aquino," dans: *Aloisiana*, II (Naples, 1961), pp. 1-95; R. Aubert, *Le problème de l'acte de foi* (Louvain, 1958(3)), pp. 43-71.

12. *In Jo.,* c. 6, lect. 5.

13. 2a 2ae, q. 1, a. 4, ad 3; III *Sent.*, d. 23, q. 2, a. 1, ad 4.

14. The same tendency is called *inclination* with respect to its efficient cause and *attraction* with respect to its final cause.

15. E. Dhanis, "Révélation explicite et implicite," *Gregorianum*, 34 (1953): 229-231; J. Alfaro, *Adnotationes in tractatum de Virtutitbus* (mimeographed, Rome, 1959), pp. 140-155; L. Malevez, Théologie dialectique théologie catholique et théologie naturelle," *Recherches de science rligieuse*, 28 (1938): 527-540; M. L. G. des Lauriers, *Dimensions de la foi* (2 vol., Paris, 1951), 2: 253-269; R. Aubert, *Le Problème de l'acte de foi* (Louvain, 1958(3)); B. Duroux, *La psychologie de la foi chez Saint Thomas d'Aquin*, pp. 32-38.

16. E. Dhanis, Révélation explicite et implicite," *Gregorianum*, 34 (1953): 203; J. Alfaro, *Adnotationes in tractatum de Virtutibus*, pp. 157-163.

17. E. Danis, "Révélation explicite et implicite," *Gregorianum*, 34 (1953)ı 231.

18. *Ibid.*, p. 231 and p. 203, note 40.

19. E. Schillebeeckx, "Parole et sacrement dans l'Église," *Lumière et Vie*, 9 (1960): 33-35.

20. E. Schillebeeckx, *ibid.*, pp. 32-39; G. Davis, "The Theology of Preaching," *The Clergy Review*, 45 (1960): 534-538.

21. Cf. 2 *Cor.* 1, 21-22.

CHAPTER VI

MIRACLE AND REVELATION

"In order for the homage of our faith to be in accord with reason, God was pleased to strengthen the inner activity of the Holy Spirit by the external truths of His revelation, divine deeds and above all by miracles and prophecies which, as an excellent sign of the all-power and infinite knowledge of God, are very certain signs of revelation, adapted to the intelligence of all".[1] The First Vatican Council calls miracles divine deeds, proofs, signs. Their function is to establish solidly "the divine origin of the Christian religion".[2] In expressing herself thus, the Church teaching office calls attention to an important function of miracle, namely, its confirmative role: God's approbation, God's seal on a word which claims to be His. The council moreover explicitly refers to the text of the Gospel of Mark on the sending of the apostles: "But they went out and preached everywhere, the Lord cooperating with them and confirming the word through the miracles which accompanied it" (Mk. 16:20). Through miracle, God attests that He is with his envoy and that the word of the envoy is really the word of God. In insisting on the confirmative role of miracle, the council obviously does not mean to exclude its other significant functions. As frequently happens in the case of such interventions, the Church teaching office confirms without excluding.

As a matter of fact, miracle is a *polyvalent* sign. Like many other Christian realities, it acts on several planes at once, it points in different directions. It is in the Gospel that this diversity of aspects appears at its best, for the miracles of Christ are the archetypes of every true miracle. All the miracles in the lives of the Saints borrow from this splendor without ever exhausting it. The same is true of the miracles of the Gospel which we shall now take up in order to study the relationship between revelation and miracle.

1. Sign of God's Agapè

To even the most inattentive examination, Christ's miracles appear first of all as works of mercy and goodness. If God, in Christ, comes towards man and leans towards him, how can this presence be anything other than grace and salvation for man? In Christ, the goodness of God our Savior and his love for men have appeared (Tit. 3:4). The miracles of Christ are a manifestation of God's Agapè, that is, His charity, active and compassionate, which stoops towards all our human misery.

At times, the initiative comes from Christ Himself, anticipating human supplication. In the miracle of the multiplication of the loaves, Christ takes the initiative, Christ "has pity" on the crowd, "because they were like sheep without a shepherd" (Mk. 6:34; 8:1-3). Luke tells how "the Lord had pity" on the widow of Naim and called her son back to life (Lk. 7:13). In the miracle of the man with the withered hand (Lk. 6:6-7), in the healing of the stooped woman (Lk. 13:11-12) and in the healing of the sick man at the pool of Bethesda (Jn. 5:5-9), it is always Christ who takes the initiative.

Other miracles, on the contrary, are presented as Christ's answer to a prayer, sometimes clearly expressed, sometimes silent, contained within a gesture, an attitude. The blind men of Jericho asked Jesus to open their eyes (Mt. 20:29-34). The Canaanite woman is healed because of her insistence (Mt. 15:21-28). The leper implores Jesus on his knees (Mk. 1:40-41). The centurion (Lk. 7:3), Jairus (Lk. 8:40-42), the father of the epileptic son (Lk. 9:38-42), Martha and Mary (Jn. 11:3), all ask Jesus to intervene in their behalf. But the woman with the hemmorhage (Mk. 5:27) and the people from the country of Genesareth (Mt. 14:36) simply touch the hem of Jesus' cloak and they are cured.

All these cures, all these raisings of the dead are acts of love. God visits us in the heart of our infirmities. He has compassion, He is moved, He is troubled in His own human heart (Mt. 11:28). The miracles, under their most obvious aspect, are the response of God's Agapè to the call of human distress. God is love, says Saint John (1 Jn. 4:8). This love, in Christ, takes on a human form, a human heart, to grasp man at his own level, at the level of his misery, and make him understand something of the intensity of the divine love.

2. Sign of the Coming of the Kingdom of Redemption

The prophets of the Old Testament announce not only the messianic era, but also the signs of this era. The messianic age would be a time of miracles. "Then," proclaims Isaiah, "the eyes of the blind will be unsealed, the ears of the deaf will be open, then the lame and crippled will leap like the deer and the tongue of the mute will cry out for joy" (Is: 35:5-6; 29:18); then "the dead shall rise again, their corpses shall come back to life" (Is. 26:19). In the thinking of the prophets, the messianic age will reproduce, on a grander scale, the marvels of exodus. The evangelists see in the miracles of Christ the realization of these prophecies, the accomplishment of God's promises, the salvation they foretold bursting upon the world.[3] This theme of the accomplishment of Scripture even seems to have inspired Saint John in his choice of miracles: signs of living water, manna, light, life.[4] The miracles of Christ, seen from this point of view, are thus bound up with the broader theme of the accomplishment of Scripture. They signify that the kingdom of God, announced by the prophets over the course of centuries, has finally arrived. In Jesus of Nazareth, the Messiah is present. His coming, longed for over so many years, has finally taken place. Thus, in the synagogue of Nazareth, Christ declares explicitly that His miracles designate Him as He who is to come (Lk. 4:16-22).[5]

Peter, in his discourse to Cornelius, sums up the career of Jesus by saying that at His baptism He was "anointed with the Holy Spirit and power" to heal and deliver all those who had fallen into the power of Satan (Acts (10:38). Healing and exorcisms, in the life of Christ, are intimately bound up with His work of salvation. They are equally important in the power conferred by Him upon His apostles: Christ gives them authority to preach, heal, and cast out devils (Mt. 10:1; Mk. 3:14; Lk. 9:1). This is because there is an intimate relationship between sin, sickness, and death. Behind the man who is sick, or possessed, or struck down by death, there is always Satan, the enemy, murderer and liar from the beginning, whose kingdom Christ has come to destroy.[6] Satan reigns through sin, and he extends his empire even over human flesh through sickness and death. Satan makes slaves of humanity like this poor woman whom he has held in bondage for eighteen years (Lk. 13:16). He who is to come, the Messiah, in order to destroy the kingdom of Satan must also triumph over sickness and death. Cures (Is. 35:5-6), and deliverance from sin (Jer. 31:34; Ez. 36:25), miracles and exorcisms must mark the coming of the messianic kingdom.[7]

Christ has come specifically as He who will destroy the reign of Satan. His whole public life is dominated by His awareness of having to carry on a personal combat against Satan. "It is in order to destroy the works of the devil that the Son of God appeared" (1 Jn. 3:8). In the temptation in the desert, His polemic with the obstinate and blind Pharisees, His encounters with the possessed, the lack of understanding and acceptance on the part of the crowds, the treason of Judas, everywhere, in different forms, we recognize the resistance of Satan.[8] But Christ is the "stronger man" of whom the parable speaks (Lk. 11:17-22; Mt. 12:29), overcoming the strong man, binding him in chains, freeing the captives he had held in his power. The change of situation prophesied by Isaiah is now effected (Is. 49:25). The words and actions of Christ are charged with a power which casts Satan out and inaugurates the kingdom of God: "If it is by the Spirit of God that I cast out demons," says Christ, "then the kingdom of God has arrived in your midst" (Mt. 12:28). Coming back from their mission, the sixty-two rejoice because they have power even over demons: "I saw Satan falling from heaven like a thunderbolt," Christ tells them (Lk. 10:17-18). At the same time that sin recedes, its effects, sickness and death, also recede. That is why Christ answers the disciples of John the Baptist: "The blind see, the lame walk, the lepers are cleansed, the deaf hear, the dead rise, the good news is announced to the poor" (Lk. 7:22). Cures and exorcisms mean that the kingdom of Satan is scattered and the reign of God has arrived. Christ is invested with a unique and irrepressible power, which annihilates his adversary and renews everything, body and soul. Wherever Christ is, the power of salvation and life of the living God is at work: it triumphs over sickness and death, just as it triumphs over sin and Satan. Christ is the "stronger" because the *Dynamis* of God dwells in Him and because He uses it at His own pleasure (Mt. 28:18).

So that the Jews will understand that the oracles of the prophets are really accomplished, that Satan is overcome and that the kingdom of God has arrived, Christ accompanies spiritual deliverance with a physical deliverance. He frees man from Satan's bondage and justifies man; and for the eyes of His spectators to bear witness to the salvation He brings, He turns a paralytic into a healthy man (Mk. 2:3-12). The miracle makes the spiritual and invisible renovation something tangible and visible. It makes the presence and salvific activity of Christ visible. His victory over sickness and death is a gauge and figure for His victory over sin and Satan. God remains faithful to the divine philanthropy of the incarnation.[9]

3. Sign of Divine Mission

In the whole biblical tradition, the principal function of miracle is to guarantee a mission as divine. It is a gesture of God attesting the authenticity of a mission that proceeds from Him. Seen under this aspect, it has something of a juridic value: it is a credential for God's envoy.[10] When the prophet presents himself as sent by God, the Jews demand proofs. Moses demands and receives from Yahweh a sign that will prove to him that Yahweh is "with him" and that "his mission comes from him" (Ex. 3:12). The prodigies accomplished by Moses make him heard among his people; they prove that Yahweh has truly "appeared," that men must "believe and hear him" (Ex. 4:1), who is the envoy of God. After the deliverance from Egypt and the passage through the Red Sea, the Jewish people "believe in Yahweh and in Moses his servant" because of the prodigies they have seen (Ex. 14:31). Throughout the whole history of prophecy, miracle is constantly invoked to distinguish between true and false prophets. Thus, Elijah, raising to life the son of the widow of Zarephath, and making fire come down from heaven on Mount Carmel, clearly proves that Yahweh is the true God (1 Kgs. 18:37-39), that he himself is Yahweh's "servant" (1 Kgs. 18:36) and that "the word of Yahweh in his mouth is truth" (1 Kgs. 17:24).[11]

"The Jews demand signs" (1 Cor. 1:22). There is something more than a national characteristic here; there is a human need. Before committing his life to any one's word, man naturally looks for a rational basis: he wants to know to what he is committing himself. When Christ presented His message, He had to meet this human need. Twice, He is asked to furnish signs that justify His actions and claims to being sent by God (Jn. 2:18; 6:30). Thus in the healing of the paralytic (Mk. 2:10), in raising Lazarus to life (Jn. 11:41-42), in His apostrophes against Bethsaida and Corozain (Mt. 11:21), He explicitly appeals to His miracles as guarantee of His mission and His power.

This juridic function of miracle is particularly stressed in the Gospel of Saint John. "Upon seeing his signs," the evangelist notes, "many of the Jews believed in him" (Jn. 2:23). Nicodemus recognizes that Christ "comes from God," for no one could work the signs which He works "if God is not with Him" (Jn. 3:2). The man born blind invokes the traditional argument against the Pharisees who are harassing him: "If this man does not come from God, he could do nothing" (Jn. 9:33). The multitude of miracles, in the eyes of many, is itself the sign: "When Christ comes," they say, "will he work more signs than this man works?" (Jn. 7:31) The triumphal entry into Jerusalem, according to Saint John, was the direct result of Christ's restoring Lazarus to life (Jn. 12:18).[12] The miracles of Christ thus are a proof that He is the envoy of God. Saint Peter, right after Pentecost, in speaking to the Jews, says of Christ: "This man whom God approved among you by the miracles and wonders and signs which God did through him" (Acts 2:22). If Christ performed cures and cast out devils, it is because "God was with him" (Acts 10:38).

The same is true of the miracles worked by the apostles: they are signs which attest to the authenticity of their mission (Mk. 16:20; Heb. 2:4). In Acts, we read that the apostles "rendered testimony to the resurrection of the Lord Jesus" "with much power" (Acts 4:33). The miraculous power of the apostles constitutes a testimony on the part of God Himself: "The Lord gave testimony to the word of his grace by permitting signs and wonders to be done by their hands" (Acts 14:3). The intervention of God *confirms* the apostolic preaching and its object, that is, the fact that Jesus is risen from the dead and that He has the power to save those who believe in him.[13]

4. Sign of Christ's Glory

From the point of view of the beneficiary, miracles are *signs*, but, from the point of view of Christ, they are more properly *works* of the Son. Miracles, envisaged as *works*, are closely bound up with Christ's own awareness of the mystery of His divine sonship and the revelation of this mystery.[14] They constitute the *testimony* of the Father in behalf of Him who is greater than Jonah and Solomon (Mt. 12:41-42), greater than Moses and Elijah (Mk. 9:2-10), greater than David (Mk. 12:35-37) and John the Baptist (Lk. 7:18-28), raised up above the prophets as a son is raised above the servants (Mk. 12:1-12). The miracles, in so far as they are the works of Christ, represent His properly divine activity as Son of God among men. Their function is to guarantee His mission as God's envoy, not, however, in the capacity of simple prophet or human messiah, but in the capacity of Son of the Father, equal to the Father, sharing knowledge with the Father (Mt. 11:27); sharing omnipotence with the Father (Mt. 28:18; Jn. 3:35). They confirm the central claim of Christ's testimony, namely, that he is the Son of the living God.

The Father "loves the Son and has given everything into his hands" (Jn. 3:35). If thus the Father gives the Son His own omnipotence, miracles are the manifest signs of the Father's approbation. They constitute the inimitable seal of the divine omnipotence on the

testimony of Him who says He is the Son of the Father; they show
Him in His glory as only-begotten Son. Through them, the Father
testifies that Christ is truthful (Jn. 6:27). Thus Christ does not cease
to refer His hearers and His opponents to His miracles as the testimony
of the Father in His behalf. "The works which the Father has given
me to accomplish, these very works that I do bear witness to me, that
the Father has sent me" (Jn. 5:36-37; 10:25). We must believe in
Christ, if not because of His words, at least because of His works
(Jn. 10:37-38). The Father's testimony through the works of power
removes every possible excuse from the Jews: their opposition to
Christ is now culpable. "If I had not done among them the works which
no other man has done, they would have no sin; but now they have
seen and they have hated both me and my Father" (Jn. 15:24; 9:41).
Just as Christ works to lead the Jews to an understanding of the
divine sonship, He also works to lead them to see in His miracles
not only signs and prodigies, but the very works of the Son of God,
living and acting in their midst.[15] But this revelation of the works of
the Son, just like the revelation of His person, met with a check
(Jn. 10:31-34). It was however destined to make known, in the
works of Christ, His glory as only Son of the Father (Jn. 1:14; 2:11;
11:40), for Christ stands out among men with the power of Yahweh,
and miracle is the striking use of that power, the action of the Word
of God made flesh.

5. Revelation of the Mystery of the Trinity

The miraculous works of Christ, in the perspective of the fourth
Gospel, are not only the seal of the Father on the word of the Son;
they also give access to the mystery of the Trinity itself. As common
activity of Father and Son, they reveal the profound unity which
joins them both. The works of Christ are at once both His works
(Jn. 5:36; 7:21; 10:25) and the works of the Father (Jn. 9:3-4;
10:32. 37; 14:10). Christ receives them from the Father, from whom
He has everything, who has the initiative in all things (Jn. 5:19-20.
30; 14:10), and who entrusts Him with the duty of accomplishing
them (Jn. 5:36); but at the same time they belong to Him, for the Father
has given the Son all power so that the Son works miracles as His
own proper works.[16] The glory of the Father and the glory of the
Son are indissolubly united. "Just as the Father raises the dead to
life, so the Son gives life to whom he will' (Jn. 5:21). "The works
that the Father has given me to accomplish," says Christ, "these
very works that I do accomplish..." (Jn. 5:36). As a result, to see

Christ's activity is to see the Father present in the Son, exercising, through the works of the Son, His own activity as Creator and Savior (Jn. 14:9-10); it means seeing, in one and the same act of knowledge, both the Son and the Father whom He makes known.[17]

Since the Father thus gives the Son His power and His works, so that miracles are works common to Father and Son, there necessarily exists between Father and Son a unique alliance, the perfect union in action and love, or to be more precise, a unity in love, a mystery of love. The miracles reveal that the Father is in the Son and the Son in the Father, united in one and the same Spirit. Christ tells Philip: "Do you not believe that I am in the Father and the Father is in me? The Father who is in me accomplishes these works. Believe me. I am in the Father and the Father is in me. At least believe because of these works" (Jn. 14:10-11; 10:37-38). "The Father and I are one" (Jn. 10:30; 17:11. 22).

The miracles of Christ must thus be compared to the great works of God in the history of Israel, that is, creation and its prodigy: they are the *magnalia Dei*, at once works of power and salvation, revealing the mystery of God. But regarding both classes of miracles, we must confess that their potentiality as vehicles of revelation appears clearly only in the light of the word which accompanies them. The works of Christ reveal the life of the Trinity, but only in so far as they are combined with the testimony of Jesus regarding Himself and His mission of salvation.[18]

6. Symbol of the Sacramentary Economy

To reduce miracle to its confirmative or juridic value would be a betrayal of Scripture. The miracle is intrinsically bound up with a message. Not only does it accompany the word which it authenticates, but it also manifests its *profound nature* in its own manner. As Saint Augustine points out: "Let us ask the miracles what they have to tell us of Christ; for the man who understands them, miracles have their own language. For since Christ himself is the Word of God, every action of this Word is also a word which speaks to us".[19]

The coming of Christ inaugurates a new world, the world of grace; it effects a revolution, the revolution of salvation through the cross. The miracle lets us see this transformation as it is effected. It is the expressive image of the spiritual gift offered to men in the Person of Christ. The marvels accomplished in the physical order are figures, symbols for the marvels of grace, for the splendor and diversity of its gifts.

In the synoptics, the symbolism of miracles already appears in outlined form. The miraculous catch of fish, in Luke, is a clear sign of the spiritual expansion of the Church through the preaching of the Gospel: "Hereafter you will be fishers of men" (Lk. 5:10). The cure of the paralytic also vindicates the truthfulness of Christ's words: "Your sins are forgiven" (Mk. 2:5). Christ comes to save, to deliver from sin. To testify to the presence of this activity of salvation, Christ prolongs it in the process of bodily salvation. He attacks first of all the root of the evil, sin, but his activity of salvation, in so far as it is tangible, symbolizes the spiritual activity of salvation at the same time that it guarantees it. It is this that is more important, and takes precedence over the other: "Which is easier to say, your sins are forgiven you, or to say take up your bed and walk?" (Mk. 2:9).[20] The visible cure "is the sign of the pardoning of sin, and this is not a purely arbitrary or artificial symbolism; there is an identity of the same act of salvation here, the pardon being the invisible face, whereas the sight of the cured paralytic is the reflection of this inner cure as it can be grasped immediately by our sense nature".[21] The cure of the leper (Mk. 1:40-45) symbolizes the return of the sinner to the society of God's kingdom: this sign is all the more expressive for the fact that leprosy cuts man off from human society, just as sin excludes him from divine society. The miracle of the withered fig tree (Mk. 11:12-14) is a parable in action: it designates and condemns the sterility of the Jewish people. The stooped woman who had been sick for eighteen years (Lk. 13:16), bound by Satan and delivered by Christ, recalls the bondage and deliverance of humanity. The deliverance of the possessed people of Gerasa, whose evil spirits invaded a herd of swine which ran headlong into the sea, is a sign of sin's power for destruction at the same time as it is a sign of the power of Christ, who comes to annihilate the power of Satan (Mt. 8:28-34). The healing of the sick by the laying on of hands (Mt. 9:18; Lk. 13:13) and the anointing of oil made by the apostles over the sick (Mk. 6:13) are a prefiguring of the sacramental anointing made by the Church in the name of Christ (Mk. 16:18; Jac. 5:14-16). For the Jews, who see the profound bond between sin, suffering, and death, this symbolism is already most expressive. Even if Christ does not always stress this relation, the broader context of His doctrine and conduct sufficiently suggests it.

But it is in the Gospel of John primarily that the symbolism of Christ's miraculous activity shines out. His Gospel is properly the Gospel of signs. The miracles there prefigure the sacramental economy. The changing of water into wine at Cana (Jn. 2) inaugurates new creation. Into the stone jars, serving for the legal purification rites, Christ pours new wine, better than the old wine and saved for the last. This new wine is a sign of the new covenant in the blood of Christ, sign of the marriage between Christ and His Church, sign of our entry into the new society by water and blood, that is, by Baptism and Eucharist.[22] The cure of the paralytic (Jn. 5) by Christ's word, forgiving his sins (Jn. 5:14), and by the water of the pool, is a symbol of man's regeneration through the words and water of baptism. The cure of the man born blind, in the pool of Siloe (Jn. 9), is a sign of baptism as illumination: Christ is the light of the world (Jn. 9:5; 1:9; 8:12). Baptism is at once purification and illumination, new birth through water and the Spirit (Jn. 3:5). The healing of the son of the royal official shows the power of Jesus' word and faith in this word (Jn. 4:50). In the multiplication of the loaves (Jn. 6), Christ invites us to believe in the sign of true bread, the "bread of God which comes down from heaven and gives life to the world (Jn. 6:32): an obvious symbol of the Eucharist which was to come. Finally, the resurrection of Lazarus (Jn. 11:1-44) represents Christ as resurrection and life, life that can restore life to what is dead. It symbolizes the total victory of Christ over death and prefigures our resurrection as well as His.

7. Sign of the Transformations of the End-time

Miracle, finally, is a *prefiguration* of the transformations which are to be effected, at the end of time, in the human body and the physical universe. For redemption is not limited to the world of the spirit: it must also invade the entire cosmos with its light and power; it must renew everything that has been touched by sin.

Miracle first of all is a sign of the liberation and glorification of the body. Christ is risen as "the first born from among the dead" (Col. 1:18), as "the prince of life" (Acts 3:15): "He has destroyed death" (2 Tim. 1:10). Now, by the resurrection, the Spirit, who is life and principle of life, has been given to men. If then this Spirit, who dwells in us through grace (1 Cor. 3:16), "has resurrected Jesus from among the dead," He "will also give life to our mortal bodies" (Rom. 8:11). Invisible now, this transformation will appear at the parousia, when the body will be glorified. "This corruptible body must put on incorruption and this mortal body must put on immortality" (1 Cor. 15:53).

Christ's miracles already announce this activity of the Spirit in all flesh. Victory over the diseases of the body prefigures the triumph of life. Life, suddenly rediscovered, is the sign of this life which Christ gives in abundance. The resurrection of Christ is the pledge and pattern for our own resurrection. The transformed body of Christ and the body of the Blessed Mother as His associate in His glory prove that the Lord "will refashion the body of our lowliness conforming it to the body of his glory by exerting the power by which he is able also to subject all things to himself" (Phil. 3:21). When all this is accomplished, flesh will be transfigured in glory.

Miracle is also the sign which announces the redemption of the universe. According to biblical mentality, there is an intimate solidarity between man and the physical universe. Man and earth from which he has been drawn (Gen. 2:7) share the same destiny. The word of God, whether it be judgment or salvation, is addressed *to man in the world*. The whole universe, bound up in the course of human destiny, shares in man's sin and his redemption. Now, according to Genesis, the harmony of creation has been disturbed by Adam's sin. The covenant has been broken between man and his environment: there is a bitter struggle between him and the beasts, between him and the earth (Hos. 4:2-3; Gen. 3:17-18; Jer. 5:6). Disorder is everywhere, in the physical world and in the human conscience. Man learns the hardship of labor, sorrow, sickness, death (Gen. 3:19).

But Christ, by His death and resurrection, has come to re-establish order wherever sin reigns. Redemption must extend its benefits even to the material universe which will rediscover its primitive splendor. The principle of harmony, in paradise, was the presence of God among men. Peace between God and man was the source of peace between man and the world. Sin, breaking the intimacy between God and man, has destroyed this harmony. But now in Christ, God once again dwells among the sons of men (Jn. 1:14). And all creation, once again, is subject to the new Adam. Nature, once again, becomes supple and obedient. The prophets had announced that the times of messianic salvation would mark a return to the peace of paradise, to perfect harmony between man, earth, and the animals (Is. 11:5-9; 35:1-2. 5-9; 41:18-19; Am. 9:13; Joel 4:18-19; Hos. 2:23-24; Ez. 34:25-27; Ps. 91:13; 85:13; Job 5:22-23). Loaves of bread multiply in the hands of the Savior (Mk. 6:30-45); the sea and the winds obey Him (Mk. 4:39); the floods bear up his feet (Mk. 6:49); and the children of new creation, the apostles, take serpents in their hands and drink deadly poisons without experiencing any ill effect (Mk. 16:17-18). These cosmic miracles are the signs that announce the transformations of the eschatological world, the renewal which must mark the terminus of the history of salvation.[23]

Saint Paul, in Rom. 8:19-21, sees man and the universe carried along by the movement of redemption towards their final glorification. "All creation eagerly aspires to the revelation of the sons of God," for it is in "the hope of being freed itself from the servitude of corruption to enter into the freedom of the glory of the sons of God" (Rom. 8:19-20). The universe is called to share in a certain fashion in the glorious state of the sons of God. It will be delivered from its actual state which is "vanity, servitude, corruption," to enter into a new condition which Saint Paul calls the "liberty of the glorious state." The actual universe is "in travail" (the travail of childbirth) towards a better state (Rom. 8:22). For Saint Paul, the universe is not destined to be annihilated, but transformed, glorified; the method of this transformation, however, escapes us.[24]

It is noteworthy that the first chapters of the Apocalypse take up the first chapters of Genesis. When everything is accomplished, flesh will be transfigured in glory. Death will be vanquished. There will no longer be any weeping, any crying, any suffering (Apoc. 21:4). There will be "a new heaven and a new earth" (Apoc. 21:1; 2 Pet. 3:12-13). The river of living water will spring up without ceasing; its banks will be covered with inviting fruit (Apoc. 22:1-2). Between Genesis and Apocalypse, which is the time of Israel and the Church, miracle is a beam of light, prefiguring the full light to come. It shows that the glorified body of Christ is at work to restore creation to its lost splendor. It announces and prefigures the definitive transformation of the universe when the power of God, after having destroyed death and sin, will establish all things in unfailing newness. Saint Ambrose puts it this way: "In Christ the world has risen, heaven has risen, earth has risen. For there will be a new heaven and a new earth".[25]

II. REVELATION AND FUNCTIONS OF MIRACLE

Briefly, according to Scripture, the miracles of Christ appear first of all as manifestation of God's *Agapè* responding to human misery. Then, in the precise context of the prophetic foretellings of the Messiah and His kingdom, they signify that the kingdom announced of old has finally arrived and that Jesus of Nazareth is the long awaited Messiah: they fulfill the Scriptures. Considered in the light of a long tradition which sees miracle as one of the principal criteria serving to establish the authenticity of a divine mission, they certify that Christ is the envoy of God and that His word is truthful; what is more, they certify that He is the Son of God, for miracle guarantees this central statement in Christ's message as true. The miracle proves that, in Christ, God is present and at work; the glory of God is proper to Him and qualifies His being. But at the same time that they are Christ's credentials as Son of God, miracles also enlighten us in the profound nature of His message; they show, on the sense plane, the invisible marvels of the new kingdom; they are the symbols of the world of grace and sacrament. Finally, they let us see, by anticipation, the glorious order of the resurrection of bodies and the transformation of the cosmos, at the end of time.

These different aspects of miracle are not independent of each other. Quite the contrary, one implies the other, explains the other, and we pass from one to another without being aware of the transition. Analysis obliges us to introduce divisions into reality, in order to better grasp its richness; but we must always put back together whatever our analysis has separated, never losing sight of the fact that all the colors of the prism issue from the same brilliant ray of light. If, however, we mean to group and systematize the data of Scripture, it seems possible to reduce the essential functions of miracle with respect to revelation to three: miracle exercises 1. a predispositive function; 2. a confirmative or juridic function; 3. a prefigurative or symbolic function.

1. Miracle first of all *disposes* us to hear the message, for it is a sign of benevolence, the *word of grace*. Miracle, actually, belongs to the genus of word. It enters into the world of signs used by persons to manifest their thinking. It is not simply a trace, a vestige of some presence, some activity, but it expresses an intention of interpersonal meeting. It is a sign from someone to someone, in the sense that we speak of "making a sign to someone." It appears as an address or a response from God. By His miracle, God addresses man, speaks to him, makes a sign to him in nature, with regard to something.[26] The content of this word, obviously, must be defined on the basis of its context. But before all further determination, miracle is a sign which expresses the benevolence of God towards men. That God actually intervenes in nature, in behalf of man, in an extraordinary manner, to heal him, to raise him from the dead, such an intervention can only mean an extraordinary benevolence of the God of love. Miracle, says Blondel, "analogically manifests the real condescension that the order of grace and charity introduces into the relationship between God and man".[27]

Most of Christ's miracles are healings and resurrections, that is, gestures of mercy and goodness. Before being any particular message, they are a word of grace, expression of love. They are like the friendly greeting that comes first and paves the way for conversation.

The Gospel makes a path for itself by way of charity. The first function of miracle, with respect to revelation, is thus to signify the presence and benevolent approach of the God of love and to dispose the soul to hear His good news.

2. In second place, the miracle exercises a *confirmative* or *juridic* function. By the physical transcendence and by the religious context which arises, miracle is presented as a sign of God. Explicitly evoked in behalf of a message which is presented as revealed, it signifies that God approves, sanctions, guarantees. The content of this word of approbation differs radically from the content of this other word which we call revelation. The envoy of God says: "This is what God invites you to believe." The miracle says: "This man is truly my envoy; he speaks in my name; what he says is truth; believe him." Revelation is communication of a message and invitation to believe this message. The miracle is the divine seal upon the message, attestation to its divine origin; it is not the message, but the sign which accredits the witness and authorizes his word. It is God's affirmation on a word which claims to be His. Let us however note the nuances of this affirmation according to the title of the man who speaks. The prophet demands signs from God which confirm his mission as God's messenger: the miracle then recommends the prophet as God's envoy and his word as God's word. Christ, however, declares Himself not only God's messenger, but Son of the Father, equal to the Father. God's affirmation, in this case, must confirm this central truth of His message, namely, that He is God, and, at the same time, all the doctrine which He announces. The Church claims to continue the existence of Christ-God: historically (apostolicity), morally (sanctity), doctrinally (continuity in faith). The miracle, in her case, must attest that God recognizes the truth of her continuity with Christ and with God; it attests the divine origin of her doctrine and her power for sanctification.

By its confirmative function, the miracle is thus the word of divine approbation; it is the seal of God's all-power, stamped on a word which claims to be His. If, as in the case of Christ and the Church, there is a further element, a miracle which is predicted, such a miracle is confirmative on two grounds: both as miracle and as the accomplishment of prophecy. The juridical argument derives new depth from the prophetic argument.

3. The confirmative funtion of miracle, isolated from the other two, would leave the miracle impoverished. In the order of word, the miracle, as a sign of divine approbation, could not ever hope to rival a message expressed in human language: it possesses neither

the richness nor the precision of language. But the confirmative function of miracle is inseparable from its *figurative* or *symbolic* function. Miracle, actually, is closely bound up with the message itself. Its paradoxical transcendence, in the order of nature, makes it marvelously fit to suggest the mystery of our elevation to a supernatural order, for it is the tangible analogue of the revealed mystery. By revelation, the universe becomes the meeting grounds between God and man; God gives it the mission of signifying this mystery, infinitely greater than that which is testified to by the order of natural laws.[28] What is more, by the multiplicity and diversity of its forms, the miracle aptly suggests the richness and diversity of the aspects of the economy of grace and sacrament. Thus, through the *message*, the significant bearing of the analogy of miracle with the world of grace becomes consistent, precise, rich, and the miracle, divine seal stamped on the message, appears no longer as something foreign, but as something related to the message.

On the other hand, the message receives from the miracle a continual accompaniment on the sense plane. The miracle is the *carnal* dimension of the *spiritual* message. In an economy of incarnation, it visualizes the word and puts it in sharp relief.[29] It makes us see what the Gospel says. The Gospel says that Christ has come to save humanity, to deliver it from sin, purify it, give it eternal life. Miracle, in healing the body, and raising the body from the dead, makes us see this spiritual deliverance and spiritual resurrection. It is a reflection in nature of the mystery of salvation. It is a foretaste of the new creation which is inaugurated and waiting for its full glorification. The miracle also demonstrates that the word of salvation is not an empty word, but a word of power, a word of act, the efficacious word of the living God. Miracle and revelation go together: they are the two faces, visible and invisible, of mystery.

Thus, miracle predisposes towards revelation; it authenticates revelation as divine word; it prefigures revelation in our world. These three functions are inseparable, and all bound up with the same reality.

---

1. Ut nihilominus fidei nostrae *obsequium rationi consentaneum* (*Rom.* 12, 1) esset, voluit Deus cum internis Spiritus Sancti auxiliis externa jungi revelationis suae argumenta, facta scilicet divina, atque imprimis miracula et prophetae, quae cum Dei omnipotentiam et infinitam scientiam luculenter commonstrent, divinae revelationis signa sunt certissima et omnium intelligentiae accommodata (D 1790).

2. *Ibid., nn.* 1813, 2145, 2305, 1638, 1639.

3. A. RICHARDSON, *The Miracle Stories of the Gospels* (London, 1956), pp. 134-135.

4. D. Mollat, "Le Semeion johannique," dans: *Sacra Pagina* (Miscellanea biblica congressu·internationalis catholici de re biblica, Paris et Gembloux, 1959), p. 214.

5. The miracles of Christ, in the Judaic context, have therefore a twofold demonstrative value: (1) by virtue of their traditional, juridical function; (2) as accomplishment of prophecies.

6. Ph. H. Menoud, "La signification du miracle dans le Nouveau Testament," *Revue d'histoire et de philosophie religieuses*, 1948-1949, no. 3, p. 180.

7. There was an idea current among Jewish apocalyptic literature that at the moment of the arrival of God's kingdom the devils would be enchained: "In those days they will be led into the abyss of fire, in torments, and they will be forever locked in their prison" (*Book of Henoc* 10:3; translation, F. Martin, Paris, 1906). *The Testament of Levi*, 18: 12, regarding the new priest raised up by God, says: "And Belial will be bound up by him and he will give power to his sons to trample on the evil spirits" (J. Bonsirven, *La Bible apocryphe en marge de l'Ancien Testament*, Paris, 1953, p. 130).

8. L. Monden, *Le miracle, signe de salut* (Bruges, 1960), p. 130.

9. On this aspect of miracle, see: C. Dumont, "Unité et diversité des signes de la révélation," *Nouvelle Revue théologique*, 80 (1958): 136-137; P. Biard, *La Puissance de Dieu* (Paris, 1960), pp. 117-120; L. Monden, *Le miracle, signe de salut*, pp. 127-132; F. Taymans, "Le miracle, signe du surnaturel," *Nouvelle Revue théologique*, 77 (1955): 230-231; A. George, "Les miracles de Jésus dans les Évangiles synoptiques," *Lumière et Vie*, no. 33, July 1957, pp. 18-20; Ph. H. Menoud, "La signification du miracle dans le Nouveau Testament," *Revue d'histoire et de philosophie religieuses*, 1948-1949, no. 3, pp. 177-181; A. Richardson, *The Miracle Stories of the Gospels* (London, 1956), pp. 38-58.

10. It corresponds, according to the expression of R. Bultmann, to the *Legitimationsfrage* (Das Evangelium des Johannes (Gottingen, 1950), pp. 88-89).

11. Miracle, however, is not the only criterion ·of the true prophet. Other criteria are: the prophet's faithfulness to the traditional religion (*Deut.* 13: 2-6), the accomplishment of his predictions (*Jer.* 28: 9; 32:-6-8; 1Kgs. 22: 28), the testimony of the prophet on the supernatural character of his vocation (*Am.* 3: 8; *Is.* 8: 11; *Jer.* 1: 4-6), to which he remains faithful even in persecution and martyrdom.

12. D. Mollat, "Le Semeion johannique," in: *Sacra Pagina*, pp. 211-212; L. Cerfaux, "Les miracles, signes messianiques de Jésus et oeuvres de Dieu," in: *L'Attente du Messie* (Coll. "Recherches bibliques," Louvain, 1958), p. 134.

13. J. Dupont, "Repentir et conversion d'après les Actes des apotres," *Sciences Ecclésiastiques*, 12 (1960): 160-162.

14. H. Van den Bussche, "La structure de Jean I-XII," in: *L'Évangile de Jean* (Coll. "Recherchs bibliques," Louvain, 1958), p. 134.

15. H. Van den Bussche, "Le structure de Jean I-XII," in: *L'Évangile de Jean*, pp. 94-96.

16. A. Vanhoye, "L'oeuvre du Christ, don du Père," *Recherches de science religieuse*, 48 (1960): 404-405.

17. L. Cerfaux, "Les miracles, signes messianiques de Jésus et oeuvres de Dieu," in: *L'Attente du Messie*, pp. 136-137.

18. H. Van den Bussche remarks in this connection: "Le miracle... n'est compris comme oeuvre du Père que par l'explication de Jésus, qui, elle, est à son tour garantie par le miracle. Miracle et discours ne font qu'un seul procédé de révélation. Le miracle se prolonge en discours et le discours fait comprendre le miracle" (La structure de I-XII," in: *L'Évangile de Jean*, p. 93).

19. (S. Aug., *In Jo. tract.* 24, 6: PL 35, col. 1953). Miracles are "the meaningful expression of a divine work, supernatural language, word of salvation addressed to us in intelligible acts. All the grand themes of the Gospel, deliverance from sin, intimacy with God through the sacrament of His Incarnate Word, redemptive meaning of the cross, glory promised and glory already present, all these themes are expressed in action in the miracles of Jesus, they become lived images and symbols full of meaning" (L. Monden, *Le miracle, signe de salut*, pp. 102-103).

20. R. Schnackenburg, *Gottes Herrschaft und Reich* (Freiburg, 1959), pp. 59-62; A. Schlier, *Machte und Gewalten im Neuen Testament* (Freiburg, 1958), pp. 37-49.

21. C. Dumont, "Unité et diversité des signes de la Révélation," *Nouvelle Revue théologique*, 80 (1958): 137.

22. D. Mollat, "Le Semeion Johannique," *Sacra Pagina*, p. 212; F. Bourassa, "Thèmes bibliques du baptême," *Sciences Ecclésiastiques*, 10, (1958): 429.

23. E. Beaucamp, *La Bible et le sens religieux de l'univers* (Paris, 1959), pp. 187-192.

24. S. Lyonnet, "La rédemption de l'univers," *Lumière et Vie*, no. 48, July-Aug. 1960, pp. 43-62.

25. *De Fide resurrectionis*, second nocturn of the fifth Sunday after Easter. See also H. Holstein, "Le miracle, signe de la Presence," *Bible et Vie chrétienne*, no. 38, March-April

1961, pp. 56-58; L. Monden, *Le miracle, signe de salut*, pp. 36-37. De Grandmaison stresses this aspect of the miracle. He shows that miracles are the sign of the presence of the Son of God in the world of sin. Under the activity of its Creator, who comes to redeem and remake what sin had enslaved and destroyed, the world rediscovers its initial splendor. Miracles are the sign of this transformation, of this return to the splendor of the first beginning. "Signs of a higher, spiritual, eternal reality, works of light and goodness, they are also works of power and, as such, they begin to inaugurate the kingdom of God which they represent so vividly. By their brilliance, they draw the attention of those who are far removed from believing, too lazy or too frivolous. But they also promte the work of re-establishing the world. The evil spirits are humiliated, effectively opposed, cast out; sicknesses, defects, the miseries of original sin are lessened, removed, overcome. Evil, in all its forms, recedes. The mastery exercised by the first man in the days of the world's innocence, a concept whose mere image enchanted the eyes of all later humanity like a beautiful dream, suddenly re-appears like the first faint trace of dawn, the humble overture of a total re-establishment, pledge of the day on which souls and bodies together will be saved, to live in God" (*Jésus-Christ* (Paris, 1928), vol. 2, p. 368).

26. E. Dhanis, "Qu'est-ce qu'un miracle?" in: *Gregorianum*, 40 (1959): 228.

27. "Miracle," *Vocabulaire philosophique* de Lalande (Paris, 1951), p. 632.

28. E. Dhanis, "Qu'est-ce qu'un miracle?" in: *Gregorianum*, 40 (1959): 232-233; L. Monden, *Le miracle, signe de salut*, p. 30.

29. F. Taymans, "Le miracle, signe du surnaturel," *Nouvelle Revue théologique*, 77 (1955): 234-235.

CHAPTER VII

CHURCH AND REVELATION

With Christ and the apostles His witnesses, revelation is completed. God no longer addresses any other word to us, but He continues to address the word which He has spoken once and for all. For the Church, which is born from the word of Christ, preserves this word and never ceases to meditate upon it, to say it over again, to explain it to the men of all centuries. Between the Church and revelation, between the Church and the word, there is thus a manifold and vital relationship. The Church depends on the word, and the word depends on the Church. These are the relationships we shall now examine. What is the relationship between word and the mystery of the Church and its growth? How can the Church, in its turn, be of service to the word? What is the nature of her activity with respect to the message of salvation and with respect to men to whom this message is addressed?

I. THE WORD CALLS THE CHURCH INTO EXISTENCE

It is the word of Christ which initiated the apostles into the secrets of the Father, and it is the same word which founded the Church by giving the apostles the threefold power to preach, sanctify, and govern. It is from the word of Christ that the apostles received the mission to invite men to faith and to incorporate them, through baptism, into the society of the Father and the Son, in the same Spirit: one faith, one baptism, one Spirit (Eph. 4:5). In one sense, we can thus affirm that the Church is *convoked and engenderd* by the word. "It is I," says Saint Paul to the Corinthians, "who, by the Gospel, have begotten you in Christ Jesus" (1 Cor. 4:15). Christians are *called* by the Gospel of Christ (Rom. 1:6). Before being a Eucharistic and baptismal community, the Church must be an evangelical community, that is, a community convoked by the word. From the very beginning, the life of the Church depends on this word which engenders and nourishes it.[1]

In the language of the *synoptics*, it is the word of God which founds the new kingdom (Mt. 13:19). The parables only describe the history of this foundation. In the parable of the sower, the word is sown in the hearts of men so that they will hear and understand (Mt. 13:23), that is, so that they will believe (Mk. 4:9; Mt. 11:15; Lk. 14:35) and produce the fruits of life (Mt. 13:23). Like leaven, the word tends to unite men in one single living bread (Mt. 13:33).

The *Acts of the Apostles* shows us the primitive Christian community called into being and nourished by the word. It is through the preaching of Peter that the community at Jerusalem was born, welcoming the word and being baptized (Acts 2:41-42). The Jews in Samaria, after the preaching of Philip who "announced the good news of the kingdom of God and the name of Jesus Christ," also accepted the word and had themselves baptized (Acts 8:12. 14). In these first times of the Church, the word manifests such a dynamism that Acts represents it as a sort of personal entity: "The word of God grew and multiplied" (Acts 12:24); the "word of the Lord spread throughout the whole region" (Acts 13:49).

For *Saint Paul*, the Church is the assembly drawn together by the divine convocation expressed in the Christian message (Rom. 1:6; 1 Cor. 1:2). It is founded on the preaching of the apostles (Eph. 2:20). The Church at Corinth is born from Paul's preaching (2 Cor. 3:3). The Ephesians, for having believed in the word of truth, the Gospel of salvation (Eph. 1:13), had been incorporated into the people of God. The word of God fructifies and develops in the entire world (Col. 1:6; 1 Thess. 1:8); it tends toward the building up of the body of Christ which is the Church, to the constitution of the perfect Man, of the whole Christ, head and members (Eph. 4:11-13).

For *Saint John*, Christ is the good shepherd who calls all His sheep so that there will be only one flock and only one shepherd (Jn. 10:16). This calling together of all man by the word is the great preoccupation of Christ: "I have given them (apostles) your word. ... Consecrate them in truth: your word is truth. ... I do not pray for them only, but also for all those who, through their word, will believe in me. May they all be one. Just as you, Father, in me, and I in you, let them be one in us" (Jn. 17:14, 17, 20-21). The word of Christ is to prolong, among men, the unity of Son and Father, in one and the same Spirit of love and truth.

This building up of humanity to the image of the society of the Trinity is a work of grace. The word convokes and begets the

Church, not by itself, but with the Spirit. From Pentecost to the second coming, the word and the Spirit work inseparably to build up the body of Christ. "The Holy Spirit is, together with the apostolic ministry or the Church institution, the agent who realizes the work of Christ".[2] What the apostles and the Church accomplish in a visible way, the Spirit accomplishes invisibly in the heart of men. This is a necessity of nature, for the word tends to build up "a chosen race, a royal priesthood, a holy nation" (1 Pet. 2:9). The people of God are convoked by a twofold call: through the preaching of the Gospel (Rom. 10:14-17; 2 Thess. 2:13-14) and the invitation of grace (Acts 16:14; Jn. 6:44; 2 Cor. 1:21-22; 4:5-6). Vocation, the divine act which follows upon election, in God, is expressed without by the word and within by an activity whose author is the Holy Spirit. Thus, the body of Christ which is the Church is constantly growing up to the final revelation of sons of God, but this mystery of growth is the fruit of the word of revelation, made fruitful by the Spirit.

II. THE CHURCH "MAKES PRESENT" THE WORD

The word of God convokes and begets the Church. But, in its turn, the Church makes the word present for the men of all time. Through the Church, Christ speaks to the men of each generation, makes known His plan of salvation and urges them to be converted (Mk. 1:14-15). The Church, according to Msgr. Martin, in the First Vatican Council, is a "sort of concrete revelation" (*quasi concreta est revelatio*).[3] Through the Church, revelation is always present and always active (Lk. 10:16; Mt. 10:40). The time of the Church is the time in which the Gospel is made known to every creature (Mk. 16:15): it is the "acceptable time," the time of salvation (2 Cor. 6:2), the *today* of God, in which each man is called to conversion (Acts 3:20; Heb. 3:7-10; 4:7). In the Apocalypse, the Church is represented as the place of God's final revelation; just as, in time, the Church is the Temple in which the word of God does not cease to echo (Eph. 2:19-20). It is the paradise from the midst of which springs forth the word which fertilizes the entire land, like a pure and unsullied fountain.[4] She is the Bride of Christ who, after having received the word of her bridegroom, constantly meditates on it in order to tell it to all men in turn, living and faithful as on the first day.[5]

The preaching of the word, for the Church, is not only an honor, but a mission, which derives from the express commandment of our Lord (Mt. 28:18-20; Mk. 16:15-16; Jn. 17:18-20). The ministry of the word proceeds from Christ, historically, juridically, actively. To preach, to evangelize, for the Church, is an obligation; for the Church is the Church of the word just as she is the Church of the sacraments. The apostle's duty is to announce the Gospel, for he is the minister of the word as well as the minister of the sacraments. The Acts of the Apostles begins with Christ's words which make the apostles His witnesses (Acts 1:8) and ends with Saint Paul preaching and teaching (Acts 28:31). The apostles have to choose between several ministries: they choose the service of the word (Acts 6:2-4). Paul declares: "Christ did not send me to baptize, but to announce the Gospel" (1 Cor. 1:17). "The Lord stood by me and strengthened me," he said, "that through me the preaching of the Gospel might be completed and that all the Gentiles might hear" (2 Tim. 4:17).

Preaching, in the actual economy of salvation, is necessary and irreplaceable; for faith is necessary for salvation and faith rests on the preaching of salvation. For Christ to be known and for the Father to be glorified, there must be mouths to announce His word. But how can men call upon a God "in whom they have not believed? And how are they to believe Him whom they have not heard? And how are they to hear, if no one preaches? ... Faith then depends on hearing, and hearing on the word of Christ" (Rom. 10:14-17). The ministry of the word belongs to the very structure of the Church. If the Church becomes silent, if the word ceases to echo throughout the world, the world will die in ignorance of the salvation which is offered to it. The preaching of the word belongs to the prophetic mission of the Church. Just as the prophets of the Old Testament were the mouth of God in Israel, the Church is Christ's mouth and the instrument of the Spirit for proclaiming the Gospel. It does not cease to announce the event of salvation so that all humanity, having heard the word of God and adhering to it through faith, can enter for all eternity into the intimacy of the Trinity's own life.

This task of making revelation *present* to all times is effected first of all through preaching, through *living*, incarnate preaching. The spoken word cannot be replaced by the written text. The word of God already possesses an objective intrinsic efficacy, which makes it analogous to sacrament;[6] but, more than in the sacrament, the person of the preacher has a role to play here. Actually, what the preacher passes on is not a pure system of thought (the material of a teaching which he could communicate without committing himself) but a *message of salvation*, bound up with an event which has changed the meaning of human existence, and first of all, his own individual existence.[7] Into the breach forced by misery and sin, Christ has introduced hope. He has come as light and life (Jn. 14:5; 9:5). By His death and resurrection, He made us into sons of the Father, called to a share in His life and glory. What the preacher announces as good news and what he testifies to as man's ultimate truth, is the very treasure of which he himself is the first beneficiary. He preaches the hope that has already enlightened and transformed his own living. And thus the hearer of his word expects to find in him a reflection of this hope. He preaches Christ, who is the all of his life. And thus, his life must show the Gospel's aptitude to transform human existence; it is in living from the Spirit of Christ that he preaches Christ effectively. Consequently, true preaching must be at once a *service* and a *testimony*, that is, a word springing from a commitment, with holiness of life for its credentials. Otherwise, the very service of the word will betray signs of sluggishness and disinterest. The servant of the word must announce Christ in the power of the Spirit who dwells in him and testifies in him. This commitment of his own person presents a spectacle of the Gospel in action, and demonstrates at once its truth and efficacy. Such a spectacle moves the man who hears him to desire a share in his universe of values which the word opens up before him. It is from this desire, made fertile by the Spirit, that faith can have its birth.[8]

This demand for a preaching authenticated by living is a logical conclusion of the fact that the essential element of the Christian message is the revelation of God's love through the love of Christ. The mystery of infinite love, as manifest in Christ, must be the goal envisioned by the Gospel preaching. Now, how can we introduce anyone to love a person excepting through a contagious love? How can we open man to the love which is offered him excepting through contact with a man who is already smitten with this love? The love of Christ must already have invaded the heart of the apostle, so that souls will see, in the preacher, the God who is loved and the God who loves. The word they hear must stir up in them the reflection of the disciples on the road to Emmaus: "Was not our heart burning within us when he spoke to us on the way and explained the Scriptures?"

III. THE CHURCH, GUARDIAN AND INTERPRETER OF THE WORD

Revelation closes with the apostles (D 2201). God has made us know once and for all his message of salvation through Christ and the apostles. The doctrine of faith has been definitively constituted by the deposition of these official witnesses. On the other hand, however, the word of God must always abide as living and alive as it was at its first beginning. The man of the twentieth century must feel that he is touched as intimately and immediately as the Jew, Greek, or Roman of the first century. It is a word addressed to a determinate milieu, at a certain moment in time, but still it must meet all men of all times, grasp them in their own particular historical situation, unique for each one, answer their questions, their uneasiness, and lead them on the path towards God. Thus we are once again confronted with the problem of the historicisation of revelation. How can the word adapt to each successive generation, without ever undergoing any deviation, any slight change in meaning, any contamination? How, over the long succession of centuries and the mixture of many civilizations, over the course of infinite changes in political, social, and economic structures, can the word always remain identical, and still always new, always present, like the first morning of Pentecost? These questions introduce us to the role of the Church with respect to the deposit of faith.

As depositary of the word, the Church has received the mission to preach the Gospel and to interpret it authentically; she is endowed with the power of understanding this word with a freshness that is always new, in order to answer the questions of each generation.[9]

In understanding the role of the magisterium, there are two excesses to be avoided: 1. The Church does not replace the sources of revelation, as many present-day Protestants think, such as G. Ebeling,[10] W. von Loewenich,[11] and W. Schweitzer,[12] who see the Catholic Church as an *absolute* which succeeds Christ and simply passes Him down in history, without any need to be taken up with Scripture or tradition; 2. going back to the sources, for the Church, is not, as L. Charlier sees it, a process of primarily historical interest, the deposit of faith being reached only in the Church's present.[13] The Church's language is quite different when she speaks about herself: she defines herself in reference to the deposit, calling herself simply *guardian* and *interpreter* (D 1793, 1800, 1836, 2145, 2307). The word comes to us through Scripture, tradition, and the magisterium, and these three are intimately bound up togther. To hear the Church means to hear the word written and handed down by tradition, such as it is understood and explained by the Church. In this sense, the magisterium, with respect to the faithful, is the proximate and universal norm of truth (D 2313). It is not the *constitutive* rule of faith, but the *directive* rule with respect to the word received from the apostles.[14]

The documents of the Church assign a threefold function to the Church magisterium with respect to the deposit of faith. It must protect, preserve holily, faithfully, as a deposit, the doctrine received from Christ and the apostles (D 792a, 1781, 1793, 1800, 1836, 2145, 2307, 2313, 2315). It must protect it, defend it against error (D 792a, 1817, 2313). Finally it must faithfully expound revealed doctrine, declaring it according to its true meaning, interpreting it authentically (D 1800, 1836, 2313, 2314, 2307). The doctrinal authority of the Church has this work of preservation, defense, and interpretation as its primary end. It is exercised through the ordinary magisterium (unanimous teaching of the bishops or doctors of the universal Church) or through the extraordinary magisterium (ecumenical council or the Pope speaking *ex cathedra*) by means of definitions.

As the depositary of God's word, just like Israel of the Old Testament, the Church must first of all preserve the deposit which has been entrusted to her. To preserve the deposit means to guard it in its integrity, to let nothing fall into oblivion, but also not to add anything to the sum of truths attested, to introduce no novelty, to invent nothing. To defend the revealed word means to protect it by answering difficulties and objections raised against it, but also, and more immediately, to proscribe errors, condemn them, to call attention to deviations, and shifts in emphasis. To *expound, declare, interpret*: these terms refer to the work of growing assimilation of the word in the Church. For the Church, who has received the word, preserves it as a living entity whose principle of assimilation is the Holy Spirit. What the Church has received is not an inert and lifeless treasure which she must preserve like a precious heirloom, but rather a living word; it is not an unproductive treasure, like the talent which the profitless servant buried in the earth, but a fount of living water from which the men of all times shall never cease to draw. Like the faithful Virgin who "preserved and meditated all these things in her heart," the Church does not cease to meditate upon the word she has received. The Bride of Christ has a contemplative soul: she never stops meditating the word of Christ, her Bridegroom, assimilating it, finding new depths within it, thanks to the unbounded discernment which comes to her from the Spirit. For this word is of an infinite richness (D 2314): it never stops stirring up the heart and the understanding. It is not a domain whose exploration will be finished someday, but rather an abyss which opens more and more as the eye grows used to its depths.

To describe this movement of assimilation of the word, this growing awareness, ever more and more precise, of the riches of revelation, the Church speaks of a passage from the implicit to the explicit,[15] from the obscure to the clear (D 2314). In the encyclical

Humani generis, we find the two expressions joined: "to the sources of revelation, God ... has joined the living magisterium of the Church to enlighten and expound whatever was to be found only *obscurely* and as it were *implicitly* in the deposit of faith".[16]

The magisterium *makes explicit* what was only implicit in the sources of revelation. Thus, in the statement: The Word was made flesh (Jn. 1:14), the following truths are implicitly contained: Christ has a human nature; He had body and soul, human intelligence and will; the humanity of Christ is adorable, Christ's heart is adorable. The progress is effected here by a simple process of unfolding, bringing to light a truth explicitly attested to by Scripture. Or else the Church magisterium casts light on what was contained only obscurely in the sources of revelation. Thus, on the basis of the scriptural data on the privileges of the Blessed Mother, through a growing penetration of the relationship between Mary and Eve, Christ and the Church, by an assiduous reflection on the grandeur and holiness of Mary, the Church grasped and defined more clearly the luminous points of which she had a feeling from the very beginning; she came to a more precise appreciation of the dimensions of certain fundamental facts (Mary, Mother of God; Mary, new Eve; Mary, Christ's associate in the victory over sin and death) and thus defined the Immaculate Conception and the Assumption of the Blessed Virgin. This is not so much a question of linear reasoning as a new awareness of perspective, a more precise perception of already existing traits, thanks to a more penetrating enlightenment.

The end result of this process is thus not the deposit of the faith objectively and definitively constituted, but rather our understanding of revelation (*quoad nos*) by an assimilation which takes place at the interior of the object of faith. It is a question of new precision, certainly, but always homogeneous with the primitive (original) truth, always situated at the interior of the object of faith, proof, thus, against any passage from the order of truths of salvation to truths of any other order, even though they are connected with dogma itself.[17] Thus, the movement of revelation which has been constituted, throughout the whole Old Testament, up to the time of Christ and the apostles, is now linked with a movement which assures the progress, not of revelation, but of the *understanding* of revelation and its mastery through formulations that are constantly clearer and more explicit.

The Church had been favored with a charism in order to preserve and authentically declare revelation. The Holy Spirit assists the Church in her mission as *custos et magistra verbi revelati* (D 1793), that is, strengthens her with a special actual assistance in order to preserve, defend, and interpret the deposit of faith. This is an infallible assistance, not merely negative, but also positive; for this charism enters in as one of the factors in dogmatic progress. Not only does the Spirit preserve the Church against error, but He also guides her towards the fullness of truth. The Church does not cease to be "taught by the Holy Spirit",[18] who is at work in her by the way of "suggestion" (D 873a, 792a) and "directs her infallibly towards a more and more perfect knowledge of revealed truth".[19] In expressing itself thus, the Church magisterium refers obviously to the passages of Saint John where he says that the Holy Spirit will "teach" the apostles and will "bring to their mind" all that Christ has said (Jn. 14:26). The Holy Spirit will guide them towards the whole truth (Jn. 16:12-13) and He will "render testimony" with regard to Christ (Jn. 15:26). These texts, in the light of Christ's promise to assist His own "until the end of the world" (Mt. 28:20) and by the promise of a Paraclete, Spirit of truth, who will be with the apostles "forever" (Jn. 14:16-17), cannot be completely understood unless the assistance promised first of all to the apostles also extends to their successors, and thus to the Church of all times.[20]

Still, the work of assimilation and interpretation of revelation, as undertaken by the magisterium with the assistance of the Holy Spirit, does not imply a new revelation. "The Holy Spirit," says the First Vatican Council, "has not been promised to the successors of Saint Peter so that, in virtue of a new revelation of which he would be the author, they might manifest a new doctrine, but rather so that in virtue of his assistanse, they would holily preserve and faithfully expound the revelation handed down by the apostles".[21] With Christ and the apostles, His witnesses, the fullness of time has arrived. The Church cannot count on new revelation on which to base her teaching; her mission is to preserve and expound revelation given once and for all. The assistance she has guaranteed is analogous to the inspiration of the light of faith. In both cases, the Spirit is at work through attraction, inclination. Never does the help of grace make itself felt and heard as the distinct word of God inviting belief in a new content of thought: it always remains hidden like those graces which are of the order of inspiration.

Thus, there is progress in the *understanding* of the word, always more profound, more detailed, more precise, but there is not ever any new message, any new mystery. There is *interpretation* of revelation, but no change in meaning. The Church, little by little, discovers the dimensions of the revealed mystery. Each epoch brings a new enlightenment, thanks to which obscure points become more manifest, and hidden details stand out in new light. But the more that is discovered the more it all remains the same: like the features of a face coming out of shadow towards the light.

The occasions for this dogmatic development can be attacks against the Church, heresies (Docetism, Arianism, Nestorianism, Protestantism), controversies among theologians, practical difficulties, the particular problems of a given era, the progress of the sciences, private revelations. But the positive factors are: 1. theological research; 2 the suggestion of the Holy Spirit in the consciousness of the faithful and in the consciousness of the magisterium; 3. the charism of infallibility.

Theological research is an understanding of the faith exercised under the control of the Spirit. This research, which enlists all the resources of human reasoning, can also count on a higher power of penetration which is the fruit of living faith and the gifts of the Spirit, whenever it is carried on in what are its best conditions, namely by a theologian who is at once teacher and confessor. The gift of intelligence, primarily, makes the mind more acute in penetrating the truths of faith.[22] The gift of wisdom infuses in the soul of the theologian, with respect to the object of faith, a connaturality of feeling which lets him judge correctly, according to the divine thinking.[23] He becomes like a friend who, in virtue of his feeling and affection, can penetrate his friend's thinking better than anyone else; the theologian possesses in himself the anointing of Christ which, like a sure instinct, directs his progress and gives it life, making it coincide with Christ's thinking and helping him to correctly grasp the implications and conclusions (1 Cor. 2:10-16; 6:17).

The Spirit's activity of inspiration is at work in accordance with individual functions: thus, it is at work in the Church taught as well as in the Church teaching. This activity of the Spirit in the body of the faithful is real and powerful. It has in fact happened that the intuition of the faithful, under the motion of the Holy Spirit, in some respects goes beyond the analysis and conclusions of theological research. Such is the case, for example, in the dogmas of the Immaculate Conception and the Assumption. The Pope has guaranteed that these two truths were a part of the faith of the universal Church, and, with his charism of infallibility, he sanctioned this universal faith.

For the principal and determining factor of dogmatic progress is always the infallible declaration of the Church magisterium. It is the charism of infallibility, given to the Church to preserve, defend, and expound the doctrine of faith which, in the last analysis, guarantees us that the truth presented as revealed is not the fruit of illuminism on the part of the faithful, nor an outburst of popular imagination, but a truth really testified by God and contained in the deposition of the apostolic witnesses.

IV. THE CHURCH, SIGN OF REVELATION

Not only does the Church make revelation constantly present by her preaching; not only does she propose and interpret it authentically for each generation, but she also constitutes, in herself, a great and perpetual motive for credibility in behalf of revelation. God, in making known His word, has never separated His word from the signs which authorize it as divine. From the very beginning, the proclamation of the Gospel was bound up with the signs of the kingdom, primarily miracles and prophecies (D 1790). These signs lose nothing of their force to establish the fact of revelation, but, normally, contemporary faith is based less upon miracles and the Scriptures as such than on the ever present sign of the Church.

The Church is thus at once the instrument which receives and actualizes the ancient signs and the instrument which, by her always contemporary presence in the world, is herself a sign that her mission and doctrine are from God. "It is to the Catholic Church alone," says the First Vatican Council, "that all the numerous and admirable signs belong which are disposed by God for making the credibility of Christian faith clearly apparent. What is more, the Church, by reason of her admirable propagation, her preeminent holiness, her inexhaustible fecundity in everything good, by reason of her Catholic unity and invisible stability, is, in herself, a great and perpetual motive of credibility and an irrefutable testimony to her divine mission. Thus it is only natural that she herself, like a standard raised up among the nations (Is. 11:12), calls to herself all those who have not yet come to believe and thus augments in her children the assurance that the faith they profess rests on a most firm foundation".[24] The Church, in herself, is a moral miracle.[25] Just as Christ *was a sign* to the men of his time by the radiation of His whole person (doctrine, witness, holiness, miracles), even so the Church, by the radiation of her whole being (spreading, unity, stability, holiness, fecundity), *is a sign* to the men of all times that she has her mission and her message from God Himself. She shares in the glory of Christ.

This aspect of the Church, which makes her a sign of revelation, is not a discovery on the part of the First Vatican Council. The argument is a traditional one in the Church. From the first centuries, the Fathers, primarily Irenaeus, Tertullian, Origen, Augustine, appealed to it to defend Christianity, its miraculous spread, the constancy of its martyrs, the brilliance of its holiness. The argument is taken up again by Savonarola, in the fifteenth century, by Bossuet and Pascal in the seventeenth century, by Fenelon in the eighteenth century, by Balmes, Lacordaire, Bautin and Dechamps in the nineteenth century, and, immediately before the Council, by J. Kleutgen and J. B. Franzelin.[26] The magisterium of the Church, however, in sanctioning the force of this argument by her own authority, has definitively consecrated it and has thus become a point of departure for a most fruitful theological reflection.[27]

The Church, as sign of revelation, can be envisaged from a dogmatic point of view and from an apologetic point of view. The dogmatic point of view sees the secret of the Church's external glory in the light of faith itself. The apologetic point of view, contemplating first of all the external brilliance of the Church, asks after the source of this brilliance; it searches for an explanation which is in proportion to the phenomena of this exceptional society. These two ways of looking at the Church are not opposite, but rather complementary. The mystery explains what is astonishing in the fact observed, whereas the miracle makes us alert to the presence of mystery.[28]

Let us examine first of all what we can discover from the *dogmatic* or descending point of view. The first society, the protoype and source of all societies, is the society of the Three Divine Persons. In this society, there is perfect unity of Father and Son in one and the same Spirit. "The Father loves the Son and has given everything over into his hands" (Jn. 3:35; 5:21, 26, 36; 17:4, 8, 11). "All that the Father has is mine," says Christ (Jn. 16:15). "All that is mine is yours, and all that is yours is mine" (Jn. 17:10). In return, Christ *loves* the Father with an unreserved love. The will of the Father is His food and drink, that is, His life (Jn. 4:32-33). It is the law of His teaching (Jn. 7:16; 12:50), of His mission (Jn. 6:38-40; 7:28; 8:42), of His sacrifice (Jn. 10:17-18; 12:27-28; 14:30-31; 19:30). Christ is the *Amen* of the Father, who always says *fiat* to the Father's will (Heb. 10:5-7; Lk. 10:21). This intimacy of life is expressed, in Saint John, in the formulas of mutual "inherence": "The Father is in me and I am in the Father" (Jn. 10:38). "The Father and I are one" (Jn. 10:30). The Spirit is the outpouring of the mutual and common love between Father and Son.

God, through Christ, wanted to introduce man into this society of love. He wanted men, scattered, divided, children of wrath and iniquity, to be gathered together and united among themselves in charity, in the image of the society of the Trinity: "That they may be one in us" (Jn. 17:11); He wanted the element of cohesion between men to be the very love with which the Father gives the Son all that He has and the Son, in like manner, gives the Father all that He has: "I have made known to them thy name, and will make it known, in order that the love with which thou hast loved me may be in them, and I in them" (Jn. 17:26). "As I have loved you, you also love one another. By this will all men know that you are my disciples, if you have love one for another" (Jn. 13:34-35; 15:12. 17; 1 Jn. 3:11. 18; 4:7-8. 11-12. 20-21; 5:1-2).

The passage of humanity from the state of dispersion and hate to the unity of charity is the fruit of Christ's death; Christ died in order "that he might gather into one, the children of God who were scattered abroad" (Jn. 11:52). Christ is the One Shepherd (Jn. 10:16) and the only gate (Jn. 10:7. 9) of the sheepfold. By His death and resurrection, He has given men the power to become sons of the Father (Eph. 1:5; Rom. 8:29; 1 Jn. 3:11. 18; 5:20), to approach the Father, in one and the same Holy Spirit (Eph. 2:18), to be able to say "Abba, Father," with the Spirit and the Son (Gal. 4:6) and to love men just as Christ and the Father loved each other (1 Jn. 3:11. 18).

To the Church He founded Christ gave, as an element of cohesion and expansion, this Spirit which unites Father and Son in their intimate life. Thus we can understand that the society of the Church, animated by such a principle, transcends the limits of *space*, (Acts 1:8), *time*, (Mt. 28:20), and *human particularisms* (Mt. 28:19). In the words of the First Vatican Council (D 1794), the Church triumphs over internal division (unity) and over external division, the effect of human particularism (Catholic unity); she triumphs over the limits of time and history (invincible stability), over the limits of material wear and tear, over the prospect of growing old, and finally over the curse of death (holiness, fecundity). In virtue of the divine principle which gives her life, that is, the Spirit of God, the Church already makes up, on earth, a sort of outline of the heavenly Jerusalem, and an anticipation of the reign of the Saints.

The presence of such a society, in the midst of human societies, stands out with unaccustomed brilliance. Now that we have contemplated the central radiance from which all these rays emerge (dogmatic point of view), we shall see how these rays lead us back to the central brilliance (apologetic point of view). In the Church society, such as it is manifest from without, what are the facts, the *observable* facts, which make the Church, among human societies, a *miraculous* society whose very existence cannot be explained without appealing to an extraordinary intervention on the part of God?

The *unity* of the Church is a first fact. Not an indiscriminate or superficial unity, but a unity in *complexity* (doctrine, worship, government), which has been maintained for over twenty centuries and which has succeeded in incorporating multitudes of men. Belonging to the Church produces a profound integration of personalities; it reaches deep within human awareness and establishes a solidarity, an unexampled sense of communion among all the members of the Church, though they be unknown to each other, isolated in space or time. This element of cohesion in the society of the Church, on the testimony of all the faithful, is Christ and his Spirit. Like an immense organism, the Church grows, but without ever losing its interior cohesion. It penetrates all human structures, but never lets itself be absorbed by them. On the other hand, we observe a most singular phenomenon whenever a branch is detached from the Church, in schism or heresy; it immediately meets with division, doctrinal variations; very frequently it falls to pieces and disappears.[29]

This unity is *dynamic* and *catholic*: it conquers space and calls together men from over all the earth. What is important in this growth of the Church is less the phenomenon in itself than its *quality*. There is actually an expansion here which is accompanied by a radical conversion of minds and a profound transformation of morals, achieved, not by force of arms or moral pressure, but by a pure attraction of love, the love of God as manifest in Christ, and this in spite of all the obstacles from within and without. Catholic expansion triumphs over all the divisions of mind and blood. It transcends biological community, overcomes the powerful bonds of family, clan, and nation, political and cultural community, and is at work to build up the community of the children of God, in Christ and through Christ. It seeks to build up, superimposed on the geography of earth, a new geography, world wide in its dimensions, reuniting all men, without distinction of color, language, race, institution, culture.[30] It builds up the body of Christ, in which there are no longer either Jews, nor Greeks, nor slaves, nor free men, but only *sons of the Father*, "all given to drink of one Spirit" (1 Cor. 12:13). The Church is built up, not by opposition, but in a union of love between all men. This material extension in unity, this unity in diversity, this universality in indivisibility and in charity, this victory over every particularism—this is a great paradox.

The Church is *stable*. It extends throughout history, but it transcends the vicissitudes of history; it preserves its inner equilibrium, despite opposition from within (conscious or unconscious error, individual or collective passion) and without (persecution, imperialism in all its forms). Whereas religions change, dissolve, and die in the course of time, or give way to a syncretism which welcomes everyone but reduces all to a common rank, the Church preserves, without contamination, a doctrinal body which is most complex and, what is more, which is opposed to human passion. This stability, moreover, is not immobility, but permanence, in equilibrium, of a living institution always growing and always in progress. Finally, this stability is perpetual, coextensive with the whole of time. Bound up in historical contexts and political structures which constantly threaten to snuff it out (Roman empire, feudal Europe, modern states), the Church always manages to be free of them.[31] Just as Israel which, thanks to the gift of prophecy, lived, and survived in the midst of the occupation forces, despite the assaults of naturalism and nationalism, the Church abides, assured of its eternity. Her stability is invincible. Such a stability and permanence appear as a sort of sharing the divine immutability; it is evidence of a vital principle which transcends time and history.[32]

The Church is *holy*, in her doctrine, in her mission, in her means of sanctification (laws, sacraments). She acts, in human society, like a ferment of continual moral and spiritual renovation, constantly infusing the elements of justice, charity, humility, purity. Never does she cease to propose the very lofty ideal of evangelical perfection, inviting the most generous of men to a full living, here below, of their life as adopted sons of God, wholly consecrated to Him by detachment from riches (poverty) and by an intimate and exclusive alliance of heart and mind with the heart and mind of God (chastity, obedience). The Church counts a heavy mass of sinners; she never ceases to implore God's pardon for them. But she also counts an important share of her members in whom a common holiness is to be found. What is more, at every age, she can count men of heroic sanctity among her ranks, men who are recruited from every class of society. This sanctity is something every man can meet for himself, if not by his personal experience at least in history; for the holiness of Augustine, Xavier, Bernard, Francis of Assisi, Thomas Aquinas, Vincent de Paul, the Curé d'Ars, belongs to the history of the world. Everyone is in a position to treasure its intensity, its fullness, its constancy, as well as its fruitfulness. The Church is fruitful "in everything good," with this fruitfulness of charity which spreads out in gestures and works of benevolence, not in any competition with civil society, but simply because the Church, living from the Spirit of God, reflects the fruitfulness and superabundance of divine life, always renewed in love. The Church, living in the charity of Christ, like

Christ, "goes her way doing good" (Acts 10:38). In the last analysis it is holiness that explains everything. For without charity there is no unity but only schism; there is no universality but only self-seeking; there is no stability but only change and death.

All these traits, taken together, make the Church an exceptional society among human societies. No society, in the recorded testimony of history, sociology, psychology, can thus offer the *simultaneous* spectacle of internal and external unity, universality, perpetuity, stability, holiness, and fecundity that the Church can offer. All this, considered *together* and *qualitatively*, completely transcends the common experience of human societies.

These facts demand an explanation, a sufficient and proportioned reason. Where does the Church get this energy, this power of cohesion, assimilation, sanctification, permanence in stability? The Church proposes as an explanation of herself both her divine origin and her divine mission. She testifies that her whole being and her whole activity proceed from a special intervention of God in Christ, Word Incarnate. She declares that she is, by the will of God, the one and only way of salvation for all men. Such an explanation is not to be rejected without examination, for it seems the only adequate explanation of the facts observed. If we admit it, everything is explained, everything becomes intelligible, even the heroism of the saints and martyrs. If not, the Church remains a puzzle. Faced with the character and importance of the facts observed, it is prudent to recognize the truth in the Church's testimony in her own behalf: her mission is from God, her doctrine is from God.

This conclusion is all the more reasonable in that there is such a marvelous harmony between the facts observed and the teaching propounded by the Church. The Church teaches that Christ is the Son of God, that He came among us to establish the kingdom of God on earth, to renew individual and social man. Now the miraculous character of the Church is a visible manifestation of this transformation she announces. Where the Church is there the sanctifying power of the Spirit is at work, renewing hearts. In the saint there is a new type for humanity, that is, a Son of God, who lives and acts under the mastery of the Spirit; a new society appears, the Church, city of God among human cities, manifesting here below some of the traits of heavenly Jerusalem: unity, stability, holiness, fruitfulness, eternity. The admirable life of the Church is thus at once the *confirmative* and *figurative* sign of revelation: it testifies to the divine origin of revelation (confirmative sign) and at the same time it symbolizes the new creation announced by revelation (figurative sign).

Thus, Church and revelation, Church and word, are two realities indissolubly joined together and giving life to each other. The Church is at once the society which calls together and which is called together. Born of the word, it is in the service of the word, it is a sign of the word. The Bride has received the Bridegroom's word and could not ever forget it again. The Bride lives from this word by waiting for the return of the Bridegroom.

1. T. Soiron, *La condition du théologien* (Paris, 1953), pp. 111-120.

2. Y. M. J. Congar, *Esquisses du mystère de l'Église* (Paris, 1953), p. 155.

3. Mansi 51: 314B.

4. Irenaeus, *Adversus Haereses*, V, 20, 2: PG 7, col. 1177-1178.

5. D 1800.

6. On the relationship between revelation and sacrament, see chapter V of this fifth part, paragraph 4.

7. D. Deden, "Le mystère paulinien," *Ephemerides theologicae lovanienses*, 13 (1936): 420-423; D. Grasso, "Il kerigma e la predicazione," *Gregorianum*, 41 (1960): 439-440; C. Dodd, *The Apostolic Preaching and its Developments* (London, 1956), pp. 7-35.

8. The preaching of the Gospel is thus efficacious in two ways: *a.* by reason of the dimension of grace which is joined with the external preaching of the message; *b.* by reason of the holiness of the preacher who acts upon his hearer as a motive of credibility, as a sign which attests the divine origin of the word he speaks.

9. K. Rahner, "Zur Frage der Dogmenentwicklung," *Schriften zur Theologie* (Einsiedeln, 1956), 1: 57-58; G. Dejaifve, "Bible, tradition et Magistère dans la théologie catholique," *Nouvelle Revue théologique*, 78 (1956): 145-146.

10. G. Ebeling, *Die Geschichtlichkeit der Kirche und ihrer Verkundigung als theologisches Problem in drei Vorlesungen* (Tubingen, 1954), pp. 44-50.

11. W. von Loewenich, *Der Moderne Katholizismus* (Witten, 1955), pp. 160-166.

12. W. Schweitzer, *Schrift und Dogme in der Oekumene* (Gutersloh, 1953), pp. 32-52.

13. L. Charlier, *Essai sur le problème théologique* (Thuillies, 1938), p. 64.

14. C. Baumgartner, "Tradition et Magistère," *Recherches de science religieuse*, 41 (1953): 171-174.

15. "Nullum sane inventum inducitur, nec quidquam additur novi ad earum summam veritatem, quae in deposito revelationis, Ecclesiae tradito, saltem implicite continentur" (Pius XI, *Mortalium animos*, AAS 20 (1928): 14).

16. "Una enim cum sacris ejusmodi fontibus Deus Ecclesiae suae Magisterium vivum dedit, ad ea quoque illustranda et enucleanda, quae in fidei deposito nonnisi obscure ac velut implicite continentur" (D 2314).

17. E. Dhanis, "Révélation explicite et implicite," *Gregorianum*, 34 (1953): 197.

18. Pius, IX, *Ineffabilis Deus*, coll. Lac., t. VI, col. 836.

19. "Universa Ecclesia, in qua viget veritatis Spiritus qui quidem eam ad revelatarum perficiendam veritatum cognitionem infallibiliter dirigit" (Pius XII, *Munificentissimus Deus*, AAS 42 (1950): 768).

20. A good number of Catholic exegetes admit that the three passages: *Jn.* 14: 16-17; 15: 26; 16: 12-13, are to be applied, not only to the apostles, but also to the Church. Cf. E. Dhanis, "Révélation explicite et implicite," *Gregorianum*, 34 (1953): 206-207, no. 52.

21. "Neque enim Petri successoribus Spiritus Sanctus promissus est, ut eo revelante novam doctrinam patefacerent, sed ut, eo assistente, traditam per apostolos revelationem seu fidei depositum sancte custodirent et fideliter exponerent" (D 1836).

22. S. Thomas, *S. th.*, 2a 2ae, q. 8, a. 1.

23. S. Thomas, *S. th.*, 2a 2ae, q. 45, a. 2, c.

24. "Ad solam enim catholicam Ecclesiam ea pertinent omnia, quae ad evidentem fidei christianae credibilitatem tam multa et tam mira divinitus sunt disposita. Quin etiam Ecclesia per se ipsa, ob suam nempe admirabilem propagationem, eximiam sanctitatem et inexhaustam in omnibus bonis foecunditatem, ob catholicam unitatem invictamque stabilitatem magnum quoddam et perpetuum est motivum credibilitatis et divinae suae legationis testimonium irrefragabile. Quo fit ut ipsa veluti signum levatum in nationes (*Is.* 11, 12) et ad se invitet, qui nondum crediderunt,

et filios suos certiores faciat, firmissimo niti fundamento fidem, quam profitentur" (D 1794).

25. By moral miracle, we understand a way of acting, individual or collective, produced in a religious context, and so completely surpassing the habitual conduct of men that the sufficient reason for it can be found only in a special intervention of God: by this intervention, God signifies the establishment of the kingdom of God among men.

26. M. GRANDMAISON, *L'Église par elle-même motif de crédibilité* (Rome, 1961), pp. 7-9; J. T. TSENG, *De Apologetica methodo quae "via empirica" audit* (Hong Kong, 1960), pp. 2-5; S. PESCE, *La Chiesa cattolica, perenne motivo di credibilità* (Catania, 1960), pp. 144-160.

27. A complete bibliography is to be found in: M. GRANDMAISON, *L'Église pare elle-même motif de crédibilité. Histoire de l'argument:* 1870-1960 (Rome, 1961), pp. 45-51. Cf. also: H. HOLSTEIN, "L'Église, signe parmi les Nations," *E'tudes*, 315 (Oct. 1962), pp. 45-59.

28. C. JOURNET, *L'Église du Verbe incarné* (2 vol., Paris, 1941, 1951), 2: 875-876.

29. C. JOURNET, *L'Église du Verbe incarné*, 2: 1269-1278.

30. C. DUMONT, "Unité et diversité des signes de la révélation," *Nouvelle Revue théologique,* 80 (1958): 148.

31. J. GUTTON, *L'Église et l'Évangile* (Paris, 1959), p. 383.

32. A. SERTILLANGES, *Le miracle de l'Église* (Paris, 1933), pp. 9 and 224.

CHAPTER VIII

REVELATION AND VISION

The God of the new covenant, like the God of the old covenant, remains a hidden God: "No one has ever seen God" (Jn. 1:18). Only Christ "who comes from God..., has seen God" (Jn. 6:46). The revelations and raptures of Saint Paul find their place at the interior of faith (2 Cor. 12:1-4). "We walk in faith, and not in the clarity of vision" (2 Cor. 5:7). Here below we live in an economy of word and hearing, testimony and faith. We have no access to God except through the mediation of signs: the sign of Christ's flesh and the signs of the human word. Revelation remains an indirect, imperfect, partial, and obscure knowledge. There is always something lost between the sign and the reality, the testimony and the presence, revelation revealed and revelation revealing. We take God's word that He Himself is Father, Son, and Spirit; but the vision of Father, Son, and Spirit remains the object of hope. The divine being, here below, remains darkness. Final revelation, clear vision, is on the other side of death.

I. FAITH, BEGINNING OF VISION

Vision, however, does have a beginning here below. Through the economy of word and faith, we enter progressively into the economy of vision, looking to the full light of our encounter and our face-to-face with the Father. Faith, actually, tends towards the luminous experience of the living God already possessed in obscurity here below. It is completely oriented towards vision. It aspires towards the unveiled contemplation of Him whom it knows to be the object of its happiness. There is, in the bosom of faith, an appetite for vision, all the more vivid in that faith is "a foretaste of future vision".[1]

1. The very fact that God comes out of His mystery and addresses man, speaking to him, has no meaning for God, unless His intention is to communicate more fully with man, unless it is His intention to

complete this intercourse inaugurated through words with the fuller gift of personal encounter. Revelation being essentially a word of friendship, it has real meaning only if God's plan is to consummate this friendship with man by a more complete gift of Himself in presence and vision. God, by the very fact that He reveals and reveals Himself, begins to give Himself, with the intention of giving Himself, someday, completely and definitively. And faith, which is adherence to the word of God inviting us to friendship and self-giving, stirs up in man the legitimate desire of arriving at that fullness of friendship and self-giving which must be realized in the transforming and beatific unity of vision. Revelation and vision are thus only two "moments" of one and the same manifestation and communication of God to man. Vision consummates what revelation inaugurates.

2. In the second place, faith inaugurates vision in the sense that it is a real, although imperfect and obscure, participation of the knowledge which God has of Himself. The word of God introduces us to the mysteries of His intimate life, initiates us into a knowledge which is the proper domain of Father, Son, and Spirit, and to which no mortal man can have access without a gratuitous and free initiative on the part of the Divine Persons (Mt. 11:25-27; 1 Cor. 2:7-10). Faith is a beginning, a foretaste of vision; it has for its material object this same mysterious reality which it will know in vision, namely the divine essence, subsisting in three persons, the divine essence subsisting in the Person of the Word hypostatically united with human nature, the divine essence actuating created intelligence in vision: in a word, the three fundamental mysteries of Christianity. This knowledge of faith, in so far as it grasps its object imperfectly and obscurely, calls for a ripening and development in full and entire knowledge. What is more, it has for its motive the very authority of Him who can neither deceive nor be deceived. And thus taking the word of God for its foundation and basis, it escapes the natural weakness of human knowledge and shares in the infallibility of divine knowledge: it enters into the immutability of vision. Without vision, faith would always be deprived of finality in some way and stop short in its forward impulse. By its material object and by its motive, it belongs to the world of vision.

3. In the third place, faith is a foretaste of vision in virtue of the attraction towards God which the grace of faith stamps within us. First Truth, as we have seen, infuses in our intellectual activity a tendency (inclination or attraction) which acts as a primary and profound instinct. In this tendency, the God of vision is known by presentiment, in a dynamic way, as the object and terminus of the

mind's movement: just as every impulse precedes and designates the goal. The activity of grace determines a dynamic tension towards the God of vision. God himself, it is true, is not actually seen, and the mind never gets farther than a mediate knowledge, but the whole dynamism of faith tends to surpass this way of knowledge; it designates as terminus of its movement God Himself, drawing us to the vision of His essence. The grace of faith is thus the beginning of vision, not in the sense that it is an imperfect vision, but in so far as it stamps the intellectual and voluntary dynamism of the soul with an impulse that is wholly oriented towards vision. It is inchoative vision by way of an active, infused, supernatural inclination towards the God of vision.[2]

4. Finally, faith, when it is nourished by charity, becomes the principle of vision. The accomplishment of God's will draws Christ's attention, who then reveals Himself to His disciple. If anyone keeps the commandments of Christ, Christ will manifest Himself (Jn. 14:21). The immanence of Christ in him, veiled until now, begins to reveal itself and, at the same time, the immanence of the Father in the Son (Jn. 14:9-10). The Spirit, who scrutinizes the depths of divinity (1 Cor. 2:10), makes the mind of the believer more and more penetrating, and makes the object of faith itself more and more luminous. By the gift of wisdom, He infuses an affective harmony which is the source of understanding. He who does the will of Christ grasps the thought of Christ, shares the tastes and inclinations of Christ. The Spirit of Christ makes him live from the thought and love of Christ. Thus, by the economy of faith, we enter progressively into the economy of vision: if we receive the word of Christ and keep it, we receive the Spirit of Christ who gives us the understanding of the Father and the Son. To certain privileged souls, God can give even more in His bounty, if He wills: this knowledge of living faith can rise to the point of extraordinary mystical graces. But never here below does the soul arrive at the point where she can tear away the veil which separates her from her Beloved.

II. DEFINITIVE REVELATION: VISION AND ENCOUNTER

Revelation par excellence belongs to eschatology. Only then "in the last days" will "the revelation of our Lord and Savior Jesus Christ" be realized in all its fullness (1 Cor. 1:7; 2 Thess. 1:7), the revelation of His glory (1 Pet. 1:7. 13; 4: 13); then will be manifest the glory of all those who are conformed to Christ (1 Pet. 1:5; Rom. 8:18. 29; 1 Cor. 1:9).

To describe this definitive revelation which will associate God and His elect in one and the same blessedness, Christ uses traditional images: kingdom, promised land, paradise, nuptials, banquet, treasure, salvation, life, resurrection, glory, etc. But, through these images, a new thinking begins to dawn: the beatitude of the kingdom will consist essentially in the vision and enjoyment of God. The vision of God, forbidden to men here below (Ex. 33:20), privilege of the Son (Jn. 6:46; 1:18) and His angels (Mt. 18:10), will become the privilege of the elect. "Blessed are the pure of heart, for they shall see God" (Mt. 5:8). Vision face to face, the final unveiling of the sacred countenance so ardently sought for in the Old Testament, will characterize eternal life.[3]

In 1 Cor. 13:12, Saint Paul contrasts the knowledge which we have of God in our present state with the knowledge we shall have in eternal happiness. "We see now through a mirror (*per speculum*), in an obscure manner (*in aenigmate*), but then face to face." Now, that is, in the knowledge of faith, we have only an imperfect knowledge of God: we see in a *mirror*, that is through an *indirect* and *enigmatic* manner, that is in an *obscure* and *symbolic* way. The vision does not see the object in itself, but only in its image; vision in an obscure manner gives only a confused image. The knowledge of the end of times, on the contrary, will be a full knowledge, "face to face," that is, an immediate, intuitive, direct, and clear knowledge. This face to face vision constitutes the supreme hope of the world to come.[4]

Saint John, in his first epistle, connects the vision of God with our divine sonship. "For now we are children of God and it has not yet appeared what we shall be. We know that, when He appears, we shall be like to Him, for we shall see Him as He is" (1 Jn. 3:2). The first revelation, imperfect, has given rise, in faith, to the beginning of our Christian being; the second revelation, perfect, in vision, will be the final fulfillment of our condition as sons. In the actual state of our sonship there is a twofold obscurity: the obscurity of what we are, in the present economy of faith, and the obscurity of what we shall be when vision bursts upon us. Our actual knowledge is not complete because our being is not complete; and it is not complete because God has not revealed Himself in vision. When God is plainly manifest, we shall see God as He is and, in the light of this revelation, we shall see what we are. Vision of God, transformation in God, revelation of our condition as sons,—these coincide.[5] Finally, in the Apocalypse, it is said that "the servants of God ... will see His face" (Apoc. 22:4). And this vision is represented as being the supreme beatitude of the elect.

The magisterium of the Church is more precise on the *object* and *mode* of this definitive revelation. The object of vision will be "the divine essence" (D 530) "of God Himself, one and triune, just as He is" (D 693). The God which vision will reveal to us and in whom we already communicate by faith, is the living and true God, Father, Son, and Spirit, the God of Abraham, Isaac, and Jacob, who spoke with Moses as a friend, at once redoubtable and fascinating, withdrawn and familiar, transcendent and very close. We shall see Him "with an intuitive vision, face to face, without the mediation of any creature" which might be interposed between the divine essence and human understanding: the divine essence will be manifest "immediately and in its nakedness" (D 530). We shall see God "clearly and openly" (D 530). This is an immediate and intuitive knowledge of God, terminating directly in the very essence of God perceived as present. The vision will be the source of eternal joy and blessedness (D 530).

To say that the eschatological revelation will be a vision of the divine essence is still not enough: the vision announced by faith comes not as a simple spectacle, of the platonic type, but rather as the mutual presence of two friends who meet each other, or like a father who stands before his son. The face-to-face meeting does away with all distance between them: there is no more tension between word and presence. The Word in person becomes presence. God stands unveiled in an interpersonal encounter and communion. The vision of God will be mutual knowledge and recognition, freely consented to, between God and man, in the most complete reciprocity: "Then I shall know," says Saint Paul "even as I am known" (1 Cor. 13:12).

In the Synoptics, the happiness promised to those who have left all to follow Christ is communion with Him, in His kingdom (Mt. 19:28). Christ concludes the last supper by promising a renewal of that banquet at the eschatological table (Mt. 26:29; Mk. 14:25). Eternal blessedness means entering into the joy of the Lord (Mt. 25:21. 23); it means being with Christ, being with the Bridegroom at the wedding feast (Mt. 25:10); it means being the table guest of Christ (Lk. 14:15; 22:30) and being served by Him (Lk. 12:37).

Saint Paul, rather than "remaining on in the flesh," desires "to be dissolved," to die, for death would permit him to be close to Christ, "to be with Christ" (Phil. 1:21-24), to "remain always with the Lord" (2 Cor. 5:8). The essential element of final happiness for the Christian will be "to be always with the Lord" (1 Thess. 4:17), to "live united to Him" (1 Thess. 5:10; 2 Thess. 2:1), to "reign with Him" (2 Tim. 2:12). Each Christian will be with Christ in a personal way, he will enjoy the society of Christ, His happiness, and His love, all in a personal way. In Saint John, our eye is focused even more on the Person of Christ, for Christ in person is life, salvation, glory (Jn. 3:15-16; 5:24-26; 11:26; 12:50). Christ wants His own to be "there where He is" (Jn. 14:3), "with Him" (Jn. 17:24).

Numerous texts, finally, insist on the *community* aspect of this encounter and vision. Just as first revelation is addressed to humanity as such (Mt. 28:19; Mk. 16:15), in view of making up the Body of Christ which is the Church (Eph. 1:22; 4:16; 5:23. 30), eschatological revelation is presented as a collective experience, as a shared joy. This idea appears primarily in a theme which is so dear to the Synoptics, that of eschatological banquet (Lk. 14:15). This banquet is a community repast which unites all the just around our Lord (Mt. 8:11-12). "You will eat and drink at my table in my kingdom," Christ promises His apostles (Lk. 22:30; Mt. 26:29). The Apocalypse represents the heavenly Jesusalem as the society of the elect "gathered" about the Lamb (Apoc. 14:1-4) and reigning with Him (Apoc. 22:5; 1:6. 9).[6]

The opposition stressed by Scripture and the Church magisterium between the economy of faith and the economy of vision does not however mean that the encounter and the vision of God will abolish all mystery. Man, seeing God, becomes like unto Him (1 Jn. 3:2), but not equal. The knowledge which God has of Himself is not only intuitive, but also exhaustive. Our knowledge, though immediate, remains none the less the knowledge of a finite and limited creature; it could not thus exhaust the divine essence. Vision will be the encounter with mystery itself in person, and not simply by way of testimony and faith. The ineffability of God will become the very object of our vision, but never, even in final revelation, will our understanding of this mystery be perfectly exhaustive. Eternal life will be like being plunged into an abyss that is always deeper and deeper; we go on from brightness to brightness, but also from abyss to abyss. The mystery will then no longer be known by the mere mediation of signs and images, but it will always remain mystery. Vision will be an unceasing initiation into the mystery of God.

III. REVELATION OF NATURE, GRACE, AND GLORY

After having compared natural revelation and the revelation of grace, then the revelation of grace and the revelation of glory, we should now like to stress the bonds which join these three forms of revelation, for there is progress and progressive depth from one to the other.

1. The objective medium of manifestation, in natural revelation, are the works of creation; in supernatural revelation it is the word and testimony of God; in the revelation of glory it is the divine essence itself.

2. A subjective light, constantly growing in intensity, accompanies this objective manifestation: the light of reason in natural revelation, the light of prophecy and the light of faith in the revelation of grace; the light of glory in the beatific vision.

3. Each level of revelation has a corresponding knowledge of God which is progressively more profound: in natural revelation, God is known as the beginning and end of the universe; in supernatural revelation, the mysteries of His inmost life are known to us, as well as His plan for salvation; in the revelation of glory, we shall see God unveiled, face to face, in the vision of His essence.

4. Each form of revelation constitutes, on the part of God, a communication and self-giving which are progressively more complete. In natural revelation, God posits the sign and gives the faculty which permits man to rise up to Him and discern His presence in the universe. In supernatural revelation, God, through His word, initiates man into what is most intimate in God, that is, the mystery of His own life and the mysterious plan of a communication of this life to man: the initiation to such a secret constitutes a self-gift of God to man. In the revelation of glory, God Himself becomes present and gives Himself wholly without any mediation.

5. Each degree of revelation implies in return, on the part of man, a self-giving which is progressively more complete. Natural revelation calls for the homage of glorification in thanksgiving. Supernatural revelation calls for faith, man's free choice which stamps a new orientation on his living, founded solely on the word of God. In the revelation of glory, the full self-gift of God calls for the full self-gift of man.[7] Steeped in this knowledge and this love of God, man, freely, fully, and with the very power of God, responds to this knowledge and love.

6. Christ, Word of God, is the principle of each revelation. All things have been created through the Word and in the Word, and particularly the light of reason which God has put in man as in His image. Christ is the principle of the revelation of grace, for He is Son, in the bosom of the Father, come to make known the Father (Jn. 1:18); He is the only way which leads to the knowledge of the

Father (Jn. 5:36-40; 8:15-20; 12:44-50; 14:1-14; 15:20-25; 16:3);
His mission is to glorify the Father by making known His name, that
is by revealing Him (Jn. 17:4. 6. 26). Finally, just as Christ is the
revealer of the Father, in His condition as slave here below, thus the
glorious Christ is once again, in the hereafter of heaven, the one
sole revealer of the Father's glory. In His priestly prayer, Christ asks
His father for the full manifestation of His glory as Son so that men,
seeing the glory of the Son, will at the same time see the glory of
the Father (Jn. 17:1. 5. 24. 26). In this manifestation of His eschatological glory Christ will manifest and reveal to men the glory of
the Father. Thus Christ will prolong His function of Word Incarnate
throughout all eternity: He will be a revealer of the Father for glorified
mankind. Just as He "revealed the name" of the Father on earth
(Jn. 17:26. 6), He will also "reveal it" in the glory of eternity (Jn.
17:26). "I have revealed your name and I shall reveal it" (Jn. 17:26).
This verse sums up the whole activity of Christ as revealer: revealer
and glorifier of the Father here on earth (Jn. 17:4. 6. 8. 14. 22. 26),
He will pursue His work further in the glory of eternity (Jn. 17:26).
During His life on earth, He revealed the Father under the veil of
signs and in the obscurity of faith; in eternity, the glorified Christ
will manifest and communicate the fullness of His eschatological
glory to the men whom the Father has given Him. Thus He will manifest
and glorify the Father. Jn. 1:14 and 17:24 are to each other[8] as the
temporal and incomplete anticipation is to the eschatological and
eternal consummation of the same reality, which is the manifestation
and communication of Christ's glory to men. The glorious Christ
will be eternally the revealer of the Father, the way that leads to
the Father.

7. Each degree of revelation prepares or at least presupposes the
preceding. Before he is open to the Word, man must first of all
recognize the existence of God, Creator and Master of the moral
order: otherwise, how can the word appear as something which is at
once free and gratuitous and demanding to be heard? The economy
of the word normally precedes the economy of vision, for it is only
fitting that man should hear God speak and choose for Him, before
enjoying His presence. Grace presupposes nature and is itself the
foundation and pledge of glory.

8. Each degree is ordered to the next higher degree: creation is
in view of the word, and the word is ordered towards vision. Revelation
broadens and makes explicit the implicit language of creation; glory is the
reality which the word announces.

9. The revelation of grace appears as a middle term between natural revelation and the revelation of glory. It presupposes and completes the former; it prepares for the latter, towards which it aspires. It shares the imperfection of the former and the perfection of the latter. But it is situated closer to glory, for, like glory, it belongs to the order of grace, incomparably elevated above nature.

---

1. *III Sent.*, d. 23, q. 2, a. 1, ad 4.

2. We have borrowed the substance of these first three considerations from P. ALFARO, *Adnotationes in tractatum de Virtutibus*, pp. 236-238.

3. A. GEORGE, "Le bonheur promis par Jésus d'après le Nouveau Testament," *Lumiére et Vie*, no. 52 (avril-mai 1961), pp. 36-37.

4. J. DUPONT, *Gnosis, La connaissance religieuse dans les épitres de S. Paul* (Louvain and Paris, 1949), pp. 105-148; N. HUGEDE, *La métaphore du miroir dans les épitres de S. Paul aux Corinthiens* (Neuchatel-Paris, 1957), pp. 98-150.

5. The text of Saint John can also be understood of Christ. It would then mean: when Christ appears, we shall be like to Him, for we shall see Him as He is. This would be a vision of Christ according to His divinity, in the glory of the Son of God (*Jn.* 1: 18; 17: 5. 24; *Apoc.* 22: 3). Cf. J. MOUROUX *L'expérience chrétienne* (Paris, 1952), pp. 171-172.

6. J. DUPONT, *L'Union avec le Christ suivant S. Paul* (Bruges, Louvain and Paris, 1952), pp. 79-100.

7. J. ALFARO, "Persona y gracia," *Gregorianum*, 41 (1960): 11-13.

8. *Jn.* 1, 14: "And the Word was made flesh, and dwelt among us. And we saw his glory." *Jn.* 17, 24: "Father, I will that where I am, they also whom thou hast given me may be with me; in order that they may behold my glory, which thou hast given me."

CHAPTER IX

THE FINALITY OF REVELATION

The way of finality is the third way suggested by the First Vatican Council to enter progressively into an understanding of the Christian mysteries. The intelligibility of the mystery, this time, is demanded from the final cause.

The finality of revelation can be envisaged either from the point of view of man, or from the point of view of God. In the theocentric perspective, we shall say that revelation is ordered towards the glory of God; in the anthropocentric perspective, we shall say that it is ordered towards the salvation of man. It is a question of perspective only, for in glorifying God, man works out his salvation; and in working out his salvation, he glorifies God.

I. REVELATION IS FOR THE SALVATION OF MAN

Revelation is ordered towards faith, and faith itself is in view of salvation. The goal of revelation, envisaged from the point of view of man, is the salvation of man; or, in more positive terms, it is vision, participation in divine life.

Revelation, we must insist, is an essentially salvific operation. God does not reveal Himself in order to satisfy our curiosity or to increase the sum total of our human knowledge, but rather to snatch man away from the death of sin and give him the gift of eternal life. Stirred up by the living God, the revealed word, preached and received in faith, begets living souls, sons of God, sharing the glory of the Three Divine Persons. To deprive revelation of its salvific character would be to deprive it of one of its fundamental dimensions; it would be a foundation for the accusations of those who see Christianity as an attempt to reduce revelation to a complex of propositions to which the human mind is forced to adhere. The idea of salvation is the *leitmotif* and the dominant idea of the whole Old Testament. Israel is the people whom God has acquired by saving them from Egypt, leading them through the Red Sea, guiding them across the desert and delivering them from the inhabitants of Canaan. The revelation of God's name is bound up with this deliverance. The message of Moses is at once the announcement of deliverance and the communication of the Name that delivered them: the two are inseparable. The proclamation of the decalogue begins with the words: "I am Yahweh your God, who has delivered you from the land of Egypt, from the house of bondage" (Ex. 20:1-2). The exodus and the divine name are only one (Ex. 3:10-15). To recall the name of Yahweh means to recall the decisive event, the grace of deliverance (Hos. 12:10; 13:4; Ez. 20:5-6; Lev. 22:33). Yahweh is always the *God who saves*; He is also the God who chastises, but, in the last analysis, only in order to save and give life.[1] The sacrifice of the passover (Ex. 12:1-14) is the memorial of salvation, that is, the passage of God who saved and always saves. Messianic expectation, in general, is rooted in this faith in the God of the covenant who never abandons the people He has adopted. The expectation of a personal Messiah is nourished from the same source; Nathan's promise to David focuses the hope of Israel on David and his offspring (2 Sam. 7:16). Despite the infidelity of the people and its princes to the conditions of the covenant, Yahweh remains faithful, always disposed to save. But, as revelation progresses, the idea of salvation becomes more profound. At the beginning, salvation is conceived of in a most material way: victory over enemies, peace and prosperity. But little by little, under the influence of the prophets and under the effect of national disaster, Israel comes to an understanding of the fact that true salvation is first of all deliverance from sin and from all forms of evil. The salvation announced by the prophets will be a redemption from sin (Is. 44:22; 45:8; 53:8). The new covenant will be made with purified hearts (Jer. 24:7; Ez. 36:23-28; Zech. 13:9), and all peoples shall have part in this salvation. Salvation will be an event of history, brought to the understanding of men by the Anointed of God, who will save Israel and all humanity through Israel.

Christ is He in whom this long awaited event takes place. In Him, the salvific goodness of God is present to humanity, makes covenant with humanity and gives men the grace of divine sonship (Gal. 4:6). Jesus means Yahweh the Savior or salvation of Yahweh. Jesus is the Lord who comes to effect salvation: He is the Savior (Mt. 1:21; Lk.

2:11. 30) and there is no other name under heaven through which we are to be saved (Acts 4:12; Rom. 10:9).

In the *Synoptics*, the preaching of Christ has for its object the inauguration of the Kingdom of God. This kingdom, begun here below through the preaching of the Gospel (Mk. 1:14-15), through deliverance from sin (Mk. 2:10-11; 14:24) and the reign of Satan (Mk. 5:1-20; Mt. 12:28), by the foundation of the Church (Mt. 16:18), will be completed in heaven where men, associates at the eternal banquet (Lk. 22:24-30; 12:37; Mk. 10:43-45), will share the very life of the Father (Mt. 25:34-41). Christ has come to call sinners (Mt. 9:13; Lk. 5:32) and save what has been lost (Lk. 4:18; Mt. 9:12). Salvation is granted to those who believe in the good news and are baptized: "Go out into the whole world, preach the good news to every creature. He who believes and is baptized will be saved; he who does not believe will be condemned" (Mt. 16:15-16). This verse explains clearly the finality of revelation: the Gospel is in view of faith, and faith is in view of salvation.

In *Acts*, the apostles testify to the work of salvation accomplished by the death and resurrection of Christ (Acts 5:30; 10:39-40). Their word has for its object the *salvation* brought by Jesus Christ (Acts 4:12; 10:36; 11:14; 13:26. 47; 15:11; 16:17. 30-31), or *life* (Acts 3:15; 5:20; 11:18; 13:46. 48). Hence the expressions: "all the words of this life" (Acts 5:20), the "message of salvation" (Acts 13:26), "the Gospel of grace" (Acts 20:24). Christ himself is "prince of life" (Acts 3:15), the "Savior" (Acts 5:31; 13:23). Outside of Him there is no salvation (Acts 4:12; 5:31; 10:43). To announce Christ or the good news of salvation is one and the same thing. Salvation is given to those who accept the word of the Gospel in faith and have themselves baptized (Acts 2:41; 18:8).

In *Saint Paul*, the theme of salvation offered to men by *faith in the Gospel* is the subject of the letter to the Romans. The Gospel is "a power of God for the salvation for all who believe, Jew first of all, then Greek" (Rom. 1:16). In the Old Testament already, salvation is bound up with the word of God (Is. 40:8; 44:26-28; 55:10-11). And thus, in the New Testament, Saint Paul links the salvation of the world with the divine energy of the word he has been commissioned to announce (Rom. 1:16); for in the Gospel the justice of God is manifest, as is His merciful will, faithful to His promises of salvation. Saint Paul states that only in the Gospel is this dynamic justice manifest to us in its true light, aimed at restoring order in a world disturbed by sin; man can enjoy the effects of this justice only through faith (Rom. 1:17).[2] Christianity is not an abstract metaphysics, but a history of salvation, ordered according to a divine plan. The epistle to the Ephesians describes the splendors of this plan. In His plan of love, God has constituted Christ as unique principle of salvation for Jew and Gentile. This plan, hidden first of all in God as a secret, then revealed and made known to man, is essentially a plan of salvation: it is destined to make us sons of the Father, co-heirs with Christ (Eph. 1:5-10; 3:6; Col. 1:25-28; Rom. 16:25-27). The Ephesians, who had heard "the word of truth, the good news of salvation," and who "have believed" (Eph. 1:13), have received the Spirit who "is the pledge of our inheritance" (Eph. 1:14). Christ is essentially, for Saint Paul, the Mediator and Savior who reconciles men with God (Rom. 4:25; 2 Cor. 5:18-20; Gal. 4:4-6). The word of Saint Paul is thus a word of "reconciliation"(2 Cor. 5:20).

The central theme of the Gospel and letters of *Saint John* can be summed up thus: the Son of the Father became incarnate to reveal and communicate eternal life to men, which is the name by which Saint John designates salvation. "For God so loved the world that He gave His only-begotten Son, that those who *believe* in Him *may not perish, but may have life everlasting.* For God did not send His Son into the world in order to judge the world, but that the world might be *saved* through Him. He who believes in Him is not judged; but he who does not believe is already judged, because he does not believe in the name of the only-begotten Son of God" (Jn. 3:16-18). The essential element of God's testimony or revelation consists in this: God has given us eternal life and this life is in His Son (1 Jn. 5:11). Through Christ, who is His Son, His word, the Father shows us the path which leads to life, for Christ is the light (Jn. 9:5; 12:35-36) and the way (Jn. 14:6) which leads to life (Jn. 12:50). Men are invited to hear and keep the word of the Son; by faith in this word they have life (Jn. 12:46-50). Christ is the Good Shepherd: to the sheep who hear His voice He gives life everlasting (Jn. 10:27-28).

This doctrine of Scripture is taken up by the magisterium of the Church, frequently in the same terms. The Lateran Council declares that the Holy Trinity "has given the human race a doctrine of salvation"[3] and that Christ has "indicated ... the way to life."[4] The Council of Trent, referring explicitly to Mk. 16:15-16, calls the Gospel the "source of all truth of salvation."[5] Through faith, it goes on to say, we believe "in the truth of revelation and the divine promises, and particularly in this truth, that God justifies simple man by His grace, by means of the redemption which is in Christ Jesus."[6] The First Vatican Council, finally, states that revelation is "absolutely necessary" because God, "in His infinite goodness, has ordered man towards a supernatural end, towards a share in the divine blessings".[7] God has willed to make man an adoptive son, called to share in the life of the Trinity; but because man is a being of intelligence and will, God has made known His plan of love so that man, conscious of his freedom, can himself choose his condition of son and freely approach the gift of vision.[8]

The salvific intention of revelation can be deduced not only from the explicit declarations of Scripture and the magisterium, but also from the following two considerations which it will be enough to recall briefly, since they have already been developed in the course of the preceding chapters: 1. This intention appears first of all in the *very fact* of revelation or the word of God to humanity. God, by revelation, comes to meet a creature, a sinful creature. Such a move on the part of God can only mean friendship and salvation. God who speaks is already God with us, God with His power of salvation. Even before it is a distinct message, revelation is already a salvific event. 2. The *message* itself, articulated to this event of salvation, is a still further manifestation of the salvific purposes of revelation. The essential mysteries that God reveals are the mysteries of the Trinity, the Incarnation, our divine sonship. In revealing the Trinity, God initiates us into the secret of His inmost life: this initiation, which is already in itself an unbelievable manifestation of friendship, is in view of a sharing in divine life. The revelation of the Incarnation shows us in Jesus Christ, Incarnate Word, the economy of love chosen by God to communicate this divine life. Revelation of our sonship shows us the nature of this communication: it is a certain extension of the life of the Divine Persons to human creation. God re-engenders His own Son in us and breathes His own Spirit into us. This elevation of mankind to the bosom and heart of God is essentially a mystery of salvation for the creature, for it makes creation share in the nature of God. If man, by faith, adheres to the mystery which is revealed, and leads the life of a son, wholly inspired by the common Spirit of the Father and the Son, he works out his salvation and *glorifies* God.

II. REVELATION IS FOR THE GLORY OF GOD

The glory of God is actually the ultimate goal of revelation. In its active form and in its accomplished form, revelation is ordered towards God's glory.

In his priestly prayer, Christ says to His Father: "I have glorified you upon earth; *I have accomplished the work which you have given me to accomplish*" (Jn. 17:4). Then He adds: "I have *manifested your name* to men" (Jn. 17:6). Christ has come upon earth to make known the Person of the Father (Jn. 17:3), the doctrine of the Father (Jn. 7:16), the words of the Father (Jn. 17:8). He has "rendered testimony" to the Father (Jn. 18:37), He has revealed His Name (Jn. 17:26). For Christ, to render testimony to the Father, to manifest His Name, to reveal His Name, means to *glorify* the Father. The apostles, in their turn, after having heard the words and testimony of Christ, believed in Him: "The words which you have given me I have given to them and they have truly admitted that I have come from you and they have believed that you have sent me" (Jn. 17:8). That is why Christ can say to the Father: "I have glorified you on earth, I have accomplished the work you have given me to do" (Jn. 17:4). In Christ and the apostles, revelation has attained its full destination. Christ, as revealer, glorified the Father, for He made manifest to men the Father's plan of grace; on the other hand, Christ and the Father have been glorified by the apostles, for they recognize the gift of revelation and salvation in Jesus Christ: they believe. "I am *glorified* in them," says Christ (Jn. 17:10).

The glory of God means, in the first place, God Himself, in the perfection of His being and in the radiance of His perfection. This perfection spreads first of all throughout the inner life of the Trinity; it is then communicated to creatures, in various degrees and orders of participation. The universe manifests the power, wisdom, and majesty of the Creator in its own way. Man, by his activity of knowledge and love, is in the image of God, in the infinite perfection of His intelligence and will. In a still more sublime way, the revelation of the Trinity, of the Incarnation, of divine sonship, manifests the infinite charity of God.

The glory of God, envisaged from the point of view of spiritual creation, means creation's recognition of the excellence of God and His gifts. Men are invited to glorify God who is manifest through the medium of creation, and make their thanks to Him (Wis. 13: 1-9; Rom. 1:18-21). More than that, they are invited to glorify God in His work of grace, that is, in the plan of salvation which He has from all eternity. The letter to the Ephesians lists all these gifts of salvation, in succeeding strophes, in tones of gratitude and admiration: predestination, sonship, redemption, revelation, election of Israel, vocation of the Gentiles. All these gifts of God, including that of revelation, are ordered, Saint Paul repeats over and over again, "towards the praise and glory of his grace" (Eph. 1:6. 12. 14).

Once again Christ is the perfect glorifier of the Father. In His hymn of jubilation (Mt. 11:25-27; Lk. 10:17-22), Christ gives thanks to the Father for being His only Son, the only one to share the intimacy of the Father and at the same time for being He in whom the Father opens up to the little ones the unfathomable riches of this intimacy. Christ's thanks spring from the spectacle of the Father's generosity, revealing and communicating the riches of His life to "the little ones." It consists in recognition of the Father's generosity and in revealing the Father to the little ones to make them His sons, capable in their turn of recognizing the Father and thanking him with a son's own words: "Abba, Father" (Gal. 4:6). In this recognition and love, men share in the perfection of God, who is love and truth: they glorify God.

The Blessed Virgin glorifies the Lord, for she accepts the angel's word in the obedience of faith (Lk. 1:27) and recognizes that the Lord has done great things for her (Lk. 1:45). Thanksgiving, in Saint Paul, is an habitual and spontaneous reflection of the soul: "I do not cease thanking," he says (1 Cor. 1:4; Eph. 1:16; Col. 1:3; 1 Thess. 1:2; 2 Thess. 1:3). Paul thanks God because in Jesus Christ we have been chosen to be saved (2 Thess. 2:13; 1 Cor. 1:4-5). He gives thanks because the faithful of his churches, the Thessalonians and the Ephesians, after having heard the word of truth, the good news of salvation, believed in it (1 Thess. 2:13; Eph. 1:13). It is in adhering to the plan of salvation by faith and in leading a life in accord with this faith that the Christian glorifies God. It is by faith, which is the communion of the human mind with the thought of God, and through charity, which instills the very love of God into the human heart, that man glorifies God. It is in leading the life of a son, in conformity with the plan of the Father as revealed by His Son, that man realizes the ultimate goal of revelation which is to make man share in the perfection of the Trinity's own life. Thus He glorifies God and at the same time realizes his own salvation; for in living fully his life of son, he effects his salvation, which is also the glory of God.

1. G. Auzou, *De la servitude au service* (Paris, 1961), p. 124.

2. A. Feuillet, "Le plan salvifique de Dieu dans l'epitre aux Romains," *Revue biblique*, 57 (1950): 338-340; S. Lyonnet, "L'histoire du salut selon le chapitre vii de l'épitre aux Romains," *Biblica*, 43 (1962): 117-151.

3. "Haec Sancta Trinitas..., primo per Moysen et sanctos Prophetas aliosque famulos suos, juxta ordinatissimam disposotionem temporum, doctrinam humano generi tribuit salutarem" (D 428).

4. "Et tandem unigenitus Dei Filius Jesus Christus... viam vitae manifestius demonstravit" (D 429).

5. "Sacrosancta oecumenica et generalis Tridentina Synodus... hoc sibi perpetuo ante oculos proponens, ut sublatis erroribus puritas ipsa Evangelii in Ecclesia conservetur, quod... Dominus noster Jesus Christus proprio ore primum promulgavit, deinde per suos Apostolos, tanquam fontem omnis et salutaris veritatis et morum disciplinae omni creaturae praedicari jussit" (D 783).

6. "Disponuntur autem ad ipsam justitiam, dum excitati divina gratia et adjuti, fidem ex auditu concipientes, libere moventur in Deum, credentes vera esse quae divinitus revelata et promissa sunt, atque illud in primis a Deo justificari impium per gratiam ejus, per redemptionem quae est in Christo Jesu" (D 798).

7. "Revelatio absolute necessaria dicenda est... quia Deus ex infinita bonitate sua ordinavit hominem ad finem supernaturalem, ad participanda scilicet bona divina, quae humanae mentis intelligentiam omnino superant" (D 1786).

8. The consideration of the finality of revelation thus necessarily involves a consideration of its necessity. If God actually decrees man's elevation to a supernatural end, the revelation of this end and the proportionate means for attaining this end appears absolutely necessary. Man, intelligent and free creature, must tend towards his end by knowing and willing this end. Now, in so far as it is supernatural, this end absolutely surpasses the powers and exigences of all created nature. The only way for man to know this end and the means he can use in the pursuit of this end is revelation. The same is not true of the religious truths of the natural order. Of himself, man can know them, for he has an innate capacity (D 1807, 1782, 1795, 2305). The revelation of these truths, however, is morally necessary so that man, "in the present condition of the human race," can know them "easily, with firm certitude, and without admixture of error" (D 1789).

CHAPTER X

UNITY AND COMPLEXITY OF REVELATION

For the theologian who seeks to sound its depths, revelation, like all the great Christian realities, appears to be extremely complex. This complexity can be seen in the paradoxes of revelation, in the number and variety of its different states, its aspects, its properties, in the variety of its media of communication and its modes of expression. And still, this very complexity resolves in harmony. Revelation, like the Trinity from which it has its source, is a mystery of unity and complexity.

I. THE ASPECTS OF REVELATION

There is, in revelation, a multiplicity of aspects that the theologian is in constant danger of overemphasizing or underestimating, or setting up in terms of contrast and opposition in an irreducible antagonism. It thus happens that revelation as doctrine is opposed to revelation as event, that revelation as encounter is opposed to revelation as truth. Rather than stress these points of opposition, we must recognize the diversity of aspects in revelation, according as we consider revelation in God, in its temporal terminus or in man's grasp of it. We may thus distinguish *four* essential aspects of revelation: it is activity of God, event of history, knowledge, encounter. All these aspects of revelation must be reunited in a synthetic and harmonious presentation.

1. Revelation is first a *mystery* and a *divine action*, that is, the transcendent activity by which God, from all eternity, decrees to save man, to intervene in his history and manifest Himself in a plan of glory. When we say that the motive of faith is God revealing Himself, we understand that faith rests on a transcendent act of the divine word: an all-knowing word, infallible, supremely truthful.

Revelation, in God, is a *free* operation, for God reveals out of love, free from the pressure of all necessity. It is an *immanent* operation: it is bound up with a decision that takes place inside God himself; only the terminus of the activity is outside God. It is an *eternal* operation, like all the divine operations. It is identical with the substance of God, for God's plan of revelation is God Himself, revealing Himself. It engages God in His entirety: it is an activity of the God of truth and love. That is why revelation is at once noetic and dynamic.

2. Revelation is an *event of history and history*. The terminus of the eternal divine activity, immanent and free, is a temporal effect. Revelation is produced in the form of interventions in history, landmarks in the story of humanity. God's activity of revelation is manifest in events whose actual content of revelation is explained by God's envoys who are sent for this mission. Divine activity is the principle of these events (exodus, the cross, etc.) and the principle of the interpretation of these events. The total event is made up of the historical fact and its interpretation, the event and the prophetic interpretation, which gives rise to the intelligibility of the event, thanks to the light received. These events are not isolated, but linked together; they have a meaning and manifest a plan. Each stage is linked to the preceding stage, taking it up again, making it more precise, pushing it a little farther. Revelation is an economy. As history progresses, the time of salvation swells with its riches. It rises slowly towards a point of fullness and concentration which is Jesus Christ. Of all the events of the history of salvation, the event of the Incarnation is the pregnant event: an event of which God Himself is the subject and whose meaning He Himself explains. In Jesus Christ, revelation culminates, as event and as history. It is accomplished.

3. Revelation is *knowledge*: testimony, message, word, doctrine. In His plan of love, God wants to associate man with His own life, but since He made man in His own image, intelligent and free, He must first of all make known His design of salvation so that man can freely adhere to this plan. As Spirit of truth, God addresses the intelligence of man. Revelation is an order of knowledge oriented towards an order of life. It is knowledge of the true God and knowledge of His plan of salvation. The activity of God, in the prophet, is the enlightening of his mind, light projected upon the events of history to let him discern their divine bearing. Christ expresses Himself in intelligible words: He speaks, preaches, teaches, testifies. The apostles, in their turn, testify, preach, and teach. The object of their testimony

and their preaching is called Gospel, good news, word of truth, message of salvation. In its actuated form, revelation is presented as the content of a word, a testimony, a deposition of witnesses, a doctrinal message. It is, however, a message which must never be separated from the person of the messenger, a message which must never become an independent reality that can be exploited by separating it from the person who has spoken it; a message which must always be referred to God's activity, testifying to Himself.

4. Revelation is *encounter*. By revelation, God addresses man, speaks to him, opens His heart to him, in a confidence of love about His personal life and His plan of salvation. This communication of God to man arrives at its destination only if it is completed in faith which is the encounter with the living and personal God in His word. This first encounter, which is a prelude to the face-to-face of vision, is the combined work of human freedom and grace.

All these aspects of revelation must be retained and never lost sight of, under pain of impoverishing or falsifying reality. A unilateral presentation of revelation as doctrine would run the risk of depersonalising revelation and cutting it out of its historical context. On the other hand, a too exclusive theory of revelation as event would lead rapidly to a purely historicising interpretation of revelation, under selling the role of witness (Christ, prophets, apostles) and the content of revelation. Finally, a revelation which is only divine activity would have no bond to join it to human awareness and would be more like a contact than an interpersonal communication of the God of truth.

II. THE PARADOXES OF REVELATION

The very multiplicity of the aspects of revelation makes it a reality whose traits frequently involve a paradox: it is at once transcendence and immanence, unity and multiplicity, discourse of truth and salvific act, doctrinal testimony and personal manifestation, progressive history and definitive truth, past event and ever actual presence, fulfillment and waiting.[1]

1. Revelation is at once *transcendence* and immanence. On the one hand it is the eternal Word of the living and uncreated God, that thrice holy and personally distinct God, "who dwells in light inaccessible," infinitely elevated above man His creature. And, on the other hand, it is incorporated into the events of history, it becomes a human dialogue with men; it uses the psyche of the prophets and expresses itself through signs and language. It comes from God, but it is

received by man, proclaimed by man. Two excesses constantly threaten revelation: the excess of a theology which absorbs the transcendence of revelation in the world of man, degrading and naturalizing the word of God, in the manner of liberal Protestantism and Modernism; or the excess of a theology which, in order not to compromise the sovereignty of God, maintains God in an inaccessible transcendence, after the manner of K. Barth, and does away with all real communication between God and man, between the activity of God and its manifestations in history: God's word never expresses itself and man can no longer grasp it, God and man both being reduced to parallel monologues. Catholic theology maintains both the transcendence and immanence of revelation, without corrupting the true notion of either. An encounter and dialogue are possible between God and man, for the analogy between the divine world and the created world, as well as man's receptivity or capacity to understand God, all authorize such a dialogue.

2. Revelation is at once *unity* and *multiplicity*. In God, revelation is a mystery of unity. The operation of the Father, Son, and Spirit is one, and one is the economy of salvation decreed by them. There are three who testify, but these three are only one. On the other hand, revelation being destined for man, it must accommodate to human conditions. Consequently, man receives a truth that is sovereignly one and simple in God in a diverse and multiple fashion. This explains the multiplicity of the media of communication: events, persons, visions, images, symbols, intuitions, dreams, ecstasies, raptures; this also explains the multiplicity of modes of expression or literary genres: history, poetry, autobiography, sapiential reflection; finally this explains the multiplicity of propositions of particular truths serving to express the unity of the divine mystery.

3. Revelation is at once *discourse of truth* and *salvific act* of the living God. It is light and power. The divine *dabar*, in this respect, goes beyond what we generally understand by the term *word*, with a noetic rather than a dynamic resonance. The word of God is a communication to man of the divine thinking, of the divine plans. But this word is charged with power. In the prophet or the apostle it acts as a consuming fire: God's envoy cannot help but testify. This word does not only make salvation known; it effects salvation. Christ proclaims the good news of salvation; at the same time He changes the situation of humanity, institutes the means that will be its salvation (Church and sacraments). The word of election, pardon, new life effects what it says. The word of God invites to the obedience

of faith through the distinct message of Christ, the apostles, or the Church. But this external proclamation is accompanied by an interior activity of grace which invites to the adherence of faith and which gives man the power to deliver himself to the living God, in Himself and for Himself. For God, there is no distance between intention and execution. What He says is accomplished, by the mere fact that it is God who says it. The word of God effects what it signifies. It is active and creative. It unsettles individual existence as well as the course of history. It tends to give life, salvation, grace. It tends to group men together and make up a kingdom of God, the Church, the holy people, the heavenly Jerusalem. It is the word of the living God. Set in motion by the Spirit of love, it is borne along by Him, alive with His breath, and thus endowed with its own efficacy.

4. Revelation is at once *doctrinal testimony* and *personal manifestation*. We have access to the mystery of God only through the mediation of signs: through the concept, image, word, writing (Scripture). In its accomplished form, divine testimony is presented as a structured complex of notions and propositions bearing on God and His plan of salvation. To take a stand against this fundamental fact would be to deny both the fact of man and the fact of Incarnation. Revelation on one hand is testimony *on* God: there is no revelation about God without revelation on God, without doctrine as a consequence. But on the other hand, revelation is the unveiling of divine reality itself. Signs and propositions are turned towards the realities they signify. Revelation is revelation of the living God, of the mysteries of His inmost life, of His plan of salvation. The message puts us in dialogue with God Himself. Correlatively, faith has its terminus, not in the words spoken, but in the Person itself: faith is the response of man to God who speaks.

5. Revelation is at once *progressive history* and *definitive truth*. Revelation is neither mythical or outside time, but part and parcel of history. It comes to us under the form of events which are intruded into the course of human history and which constitute the history of salvation. This is a homogeneous history which is presented as an economy, that is, as the effect of a disposition of divine wisdom. The center of this economy is Christ who prepares, announces, and, little by little, reveals everything. On the other hand, this revelation, communicated by way of human history, and to this degree incorporated into history and bound up with the conditions of history, stands out, once it is completed, as the absolute truth about man and God. On the plane of the relationship between God and man (not on

the plane of purely human and earthly values), it is declared to be definitive, immutable truth, valid for all men of all centuries; a truth which the Church has for its mission to propose, to sound its depths, to interpret, but not to modify or to suppress.

6. Revelation is at once *past event* and *actual presence.* Revelation is terminated as a series of events in which it is proposed or as a deposition of chosen witnesses. But this "once and for all" of the events of salvation does not exclude the "right now," the "today" of God's activity stirring up our faith and love. The call of Christ does not cease to echo, just as living, just as present as at the time of Christ and the apostles. Christ is still present in His truth and in His efficacy. The word is consigned to Scripture and preached by the Church only to reach all generations of men. God, through the voice of his Bride, does not cease to speak with us. The word is written so that it will last, so that it will not solidify and die. It springs up at each instant of time, just as fresh as on the first morning, always contemporary, always present. That is why liturgy is constantly repeated: today Christ is born, today Christ has died for our sins, today Christ has risen from the dead. Through the Church, God speaks to each man to introduce and associate him into the mystery of salvation. Today, the word echoes for each one of us; today, in each one of us, is accomplished what the word announces.

7. Revelation is at once *completion* and *expectation.* In Jesus Christ, revelation reaches its fullness: the decisive event is at the heart of history; the Gospel fulfills Scripture. Revelation is no longer something to be expected, but rather something to be proclaimed as a good news, something to be received in faith. The word of the Church is the definitive and efficacious proclamation of salvation. And still the Church always announces that the Lord is coming, that He is going to come. This means that the final act of revelation has not yet been produced, namely, the coming of Christ in His glory as Son of God and Savior, as well as the manifestation of the sons of the Father who have been won by the Son in the spirit of love. The Church waits for the return of the Bridegroom and the brilliant manifestation of the realities that exist behind the veil of faith.

III. REVELATION AS ACTION OF THE TRINITY

The complexity of revelation can be ultimately understood if it is bound up with the theology of the trinitarian missions and the doctrine of appropriation.

Revelation is the work of the whole Trinity: Father, Son, and Spirit. The spiritual fecundity of the Trinity is at work in accordance with the twofold line of thought and love: hence the "speaking" of the Word and the "spiration" of the Spirit. The speaking *ad intra* is prolonged by a speaking *ad extra,* and this is revelation. This speaking is a speaking out of love, just as the speaking *ad intra.* The word of Christ has its origin in the communion of life between Father and Son, and that is why it is the Word of God. The Spirit prolongs the mission of Christ, but He does not prolong it by speaking of Himself; He casts light on the word of Christ in communion of life with the Son, who is also in communion with the Father. The Word of the Spirit is that of the Son, and the Word of the Son is that of the Father. The only word of God belongs to the Father, to the Son, and to the Spirit. It has its origin in the unity of life within the Trinity. It is not the truth of one Person, but the truth of the Three Persons. It has its roots in the community of life of the Three Persons and expresses this community.

Even though the Father, Son, and the Spirit are one and the same single principle of revelation, it does not follow that the Trinity as such has no influence whatsoever on revelation. Each of the Persons acts according to the effects which correspond mysteriously to what are, respectively Father, Son, and Spirit, in the bosom of the Trinity.

As in all things, it is the Father who takes the initiative, for the Son receives everything from the Father, nature and mission. He is begotten of the Father, from the substance of the Father, true God from true God, consubstantial with the Father. It is the Father who sends the Son as Revealer of His plan of love (Jn. 4:9-10; Jn. 3:16); it is the Father who testifies in behalf of the Son and His mission of revelation through the works which He gives the Son to accomplish (Jn. 10:25; 5:36-37; 15:24; 9:41); it is the Father who draws men towards the Son by the interior attraction which He produces in human hearts (Jn. 6:44).

The Son, already the eternal Word of the Father, in the bosom of the Trinity, the Uncreated Word, in whom the Father expresses himself adequately, is ontologically qualified to be the supreme revelation of the Father and His plan of salvation. Already Son of the Father, He who always does the will of the Father and in whom the Father is well pleased, He is ontologically designated to initiate men into their life as sons. Christ is thus the perfect Revealer. Now the plan of the Father is the extension of the very life of the Trinity to all humanity. Through Christ, the Father means to associate us with the relationship of sonship and spiration in the life of the Trinity. He wants to beget His own Son in each human person, to breathe His own Spirit into them and join Himself to them in the most intimate communion, so that all will be one, as the Father and Son are one, in one and the same Spirit of love. And the Son comes, giving testimony of the Father and his plan of love: "For God so loved the world that He gave His only-begotten Son so that every man who believes in Him will not perish but will have life everlasting" (Jn. 3:16). If we accept the testimony that the Father addresses to us through His Son, the Father will make us His own children: "To all those who received Him (the Word), He gave the power to become sons of God" (Jn. 1:12). As a result of the presence of the Son in us, we receive a spirit of sonship, a spirit of love: "God has sent the Spirit of his Son into our hearts, which cries out Abba Father" (Gal. 4:6).

Whereas the Son "makes known," the Spirit "inspires".[2] He is the breath and the warmth of divine thought: he gives power and efficacy to the word. Christ has posited the objective reality of grace and truth, of salvation and revelation. The Spirit *applies* this to us and makes it *interior*. He makes the word soluble in the soul through the anointing He spreads there, for without the Spirit, transforming the understanding and the heart, how could man open his mind to something that is foreign to him? Christ proposes the word of God: the Spirit repeats it, insinuates it, makes it penetrate and abide. It is the Spirit who makes effective the gift of revelation.

The Spirit makes the message interior. It is also He who makes revelation something *actual*. He does not innovate, but he brings everything to its accomplishment. He does not pronounce any new revelation, but he opens all the depths of the first revelation. To the apostles He gives the living memory and understanding of the words of Christ (Jn. 14:26; 16:12-13). Through the assistance He gives the Church, He makes the revelation of the past actual for each generation. He constantly explains and interprets what is from Christ. And it is He, the Spirit of Christ, whose mission is to serve the word of Christ, who assures the continuity and faithfulness of this growing penetration, calling attention to what the Church had not yet observed, showing how new things are bound up with old things. To the questions of each age, the Spirit answers by a suggestion, which is His gift.

It is thus that the Father, by the combined activity of Word and Spirit, as with two arms of love, reveals Himself to humanity and draws humanity to Himself. The movement of love through which the Father reveals Himself to men through Christ and the return of this love which men make to Him by faith and by charity, appear as immersed in the flux and reflux of love which unite Father and Son in one Spirit. Revelation is an activity which involves both Trinity and humanity, setting up an uninterrupted dialogue between the Father and His children who are acquired through the blood of Christ. This dialogue unfolds at one and the same time on the plane of historical event and on the plane of eternity. It is inaugurated by the word and will be completed in vision, in a living encounter, face to face.

1. We could add still other characteristics of revelation which have been frequently stressed throughout the course of this study; revelation is gratuitous, inter-personal, social, hierarchical, salvific, ecclesial; progressive, historic, definitive, eschatological. In order to avoid repetition, we have thought it best in this chapter, to concentrate only on those characteristics whose contradiction is more obvious and might occasion more difficulty.

2. Saint Thomas notes: "The Holy Spirit is the Spirit of truth...; to those to whom he is sent he *inspires* the truth, just as the Son, sent from the Father, *makes known* the Father" (*In Iam ad Cor.*, c. 2, lect. 2).

CHAPTER XI

REVELATION AND ITS TRANSMISSION
ACCORDING TO THE CONSTITUTION "DEI VERBUM"

On November 14, 1962, the Second Vatican Council, began examining the schema *De Fontibus Revelationis.* The examination continued until November 21. In this first schema, composed of five chapters (1. The Twofold Source of Revelation; 2. Inspiration, Inerrancy, Literary Genre; 3. Old Testament; 4. New Testament; 5. Sacred Scripture in the Church), the passages which directly concerned revelation treated of the fact of revelation and its transmission, the role of Christ and the apostles in the economy of revelation, the twofold source of revelation, and the role of the Magisterium with reference to the deposit of faith.

First there were some general observations on the schema taken as a whole. From the very outset of the discussion, two distinct attitudes were observable among the Fathers: one group accepted the schema substantially but with reservations; while the other group declared the schema to be unacceptable as such and demanded that it be replaced by a more concise, more pastoral, and more ecumenical text.

Among the problems taken up in greater detail, the question of the relationship between Scripture and Tradition received special attention. What is this relationship and what are the terms in which it should be expressed? Concern for the ecumenical dialogue made the problem even more delicate. For Protestants, the schema on revelation immediately took on the force of a symbol: they were prepared to judge the Council largely on the basis of its attitude on this question. In the face of all the painstaking theological research involved, as well as the difficulties involved in elaborating an exact formulation, a good number of the Fathers asked if it were really opportune for the Council to take position on a question that was still disputed.

Since the first schema had thus met with strong resistance by an important majority of the Fathers and since, as a consequence, the formal discussion of the individual chapters promised to be laborious, lengthy, and without great hope of success, Pope John XXIII decided, on November 20, to have the schema revised by a special commission before continuing the examination of its individual details. This mixed commission, composed of seven cardinals named by the Pope, ten members of the theological commission, and ten members of the secretariat for unity, was named on November 25, 1962.

Tuesday, November 20, the day on which Pope John decided to send the schema before this mixed commission, was a turning point in the Council. Since that day, the problem of the material content of Scripture and Tradition remains an *open* problem, one which theologians and exegetes can continue to explore in depth. The Council, for its part, chose to explore a different route, stressing rather the organic unity of Scripture and Tradition, as well as the intimate relationship between Scripture, Tradition, and the Church.

In the course of the second session of the Council, there was complete silence regarding the schema on revelation. The mixed commission completed its work in March of 1963 and the Fathers were informed of the results in May of the same year. At that time, a good number of them expressed their desire to see Tradition and Revelation itself taken up in a more developed manner in the text. On March 7, 1964, the theological commission set up a sub-commission to amend the schema along these lines. This sub-commission divided the first chapter (God's revealed word) into two chapters: I. *Revelation itself,* II. *Handing on Divine Revelation.* These two new chapters were examined by the theological commission in plenary session, from June 1 to June 6, 1964. The first chapter was accepted without difficulty. The second was accepted by a majority of 17 to 7, the opposition objecting that the text did not state that there are more truths in Tradition than in Scripture.

The new schema was discussed in the course of the third session of the Council, from September 30 to October 6, 1964, and this time the delicate balance which had been achieved by the commission and sub-commission was not called into question. As a whole, the text pleased the Fathers by its balance, its biblical flavor, its Christocentric character, the large treatise on Tradition, and finally by the freedom granted to theologians in the investigation of disputed questions.

As soon as the Council's discussion had been completed, the commission went back to work to incorporate the observations made by the Fathers, particularly on Chapters I and II, the most important in the schema. The result of their work was submitted to the Fathers on the last day of the third session.

Finally, the revised text was submitted to a vote of the Council assembly at the beginning of the fourth session, September 20 to 22, 1965. The modifications of detail suggested by the Fathers, without changing the substance of the text, improved it considerably in its expression. Having been voted upon chapter by chapter on October 29, 1965, and approved almost unanimously, the Constitution *Dei Verbum* was officially promulgated by Pope Paul VI on November 18, 1965.

It is not our intention here to analyse the whole Constitution, nor to examine the history of the different schemas which preceded the text voted upon by the Fathers of the Council. We shall consider only Chapters I and II, which concern revelation and its handing on, and particularly Chapter I, which describes revelation in itself. We shall make a detailed analysis of the first ten paragraphs which compose Chapters I and II of *Dei Verbum*, and then comment on the first two chapters as a whole.[1] This commentary on the Second Vatican Council's teaching on revelation will constitute a sort of synthesis of our work.

1. Preface

1. *Dei Verbum*: These words will serve from now on as the title of sancta Synodus verbis S. Joannis obsequitur dicentis: "Annuntiamus vobis vitam aeternam, quae erat apud Patrem et apparuit nobis: quod vidimus et audivimus vobis, ut et vos societatem habeatis nobiscum, et societas nostra sit cum Patre et cum Filio eius Iesu Christo" (1 *Jn*. 1:2-3).

2. Propterea, Conciliorum Tridentini et Vaticani I inhaerens vestigiis, genuinam de divina revelatione ac de eius transmissione doctrinam proponere intendit, ut salutis praeconio mundus universus audiendo credat, credendo speret, sperando amet.

1. Hearing the word of God with reverence and proclaiming it with faith, the Sacred Synod takes its direction from these words of St. John: "We announce to you the eternal life which dwelt with the Father and was made visible to us. What we have seen and heard we announce to you, so that you may have fellowship with us and our common fellowship be with the Father and his son Jesus Christ" (1 *Jn*. 1:2-3).

2. Therefore, following in the footsteps of the Council of Trent and Vatican I, this present Council wishes to set forth authentic

doctrine on divine revelation and how it is handed on, so that by hearing the message of salvation the whole world may believe, by believing it may hope, and by hoping it may love.

Although sober, the introduction is profound. Both solemn and religious, the tone of this first paragraph is amply justified by the fact that the Constitution *Dei Verbum* is logically presented as the first great document produced by Vatican II. Indeed, these words also serve as an introduction to the whole of the Council's work. Here is stated the theme of the Constitution, a theme which the following chapters will further develop.

1. *Dei Verbum*: These words will serve from now on as the title of the Constitution. They distinguish it from other conciliar documents and at the same time express the whole of its content. The Living God has *spoken* to humanity. This phrase, the *Word of God*, refers first of all to revelation, that first intervention by which God steps out of his mystery and speaks to humanity to disclose to it the secrets of divine life and to communicate to it his plan of salvation. This is the great fact which dominates the two Testaments and from which the Church draws her life. This word of God, spoken once and for all, endures throughout the ages, through Tradition and Scripture, always living and relevant.

The attitude of the Council toward the word of God is the same described in Chapter II as that of the Magisterium of the Church: it *hears* and *proclaims* the word of God. Like the whole Christian people, whose faith it shares, it first of all receives the word of the Lord with faith and reverence; but also, in virtue of the prophetic mission received from Christ, it is the herald of this word which it proclaims with the confidence of the apostles. The word *fidenter*, which qualifies this proclamation, calls to mind the *parrèsia* or attitude of confidence and assurance of the apostolic preaching (*Acts* 4:29-31; 9:28; 19:8). As the minister of God's word, the Council respectfully recalls (*obsequitur*) the beginning of St. John's first epistle: "We announce to you the eternal life which dwelt with the Father and was made visible to us. What we have seen and heard we announce to you, so that you may have fellowship with us and our common fellowship be with the Father and his Son Jesus Christ" (1 *Jn.* 1:2-3). This text announces in biblical terms everything that is essential to the Constitution. Life, which was in God, together with the Father, *was made visible to us*. God has stepped out of his Mystery and, thanks to the sign of Christ's humanity, John has been able to see and hear the Word of life. John announces what he has seen and heard, so that all men, by faith in his testimony, will share in his experience and, together with him, enter into communion of life with the Father and His Son Jesus Christ. Epiphany of God in Jesus Christ, mediation of the apostolic testimony, participation by man in the life of the Trinity: this text of St. John's describes the whole movement of revelation: the *life in God*, the life which *descends* towards man and, in Jesus Christ, is *manifest* to man in order to effect his return to Life. The text, in its compactness and power of suggestion, is a sort of *leitmotif* for the whole Constitution, and especially for the first chapter.

2. The second sentence indicates the *purpose* of the Constitution. The Council proposes to explain the true doctrine on revelation and its transmission. In this, it continues, yet develops, the work undertaken by the Councils of Trent and Vatican I. The reference to St. Augustine, which concludes the introduction, further emphasizes the pastoral preoccupation which inspires all the efforts of the Council.

CHAPTER I. REVELATION ITSELF

2. *Nature and Object of Revelation*

1. Placuit Deo in sua bonitate et sapientia seipsum revelare et notum facere sacramentum voluntatis suae (cf. *Eph.* 1:9), quo homines per Christum, Verbum carnem factum, in Spiritu Sancto accessum habent ad Patrem et divinae naturae consortes efficiuntur (cf. *Eph.* 2:18; 2 Pet. 1:4).

2. Hac itaque revelatione Deus invisibilis (cf. *Col.* 1:15; 1 *Tim.* 1, 17) ex abundantia caritatis suae homines tamquam amicos alloquitur (cf. *Ex.* 33:11; *Jn.* 15:14-15) et cum eis conversatur (cf. *Bar.* 3, 38), ut eos ad societatem secum invitet in eamque suscipiat.

3. Haec revelationis oeconomia fit gestis verbisque intrinsece inter se connexis, ita ut opera, in historia salutis a Deo patrata, doctrinam et res verbis significatas manifestent ac corroborent, verba autem opera proclament et mysterium in eis contentum elucident.

4. Intima autem per hanc revelationem tam de Deo quam de hominis salute veritas nobis in Christo illucescit, qui mediator simul et plenitudo totius revelationis existit.

1. In his goodness and wisdom God chose to reveal himself and to make known to us the hidden purpose of his will (see *Eph.* 1:9) by which through Christ, the word made flesh, man might in the Holy Spirit have access to the Father and come to share in the divine nature (see *Eph.* 2:18; 2 *Pet.* 1:4).

2. Through this revelation, therefore, the invisible God (see *Col.* 1:15; 1 *Tim.* 1:17) out of the abundance of his love speaks to men as friends (see *Ex.* 33:11; *Jn.* 15:14-15) and lives among them (see *Bar.* 3:38), so that he may invite and take them into fellowship with himself.

3. This plan of revelation is realized by deeds and words having an inner unity: the deeds wrought by God in the history of salvation manifest and confirm the teaching and realities signified by the words, while the words proclaim the deeds and clarify the mystery contained in them.

4. By this revelation then, the deepest truth about God and the salvation of man shines out for our sake in Christ, who is both the mediator and the fullness of all revelation.

1. The revelation here described is revelation in its active and constitutive phase. It is also revelation in the whole economy of its concrete realization by means of history and the Incarnation. The Constitution states first of all the fact and the object of revelation.

Revelation, like the whole work of salvation, must be called an effect of God's good will: *placuit*. It is *grace*. It is free initiative on the part of God, and not the result of any constraint or previous request on the part of man. It is a work of love and proceeds from the goodness and wisdom of God. The text takes up the words of Vatican I, but it adopts a more *personalized* formulation. Instead of the phrase *placuit ejus sapientiae et bonitati*, it says: *placuit Deo, in sua bonitate et sapientia*, and it speaks first of God's *goodness* and then of his wisdom.

With respect to the object of revelation, the text also follows Vatican I, but whereas Vatican I said: *seipsum ac aeterna voluntatis suae decreta revelare*, Vatican II repeats the verb and replaces the words *decreta* by the Pauline term *sacramentum* ("mysterium" in the Greek text), which is more biblical and more concrete: *seipsum revelare et notum facere sacramentum voluntatis suae*. In saying that the object of revelation is God himself, the text thus personalizes revelation: before making known something, that is, his plan for salvation, God reveals someone, himself. The Pauline mystery brings out this plan of salvation, hidden in God from all eternity, and now unveiled, the plan in which God establishes Christ as the center of the new economy and constitutes him, by his death and resurrection, the one and only principle of salvation, for Jew and Gentile alike, Head of all, both angels and men. This mystery is the overall divine plan which essentially goes back to Christ, with his unfathomable riches, his treasures of wisdom and knowledge. Concretely, this mystery is Christ. By using this Pauline terminology of *mystery*, with this fullness of meaning and manifold overtones which it takes on in the letter to the Ephesians (Ch. 1), the Council gives the most complete, the richest, and the most suggestive expression of the object of revelation.

The second part of the sentence explains the content of God's salvific plan for humanity. God's plan is that mankind, through Christ, Incarnate Word, approach the Father (*Eph.* 2:18) in the Spirit and become sharers in the divine nature (2 *Pet.* 14). The divine plan, expressed in terms of interpersonal relations, includes the three principal mysteries of Christianity: Trinity, Incarnation, Grace.

2. After having stated the fact and object of revelation, the Council clarifies its nature. By revelation, the *invisible* and hidden God (*Col.* 1:15; 1 *Tim.* 1:17), whom no one can see without passing through the portals of death, the transcendent and thrice-holy God, *out of the abundance of his love* (for God is Love: 1 *Jn.* 4:8) steps out from his mystery. God breaks the silence: he speaks to man, calls him, establishes a friendly *dialogue* with him, as he did with Moses (*Ex.* 33:11) and with the apostles (*Jn.* 15:14-15).

God enters into *conversation* with man in order to invite him to share in the society of the Divine Persons and to introduce him into this society. The text of *Baruch* 3:38, to which the Council refers, and which is used in the liturgy (for example, in the sixth prophecy of the old office for Holy Saturday), shows how Wisdom has come down from heaven to live among men by its incarnation in the Jewish Law. The Council already alludes to this fullness of revelation in which the Personal Wisdom of God, through the Incarnation, makes its way into human existence, lives with men, a man among men, and converses with them. Jesus Christ is the wisdom of God who has appeared on earth and conversed with men. This theme, merely touched upon here, will be taken up again in paragraph IV.

In defining revelation, the Council thus retains the analogy of word, present throughout the whole of the Old and New Testament (*Heb.* 1:1), commonly found in the documents of the Magisterium[2] and the whole theological tradition of the Church. God has *spoken* to humanity; it is by his word that the Invisible has made himself known and the Transcendent has become near to us. The present economy is an economy of word and faith. The economy of vision belongs to the time after death. Our God is the God of the word: he speaks to Abraham, to Moses, to the prophets, and, through them, he speaks to his people. Through Christ, God speaks to the apostles and to us; for in Christ it is the Son Himself who speaks.

This word by which God somehow bridges the infinite distance which separates him from man in order to meet him can only be a word of friendship: it proceeds from love, develops in friendship, and pursues a work of love: *ex abundantia caritatis . . . tamquam amicos . . . ut ad societatem secum. . . .* If God enters into communication with man his creature, this can only be, in the last analysis, in order to establish bonds of friendship with him and to associate him in his own innermost life: to invite him into it. The revelation that proceeds from love pursues a work of love, and seeks to introduce man into this society of love which is the Trinity. The text thus echoes the theme announced in the introduction.

3. The analogy of word, which serves to represent revelation, does not as yet say anything about the *concrete disposition* adopted by God to enter into personal encounter with man. A man, for example, can communicate in many different ways: by gesture, by word, by gesture and word together, by oral signs or written symbols. So too, in many different ways can God communicate with man. Thus it is important for an understanding of revelation to describe the *economy* actually adopted by God in speaking to humanity. Addressing man, who is a being of flesh and spirit immersed in a world of matter and time, God communicated by way of the Incarnation and history. This is the first time that any document of the Church's Magisterium has thus described the economy of revelation in its *concrete realization* and in this active phase which brings it into existence.

The Council states first of all that revelation is effected by an intimate union of deeds and words. By *gesta* (a word that has a more personalist connotation than *facta*), we must understand the salvific acts of God, that is, all those works accomplished by God which constitute salvation history. Some are directly accomplished by God, others through the instrumentality of the prophets. Some result from his ordinary Providence, others appear as genuine miracles. But all of them, properly speaking, are manifestations of the divine activity in the history of salvation, ordered according to an all-wise dispensation (economy) willed by God. Examples of these deeds or works of God in the Old Testament are the events of the Exodus, the establishment of the royal line in Israel, judgments of God manifested by the defeat of armies, the Exile, the Captivity and the Restoration. New Testament examples are the actions of Christ's life and particularly his miracles, his death and resurrection. The *words* are the words of Moses and the prophets who interpret God's actions in history, the words of Christ explaining the meaning of his own actions, and finally, the words of the apostles, witnesses and authorized interpreters of Christ's life.

Having thus asserted the intimate union of word and work in the economy of revelation, a union not unlike the union which exists between body and soul, the Council briefly explains how words and works are intimately interdependent and mutually serve each other. The *works* accomplished by God "in the history of salvation, manifest and confirm the teaching and realities (the plan and salvific actions of God) signified by the words." God actually manifests His plan for salvation in the very act by which He accomplishes. The God who reveals is a God who makes a place for Himself in history and stands revealed as effecting the salvation of His people. Thus, the deliverance from the yoke of Egypt is a clear sign of the intervention of God the Savior and of salvation itself; the cure of the paralytic is a clear sign of the power of Christ to liberate and of the very liberation from sin which he works in the soul. The resurrection expresses his sovereign power over life and death. On the other hand, these same works also *confirm*, that is, support, corroborate, and attest both the teaching and the mysterious underlying reality which is hidden in the works and signified by the words. Thus, the Exodus confirms the promise Yahweh made to Moses that he would save his people; the cure of the paralytic is both a sign and a proof of the validity of the word of the Son of God who dares to forgive sins; the resurrection confirms the truth of Christ's testimony and the reality of his mission as Son of God, come to save mankind from sin and death.

The events, however, frequently remain opaque; works are often marred or threatened by ambiguity and equivocation. The word must come into play to dissipate this ambiguity and establish the authentic and mysterious meaning of the divine activity: "The words *proclaim* the deeds and *clarify* the mystery contained in them." If it is true, for example, that Christ's acts of healing and pardon admirably express the love he has come to reveal, his death still remains an event which is subject to a variety of interpretations. It is the word of Christ, living on in the word of his apostles, which reveals the unheard-of dimensions of this death and, at one and the same time, proposes both the event itself and its salvific bearing on our belief. It is Peter's preaching that witnesses to the fact that the apostles on Pentecost morning were not drunk, but under the influence of the Holy Spirit who had descended upon them (*Act.* 2:15-18), and that Christ's resurrection is not only a miracle, but also the mystery of Christ's enthronement as Messiah and Lord (*Act.* 2:33-36). The same is true of the Exodus. Without Moses' word, speaking in the name of God, to interpret this migration as a deliverance in view of a future covenant, the event is no longer pregnant with that fullness of meaning which could transform it into the foundation of Israel's religion. The events are charged with a religious meaning which the words are meant to proclaim and clarify.

With respect to this intimate and vital union between word and work, there are two important remarks to be made: a) The union in question here is a union of *nature*, not always a union in *time*. Sometimes there is simultaneity of deed and word, e.g. in the cure of the paralytic where the words accompany the deed. Sometimes the event precedes the words, e.g. the creation of the world, the establishment of the royal line in Israel. Then again, the word may at times precede the event, e.g. the description of the Messiah as a Suffering Servant (cf. *Is.* 48:3-8; *Amos* 3:7). b) We must also note that the proportion between word and work can be variable. Sometimes words are prevalent, e.g. in the Wisdom Books, in the Sermon on the Mount, but sometimes, too, deeds are prevalent, e.g. in the Historical Books, in the events of the passion, death, and resurrection of Christ.

By insisting on the works and words as the constitutive elements of revelation and upon their intimate union, the Council emphasizes the historical and sacramental character of revelation: events explained by the word of the prophets, Christ, and the apostles. The *historical* character of revelation appears in the activity of God himself who steps out of his mystery and takes a hand in human history, in the succession of events or interventions of God which all take place in a coherent and very wise plan which is, properly speaking, the economy of revelation and salvation, and finally, in the interpretation of these events by the word which in itself constitutes an event. The *sacramental* character of revelation appears in the interpenetration and mutual support that exists between word and work. God performs the act of salvation and at the same time develops its meaning; He intervenes in history and tells us of the import of His intervention; He acts and comments on His action. This general structure of revelation, asserted once again in Chapter IV with respect to the Old Testament,[3] and in Chapter V with respect to the New Testament,[4] is enough to distinguish Christian revelation from every other form of revelation of a purely philosophical or gnostic type.

4. It is through this revelation that the deepest truth about God and man *shines out for our sake in Christ*. In Christ is revealed who God is: the Father who has created us and who loves us as his children; the Son or Word, who calls and invites us to a communion of life with the Trinity; the Spirit who vivifies and sanctifies. In Christ, the truth about man is also revealed: he is called and chosen by God from the creation of the world to be the adopted son of the Father in Christ.

Christ is at once Mediator and Fullness of revelation. He is the *means* chosen by God to reveal who he is (Father, Son, Spirit) and what we are (sinners called to divine life). Christ is the means revealing to us Life and the way to Life. "I am the way; I am the truth and I am the life; no one comes to the Father except by me" (*Jn.* 14:6). And again: "no one knows the Son but the Father, and no one knows the Father but the Son and those to whom the Son may choose to reveal him" (*Mt.* 11:27). "No one has ever seen God; but God's only Son, he who is nearest to the Father's heart, he has made him known" (*Jn.* 1:18). Christ is also the fullness[5] of revelation, that is, God revealing and God revealed, author and object of revelation, he who reveals the mystery and is the mystery himself in person (*Jn.* 14:6; 2 *Cor.* 4:4-6; *Eph.* 1:3-14; *Col.* 1:26-27; 1 *Tim.* 3:16). He is in person the truth he announces and preaches. As a result, this truth which shines in him does not merely engage the adherence of our mind; it demands to play a role in our whole life, to transform our life and to transform us into Christ. Through union with Christ it tends towards communion with the Father, the Son, and the Spirit.

3. *Preparation for Revelation of the Good News*

1. Deus, per Verbum omnia creans (cf. *Jn.* 1:3) et conservans, in rebus creatis perenne sui testimonium hominibus praebet (cf. *Rom.* 1:19-20), et viam salutis supernae aperire intendens, insuper protoparentibus inde ab initio semetipsum manifestavit.

2. Post eorum autem lapsum eos, redemptione promissa, in spem salutis erexit (cf. *Gen.* 3:15), et sine intermissione generis humani curam egit, ut omnibus qui secundum patientiam boni operis salutem quaerunt, vitam aeternam daret (cf. *Rom.* 2:6-7).

3. Suo autem tempore Abraham vocavit, ut faceret eum in gentem magnam (cf. *Gen.* 12:2), quam post Patriarchas per Moysen et Prophetas erudivit ad se solum Deum vivum et verum, providum Patrem et iudicem iustum agnoscendum, et ad promissum Salvatorem expectandum, atque ita per saecula viam Evangelio praeparavit.

1. God, who through the Word creates all things (see *Jn.* 1:3) and keeps them in existence, gives men an enduring witness to himself in created realities (see *Rom.* 1:19-20). Planning to make known the way of heavenly salvation, he went further and from the start manifested himself to our first parents.

2. Then after their fall, his promise of redemption aroused in them the hope of being saved (see *Gen.* 3:15), and from that time on

he ceaselessly kept the human race in his care, to give eternal life to those who perseveringly do good in search of salvation (see *Rom.* 2:6-7).

3. Then, at the time he had appointed, he called Abraham in order to make of him a great nation (see *Gen.* 12:2). Through the patriarchs, and after them through Moses and the prophets, he taught this people to acknowledge himself the one living and true God, provident Father and just judge, and to wait for the Savior promised by him, and in this manner prepared the way for the gospel down through the centuries.

1. The first sentence affirms and dintinguishes a double manifestation on the part of God: one by the testimony of the created world, addressed to all men; the other by positive revelation, addressed to our first parents. The same God who made the cosmos has also manifested himself in human history.

The text describes in a few words God's first manifestation, creation. It is through his Word that God has created (*Jn.* 1:3) and sustains all things, just as it is through his Word that God has spoken to humanity (paragraph 4). The created universe constitutes a first presence and a first manifestation of God: it is a permanent testimony of himself to humanity inscribed in the universe he has created (*Rom.* 1:19-20). The Council merely states this fact without pausing to explain it.

The same God who has manifested himself to humanity by his creative Word is also the saving God who, in order to open to mankind the way of salvation, has manifested himself to our first parents by an historical and personal revelation. The Council however does not specify the relationship between these two manifestations of God, the one natural, the other supernatural. It does not say whether in the divine intention the one is ordered to the other, nor whether the first is already permeated by grace. It immediately begins a summary description of the stages of Old Testament revelation: the promise made to our first parents, the call of Abraham, and the instruction of the chosen people through Moses and the prophets.

2. After the fall of our first parents God *aroused* in them the hope of a future salvation (*Gen.* 3:15) by the promise of redemption. This glimmer of salvation, first evoked by Genesis, is the Protoevangelium. With this promise, which is of universal salvific bearing, the history of salvation is under way, and God leaves no one outside of salvation. Even though the people of Israel was constituted the chosen depositary of this promise, God has never ceased (*sine intermissione*) to keep

the whole of mankind in his care (*curam egit*) and to give eternal life to all those who, persevering in good, seek salvation (*Rom.* 2:6-7).

3. The last sentence quickly scans over two millenia of history, from Abraham to Christ. God called Abraham, formed and instructed Israel to be his chosen people, and thus prepared the way for the gospel.

At a time of his own choosing, God *called Abraham* to make for himself a great nation (*Gen.* 12:2-3). This people, after the patriarchal age, was instructed by God through Moses and the prophets. The verb *erudire* implies both instruction and formation. God formed the Jewish people to recognize him as *the living and true God*, as a *Father who cares* for his children, as a *Judge* of great justice, and to wait for the promised Savior. The Council thus affirms the essential content of the Old Testament revelation: on the one hand, *knowledge of the one God*, that is, the God of truth and life, love and justice; and, on the other hand, *longing for the promised Savior*. The last clause of this sentence presents the Old Testament revelation as a thorough pedagogy which lasted over many centuries, on the course of which God formed his people and outlined the path for his gospel.

4. *Christ, Who Brings Revelation to Fulfillment*

1. Postquam vero multifariam multisque modis Deus locutus est in Prophetis, "novissime diebus istis locutus est nobis in Filio" (*Heb.* 1:1-2).

2. Misit enim Filium suum, aeternum scilicet Verbum, qui omnes homines illuminat, ut inter homines habitaret iisque intima Dei enarraret (cf. *Jn.* 1:1-18).

3. Iesus Christus ergo, Verbum caro factum, "homo ad homines" missus, "verba Dei loquitur" (*Jn.* 3:34), et opus salutare consummat quod dedit ei Pater faciendum (cf. *Jn.* 5:36; 17:4).

4. Quapropter Ipse, quem qui videt, videt et Patrem (cf. *Jn.* 14:9), tota suiipsius praesentia ac manifestatione, verbis et operibus, signis et miraculis, praesertim autem morte sua et gloriosa ex mortuis resurrectione, misso tandem Spiritu veritatis, revelationem complendo perficit ac testimonio divino confirmat, Deum nempe nobiscum esse ad nos ex peccati mortisque tenebris liberandos et in aeternam vitam resuscitandos.

5. Oeconomia ergo christiana, utpote foedus novum et definitivum, numquam praeteribit, et nulla iam nova revelatio publica expectanda est ante gloriosam manifestationem Domini Nostri Iesu Christi (cf. 1 *Tim.* 6:14 and *Tit.* 2:13).

1. Then, after speaking in many and varied ways through the prophets, "now at last in these days God has spoken to us in his Son" (*Heb.* 1:1-2).

2. For he sent his Son, the eternal Word, who enlightens all men, so that he might dwell among men and tell them of the innermost being of God (see *Jn.* 1:1-18).

3. Jesus Christ, therefore, the Word made flesh, sent as "a man to men, speaks the words of God" (*Jn.* 3:34), and completes the work of salvation which his Father gave him to do (see *Jn.* 5:36; 17:4).

4. To see Jesus is to see his Father (*Jn.* 14:9). For this reason Jesus perfected revelation by fulfilling it through his whole work of making himself present and manifesting himself: through his words and deeds, his signs and wonders, but especially through his death and glorious resurrection from the dead and final sending of the Spirit of truth. Moreover he confirmed with divine testimony what revelation proclaimed, that God is with us to free us from the darkness of sin and death, and to raise us up to life eternal.

5. The Christian dispensation, therefore, as the new and definitive covenant, will never pass away and we now await no further new public revelation before the glorious manifestation of our Lord Jesus Christ (see 1 *Tim.* 6:14 and *Tit.* 2:13).

The paragraph returns to the theme of Christ the Mediator and Fullness of revelation, but this time in the context of the *history* of revelation.

1. The text of the Epistle to the Hebrews states, in this historical perspective, that Christ is the *peak* of revelation. It brings out the superiority of the new revelation over the old, as well as the relation between the two phases of salvation history. Between the two economies there is both continuity and difference. The element of continuity is God and his *word*, the word of the Son being the continuation and fulfillment of the word spoken through the instrumentality of the prophets. There is continuity, but also *difference* and greater excellence. There is difference in the eras, the manner of revelation (intermittent and fragmentary word in the Old Testament; the unique and total word of the Son in the New Testament), the forms of revelation, the people addressed, and the mediators. It is the person of the Son who, in the last analysis, constitutes *the superior excellence* of the new revelation as compared to the old. Because Christ is Son, revelation attains its peak in him.[6]

2. The text then explains why Christ is thus the peak of revelation.

God has sent us His Son, that is, His eternal *Word*: this Son, this Word of God, who is already the light of men through the fact of creation, has been sent by God to *dwell* among men and *tell* us the secret of this divine life to which he invites us and wants to introduce us: "No one has ever seen God: the only-begotten Son of God, who is in the bosom of the Father, he reveals him" (Jn 1:18). This is the deeper meaning and fulfillment of the text of Baruch 3:38, quoted above. Christ is the Wisdom of God living among men and conversing with them. As the Son of God, the eternal Word of the Father, the Light of men, he is ontologically qualified to reveal God and his mystery.

3. The third sentence contains the central insight of the whole paragraph and even of the whole chapter. It takes up again what has just been said concerning the Son sent among men, insisting on the fullness and reality of the Incarnation in the economy of revelation. Jesus Christ, the substantial Word of God, in whom God speaks Himself and all creation (*ad intra et ad extra*), is the same Word who, through his Incarnation, speaks to us as a man to men. The close relationship between the *Word* and the *words* of God he pronounces in the form of *human flesh* is a striking emphasis of this *humanization* of the Son of God who, as true man, has a perfect right to use the means of expression proper to human nature. Jesus Christ, the Council says, is thus the Word of God made flesh (*Verbum caro factum*), become one of us, that is, *man*, and sent to *men* to meet us and speak to us on our own level (*homo ad homines missus*). Jesus Christ is the Word of God who is all truth, "pronounces the words of God" (*verba Dei loquitur*: Jn. 3:34) and "fulfills the work of salvation which his Father has given him to do" (Jn. 5:36; 17:4). Revelation actually belongs to this work of salvation which the Father has entrusted to his Son. In his priestly prayer, Christ says to his Father: "I have glorified you on earth, I have completed the work you have given me to do" (Jn. 17:4), and then he adds at once: "I have manifested your Name to men" (Jn. 17:6). And further on: "I have revealed your Name to them and I shall reveal it to them so that the love with which you have loved me will be in them and I will be in them" (Jn. 17:26).

4. Since Christ is thus the Son of God, the eternal Word made flesh, it follows that he is at once both the supreme Revealer and the supreme Object of revelation. In him revelation attains its *fulfillment* (*complendo*) and *completion* (*perficit*). The Council applies to Christ what has been said in paragraph 2 about the general structure of revelation.[7] Christ exercised his role as Revealer in all the ways that are consistent with his incarnation: by his full presence and self-manifestation,[8] through his signs and wonders,[9] his words and deeds, chief

among them his death and resurrection, and finally, through the sending of the Spirit of truth. The expression "by his full presence and self-manifestation," which is equivalent to the Greek term *epiphany* (2 *Tim.* 1:10), means that revelation in Christ, the incarnate Word, has enlisted all the resources of human expression, the *facere* as well as the *docere* (*Acts* 1:1), to manifest the Son of God and, in him, the Father; for he who sees Christ sees the Father (*Jn.* 14:9). In the same vein, St. Ignatius of Antioch said: "There is but one God, manifested by Jesus Christ his Son, who is his Word emerged from silence" (*Magn.* 7, 2). And St. Irenaeus: "through the Son made visible and tangible, the Father has appeared" (*Adv. Haer.* IV, 6, 6). The Incarnation of the Son concretely understood is the revelation of the Son, and through him, of the Father. It is thus through his actions, his deeds, his attitudes, his whole behavior, as well as by his words, that Christ exercised his role as Revealer. The mission of the Spirit equally belongs to Christ's role as Revealer insofar as it guides this work to its completion, for although the Spirit brings no new objects of revelation, it is still the Spirit who introduces us into the whole truth of Christ and thus brings all things to their fulfillment. It is he, the Spirit, who gives the apostles their living memory and understanding of the words and deeds of Christ (*Jn.* 14:26; 16:12-13). Again, this is an expression of the trinitarian dimension of revelation.

The Council stresses the twofold role realized by the same realities in the life of Christ. Christ's words, actions, miracles, life, passion, death, and resurrection, which belong to the very economy of revelation, also have an *apologetic* value. Since Christ lived among men as the Son of the Father, his message, his works, his whole behavior as Incarnate Word *radiate* a light which is, properly speaking, his *glory* and which designates him as Son of the Father.[10] The sublimity of his teaching, the wisdom and the holiness of his life, the power manifested in his miracles and resurrection, the abundance of charity demonstrated by his death: this whole radiance of Christ's being and activity constitutes a *divine testimony* (*Jn.* 5:36-37; 10:37-38) which confirms revelation and clearly shows its credibility. For this radiance attests that Christ is *truly* in our midst, Emmanuel, God-with-us, acting and conversing with us, in order to free us from the shadow of sin and death and lead us up to everlasting life.

5. The last sentence of this paragraph is a conclusion to everything said about Christ. Since Christ is the eternal Word of God, the only Son of the Father, sent to man to reveal the intimate life of God, the new and definitive *covenant* brought by him could not possibly be considered as something merely transitory. This economy will not pass

away, will not ever be supplanted by a more perfect one. Thus we are not to await a new public revelation (this does not exclude private revelation) before the glorious epiphany of Christ, his manifestation in glory and not in the condition of mere slave (1 *Tim.* 6:16; *Tit.* 2:13). Since God has spoken his only Word, complete and entire (insofar as we can grasp it in our earthly condition), what more could he say? Likewise, having given us his only Son, what more could he give us? We could not possibly imagine a new revelation in the future anymore than a new Incarnation of the Son of God. The New Testament is *novum et definitivum.* Jesus Christ is the final word of revelation: in him everything is accomplished, our salvation and his manifestation.

5. *Faith, Accepting Revelation*

1. Deo revelanti praestanda est "oboeditio fidei" (*Rom.* 16:26; cf. *Rom.* 1:5; 2 *Cor.* 10:5-6), qua homo se totum libere Deo committit "plenum revelanti Deo intellectus et voluntatis obsequium" praestando et voluntarie revelationi ab Eo datae assentiendo.

2. Quae fides ut praebeatur, opus est praeveniente et adiuvante gratia Dei et internis Spiritus Sancti auxiliis, qui cor moveat et in Deum convertat, mentis oculos aperiat, et det "omnibus suavitatem in consentiendo et credendo veritati."

3. Quo vero profundior usque evadat revelationis intelligentia, idem Spiritus Sanctus fidem iugiter per dona sua perficit.

1. "The obedience of faith" (*Rom.* 16:26; see 1:5; 2 *Cor.* 10:5-6) is to be given to God who reveals, an obedience by which man commits his whole self freely to God, "offering the full submission of intellect and will to God who reveals," and freely assenting to the truth revealed by him.

2. To make this act of faith, the grace of God and the interior help of the Holy Spirit must precede and assist, moving the heart and turning it to God, opening the eyes of the mind and giving "joy and ease to everyone in assenting to the truth and believing it."

3. To bring about an ever deeper understanding of revelation the same Holy Spirit constantly brings faith to completion by his gifts.

1. Faithful to the concept of revelation just elaborated, and also in an effort to stress the *theological* character of faith, the Council declares first of all that the object of faith is God himself as Revealer. This God who reveals, this God who speaks, must be *believed* and *obeyed*: such

is the constant assertion of revelation itself (*Rom.* 16:26; 1:5; 2 *Cor.* 10:5-6; *Eph.* 1:13; 1 *Cor.* 15:11; *Mk.* 16:15-16) and the Church's Magisterium.[11]

The Council describes this faith as establishing a living relationship, *person to person*, between God and man, in a complete and total adherence which involves knowledge and love: man freely commits his whole self to God. Thus, through revelation, God *comes* toward man, *condescends*, and opens to him the secrets of his intimate life with a view toward reciprocal love. Through faith, man *turns* toward God and gives himself to God in friendship. The end of the sentence explains the meaning of man's self-surrender to God. By faith, man renders to God the full homage of his intellect and will, and gives free assent to what he has revealed. The Council thus avoids two incomplete conceptions of faith: that of faith-homage, personal but without content; and that of faith-assent, doctrinal but depersonalized. Christian faith is inseparably both gift and assent.

2. Man's response to revelation is not the simple result of human activity, *but a gift of God*. It is not enough for the gospel teaching to echo in his ear: the action of grace must also precede and assist,[12] moving him to believe (*ad credendum*) and giving him delight *in* believing (*in credendo*). This activity of grace is then described in biblical and more personalized terms. Concretely, it involves the help of the Holy Spirit,[13] the effect of which is to *move* the human heart and *turn* it to God, to *open the eyes of the mind* and *incline* the powers of the will. It is the Spirit who gives "joy and ease to everyone in assenting to the truth and believing it".[14] Scripture frequently stresses the necessity of this activity of grace which opens the mind to the light that comes from on high (*Mt.* 16:17; 11:25; *Acts* 16:14; 2 *Cor.* 4:6) and draws man toward Christ (*Jn.* 6:44). This interior activity is the testimony of the Spirit (1 *Jn.* 5:6) which is at work within man to make him recognize the truth of Christ.

3. It is once again to the Spirit and his gifts that we must attribute the deeper appreciation and understanding of revelation. The gift of faith is a seed which is destined to ripen and grow indefinitely. This deeper penetration of faith, which leads to a higher knowledge of God and His mystery, is the work of the Spirit.

6. Revealed Truths

1. Divina revelatione Deus seipsum atque aeterna voluntatis suae decreta circa hominum salutem manifestare ac communicare

voluit, "ad participanda scilicet bona divina, quae humanae mentis intelligentiam omnino superant."

2. Confitetur Sacra Synodus, "Deum, rerum omnium principium et finem, naturali humanae rationis lumine e rebus creatis certo cognosci posse" (cf. Rom. 1:20); eius vero revelationi tribuendum esse docet, "ut ea, quae in rebus divinis humanae rationi per se impervia non sunt, in praesenti quoque generis humani conditione ab omnibus expedite, firma certitudine et nullo admixto errore cognosci possint."

1. Through divine revelation, God chose to show forth and communicate himself and the eternal decisions of his will regarding the salvation of men. That is to say, he chose "to share with them those divine treasures which totally transcend the understanding of the human mind."

2. A Sacred Synod affirms that "God, the beginning and end of all things, can be known with certainty from created reality by the light of human reason" (see Rom. 1:20); but teaches that it is through his revelation "that those religious truths which are by their nature accessible to human reason can be known by all men with ease, with solid certitude and with no trace of error, even in this present state of the human race."

1. Having spoken of faith, the Council now speaks of revealed truths, truths which are to be believed: first of all mysteries, and then truths whose revelation is morally necessary in the present state of humanity. The text returns to the assertion of Vatican I, but introduces two important refinements. The actual formula uses two verbs: *manifestare et communicare*, instead of the simple *revelare* of Vatican I, to show that revelation is both manifestation and communication of life. For the word of God does more than simply announce salvation, it brings salvation. Secondly, the Council specifies that the eternal *decisions* in question concern man's salvation. It is a question, then, of those decisions which have for their object our elevation to the supernatural order, namely the Incarnation and Redemption. Speaking of these decisions without further precision, the First Vatican Council implied that these divine decisions concern both the natural as well as the supernatural order. Thus we see that, according to Vatican II, God does not reveal himself and does not make any revelation in order to satisfy the curiosity of man, but rather to *save* him, that is to rescue him from the death of sin and give him a share in a divine destiny completely surpassing the capacity of human understanding.

2. Having spoken of the primary object of revelation and its mysteries, the Council goes on to speak of those truths concerning God which remain accessible to human reason even after original sin, notably our knowledge of God as beginning and end of all things. This God, the Council stresses—with a solemnity justified by the historical context of contemporary atheism—can be known by the light of human reason reflecting on the world, for the created world speaks of its author with irresistible force. We must credit revelation with the fact that these religious truths can now be "known by all men with ease, with solid certitude and with no trace of error".[15]

The Council, in this paragraph, thus considers the object of revelation *in itself* (God and His decisions), *in its proportion to the human mind* (mysteries which surpass the grasp of our mind, and truths accessible to natural reason) and *in its finality* (human salvation, participation in the divine life). Just as it opened by a statement of its fidelity to Vatican I, this first chapter now closes by returning to its doctrine and terminology.

CHAPTER II. HANDING ON DIVINE REVELATION

7. *The Apostles and Their Successors, Heralds of the Gospel*

1. Quae Deus ad salutem cunctarum gentium revelaverat, eadem benignissime disposuit ut in aevum integra permanerent omnibusque generationibus transmitterentur.

2. Ideo Christus Dominus, in quo summi Dei tota revelatio consummatur (cf. 2 *Cor.* 1:20; 3:16—4:6), mandatum dedit Apostolis ut Evangelium, quod promissum ante per Prophetas Ipse adimplevit et proprio ore promulgavit, tamquam fontem omnis et salutaris veritatis et morum disciplinae omnibus praedicarent, eis dona divina communicantes.

3. Quod quidem fideliter factum est, tum ab Apostolis, qui in praedicatione orali, exemplis et institutionibus ea tradiderunt quae sive ex ore, conversatione et operibus Christi acceperant, sive a Spiritu Sancto suggerente didicerant, tum ab illis Apostolis virisque apostolicis, qui, sub inspiratione eiusdem Spiritus Sancti, nuntium salutis scriptis mandaverunt.

4. Ut autem Evangelium integrum et vivum iugiter in Ecclesia servaretur, Apostoli successores reliquerunt Episcopos, ipsis "suum ipsorum locum magisterii tradentes."

5. Haec igitur Sacra Traditio et Sacra utriusque Testamenti Scriptura veluti speculum sunt in quo Ecclesia in terris peregrinans

contemplatur Deum, a quo omnia accipit, usquedum ad Eum videndum facie ad faciem sicuti est perducatur (cf. 1 Jn. 3:2).

1. In his gracious goodness, God has seen to it that what he
had revealed for the salvation of all nations would abide perpetually
in its full integrity and be handed on to all generations.

2. Therefore Christ the Lord in whom the full revelation of the
supreme God is brought to completion (see 2 *Cor.* 1:20; 3:16—
4:6), commissioned the apostles to preach to all men that gospel
which is the source of all saving truth and moral teaching, and to
impart to them heavenly gifts. This gospel had been promised in
former times through the prophets, and Christ himself had fulfilled
it and promulgated it with his lips.

3. This commission was faithfully fulfilled by the apostles who,
by their oral preaching, by example, and by observances handed
on what they had received from the lips of Christ, from living with
him, and from what he did, or what they had learned through the
prompting of the Holy Spirit. The commission was fulfilled, too, by
those apostles and apostolic men who under the inspiration of the
same Holy Spirit committed the message of salvation to writing.

4. But in order to keep the gospel forever whole and alive within
the Church, the apostles left bishops as their successors, "handing
over" to them "the authority to teach in their own place."

5. This Sacred Tradition, therefore, and Sacred Scripture of
both the Old and the New Testaments are like a mirror in which
the pilgrim Church on earth looks at God, from whom she has
received everything, until she is brought finally to see him as he is,
face to face (see 1 *Jn.* 3:2).

1. Having spoken of revelation in itself, the Council takes up the
problem of its transmission or handing on. The first sentence of paragraph 7 expresses the object of Chapter II as a whole: it is God's will
that His revelation *abide* in its *full integrity* over the course of the
centuries and be *handed on* to all generations. The present chapter
will consider this transmission of revelation under the form of Tradition
and Scripture, their mutual relationship, and their common relationship
to the Church and to the Magisterium.

2. This intention on the part of God was clearly indicated by Christ
in the express command he gave his apostles to preach to all men the
gospel promised by the prophets, *fulfilled* in him and promulgated from
his lips, as the *source* of all saving truth and all human morality. Vatican
II takes up the text of the Council of Trent, but with two important

additions. The Council insists once again on the fact that in Christ *all* revelation is completed, that Christ has *fulfilled* the gospel promised of old, and that as a consequence his command to the apostles to preach the gospel extends to the *totality* of revelation, Old Testament as well as New. This assertion is emphasized in the same paragraph by the expression *utriusque Testamenti*. The Council notes that the apostles communicate not only the gospel itself, but also the spiritual wealth which they have received and which is linked to the gospel (such as charisms, sacraments, etc.) since revelation is at once both manifestation and communication of salvation.

3. This commandment of Christ to his apostles that they should preach the gospel was faithfully carried out. It was carried out first of all by the preaching and testimony of the apostles themselves. It was always understood in a *concrete* manner, including not only words but also examples and ways of acting, usages, institutions and rites. In a word it included everything the apostles had *received from Christ* *through* his conversation and his activity, as well as everything they had *learned from the Holy Spirit* by his promptings concerning the words and works of Christ. The testimony of the apostles thus goes far beyond oral preaching. It also includes the whole domain of cult and sacrament (especially Baptism and Eucharist) and the whole domain of moral conduct and the moral direction of Christian communities. The apostles testified to Christ's mystery by communicating and pro-longing it among men in keeping with Our Lord's command. Secondly, the commandment of Christ has been faithfully carried out by making a written record of the Good News of salvation, under the inspiration of the Holy Spirit, either by the apostles or by their disciples. Revelation has thus been handed on in two ways: by Tradition, and by Scripture. Vatican II speaks first of all of Tradition, and then of Scripture (contrary to the order adopted by the Council of Trent). In this it follows the actual order of events. For as a matter of fact, Tradition did precede Scripture.

4. Having thus discussed the handing on of revelation by Christ and the Holy Spirit to the apostles (vertical transmission), and by the apostles to the Church (horizontal transmission), the text goes on to say that this horizontal transmission is perpetuated in the Church by the successors of the apostles. These are the bishops, to whom the apostles handed over their own teaching mission so that the gospel would be preserved *integral and living* throughout the centuries. The role of the bishops is to faithfully hand on everything they have received from the apostles, either by preaching (understood concretely as ex-plained above) or by Scripture.

5. The last sentence draws conclusions from the above. Since all revelation is handed down to us by Tradition and Scripture, it follows that Tradition and Scripture are a sort of mirror, in which the Church, on her way toward her heavenly home, progressively enters into the economy of vision, waiting for the full light of face to face encounter with the Father. Faith is a foretaste of the eschatological vision.[16] This mention of the Church prepares the way for the last paragraph of the chapter in which the common relationship of Tradition and Scripture to the Church and to the Magisterium will be examined.

8. Sacred Tradition

1. Itaque praedicatio apostolica, quae in inspiratis libris speciali modo exprimitur, continua successione usque ad consummationem temporum conservari debebat.

2. Unde Apostoli, tradentes quod et ipsi acceperunt, fideles monent ut teneant traditiones quas sive per sermonem sive per epistolam didicerint (cf. 2 Thess. 2:15), utque pro semel sibi tradita fide decertent (cf. Jud. 3).

3. Quod vero ab Apostolis traditum est, ea omnia complectitur quae ad Populi Dei vitam sancte ducendam fidemque augendam conferunt, sicque Ecclesia, in sua doctrina, vita et cultu, perpetuat cunctisque generationibus transmittit omne quod ipsa est, omne quod credit.

4. Haec quae est ab Apostolis Traditio sub assistentia Spiritus Santi in Ecclesia proficit: crescit enim tam rerum quam verborum traditorum perceptio, tum ex contemplatione et studio credentium, qui ea conferunt in corde suo (cf. Lk. 2:19 and 51), tum ex intima spiritualium rerum quam experiuntur intelligentia, tum ex praeconio eorum qui cum episcopatus successione charisma veritatis certum acceperunt.

5. Ecclesia scilicet, volventibus saeculis, ad plenitudinem divinae veritatis iugiter tendit, donec in ipsa consummentur verba Dei.

6. Sanctorum Patrum dicta huius Traditionis vivificam testificantur praesentiam, cuius divitiae in praxim vitamque credentis et orantis Ecclesiae transfunduntur.

7. Per eandem Traditionem integer Sacrorum Librorum canon Ecclesiae innotescit, ipsaeque Sacrae Litterae in ea penitius intelliguntur et indesinenter actuosae redduntur; sicque Deus, qui olim locutus est, sine intermissione cum dilecti Filii sui Sponsa colloquitur, et Spiritus Sanctus, per quem viva vox Evangelii in Ecclesia, et per

ipsam in mundo resonat, credentes in omnem veritatem inducit, verbumque Christi in eis abundanter inhabitare facit (cf. *Col.* 3:16).

1. And so the apostolic preaching, which is expressed in a special way in the inspired books, was to be preserved by an unending succession of preachers until the end of time.

2. Therefore the apostles, handing on what they themselves had received, warn the faithful to hold fast to the traditions which they have learned either by preaching or by letter (see 2 *Thess.* 2:15), and to fight in defense of the faith handed on once and for all (see *Jud.* 3).

3. Now what was handed on by the apostles includes everything which contributes toward the holiness of life and increase in faith of the people of God; and so the Church, in her teaching, life and worship, perpetuates and hands on to all generations all that she herself is, all that she believes.

4. This tradition which comes from the apostles develops in the Church with the help of the Holy Spirit. For there is a growth in the understanding of the realities and words which have been handed down. This happens through the contemplation and study made by believers, who treasure these things in their hearts (see *Lk.* 2:19 and 51), through a penetrating understanding of the spiritual realities which they experience, and through the preaching of those who have received through episcopal succession the sure gift of truth.

5. For as the centuries succeed one another, the Church constantly moves forward toward the fullness of divine truth until the words of God reach their complete fulfillment in her.

6. The words of the Holy Fathers are witness to the presence of this living tradition, whose wealth is poured into the practice and life of the believing and praying Church.

7. Through the same Tradition the Church's full canon of the sacred books is known, and the sacred writings themselves are more profoundly understood and unceasingly made active in her; and thus God, who spoke of old, uninterruptedly converses with the bride of his beloved Son; and the Holy Spirit, through whom the living voice of the gospel resounds in the Church, and through her, in the world, leads those who believe into all truth and makes the word of Christ dwell abundantly in them (See *Col.* 3:16).

This is the first time that any document of the extraordinary Magisterium has proposed such an elaborate text on the nature, object and importance of Tradition.

1. The apostolic preaching, expressed in a special way in the inspired books, was to be *preserved* in continuous succession until the end of time.

2. That is why the apostles, in handing on what they themselves had received, exhort the faithful to hold fast to the traditions which they have learned by word of mouth or by letter (2 *Thess.* 2:15), and to join the struggle in defense of the faith entrusted to the people.

3. Having treated of Tradition in the active sense (transmission of revelation), the Council treats of Tradition in the passive sense (that which has been transmitted). It states the object of Tradition and its extent. What has been handed down by the apostles embraces everything that contributes to the *holiness of life* and the *increase in Faith* of the People of God; in other words, everything that concerns faith and morals in the Christian people. This coincides with the statement of the Council of Trent that the gospel (revelation) is the source of every saving truth and moral teaching. In this way, the Church, in her teaching, life and liturgy, perpetuates and hands down to every generation all she is and all that she believes. Tradition is not only verbal, but *real*. Consequently, it is passed down not only by way of instruction, but also by means of institution, cult, rites, etc. Tradition perpetuates not only the faith of the Church, but also her *life*.

4. The Council next considers Tradition from a *dynamic* point of view. Since divine Tradition stemming from the apostles is a living reality in the Church from which she draws her life, we might say that in one sense this Tradition is continually developing in her under the action and assistance of the Holy Spirit. Still, it is not the apostolic Tradition itself, but rather our penetration of these inherited words and realities which develops and grows. Factors in this growth are contemplation and study on the part of the faithful (*Lk.* 2:19 and 51), the day to day experience of spiritual realities, with the rich understanding to which it leads,[17] and lastly, the preaching of those who have received the charism of teaching through episcopal consecration.

5. Thus, throughout the centuries, under the living impulse she receives from Tradition, the Church will never cease to offer the fullness of divine truth until the words of God are accomplished in her. Both active and passive, the Church not only bears Tradition but also finds herself borne by it, for in it lies her life.

6. It follows that a truth handed down by Tradition could never be known or understood in its full richness through a single Church document or testimony, but only by the sum total of all the testimony and forms of expression in which it lives: the writings of the Fathers, the liturgy, the practice of the Church and theological speculation. The

work of the Fathers is a primary witness of this *life-giving* Tradition, whose richness is poured into the life and practice of the early Church's creed and prayers. The Fathers are *witnesses* of Tradition. Their value stems less from their proximity to the apostolic age than from the fact that their writings have systematized the revelation which they received, believed and lived in the Church. The liturgy also constitutes a privileged witness to Tradition, assimilating its wealth so completely that it would be difficult to find a single truth of faith that is not somehow expressed in the liturgy.

7. The last sentence of this paragraph demonstrates the importance of Tradition with respect to Scripture. This importance stems from the following facts: *a*) it is through Tradition that the canon of inspired books is known to us in its *fullness*. On this point, the Council recognizes that the objective content of Tradition surpasses that of Scripture; *b*) it is also through Tradition that Scripture is more profoundly understood; *c*) finally, it is through Tradition that Scripture is constantly actual and actualized. It is through Tradition, the Council concludes (in a very Trinitarian setting), that God continues a permanent dialogue with the Church, the Bride of his Son, while the Holy Spirit, through whom the voice of the gospel echoes in the Church and, through the Church, in the whole world, leads the believers toward the fullness of truth and fills each of them abundantly with the Word of Christ (*Col.* 3:16).

9. *Mutual Relationship between Tradition and Scripture*

1. Sacra Traditio ergo et Sacra Scriptura arcte inter se connectuntur atque communicant.

2. Nam ambae, ex eadem divina scaturigine promanantes, in unum quodammodo coalescunt et in eundem finem tendunt.

3. Etenim Sacra Scriptura est locutio Dei quatenus divino afflante Spiritu scripto consignatur; Sacra autem Traditio verbum Dei, a Christo Domino et a Spiritu Sancto Apostolis concreditum, successoribus eorum integre transmittit, ut illud, praelucente Spiritu veritatis, praeconio suo fideliter servent, exponant atque diffundant; quo fit ut Ecclesia certitudinem suam de omnibus revelatis non per solam Scripturam hauriat.

4. Quapropter utraque pari pietatis affectu ac reverentia suscipienda et veneranda est.

1. Hence there exists a close connection and communication between Sacred Tradition and Sacred Scripture.

2. For both of them, flowing from the same divine well-spring, in a certain way merge into a unity and tend toward the same end.

3. For Sacred Scripture is the word of God inasmuch as it is consigned to writing under the inspiration of the divine Spirit, while Sacred Tradition takes the word of God, entrusted by Christ the Lord and the Holy Spirit to the apostles, and hands it on to their successors in its full purity, so that led by the light of the Spirit of truth, they may in proclaimng it preserve this word of God faithfully, explain it, and make it more widely known. Consequently it is not from Sacred Scripture alone that the Church draws her certainty about everything which has been revealed.

4. Therefore both Sacred Tradition and Sacred Scripture are to be accepted and venerated with the same sense of loyalty and reverence.

The Council has deliberately avoided the problem (not yet theologically resolved) of the material content of Tradition and Scripture. Does Tradition enjoy a more extensive *object content* than Scripture? Is it not correct to say that there is nothing in Tradition which is not in some way also contained in Scripture?[18] Apart from the question of the canon of inspired books, the Council thought it inopportune to add any other determination regarding the quantitative object of Tradition and Scripture. It insisted rather, and with good reason—for the matter is of primary importance to the present-day ecumenical dialogue—on the relation and mutual cooperation between Tradition and Scripture.

1. As a conclusion to the preceding paragraphs, the first sentence states that Tradition and Scripture are *closely connected* and in *mutual relationship*. It would be an error to consider them as two parallel and independent forms of revelation, to assert the existence of one and deny the existence of the other, or to ignore their mutual relationship. Scripture and tradition are inseparable and together constitute an organic whole whose elements are interdependent.

2. The Council states precisely why Scripture and Tradition are so closely united: *a*) both spring from the same stream of living water —revelation; *b*) both, in a sense, fuse together into a whole, since each expresses the same unique mystery, although in a different form; *c*) the two cooperate toward one and the same end, namely, human salvation. This last is explained in the following paragraph.

3. The third sentence gives the final reason for the close bond between Tradition and Scripture: each of them is equally the *word of God*. Scripture is the word of God insofar as it is consigned to writing

under the inspiration of the Holy Spirit. Tradition is also the word of
God entrusted by Christ and the Holy Spirit to the apostles and handed
on *in its full purity* to their successors, so that in the light of the Holy
Spirit, their preaching will faithfully preserve, explain and spread the
word received by the apostles. It follows from this that the *certainty*
which the Church has concerning everything God has revealed (and
which consequently she can or does propose as such to the faith of her
children) does not derive from *Sacred Scripture alone*, since the
Church never ceases to possess in its entirety (*integre transmittitur*)
the living word which she received in the beginning. Furthermore,
when the Church hesitates to pronounce herself on a particular point
because Scripture does not seem suffleiently clear and explicit, she can
find in the Tradition of which she is the guardian a source of enlightenment and assurance. Tradition and Scripture complete one another,
not so much in a quantitative sense, but rather in the sense that each
sheds light upon the other. In making this distinction, a simple consequence of all that precedes, the Council does not surreptitiously
reintroduce the question of the two sources, but it affirms a fact
universally recognized by theologians and at the same time confirms
a constant practice in the Church.

4. The last sentence concludes with the words of the Council of Trent.
Since Tradition and Scripture hand down and preserve divine revelation
under the two forms in which it has appeared, and both tend toward
the same ultimate goal, namely, the salvation of mankind, it follows that
both are to be received and venerated with the same sense of loyalty
and reverence.

10. Common Relationship of Tradition and Scripture to the Church and Magisterium

1. Sacra Traditio et Sacra Scriptura unum verbi Dei sacrum
depositum constituunt Ecclesiae commissum, cui inhaerens tota plebs
sancta Pastoribus suis adunata in doctrina Apostolorum et communione, fractione panis et orationibus iugiter perseverat (cf. *Act.*
2:42), ita ut in tradita fide tenenda, exercenda profitendaque
singularis fiat Antistitum et fidelium conspiratio.

2. Munus autem authentice interpretandi verbum Dei scriptum
vel traditum, soli vivo Ecclesiae Magisterio concreditum est, cuius
auctoritas in nomine Iesu Christi exercetur.

3. Quod quidem Magisterium non supra verbum Dei est, sed
eidem ministrat, docens nonnisi quod traditum est, quatenus illud,

ex divino mandato et Spiritu Sancto assistente, pie audit, sancte custodit et fideliter exponit, ac ea omnia ex hoc uno fidei deposito haurit quae tamquam divinitus revelata credenda proponit.

4. Patet igitur Sacram Traditionem, Sacram Scripturam et Ecclesiae Magisterium, iuxta sapientissimum Dei consilium, ita inter se connecti et consociari, ut unum sine aliis non consistat, omniaque simul, singula suo modo, sub actione unius Spiritus Sancti, ad animarum salutem efficaciter conferant.

1. Sacred Tradition and Sacred Scripture form one sacred deposit of the word of God, committed to the Church. Holding fast to this deposit the entire holy people united with their shepherds remain always steadfast in the teaching of the apostles, in the common life, in the breaking of the bread and in prayers (see *Acts* 2:42, Greek text), so that holding to, practicing and professing the heritage of the faith, it becomes on the part of the bishops and faithful a single common effort.

2. But the task of authentically interpreting the word of God, whether written or handed on, has been entrusted exclusively to the living teaching office of the Church, whose authority is exercised in the name of Jesus Christ.

3. This teaching office is not above the word of God, but serves it, teaching only what has been handed on, listening to it devoutly, guarding it scrupulously and explaining it faithfully in accord with a divine commission and with the help of the Holy Spirit; it draws from this one deposit of faith everything which it presents for belief as divinely revealed.

4. It is clear, therefore, that Sacred Tradition, Sacred Scripture and the teaching authority of the Church, in accord with God's most wise design, are so linked and joined together that one cannot stand without the others, and that all together and each in its own way under the action of the one Holy Spirit contribute effectively to the salvation of souls.

This paragraph is made up of two parts. The first discusses the relationship of Tradition and Scripture to *the entire Church*: faithful and hierarchy. The second treats the relationship of Tradition and Scripture to the Church's *Magisterium*. It is most important to establish the correct relationship of Tradition and Scripture to the Magisterium, for Protestants frequently have the impression that we subordinate Scripture to the Magisterium and that we confuse the Magisterium with Tradition.

The one deposit of revelation, made up of Tradition and Scripture, has been entrusted to the whole Church, not only that the whole Church be its official interpreter—this role belongs only to the Magisterium—but that the whole Church draws from it her *life*. The entire Christian people, united with its shepherds and faithfully attached to this unique and sacred deposit of the word of God, perseveres in the teaching of the apostles, in full harmony of mind and heart with them, in the breaking of bread and in prayer, so that there will be a union of the faithful and their spiritual leaders in the application, exercise, and profession of this Faith which is their common inheritance. Living thus in the Faith handed down by the apostles, the Church of every generation imitates the apostolic Church in her attachment to revelation. Although not a doctrinal innovation, the statement of this first part of the paragraph does however represent progress over the earlier documents, primarily those of Vatican I and the encyclical *Humani Generis*, which were content to consider the relationship of Scripture and Tradition only to the Magisterium of the Church.

2. The second part of the paragraph describes the role which belongs exclusively to the ordinary or extraordinary Magisterium of the Church, that is, *authentic interpretation* of the deposit of Faith. The Council takes up the teaching of Humani Generis,[19] explaining precisely why this function belongs only to the Magisterium. It is only to the Magisterium of the Church, whose authority is exercised in his name, that Christ has entrusted the role of authoritatively interpreting the word of God, whether written or handed down by Tradition.

3. The next sentence more fully explains the position of the Magisterium with respect to revelation. Depending upon the point of view, this position is one of dependence or transcendence. In a general way, however, we must say that the Magisterium *is not above* the word of God, but *serves* the word of God. In environments foreign to Catholic thinking, people frequently have the impression that the Church is an *absolute* which inherits the sovereignty of Scripture and substitutes for it. The Church Magisterium here defines itself much more modestly as the *servant* of God's word, teaching nothing more than what has been handed down to her. The Church is not the *domina*, but rather the *ancilla* of God's word. This is a valuable statement for the ecumenical dialogue of our day: it is the first time that any Council text has thus expressed itself.

This role is then explained in detail. The Magisterium, by reason of the express mandate it has received from Christ, and with the assistance of the Holy Spirit, hears with filial devotion, guards as sacred, faithfully explains and draws from the one and only deposit of faith everything that it proposes for belief as divinely revealed. *a*) The Magisterium *listens devoutly* to the living voice of the gospel resounding in her ear. The Magisterium as such is a believer, one of the faithful, and thus the first to listen to God's word. Like the Blessed Virgin who treasured in her heart every word falling from the lips of Christ, the Magisterium is ever attentive to the word of God. *b*) The Magisterium *scrupulously* guards the word of God. This expression, borrowed from Vatican I,[20] is traditional and comes up frequently in many documents of the Magisterium in an identical or equivalent form.[21] Scrupulously guarding the deposit of the word of God means losing nothing of it, deleting nothing from it, and adding nothing to it. Just as there is nothing to add to Scripture, neither is there anything to add to Tradition. Just as the efforts of the Church in scrutinizing Scripture do not claim to enrich the treasure of Scripture, neither does the living Tradition of the Church, expressed in different forms from one age to another, claim to enrich the treasure Tradition received from the apostles. What is perfected in the course of the centuries is not revelation itself, but the *understanding* we have of it. It is the successive series of *explanations* which we make in our efforts to discover its inexhaustible riches and in so doing to enlighten future generations. Finally, it is the *formulations* which we multiply in our attempt to express this whole effort of assimilating God's word in human terms. The role of *custos* or guardian of revelation also implies the role of protecting the word of God against deviation, subtle innovation, and heresy. *c*) The Magisterium also must *faithfully explain* the word of God.[22] In effect, the role of safeguarding and protecting the word does not exhaust the mission of the Church with regard to God's revealed word: it must also propose this word to men of all times. This means that the Church must declare its authentic meaning, explaining and casting light on everything that is obscure. This faithful exposition of God's word is the basis for the whole *teaching office* of the Church, its ordinary and extraordinary Magisterium. *d*) Finally, the Council says, the Magisterium draws upon this fountain of living and everflowing water of God's word for everything that it proposes to the belief of its faithful as divinely revealed.[23] It proposes nothing not already contained in the one deposit of faith. Dogmatic development, which is an attempt to propose and formulate the word of God in a faithful, more precise, and richer way, is always at work within the object of Faith.

4. The last sentence of this paragraph concludes what has been said about Scripture, Tradition and the Church Magisterium, stating that in the infinitely wise plan of God, the three are *inseparable*.

They are so intimately bound up *together* and mutually associated that no one of the three has any *solidity* without the others. These three realities taken together, each in its own way, under the action of one and the same Spirit, efficaciously cooperate in the salvation of souls. Just as Tradition and Scripture are inseparable from each other, so are they inseparable from the Church's Magisterium. They are bound together in mutual service.

The Constitution of Vatican II on revelation has not had a simple history. It was one of the first to be proposed to the discussion of the Fathers of the Council, and one of the last to be voted upon. And before receiving its final approval, it had to overcome much resistance, weather many storms and even survive shipwreck. The definitive text voted by the Fathers of the Council represents the fifth official draft. The resistance encountered should not surprise us too much. On the doctrinal level, this Constitution, together with the Constitution on the Church, is the most important document of the Council by reason of the seriousness of the problems taken up as well as by the consequences it will have on ecumenical dialogue.

This is the first time that a Council has studied the *fundamental and absolutely primary categories* of Christianity in such a deliberate and methodical way: Revelation, Tradition, and Inspiration. These notions, present throughout the whole of Christianity and implied in every theological discussion, are also the most difficult to define, precisely because they are the *most general and fundamental.* They are to theology what the notions of knowledge, being, and activity are to philosophy. We live in these realities, but they are the last to form the object of our critical reflection. We might add that the Council's difficulties in this area are largely due to the fact that theological reflection on these fundamental points had not everywhere arrived at its full degree of maturity. It is impossible to present a coherent doctrinal treatment of points that theological research itself has frequently only outlined. This incomplete state of research, as well as the ignorance in more than one Catholic circle of the results *already* achieved, partially explains the groping of the Council, the toil of revision, and the extreme conciseness of the text.

On the ecumenical level, the importance of this Constitution can hardly be exaggerated. By giving a balanced description of the various aspects of revelation, by better defining the position of Magisterium with respect to Scripture and Tradition, by giving greater refinement to the notions of Inspiration and Inerrancy, by sanctioning the importance of literary genres in the understanding of sacred texts, by insisting on the profound unity of the two Testaments and the necessity of their mutual clarification, by restoring Scripture to its rightful place in the teaching and the liturgical life of the Church, as well as in the piety of the faithful, the Council has done away with much ambiguity and incorporated into the texts themselves a harmony already frequently found in Christian practice.

As far as revelation itself is concerned, the text of the Constitution is on the whole remarkable. We might emphasize some of its particular merits:

1. The Constitution furnishes the *solid basis for a dogmatic treatise on revelation*. All the essential points are touched upon: the nature, object, and finality of revelation, the economy, progress, and pedagogy of revelation, the central position of Christ as God revealing and God revealed, the response of faith, the handing down of revelation and the forms of this transmission, the relationship of Scripture and Tradition to the Church and her Magisterium. The text does not neglect a single one of the aspects of this complex reality: revelation is divine activity, an intervention of God in history and a history in itself, an interpersonal communication of the order of word, an encounter with the living God demanding the adherence of our whole person and assent of our whole mind to the message of salvation. It also points out the condescension of God who, in order to reveal himself, chooses the way of history and flesh: the distinctive characteristic of Christian revelation.

2. Notwithstanding certain shortcomings of detail, the *arrangement* is solid, concise, and well constructed. The paragraph titles clearly outline the progress of the thought, which is dynamic: the purpose of the Constitution (1), the nature, object, and the economy of revelation (2), revelation in its preparation (3), revelation in its peak and fullness (4), our response to revelation (5), revealed truths to be believed (6), the apostles and their successors, heralds of the gospel (7), Tradition itself (8), the mutual relationship between Tradition and Scripture (9), the common relationship of Scripture and Tradition to Church and Magisterium (10).

3. The text intends a *calm exposition* of the Church's teaching. There is no question of anathemas, nor even of polemics. The Council's intention was primarily to study those points which are peacefully accepted, leaving theologians free to discuss problems not yet resolved. A typical example of this freedom is the question of the objective material content of Scripture and Tradition.

4. The tone of the Constitution is profoundly *religious*. Everywhere there is evidence of the contemplative and apostolic presence of the Bride of Christ, who never ceases to ponder the word of her Bridegroom, and who breaks for her children the bread of the word as well as the bread of the Eucharist. This religious character stems in large part from the abundant use of texts from Scripture, so well incorporated that they seem the natural means for expressing the thought of the Church. These texts are a sort of backbone to the Constitution. The biblical character of the Constitution is apparent primarily in Chapter I which contains, in the body and notes, thirty-two biblical references divided as follows: four to the Old Testament, one to the Synoptic Tradition, fourteen to St. Paul, eleven to St. John, one to St. Peter, and one to the Letter to the Hebrews.[24] This sequence of texts is in itself a rich doctrinal treatise. As a matter of fact, the great majority of important Scriptural texts on revelation have been utilized.

5. The text is conceived and elaborated in a *Trinitarian perspective*. This aspect of the Constitution, which we have stressed in the course of our analysis, is manifest particularly in the introduction, in the first sentence of paragraph 2 on the nature of revelation, in the fourth sentence of paragraph 4 on the economy of revelation in Christ, in paragraph 8 on Tradition, and in paragraph 9 on the mutual relationship between Scripture and Tradition.

6. The constant reference to the Divine Persons in the description of the activity of revelation helps to establish the *personalist* overtone which the Fathers of the Council wanted to incorporate into the text. The terms word, conversation, dialogue, society, communication, participation, friendship, love, which stand out everywhere in the text, are in themselves an obvious sign of this intention. Revelation is presented as a free initiative on the part of the living God; as the manifestation of his personal mystery. God enters into a person-to-person relationship with man: the divine I calls to the human Thou, speaks to him, carries on dialogue with him, reveals the mystery of his own intimate life in view of a communion of thought and love with the Divine Persons. By faith, man responds to this initiative of love and surrenders his whole self. Described thus, revelation is at once personalized *and* personalizing.

7. Another aspect of the Constitution, equally intended by the Fathers, is its *Christocentric* character. It is Christ who forms the unity of the economy and object of revelation. This object of revelation is God himself, intervening in human history and manifesting himself in and through Jesus Christ. The mystery, concretely, is Christ, Author and Consummator of our faith, Revealer and Mystery revealed,

as well as the Sign of revelation. This Christocentric character, already proclaimed in the introduction, appears primarily in paragraph 2 (homines per Christum; veritas in Christo illucescit), in paragraph 4 (locutus est in Filio; Jesus Christus Verbum caro factum), and in paragraph 7 (Christus, in quo tota revelatio consummatur). In this respect, it is enlightening to compare two similar sentences from Vatican I and Vatican II on the very fact of revelation. We immediately note that the *Theocentric* character of Vatican I has been replaced by the *Christocentric* character of Vatican II:

VATICAN I	VATICAN II
Placuisse ejus [Dei] sapientiae et bonitati, alia eaque supernaturali via, seipsum ac aeterna voluntatis suae decreta humano generi revelare.	Placuit Deo in sua bonitate et sapientia seipsum revelare et notum facere sacramentum voluntatis suae, quo homines, *per Christum, Verbum carnem* factum, in Spiritu Sancto accessum habent ad Patrem et divinae naturae consortes efficiuntur.
. . . it was good pleasure of his wisdom and goodness to reveal himself and the eternal decrees of his will to the human race in another and supernatural way.	In his goodness and wisdom God chose to reveal himself and to make known the hidden purpose of his will by which *through Christ, the Word made flesh,* man might in the Holy Spirit have access to the Father and come to share in the divine nature.

8. Finally, one last trait which is also characteristic of the present Constitution is the position given to the *Church*. It is in the Church that the gospel is preserved living and intact (7); it is the Church which perpetuated and hands down the treasure received from the apostles by her teaching, life, and cult (8); it is the Church which tends by her contemplation, study, and life, towards the fullness of truth in God's word (8); it is with the Church as Bride that God constantly carries on a dialogue over the course of the ages and through whom the word of God echoes over all the universe (8); it is the Church which through her Magisterium interprets God's word; she

is the servant, preserving it scrupulously, explaining it faithfully, and proposing it infallibly.

1. To facilitate study we have numbered the sentences of each paragraph.

2. For example, the encyclical "Qui pluribus" (D 1637), Vatican I (D 1785), the Oath against Modernism (D 2145), the encyclical "Mit brennender Sorge" (A.A.S. 29 [1937] 156), the encyclical "Mortalium animos" (A.A.S. [1928] 8)

3. "Amantissimus Deus... ita Se tanquam unicum Deum verum et vivum *verbis ac gestis revelavit* ut Israel, quae divinae essent cum hominibus viae experiretur easque, ipso Deo per os Prophetarum loquente, penitus et clarius in dies intelligeret atque latius in gentes exhiberit" (cap. IV, n. 14).

4. "Christus Regnum Dei in terris instauravit, *factis et verbis* Patrem suum ac Seipsum *manifestavit*, atque morte, resurrectione et gloriosa ascensione missioneque Spiritus Sancti opus suum complevit" (cap. V, n. 17).

5. One of the first times the expression appears is in the encyclical "Mit brennender Sorge": "In Jesus Christus, dem menschgewordenen Gottessohn, ist die Fülle der göttlichen Offenbarung erschienen" (A.A.S. 29 [1937] 150).

6. R. SCHNACKENBURG, "Zum Offenbarungsgedanken in der Bibel," *Biblishche Zeitschrift*, 7 (1963): 2-23.

7. The order is that of the historical manifestation of Christ: deeds, death, resurrection, mission of the Spirit.

8. The preceding schema had said: *tota sua persona*. The Council preferred the present expression to avoid christological difficulties.

9. Signs and miracles are not pure synonyms: if it is true that miracles are signs, there are also—for example, Christ's gestures of goodness and mercy toward sinners—which are not miracles.

10. The signs of revelation are not exterior to Christ. They are Christ himself, in the radiation of his power, his holiness and his wisdom. In this radiation, we perceive his glory as Son of the Father: we pass directly from the reflection to the source.

11. D 1637, 1789, 2145.

12. D 798, 1789.

13. D 1790.

14. D 1791 and 180.

15. D 1785, 1786.

16. S. THOMAS, *III Sent.*, d. 23, q. 2, a. 1, ad 4.

17. For example, the understanding born of the sacramental life.

18. On this problem, see the excellent exposition of J. Dupont, "Écriture et Tradition," *Nouvelle Revue Théologique* 85 (1963): 337-356, 449-468.

19. D 2314.

20. D 1800.

21. D 1781, 1793, 1800, 1836, 2145, 2315.

22. D 1800, 1836, 2307, 2313, 2314.

23. D 2314.

24. The scriptural references of the first chapter are the following: *Gen.* 3:15; 12:2-3; *Ex.* 33: 11; *Bar.* 3:38; *Mt.* 11:27; *Rom.* 1:5; 1:19-20; 2:6-7; 16:26; 2 *Cor.* 3:16; 4:6; 10:5-6; *Eph.* 1:9; 1:3-14; 2:18; *Col.* 1:15; 1 *Tim.* 1:17; 6:14; *Tit.* 2:13; *Heb.* 1:1-2; *Jo.* 1:3; 1:14; 1:17; 1:1-18; 3:34; 5:36; 14:6; 14:9; 15:14-15; 17:1-3; 1 *Jo.* 1:2-3; 2 *Pet.* 1:4.

bibliography

BIBLIOGRAPHY

I. BOOKS

The works listed here deal specifically with revelation or devote the equivalent of one or more chapters to the topic. Numerous works which treat of revelation in a summary fashion have been referred to already in the footnotes. The present list does not include the many treatises and manuals on revelation used in theology courses. The most recent books and articles on the subject are listed at the end of this Bibliography.

Aeby, G., *Les missions divines, de Saint Justin à Origène*, Fribourg, 1958.

Alfaro, J., *Adnotationes in tractatum de virtutibus*, PUG, Romae, 1959.

Asting, R., *Die Verkundigung des Wortes Gottes im Urchristentum dargestellt an den Begriffen Wort Gottes, Evangelium und Zeugnis*, Stuttgart, 1939.

Auzou, G., *Word of God*, St. Louis, 1960.

Baierl, J., *The Theory of Revelation*, New York, 1927.

Baillie, J. et Martin, H., ed., *Revelation, A Symposium*, London, 1937.

Baillie, J., *The Idea of Revelation in Recent Thought*, London, 1956.

Barsotti, D., *Il Mistero cristiano e la Parola di Dio*, Firenze, 1954. Trad. fr., *La Parole de Dieu dans le mystère chrétien*, Paris, 1954.

Barth, K., *Die christliche Dogmatik im Entwurf*, I: *Die Lehre vom Worte Gottes*, München, 1927.

Barth, K., *Die kirchliche Dogmatik*, I: *Die Lehre vom Worte Gottes*, München, 1932. Trad. fr., *Dogmatique*, I: *La Doctrine de la Parole de Dieu*, Genève, 1953-1954.

Barth, K., *Word of God and Man*, Magnolia, Mass., 1958.

Barth, K., *Daschristliche Verständnis der Offenbarung*, München, 1948.

Besnard, A.-M., *Le mystère du Nom*, Paris, 1962, pp. 15-90.

Beumer, J., *Die mündliche überlieferung als Glaubensquelle* (Handbuch der Dogmengeschichte), Freiburg, 1962, pp. 74-88.

Boismard, M.E., *Le Prologue de Saint Jean*, Paris, 1952, pp. 109-123.

Boman, T., *Das Hebräische Denken im Vergleich mit dem Griechischen*, Göttingen, 1957.

Botterweck, G. J., *Gott Erkennen im Sprachgebrauch des A. T.* Bonn, 1951.

Brox, N., *Zeuge und Märtyrer*, München, 1961.

Brunner, E., *Wahrheit als Begegnung*, Berlin, 1938.

Brunner, E., *Offenbarung und Vernunft*, Zürich, 1941. Eng. trans., *Revelation and Reason*, Philad., 1946.

Brunner, E., *Dogmatik*, I: *Die Christliche Lehre von Gott*, Zürich, 1946.

Büchsel, F., *Theologie des Neuen Testaments, Geschichte des Wortes Gottes im NT*, Gütersloh, 1937.

Bulgakow, P. S., *Dialog zwischen Gott und Mensch, Ein Beitrag zum Christlichen Offenbarungsbegriff*, Marburg, 1961.

Bulst, W., *Offenbarung, Biblischer und Theologischer Begriff*, Düsseldorf, 1960.

Bultmann, R., *Der Begriff der Offenbarung im Neuen Testament*, Tübingen, 1929.

Burnier, E., *La notion de témoignage dans le Nouveau Testament*, Lausanne, 1939.

Cahill, J., *Eschatological Occurrence, A critical Examination of Rudolf Bultmann's Concept of Revelation*, Dissertatio ad lauream, PUG, Rome, 1960.

Caiazzo, S., *Il concetto di rivelazione, Idea centrale della Teologia di E. Brunner*, Dissertatio ad lauream, PUG, Roma, 1959

Cerfaux, L., *Le Christ dans la théologie de S. Paul*, Paris, 1954, pp. 229-242, 303-328.

Charlier, L., *Essai sur le problème théologique*, Thuillies, 1938, pp. 66-80.

Crouzel, H., *Origène et la connaissance mystique*, Bruges, 1961.

Cullmann, O., *Christ and Time*, Philadelphia, 1964.

Cullmann, O., *Christology of the New Testament*, Philadelphia, 1964.

Daniélou, J., Bouyer, L., et Alii, *Parole de Dieu et Liturgie*, Coll. "Lex Orandi," Paris, 1958.

Daniélou, J., *Message évangélique et culture hellénistique*, Paris-Tournai-New York-Rome, 1961.

Decker, B., *Die Entwicklung der Lehre von der prophetischen Offenbarung von Wilhelm von Auxerre bis zu Thomas von Aquin*, Breslau, 1940.

De Saussure, J., *Révélation et inspiration*, Genève, 1952.

Dewailly, L.-M., *Jésus-Christ, Parole de Dieu*, Paris, 1945.

Dewailly, L.-M., *Envoyés du Père. Mission et apostolicité*, Paris, 1960.

Dewailly, L.-M., *La jeune Eglise de Thessalonique*, Paris, 1963, pp. 24-48.

Dieckmann, H., *De Revelatione christiana*, Freiburg, 1930, pp. 135-141.

Dilschneider, O. A., *Christus Praesens. Grundriss einer Dogmatik der Offenbarung*, 2 vol., Gütersloh, 1948.

Dodd, C. H., *Bible Today*, Cambridge, 1960.

Dupont, J., *Gnosis. La connaissance religieuse dans les épîtres de S. Paul*, Louvain-Paris, 1949, pp. 187-194, 493-498.

Dürr, L., *Die Wertung desgöttlichen Wortes im A. T. und im Antiken Orient*, Leipzig, 1938.

Eichrodt, W., *Theologie des Alten Testaments*, 3 vol., Berlin, 1948, t. 2, pp. 32-38.

Etspüler, P. J., *Das göttliche Wort im Künder der christlichen Wahrheit nach dem hl. Bonaventura*, Porto Alegre, 1961.

Fairweather, A. M., *The Word as Truth, A Critical Examination of the Christian Doctrine of Revelation in the Writings of Thomas Aquinas and Karl Barth*, London, 1944.

Fehr, J., *Das Offenbarungsproblem in dialektischer und thomistischer Theologie*, Fribourg-Leipzig, 1939.

Féret, H. M., *Connaissance biblique de Dieu*, Paris, 1955.

Fischer, É., Bouyer, L., éd., *Parole de Dieu et sacerdoce*, Paris-Tournai-Rome-New York, 1962.

Fitzgerald, E., *Christ and the Prophets, A Study in Origen's Teaching on the Economy of the Old Testament*, Dissertatio ad lauream, PUG, Rome, 1961.

Ford, J., *St. Irenaeus and Revelation, A Theological Perspective*, Dissertatio ad lauream, PUG, Rome, 1961.

Fülling, E., *Geschichte als Offenbarung*, Berlin, 1956.

Gardeil, A., *Le Donné révélé et la théologie*, Paris, 1909, chapitre II.

Garrigou-Lagrange, R., *De Revelatione per Ecclesiam catholicam proposita*, 2 vol., Romae, 1950, t. I, pp. 130-160.

Geiselmann, J. R., *Jesus der Christus. Die Urform des Apostolischen Kerygmas als Norm unserer Verkündigung und Theologie von Jesus Christus*, Stuttgart, 1951.

Gewiess, J., *Die Urapostolische Heilsverkündigung nach der Apostelgeschichte*, Breslau, 1939.

Gils, F., *Jésus Prophète d'après les Synoptiques*, Louvain, 1957.

Gloege, G., *Offenbarung und Ueberlieferung*, Hamburg, 1954.

Gondal, I. L., *Mystère et Révélation*, Paris, 1905.

González Morfín, A., *JesuCristo-Palabra y palabra de JesuCristo*, Mexico, 1962.

Grether, O., *Name und Wort Gottes im Alten Testament, Giessen*, 1934. 136.

Grelot, P., *Sens chrétien de l'Ancien Testament*, Tournai, 1962, pp. 126-

Guardini, R., *Die Offenbarung, ihr Wesen und ihre Formen*, Würzburg, 1940.

Guitton, J., *Le problème de Jésus et les fondements du témoignage chrétien*, Paris, 1950, pp. 153-178.

Hamer, J., *Karl Barth*, Westminster, 1962.

Hänel, J., *Das Erkennen Gottes bei den Schriftpropheten*, Stuttgart, 1923.

Harl, M., *Origène et la fonction révélatrice du Verbe incarné*, Paris, 1958.

Hasler, E., *Gesetz und Evangelium in der Alten Kirche bis Origenes*, Zürich-Frankfurt, 1953, pp. 74-102.

Hempel, J., *Gott und Mensch im Alten Testament*, Stuttgart, 1927.

Henry, A.-M., éd., *L'annonce de l'Évangile aujourd'hui*, Paris, 1962.

Henry, C.F.H., ed., *Revelation and the Bible*, London, 1959, pp. 11-105.

Herrmann, W., *Offenbarung und Wunder*, Giessen, 1908.

Houssiau, A., *La christologie de S. Irénée*, Louvain Gembloux, 1955.

Huber, H., *Der Begriff der Offenbarung im Johannes-Evangelium*, Göttingen, 1934.

Jacob, E., *Théologie de l'Ancient Testament*, Paris, 1955, pp. 103-109, 148-184.

Jewett, J.K., *Emil Brunner's Concept of Revelation*, London, 1954.

Jungmann, J. A., *Die Frohbotschaft und unsere Glaubensverkündigung*, Regensburg, 1936.

Koehler, L., *Old Testament Theology*, London, 1957, pp. 99-126.

König, F. E., *De Offenbarungsbegriff des Alten Testaments*, 2 vol., Leipzig, 1882.

Lawton, J.S., *Miracles and Revelation*, London, 1959, p. 217-228.

Lebreton, J., *Histoire du dogme de la Trinité*, 2 vol., Paris, 1928.

Léonard, A., Larcher, C., Dupont, J. et Alii, *La Parole de Dieu en Jésus-Christ*, Paris, 1961.

Loisy, A., *Autour d'un petit livre*, Paris, 1903.

Lossky, V. *Vision de Dieu*, Paris, 1962.

Löwenich, W., *Was heisst Offenbarung? Gottes Wort und menschliche Rede im A.T. und N.T.*, Berlin, 1938.

McDonald, H. D., *Ideas of Revelation, An Historical Study, A.D. 1700 to A.D. 1860*, London, 1959.

McDonald, H. D., *Theories of Revelation, An Historical Study, A.D. 1860 to A.D. 1960*, London, 1963.

McKenzie, J. L., *The Two-edged Sword*, Milwaukee, 1956, pp. 22-44.

Mendenhall, G. E., *Law and Covenant in Israel and the Ancient Near East*, Pittsburgh, 1955.

Molland, E., *The Conception of the Gospel in the Alexandrian Theology*, Oslo, 1938.

Monsma, P. H., *Karl Barth's Idea of Revelation*, Somerville, N.J., 1937.

Mouroux, J., *L'expérience chrétienne*, Paris, 1952.

Mouroux, J., *Mystery of Time*, New York, 1964.

Neher, A., *L'essence du prophétisme*, Paris, 1955.

Niebecker, H., *Wesen und Wirklichkeit der übernatürlichen Offenbarung*, Freiburg, 1940.

Niebuhr, H. R., *The Meaning of Revelation*, New York, 1955.

Noack, H., *Sprache und Offenbarung*, Gütersloh, 1960, pp. 172-221.

Noth, M., *Geschichte und Gottes Wort im A.T.*, Krefeld, 1949.

Nötscher, F., *Das Angesicht Gottes schauen*, Würzburg, 1924.

Nyssens, A., *La plénitude de vérité dans le Verbe incarné. Doctrine de S. Thomas d'Aquin*, Baudouinville, 1961.

Pannenberg, W., Rendtorff, R. et Alii, *Offenbarung als Geschichte*, Göttingen, 1961.

Przywara, E., *Logos*, Düsseldorf, 1964, pp. 31-51.

Rahner, H., *Eine Theologie der Verkündigung*, Freiburg, 1939. Trad. ital., *Teologia e Kerygma*, Brescia, 1958.

Rahner, K., *Hearers of the Word*, New York.

Rahner, K., *Visionen und Prophezeiungen*, Freiburg, 1958.

Ramm, B., *Special Revelation and the Word of God*, Grand Rapids, Michigan, 1961.

Ratzinger, J., Fries, H., hrsg., *Einsicht und Glaube*, Freiburg-Basel-Wien, 1962, pp. 15-27, 75-97.

Rétif, A., *Foi au Christ et Mission*, Paris, 1953.

Richardson, A., *Christian Apologetics*, London, 1955, pp. 110-153.

Rigaux, B., S. Paul, *Les épîtres aux Thessaloniciens*, Paris, 1956, pp. 153-194.

Rivière, J., *Le Modernisme dans l'Église*, Paris, 1929.

Robinson, H. W., *Record and Revelation*, Oxford, 1938.

Robinson, H. W., *Inspiration and Revelation in the Old Testament*, Oxford, 1946.

Robinson, H. W., *Redemption and Revelation*, London, 1947.

Rowley, H. H., *The Faith of Israel*, London, 1956, pp. 23-47.

Sabatier, A., *Esquisse d'une philosophie de la religion d'après la psychologie et l'historire*, Paris, 1897, pp. 3-61.

Schlier, H., *Wort Gottes*, Würzburg, 1958.

Schreiner, H., *Die Verkündigung des Wortes Gottes*, Hamburg, 1949.

Schrey, H.-H., *Existenz und Offenbarung*, Tübingen, 1947.

Schulte, H., *Der Begriff der Offenbarung im Neuen Testament*, München, 1949.

Scott, E. F., *The New Testament Idea of Revelation*, New York-London, 1935.

Scott, R. B. Y., *The Relevance of the Prophets*, New York, 1960.[10]

Seidensticker, P., *Propheten und Evangelisten. Zeugen und Zeugnisse der Heilsgeschichte*, Paderborn, 1962.

Semmelroth, O., *Wirkendes Wort*, Frankfurt, 1962.

Seynaeve, J., *Cardinal Newman's Doctrine on Holy Scripture*, Louvain-Oxford-Tielt, 1953, pp. 30-37, 205-214.

Simpson, C. A., *Revelation and Response in the Old Testament*, New York, 1947.

Söhngen, G., *Die Einheit in der Theologie*, München, 1952, pp. 316 ss.

Soiron, T., *Die Verkündigung des Wortes Gottes*, Freiburg, 1943.

Synave, P., Benoit, P., *Prophecy and Inspiration*, New York, 1961.

Temple, W., *Nature, Man and God*, London, 1953, pp. 301-325.

Thomson, J. G. S. S., *The Old Testament View of Revelation*, Grand Rapids, Michigan, 1960.

Thornton, L. S., *Revelation and the Modern World*, London, 1950.

Tillich, P., *Systematic Theology*, Chicago, 1956,[5] t. 1, pp. 71-159.

Tyrrell, G., *Through Scylla and Charybdis*, London, 1907, pp. 264-354.

Vacant, A., *Études théologiques sur les Constitutions du Concile du Vatican*, 2 vol., Paris, 1895.

Van Den Eynde, D., *Les normes de l'enseignement chrétien dans la littérature patristique des trois premiers siècles*, Gembloux, 1933.

Van Imschoot, P., *Théologie de l'Ancien Testament*, 2 vol., Paris-Tournai-New York-Rome, 1954 et 1956, t. 1, pp. 142-255.

Vellico, A., *La Rivelazione e le sue fonti nel 'De Praescriptione haereticorum' di Tertulliano*, Roma, 1935.

Vögelin, E., *Israel and Revelation*, Bâton-Rouge, Louisiana, 1956.

Volk, H., *Zur Theologie des Wortes Gottes*, Münster, 1962.

von Balthasar, H. U., *Verbum Caro*, Einsiedeln, 1960, pp. 11-155.

Vriezen, T. C., *An Outline of the Old Testament Theology*, Oxford, 1958, pp. 233-267.

Walgrave, J. H., *Newman the Theologian*, New York, 1960.

Warfield, B. B., *Revelation and Inspiration*, London, 1927.

Wolff, J., *Der Begriff der Offenbarung*, Bonn, 1949.

Wright, G. E., *God Who Acts*, London, 1952.

Xiberta, M., *Introductio in sacram Theologiam*, Matriti, 1949, pp. 92-120.

II. ARTICLES

Alfaro, J., "Cristo glorioso, Revelador del Padre," *Gregorianum*, 39 (1958): 222-271.

Alfaro, J., "Persona y gracia," *Gregorianum*, 41 (1960): 5-29.

Alfaro, J., "Supernaturalitas fidei juxta S. Thomam," *Gregorianum*, 44 (1963): 501-542; 731-787.

Alszeghy, Z., Flick, M., "Il problema teologico della predicazione," *Gregorianum*, 40 (1959): 671-744.

Althaus, P., "Die Inflation des Begriffes 'Offenbarung' in der gegenwärtigen Theologie," Zeitschrift für Systematische Theologie, 18 (1941): 134-149.

Aubert, R., "Le concile du Vatican et la connaissance naturelle de Dieu," *Lumière et Vie*, n. 14 (1954), pp. 21-53.

Barucq, A., "Oracle et divination," *Suppl. Dict. de la Bible*, 6: 752-787.

Bea, A., "Inspiration et Révélation," *Suppl. Dict. de la Bible*, 4: 504-505.

Benoit, P., "Révélation et Inspiration," *Revue Biblique*, 70 (1963): 321-370.

Berkouwer, G. C., "Revelation: The Christian View," *Christ Today*, 3 (1958): 1, 15 ss; 2, 22 ss.

Beumer, J., "Der Neutest. Offenbarungsbegriff und seine Verwendwung in der Apologetik," *Wissenschaft und Weisheit*, 22 (1959): 92- 100.

Blank, J., "Der Johanneische Wahrheitsbegriff," *Biblische Zeitschrift*, 7 (1962: 163-173.

Bornkamm, G., art. "*Mustèrion*," *Theol. Wörterbuch*, 4: 809-834.

Bouyer, L., "La doctrine de la Parole de Dieu," *Bible et Vie chrétienne*, 9 (1955): 102-107.

Boyer, C., "Qu'est-ce que la théologie? Réflexions sur une controverse récente," *Gregorianum*, 21 (1940): 255-266.

Brinktrine, J., "Der Begriff der Offenbarung im Neuen Testament," *Theologie und Glaube*, 1942, pp. 76-83.

Bultmann, R., "Der Begriff des Wortes Gottes im Neuen Testament," dans: *Glauben und Verstehen*, Tübingen, 1954, pp. 268-293.

Bultmann, R., "Welchen Sinn hat es, von Gott zu reden," dans: *Glauben und Verstehen*, Tübingen, 1954, pp. 26-37.

Burrows, M., "The Origin of the Term Gospel," *Journal of bibl. Litt.*, 1925, pp. 21-33.

Cerfaux, L., "Témoins du Christ d'après le Livre des Actes," dans: *Recueil Cerfaux*, 2 vol., Gembloux, 1954, t. 2, pp. 157-174.

Charlier, L., "Le Christ, Parole de Dieu," dans: *La Parole de Dieu en Jésus-Christ*, Paris, 1961, pp. 121-139.

Chenu, M.-D., "Position de la théologie," *Rev. des sc. ph. et th.*, 24 (1935): 232-257.

Colombo, C., "Rivelazione," *Enc. Cattolica*, 10 (1953): 1018-1025.

Coppens, J., "Le mystère dans la théologie paulinienne et ses parallèles qumrâniens," dans: *Littérature et théologie pauliniennes*, Coll. "Recherches bibliques" V, Bruges, 1960, pp. 142-165.

Daniélou, J., "Le kérygme selon le christianisme primitif," dans: *L'annonce de l'Évangile aujourd'hui*, Paris, 1962, pp. 67-86.

Davis, C., "The Theology of Preaching," *The Clergy Review*, 45 (1960): 524-545.

Decker, B., "Die Analyse des Offenbarungsvorganges beim hl. Thomas im Lichte vorthomistischer Prophetietraktate," *Angelicum*, 16 (1939): 195-244.

Deden, D., "Le mystère paulinien," *Eph. theol. lov.*, 13 (1936): 403-442.

de Ghellinck, J., "Pour l'histoire du mot revelare," *Rech. de sc. rel.*, 6 (1916): 149-157.

De Grandmaison, L., "Modernisme," *Dict. apol. de la foi cathol.*, 3: 602-603.

De Grandmaison, L., "Le développement du dogme chrétien," *Revue pratique d'apologétique*, 6 (1908): 81-104, 401-436.

de la Potterie, I., "La notion de témoignage dans S. Jean," dans: *Sacra Pagina*, 2 vol., Paris-Gembloux, 1959, t. 2, pp. 192-208.

de la Potterie, I., "L'arrière-plan du thème johannique de la vérité," dans: *Studia Evangelica*, Berlin, 1959, pp. 277-294.

de Lubac, H., "Le problème du développement du dogme," *Rech. de sc. rel.*, 35 (1948) : 130-160.

Demann, P., "Foi juive et foi chrétienne," *Cahiers Sioniens*, 6 (1952) : 89-103.

Dewailly, L.-M., "Course et gloire de la Parole, 2 Thess. 3, 1" *Revue biblique*, 71 (1964) : 25-42.

Dhanis, E., "Révélation explicite et implicite," *Gregorianum*, 34 (1953) : 187-238.

Didiot, J., "Révélation divine," *Dict. apol. de la foi cathol.*, 4: 1004-1009.

Dodd, C. H., "Le kérygme apostolique dans le quatrième Évangile," *Rev. d'hist. et de phil. rel.*, 31 (1951) : 265-275.

Dunas, N., "Pour une proposition kérygmatique de l'Évangile aujourd'hui," dans: *L'annonce de l'Évangile aujourd'hui*, Paris, 1962, pp. 233-314.

Dupont, J., "La parole de Dieu suivant S. Paul," dans: *La Parole de Dieu en Jésus-Christ*, Paris, 1961, pp. 68-84.

Durand, A., "Incarnation et christocentrisme," *Nouv. Rev. théol.*, 69 (1947) : 475-486.

Eichrodt, W., "Offenbarung und Geschichte im Alten Testament," *Theol. Zeitschrift*, 4 (1948) : 321-331.

Eichrodt, W., "Heilserfahrung und Zeitverständnis im AT," *Theol. Zeitschrift*, 12 (1956) : 103-125.

Eichrodt, W., "Offenbarung im AT," *Die Religion in Geschichte und Gegenwart*, 3e éd., 4: 1599-1601.

Escoula, L., "Saint Irénée et la connaissance naturelle de Dieu," *Rev. des sc. rel.*, 20 (1940) : 252-271.

Fehr, J., "Die Offenbarung als Wort Gottes bei Karl Barth und Thomas von Aquin," *Divus Thomas*, 15 (1937) : 55-64.

Feuillet, A., "La connaissance naturelle de Dieu par les hommes d'après Rom. 1, 18-29," *Lumière et Vie*, n. 14 (1954), pp. 207-222.

Feuillet, A., Grelot, P., "Parole de Dieu," *Vocabulaire de théologie biblique*, Paris, 1962, col. 750-758.

Frey, J. B., "La révélation d'après les conceptions juives au temps de Jésus-Christ," *Revue Biblique*, 25 (1916): 472-510.

Freidrich, G., art. *"Evangelizomai, evangelion,"* *Theol. Wörterbuch*, 2: 705-735.

Friedrich, G., art. *"Kèrussô, kèrugma,"* *Theol. Wörterbuch*, 3:701-717.

Fries, H., "Vom Hören des Wortes Gottes. Eine Fundamentaltheologische Überlegung," in: *Einsicht und Glaube*, Friburg-Basel-Wien, 1962, pp. 15-27.

Geiselmann, J. R., "Offenbarung," in: *Handbuch theologischer Grundbegriffe*, 2 vol., München, 1963, vol. 2, pp. 242-250.

Gelineau, J., "L'annonce de la Parole de Dieu dans le mystère du culte," dans: *La Parole de Dieu en Jésus-Christ*, Paris, 1961, pp. 202-209.

Giblet, J., "La théologie johannique du Logos," dans: *La Parole de Dieu en Jésus-Christ*, Paris, 1961, pp. 85-119.

Gloege, G., "Christliche Offenbarung, dogmatisch," *Die Religion in Geschichte und Gegenwart*, 3e éd., 4: 1609-1613.

Goudge, H. L., "Revelation," *Encyclopaedia of Religion and Ethics*, 10: 745-749.

Grasso, D., "Il kerigma e la predicazione," *Gregorianum*, 41 (1960): 424-450.

Grasso, D., "Evangelizzazione, catechesi, omilia," *Gregorianum*, 42 (1961): 242-267.

Guardini, R., "Le mythe et la vérité de la révélation," *Rech. de sc. rel.*, 37 (1950): 161-175.

Guardini, R., "Revelation and History," in: *The Faith and Modern Man*, Washington, 1952, pp. 82-101.

Haag, H., "Offenbarung in der hebräischen Bibel," *Theol. Zeitschrift* 16 (1960): 281-284.

Hamer, J., "Parole de Dieu ou parole sur Dieu dans la pensée de Karl Barth," dans: *La Parole de Dieu en Jésus-Christ*, Paris, 1961, pp. 281-287.

Henry, A.-M., "Le kérygme dans le ministère de la parole," dans: *L'annonce de l'Évangile aujourd'hui*, Paris, 1962, pp. 87-116.

Holstein, H., "La tradition des apôtres chez S. Irénée," *Rech. de sc. rel.*, 36 (1949) : 229-270.

Holstein, H., "Les témoins de la révélation d'après S. Irénée," *Rech. de sc. rel.*, 41 (1953) : 410-420.

Holstein, H., "La Révélation du Dieu vivant," *Nouv. Rev. théol.*, 81 (1959) : 157-168.

Holstein, H., "Prédication apostolique et Magistère," dans: *La Parole de Dieu en Jésus-Christ*, Paris, 1961, pp. 157-169.

Holth, S., "The Christian Doctrine of Revelation," *South-East Asia Journal of Theology*, 2, 4 (1961) : 20-30.

Hooke, S. H., *Alpha and Omega, A study in the Pattern of Revelation*, Welwyn (Hertfordshire, 1961.

Jacob, E., Biber, C., "Révélation," *Vocabulaire biblique*, Neuchâtel, 1954, pp. 254-258.

Jung, N., "Révélation," *Dict. de théol. cathol.*, 13 (2) : 2580-2618.

Kantzer, K. S., "Revelation and Inspiration in Neo-Orthodox Theology," *Bibliotheca Sacra, A Theological Quarterly*, 115 (1958) : 120-127, 218-228, 302-312; 116 (1959) : 15-29.

Kittel, G., art. "*Akoûo*," *Theol. Wörterbuch*, 1: 216-225.

Kittel, G., "Wort und Reden im NT," *Theol. Wörterbuch*, 4: 100-140.

Knox, D. B., "Propositional Revelation the Only Revelation," *The Reformed Theological Review*, 19 (1960) : 1-9.

Kock, R., "Die Verkündigung des Wortes Gottes in der Urkirche," *Anima*, 1955, pp. 256-265.

Lanne, D. E., "Le ministère apostolique dans l'œuvre de S. Irénée," *Irénikon*, 25 (1952) : 113-141.

Larcher, C., "De la nature à son Auteur d'après le livre de la Sagesse 13, 1-9," *Lumière et Vie*, n. 14 (1954), pp. 197-206.

Larcher, C., "La parole de Dieu en tant que révélation dans l'Ancien Testament," dans: *La Parole de Dieu en Jésus-Christ*, Paris, 1961, pp. 35-67.

Latourelle, R., "Notion de révélation et Magistère de l'Église," *Sciences Ecclésiastiques,* 9 (1957): 201-261.

Latourelle, R., "L'idée de révélation chez les Pères de l'Église," *Sciences Ecclésiastiques,* 11 (1959): 297-344.

Latourelle, R., "La révélation comme parole, témoignage et rencontre," *Gregorianum,* 43 (1962): 39-54.
195-211.

Latourelle, R., "Miracle et révélation," *Gregorianum,* 43 (1962): 492-

Latourelle, R., "Église et Parole," *Sciences Ecclésiastiques,* 14 (1962): 509.

Latourelle, R., "Révélation, Histoire et Incarnation," *Gregorianum,* 44 (1963): 225-262.

Lebreton, J., "La connaissance de Dieu chez S. Irénée," *Rech. de sc. rel.,* 16 (1920): 385-406.

Lebreton, J., "L'Encyclique et la théologie moderniste," *Dict. apol. de la foi cathol.,* 3: 665-695.

Leenhardt, F. J., "La signification de la notion de parole dans la pensée chrétienne," *Rev. d'hist. et de phil. rel.,* 35 (1955): 261-273.

Léonard, A., "La parole de Dieu, mystère et événement, vérité et présence," dans: *La Parole de Dieu en Jésus-Christ,* Paris, 1961, pp. 307-310.

Léonard, A., "Vers une théologie de la parole de Dieu," dans: *La Parole de Dieu en Jésus-Christ,* Paris, 1961, pp. 11-32.

Lewis, H. D., "Revelation without Content," *The Hibbert Journal,* 48 (1950): 379-382.

Liégé, P.-A., "De la parole à la catéchèse," *Lumière et Vie,* n. 36 (déc. 1957), pp. 56-72.

Liégé, P.-A., "Évangélisation," *Catholicisme,* 4: 755-764.

Liégé, P.-A., "Le ministère de la Parole: du kérygme à la catéchèse," dans: *La Parole de Dieu en Jésus-Christ,* Paris, 1961, pp. 170-184.

Malevez, L., "Théologie dialectique, théologie catholique et théologie naturelle," *Rech. de sc. rel.,* 28 (1938): 385-429, 527-569.

Malevez, L., "Révélation et Témoignage," *Mélanges de sc. rel.*, 6 (1949) : 217-232.

Marc, A., "L'idée de révélation," *Gregorianum*, 34 (1953) : 390-420.

Marlé, R., "La théologie bultmannienne de la Parole de Dieu," dans: *La Parole de Dieu en Jésus-Christ*, Paris, 1961, pp. 268-280.

Martelet, G., "L'homme comme parole et Dieu comme révélation," *Cahiers d'études biologiques*, n. 6-7 (1960), pp. 162-184.

Masson, C., "Le témoignage de Jean," *Rev. de th. et de ph.*, 1950, pp. 120-127.

McKenzie, J. L., "The Word of God in the Old Testament," *Theological Studies*, 21 (1960) : 183-206.

Menoud, Ph.-H., "Jésus et ses témoins," *Église et Théologie*, juin 1960, pp. 1-14.

Menoud, Ph.-H., "Révélation et tradition," *Verbum Caro*, 1953, pp. 2-10.

Michel, A., "Prophétie," *Dict. de théol. cathol.*, 13 (1) : 708-737.

Moeller, C., "Théologie de la parole et œcuménisme," *Irénikon*, 24 (1951) : 313-343.

Mohrmann, C., "Epiphaneia," *Rev. des sc. ph. et th.*, 37 (1953) : 644-670.

Mohrmann, C., "Praedicare-Tractare-Sermo. Essai sur la terminologie paléochrétienne," *La Maison-Dieu*, 1954, pp. 97-108.

Moingt, J., "La gnose de Clément d'Alexandrie dans ses rapports avec la foi et la philosophie," *Rech. de sc. rel.*, 37 (1950) : 195-251, 398-421, 537-564; 38 (1951) : 82-118.

Mollat, D., "Évangile," *Dict. de spiritualité*, 4: 1745-1772.

Mollat, D., "Le Semeion johannique," dans: *Sacra Pagina*, Paris-Gembloux, 1959, pp. 219-228.

Mowinckel, S., "La connaissance de Dieu chez les prophètes de l'Ancien Testament," *Rev. d'hist. et de phil. rel.*, 22 (1942) : 69-106.

Ochagavia, J., "The Notion of Revelation," *The Theologian*, 11 (1956) : 1-10.

Oepke, A., art. "*Apokaluptô, apokalupsis*," *Theol. Wörterbuch*, 3: 565-597.

Orbe, A., "La excelencia de los profetas según Orígenes," *Estudios Biblicos*, 14 (1955): 191-221.

Packer, J. I., "Contemporary Views of Revelation," *Christ Today*, 3 (1958): 4, 3-6; 5, 15 ss.

Peter, F. J., "Revelation and Propositions," *Evangelical Quarterly*, 33 1961): 67-80.

Piper, O. A., "Offenbarung in NT," *Die Religion in Geschichte und Gegenwart*, 3ᵉ éd., 4: 1603-1605.

Procksch, O., "Wort Gottes im AT," *Theol. Wörterbuch*, 4: 89-100.

Prümm, K., "Mysterion von Paulus bis Origenes," Zeitschrift für Kath. *Theol.*, 61 (1937): 391-425.

Prümm, K., "Göttliche Planung und menschliche Entwicklung nach Irenäus Adversus Haereses," *Scholastik*, 13 (1938): 206-224, 342-366.

Prümm, K., "Zur Phänomenologie des paulinischen Mysterion," *Biblica*, 37 (1956): 135-161.

Prümm, K., "Mystères," *Suppl. au Dict. de la Bible*, 6: 1-225.

Prümm, K., "Phänomenologie der Offenbarung laut 2 Kor," *Biblica*, 43 (1962): 396-416.

Quinn, E., "Revelation: Propositions or Encounter," *The Downside Review*, 79 (1961): 10-21.

Rahner, K., "Dieu dans le Nouveau Testament. La signification du mot Theos," dans: *Écrits théologiques*, Bruges, 1959, t. 1, pp. 15-111.

Rengstorf, K. H., art. "*Didaskô, didaskalos*," *Theol. Wörterbuch*, 2: 138-168.

Rigaux, B., Grelot, P., "Révélation," *Vocabulaire de théologie biblique*, Paris, 1962, col. 925-935.

Rivière, J., "Révélation," *Dict. pr. des connaissances rel.*, 5: 1252-1261.

Robert, A., Starcky, J., "La parole divine dans l'A. et le N.T.," *Suppl. au Dict. de la Bible*, 5: 425-497.

Rolland, E., "La Révélation," dans: M. Brillant et M. Nédoncelle, éd., *Apologétique*, Paris, 1939, pp. 197-229.

Rose, D. G., "The Biblical Idea of Revelation: Its Relevance for Constructive Theology," *Encounter*, 21, 2 (1960): 201-217.

Rowley, H. H., "The Nature of the Old Testament Prophecy in the Light of Recent Study," in: *The Servant of the Lord and other Essays in the Old Testament*, London, 1952, pp. 91-128.

Schillebeeckx, E., "Parole et sacrement dans l'Église," *Lumière et Vie*, 9 (1960): 25-45.

Schlier, H., "La notion paulinienne de la parole de Dieu," dans: *Littérature et théologie pauliniennes*, Coll. "*Recherches bibliques*" V, Bruges, 1960, pp. 127-141.

Schnackenburg, R., "Zum Offenbarungsgedanken in der Bibel," *Biblische Zeitschrift*, 7 (1963): 2-23.

Spacil, T., "Doctrina Theologiae Orientis separati, pars prima: De Revelatione, de Fide," *Orientalia christiana*, n. 88, sept. 1953, pp. 153-390.

Spicq, C., "Le mystère chrétien," dans: *Les Épitres pastorales*, Paris, 1947, pp. 116-125.

Strathmann, H., art. "*Martus, martureô, marturia,*" *Theol. Wörterbuch*, 4: 492-514.

Straubinger, H., "Offenbarung," *Lexikon für Theol. und Kirche*, 7 (1935): 682-685.

Thils, G., "La définition de l'Immaculée Conception et l'idée de révélation," *Eph. theol. lov.*, 31 (1955): 34-45.

Torres Capellán, A., "Palàbra y Revelación," *Burgense*, 1 (1960): 143-190.

Trépanier, B., "L'idée de témoin dans les écrits johanniques," *Rev. de l'Univ. d'Ottawa*, 15 (1945): 5*-63.*

Trémel, Y.-B., "Du kérygme des apôtres à celui d'aujourd'hui," dans: *L'annonce de l'Évangile aujourd'hui*, Paris, 1962, pp. 19-54.

Ubieta, J. A., "El Kerygma apostólico y los Evangelios," *Estudios Bíblicos*, 18 (1959): 21-61.

Vanhoye, A., "Notre foi, oeuvre divine d'après le quatrième Évangile," *Christus*, n. 6, avril 1955, pp. 150-171.

Vanhoye, A., "Notre foi, oeuvre divine d'après le quatrième Evangile," *Nouvelle Revue théologique*, 86 (1964): 337-354.

Vereno, M., Schnackenburg, R., Fries, H., art. "Offenbarung," *Lexikon für Theologie und Kirche*, 7: col. 1104-1115.

Verrièle, A., "Le plan du salut d'après S. Irénée," *Rev. des sc. rel.*, 14 (1934): 493-524.

von Balthasar, H. U., "Dieu a parlé un langage d'homme," dans: *Parole de Dieu et Liturgie*, Paris, 1958, pp. 71-103.

von Balthasar, H. U., "Parole et histoire," dans: *La Parole de Dieu en Jésus-Christ*, Paris, 1961, pp. 227-240.

von Rad, G., "Kritische Vorarbeiten zu einer Theologie des A.T.," dans: *Theologie und Liturgie*, Kassel, 1932, pp. 9-34.

von Rad, G., "Gesetz und Evangelium im A.T.," *Theol. Blätter*, 16 (1937): 41-47.

von Rad, G., "Grundprobleme einer biblischen Theologie des A.T.," *Theol. Lit Zeitung*, 68 (1943): 225-234.

Wennemer, K., "Theologie des Wortes im Johannesevangelium," *Scholastik*, 38 (1963): 1-17.

White, V., "Le concept de révélation chez S. Thomas," *L'Année théologique*, 11 (1950): 1-17, 109-132.

Zimmermann, H., "Das absolute *egô eimi* als die Neutestamentliche Offenbarungsformel," *Biblische Zeitschrift*, 4, (1960): 54-70.

index

INDEX